M000117830

ADOBE® COLDFUSION® 9
Getting Started

web application construction kit
VOLUME 1

Ben Forta and Raymond Camden
with Charlie Arehart

Adobe ColdFusion 9 Web Application Construction Kit, Volume 1: Getting Started
Ben Forta and Raymond Camden with Charlie Arehart

This Adobe Press book is published by Peachpit.
For information on Adobe Press books, contact:

Peachpit
1249 Eighth Street
Berkeley, CA 94710
510/524-2178
510/524-2221 (fax)

For the latest on Adobe Press books, go to www.adobepress.com
To report errors, please send a note to errata@peachpit.com
Peachpit is a division of Pearson Education

Copyright ©2010 by Ben Forta

Series Editor: Karen Reichstein
Editor: Judy Ziajka
Technical Reviewer: Terry Ryan
Production Editor: Tracey Croom
Compositor: Maureen Forys, Happenstance Type-O-Rama
Proofreader: Liz Welch
Indexer: Ron Strauss
Cover design: Charlene Charles-Will

NOTICE OF RIGHTS

All rights reserved. No part of this book may be reproduced or transmitted in any form by any means, electronic, mechanical, photocopying, recording, or otherwise, without the prior written permission of the publisher. For information on getting permission for reprints and excerpts, contact permissions@peachpit.com.

NOTICE OF LIABILITY

The information in this book is distributed on an "As Is" basis, without warranty. While every precaution has been taken in the preparation of the book, neither the author nor Peachpit shall have any liability to any person or entity with respect to any loss or damage caused or alleged to be caused directly or indirectly by the instructions contained in this book or by the computer software and hardware products described in it.

TRADEMARKS

Adobe, ColdFusion, Dreamweaver, Flash, and Flex are registered trademarks of Adobe Systems, Inc., in the United States and/or other countries. All other trademarks are the property of their respective owners. Many of the designations used by manufacturers and sellers to distinguish their products are claimed as trademarks. Where those designations appear in this book, and Peachpit was aware of a trademark claim, the designations appear as requested by the owner of the trademark. All other product names and services identified throughout this book are used in editorial fashion only and for the benefit of such companies with no intention of infringement of the trademark. No such use, or the use of any trade name, is intended to convey endorsement or other affiliation with this book.

ISBN 13: 978-0-321-66034-3
ISBN 10: 0-321-66034-X

Biographies

Ben Forta

Ben Forta is director of platform evangelism for Adobe Systems Incorporated and has more than two decades of experience in the computer software industry in product development, support, training, and marketing. Ben is the author of the best-selling ColdFusion book series of all time, *ColdFusion Web Application Construction Kit*, as well as books on SQL, JavaServer Pages, Windows development, regular expressions, and more. More than a half million Ben Forta books have been printed in more than a dozen languages worldwide. Ben helped create the official Adobe ColdFusion training material, as well as the certification tests and study guides for those tests. He writes regular columns on ColdFusion and Internet development and spends a considerable amount of time lecturing and speaking on application development worldwide. Ben welcomes your email at ben@forta.com and invites you to visit his Web site at http://forta.com/ and his blog at http://forta.com/blog.

Raymond Camden

Raymond Camden is a software consultant focusing on ColdFusion and rich Internet application development. A longtime ColdFusion user, Raymond has worked on numerous ColdFusion books, including *ColdFusion Web Application Construction Kit*, and has contributed to the *Fusion Authority Quarterly Update* and the *ColdFusion Developers Journal*. He also presents at conferences and contributes to online Webzines. He founded many community Web sites, including CFLib.org, ColdFusionPortal.org, and ColdFusionCookbook.org, and is the author of open source applications, including the popular BlogCFC (www.blogcfc.com) blogging application. Raymond is an Adobe Community Professional. He is the happily married proud father of three kids and is something of a *Star Wars* nut. Raymond can be reached at his blog (www.coldfusionjedi.com) or via email at ray@camdenfamily.com.

Charlie Arehart

A veteran ColdFusion developer and troubleshooter since 1997 with more than 25 years in IT, Charlie Arehart is a longtime contributor to the ColdFusion community and a recognized Adobe Community Professional. As an independent consultant, he provides short-term troubleshooting and tuning assistance and training and mentoring for organizations of all sizes and ColdFusion experience levels (carehart.org/consulting). Besides running the 2000-member Online ColdFusion Meetup (coldfusionmeetup.com, an online CF user group), he hosts the UGTV repository of recorded presentations from hundreds of speakers (carehart.org/ugtv) and the CF411 site with more than 1000 tools and resources for ColdFusion developers (cf411.com). A certified Advanced ColdFusion Developer and an instructor for each version since ColdFusion 4, Charlie has spoken at each of the major ColdFusion conferences worldwide and is a contributor to all three volumes of *Adobe ColdFusion 9 Web Application Construction Kit*.

Acknowledgments

Ben Forta

Thanks to my co-authors, Ray Camden and Charlie Arehart, for their outstanding contributions. Although this book is affectionately known to thousands as "the Ben Forta book," it is, in truth, as much theirs as it is mine. An extra thank you to Ray Camden for once again bravely accepting the role of lead co-author. Thanks to fellow Adobe Platform Evangelist Terry Ryan for his thorough technical review. Thanks to Nancy Ruenzel and the crew at Peachpit for allowing me the creative freedom to build these books as I see fit. Thanks to Karen Reichstein for bravely stepping in as acquisitions editor on this revision, and to Judy Ziajka for so ably shepherding this book through the publication process yet again. Thanks to the thousands of you who write to me with comments, suggestions, and criticism (thankfully not too much of the latter)—I do read each and every message (and even attempt to reply to them all, eventually), and all are appreciated. And last, but by no means least, a loving thank you to my wife Marcy and our children for putting up with (and allowing) my often hectic work schedule. Their love and support make all that I do possible.

Raymond Camden

I'd like to thank Ben and Adobe Press for once again asking me to be a part of this incredible series. It is both an honor and a privilege! I'd also like to thank Adobe, specifically Adam Lehman and the engineers. Thanks for having me as part of the ColdFusion 9 beta process and allowing me to help shape the product I love. I promise I'll ask only half as many annoying questions for ColdFusion 10.

Charlie Arehart

First, I want to thank Ben for having me as a contributor to this series. With so many excellent authors among the current and past contributors, I really feel privileged. I also want to thank him for all his contributions to the community. Again, as with my fellow authors, I follow in the footsteps of giants. In that regard, I want to acknowledge the awesome ColdFusion community. I've so enjoyed being a part of it, as both beneficiary and contributor, since 1997. This book's for you.

Dedications

Ben Forta

To the ColdFusion community, a loyal and passionate group that I've been proud to call my friends for a decade and a half.

Raymond Camden

As always, for my wife. Thank you, Jeanne, for your love and support.

Charlie Arehart

I'd like to dedicate this book to my wife of 10 years and the love of my life, Kim. I couldn't do all I do without your patience, support, and encouragement. Thank you, my love. God truly blessed me when He brought you into my life.

CONTENTS AT A GLANCE

CONTENTS

PART 1

Getting Started

CHAPTER 1

Introducing ColdFusion

Understanding ColdFusion

Millions of Web sites exist that attract millions of visitors daily. Many Web sites are being used as electronic replacements for newspapers, magazines, brochures, and bulletin boards. The Web offers ways to enhance these publications using audio, images, animation, multimedia, and even virtual reality.

These sites add value to the Net because information is knowledge, and knowledge is power. All this information is literally at your fingertips. But because of the underlying technology that makes the Web tick, sites can be much more than electronic versions of paper publications. Users can interact with you and your company, collect and process mission-critical information in real time (allowing you to provide new levels of user support), and much more.

The Web isn't merely the electronic equivalent of a newspaper or magazine—it's a communication medium limited only by the innovation and creativity of Web site designers.

The Dynamic Page Advantage

Dynamic pages—pages that contain dynamic content—are what bring the Web to life. Linking your Web site to live data is a tremendous advantage, but the benefits of database interaction go beyond extending your site's capabilities.

To see why dynamic Web pages are becoming the norm, compare them to static pages:

- **Static Web pages.** Static Web pages are made up of text, images, and HTML formatting tags. These pages are manually created and maintained so that when information changes, so must the page. This usually involves loading the page into an editor, making the changes, reformatting text if needed, and then saving the file. And not everyone in the organization can make these changes. The webmaster or Web design team is responsible for maintaining the site and implementing all changes and enhancements. This often means that by the time information finally makes it onto the Web site, it's out of date.

- **Dynamic Web pages.** Dynamic Web pages contain very little text. Instead, they pull needed information from other applications. Dynamic Web pages communicate with databases to extract employee directory information, spreadsheets to display accounting figures, client-server database management systems to interact with order processing applications, and more. A database already exists. Why re-create it for Web page publication?

Creating dynamic pages lets you create powerful applications that can include features such as these:

- Querying existing database applications for data

- Creating dynamic queries, facilitating more flexible data retrieval

- Generating and working with email, instant messaging, text messaging, and more

- Executing conditional code on the fly to customize responses for specific situations

- Enhancing the standard HTML form capabilities with data validation functions

- Dynamically populating form elements

- Customizing the display of dates, times, and currency values with formatting functions

- Using wizards to ease the creation of data entry and data drill-down applications

- Creating printable content

- Data-driven reports in Adobe PDF formats

- Shopping carts and e-commerce sites

- Data syndication and affiliate programs

Understanding Web Applications

Web sites are powered by Web servers, and Web servers do just that: they serve. Web browsers make requests, and Web servers fulfill those requests—they serve up the requested information to the browser. These are usually HTML files, as well as the other file types discussed previously.

And that's really all Web servers do. In the grand scheme of things, Web servers are actually pretty simple applications—they sit and wait for requests that they attempt to fulfill as soon as they arrive. Web servers don't let you interact with a database; they don't let you personalize Web pages; they don't let you process the results of a user's form submission. They do none of that; all they do is serve pages.

So how do you extend your Web server to do all the things listed above? That's where Web application servers come into play. A *Web application server* is a piece of software that extends the Web server, enabling it to do things it can't do by itself—kind of like teaching an old dog new tricks.

Here's how it all works. When a Web server receives a request from a Web browser, it looks at that request to determine whether it is a simple Web page or a page that needs processing by a Web application server. It does this by looking at the MIME type (or file extension). If the MIME type indicates that the file is a simple Web page (for example, it has an .htm extension), the Web server fulfills the request and sends the file to the requesting browser as is. But if the MIME type indicates that the requested file is a page that needs processing by a Web application server (for example, it has a .cfm extension), the Web server passes it to the appropriate Web application server and returns the results it gets back rather than the actual page itself.

In other words, Web application servers are *page preprocessors*. They process the requested page before it's sent back to the client (the browser), and in doing so they open the door to developers to do all sorts of interesting things on the server, such as:

- Creating guest books

- Conducting surveys

- Changing your pages on the fly based on date, time, first visit, and whatever else you can think of

- Personalizing pages for your visitors

- In fact, all the features listed previously

What Is ColdFusion?

Initially, developing highly interactive and data-rich sites was a difficult process. Writing custom Web-based applications was a job for experienced programmers only. A good working knowledge of Unix was a prerequisite, and experience with traditional development or scripting languages was a must.

But all that has changed. Adobe ColdFusion enables you to create sites every bit as powerful and capable, without a long and painful learning curve. In fact, rather than being painful, the process is actually fun!

So, what exactly is ColdFusion? Simply put, ColdFusion is an application server—one of the very best out there, as well as the very first. (ColdFusion actually defined the application server category back in 1995.)

ColdFusion doesn't require coding using traditional programming languages, although traditional programming constructs and techniques are fully supported. Instead, you create applications by extending your standard HTML files with high-level formatting functions, conditional operators, and database commands. These commands are instructions to the ColdFusion processor and form the blocks on which to build industrial-strength applications.

Creating Web applications this way has significant advantages over conventional application development:

- ColdFusion applications can be developed rapidly because no coding is required, other than use of simple HTML style tags.

- ColdFusion applications are easy to test and roll out.

- The ColdFusion language contains all the processing and formatting functions you'll need (and the capability to create your own functions if you run into a dead end).

- ColdFusion applications are easy to maintain because no compilation or linking step is required. (Files actually are compiled, but that happens transparently, as I'll explain shortly.) The files you create are the files used by ColdFusion.

- ColdFusion provides all the tools you need to troubleshoot and debug applications, including a powerful development environment and debugger.

- ColdFusion comes with all the hooks necessary to link to almost any database application and any other external system.

- ColdFusion is fast, thanks to its scalable, multithreaded, service-based architecture.

- ColdFusion is built on industry-standard Java architecture, and supports all major standards and initiatives.

ColdFusion and Your Intranet, Extranet, and Portal

Everything explained here applies not just to Internet Web sites. Indeed, the benefits of Cold-Fusion apply to intranets, extranets, and portals, too.

Most companies have masses of information stored in various systems. Users often don't know what information is available or even how to access it.

ColdFusion bridges the gap between existing and legacy applications and your employees. It gives employees the tools to work more efficiently.

ColdFusion Explained

You're now ready to take a look at ColdFusion so you can understand what it is and how it works its magic.

And if you're wondering why you went through all this discussion about the Internet and Web servers, here's where it will all fit together.

The ColdFusion Application Server

ColdFusion is an application server—a piece of software that (usually) resides on the same computer as your Web server, enabling the Web server to do things it wouldn't normally know how to do.

ColdFusion is actually made up of several pieces. The ColdFusion Application Server is the program that actually parses (reads and compiles) and processes any supplied instructions.

Instructions are passed to ColdFusion using *templates*. A template looks much like any HTML file, with one big difference. Unlike HTML files, ColdFusion templates can contain special tags that instruct ColdFusion to perform specific operations. Here is a sample ColdFusion template that you'll use later in this book.

```
<!--- Get movies sorted by release date --->
<cfquery datasource="ows" name="movies">
 SELECT MovieTitle, DateInTheaters
 FROM Films
 ORDER BY DateInTheaters
</cfquery>


<!--- Create HTML page --->
<HTML>
<HEAD>
<TITLE>Movies by Release Date</TITLE>
</HEAD>


<BODY>


<H1>Movies by Release Date</H1>


<!--- Display movies in list format --->
<UL>
<cfoutput query="movies">
 <LI><STRONG>#Trim(MovieTitle)#</STRONG> - #DateFormat(DateInTheaters)#</LI>
</cfoutput>
</UL>


</BODY>


</HTML>
```

Earlier in this chapter, I said that Web servers typically return the contents of a Web page without paying any attention to the file contents.

That's exactly what ColdFusion *doesn't* do. When ColdFusion receives a request, it parses the template looking for special ColdFusion tags (they all begin with CF) or ColdFusion variables and functions (always surrounded by number [#] signs). HTML or plain text is left alone and is output to the Web server untouched. Any ColdFusion instructions are processed, and any existing results are sent to the Web server. The Web server can then send the entire output back to the requester's browser. As explained earlier, the request file type tells the Web server that a request is to be handled by an application server. All ColdFusion files have an extension of .cfm or .cfml, like this:

```
http://www.forta.com/books/index.cfm
```

When ColdFusion is installed, it configures your Web server so it knows that any file with an extension of .cfm (or .cfml) is a ColdFusion file. Then, whenever a ColdFusion file is requested, the Web server knows to pass the file to ColdFusion for processing rather than return it.

It's worth noting that ColdFusion doesn't actually need a Web server because it has one built in. So as not to conflict with any other installed Web servers (like Apache and Microsoft IIS) the internal

Web server runs on port 8500 or 8300 (depending on the type of installation performed) instead of the default port 80. During ColdFusion installation you'll be asked whether you want to run Cold-Fusion in stand-alone mode (bound to the integrated Web server) or using an existing Web server. If you opt to use the internal Web server you'll need to specify the port number in all URLs.

NOTE

The examples in this book use the internal Web server, so they include the port number. If you're using an external Web server, just drop the port number from the URLs.

CAUTION

Adobe doesn't recommend that the internal Web server (stand-alone mode) be used on production boxes. ColdFusion's integrated HTTP server is intended for use on development boxes only.

The ColdFusion Markup Language

I said earlier that ColdFusion is an application server; that's true, but that's not all it is. In fact, ColdFusion is two distinct technologies:

- The ColdFusion Application Server
- The CFML language (including `<cfscript>`)

Although the ColdFusion Application Server itself is important, ColdFusion's power comes from its capable and flexible language. ColdFusion Markup Language (CFML) is modeled after HTML, which makes it very easy to learn.

CFML extends HTML by adding tags with the following capabilities:

- Read data from, and update data to, databases and tables
- Create dynamic data-driven pages
- Perform conditional processing
- Populate forms with live data
- Process form submissions
- Generate and retrieve email messages
- Interact with local files
- Perform HTTP and FTP operations
- Perform credit-card verification and authorization
- Read and write client-side cookies

And that's not even the complete list.

The majority of this book discusses ColdFusion pages (often called templates) and the use of CFML.

Linking to External Applications

One of ColdFusion's most powerful features is its capability to connect to data created and maintained in other applications. You can use ColdFusion to retrieve or update data in many applications, including the following:

- Corporate databases

- Client-server database systems (such as Microsoft SQL Server and Oracle)

- Spreadsheets

- XML data

- Contact-management software

- ASCII-delimited files

- Images

- JavaBeans, JSP tag libraries, and EJBs

- .NET classes and assemblies

- Web Services

Extending ColdFusion

As installed, ColdFusion will probably do most of what you need, interacting with most of the applications and technologies you'll be using. But in the event that you need something more, ColdFusion provides all the hooks and support necessary to communicate with just about any application or service in existence. Integration is made possible via:

- C and C++

- Java

- .NET

- COM

- CORBA

- XML

- Web Services

These technologies and their uses are beyond the scope of this book and are covered in detail in the sequels, *ColdFusion Web Application Construction Kit, Volume 2: Application Development*, and *ColdFusion Web Application Construction Kit, Volume 3: Advanced Application Development*.

Inside ColdFusion 9

ColdFusion 9 is the most remarkable ColdFusion to date, and is built on top of ColdFusion MX, the first completely redesigned and rebuilt ColdFusion since the product was first created back in 1995. Understanding the inner workings of ColdFusion isn't a prerequisite to using the product, but knowing what ColdFusion is doing under the hood will help you make better use of this remarkable product.

I said earlier that ColdFusion is a page preprocessor—it processes pages and returns the results as opposed to the page itself. To do this ColdFusion has to read each file, check and validate the contents, and then perform the desired operations. But there is actually much more to it than that. In fact, within ColdFusion is a complete J2EE (Java 2 Enterprise Edition) server that provides the processing power ColdFusion needs.

NOTE

Don't worry. You don't need to know any Java at all to use ColdFusion.

First, a clarification. When people talk about Java they generally mean two very different things:

- The Java language is just that, a programming language. It is powerful and not at all easy to learn or use.

- The Java platform, a complete set of building blocks and technologies to build rich and powerful applications.

Of the two, the former is of no interest (well, maybe little interest) to ColdFusion developers. After all, why write complex code in Java to do what CFML can do in a single tag? But Java the platform? Now that's compelling. The Java platform provides the wherewithal to:

- Access all sorts of databases

- Interact with legacy systems

- Support mobile devices

- Use directory services

- Create multilingual and internationalized applications

- Leverage transactions, queuing, and messaging

- Create robust and highly scalable applications

In the past you'd have had to write Java code in order to leverage the Java platform, but not any more. ColdFusion runs on top of the Java platform, providing the power of underlying Java made accessible via the simplicity of CFML.

NOTE

By default, the Java engine running ColdFusion is Adobe's own award-winning J2EE server, JRun. ColdFusion can also be run on top of third-party J2EE servers like IBM WebSphere, BEA WebLogic, and JBoss. See Appendix A, "Installing ColdFusion and ColdFusion Builder," for more information.

But don't let the CFML (and CFM files) fool you—when you create a ColdFusion application you are actually creating a Java application. In fact, when ColdFusion processes your CFM pages it creates Java source code and compiles it into Java byte code for you, all in the background.

This behavior was first introduced in ColdFusion MX. Using ColdFusion you can truly have the best of both worlds—the power of Java, and the simplicity of ColdFusion, and all without having to make any sacrifices at all.

Powered by ColdFusion

You were probably planning to use ColdFusion to solve a particular problem or fill a specific need. Although this book helps you do just that, I hope that your mind is now racing and beginning to envision just what else ColdFusion can do for your Web site.

In its relatively short life, ColdFusion has proven itself to be a solid, reliable, and scalable development platform. ColdFusion 9 is the eleventh major release of this product, and with each release it becomes an even better and more useful tool. It is easy to learn, fun to use, and powerful enough to create real-world, Web-based applications. With a minimal investment of your time, your applications can be powered by ColdFusion.

CHAPTER 2

Accessing the ColdFusion Administrator

The ColdFusion server is a piece of software—an application. As explained in Chapter 1, "Introducing ColdFusion," the software usually runs on a computer running Web server software. Production servers (servers that run finished and deployed applications) usually are connected to the Internet with a high-speed always-on connection. Development machines (used during the application development phase) often are stand-alone computers or workstations on a network and usually run locally installed Web server software and ColdFusion.

TIP

If you're serious about ColdFusion development, you should install a server locally. Although you can learn ColdFusion and write code using a remote server, not having access to the server will complicate both your learning and your ongoing project development.

The ColdFusion Application Server software—I'll just call it ColdFusion for readability's sake—has all sorts of configuration and management options. Some must be configured before features will work (for example, connections to databases). Others are configured only if necessary (for example, the extensibility options). Still others are purely management and monitoring related (for example, log file analysis).

All these configuration options are managed via a special program, the ColdFusion Administrator. The Administrator is a Web-based application; you access it using any Web browser, from any computer with an Internet connection. This is important because:

- Local access to the production computer running ColdFusion is often impossible (especially if hosting with an ISP or in an IT department).

- ColdFusion servers can be managed easily, without needing to install special client software.

- ColdFusion can be managed from any Web browser, even those running on platforms not directly supported by ColdFusion, and even on browsers not running on PCs.

Of course, such a powerful Web application needs to be secure—otherwise, anyone would be able to reconfigure your ColdFusion server! At install time, you were prompted for a password with which to secure the ColdFusion Administrator. Without that password, you won't be able to access the program.

NOTE

In addition to the Web-based ColdFusion Administrator, developers and administrators can create their own Administration screens, consoles, and applications using a special Administrative API. This feature is beyond the scope of this book and is covered in *Adobe ColdFusion Web Application Construction Kit, Volume 3: Advanced Application Development*.

TIP

Many ColdFusion developers abbreviate ColdFusion Administrator to CF Admin. So if you hear people talking about "CF Admin," you'll know what they're referring to.

Logging Into (and Out of) the ColdFusion Administrator

When ColdFusion is installed (on Windows), a program group named Adobe, ColdFusion 9 is created. Within that group is an option named Administrator that, when selected, launches the ColdFusion Administrator.

NOTE

Depending on installation options selected, the menu item might be named Administrator or ColdFusion 9 Administrator.

It's important to note that this menu option is just a shortcut; you can also access the ColdFusion Administrator by specifying the appropriate URL directly. This is especially important if Cold-Fusion isn't installed locally, or if you simply want to bookmark the Administrator directly.

The URL for the local ColdFusion Administrator is
`http://localhost/CFIDE/administrator/index.cfm`.

As explained in Chapter 1, ColdFusion has an integrated (stand-alone) Web server that may be used for development. That server is usually on port `8500` or `8300` (instead of the default Web port of `80`), so any URLs referring to the integrated Web server must specify that port. As such, the URL for the local ColdFusion Administrator (when using the integrated Web server) is

`http://localhost:8500/CFIDE/administrator/index.cfm`

or

`http://localhost:8300/CFIDE/administrator/index.cfm`

NOTE

If, for some reason `localhost` doesn't work, the IP address `127.0.0.1` can be used instead:
`http://127.0.0.1:8500/CFIDE/administrator/index.cfm`.

TIP

To access the ColdFusion Administrator on a remote server, use the same URL but replace `localhost` with the DNS name (or IP address) of that remote host.

Using the Program Group option or any of the URLs listed previously, start your ColdFusion Administrator. You should see a login screen. Enter your password, then click the Login button. Assuming your password is correct (you'll know if it isn't), you'll see the Administrator Welcome page, as shown in Figure 2.1.

Figure 2.1

The Administrator Welcome page.

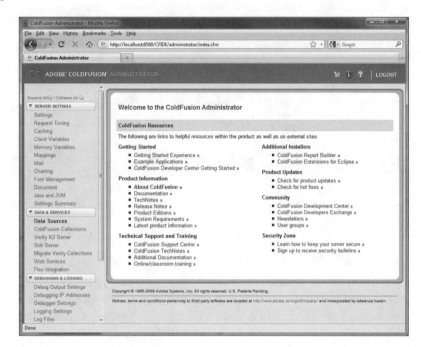

NOTE

The ColdFusion Administrator password is initially set during ColdFusion installation.

NOTE

The exact contents of the Administrator Welcome page will vary, depending on the installation type and edition being used.

The Administrator screen is divided into several regions:

- The top of the screen contains a ColdFusion logo (use this to get back to the home page if you get lost), a resources icon, a system information icon (used to obtain system configuration information), a Logout link, and a help icon (this provides additional context-sensitive help as necessary).

- The left side of the screen contains menus that may be expanded to display the administrative and configuration options.

- To the right of the menus is the main Administrator screen, which varies based on the menu options selected. When at the home page, this screen contains links to documentation, online support, training, product registration, community sites, the Security Zone, and much more.

NOTE

Use the System Information link at the top of the ColdFusion Administrator screen to install or change your ColdFusion license and serial number (perhaps to upgrade from Standard to Enterprise).

Try logging out of the Administrator (use the Logout button) and then log in again. You should get in the habit of always logging out of the Administrator when you are finished using it.

TIP

If you are logged into the Administrator, your login will time out after a period of inactivity (forcing you to log in again), but don't rely on this. If you leave your desk, or you work in an environment where others can access your computer, always explicitly log out of the ColdFusion Administrator when you're finished or when you leave.

Using the ColdFusion Administrator

Let's take a brief look at the Administrator, and then configure the few options needed so that you can begin development. If you have logged out of the ColdFusion Administrator (or if you have yet to log in), log in now.

Creating a Data Source

One of the most important uses of the ColdFusion Administrator is to create and define *data sources*, which are connections that ColdFusion uses to interact with databases. Data sources are defined using the Data Sources menu option (it's in the section labeled Data & Services).

You'll need a data source ready and configured for just about every lesson in this series, so we'll walk through the process of creating a data source named ows right now.

➜ Data sources and databases will be explained in detail in Chapter 5, "Reviewing the Databases," and Chapter 6, "Introducing SQL."

Here are the steps to follow to create the ows data source using the ColdFusion Administrator:

NOTE

If you haven't yet installed the sample file and databases, see the end of Appendix A, "Installing ColdFusion and ColdFusion Builder."

1. Log into the ColdFusion Administrator.

2. Select the Data Sources menu option (it's in the section labeled Data & Services).

   All defined data sources are listed in this screen, and they can be added and edited here as well.

3. At the top of the screen, enter ows as the name for the new data source and set the driver type to `Apache Derby Embedded`; then click the Add button.

The Data Sources definition screen (seen in Figure 2.2) prompts for any information necessary to define the data source.

4. The only field necessary for an Apache Derby Embedded data source is the name of the database folder. If you saved the database under the ColdFusion DB folder (as recommended in Appendix A), you'll just need to enter the folder name ows here. If you saved the database to another location, provide the full path to the ows data folder in this field. You also can click the Browse Server button to display a tree control created using a Java applet that can be used to browse the server's hard drive to locate the file interactively.

Figure 2.2

Data source options vary based on the data-source type selected.

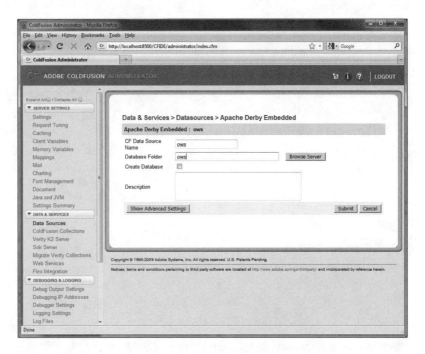

5. After you have filled in any required fields, click the Submit button to create the new data source. The list of data sources will be redisplayed, and the new ows data source will be listed with a status of OK. The screen will report that the data source was successfully updated. If an error status message is returned, click ows to make any necessary corrections.

NOTE

The options required in a data source definition vary based on the driver used. Thus, the screen used to create and edit data sources varies based on the driver used.

Defining a Mail Server

In Chapter 20, "Interacting with Email," you will learn how to generate email messages with ColdFusion. ColdFusion doesn't include a mail server; therefore, to generate email the name of a mail server (an SMTP server) must be provided.

NOTE

> If you don't have access to a mail server or don't know the mail server name, don't worry. You won't be using this feature for a while, and omitting this setting now won't keep you from following along in the next lessons.

To set up your SMTP mail server, do the following:

1. In the ColdFusion Administrator, select the Mail menu option (it's in the section labeled Server Settings).

2. The first field, titled Mail Server, prompts for the mail server host (either the DNS name or IP address). Provide this information as requested.

3. Before you submit the form, you always should ensure that the specified mail server is valid and accessible. To do this, check the Verify Mail Server Connection checkbox lower down the page.

4. Click the Submit Changes button (there is one at both the top and the bottom of the screen). Assuming the mail server was accessible, you'll see a success message at the top of the screen. You'll see an error message if the specified server could not be accessed.

   You have now configured your mail server and can use ColdFusion to generate SMTP email.

Enabling Debugging

The debugging screens are another important set of screens that you should be familiar with, starting with the Debugging Output Settings screen. To access this screen, select Debugging Output Settings (it's in the section labeled Debugging & Logging).

I don't want you to turn on any of these options now, but I do want you to know where these options are and how to get to them, so that you'll be ready to use them in Chapter 10, "Creating Data-Driven Pages."

Now go to the Debugging IP Address screen. To get to it, select the Debugging IP Addresses option; it's also in the section labeled Debugging & Logging. This screen is used to define the IP addresses of clients that will receive debug output (this will make more sense in later chapters, I promise). Ensure that the addresses 127.0.0.1 and 0:0:0:0:0:0:0:1 are listed; if they're not, add them. If you don't have a locally installed ColdFusion (and are accessing a remote ColdFusion server), add your own IP address, too, by clicking the Add Current button.

Debugging and the generated debug output are an important part of application development, as you'll see later in the book.

→ Chapter 17, "Debugging and Troubleshooting," covers the debugging options in detail.

Viewing Settings

The final screen I'd like to show you is the Settings Summary screen. As its name implies, this reports all ColdFusion settings, including all defined data sources. To access this screen, select the Settings Summary menu option; it's in the Server Settings section. The ColdFusion Administrator will read all settings and then generate a complete report. Settings are also linked, allowing quick access to the appropriate screens if changes are to be made.

TIP

It's a good idea to keep a copy of this screen so that you'll have all the settings readily available if you ever have to restore them.

For now, you are finished with the ColdFusion Administrator. So log out and proceed to the next chapter.

TIP

To log out of the ColdFusion Administrator, click the Logout button at the top right.

NOTE

Feel free to browse through the other administrator screens, but resist the urge to make changes to any settings until you have studied Chapter 25, "ColdFusion Server Configuration," in *Adobe ColdFusion 9 Web Application Construction Kit, Volume 2: Application Development.*

CHAPTER 3

Introducing ColdFusion Builder

ColdFusion applications are made up of files—lots and lots of files. These files are plain text files containing CFML, HTML, SQL, JavaScript, CSS, and more. Because they are plain text files, ColdFusion developers are free to use any editor they like to write and edit their applications.

CAUTION

Although you can indeed use any editor, you must use editors that save files as plain text. This means that you should not use word processors (like Microsoft Word) to edit source code.

One of the most exciting and eagerly anticipated additions in ColdFusion 9 is the ColdFusion Builder, a new development environment designed specifically for us ColdFusion developers.

NOTE

You'll need to have ColdFusion Builder installed before working through this chapter. For installation instructions and notes, see Appendix A, "Installing ColdFusion and ColdFusion Builder."

The Relationship Between ColdFusion Builder and Eclipse

ColdFusion Builder is an integrated development environment, or IDE. That's important. Cold-Fusion Builder is more than a text editor. Rather, it is a complete workspace for ColdFusion development, supporting ColdFusion itself and lots of related and supported products and technologies.

ColdFusion is built on top of Eclipse. Eclipse is an open source, Java-based application development environment, and it is used by millions of developers working in all sorts of programming languages. ColdFusion development using Eclipse has long been supported by the ColdFusion community, and now ColdFusion Builder provides an official ColdFusion development environment built on this same trusted platform.

NOTE

> Eclipse is not an Adobe product: it is an open source technology supported by Adobe and many other organizations and individuals. To learn more about Eclipse, visit http://eclipse.org/.

ColdFusion Builder is designed to be installed and used in either of two ways:

- If you have no prior experience with Eclipse and do not have an existing Eclipse installation, then you can just install and use ColdFusion Builder as a standalone application without paying any attention to the Eclipse internals until you are ready to do so.

- If you already use Eclipse (or other Eclipse-based tools, such as Adobe Flash Builder), then ColdFusion Builder can be installed as a plug-in inside that existing Eclipse application. This way, you'll have a single integrated development environment for all projects.

Eclipse is a code-centric tool, and it is designed for experienced coders. Eclipse lacks the design tools that many users love in Adobe Dreamweaver, but by concentrating on just what hard-core coders need, it does a better job of addressing this group's unique requirements.

NOTE

> Adobe Flash Builder is also built on Eclipse. Many ColdFusion developers also write Flex applications, and so Adobe Flash Builder and ColdFusion Builder, both built on Eclipse, can provide a single environment to work on both.

Getting Started with ColdFusion Builder

When you launch ColdFusion Builder, you will see a screen similar to the one in Figure 3.1. (The exact screen layout may differ depending on the operating system you're using and the plug-ins that you have installed.)

NOTE

> Not seeing a screen like the one in Figure 3.1? Depending on how ColdFusion Builder and Eclipse are configured, you may be presented with an Eclipse splash screen. If this is the case, just click the X button in the tab above the splash screen.

A Note About Perspectives

As already noted, ColdFusion Builder is built on Eclipse, and Eclipse can be used for many types of languages and development, and each language has different editor needs. To address all the different requirements of different languages, Eclipse supports a feature called *perspectives*.

A perspective is a simply a group of configuration settings that you can activate as needed. As a rule, when writing ColdFusion code, you'll want to use the ColdFusion perspective. When you start ColdFusion Builder you should automatically be in the ColdFusion perspective, and so more often than not, you can ignore perspectives altogether. But just in case, here's what you need to know.

Figure 3.1

The ColdFusion Builder screen features the editor and supporting panels.

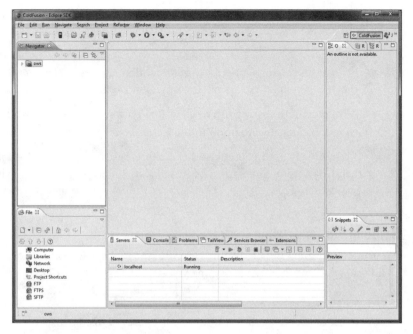

The current perspective is displayed at the top right of the ColdFusion Builder screen. If you see a little CF icon with the word *ColdFusion* next to it, then you should be good to go. If you need to change the current perspective, use the Window > Open Perspective menu options. The Cold-Fusion perspective will be listed under Other. In addition, recently used perspectives are usually displayed at the top right of the screen for easy selection.

The ColdFusion Builder Screen

The ColdFusion Builder screen, seen in Figure 3.1, is divided into paneled sections:

- The Navigator panel (shown on the left in Figure 3.1, though it can be moved elsewhere) is used to browse and open projects and files.

- Beneath the Navigator panel is the File panel, which provides access to folders, files, FTP, and more.

- The top-right side of the screen is a window containing three panels that can be selected by their named tabs. The Outline panel shows the code outline for the open and selected file (and is therefore empty if no file is open). The RDS Dataview panel provides access to all ColdFusion data sources. The RDS Fileview panel provides access to files and folders on the ColdFusion server (this panel is only really of use when you're working with a remote ColdFusion server).

- At the bottom right is the Snippets panel, which can be used to store and access reusable chunks of code.

- The large area in the middle of the screen is the actual ColdFusion Builder editor window. When you are working in a file, CFML toolbars and buttons will be displayed at the top of this area.

- Beneath the editor area is a block containing a series of very important tabs. We'll use the Servers tab in a moment, and others in later chapters.

- At the top of the screen are toolbars and buttons used to open and save files, and more.

TIP

Panels can be moved around and repositioned as desired. For example, I personally like my editor window to be as big as possible, so I moved my Outline and Snippets panels into tabs alongside my File panel, and my two RDS panels into tabs below the editor. Feel free to move panels as you see fit.

Defining the ColdFusion Server

For many ColdFusion Builder features to work, the tool needs to know how to connect to your ColdFusion Server. Thus, the first thing you should do is define your ColdFusion Server.

Here are the steps to define your local ColdFusion Server:

1. Click the Servers tab beneath the editor area. This tab displays a list of defined servers and will initially be empty.

2. Locate the Add Server button in the toolbar right below the tabs; it's the one with a picture of a computer with a yellow + sign on it. Click the Add Server button to display the Add Server window.

3. Select ColdFusion and click OK to display the New ColdFusion Server Setup window (shown in Figure 3.2).

4. Some of the fields in the New ColdFusion Server Setup window apply only to J2EE configuration installations. For typical local ColdFusion development installations, specify the following:

   Server Name: `localhost`

   Host Name: `localhost`

   WebServer Port: `8500`

   RDS Password: The RDS password provided at ColdFusion installation time

5. Click Next to display the Local Server Settings window.

6. In the Server Home field, enter the root of the ColdFusion installation. On Windows computers, the root will usually be `C:\ColdFusion9`. The Document Root field should be filled in automatically (if the Server Home specification is correct). Set the version to `9` (or `9.0.x`).

Figure 3.2

The first thing you should do upon running ColdFusion Builder is define your ColdFusion Server connection.

7. Click Next to display the Install Extensions window.

8. Make sure Install Extensions is checked and click Finish.

   You should see your localhost server now listed on the Servers tab, and the Status area should say Running (indicating that ColdFusion Server is running and ColdFusion Builder can connect to it).

You can verify that ColdFusion Builder is communicating with ColdFusion Server by opening the RDS Dataview tab and expanding the localhost data source entered there. If that data source is present, and if you can expand it to see the tables and their contents, then all is well.

TIP

You can right-click servers listed on the Servers tab to quickly access the ColdFusion Administrator, stop and start ColdFusion, and more.

NOTE

If you develop on multiple ColdFusion servers (perhaps one local, one for testing, and others), you can define each of those ColdFusion servers within ColdFusion Builder. This way, you can write and test using them all.

Creating a Project

ColdFusion development almost never involves a single file. Rather, ColdFusion applications are usually large (and ever growing) collections of files and folders. In ColdFusion Builder, each application you work on is defined as a *project*, and you can define as many projects as you need.

All the lessons in these books build parts of an application for Orange Whip Studios, or OWS. Therefore, we'll create a project named ows. Here are the steps:

1. Locate the ColdFusion Builder File menu and choose File > New > ColdFusion Project to display the New ColdFusion Project window. (You can also right-click in the Navigator panel and choose New > ColdFusion Project.)

2. Specify OWS as the project name.

3. Uncheck the Use Default Location option, and for the Project Location specify the application path (on a Windows computer with the default configuration, the path should be C:\ColdFusion9\wwwroot\OWS). Then click Next.

4. You now need to specify the ColdFusion Server to use for this project. Select Localhost (the server you just defined) from the Servers drop-down list. Then click Next.

5. The final screen will ask you about additional sources and applications. Leave these all as set and click Finish.

You now have a project set up for use with the applications in this book. The new project will automatically be opened in the Navigator panel. If ever the project is not opened, you can open it by right-clicking it in the Navigator panel and choosing Open Project, or by double-clicking it.

Working with Files

Now that you've successfully defined the ows project, here are a few basic file access techniques that you should know.

Creating Folders

To create new folders in ColdFusion Builder, select the folder to contain the new folder, right-click (Windows) or Control-click (Mac), and choose New > Folder. You'll be prompted for the folder name; enter it and then click Finish.

Creating Files

To create new files in ColdFusion Builder, select the folder to contain the new file, right-click (Windows) or Control-click (Mac), and choose New > ColdFusion Page. You'll be prompted for the file name; enter it and then click Finish.

TIP

As explained in Chapter 1, ColdFusion files need a .cfm extension. However, when you enter the file name, you can omit the extension and ColdFusion Builder will add it for you.

Saving, Closing, and Opening Files

To save a file, do one of the following:

■ Press Ctrl-S (Windows) or Command-S (Mac).

- Choose Save from the File menu.
- Click the Save button on the toolbar (it is a picture of a diskette).

To close a file, do one of the following:

- Press Ctrl-W (Windows) or Command-W (Mac).
- Choose Close from the File menu.

TIP

Windows users can press Ctrl-F4 to close an open file.

To open a file, do one of the following:

- Choose Open from the File menu.
- Double-click the file in the Navigator panel.

And with that, you're ready to begin ColdFusion development using ColdFusion Builder.

CHAPTER 4

Previewing ColdFusion

Preparing to Learn ColdFusion

You're just about ready to go. But before you do, you need to know a little about the sample applications you'll be using.

Orange Whip Studio is a low-budget movie studio waiting for its first big break. To help it get there, you need to create a series of Web applications. These include:

- A public Web site that will allow viewers to learn about the movies

- Intranet screens for movie management (budgets, actors, directors, and more)

- A public e-commerce site allowing fans to purchase movie goodies and memorabilia

Your job throughout this book is to build these and other applications.

TIP

Most of the applications created in this book share common resources (images and data, for example) but are actually stand-alone, meaning they don't require components or code created elsewhere. Although this isn't typical of real-world application development, in this book it is deliberate and by design.

Here are a few things you must know about how to manage code and resources:

- You'll create and store the Orange Whip Studio applications in a folder named `ows` beneath the Web root. This is the folder for you created a project in Chapter 3, "Introducing ColdFusion Builder."

- The ows folder contains a folder named `images`, which—this should come as no surprise— contains images used in many of the applications.

- The database used by our application resides in a special folder under the ColdFusion root.

- Web applications are usually organized into a directory structure that maps to application features or sections. However, you won't do that here. To simplify the learning process, you'll create a folder beneath ows for each chapter in the book: 4 for Chapter 4, 5 for Chapter 5, and so on. The files you create in each chapter should go in the appropriate folders.

Assuming you are running ColdFusion locally (this is advised), and assuming you installed the files in the default locations, the URL to access the ows folder will be `http://localhost:8500/ows/` if you're using the integrated HTTP server, or `http://localhost/ows/` if you're using an external HTTP server. You would then access folders beneath ows, such as the folder for this chapter, as `http://localhost:8500/ows/4/` or `http://localhost/ows/4/` (again, depending on whether you're using ColdFusion's integrated HTTP server).

NOTE

Once again, `8500` is the default port used by ColdFusion's integrated Web server. The default port used by the integrated Web server in a JRun/ColdFusion installation is `8300`. If you are using an external Web server (IIS or Apache, for example) then the default port of `80` will likely be used (and can also be entirely omitted from URLs).

TIP

If you have problems resolving host `localhost`, try using IP address `127.0.0.1` instead. `127.0.0.1` is a special IP address that always refers to your own host, and `localhost` is the host name that should always resolve to `127.0.0.1`.

Your First ColdFusion Application

Let's start with a really simple example, just to get comfortable using ColdFusion Builder. Here are the steps:

1. Create a new folder in the ows project named 4 (to indicate Chapter 4, this chapter). (If you need a reminder about how to do this, see section "Working with Files" in Chapter 3).

2. Create a new file in the 4 folder and name it `welcome.cfm`.

3. Your new file will automatically be opened, ready for you to write your code. Enter the following code (don't worry about what it all means just yet; we'll have plenty of time to review CFML in detail in upcoming chapters):

```
It is #DateFormat(Now())#<br>
Welcome to ColdFusion!
```

Notice that as you typed, ColdFusion Builder provided assistance. For example, when you typed the #, the matching # was automatically inserted. Also, notice the automatic color coding, with different language elements colored differently.

4. This code needs to be within `<cfouput>` tags. Select and highlight both lines and then click the Wrap In Cfoutput button above the editor area (it's the fourth button from the left, the one that looks like a computer monitor). ColdFusion Builder will insert the `<cfoutput>` and `</cfoutput>` tags for you. You could also have used the keyboard shortcut Ctrl-Shift-O. And yes, you could have written the tags yourself, of course.

5. Open the Outline panel and see how your code outline has automatically been populated. Expand the list and click each item, noticing what gets selected in the editor window. This particular outline is small and not overly useful, but as your code grows in length and complexity, the Outline panel provides an easy way to see how tags are nested and allows you to click elements to quickly jump to them.

6. Run the code. Look at the bottom of the editor window area. You'll see a series of tabs. The leftmost one is named Source, and it is currently selected. To the right you'll see one or more tabs with names of Web browsers (Internet Explorer, Firefox, and others, depending on your operating system and on the browsers you have installed). Click a browser tab to run your code in that browser. You should see a welcome message containing today's date.

TIP

Experienced developers regularly test their code in multiple Web browsers, just to make sure everything works properly regardless of the browser used.

ColdFusion Builder lets you run your applications right within the development environment using embedded Web browsers. But, of course, you can also test your code using an actual Web browser. For example, to run welcome.cfm in your Web browser, open that browser, and go to `http://localhost:8500/ows/4/welcome.cfm`.

A More Complete Example

Here is a more complete example, one that is composed of multiple files (as is usually the case). I won't go into the details of the code itself; for now, concentrate on creating and executing CFM files so they work. If you can get all these to function, you'll have a much easier time working through the book.

The `bday` application is really simple; it prompts you for your name and date of birth and calculates your age, using simple date arithmetic. The application is made up of two files:

- `bday1.cfm` (shown in Listing 4.1) is the form that prompts for the name and date of birth.
- `bday2.cfm` (shown in Listing 4.2) processes the form and displays the results.

Using Dreamweaver, create these two new files, saving them both in the 4 directory. Then enter the code that follows in each file exactly as it appears here—your files should contain this code and nothing else.

Listing 4.1 bday1.cfm

```
<html>
<body>
<form action="bday2.cfm" method="post">
Name: <input type="text" name="name">
<br>
Date of birth: <input type="text" name="dob">
<br>
<input type="submit" value="calculate">
</form>
</body>
</html>
```

The code in bday1.cfm is simple HTML—there's no ColdFusion code at all. In fact, you could have named the file with an .html extension and it would have worked properly.

bday1.cfm contains an HTML form with two form fields: name for the username and dob for the date of birth.

Listing 4.2 bday2.cfm

```
<html>
<body>
<cfoutput>
Hello #FORM.name#,
you are #DateDiff("YYYY", FORM.dob, Now())#.
</cfoutput>
</body>
</html>
```

The code in bday2.cfm is a mixture of HTML and CFML. The name form field displays the Hello message, and the dob field calculates the age.

To try the application, run file bday1.cfm. (Don't run file bday2.cfm or you'll receive an error message.) You can run it either within ColdFusion Builder (just click the browser tab below the editor) or in your Web browser at the following URL:

```
http://localhost:8500/ows/4/bday1.cfm
```

NOTE

If you aren't using the integrated HTTP server, adjust the URL accordingly.

A form will prompt you for your name and date of birth. Fill in the two fields, and then click the form submission button to display your age.

Browsing the Examples and Tutorials

ColdFusion comes with extensive examples, tutorials, and help. These are installed along with ColdFusion (assuming that they were actually selected during the installation). The Getting Started applications are available via links in the ColdFusion Administrator welcome screen.

Two of the options on this page deserve special mention:

- Select Explore Real-World Example Applications to browse two applications that demonstrate lots of ColdFusion functionality, along with the code used to build them.

- Select Code Snippets by Feature and Task to display a Code Snippet Explorer that provides you with instant access to ColdFusion code used to perform various tasks, as well as narrated and interactive tutorials.

Conclusion

Hopefully this chapter has given you a taste for what is to come. But before we continue learning ColdFusion, we need to take a little detour into the world of databases and SQL.

CHAPTER **5**

Reviewing the Databases

Database Fundamentals

You have just been assigned a project: you must create and maintain a list of all the movies produced by your employer, Orange Whip Studios.

What do you use to maintain this list? Your first thought might be to use a word processor. You could create the list, one movie per line, and manually enter each movie's name so the list is alphabetical and usable. Your word processor provides you with sophisticated document-editing capabilities, so adding, removing, or updating movies is no more complicated than editing any other document.

Initially, you might think you have found the perfect solution—that is, until someone asks you to sort the list by release date and then alphabetically for each date. Now you must re-create the entire list, again sorting the movies manually and inserting them in the correct sequence. You end up with two lists to maintain. You must add new movies to both lists and possibly remove movies from both lists as well. You also discover that correcting mistakes or even just making changes to your list has become more complicated because you must make every change twice. Still, the list is manageable. You have only the two word-processed documents to be concerned with, and you can even open them both at the same time and make edits simultaneously.

The word processor isn't the perfect solution, but it's still a manageable solution—that is, until someone else asks for the list sorted by director. As you fire up your word processor yet again, you review the entire list-management process in your mind. New movies must now be added to all three lists. Likewise, any deletions must be made to the three lists. If a movie tag line changes, you must change all three lists.

And then, just as you think you have the entire process worked out, your face pales and you freeze. What if someone else wants the list sorted by rating? And then, what if yet another department needs the list sorted in some other way? You panic, break out in a sweat, and tell yourself, "There must be a better way!"

This example is a bit extreme, but the truth is that a better way really does exist. You need to use a database.

Databases: A Definition

Let's start with a definition. A *database* is simply a structured collection of similar data. The important words here are *structured* and *similar*, and the movie list is a perfect example of both.

Imagine the movie list as a two-dimensional grid or table, similar to that shown in Figure 5.1. Each horizontal row in the table contains information about a single movie. The rows are broken up by vertical columns. Each column contains a single part of the movie record. The `MovieTitle` column contains movie titles, and so on.

Figure 5.1

Databases display data in an imaginary two-dimensional grid.

Movies

Movie Title	Rating	Budget
Being Unbearably Light	5	300000
Charlie's Devils	1	750000
Closet Encounters of the Odd Kind	5	350000
Four Bar-Mitzvahs and a Circumcision	1	175000

The movie list contains similar data for all movies. Every movie record, or row, contains the same type of information. Each has a title, tag line, budget amount, and so on. The data is also structured in that the data can be broken into logical columns, or fields, that contain a single part of the movie record.

Here's the rule of thumb: any list of information that can be broken into similar records of structured fields should probably be maintained in a database. Product prices, phone directories, invoices, invoice line items, vacation schedules, and lists of actors and directors are all database candidates.

Where Are Databases Used?

You probably use databases all the time, often without knowing it. If you use a software-based accounting program, you are using a database. All accounts payable, accounts receivable, vendor, and customer information is stored in databases. Scheduling programs use databases to store appointments and to-do lists. Even email programs use databases for directory lists and folders.

These databases are designed to be hidden from you, the end user. You never add accounts receivable invoice records into a database yourself. Rather, you enter information into your accounting program, and it adds records to the database.

Clarification of Database-Related Terms

Now that you understand what a database is, I must clarify some important database terms for you. In the SQL world (you will learn about SQL in depth in Chapter 6, "Introducing SQL"), this collection of data is called a *table*. The individual records in a table are called *rows*, and the fields that make up the rows are called *columns*. A collection of tables is called a *database*.

Picture a filing cabinet. The cabinet houses drawers, each of which contains groups of data. The cabinet is a way to keep related but dissimilar information in one place. Each cabinet drawer contains a set of records. One drawer might contain employee records, and another drawer might contain sales records. The individual records within each drawer are different, but they all contain the same type of data, in fields.

The filing cabinet shown in Figure 5.2 is the database—a collection of drawers or tables containing related but dissimilar information. Each drawer contains one or more records, or rows, made up of different fields, or columns.

Figure 5.2

Databases store information in tables, columns, and rows, the way records are filed in a filing cabinet.

Data Types

Each row in a database table is made up of one or more columns. Each column contains a single piece of data, part of the complete record stored in the row. When a table is created, each of its columns needs to be defined. Defining columns involves specifying the column's name, size, and data type. The data type specifies what data can be stored in a column.

Data types specify the characteristics of a column and instruct the database as to what kind of data can be entered into it. Some data types allow the entry of free-form alphanumeric data. Others restrict data entry to specific data, such as numbers, dates, or true or false flags. A list of common data types is shown in Table 5.1.

Table 5.1   Common Database Data Types and How They Are Used

DATA TYPE	RESTRICTIONS	TYPICAL USE
Character	Upper and lowercase text, numbers, symbols	Names, addresses, descriptions
Numeric	Positive and negative numbers, decimal points	Quantities, numbers
Date	Dates, times	Dates, times
Money	Positive and negative numbers, decimal points	Prices, billing amounts, invoice line items
Boolean	Yes and No or True and False	On/off flags, switches
Binary	Nontext data	Pictures, sound, and video data

There are several reasons for using data types, instead of just entering all data into simple text fields. One of the main reasons is to control or restrict the data a user can enter into that field. A field that has to contain a person's age, for example, could be specified as a numeric field. This way, the user can't enter letters into it—only the digits 0 through 9. This restriction helps keep invalid data out of your database.

Various data types are also used to control how data is sorted. Data entered in a text field is sorted one character at a time, as if it were left justified. The digit 0 comes before 1, which comes before 9, which comes before a, and so on. Because each character is evaluated individually, a text field containing the number 10 is listed after 1 but before 2 because 10 is greater than 1 but less than 2, just as a 0 is greater than a but less than b. If the value being stored in this column is a person's age, correctly sorting the table by that column would be impossible. Data entered into a numeric field, however, is evaluated by looking at the complete value rather than a character at a time; 10 is considered greater than 2. Figure 5.3 shows how data is sorted if numbers are entered into a text field.

Figure 5.3

Unless you use the correct data type, data may not be sorted the way you want.

1000
2
248
39
7

The same is true for date fields. Dates in these fields are evaluated one character at a time, from left to right. The date 02/05/07 is considered less than the date 10/12/99 because the first character of the date 02/05/07—the digit 0—is less than the first character of the date 10/12/99—the digit 1. If the same data is entered in a date field, the database evaluates the date as a complete entity and therefore sorts the dates correctly.

The final reason for using various data types is the storage space that plain-text fields take up. A text field big enough to accommodate up to 10 characters takes up 10 bytes of storage. Even if only

2 characters are entered into the field, 10 bytes are still stored. The extra space is reserved for possible future updates to that field. Some types of data can be stored more efficiently when not treated as text. For example, a 4-byte numeric field can store numeric values from 0 to over 4,000,000,000! Storing 4,000,000,000 in a text field requires 10 bytes of storage. Similarly, a 4-byte date/time field can store the date and time with accuracy to the minute. Storing that same information in a text field would take a minimum of 14 bytes or as many as 20 bytes, depending on how the data is formatted.

TIP

In addition to what has been said about picking the appropriate data types, it's important to note that picking the wrong type can have a significant impact on performance.

NOTE

Different database applications use different terms to describe the same data type. For example, Microsoft Access uses the term text to describe a data type that allows the entry of all alphanumeric data. Microsoft SQL Server calls this same data type char and uses text to describe variable-length text fields. After you determine the type of data you want a column to contain, refer to your database application's manuals to ensure that you use the correct term when making data type selections.

When you're designing a database, you should give careful consideration to data types. You usually can't easily change the type of a field after the table is created. If you do have to change the type, you might have to create a new table and write routines to convert the data from one table to the new one.

Planning the size of fields is equally important. With most databases, you can't change the size of a field after the table is created. Getting the size right the first time and allowing some room for growth can save you much aggravation later.

CAUTION

When you're determining the size of data fields, always try to anticipate future growth. If you're defining a field for phone numbers, for example, realize that not all phone numbers follow the three-digit area code plus seven-digit phone number convention used in the United States and Canada. Paris, France, for example, has eight-digit phone numbers, and area codes in small towns in England can contain four or five digits.

Using a Database

Back to the example. At this point, you have determined that a film database will make your job easier and might even help preserve your sanity. You create a table with columns for movie title, tag line, release date, and the rest of the required data. You enter your movie list into the table, one row at a time, and are careful to put the correct data in each column.

Next, you instruct the database application to sort the list by movie title. The list is sorted in a second or less, and you print it out. Impressed, you try additional sorts—by rating and by budgeted amount.

You now have two or more lists, but you had to enter the information only once; because you were careful to break the records into multiple columns, you can sort or search the list in any way necessary. You just need to reprint the lists whenever your records are added, edited, or deleted. And the new or changed data is automatically sorted for you.

A Database Primer

You have just seen a practical use for a database. The movie list is a simple database that involves a single table and a small set of columns. Most well-designed database applications require many tables and ways to link them. You'll revisit the movie list when we discuss relational databases.

Your first table was a hit. You have been able to accommodate any list request, sorted any way anyone could need. But just as you are beginning to wonder what you're going to do with all your newfound spare time, your boss informs you that he'll need reports sorted by the director name.

"No problem," you say. You open your database application and modify your table. You add two new columns, one for the director's first name and one for the last name. Now, every movie record can contain the name of the director, and you even create a report of all movies including director information. Once again, you and your database have saved the day, and all is well—or so you think.

Just when things are looking good, you get a memo asking you to include movie expenses in your database so as to be able to run reports containing this information.

You think for a few moments and come up with two solutions to this new problem. The first solution is simply to add lots more columns to the table, three for each expenses item (date, description, and amount).

But you realize this isn't a long-term solution at all. How many expenses should you allow space for? Every movie can, and likely will, have a different set of expenses, and you have no way of knowing how many you should accommodate for. Inevitably, whatever number you pick won't be enough at some point. In addition, adding all these extra columns, which won't be used by most records, is a tremendous waste of disk space. Furthermore, data manipulation becomes extremely complicated if data is stored in more than one column. If you need to search for specific expenses, you'd have to search multiple columns. This situation greatly increases the chance of incorrect results. It also makes sorting data impossible because databases sort data one column at a time, and you have data that must be sorted together spread over multiple columns.

NOTE
An important rule in database design is that if columns are seldom used by most rows, they probably don't belong in the table.

Your second solution is to create additional rows in the table, one for each expense for each movie. With this solution, you can add as many expenses as necessary without creating extra columns.

This solution, though, isn't workable. Although it does indeed solve the problem of handling more than a predetermined number of expenses, doing so introduces a far greater problem. Adding additional rows requires repeating the basic movie information—things such as title and tag line—over and over, for each new row.

Not only does reentering this information waste storage space, it also greatly increases the likelihood of your being faced with conflicting data. If a movie title changes, for example, you must be sure to change every row that contains that movie's data. Failing to update all rows would result in queries and searches returning conflicting results. If you do a search for a movie and find two rows, each of which has different ratings, how would you know which is correct?

This problem probably isn't too serious if the conflicting data is the spelling of a name, but imagine that the data is customer-billing information. If you reenter a customer's address with each order and then the customer moves, you could end up shipping orders to an incorrect address.

You should avoid maintaining multiple live copies of the same data whenever possible.

NOTE
> Another important rule in database design is that data should never be repeated unnecessarily. As you multiply the number of copies you have of the same data, the chance of data-entry errors also multiplies.

TIP
> One point worth mentioning here is that the "never duplicate data" rule does not apply to backups of your data. Backing up data is incredibly important, and you can never have too many backup plans. The rule of never duplicating data applies only to live data—data to be used in a production environment on an ongoing basis.

And while you are thinking about it, you realize that even your earlier solution for including director names is dangerous. After all, what if a movie has two directors? You've allocated room for only one name.

Understanding Relational Databases

The solution to your problem is to break the movie list into multiple tables. Let's start with the movie expenses.

The first table, the movie list, remains just that—a movie list. To link movies to other records, you add one new column to the list, a column containing a unique identifier for each movie. It might be an assigned movie number or a sequential value that is incremented as each new movie is added to the list. The important thing is that no two movies have the same ID.

TIP
> It's generally a good idea never to reuse record-unique identifiers. If the movie with ID number 105 is deleted, for example, that number should never be reassigned to a new movie. This policy guarantees that there is no chance of the new movie record getting linked to data that belonged to the old movie.

Next, you create a new table with several columns: movie ID, expense date, expense description, and expense amount. As long as a movie has no associated expenses, the second table—the expenses table—remains empty. When an expense is incurred, a row is added to the expenses table. The row contains the movie that uniquely identifies this specific movie and the expense information.

The point here is that no movie information is stored in the expenses table except for that movie ID, which is the same movie ID assigned in the movie list table. How do you know which movie the record is referring to when expenses are reported? The movie information is retrieved from the movie list table. When displaying rows from the expenses table, the database relates the row back to the movie list table and grabs the movie information from there. This relationship is shown later in this chapter, in Figure 5.4.

Figure 5.4

The foreign key values in one table are always primary key values in another table, which allows tables to be *related* to each other.

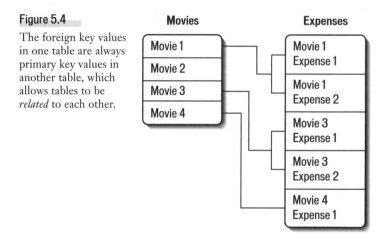

This database design is called a *relational database*. With it you can store data in various tables and then define *links*, or *relationships*, to find associated data stored in other tables in the database. In this example, a movie with two expenses would have two rows in the expenses table. Both of these rows contain the same movie ID, and therefore both refer to the same movie record in the movie table.

NOTE
The process of breaking up data into multiple tables to ensure that data is never duplicated is called normalization.

Primary and Foreign Keys

Primary key is the database term for the column(s) that contains values that uniquely identify each row. A primary key is usually a single column, but doesn't have to be.

There are only two requirements for primary keys:

- **Every row must have a value in the primary key.** Empty fields, sometimes called null fields, are not allowed.

- **Primary key values can never be duplicated.** If two movies were to have the same ID, all relationships would fail. In fact, most database applications prevent you from entering duplicate values in primary key fields.

When you are asked for a list of all expenses sorted by movie, you can instruct the database to build the relationship and retrieve the required data. The movie table is scanned in alphabetical order, and as each movie is retrieved, the database application checks the expenses table for any rows that have a movie ID matching the current primary key. You can even instruct the database to ignore the movies that have no associated expenses and retrieve only those that have related rows in the expenses table.

TIP

Many database applications support a feature that can be used to auto-generate primary key values. Microsoft Access refers to this as an Auto Number field, SQL Server uses the term Identity, and other databases use other terms for essentially the same thing. Using this feature, a correct and safe primary key is automatically generated every time a new row is added to the table.

NOTE

Not all data types can be used as primary keys. You can't use columns with data types for storing binary data, such as sounds, images, variable-length records, or OLE links, as primary keys.

The movie ID column in the expenses table isn't a primary key. The values in that column are not unique if any movie has more than one expense listed. All records of a specific movie's expenses contain the same movie ID. The movie ID is a primary key in a different table—the movie table. This is a *foreign key*. A foreign key is a non-unique key whose values are contained within a primary key in another table.

To see how the foreign key is used, assume that you have been asked to run a report to see which movies incurred expenses on a specific date. To do so, you instruct the database application to scan the expenses table for all rows with expenses listed on that date. The database application uses the value in the expenses table's movie ID foreign key field to find the name of the movie; it does so by using the movie table's primary key. This relationship is shown in Figure 5.4.

The relational database model helps overcome scalability problems. A database that can handle an ever-increasing amount of data without having to be redesigned is said to *scale well*. You should always take scalability into consideration when designing databases.

Now you've made a significant change to your original database, but what you've created is a manageable and scalable solution. Your boss is happy once again, and your database management skills have saved the day.

Different Kinds of Relationships

The type of relationship discussed up to this point is called a *one-to-many* relationship. This kind of relationship allows an association between a single row in one table and multiple rows in another table. In the example, a single row in the movie list table can be associated with many rows in the expenses table. The one-to-many relationship is the most common type of relationship in a relational database.

Two other types of relational database relationships exist: one-to-one and many-to-many.

The *one-to-one relationship* allows a single row in one table to be associated with no more than one row in another table. This type of relationship is used infrequently. In practice, if you run into a situation in which a one-to-one relationship is called for, you should probably revisit the design. Most tables that are linked with one-to-one relationships can simply be combined into one large table.

The *many-to-many relationship* is also used infrequently. The many-to-many relationship allows one or more rows in one table to be associated with one or more rows in another table. This type of relationship is usually the result of bad design. Most many-to-many relationships can be more efficiently managed with multiple one-to-many relationships.

Multi-Table Relationships

Now that you understand relational databases, let's look at the directors problem again. You will recall that the initial solution was to add the directors directly into the movie table, but that was not a viable solution because it would not allow for multiple directors in a single movie.

Actually, an even bigger problem exists with the suggested solution. As I said earlier, relational database design dictates that data never be repeated. If the director's name was listed with the movie, any director who directed more than one movie would be listed more than once.

Unlike expenses—which are always associated with a single movie—directors can be associated with multiple movies, and movies can be associated with multiple directors. Two tables won't help here.

The solution to this type of relationship problem is to use three database tables:

- Movies are listed in their own table, and each movie has a unique ID.

- Directors are listed in their own table, and each director has a unique ID.

- A new third table is added, which relates the two previous tables.

For example, if movie number 105 was directed by director ID number 3, a single row would be added to the third table. It would contain two foreign keys, the primary keys of each of the movie and director tables. To find out who directed movie number 105, all you'd have to do is look at that third table for movie number 105 and you'd find that director 3 was the director. Then, you'd look at the directors table to find out who director 3 is.

That might sound overly complex for a simple mapping, but bear with me—this is all about to make a lot of sense.

If movie number 105 had a second director (perhaps director ID 5), all you would need to do is add a second row to that third table. This new row would also contain 105 in the movie ID column, but it would contain a different director ID in the director column. Now you can associate two, three, or more directors with each movie. You associate each director with a movie by simply adding one more record to that third table.

And if you wanted to find all movies directed by a specific director, you could do that too. First, you'd find the ID of the director in the directors table. Then, you'd search that third table for all movie IDs associated with the director. Finally, you'd scan the movies table for the names of those movies.

This type of multi-table relationship is often necessary in larger applications, and you'll be using it later in this chapter. Figure 5.5 summarizes the relationships used.

Figure 5.5

To relate multiple rows to multiple rows, you should use a three-way relational table design.

To summarize, two tables are used if the rows in one table might be related to multiple rows in a second table and when rows in the second table are only related to single rows in the first table. If rows in both tables might be related to multiple rows, however, three tables must be used.

Indexes

Database applications make extensive use of a table's primary key whenever relationships are used. It's therefore vital that accessing a specific row by primary key value be fast. When data is added to a table, you have no guarantee that the rows are stored in any specific order. A row with a higher primary key value could be stored before a row with a lower value. Don't make any assumptions about the actual physical location of any rows within your table.

Now take another look at the relationship between the movie list table and the expenses table. You have the database scan the expenses table to learn which movies have incurred expenses on specific dates; only rows containing that date are selected. This operation, however, returns only the movie IDs—the foreign key values. To determine to which movies these rows are referring, you have the database check the movie list table. Specific rows are selected—the rows that have this movie ID as their primary-key values.

To find a specific row by primary-key value, you could have the database application sequentially read through the entire table. If the first row stored is the one needed, the sequential read is terminated. If not, the next row is read, and then the next, until the desired primary key value is retrieved.

This process might work for small sets of data. Sequentially scanning hundreds, or even thousands of rows is a relatively fast operation, particularly for a fast computer with plenty of available system memory. As the number of rows increases, however, so does the time it takes to find a specific row.

The problem of finding specific data quickly in an unsorted list isn't limited to databases. Suppose you're reading a book on mammals and are looking for information on cats. You could start on the first page of the book and read everything, looking for the word *cat*. This approach might work if you have just a few pages to search through, but as the number of pages grows, so does the difficulty of locating specific words and the likelihood that you will make mistakes and miss references.

To solve this problem, books have indexes. An index allows rapid access to specific words or topics spread throughout the book. Although the words or topics referred to in the index are not in any sorted order, the index itself is. *Cat* is guaranteed to appear in the index somewhere after *bison*, but before *cow*. To find all references to *cat*, you would first search the index. Searching the index is a quick process because the list is sorted. You don't have to read as far as *dog* if the word you're looking for is *cat*. When you find *cat* in the index list, you also find the page numbers where cats are discussed.

Databases use indexes in much the same way. Database indexes serve the same purpose as book indexes—allowing rapid access to unsorted data. Just as book indexes list words or topics alphabetically to facilitate the rapid location of data, so do database table indexes list the values indexed in a sorted order. Just as book indexes list page numbers for each index listing, database table indexes list the physical location of the matching rows, as shown in Figure 5.6. After the database application knows the physical location of a specific row, it can retrieve that row without having to scan every row in the table.

Figure 5.6

Database indexes are lists of rows and where they appear in a table.

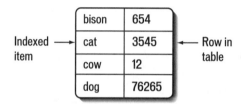

There are two important differences between an index at the back of a book and an index to a database table. First, an index to a database table is *dynamic*. This means that every time a row is added to a table, the index is automatically modified to reflect this change. Likewise, if a row is updated or deleted, the index is updated to reflect this change. As a result, the index is always up to date and always useful. Second, unlike a book index, the table index is never explicitly browsed by the end user. Instead, when the database application is instructed to retrieve data, it uses the index to determine how to complete the request quickly and efficiently.

The database application maintains the index and is the only one to use it. You, the end user, never actually see the index in your database, and in fact, most modern database applications hide the actual physical storage location of the index altogether.

When you create a primary key for a table, it's automatically indexed. The database assumes the primary key will be used constantly for lookups and relationships and therefore does you the favor of creating that first index automatically.

When you run a report against the expenses table to find particular entries, the following process occurs. First, the database application scans the expenses table to find any rows that match the desired date. This process returns the IDs of any matching expenses. Next, the database application retrieves the matching movie for each expense row it has retrieved. It searches the primary key index to find the matching movie record in the movie list table. The index contains all movie IDs in order and, for each ID, lists the physical location of the required row. After the database application finds the correct index value, it obtains a row location from the index and then jumps directly to that location in the table. Although this process might look involved on paper, it actually happens very quickly and in less time than any sequential search would take.

Using Indexes

Now revisit your movies database. Movie production is up, and the number of movies in your movies table has grown, too. Lately, you've noticed that database operations are taking longer than they used to. The alphabetical movie list report takes considerably longer to run, and performance drops further as more movies are added to the table. The database design was supposed to be a scalable solution, so why is the additional data bringing the system to its knees?

The solution here is the introduction of additional indexes. The database application automatically creates an index for the primary key. Any additional indexes have to be explicitly defined. To improve sorting and searching by rating, you just need an index on the rating column. With this index, the database application can instantly find the rows it's looking for without having to sequentially read through the entire table.

The maximum number of indexes a table can have varies from one database application to another. Some databases have no limit at all and allow every column to be indexed. That way, all searches or sorts can benefit from the faster response time.

CAUTION

Some database applications limit the number of indexes any table can have. Before you create dozens of indexes, check to see whether you should be aware of any limitations.

Before you run off and create indexes for every column in your table, you have to realize the trade-off. As we saw earlier, a database table index is dynamic, unlike an index at the end of a book. As data changes, so do the indexes—and updating indexes takes time. The more indexes a table has, the longer write operations take. Furthermore, each index takes up additional storage space, so unnecessary indexes waste valuable disk space.

So when should you create an index? The answer is entirely up to you. Adding indexes to a table makes read operations faster and write operations slower. You have to decide the number of indexes to create and which columns to index for each application. Applications that are used primarily for data entry have less need for indexes. Applications that are used heavily for searching and reporting can definitely benefit from additional indexes.

In our example, you should probably index the movie list table by rating because you often will be sorting and searching by movie rating. Likewise, the release date column might be a candidate for indexing. But you will seldom need to sort by movie summary, so there's no reason to index the summary column. You still can search or sort by summary if the need arises, but the search will take longer than a rating search. Whether you add indexes is up to you and your determination of how the application will be used.

TIP

With many database applications, you can create and drop indexes as needed. You might decide that you want to create additional temporary indexes before running a batch of infrequently used reports. They enable you to run your reports more quickly. You can drop the new indexes after you finish running the reports, which restores the table to its previous state. The only downside to doing so is that write operations are slower while the additional indexes are present. This slowdown might or might not be a problem; again, the decision is entirely up to you.

Indexing on More than One Column

Often, you might find yourself sorting data on more than one column; an example is indexing on last name plus first name. Your directors table might have more than one director with the same last name. To correctly display the names, you need to sort on last name plus first name. This way, Jack Smith always appears before Jane Smith, who always appears before John Smith.

Indexing on two columns—such as last name plus first name—isn't the same as creating two separate indexes (one for last name and one for first name). You have not created an index for the first name column itself. The index is of use only when you're searching or sorting the last name column, or both the last name and first name.

As with all indexes, indexing more than one column often can be beneficial, but this benefit comes with a cost. Indexes that span multiple columns take longer to maintain and take up more disk space. Here, too, you should be careful to create only indexes that are necessary and justifiable.

Understanding the Various Types of Database Applications

All the information described to this point applies equally to all databases. The basic fundamentals of databases, tables, keys, and indexes are supported by all database applications. At some point, however, databases start to differ—in price, performance, features, security, scalability, and more.

One decision you should make very early in the process is whether to use a *shared-file* database, such as Microsoft Access, or a *client-server* database application, such as Microsoft SQL Server and Oracle. Each has advantages and disadvantages, and the key to determining which will work best for you is understanding the difference between shared-file database applications and client-server systems.

Shared-File Databases

Databases such as Microsoft Access and FileMaker are shared-file databases. They store their data in data files that are shared by multiple users. These data files usually are stored on network drives so they are easily accessible to all users who need them, as shown in Figure 5.7.

Figure 5.7

The data files in a Shared-File database are accessed by all users directly.

PC Running
Microsoft Access

File Server
With Shared
Data File

PC Running
Microsoft Access

PC Running
Microsoft Access

When you access data from a Microsoft Access table, for example, that data file is opened on your computer. Any data you read is also read by Microsoft Access running on your computer. Likewise, any data changes are made locally by the copy of Microsoft Access running on your computer.

Considering this point is important when you're evaluating shared-file database applications. The fact that every running copy of Microsoft Access has the data files open locally has serious implications:

- **Shared data files are susceptible to data corruption.** Each user accessing the tables has the data files open locally. If the user fails to terminate the application correctly or the computer hangs, those files don't close gracefully. Abruptly closing data files like this can corrupt the file or cause garbage data to be written to it.

- **Shared data files create a great deal of unnecessary network traffic.** If you perform a search for specific expenses, the search takes place on your own computer. The database application running on your computer has to determine which rows it wants and which it does not. The application has to know of all the records—including those it will discard for this particular query—for this determination to occur. Those discarded records have to travel to your computer over a network connection. Because the data is discarded anyway, unnecessary network traffic is created.

- **Shared data files are insecure.** Because users have to open the actual data files they intend to work with, they must have full access to those files. This also means that users can either intentionally or accidentally delete the entire data file with all its tables.

This isn't to say that you should never use shared-file databases. The following are some reasons to use this type of database:

- **Shared-file databases are inexpensive.** Unless you choose an open source database such as MySQL, the software itself costs far less than client-server database software. And unlike client-server software, shared-file databases don't require dedicated hardware for database servers.

- **Shared-file databases are easier** to learn and use than client-server databases.

Client-Server Databases

Databases such as Microsoft SQL Server, Oracle, and MySQL are client-server databases. Client-server applications are split into two distinct parts. The *server* portion is a piece of software that is responsible for all data access and manipulation. This software runs on a computer called the *database server*. In the case of Microsoft SQL Server, it's a computer running Windows and the SQL Server software.

Only the server software interacts with the data files. All requests for data, data additions and deletions, and data updates are funneled through the server software. These requests or changes come from computers running client software. The *client* is the piece of software the user interacts with. If you request a list of movies sorted by rating, for example, the client software submits that request over the network to the server software. The server software processes the request; it filters, discards, and sorts data as necessary, and sends the results back to your client software. This process is illustrated in Figure 5.8.

Figure 5.8

Client-server databases enable clients to perform database operations that are processed by the server software.

PC Running Database Client   Database Server   PC Running Microsoft Access   PC Running Database Client

Data

All this action occurs transparently to you, the user. The fact that data is stored elsewhere or that a database server is even performing all this processing for you is hidden. You never need to access the data files directly. In fact, most networks are set up so that users have no access to the data, or even the drives on which it's stored.

Client-server database servers overcome the limitations of shared-file database applications in the following ways:

- **Client-server database files are less susceptible to data corruption caused by incorrect application termination.** If a user fails to exit a program gracefully, or if their computer locks up, the data files do not get damaged. That is because the files are never actually open on that user's computer.

- **Client-server database servers use less network bandwidth.** Because all data filtering occurs on the server side, all unnecessary data is discarded before the results are sent back to the client software. Only the necessary data is transmitted over the network.

- **End users in a client-server database environment need never have access to the actual physical data files.** This lack of access helps ensure that the files are not deleted or tampered with.

- **Client-server databases offer greater performance.** This is true of the actual database server itself. In addition, client-server databases often have features not available in shared-file databases that can provide even greater performance.

As you can see, client-server databases are more secure and more robust than shared-file databases—but all that extra power and security comes with a price:

- **Running client-server databases is expensive.** The software itself is far more expensive than shared-file database applications. In addition, you need a database server to run a client-server database. It must be a high-powered computer that is often dedicated for just this purpose.

- **Client-server databases are more difficult to set up, configure, and administer.** Many companies hire full-time database administrators to do this job.

Which Database Product to Use?

Now that you have learned the various types of database systems you can use, how do you determine which is right for your application?

Unfortunately, this question has no simple answer. You really need to review your application needs, the investment you are willing to make in the system, and which systems you already have in place.

To get started, try to answer as many of the following questions as possible:

- Do you have an existing database system in place? If yes, is it current technology that is still supported by the vendor? Do you need to link to data in this system, or are you embarking on a new project that can stand on its own feet?

- Do you have any database expertise or experience? If yes, with which database systems are you familiar?

- Do you have database programmers or administrators in-house? If yes, with which systems are they familiar?

- How many users do you anticipate will use the system concurrently?

- How many records do you anticipate your tables will contain?

- How important is database uptime? What is the cost associated with your database being down for any amount of time?

- Do you have existing hardware that can be used for a database server?

These questions are not easy to answer, but the effort is well worth your time. The more planning you do up front, the better chance you have of making the right decision. Getting the job done right the first time will save you time, money, and aggravation later.

Of course, there is no way you can anticipate all future needs. At some point you might, in fact, need to switch databases. If you ever have to migrate from one database to another, contact the database vendor to determine which migration tools are available. As long as you select known and established solutions from reputable vendors, you should be safe.

TIP

As a rule, shared-file databases should never be used on production servers. Most developers opt to use client-server databases for production applications because of the added security and scalability. But shared-file databases are often used on development and testing machines because they are cheaper and easier to use. This is a good compromise, and one that is highly recommended if it isn't possible to run client-server databases on all machines—client-server on production machines, shared-file on development machines (if necessary).

ColdFusion comes with a built-in DBMS called Apache Derby (a free, open source, Java application). Derby can be used in two ways: as a file-based database that uses local files (this is called Apache Derby Embedded) and as a client-server database that accesses a Derby server. The database for all examples in this book uses Apache Derby Embedded.

Understanding the OWS Database Tables

Now that you've reviewed the important database fundamentals, let's walk through the tables used in the Orange Whip Studios application (the database you'll be using throughout this book).

NOTE

Tables and table creation scripts for additional databases can be found on the book Web site at
`http://www.forta.com/ books/032151548X`.

The database is made up of 12 tables, all of which are related.

NOTE

What follows isn't a complete definition of the tables; it's a summary intended to provide a quick reference that will be of use to you when building the applications. You might want to bookmark this page for future reference.

→   See Appendix B, "Sample Application Data Files," for a more thorough description of the tables used.

The Films Table

The Films table (Table 5.2) contains the movies list. The primary key for this table is the FilmID column.

This table contains a single foreign key:

- The RatingID column is related to the primary key of the FilmsRatings table.

Table 5.2   The Films Table

COLUMN	DATA TYPE	DESCRIPTION AND SIZE
FilmID	Numeric	Unique ID for each movie; can be populated manually when rows are inserted or automatically (if defined as an Auto Number field)
MovieTitle	Text	Movie title
PitchText	Text	Movie pitch text; the tag line

Table 5.2 (CONTINUED)

COLUMN	DATA TYPE	DESCRIPTION AND SIZE
AmountBudgeted	Numeric, currency	Amount budgeted for movie (may not be equal to the actual cost plus expenses)
RatingID	Numeric	ID of associated rating in the FilmsRatings table
Summary	Memo or long text	Full movie summary stored in a variable-length text field (to enable longer summaries)
ImageName	Text	File name of associated image (if there is one)
DateInTheaters	Date	Expected movie release date

The Expenses Table

The Expenses table (Table 5.3) contains the expenses associated with any movies listed in the Films table.

Table 5.3 The Expenses Table

COLUMN	DATA TYPE	DESCRIPTION AND SIZE
ExpenseID	Numeric	Unique ID for each expense; can be populated manually when rows are inserted or automatically (if defined as an Auto Number field)
FilmID	Numeric	ID of associated movie
ExpenseAmount	Numeric, or currency	Expense amount
Description	Text	Expense description
ExpenseDate	Date	Expense date

The primary key for this table is the ExpenseID column.

This table contains a single foreign key:

- The FilmID column is related to the primary key of the Films table.

The Directors Table

The Directors table (Table 5.4) contains the list of directors. This table is related to the Films table via the FilmsDirectors table.

Table 5.4 The Directors Table

COLUMN	DATA TYPE	DESCRIPTION AND SIZE
DirectorID	Numeric	Unique ID for each director; can be populated manually when rows are inserted or automatically (if defined as an Auto Number field)

Table 5.4 (CONTINUED)

COLUMN	DATA TYPE	DESCRIPTION AND SIZE
FirstName	Text	Director's first name
LastName	Text	Director's last name

The primary key for this table is the DirectorID column.

This table contains no foreign keys.

The FilmsDirectors Table

The FilmsDirectors table (Table 5.5) is used to relate the Films and Directors tables (so as to associate directors with their movies).

Table 5.5 The FilmsDirectors Table

COLUMN	DATA TYPE	DESCRIPTION AND SIZE
FDRecID	Numeric	Unique ID for each row; can be populated manually when rows are inserted or automatically (if defined as an Auto Number field)
FilmID	Numeric	ID of associated movie
DirectorID	Numeric	ID of associated director
Salary	Numeric, or currency	Director's salary

- The FilmID column is related to the primary key of the Films table.

- The DirectorID column is related to the primary key of the Directors table.

The Actors Table

The Actors table (Table 5.6) contains the list of actors. This table is related to the Films table via the FilmsActors table.

Table 5.6 The Actors Table

COLUMN	DATA TYPE	DESCRIPTION AND SIZE
ActorID	Numeric	Unique ID for each actor; can be populated manually when rows are inserted or automatically (if defined as an Auto Number field)
NameFirst	Text	Actor's first name
NameLast	Text	Actor's last name
Age	Numeric	Actor's age
NameFirstReal	Text	Actor's real first name

Table 5.6 (CONTINUED)

COLUMN	DATA TYPE	DESCRIPTION AND SIZE
NameLastReal	Text	Actor's real last name
AgeReal	Numeric	Actor's real age (this one actually increases each year)
IsEgomaniac	Bit or Yes/No	Flag specifying whether actor is an egomaniac
IsTotalBabe	Bit or Yes/No	Flag specifying whether actor is a total babe
Gender	Text	Actor's gender (M or F)

The primary key for this table is the ActorID column.

This table contains no foreign keys.

The FilmsActors Table

The FilmsActors table (Table 5.7) is used to relate the Films and Actors tables (so as to associate actors with their movies).

Table 5.7 The FilmsActors Table

COLUMN	DATA TYPE	DESCRIPTION AND SIZE
FARecID	Numeric	Unique ID for each row; can be populated manually when rows are inserted or automatically (if defined as an Auto Number field)
FilmID	Numeric	ID of associated movie
ActorID	Numeric	ID of associated actor
IsStarringRole	Bit or Yes/No	Flag specifying whether this is a starring role
Salary	Numeric or currency	Actor's salary

The primary key for this table is the FARecID column.

This table contains two foreign keys:

- The FilmID column is related to the primary key of the Films table.
- The ActorID column is related to the primary key of the Actors table.

The FilmsRatings Table

The FilmsRatings table (Table 5.8) contains a list of film ratings used in the Films table (which is related to this table).

Table 5.8   The `FilmsRatings` Table

COLUMN	DATA TYPE	DESCRIPTION AND SIZE
RatingID	Numeric	Unique ID for each rating; can be populated manually when rows are inserted or automatically (if defined as an Auto Number field)
Rating	Text	Rating description

The primary key for this table is the `RatingID` column.

This table contains no foreign keys.

The `UserRoles` Table

The `UserRoles` table (Table 5.9) defines user security roles used by secured applications. This table isn't related to any of the other tables.

Table 5.9   The `UserRoles` Table

COLUMN	DATA TYPE	DESCRIPTION AND SIZE
UserRoleID	Numeric	Unique ID of user roles; can be populated manually when rows are inserted or automatically (if defined as an Auto Number field)
UserRoleName	Text	User role name (title)
UserRoleFunction	Text	User role description

The primary key for this table is the `UserRoleID` column.

This table contains no foreign keys.

The `Contacts` Table

The `Contacts` table (Table 5.10) contains a list of all contacts (including customers).

Table 5.10   The `Contacts` Table

COLUMN	DATA TYPE	DESCRIPTION AND SIZE
ContactID	Numeric	Unique ID for each contact; can be populated manually when rows are inserted or automatically (if defined as an Auto Number field)
FirstName	Text	Contact first name
LastName	Text	Contact last name
Address	Text	Contact address
City	Text	Contact city
State	Text	Contact state (or province)

Table 5.10 (CONTINUED)

COLUMN	DATA TYPE	DESCRIPTION AND SIZE
Zip	Text	Contact ZIP code (or postal code)
Country	Text	Contact country
Email	Text	Contact email address
Phone	Text	Contact phone number
UserLogin	Text	Contact login name
UserPassword	Text	Contact login password
MailingList	Bit or Yes/No	Flag specifying whether this contact is on the mailing list
UserRoleID	Numeric	ID of associated security level

The primary key for this table is the ContactID column.

This table contains a single foreign key:

- The UserRoleID column is related to the primary key of the UserRoles table.

The Merchandise Table

The Merchandise table (Table 5.11) contains a list of merchandise for sale. Merchandise is associated with movies, so this table is related to the Films table.

Table 5.11 The Merchandise Table

COLUMN	DATA TYPE	DESCRIPTION AND SIZE
MerchID	Numeric	Unique ID for each item of merchandise; can be populated manually when rows are inserted or automatically (if defined as an Auto Number field)
FilmID	Numeric	ID of associated movie
MerchName	Text	Item name
MerchDescription	Text	Item description
MerchPrice	Numeric or currency	Item price
ImageNameSmall	Text	File name of small image of item (if present)
ImageNameLarge	Text	File name of large image of item (if present)

The primary key for this table is the MerchID column.

This table contains a single foreign key:

- The FilmID column is related to the primary key of the Films table.

The MerchandiseOrders Table

The MerchandiseOrders table (Table 5.12) contains the orders for movie merchandise. Orders are associated with contacts (the buyer), so this table is related to the Contacts table.

Table 5.12 The MerchandiseOrders Table

COLUMN	DATA TYPE	DESCRIPTION AND SIZE
OrderID	Numeric	Unique ID of order (order number); can be populated manually when rows are inserted or automatically (if defined as an Auto Number field)
ContactID	Numeric	ID of associated contact
OrderDate	Date	Order date
ShipAddress	Text	Order ship to address
ShipCity	Text	Order ship to city
ShipState	Text	Order ship to state (or province)
ShipZip	Text	Order ship to ZIP code (or postal code)
ShipCountry	Text	Order ship to country
ShipDate	Date	Order ship date (when shipped)

The primary key for this table is the OrderID column.

This table contains a single foreign key:

- The ContactID column is related to the primary key of the Contacts table.

The MerchandiseOrdersItems Table

The MerchandiseOrdersItems table (Table 5.13) contains the individual items within an order. Order items are associated with an order and the merchandise being ordered, so this table is related to both the MerchandiseOrders and Merchandise tables.

Table 5.13 The MerchandiseOrdersItems Table

COLUMN	DATA TYPE	DESCRIPTION AND SIZE
OrderItemID	Numeric	Unique ID of order items; can be populated manually when rows are inserted or automatically (if defined as an Auto Number field)
OrderID	Numeric	ID of associated order
ItemID	Numeric	ID of item ordered
OrderQty	Numeric	Item quantity
ItemPrice	Numeric or currency	Per-item price

The primary key for this table is the OrderItemID column.

This table contains two foreign keys:

- The OrderID column is related to the primary key of the MerchandiseOrders table.
- The ItemID column is related to the primary key of the Merchandise table

CHAPTER 6

Introducing SQL

SQL—pronounced "sequel" or "S-Q-L"—is an acronym for Structured Query Language, a language you use to access and manipulate data in a relational database. It was designed to be easy to learn and extremely powerful, and its mass acceptance by many database vendors proves that it has succeeded in both.

In 1970, Dr. E. F. Codd, the man called the father of the relational database, described a universal language for data access. In 1974, engineers at IBM's San Jose Research Center created the Structured English Query Language, or SEQUEL, built on Codd's ideas. This language was incorporated into System R, IBM's pioneering relational database system.

Toward the end of the 1980s, two of the most important standards bodies, the American National Standards Institute (ANSI) and the International Standards Organization (ISO), published SQL standards, opening the door to mass acceptance. With these standards in place, SQL was poised to become the de facto standard used by every major database vendor.

Although SQL has evolved a great deal since its early SEQUEL days, the basic language concepts and its founding premises remain the same. The beauty of SQL is its simplicity. But don't let that simplicity deceive you. SQL is a powerful language, and it encourages you to be creative in your problem solving. You can almost always find more than one way to perform a complex query or to extract desired data. Each solution has pros and cons, and no solution is explicitly right or wrong.

Lest you panic at the thought of learning a new language, let me reassure you: SQL is easy to learn. In fact, you need to learn only four statements to be able to perform almost all the data manipulation you will need on a regular basis. Table 6.1 lists these statements.

Table 6.1 SQL-Based Data Manipulation Statements

STATEMENT	DESCRIPTION
SELECT	Queries a table for specific data.
INSERT	Adds new data to a table.

Table 6.1 (CONTINUED)

STATEMENT	DESCRIPTION
UPDATE	Updates existing data in a table.
DELETE	Removes data from a table.

Each of these statements takes one or more keywords as parameters. By combining various statements and keywords, you can manipulate your data in as many ways as you can imagine.

ColdFusion provides you with all the tools you need to add Web-based interaction to your databases. ColdFusion itself has no built-in database, however. Instead, it communicates with whatever database you select, passing updates and requests and returning query results.

TIP

This chapter (and the next) is by no means a complete SQL tutorial, so a good book on SQL is a must for ColdFusion developers. If you want a crash course on all the major SQL language elements, you might want to pick a copy of my book *Teach Yourself SQL in 10 Minutes* (ISBN: 0-672-32567-5).

Understanding Data Sources

As explained in Chapter 5, "Reviewing the Databases," a database is a collection of tables that store related data. Databases are generally used in one of two ways:

- Directly within a DBMS application such as Microsoft Access, MySQL, Query Browser, or SQL Server's Enterprise Manager. These applications tend to be very database specific (they are usually designed by the database vendor for use with specific databases).

- Via third-party applications, commercial or custom, that know how to interact with existing external databases.

ColdFusion is in the second group. It isn't a database product, but it lets you write applications that interact with databases.

How do third-party applications interact with databases, which are usually created by other vendors? That's where data sources come in to the picture. But first, we need to look at the *database driver*. Almost every database out there has available database drivers—special bits of software that provide access to the database. Each database product requires its own driver (the Oracle driver, for example, won't work for SQL Server), although a single driver can support multiple databases (the same SQL Server driver can access many different SQL Server installations).

There are two primary standards for databases drivers:

- ODBC has been around for a long time, and is one of the most widely used database driver standards. ODBC is primarily used on Windows, although other platforms are supported, too.

- JDBC is Java's database driver implementation, and is supported on all platforms and environments running Java.

NOTE

ColdFusion 5 and earlier used ODBC database drivers. ColdFusion MX and later, which are Java based, primarily use JDBC instead.

Regardless of the database driver or standard used, the purpose of the driver is the same—to hide databases differences and provide simplified access to databases. For example, the internal workings of Microsoft Access and Oracle are very different, but when accessed via a database driver they look the same (or at least more alike). This allows the same application to interact with all sorts of databases, without needing to be customized or modified for each one. Database drivers are very database specific, so access to databases need not be database specific at all.

Of course, different database drivers need different information. For example, the Microsoft Access and Apache Derby Embedded drivers simply need to know the name and location of the data files to be used, whereas the Oracle and SQL Server database drivers require server information and an account login and password.

This driver-specific information could be provided each time it's needed, or a data source could be created. A data source, like the one we created in Chapter 2, "Accessing the ColdFusion Administrator," is simply a driver plus any related information stored for future use. Client applications, like ColdFusion, use data sources to interact with databases.

Preparing to Write SQL Queries

You already have a data source, so all you need is a client application with which to access the data. Ultimately, the client you will use is ColdFusion via CFML code; after all, that is why you're reading this book. But to start learning SQL, we'll use something simpler: a SQL Query Tool (written in ColdFusion). The tool can be accessed from inside ColdFusion Builder by opening and running `index.cfm`, which is in the `sql` folder under the `ows` folder. Alternatively, it can be accessed via a Web browser using the following URL:

```
http://localhost:8500/ows/sql/index.cfm
```

NOTE

If you are using the integrated server in a multi-server installation, use port **8300** instead of **8500**.

The SQL Query Tool, shown in Figure 6.1, allows you to enter SQL statements in the box provided; they are executed when the Execute button is clicked. Results are displayed in the bottom half of the screen.

CAUTION

The SQL Query Tool is provided here as a convenience to you. It is intended for use on development computers and should never be installed on live (production) servers—and I do mean NEVER!

NOTE

The SQL Query Tool allows SQL statements to be executed against databases. This type of tool is dangerous, as it could be used to delete or change data (accidentally or maliciously). To help prevent this, SQL Query Tool has several built-in security measures: by default it only allows **SELECT** statements; it has a hard-coded data source; and it only allows SQL statements to be executed locally (local IP address only). To use SQL Query Tool remotely, you must explicitly allow your own IP address access to the tool by modifying the `Application.cfc` file specifying the address in the `ip_restrict` variable. If you modify these `Application.cfc` settings only to find that access is still blocked, then add `?reset` to the URL (after `index.cfm`) to force the code to read your changes.

Figure 6.1

The SQL Query Tool allows SQL statements to be entered manually and then executed.

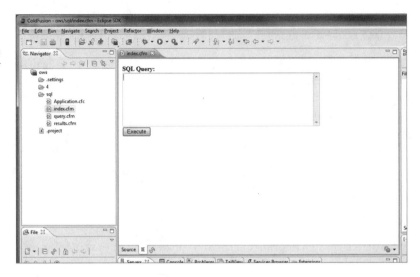

Creating Queries

With all the preliminaries taken care of, you can roll up your sleeves and start writing SQL. The SQL statement you will use most is the SELECT statement. As its name implies, you use SELECT to select data from a table.

Most SELECT statements require at least the following two parameters:

- What data you want to select, known as the select list. If you specify more than one item, you must separate each with a comma.

- The table (or tables) from which to select the data, specified with the FROM keyword.

The first SQL SELECT you will create is a query for a list of movies in the Films table. Type the code in Listing 6.1 in the SQL Query box and then execute the statement by clicking the Execute button.

Listing 6.1 Simple SELECT Statement

```
SELECT
MovieTitle
FROM Films
```

That's it! You've written your first SQL statement. The results will be shown as seen in Figure 6.2.

TIP

You can enter SQL statements on one long line or break them up over multiple lines. All white-space characters (spaces, tabs, newline characters) are ignored when the command is processed. Breaking a statement into multiple lines and indent parameters makes it easier to read and debug.

Figure 6.2

The SQL Query Tool displays query results in the bottom half of the screen along with the SQL used and the number of rows returned.

Here's another example. Type the code in Listing 6.2, then click the Execute button to display two columns.

Listing 6.2 Multi-column SELECT Statement

```
SELECT
MovieTitle, PitchText
FROM Films
```

Before you go any further, take a closer look at the SQL code in Listing 6.2. The first parameter you pass to the SELECT statement is a list of the two columns you want to see. A column is specified by its name (for example, MovieTitle) or as table.column (such as Films.MovieTitle, where Films is the table name and MovieTitle is the column name).

Because you want to specify two columns, you must separate them with commas. No comma appears after the last column name, so if you have only one column in your select list, you don't need a comma.

Right after the select list, you specify the table on which you want to perform the query. You always precede the table name with the keyword FROM. The table is specified by name, in this case Films.

NOTE

SQL statements aren't case sensitive, so you can specify the SELECT statement as SELECT, select, Select, or however you want. Common practice, however, is to enter all SQL keywords in uppercase and parameters in lowercase or mixed case. This way, you can read the SQL code and spot typos more easily.

Now modify the SELECT statement so it looks like the code in Listing 6.3, then execute it.

Listing 6.3 SELECT All Columns

```
SELECT
*
FROM Films
```

This time, instead of specifying explicit columns to select, you use an asterisk (*). The asterisk is a special select list option that represents all columns. The data pane now shows all the columns in the table in the order in which they are returned by the database table itself.

CAUTION

Don't use an asterisk in the select list unless you really need every column. Each column you select requires its own processing, and retrieving unnecessary columns can dramatically affect retrieval times as your tables get larger.

Sorting Query Results

When you use the SELECT statement, the results are returned to you in the order in which they appear in the table. This is usually the order in which the rows were added to the table. Since that probably isn't the order you want, here is how to sort the query results. To sort rows, you need to add the ORDER BY clause. ORDER BY always comes after the table name; if you try to use it before, you generate a SQL error.

Now click the SQL button, enter the SQL code shown in Listing 6.4, and then click OK.

Listing 6.4 SELECT with Sorted Output

```
SELECT MovieTitle, PitchText, Summary
FROM Films
ORDER BY MovieTitle
```

Your output is then sorted by the MovieTitle column.

What if you need to sort by more than one column? No problem. You can pass multiple columns to the ORDER BY clause. Once again, if you have multiple columns listed, you must separate them with commas. The SQL code in Listing 6.5 demonstrates how to sort on more than one column by sorting by RatingID, and then by MovieTitle within each RatingID.

Listing 6.5 SELECT with Output Sorted on More than One Column

```
SELECT RatingID, MovieTitle, Summary
FROM Films
ORDER BY RatingID, MovieTitle
```

You also can use ORDER BY to sort data in descending order (Z–A). To sort a column in descending order, just use the DESC (short for descending) parameter. Listing 6.6 retrieves all the movies and sorts them by title in reverse order.

Listing 6.6 SELECT with Output Sorted in Reverse Order

```
SELECT MovieTitle, PitchText, Summary
FROM Films
ORDER BY MovieTitle DESC
```

Filtering Data

So far, your queries have retrieved all the rows in the table. You also can use the SELECT statement to retrieve only data that matches specific search criteria. To do so, you must use the WHERE clause and provide a restricting condition. If a WHERE clause is present, when the SQL SELECT statement is processed, every row is evaluated against the condition. Only rows that pass the restriction are selected.

If you use a WHERE clause, it must appear after the table name. If you use both the ORDER BY and WHERE clauses, the WHERE clause must appear after the table name but before the ORDER BY clause.

Filtering on a Single Column

To demonstrate filtering, modify the SELECT statement to retrieve only movies with a RatingID of 1. Listing 6.7 contains the SELECT statement.

Listing 6.7 SELECT with WHERE Clause

```
SELECT MovieTitle, PitchText, Summary
FROM Films
WHERE RatingID=1
ORDER BY MovieTitle DESC
```

Filtering on Multiple Columns

The WHERE clause also can take multiple conditions. To search for Ben Forta, for example, you can specify a search condition in which the first name is Ben and the last name is Forta, as shown in Listing 6.8.

Listing 6.8 SELECT with Multiple WHERE Clauses

```
SELECT FirstName, LastName, Email
FROM Contacts
WHERE FirstName='Ben' AND LastName='Forta'
```

CAUTION

Text passed to a SQL query must be enclosed within quotation marks. If you omit the quotation marks, the SQL parser thinks that the text you specified is the name of a column, and you receive an error because that column doesn't exist. Pure SQL allows strings to be enclosed within single quotation marks ('like this') or within double quotation marks ("like this"). But when passing text in a SQL statement to an ODBC or JDBC driver, you must use single quotation marks. If you use double ones, the parser treats the first double quotation mark as a statement terminator, and ignores all text after it.

The AND and OR Operators

Multiple WHERE clauses can be evaluated as AND conditions or OR conditions. The example in Listing 6.8 is an AND condition. Only rows in which both the last name is Forta *and* the first name is Ben will be retrieved. If you change the clause to the following, contacts with a first name of Ben will be retrieved (regardless of last name) and contacts with a last name of Forta will be retrieved (regardless of first name):

```
WHERE FirstName='Ben' OR LastName='Forta'
```

You can combine the AND and OR operators to create any search condition you need. Listing 6.9 shows a WHERE clause that can be used to retrieve only Ben Forta and Rick Richards.

Listing 6.9   Combining WHERE Clauses with AND and OR Operators

```
SELECT FirstName, LastName, Email
FROM Contacts
WHERE FirstName='Ben' AND LastName='Forta'
 OR FirstName='Rick' AND LastName='Richards'
```

Evaluation Precedence

When a WHERE clause is processed, the operators are evaluated in the following order of precedence:

- Parentheses have the highest precedence.

- The AND operator has the next level of precedence.

- The OR operator has the lowest level of precedence.

What does this mean? Well, look at the WHERE clause in Listing 6.9. The clause reads WHERE FirstName='Ben' AND LastName='Forta' OR FirstName='Rick' AND LastName='Richards'. AND is evaluated before OR so this statement looks for Ben Forta and Rick Richards, which is what we wanted.

But what would be returned by a WHERE clause of WHERE FirstName='Rick' OR FirstName='Ben' AND LastName= 'Forta'? Does that statement mean *anyone whose first name is either Rick or Ben, and whose last name is Forta*, or does it mean *anyone whose first name is Rick, and also Ben Forta*? The difference is subtle, but if the former is true, then only contacts with a last name of Forta will be retrieved, whereas if the latter is true, then any Rick will be retrieved, regardless of last name.

So which is it? Because AND is evaluated first, the clause means *anyone whose first name is Rick, and also Ben Forta*. This might be exactly what you want—and then again, it might not.

To prevent the ambiguity created by mixing AND and OR statements, parentheses are used to group related statements. Parentheses have a higher order of evaluation than both AND and OR, so they can be used to explicitly match related clauses. Consider the following WHERE clauses:

```
WHERE (FirstName='Rick' OR FirstName='Ben') AND (LastName='Forta')
```

This clause means anyone whose first name is either Rick or Ben, and whose last name is Forta.

```
WHERE (FirstName='Rick') OR (FirstName='Ben' AND LastName='Forta')
```

This clause means *anyone whose first name is Rick, and also Ben Forta*.

As you can see, the exact same set of WHERE clauses can mean very different things depending on where parentheses are used.

TIP

Always using parentheses whenever you have more than one **WHERE** clause is good practice. They make the SQL statement easier to read and easier to debug.

WHERE **Conditions**

In the examples so far, you have used only the = (equal to) operator. You filtered rows based on their being equal to a specific value. Many other operators and conditions can be used with the WHERE clause; they're listed in Table 6.2.

Feel free to experiment with different SELECT statements, using any of the WHERE clauses listed here. The SQL Query tool is safe. By default, it won't update or modify data (by default), so there's no harm in using it to play around with statements and clauses.

Table 6.2 WHERE Clause Search Conditions

CONDITION	DESCRIPTION
=	Equal to. Tests for equality.
<>	Not equal to. Tests for inequality.
<	Less than. Tests that the value on the left is less than the value on the right.
<=	Less than or equal to. Tests that the value on the left is less than or equal to the value on the right.
>	Greater than. Tests that the value on the left is greater than the value on the right.
>=	Greater than or equal to. Tests that the value on the left is greater than or equal to the value on the right.
EXISTS	Tests for the existence of rows returned by a subquery.
BETWEEN	Tests that a value is in the range between two values; the range is inclusive.
IN	Tests to see whether a value is contained within a list of values.
IS NULL	Tests to see whether a column contains a NULL value.
IS NOT NULL	Tests to see whether a column contains a non-NULL value.
LIKE	Tests to see whether a value matches a specified pattern.
NOT	Negates any test.

Testing for Equality: =

You use the = operator to test for value equality. The following example retrieves only contacts whose last name is Smith:

```
WHERE LastName = 'Smith'
```

Testing for Inequality: <>

You use the <> operator to test for value inequality. The following example retrieves only contacts whose first name is not Kim:

```
WHERE FirstName <> 'Kim'
```

Testing for Less Than: <

By using the < operator, you can test that the value on the left is less than the value on the right. The following example retrieves only contacts whose last name is less than C, meaning that their last name begins with an A or a B:

```
WHERE LastName < 'C'
```

Testing for Less Than or Equal To: <=

By using the <= operator, you can test that the value on the left is less than or equal to the value on the right. The following example retrieves actors aged 21 or less:

```
WHERE Age <= 21
```

Testing for Greater Than: >

You use the > operator to test that the value on the left is greater than the value on the right. The following example retrieves only movies with a rating of 3 or higher (greater than 2):

```
WHERE RatingID > 2
```

Testing for Greater Than or Equal To: >=

You use the >= operator to test that the value on the left is greater than or equal to the value on the right. The following example retrieves only contacts whose first name begins with the letter J or higher:

```
WHERE FirstName >= 'J'
```

BETWEEN

Using the BETWEEN condition, you can test whether a value falls into the range between two other values. The following example retrieves only actors aged 20 to 30. Because the test is inclusive, ages 20 and 30 are also retrieved:

```
WHERE Age BETWEEN 20 AND 30
```

The BETWEEN condition is actually nothing more than a convenient way of combining the >= and <= conditions. You also could specify the preceding example as follows:

```
WHERE Age >= 20 AND Age <= 30
```

Using the BETWEEN condition makes the statement easier to read.

EXISTS

Using the EXISTS condition, you can check whether a subquery returns any rows.

IN

You can use the IN condition to test whether a value is part of a specific set. The set of values must be surrounded by parentheses and separated by commas. The following example retrieves contacts whose last name is Black, Jones, or Smith:

```
WHERE LastName IN ('Black', 'Jones', 'Smith')
```

The preceding example is actually the same as the following:

```
WHERE LastName = 'Black' OR LastName = 'Jones' OR LastName = 'Smith'
```

Using the IN condition has two advantages. First, it makes the statement easier to read. Second, and more importantly, you can use the IN condition to test whether a value is within the results of another SELECT statement (providing a complete SELECT statement in between (and) so as to match whatever that statement returned).

IS NULL and IS NOT NULL

A NULL value is the value of a column that is empty. The IS NULL condition tests for rows that have a NULL value; that is, the rows have no value at all in the specified column. IS NOT NULL tests for rows that have a value in a specified column.

The following example retrieves all contacts whose Email column is empty:

```
WHERE Email IS NULL
```

To retrieve only the contacts who have an email address, use the following example:

```
WHERE Email IS NOT NULL
```

LIKE

Using the LIKE condition, you can test for string pattern matches using wildcards. Two wildcard types are supported. The % character means that anything from that position on is considered a match. You also can use [] to create a wildcard for a specific character.

The following example retrieves actors whose last name begins with the letter S. To match the pattern, a last name must have an S as the first character.

```
WHERE LastName LIKE 'S%'
```

To retrieve actors with an S anywhere in their last names, you can use the following:

```
WHERE LastName LIKE '%S%'
```

You also can retrieve just actors whose last name ends with S, as follows:

```
WHERE LastName LIKE '%S'
```

The LIKE condition can be negated with the NOT operator. The following example retrieves only actors whose last name doesn't begin with S:

```
WHERE LastName NOT LIKE 'S%'
```

Using the LIKE condition, you also can specify a wildcard on a single character. If you want to find all actors named Smith but aren't sure whether the one you want spells his or her name Smyth, you can use the following:

```
WHERE LastName LIKE 'Sm[iy]th'
```

This example retrieves only names that start with Sm, then have an i or a y, and then a final th. As long as the first two characters are Sm and the last two are th, and as long as the middle character is i or y, the name is considered a match.

TIP

Using the powerful LIKE condition, you can retrieve data in many ways. But everything has its price, and the price here is performance. Generally, LIKE conditions take far longer to process than other search conditions, especially if you use wildcards at the beginning of the pattern. As a rule, use LIKE and wildcards only when absolutely necessary.

For even more powerful searching, LIKE may be combined with other clauses using AND and OR. And you may even include multiple LIKE clauses in a single WHERE clause.

SQL Data Manipulation

Chapter 6, "Introducing SQL," introduced data drivers, data sources, SQL, and data retrieval (using the SELECT statement). You'll probably find that you spend far more time retrieving data than you do inserting, updating, or deleting it (which is why we concentrated on SELECT first).

NOTE

As in the previous chapter, the SQL Query Tool in the ows/sql directory will be used to execute the SQL statements. For security's sake (to prevent accidental data changes) the SQL Query Tool by default allows execution of SELECT statements, but no other SQL statements.

To change this behavior, edit the Application.cfc file in the ows/sql directory. You will see a series of variables that are set, one of which is THIS.select_only. This flag is set to yes (the default setting) instructing the utility to execute only SELECT statements. Change this value to no before proceeding (and save the updated Application.cfc file) with the examples in this chapter (or an error will be thrown). You may need to add ?reset to the index.cfm URL to force changes to be seen.

When you're done, set the flag back to yes, just to be safe.

Adding Data

You will need to insert data into tables at some point, so let's look at data inserting using the INSERT statement.

NOTE

In this chapter, you will add, update, and delete rows from tables in the ows data source. The reason you delete any added rows is to ensure that any example code and screen shots later in the book actually look like the way they're supposed to. Feel free to add more rows if you'd like, but if you don't clean up when you're finished, your screens will look different from the ones shown in the figures. This isn't a problem, just something to bear in mind.

Using the INSERT Statement

You use the INSERT statement to add data to a table. INSERT is usually made up of three parts:

- The table into which you want to insert data, specified with the INTO keyword.

- The column(s) into which you want to insert values. If you specify more than one item, each must be separated by a comma.

- The values to insert, which are specified with the VALUES keyword.

The Directors table contains the list of movie directors working with or for Orange Whip Studios. Directors can't be assigned projects (associated with movies) if they aren't listed in this table, so any new directors must be added immediately.

→ See Appendix B, "Sample Application Data Files," for an explanation of each of the data files and their contents.

Now you're ready to add the new director. The following code contains the SQL INSERT statement:

```
INSERT INTO Directors(FirstName, LastName)
VALUES('Benjamin', 'FORTA')
```

Enter this statement into the SQL Query field as seen in Figure 7.1. Feel free to replace my name with your own. When you're finished, click the Execute button to insert the new row. Assuming no problems occur, you should see a confirmation screen like the one at the bottom of Figure 7.1.

Figure 7.1

Type the statement in the SQL Query field and then click Execute.

TIP

How can you tell if an INSERT succeeds or fails? Well, no news is good news. If no error is returned, the INSERT has succeeded. If an error has occurred, it will be displayed.

Understanding INSERT

Now that you've successfully inserted a row using the SQL INSERT statement, take a minute to look at the statement's syntax.

The first line of your statement reads:

```
INSERT INTO Directors(FirstName, LastName)
```

The text immediately following the INTO keyword is the name of the table into which the new row is being inserted—in this case, the Directors table.

Next, the columns being added are specified. The columns are listed within parentheses, and since multiple columns are specified, they are separated by a comma. A row in the Directors table requires both a FirstName and a LastName, so the INSERT statement specifies both columns.

NOTE

When you insert a row into a table, you can provide values for as few or as many columns as you like. The only restriction is that any columns defined as NOT NULL columns—meaning they can't be left empty—must have values specified. If you don't set a value for a NOT NULL column, the database driver returns an error message and the row is not inserted.

The next line reads:

```
VALUES('Benjamin', 'FORTA')
```

A value must be specified for every column listed whenever you insert a row. Values are passed to the VALUES keyword; all values are contained within parentheses, just like their column names. Two columns are specified, so two values are passed to the VALUES keyword.

NOTE

When inserting rows into a table, columns can be specified in any order. But be sure that the order of the values in the VALUES keyword exactly matches the order of the columns after the table name, or you'll insert the wrong data into the columns.

To verify that the new director was added to the table, retrieve the complete list of directors using the following SQL statement:

```
SELECT * FROM Directors
```

As explained in Chapter 6, SELECT * means select all columns. You should see the new row that was added to the table. Make a note of the DirectorID value, which you'll need later to update or delete this row (and the ID generated for you may not be the same as the 14 generated for me).

NOTE

In the previous INSERT statement, no value was provided for the DirectorID column. So where did that value come from? The Directors table was set up to automatically assign primary key values every time a new row is inserted. This is a feature supported by many databases—Access calls these AutoNumber columns, SQL Server and Derby use the term Identity, and other databases have their own names. As a result, you don't have to worry about creating unique values because the database does that for you.

TIP

INSERT can usually insert only one row at a time, and so multiple insertions require multiple INSERT statements. However, some DBMSs, including Derby, allow multiple VALUE clauses to be passed to INSERT. If you look at the scripts used to populate the example tables, you will see how this syntax is used.

Modifying Data

You use the SQL UPDATE statement to update one or more columns. This usually involves specifying the following:

- The table containing the data you want to update.

- The column or columns you want to update, preceded by the SET keyword. If you specify more than one item, each must be separated by a comma.

- An optional WHERE clause to specify which rows to update. If no WHERE clause is provided, all rows are updated.

Try updating a row. Enter the following SQL statement (ensuring that the ID number used in the WHERE clause is the DirectorID you noted earlier).

```
UPDATE Directors
SET FirstName='Ben'
WHERE DirectorID = 14
```

Click Execute to perform the update. Again, no results will be displayed, as UPDATE doesn't return data (although the SQL, execution time, and other information will indeed be displayed).

If you now select the contents of the Directors table, you see that the new director's first name has been changed.

Understanding UPDATE

Now, take a closer look at the SQL statement you just used. The first line issued the UPDATE statement and specified the name of the table to update. As with the INSERT and DELETE statements, the table name is required.

You next specified the column you wanted to change and its new value:

```
SET FirstName='Ben'
```

This is an instruction to update the FirstName column with the text Ben. The SET keyword is required for an UPDATE operation, because updating rows without specifying what to update makes little sense.

The SET keyword can be used only once in an UPDATE statement. If you are updating multiple columns—for example, to change Benjamin to Ben and to set the LastName to Forta in one operation—the SET keyword would look like this:

```
SET FirstName='Ben', LastName='Forta'
```

When updating multiple columns, each column must be separated by a comma. The complete (revised) UPDATE statement would then look like this:

```
UPDATE Directors
SET FirstName='Ben', LastName='Forta'
WHERE DirectorID = 14
```

The last line of the code listing specifies a WHERE clause. The WHERE clause is optional in an UPDATE statement. Without it, all rows will be updated. The following code uses the primary key column to ensure that only a single row gets updated:

```
WHERE DirectorID = 14
```

To verify that the updates worked, try retrieving all the data from the Directors table. The results should reflect the changes made.

CAUTION

Be sure to provide a WHERE clause when using the SQL UPDATE statement; otherwise, all rows will be updated.

Making Global Updates

Occasionally, you will want to update all rows in a table. To do this, you use UPDATE, too—you just omit the WHERE clause, or specify a WHERE clause that matches multiple rows.

When updating multiple rows using a WHERE clause, always be sure to test that WHERE clause with a simple SELECT statement before executing the UPDATE. If the SELECT returns the correct data (i.e., the data you want updated), you'll know that it is safe to use with UPDATE. If you don't, you might update the wrong data!

TIP

Before executing INSERT, UPDATE, or DELETE operations that contain complex statements or WHERE conditions, you should test the statement or condition by using it in a SELECT statement. If SELECT returns incorrect statement results or an incorrect subset of data filtered by the WHERE clause, you'll know that the statement or condition is incorrect. Unlike INSERT, UPDATE, and DELETE, the SELECT statement never changes any data. So if an error exists in the statement or condition, you'll find out about it before any damage is done.

Deleting Data

Deleting data from a table is even easier than adding or updating data—perhaps too easy.

You use the SQL DELETE statement to delete data. The statement takes only two parameters—one required and one optional:

- The name of the table from which to delete the data must be specified immediately following the words DELETE FROM.

- An optional WHERE clause can be used to restrict the scope of the deletion process.

The DELETE statement is dangerously easy to use. Look at the following line of code (but don't execute it):

```
DELETE FROM Directors
```

This statement removes all directors from the Directors table, and does it without any warnings or confirmation.

TIP

Some databases, in particular client-server databases (such as Microsoft SQL Server and Oracle), offer safeguards against accidental or malicious deletions. There generally are two approaches to preventing mass deletion. One is to create a trigger (a piece of code that runs on the server when specific operations occur) that verifies every DELETE statement and blocks any DELETE without a WHERE clause. A second is to restrict the use of DELETE without a WHERE clause based on login name. Only certain users, usually those with administrative rights, are granted permission to execute DELETE without a WHERE clause. Any other user attempting a mass DELETE will receive an error message, and the operation will abort. Not all database systems support these techniques. Consult the database administrator's manuals to ascertain which safeguards are available to you.

The DELETE statement is most often used with a WHERE clause. For example, the following SQL statement deletes a single director (the one you just added) from the Directors table:

```
DELETE FROM Directors
WHERE DirectorID=14
```

To verify that the row was deleted, retrieve all the directors one last time.

As with all WHERE clauses, the DELETE statement's WHERE clause can be a SELECT statement that retrieves the list of rows to delete. If you do use a SELECT statement for a WHERE clause, be careful to test the SELECT statement first to ensure that it retrieves all the values you want, and only those values.

TIP

Feel free to INSERT, UPDATE, and DELETE rows as necessary, but when you're finished either clean up the changes or just copy overwrite the data file with the original (to restore it to its original state).

NOTE

Primary key values are never reused. If you INSERT rows after you have performed delete operations, the new rows will be assigned brand-new IDs, and the old (deleted) IDs will not be reused. This behavior is a required part of how relational databases work, and was explained in Chapter 5, "Reviewing the Databases."

PART 2

Using ColdFusion

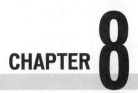

CHAPTER **8**

The Basics
of CFML

Working with Templates

Back in Chapter 4, "Previewing ColdFusion," we walked through the process of creating several simple applications. ColdFusion applications are made up of one or more files, each with a .cfm extension. These files often are referred to as *templates* or *pages*—you'll see the terms used somewhat interchangeably. Just so you know, they all refer to the same thing. I'll explain why the term templates is used in a few moments.

> **NOTE**
>
> As explained in Chapter 2, "Accessing the ColdFusion Administrator," the URL used with ColdFusion will vary based on whether or not an external Web server is being used. For the sake of simplicity, all URLs used in this and future chapters assume that Cold-Fusion is being used in conjunction with the integrated Web server ("stand-alone" mode). As such, you'll see the port address :8500 specified in all URLs (both in the content and the figures). If you are not using the integrated Web server, simply omit the :8500 from any URLs.

Creating Templates

As already explained, ColdFusion templates are plain text files. As such, they can be created using many different programs. We'll continue to use ColdFusion Builder as we work through these lessons, but there are other options, including Adobe Dreamweaver, which is very popular among Web developers and designers.

> **NOTE**
>
> There are two other file extensions used with ColdFusion, .cfc and .cfr. We'll look at those files in future chapters.

The following code is the contents of a simple ColdFusion file named hello1.cfm. Actually, at this point no ColdFusion code exists in the listing—it is all straight HTML and text, but we'll change that soon. Launch ColdFusion Builder (if it is not already open), create a 8 folder under ows, create a new file named hello1.cfm, and type the code as shown in Listing 8.1.

Listing 8.1 `hello1.cfm`

```
<html>
<head>
 <title>Hello 1</title>
</head>

<body>

Hello, and welcome to ColdFusion!

</body>
</html>
```

TIP

Tag case is not important, so **<BODY>** or **<body>** or **<Body>** can be used—it's your choice.

Executing Templates

Now, let's test the code. There are several ways to do this. The simplest is to just click the browser tab under the editor window in ColdFusion Builder.

You may also execute the page directly yourself. Simply open your Web browser and go to this URL:

```
http://localhost:8500/ows/8/hello1.cfm
```

TIP

Not using the integrated Web server? See the note at the start of this chapter.

You should see a page like the one in Figure 8.1. I admit that this is somewhat anticlimactic, but wait; it'll get better soon enough.

Figure 8.1

ColdFusion-generated output usually is viewed in any Web browser.

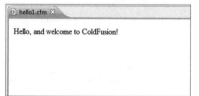

Templates Explained

I promised to explain why ColdFusion files are often referred to as templates. Chapter 1, "Introducing ColdFusion," explains that ColdFusion pages are processed differently from Web pages. When requested, Web pages are sent to the client (the browser) as is, whereas ColdFusion files are processed and the generated results are returned to the client instead.

In other words, ColdFusion files are never sent to the client, but what they create is. And depending on what a ColdFusion file contains, it likely will generate multiple different outputs all from that same single .cfm file—thus the term *template*.

Using Functions

This is where it starts to get interesting. CFML (the ColdFusion Markup Language) is made up of two primary language elements:

- **Tags.** These perform operations, such as accessing a database, evaluating a condition, and flagging text for processing.

- **Functions.** These return (and possibly process) data and do things such as getting the current date and time, converting text to uppercase, and rounding a number to its nearest integer.

Writing ColdFusion code requires the use of both tags and functions. The best way to understand this is to see it in action. Here is a revised hello page. Type Listing 8.2 in a new page (or use Save As to save a copy of the previous page and then edit the page), and save it as `hello2.cfm` in the `ows/8` directory.

Listing 8.2   `hello2.cfm`

```
<html>
<head>
 <title>Hello 2</title>
</head>

<body>

Hello, and welcome to ColdFusion!
<br>
<cfoutput>
It is now #Now()#
</cfoutput>

</body>
</html>
```

After you have saved the page, try it by browsing it either in a Web browser or right within ColdFusion Builder. (If using a Web browser the URL will be `http://localhost:8500/ows/8/hello2.cfm`.) The output should look similar to Figure 8.2 (except that your date and time will probably be different).

Figure 8.2

ColdFusion code can contain functions, including one that returns the current date and time.

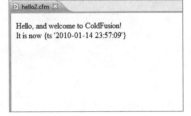

```
hello2.cfm

Hello, and welcome to ColdFusion!
It is now {ts '2010-01-14 23:57:09'}
```

Before we go any further, let's take a look at Listing 8.2. You will recall that when ColdFusion processes a .cfm file, it looks for CFML code to be processed and returns any other code to the client as is. So, the first line of code is

```
<html>
```

That is not CFML code—it's plain HTML. Therefore, ColdFusion ignores it and sends it on its way (to the client browser). The next few lines are also HTML code:

```
<title>Hello 2</title>
</head>

<body>

Hello, and welcome to ColdFusion!
<br>
```

No ColdFusion language elements exist there, so ColdFusion ignores the code and sends it to the client as is.

But the next three lines of code are not HTML:

```
<cfoutput>
It is now #Now()#
</cfoutput>
```

`<cfoutput>` is a ColdFusion tag (all ColdFusion tags begin with CF). `<cfoutput>` is used to mark a block of code to be processed by ColdFusion. All text between the `<cfoutput>` and `</cfoutput>` tags is parsed, character by character, and any special instructions within that block are processed.

In the example, the following line was between the `<cfoutput>` and `</cfoutput>` tags:

```
It is now #Now()#
```

The text It is now is not an instruction, so it is sent to the client as is. But the text #Now()# *is* a ColdFusion instruction—instructions within strings of text are delimited by number signs (the # character). #Now()# is an instruction telling ColdFusion to execute a function named Now()—a function that returns the current date and time. Thus the output in Figure 8.3 is generated.

Figure 8.3

Number signs (#) are needed around all expressions; otherwise, the expression is sent to the client instead of being processed.

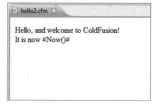

The entire block of text from `<cfoutput>` until `</cfoutput>` is referred to as a `<cfoutput>` *block*. Not all the text in a `<cfoutput>` block need be CFML functions. In the previous example, literal text was used, too, and that text was sent to the client untouched. As such, you also could have entered the code like this:

```
It is now <cfoutput>#Now()#</cfoutput>
```

Only the #Now()# expression needs ColdFusion processing, so only it really needs to be within the <cfoutput> block. But what if you had not placed the expression within a <cfoutput> block? Try it; remove the <cfoutput> tags, save the page, and execute it. You'll see output similar to that in Figure 8.3—obviously not what you want. Because any content not within a <cfoutput> block is sent to the client as is, using Now() outside a <cfoutput> block causes the text Now() to be sent to the client instead of the data returned by Now(). Why? Because if it is outside a <cfoutput> block (and not within any other CFML tag), ColdFusion will never process it.

Omitting the number signs has a similar effect. Put the <cfoutput> tags back where they belong, but change #Now()# to Now() (removing the number signs from before and after it). Then save the page, and execute it. The output will look similar to Figure 8.4. Why? Because all <cfoutput> does is flag a block of text as needing processing by ColdFusion. However, ColdFusion does not process *all* text between the tags—instead, it looks for expressions delimited by number signs, and any text *not* within number signs is assumed to be literal text that is to be sent to the client as is.

Figure 8.4

If expressions are sent to the browser, it usually means you have omitted the <cfoutput> tags.

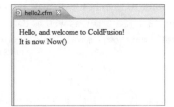

hello2.cfm

Hello, and welcome to ColdFusion!
It is now Now()

NOTE

<cfoutput> has another important use when working with database-driven content. More information about that can be found in Chapter 10, "Creating Data-Driven Pages."

Now() is a function, one of many functions supported in CFML. Now() is used to retrieve information from the system (the date and time), but the format of that date is not entirely readable. Another function, DateFormat(), can help here. DateFormat() is one of ColdFusion's output formatting functions, and its job is to format dates so they are readable in all types of formats. Here is a revision of the code you just used (see Listing 8.3); save it as hello3.cfm and browse the file to see output similar to what is shown in Figure 8.5.

Figure 8.5

ColdFusion features a selection of output formatting functions that can be used to better control generated output.

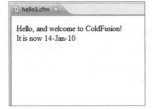

hello3.cfm

Hello, and welcome to ColdFusion!
It is now 14-Jan-10

Listing 8.3 `hello3.cfm`

```
<html>
<head>
 <title>Hello 3</title>
</head>

<body>

Hello, and welcome to ColdFusion!
<br>
<cfoutput>
It is now #DateFormat(Now())#
</cfoutput>

</body>
</html>
```

`DateFormat()` is an example of a function that accepts (and requires) that data must be passed to it—after all, it needs to know which date you want to format for display. `DateFormat()` can accept dates as hard-coded strings (as in `#DateFormat("8/17/2010")#`), as well as dates returned by other expressions, such as the `Now()` function. `#DateFormat(Now())#` tells ColdFusion to format the date returned by the `Now()` function.

NOTE

Passing a function as a parameter to another function is referred to as "nesting." In this chapter's example, the `Now()` function is said to be nested in the `DateFormat()` function.

`DateFormat()` takes a second optional attribute, too: a format mask used to describe the output format. Try replacing the `#DateFormat(Now())#` in your code with any of the following, and try each to see what they do:

- `#DateFormat(Now(), "MMMM-DD-YYYY")#`

- `#DateFormat(Now(), "MM/DD/YY")#`

- `#DateFormat(Now(), "DDD, MMMM DD, YYYY")#`

Parameters passed to a function are always separated by commas. Commas are not used if a single parameter is passed, but when two or more parameters exist, every parameter must be separated by a comma.

You've now seen a function that takes no parameters, a function that takes a required parameter, and a function that takes both required and optional parameters. All ColdFusion functions, and you'll be using many of them, work the same way—some take parameters, and some don't. But all functions, regardless of parameters, return a value.

NOTE

It is important to remember that # is not part of the function. The functions you used here were `DateFormat()` and `Now()`. The number signs were used to delimit (mark) the expressions, but they are not part of the expression itself.

I know I've already said this, but it's worth repeating: CFML code is processed on the server, not on the client. The CFML code you write is *never* sent to the Web browser. What is sent to the browser? Most browsers feature a View Source option that displays code as received. If you view the source of for page `hello3.cfm` you'll see something like this:

```
<html>
<head>
 <title>Hello 3</title>
</head>

<body>

Hello, and welcome to ColdFusion!
<br>

It is now 02-Jul-10



</body>
</html>
```

As you can see, there is no CFML code here at all. The `<cfoutput>` tags, the functions, the number signs—all have been stripped out by the ColdFusion Server, and what was sent to the client is the output that they generated.

TIP

Viewing the generated source is an invaluable debugging trick. If you ever find that output is not being generated as expected, viewing the source can help you understand exactly what was generated and why.

Using Variables

Now that you've had the chance to use some basic functions, it's time to introduce variables. Variables are an important part of just about every programming language, and CFML is no exception. A *variable* is a container that stores information in memory on the server. Variables are named, and the contents of the container are accessed via that name. Let's look at a simple example. Type the code in Listing 8.4 into a new file (feel free to use your own name instead of mine), save it as `hello4.cfm`, and browse it. You should see a display similar to the one shown in Figure 8.6.

Figure 8.6

Variables are replaced by their contents when content is generated.

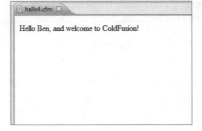

Listing 8.4 `hello4.cfm`

```
<html>
<head>
 <title>Hello 4</title>
</head>

<body>

<cfset FirstName="Ben">

<cfoutput>
Hello #FirstName#, and welcome to ColdFusion!
</cfoutput>

</body>
</html>
```

This code is similar to the previous code listings. It starts with plain HTML, which is sent to the client as is. Then a new tag is used, `<cfset>`:

```
<cfset FirstName="Ben">
```

`<cfset>` is used to set variables. Here, a variable named `FirstName` is created, and a value of `Ben` is stored in it. After it's created, that variable will exist until the page has finished processing and can be used, as seen in the next line of code:

```
Hello #FirstName#, and welcome to ColdFusion!
```

This line of code was placed in a `<cfoutput>` block so ColdFusion will know to replace `#FirstName#` with the contents of `FirstName`. The generated output is then:

```
Hello Ben, and welcome to ColdFusion!
```

Variables can be used as many times as necessary, as long as they exist. Try moving the `<cfset>` statement after the `<cfoutput>` block, or delete it altogether. Executing the page now will generate an error, similar to the one seen in Figure 8.7. This error message is telling you that you referred to (tried to access) a variable that doesn't exist. The error message includes the name of the variable that caused the problem, as well as the line and column in your code, to help you find and fix the problem easily. More often than not, this kind of error is caused by typos.

NOTE

If the error message doesn't contain line numbers (or displays less detail than seen in Figure 8.7), you'll need to access the ColdFusion Administrator (as explained in Chapter 2), go to the Debugging Output Settings page, and turn on Enable Robust Exception Information.

NOTE

Regular variables exist only in the page that creates them. If you define a variable named `FirstName` in one page, you can't use it in another page unless you explicitly pass it to that page (see Chapter 10). An exception to this rule does exist. In Chapter 19, "Working with Sessions," you learn how to create and use variables that persist across requests. (Each page access is known as a request.)

Figure 8.7

ColdFusion produces an error if a referenced variable doesn't exist.

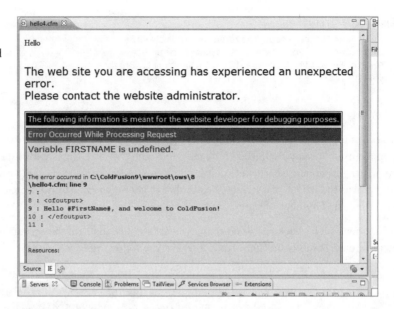

Here is a new version of the code, this time using the variable `FirstName` six times. Save Listing 8.5 as `hello5.cfm`, and then try this listing for yourself (feel free to replace my name with your own). The output is shown in Figure 8.8.

Figure 8.8

There is no limit to the number of functions that can be used in one page, which enables you to render content as you see fit.

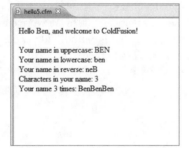

Listing 8.5 `hello5.cfm`

```
<html>
<head>
 <title>Hello 5</title>
</head>

<body>

<cfset firstName="ben">
<cfoutput>
Hello #firstName#, and welcome to ColdFusion!<p>
Your name in uppercase: #UCase(firstName)#<br>
Your name in lowercase: #LCase(firstName)#<br>
```

Listing 8.5   (CONTINUED)

```
Your name in reverse: #Reverse(firstName)#<br>
Characters in your name: #Len(firstName)#<br>
Your name 3 times: #RepeatString(firstName, 3)#<br>
</cfoutput>

</body>
</html>
```

Let's take a look at the previous code. A `<cfset>` is used to create a variable named `FirstName`. That variable is used once by itself (the Hello message), and then five times with functions. `UCase()` converts a string to uppercase, `LCase()` converts a string to lowercase, `Reverse()` reverses the string, `Len()` returns the length of a string (the number of characters in it), and `RepeatString()` repeats a string a specified number of times.

But functions such as `UCase()` don't truly convert strings; instead, they return converted strings. The difference is subtle but important. Look at the following line of code:

```
Your name in uppercase: #UCase(firstName)#
```

`UCase()` returns `FirstName` converted to uppercase, but the contents of `FirstName` itself are intact and are not converted to anything at all. `FirstName` was not modified; a copy was made and modified instead, and that copy was returned. To save the uppercase `FirstName` to a variable, you must do something like this:

```
<CFSET UpperFirstName=UCase(FirstName)>
```

Here a new variable, `UpperFirstName`, is created. `UpperFirstName` is assigned the value that is returned by `UCase(FirstName)`, the uppercase `FirstName`. And this new variable can be used like any other variable, and as often as necessary. Listing 8.6 is a modified version of Listing 8.5. Try it for yourself—the output will be exactly the same as in Figure 8.8.

Listing 8.6   hello6.cfm

```
<html>
<head>
 <title>Hello 6</title>
</head>

<body>

<cfset firstName="ben">
<cfset upperFirstname=UCase(firstName)>
<cfset lowerFirstname=LCase(firstName)>
<cfset reverseFirstname=Reverse(firstName)>
<cfset lenFirstName=Len(firstName)>
<cfset repeatFirstName=RepeatString(firstName, 3)>

<cfoutput>
Hello #FirstName#, and welcome to ColdFusion!<p>
Your name in uppercase: #upperFirstName#<br>
Your name in lowercase: #lowerFirstName#<br>
Your name in reverse: #reverseFirstName#<br>
Characters in your name: #lenFirstName#<br>
```

Listing 8.6 (CONTINUED)

```
Your name 3 times: #repeatFirstName#<br>
</cfoutput>

</body>
</html>
```

This code deserves a closer look. Six `<cfset>` tags now exist, and six variables are created. The first creates the `firstName` variable, just like in the previous examples. The next creates a new variable named `upperFirstName`, which contains the uppercase version of `firstName`. And then `lowerFirstName`, `reverseFirstName`, `lenFirstName`, and `repeatFirstName` are each created with additional `<cfset>` statements.

The `<cfoutput>` block here contains no functions at all. Rather, it just displays the contents of the variables that were just created. In this particular listing there is actually little value in doing this, aside from the fact that the code is a bit more organized this way. The real benefit in saving function output to variables is realized when a function is used many times in a single page. Then, instead of using the same function over and over, you can use it once, save the output to a variable, and just use that variable instead.

One important point to note here is that variables can be overwritten. Look at the following code snippet:

```
<cfset firstName="Ben">
<cfset firstName="Ray">
```

Here, `firstName` is set to `Ben` and then set again to `Ray`. Variables can be overwritten as often as necessary, and whatever the current value is when accessed (displayed, or passed to other functions), that's the value that will be used.

Knowing that, what do you think the following line of code does?

```
<cfset firstName=UCase(FirstName)>
```

This is an example of variable overwriting, but here the variable being overwritten is the variable itself. I mentioned earlier that functions such as `UCase()` don't convert text; they return a converted copy. So how could you really convert text? By using code such as the line just shown. `<cfset firstName=UCase(firstName)>` sets `firstName` to the uppercase version of `firstName`, effectively overwriting itself with the converted value.

Variable Naming

This would be a good place to discuss variable naming. When you create a variable you get to name it, and the choice of names is up to you. However, you need to know a few rules about variable naming:

- Variable names can contain alphanumeric characters but can't begin with a number (so `result12` is okay, but `4thresult` is not).

- Variable names can't contain spaces. If you need to separate words, use underscores (for example, `monthly_sales_figures` instead of `monthly sales figures`).

- Aside from the underscore, non-alphanumeric characters can't be used in variable names (so `Sales!`, `SSN#`, and `first-name` are all invalid).

- Variable names are case insensitive (`FirstName` is the same as `FIRSTNAME`, which is the same as `firstname`, which is the same as `firstName`).

Other than that, you can be as creative as necessary with your names. Pick any variable name you want; just be careful not to overwrite existing variables by mistake.

TIP

Avoid the use of abbreviated variable names, such as `fn` or `c`. Although these are valid names, what they stand for is not apparent just by looking at them. Yes, `fn` is fewer keystrokes than `FirstName`, but the first time you (or someone else) must stare at the code trying to figure out what a variable is for, you'll regret saving that little bit of time. As a rule, make variable names descriptive.

Using Prefixes

ColdFusion supports many variable types, and you'll become very familiar with them as you work through this book. For example, local variables (the type you just created) are a variable type. Submitted form fields are a variable type, as are many others.

ColdFusion variables can be referenced in two ways:

- The variable name itself

- The variable name with the type as a prefix

For example, the variable `firstName` that you used a little earlier is a local variable (local to this page only; type `VARIABLES`). That variable can be referred to as `firstName` (as you did previously) and as `VARIABLES.firstName`. Both are valid, and both will work (you can edit file `hello6.cfm` to use the `VARIABLES` prefix to try this).

So should you use prefixes? Well, there are pros and cons. Here are the pros:

- Using prefixes improves performance. ColdFusion will have less work to do finding the variable you are referring to if you explicitly provide the full name (including the prefix).

- If multiple variables exist with the same name but are of different types, the only way to be 100 percent sure that you'll get the variable you want is to use the prefix.

As for the cons, there is just one:

- If you omit the prefix, multiple variable types will be accessible (perhaps form fields and URL parameters, which are discussed in the following chapters). If you provide the type prefix, you restrict access to the specified type, and although this does prevent ambiguity (as just explained), it does make your code a little less reusable.

The choice is yours, and there is no real right or wrong. You can use prefixes if you see fit, and not use them if not. If you don't specify the prefix, ColdFusion will find the variable for you. And if multiple variables of the same name do exist (with differing types) then a predefined order of precedence is used. (Don't worry if these types are not familiar yet; they will become familiar soon enough, and you can refer to this list when necessary.) Here is the order:

- Function local (user-defined functions and CFC methods)

- Thread local (within a `<CFTHREAD>` statement)

- Query results

- Function `ARGUMENTS`

- Local variables (`VARIABLES`)

- `CGI` variables

- `FILE` variables

- `URL` parameters

- `FORM` fields

- `COOKIE` values

- `CLIENT` variables

In other words, if you refer to `#firstName#` (without specifying a prefix) and that variable exists both as a local variable (`VARIABLES.firstName`) and as a `FORM` field (`FORM.firstName`), `VARIABLES.firstName` will be used automatically.

NOTE

An exception to this does exist. Some ColdFusion variable types must always be accessed with an explicit prefix; these are covered in later chapters.

Working with Expressions

I've used the term *expressions* a few times in this chapter. What is an expression? The official Cold-Fusion documentation explains that expressions are "language constructs that allow you to create sophisticated applications." A better way to understand it is that expressions are strings of text made up of one or more of the following:

- Literal text (strings), numbers, dates, times, and other values

- Variables

- Operators (+ for addition, & for concatenation, and so on)

- Functions

So, UCase(FirstName) is an expression, as are "Hello, my name is Ben", 12+4, and DateFormat(Now()). And even though many people find it hard to articulate exactly what an expression is, realize that expressions are an important part of the ColdFusion language.

Building Expressions

Expressions are entered where necessary. Expressions can be passed to a <cfset> statement as part of an assignment, used when displaying text, and passed to almost every single CFML tag (except for the few that take no attributes).

Simple expressions can be used, such as those discussed previously (variables, functions, and combinations thereof). But more complex expressions can be used, too, and expressions can include arithmetic, string, and decision operators. You'll use these in the next few chapters.

When using expressions, number signs are used to delimit ColdFusion functions and variables within a block of text. So, how would you display the # itself? Look at the following code snippet:

```
<cfoutput>
#1: #FirstName#
</cfoutput>
```

You can try this yourself if you so feel inclined; you'll see that ColdFusion generates an error when it processes the code (see Figure 8.9).

Figure 8.9

Number signs in text must be escaped; otherwise, ColdFusion produces an error.

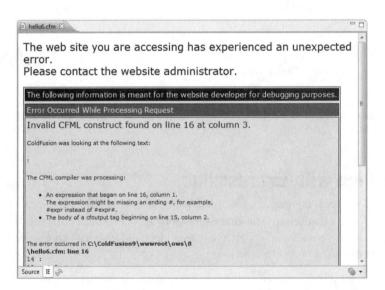

What causes this error? When ColdFusion encounters the # at the start of the line, it assumes you are delimiting a variable or a function and tries to find the matching # (which of course does not exist, as this is not a variable reference at all). The solution is to *escape* the number sign (flag it as being a real number sign), as follows:

```
<cfoutput>
##1: #FirstName#
</cfoutput>
```

When ColdFusion encounters ##, it knows that # is not delimiting a variable or function. Instead, it correctly displays a single #.

When to Use #, and When Not To

Before we go any further, let's clarify exactly when number signs are needed and when they're not.

Simply put, number signs are needed to flag functions and variables within a string of text.

In this first example, the number signs are obviously needed:

```
Hello #VARIABLES.FirstName#
```

But what about when a variable is used within a tag, like this?

```
<cfset UpperFirstName=UCase(FirstName)>
```

Here number signs are not necessary because ColdFusion assumes that anything passed to a tag is a function or variable unless explicitly defined as a string. So the following is incorrect:

```
<cfset #UpperFirstName#=#UCase(FirstName)#>
```

This code will actually work (ColdFusion is very forgiving), but it is still incorrect and should not be used.

This next example declares a variable and assigns a value that is a string, so no number signs are needed here:

```
<cfset FirstName="Ben">
```

But if the string contains variables, number signs would be necessary. Look at this next example: FullName is assigned a string, but the string contains two variables (FirstName and LastName) and those variables must be enclosed within number signs (otherwise ColdFusion will assign the text, not the variable values):

```
<cfset FullName="#FirstName# #LastName#">
```

Incidentally, the previous line of code is functionally equivalent to the following:

```
<cfset FullName=FirstName & " " & LastName>
```

Here number signs are not necessary because the variables are not being referred to within a string.

Again, the rule is: Only use number signs when referring to variables and functions within a block of text. It's as simple as that.

Using ColdFusion Data Types

The variables you have used thus far are simple variables, are defined, and contain a value. ColdFusion supports three advanced data types that I'll briefly introduce now: lists, arrays, and structures.

> **NOTE**
>
> This is just an introduction to lists, arrays, and structures. All three are used repeatedly throughout the rest of this book, so don't worry if you do not fully understand them by the time you are done reading this chapter. Right now, the intent is to ensure that you know these exist and what they are. You'll have lots of opportunities to use them soon enough.

Lists

Lists are used to group together related information. Lists are actually strings (plain text)—what makes them lists is that a delimiter is used to separate items within the string. For example, the following is a comma-delimited list of five U.S. states:

```
California,Florida,Michigan,Massachusetts,New York
```

The next example is also a list. Even though it might not look like a list, a sentence is a list delimited by spaces:

```
This is a ColdFusion list
```

Lists are created just like any other variables. For example, this next line of code uses the `<cfset>` tag to create a variable named `fruit` that contains a list of six fruits:

```
<cfset fruit="apple,banana,cherry,grape,mango,orange">
```

The code in Listing 8.7 demonstrates the use of lists. Type the code and save it as `list.cfm` in the 8 directory; then execute it. You should see an output similar to the one shown in Figure 8.10.

Figure 8.10

Lists are useful for grouping related data into simple sets.

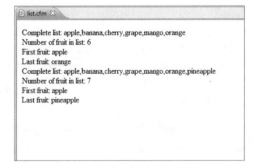

```
list.cfm
Complete list: apple,banana,cherry,grape,mango,orange
Number of fruit in list: 6
First fruit: apple
Last fruit: orange
Complete list: apple,banana,cherry,grape,mango,orange,pineapple
Number of fruit in list: 7
First fruit: apple
Last fruit: pineapple
```

Listing 8.7 `list.cfm`

```
<html>
<head>
 <title>List Example</title>
</head>
```

Listing 8.7 (CONTINUED)

```
<body>

<cfset fruit="apple,banana,cherry,grape,mango,orange">
<cfoutput>
Complete list: #fruit#<BR>
Number of fruit in list: #ListLen(fruit)#<BR>
First fruit: #ListFirst(fruit)#<BR>
Last fruit: #ListLast(fruit)#<BR>
<cfset fruit=ListAppend(fruit, "pineapple")>
Complete list: #fruit#<BR>
Number of fruit in list: #ListLen(fruit)#<BR>
First fruit: #ListFirst(fruit)#<BR>
Last fruit: #ListLast(fruit)#<BR>
</cfoutput>

</body>
</html>
```

Let's walk through the code in Listing 8.7. A <cfset> is used to create a list. As a list is simply a string, a simple variable assignment can be used.

Next comes the <cfoutput> block, starting with displaying #fruit# (the complete list). The next line of code uses the ListLen() function to return the number of items in the list (there are six of them). Individual list members can be retrieved using ListFirst() (used here to get the first list element), ListLast() (used here to get the last list element), and ListGetAt() (used to retrieve any list element, but not used in this example).

Then another <cfset> tag is used, as follows:

```
<cfset fruit=ListAppend(fruit, "pineapple")>
```

This code uses the ListAppend() function to add an element to the list. You will recall that functions return copies of modified variables, not modified variables themselves. So the <cfset> tag assigns the value returned by ListAppend() to fruit, effectively overwriting the list with the new revised list.

Then the number of items, as well as the first and last items, is displayed again. This time 7 items are in the list, and the last item has changed to pineapple.

As you can see, lists are very easy to use and provide a simple mechanism for grouping related data.

NOTE

I mentioned earlier that a sentence is a list delimited by spaces. The default list delimiter is indeed a comma. Actually, though, any character can be used as a list delimiter, and every list function takes an optional delimiter attribute if necessary.

Arrays

Arrays, like lists, store multiple values in a single variable. But unlike lists, arrays can contain far more complex data (including lists and even other arrays).

Unlike lists, arrays support multiple dimensions. A single-dimensional array is actually quite similar to a list: It's a linear collection. A two-dimensional array is more like a grid (imagine a spreadsheet), and data is stored in rows and columns. ColdFusion also supports three-dimensional arrays, which can be envisioned as cubes of data.

If this all sounds somewhat complex, well, it is. Arrays are not as easy to use as lists, but they are far more powerful (and far quicker). Here is a simple block of code that creates an array and displays part of it; the output is shown in Figure 8.11. To try it out, type the code in Listing 8.8 and save it as array1.cfm.

Figure 8.11

Arrays treat data as if they were in a one-, two-, or three-dimensional grid.

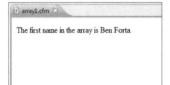

Listing 8.8 array1.cfm

```
<html>
<head>
 <title>Array Example 1</title>
</head>

<body>

<cfset names=ArrayNew(2)>
<cfset names[1][1]="Ben">
<cfset names[1][2]="Forta">
<cfset names[2][1]="Ray">
<cfset names[2][2]="Camden">
<cfset names[3][1]="Leon">
<cfset names[3][2]="Chalnick">

<cfoutput>
The first name in the array is #names[1][1]# #names[1][2]#
</cfoutput>

</body>
</html>
```

Arrays are created using the ArrayNew() function. ArrayNew() requires that the desired dimension be passed as a parameter, so the following code creates a two-dimensional array named names:

```
<cfset names=ArrayNew(2)>
```

Array elements are set using <cfset>, just like any other variables. But unlike other variables, when array elements are set the element number must be specified using an index (a relative position starting at 1). So, in a one-dimensional array, names[1] would refer to the first element and names[6] would refer to the sixth. In two-dimensional arrays, both dimensions must be specified, as seen in these next four lines (taken from the previous code listing):

```
<cfset names[1][1]="Ben">
<cfset names[1][2]="Forta">
<cfset names[2][1]="Ray">
<cfset names[2][2]="Camden">
```

names[1][1] refers to the first element in the first dimension—think of it as the first column of the first row in a grid. names[1][2] refers to the second column in that first row, and so on.

When accessed, even for display, the indexes must be used. Therefore, the following line of code

```
The first name in the array #names[1][1]# #names[1][2]#
```

generates this output:

```
The first name in the array Ben Forta
```

For a better view into an array, you can use a tag named <cfdump>. Listing 8.9 contains the code for array2.cfm (the same as array1.cfm, but with different output code). The output is shown in Figure 8.12.

Figure 8.12

<cfdump> is a great way to inspect array contents.

Listing 8.9 array2.cfm

```
<html>
<head>
 <title>Array Example 2</title>
</head>

<body>

<cfset names=ArrayNew(2)>
<cfset names[1][1]="Ben">
<cfset names[1][2]="Forta">
<cfset names[2][1]="Ray">
<cfset names[2][2]="Camden">
<cfset names[3][1]="Charlie">
<cfset names[3][2]="Arehart">

<cfdump var="#names#">
</body>
</html>
```

We'll take a look at `<cfdump>` again in a moment. But for now, as you can see, although they're not as easy to use as lists, arrays are a very flexible and powerful language feature.

As you have seen, arrays are first created using `ArrayNew()`, and then elements are added as needed. Thus far, elements were added to specific array locations ([2][1], for example). Array elements can also be appended using `ArrayAppend()`, as seen here:

```
<cfset names=ArrayNew(1)>
<cfset ArrayAppend(names, "Ben")>
<cfset ArrayAppend(names, "Ray")>
<cfset ArrayAppend(names, "Charlie")>
```

This example creates a single-dimensional array and then appends three elements to it.

When working with single-dimensional arrays, ColdFusion provides a shortcut syntax that can create and populate an array in a single step. The following snippet is functionally identical to the previous example:

```
<cfset names=["Ben","Ray","Charlie"]>
```

As you can see, single-dimensional arrays can be created and populated without the use of any array functions at all.

TIP

ColdFusion can process arrays far more quickly than it can lists. For very short sets of data, you'll probably not see much of a difference between arrays and lists, but as the amount of data in sets grows, the performance benefit of arrays of lists will become more apparent.

Structures

Structures are the most powerful and flexible data type within ColdFusion, so powerful in fact that many internal variables are actually structures.

Simply put, structures provide a way to store data within data. Unlike arrays, structures have no special dimensions and are not like grids. Rather, they can be thought of as top-level folders that can store data, or other folders, which in turn can store data, or other folders, and so on. Structures can contain lists, arrays, and even other structures.

To give you a sneak peek at what structures look like, here is some code. Give it a try yourself; save the file as `structure.cfm` (see Listing 8.10), and you should see output as shown in Figure 8.13.

Figure 8.13

Structures are one of the most important data types in ColdFusion and are used internally extensively.

Listing 8.10 structure.cfm

```
<html>
<head>
 <title>Structure Example</title>
</head>

<body>

<cfset contact=StructNew()>
<cfset contact.FirstName="Ben">
<cfset contact.LastName="Forta">
<cfset contact.EMail="ben@forta.com">

<cfoutput>
e-mail:
<a href="mailto:#contact.EMail#">#contact.FirstName# #contact.LastName#</a>
</cfoutput>

</body>
</html>
```

Structures are created using StructNew(), which—unlike ArrayNew()—takes no parameters. After a structure is created, variables can be set inside it. The following three lines of code all set variables with the contact structure:

```
<cfset contact.FirstName="Ben">
<cfset contact.LastName="Forta">
<cfset contact.EMail="ben@forta.com">
```

To access structure members, simply refer to them by name. #contact.FirstName# accesses the FirstName member of the contact structure. Therefore, the code

```
<a href="mailto:#contact.EMail#">#contact.FirstName# #contact.LastName#</a>
```

generates this output:

```
<a href="mailto:ben@forta.com">Ben Forta</a>
```

And that's just scratching the surface. Structures are incredibly powerful, and you'll use them extensively as you work through this book.

Like arrays, structures can be implicitly created and populated without the need to use StructNew(). The following snippet replaces the four <cfset> statements in the previous example:

```
<cfset contact={FirstName="Ben",
                LastName="Forta",
                EMail="ben@forta.com"}>
```

For simplicity's sake, I have described only the absolute basic form of structure use. ColdFusion features an entire set of structure manipulation functions that can be used to better take advantage of structures—you use some of them in the next chapter, "Programming with CFML."

"Dumping" Expressions

I showed you a tag named <cfdump> in Listing 8.9. This tag is never used in live applications, but it's an invaluable testing and debugging tool. <cfdump> lets you display any expression in a cleanly formatted table. You saw an example of dumping an array previously; now let's try another example. Type the following code into a new document (see Listing 8.11), save it as cfdump1.cfm, and then execute it in your browser. The output is shown in Figure 8.14.

Figure 8.14

<cfdump> is an invaluable diagnostics and debugging tool capable of displaying all sorts of data in a clean and easy-to-read format.

Listing 8.11 cfdump1.cfm

```
<html>
<head>
 <title>&lt;cfdump&gt; Example 1</title>
</head>

<body>

<cfset contact=StructNew()>
<cfset contact.FirstName="Ben">
<cfset contact.LastName="Forta">
<cfset contact.EMail="ben@forta.com">

<cfdump var="#contact#">

</body>
</html>
```

In this listing we've removed the <cfoutput> block. Instead, a <cfdump> tag is being used to dump (display) the contents of the contact structure. As you can see in Figure 8.14, <cfdump> creates a nicely formatted table containing the data contained within the structure. Our structure was pretty simple (three members, and no nested data types) but as the variables and data types you work with grow in complexity you'll find <cfdump> to be an invaluable utility tag.

Here is one final <cfdump> example, this time dumping the contents of two special variable scopes. SERVER is a structure (that contains two other structures) containing ColdFusion and operating system information. CGI is a structure that contains all sorts of data provided by the Web browser, Web server, and ColdFusion. Type the following code into a new document (see Listing 8.12), save it as cfdump2.cfm, and then execute it in your browser. The output is shown in Figure 8.15.

Figure 8.15

<cfdump> can display all ColdFusion data types, including nested data types.

Listing 8.12 cfdump2.cfm

```
<html>
<head>
 <title>&lt;cfdump&gt; Example 2</title>
</head>

<body>

<h1>SERVER</h1>
<cfdump var="#SERVER#">
<h1>CGI</h1>
<cfdump var="#CGI#">

</body>
</html>
```

TIP

The <cfdump> tag actually does more than just paint an HTML table. Try clicking any of the boxes with colored backgrounds; you'll be able to collapse and expand them as needed. When working with very large complex expressions this feature is incredibly useful, and to make it work ColdFusion automatically generates DHTML code (with supporting JavaScript) all automatically. To appreciate just how much work this little tag does, use View Source in your Web browser.

Commenting Your Code

The last introductory topic I want to mention is commenting your code. Many books leave this to the very end, but I believe it is so important that I am introducing the concept right here—before you start real coding.

The code you have worked with thus far has been short, simple, and pretty self-explanatory. But as you start building bigger and more complex applications, your code will become more involved and more complex, and comments become vital. Here is why you should comment your code:

- If you make code as self-descriptive as possible, when you revisit it at a later date you'll remember what you did, and why.

- This is even truer if others have to work on your code. The more detailed and accurate comments are, the easier (and safer) it will be to make changes or corrections when necessary.

- Commented code is much easier to debug than uncommented code.

- Commented code tends to be better organized.

And that's just the start of it.

Listing 8.13 is a revised version of `hello6.cfm`; all that has changed is the inclusion of comments. And as you can see from Figure 8.16, this has no impact on generated output whatsoever.

Figure 8.16

ColdFusion comments in your code are never sent to the client browser.

> hello7.cfm
>
> Hello ben, and welcome to ColdFusion!
>
> Your name in uppercase: BEN
> Your name in lowercase: ben
> Your name in reverse: neb
> Characters in your name: 3
> Your name 3 times: benbenben

Listing 8.13 `hello7.cfm`

```
<!---
Name:        hello7.cfm
Author:      Ben Forta (ben@forta.com)
Description: Demonstrate use of comments
Created:     07/01/2010
--->
<html>
<head>
 <title>Hello 7</title>
</head>

<body>

<!--- Save name --->
<cfset firstName="ben">

<!--- Save converted versions of name --->
<cfset upperFirstname=UCase(firstName)>
<cfset lowerFirstname=LCase(firstName)>
<cfset reverseFirstname=Reverse(firstName)>
<!--- Save name length --->
<cfset lenFirstName=Len(firstName)>
```

Listing 8.13 (CONTINUED)

```
<!--- Save repeated name --->
<cfset repeatFirstName=RepeatString(firstName, 3)>

<!--- Display output --->
<cfoutput>
Hello #FirstName#, and welcome to ColdFusion!<p>
Your name in uppercase: #upperFirstName#<br>
Your name in lowercase: #lowerFirstName#<br>
Your name in reverse: #reverseFirstName#<br>
Characters in your name: #lenFirstName#<br>
Your name 3 times: #repeatFirstName#<br>
</cfoutput>

</body>
</html>
```

Comments are typed between <!--- and ---> tags. Comments should never be nested and should never be mismatched (such as having a starting tag without an end tag, or vice versa).

NOTE

ColdFusion uses <!--- and ---> to delimit comments. HTML uses <!-- and --> (two hyphens instead of three). Within ColdFusion code, always use ColdFusion comments and not HTML comments. The latter will be sent to the client (they won't be displayed, but they will still be sent), whereas the former won't.

CAUTION

Be sure not to mix comment styles, using two hyphens on one end of the comment and three on the other. Doing so could cause your code to not be executed as expected.

TIP

Commenting code is a useful debugging technique. When you are testing code and need to eliminate specific lines, you can comment them out temporarily by wrapping them within <!--- and ---> tags.

Working with Conditional Processing

Chapter 8, "The Basics of CFML," introduced two ColdFusion tags (`<cfoutput>` and `<cfset>`), functions, and variables. This chapter takes CFML one big step further, adding conditional and programmatic processing, the stuff that starts to add real power to your code.

The code you wrote in the last chapter was linear—ColdFusion started at the top of the page and processed every line in order. And although that works for simple applications, more often than not you'll need to write code that does various things based on conditions, such as:

- Displaying different messages based on the time of day or day of the week

- Personalizing content based on user login

- Informing users of the status of searches or other operations

- Displaying (or hiding) options based on security level

All these require intelligence within your code to facilitate decision making. Conditional processing is the mechanism by which this is done, and ColdFusion supports two forms of conditional processing:

- If statements, created using `<cfif>` and related tags

- Switch statements, created using `<cfswitch>` and `<cfcase>`

Let's start by taking a look at these in detail.

If Statements

If statements are a fundamental part of most development languages. Though the syntax varies from one language to the next, the basic concepts and options are the same. If statements are used to create conditions that are evaluated, enabling you to perform actions based on the result.

The conditions passed to if statements always evaluate to TRUE or FALSE, and any condition that can be expressed as a TRUE / FALSE (or YES / NO) question is valid. Here are some examples of valid conditions:

- Is today Monday?
- Does variable FirstName exist?
- Were any rows retrieved from a database?
- Does variable one equal variable two?
- Is a specific word in a sentence?

More complex conditions (multiple conditions) are allowed, too:

- Is today Sunday or Saturday?
- Was a credit card number provided, and if yes, has it been validated?
- Does the currently logged-in user have a first name of Ben and a last name of Forta, or a first name of Ray and a last name of Camden?

The common denominator here is that all these conditions can be answered with TRUE or FALSE, so they are all valid conditions.

NOTE

In ColdFusion, the words TRUE and FALSE can be used when evaluating conditions. In addition, YES can be used in lieu of TRUE, and NO can be used in lieu of FALSE. It is also worth noting that all numbers are either TRUE or FALSE: 0 is FALSE, and any other number (positive or negative) is TRUE.

Basic If Statements

ColdFusion if statements are created using the <cfif> tag. <cfif> takes no attributes; instead, it takes a condition. For example, the following <cfif> statement checks to see whether a variable named FirstName contains the value Ben:

```
<cfif FirstName IS "Ben">
```

The keyword IS is an operator used to test for equality. Other operators are supported, too, as listed in Table 9.1.

Table 9.1   CFML Evaluation Operators

OPERATOR	SHORTCUT	DESCRIPTION
EQUAL	IS, EQ	Tests for equality
NOT EQUAL	IS NOT, NEQ	Tests for nonequality
GREATER THAN	GT	Tests for greater than
GREATER THAN OR EQUAL TO	GTE	Tests for greater than or equal to
LESS THAN	LT	Tests for less than
LESS THAN OR EQUAL TO	LTE	Tests for less than or equal to
CONTAINS		Tests whether a value is contained within a second value
DOES NOT CONTAIN		Tests whether a value is not contained within a second value

As seen in Table 9.1, most CFML operators have shortcut equivalents that you can use. The IS operator used in the previous code example is actually a shortcut for EQUAL, and that condition is:

```
<cfif FirstName EQUAL "Ben">
```

To test whether FirstName is not Ben, you could use the following code:

```
<cfif FirstName IS NOT "Ben">
```

or

```
<cfif FirstName NEQ "Ben">
```

or

```
<cfif FirstName NOT EQUAL "Ben">
```

or even

```
<cfif NOT FirstName IS "Ben">
```

In this last snippet, the NOT operator is used to negate a condition.

Ready to try <cfif> yourself? What follows is a simple application that checks to see whether today is the weekend (Listing 9.1). Save the file as if1.cfm, and execute it from within ColdFusion Builder or your Web browser (if the latter then the URL to use will be http://localhost:8500/ows/9/if1.cfm if the integrated Web server is being used). The output is shown in Figure 9.1 (if today is Sunday).

Figure 9.1

You can use <cfif> statements to display output conditionally.

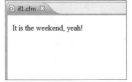

Listing 9.1   if1.cfm

```
<!---
Name:        if1.cfm
Author:      Ben Forta (ben@forta.com)
Description: Demonstrate use of <cfif>
Created:     01/01/2010
--->

<html>
<head>
 <title>If 1</title>
</head>

<body>

<!--- Is it the weekend? --->
<cfif DayOfWeek(Now()) IS 1>
 <!--- Yes it is, great! --->
 It is the weekend, yeah!
</cfif>

</body>
</html>
```

TIP

Don't forget to create the **9** directory under **ows**; all the code created in this chapter should go in that directory.

The code in Listing 9.1 should be self-explanatory. A comment header describes the code, and the standard HTML <head> and <body> tags are used to create the page. Then comes the <cfif> statement:

```
<cfif DayOfWeek(Now()) IS 1>
```

As you already have seen, Now() is a function that returns the current system date and time. DayOfWeek() is a function that returns the day of the week for a specified date (a variable, a literal, or another function). DayOfWeek(Now()) returns the current day of the week: 1 for Sunday, 2 for Monday, 3 for Tuesday, and so on. The condition DayOfWeek(Now()) IS 1 then simply checks to see whether it is Sunday. If it is Sunday, the condition evaluates to TRUE; if not, it evaluates to FALSE.

If the condition is TRUE, the text between the <cfif> and </cfif> tags is displayed. It's as simple as that.

Multiple-Condition If Statements

A couple of problems exist with the code in Listing 9.1, the most important of which is that weekends include both Sundays and Saturdays. Therefore, the code to check whether it is the weekend needs to check for both days.

Here is a revised version of the code (see Listing 9.2); save this file as if2.cfm, and then execute it.

TIP

So as not to have to retype all the code as you make changes, use ColdFusion Builder's File > Save As menu option to save the file with the new name, and then edit the newly saved file.

Listing 9.2 if2.cfm

```
<!---
Name:        if2.cfm
Author:      Ben Forta (ben@forta.com)
Description: Demonstrate use of multiple conditions
Created:     01/01/2010
--->

<html>
<head>
 <title>If 2</title>
</head>

<body>

<!--- Is it the weekend? --->
<cfif (DayOfWeek(Now()) IS 1) OR (DayOfWeek(Now()) IS 7)>
 <!--- Yes it is, great! --->
 It is the weekend, yeah!
</cfif>

</body>
</html>
```

The code is the same as Listing 9.1, except for the `<cfif>` statement itself:

```
<cfif (DayOfWeek(Now()) IS 1) OR (DayOfWeek(Now()) IS 7)>
```

This statement contains two conditions, one that checks whether the day of the week is 1 (Sunday), and one that checks whether it is 7 (Saturday). If it is Sunday or Saturday, the message is displayed correctly. Problem solved.

To tell ColdFusion to test for either condition, the OR operator is used. By using OR if either of the specified conditions is TRUE, the condition returns TRUE. FALSE is returned only if *neither* condition is TRUE. This is in contrast to the AND operator, which requires that *both* conditions be TRUE and returns FALSE if only one or no conditions are TRUE. Look at the following code snippet:

```
<cfif (FirstName IS "Ben") AND (LastName IS "Forta")>
```

For this condition to be TRUE, the FirstName must be Ben and the LastName must be Forta. Ben with any other LastName or Forta with any other FirstName fails the test.

AND and OR are logical operators (sometimes called *Boolean* operators). These two are the most frequently used logical operators, but others are supported, too, as listed in Table 9.2.

Table 9.2 CFML Logical Operators

OPERATOR	DESCRIPTION
AND	Returns TRUE only if both conditions are TRUE
OR	Returns TRUE if at least one condition is TRUE
XOR	Returns TRUE if either condition is TRUE, but not if both or neither are TRUE

Table 9.2 (CONTINUED)

OPERATOR	DESCRIPTION
EQV	Tests for equivalence and returns TRUE if both conditions are the same (either both TRUE or both FALSE, but not if one is TRUE and one is FALSE)
IMP	Tests for implication; returns FALSE only when the first condition is TRUE and the second is FALSE
NOT	Negates any other logical operator

TIP

You probably noticed that when multiple conditions (either AND or OR) were used, each condition was enclosed within parentheses. This is not required but is generally good practice. Not only does it make the code cleaner and easier to read, but it also prevents bugs from being introduced by expressions being evaluated in ways other than you expected. For example, if both AND and OR are used in a condition, AND is always evaluated before OR, which might or might not be what you want. Parentheses are evaluated before AND, so by using parentheses you can explicitly manage the order of evaluation.

If and Else

The code in Listing 9.2 is logically correct: If it is Sunday or Saturday, then it is indeed the weekend, and the weekend message is displayed. But what if it is not Sunday or Saturday? Right now, nothing is displayed at all; so let's fix that.

Listing 9.3 contains the revised code, capable of displaying a non-weekend message if necessary (see Figure 9.2). Save this code as if3.cfm, and then execute it.

Figure 9.2

The <cfelse> statement enables the creation of code to be executed when a <cfif> test fails.

Listing 9.3 if3.cfm

```
<!---
Name:        if3.cfm
Author:      Ben Forta (ben@forta.com)
Description: Demonstrate use of <cfif> and <cfelse>
Created:     01/01/2010
--->

<html>
<head>
 <title>If 3</title>
</head>
```

Listing 9.3 (CONTINUED)

```
<body>

<!--- Is it the weekend? --->
<cfif (DayOfWeek(Now()) IS 1) OR (DayOfWeek(Now()) IS 7)>
 <!--- Yes it is, great! --->
 It is the weekend, yeah!
<cfelse>
 <!--- No it is not :-( --->
 No, it's not the weekend yet, sorry!
</cfif>

</body>
</html>
```

The only real difference between Listings 9.2 and 9.3 is the introduction of a new tag—<cfelse>.
<cfif> is used to define code to be executed when a condition is TRUE, and <cfelse> defines code to
be executed when a condition is FALSE. <cfelse> takes no attributes and can be used only between
<cfif> and </cfif> tags. The new code will now display It is the weekend, yeah! if it is Sunday or
Saturday and No, it's not the weekend yet, sorry! if not. Much better.

But before you move on, Listing 9.4 contains one more refinement—a cleaner <cfif> statement.
Save Listing 9.4 as if4.cfm, and then execute it (it should do exactly what Listing 9.3 did).

Listing 9.4 if4.cfm

```
<!---
Name:       if4.cfm
Author:     Ben Forta (ben@forta.com)
Description: Demonstrate saving <cfif> results
Created:    01/01/2010
--->

<html>
<head>
<title>If 4</title>
</head>

<body>

<!--- Is it the weekend? --->
<cfset weekend=(DayOfWeek(Now()) IS 1) OR (DayOfWeek(Now()) IS 7)>

<!--- Let the user know --->
<cfif weekend>
 <!--- Yes it is, great! --->
 It is the weekend, yeah!
<cfelse>
 <!--- No it is not :-( --->
 No, it's not the weekend yet, sorry!
</cfif>

</body>
</html>
```

The more complex conditions become, the harder they are to read, so many developers prefer to save the results of executed conditions to variables for later use. Look at this line of code (from Listing 9.4):

```
<cfset weekend=(DayOfWeek(Now()) IS 1) OR (DayOfWeek(Now()) IS 7)>
```

Here, `<cfset>` is used to create a variable named `weekend`. The value stored in this variable is whatever the condition returns. So, if it is a weekend (Sunday or Saturday), `weekend` will be `TRUE`, and if it is not a weekend then `weekend` will be `FALSE`.

→   See Chapter 8 for detailed coverage of the `<cfset>` tag.

The `<cfset>` statement could be broken down further if required, like this:

```
<!--- Get day of week --->
<cfset dow=DayOfWeek(Now())>
<!--- Is it the weekend? --->
<cfset weekend=(dow IS 1) OR (dow IS 7)>
```

The end result is the same, but this code is more readable.

After `weekend` is set, it can be used in the `<cfif>` statement:

```
<cfif weekend>
```

If `weekend` is `TRUE`, the first block of text is displayed; otherwise, the `<cfelse>` text is displayed.

But what is `weekend` being compared to? In every condition thus far, you have used an operator (such as `IS`) to test a condition. Here, however, no operator is used. So what is `weekend` being tested against?

Actually, `weekend` is indeed being tested; it is being compared to `TRUE`. Within a `<cfif>` the comparison is optional, and if it's omitted, a comparison to `TRUE` is assumed. So, `<cfif weekend>` is functionally the same as

```
<cfif weekend IS TRUE>
```

The `weekend` variable contains either `TRUE` or `FALSE`. If it's `TRUE`, the condition is effectively

```
<cfif TRUE IS TRUE>
```

which obviously evaluates to `TRUE`. But if `weekend` is `FALSE`, the condition is

```
<cfif FALSE IS TRUE>
```

which obviously is `FALSE`.

I said that `weekend` contained either `TRUE` or `FALSE`, but you should feel free to test that for yourself. If you add the following line to your code, you'll be able to display the contents of `weekend`:

```
<cfoutput>#weekend#</cfoutput>
```

As you can see, you have a lot of flexibility when it comes to writing `<cfif>` statements.

Multiple If Statements

There's one more feature of <cfif> that you need to look at—support for multiple independent conditions (as opposed to one condition made up of multiple conditions).

The best way to explain this is with an example. In the previous listings, you displayed a message on weekends. But what if you wanted to display different messages on Sunday and Saturday? You could create multiple <cfif> </cfif> blocks, but there is a better way.

Listing 9.5 contains yet another version of the code; this time the file name should be if5.cfm.

Listing 9.5 if5.cfm

```
<!---
Name:        if5.cfm
Author:      Ben Forta (ben@forta.com)
Description: Demonstrate <cfelseif> use
Created:     01/01/2010
--->

<html>
<head>
 <title>If 5</title>
</head>

<body>

<!--- Get day of week --->
<cfset dow=DayOfWeek(Now())>

<!--- Let the user know --->
<cfif dow IS 1>
 <!--- It's Sunday --->
 It is the weekend! But make the most of it, tomorrow it's back to work.
<cfelseif dow IS 7>
 <!--- It's Saturday --->
 It is the weekend! And even better, tomorrow is the weekend too!
<cfelse>
 <!--- No it is not :-( --->
 No, it's not the weekend yet, sorry!
</cfif>

</body>
</html>
```

Let's take a look at the previous code. A <cfset> is used to create a variable named dow, which contains the day of the week (the value returned by DayOfWeek(Now()), a number from 1 to 7).

The <cfif> statement checks to see whether dow is 1, and if TRUE, displays the Sunday message (see Figure 9.3). Then a <cfelseif> is used to provide an alternative <cfif> statement:

```
<cfelseif dow IS 7>
```

Figure 9.3

If dow is 1, the Sunday message is displayed.

The <cfelseif> checks to see whether dow is 7, and if TRUE, displays the Saturday message (see Figure 9.4). Finally, <cfelse> is used to display text if neither the <cfif> nor the <cfelseif> is TRUE. <cfelseif> is essentially a combined <cfelse> and <cfif>; hence its name.

Figure 9.4

If dow is 7, the Saturday message is displayed.

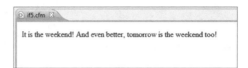

Saving conditions' results to variables, as you did here with the dow variable and previously with weekend, instead of repeating code makes your code more readable. But it also has another benefit. If you use the exact same expressions (getting the day of the week, say) in multiple places, you run the risk that one day you'll update the code and not make all the changes in all the required locations. If just a single expression must be changed, that potential problem is avoided.

No limit exists to the number of <cfelseif> statements you use within a <cfif> tag, but you can never use more than one <cfif> or <cfelse>.

NOTE

Use of <cfelseif> and <cfelse> is optional. However, if <cfelse> is used, it must always be the last tag before the </cfif>.

Putting It All Together

<cfif> is one of the most frequently used tags in CFML. So before we move on to the next subject, let's walk through one more example—a slightly more complex one.

Guess the Number is a simple game: *I'm thinking of a number between 1 and 10; guess what number I am thinking of.* ColdFusion selects a random number, you guess a number, and ColdFusion will tell you whether you guessed the correct one.

Listing 9.6 contains the code for guess1.cfm. Save it in the 9 directory, but don't execute it from within ColdFusion Builder. Instead, use this URL to execute it:

```
http://localhost:8500/ows/9/guess1.cfm?guess=n
```

Replace n with a number from 1 to 10. For example, if you guess 5, use this URL:

```
http://localhost:8500/ows/9/guess1.cfm?guess=5
```

You must pass the guess URL parameter, or an error will be thrown. When you pass that parameter you'll see an output similar to the ones shown in Figures 9.5 and 9.6. (Actually, if you reload the page often enough, you'll see both figures.)

Figure 9.5

URL.guess matched the number ColdFusion picked.

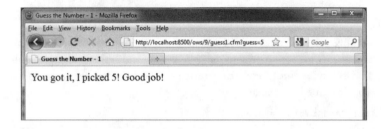

Figure 9.6

URL.guess did not match the number ColdFusion picked.

Listing 9.6 guess1.cfm

```
<!---
Name:        guess1.cfm
Author:      Ben Forta (ben@forta.com)
Description: if statement demonstration
Created:     01/01/2010
--->

<html>
<head>
 <title>guess the number - 1</title>
</head>

<body>

<!--- Pick a random number --->
<cfset RandomNumber=RandRange(1, 10)>

<!--- Check if matched --->
<cfif RandomNumber IS URL.guess>
 <!--- It matched --->
 <cfoutput>
 You got it, I picked #RandomNumber#! Good job!
 </cfoutput>
<cfelse>
 <!--- No match --->
 <cfoutput>
 Sorry, I picked #RandomNumber#! Try again!
```

Listing 9.6   (CONTINUED)

```
  </cfoutput>
  </cfif>

  </body>
  </html>
```

The first thing the code does is pick a random number. To do this, the RandRange() function is used. RandRange() takes two parameters (the range) and returns a random number within that range. The following line of code thus returns a random number from 1 to 10 (inclusive) and saves it in a variable named RandomNumber:

```
<cfset RandomNumber=RandRange(1, 10)>
```

Next, the randomly generated number is compared to the guessed number (which was passed as a URL parameter) using the following <cfif> statement:

```
<cfif RandomNumber IS URL.guess>
```

URL.guess is the variable containing the guess value provided in the URL. If the two match, the first message is displayed; if they don't, the second message is displayed.

→   URL variables and their use are covered in detail in Chapter 10, "Creating Data-Driven Pages." For now, it's sufficient to know that variables passed as parameters to a URL are accessible via the URL scope.

But what if no guess parameter was specified? You will recall from Chapter 8 that referring to a variable that doesn't exist generates an error. Therefore, you should modify the code to check that URL.guess exists before using it. Listing 9.7 contains the modified version of the code; save this file as guess2.cfm.

NOTE

This is why I said not to try guess1.cfm from within ColdFusion Builder. If you had, the code would have been executed without allowing you to pass the necessary URL parameter, and an error would have been generated.

Listing 9.7   guess2.cfm

```
<!---
Name:        guess2.cfm
Author:      Ben Forta (ben@forta.com)
Description: if statement demonstration
Created:     01/01/2010
--->

<html>
<head>
 <title>Guess the Number - 2</title>
</head>

<body>

<!--- Pick a random number --->
<cfset RandomNumber=RandRange(1, 10)>

<!--- Check if number was passed --->
```

Listing 9.7 (CONTINUED)

```
<cfif IsDefined("URL.guess")>

  <!--- Yes it was, did it match? --->
  <cfif RandomNumber IS URL.guess>
  <!--- It matched --->
  <cfoutput>
  You got it, I picked #RandomNumber#! Good job!
  </cfoutput>
  <cfelse>
  <!--- No match --->
  <cfoutput>
  Sorry, I picked #RandomNumber#! Try again!
  </cfoutput>
  </cfif>

<cfelse>

  <!--- No guess specified, give instructions --->
  You did not guess a number.<BR>
  To guess a number, reload this page adding
  <B>?guess=n</B> (where n is the guess, for
  example, ?guess=5). Number should be between
  1 and 10.

</cfif>

</body>
</html>
```

Listing 9.7 introduces a new concept in <cfif> statements—nested <cfif> tags (one set of <cfif> tags within another). Let's take a look at the code. The first <cfif> statement is

```
<cfif IsDefined("URL.guess")>
```

IsDefined() is a CFML function that checks whether a variable exists. IsDefined("URL.guess") returns TRUE if guess was passed on the URL and FALSE if not. Using this function, you can process the guess only if it actually exists. So the entire code block (complete with <cfif> and <cfelse> tags) is within the TRUE block of the outer <cfif>, and the original <cfif> block is now nested—it's a <cfif> within a <cfif>.

This also enables you to add another <cfelse> block, on the outer <cfif>. Remember, the outer <cfif> checks whether URL.guess exists, so <cfelse> can be used to display a message if it doesn't. Therefore, not only will the code no longer generate an error if guess was not specified, it will also provide help and instruct the user appropriately (see Figure 9.7).

NOTE

The code in Listing 9.7 clearly demonstrates the value of indenting your code. The code within each <cfif> block is indented, and the deeper the nesting, the further the indentation. This type of formatting is extremely popular among professional developers because it makes finding matching (or mismatched) code blocks much easier.

Figure 9.7

By checking for the existence of expected variables, your applications can provide assistance and instructions if necessary.

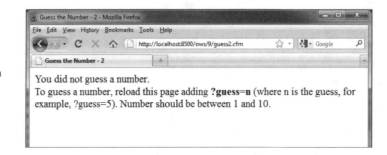

As a rule, nesting should be avoided unless absolutely necessary. And nesting really isn't necessary in this game. Listing 9.8 takes the game code one step further, this time using `<cfelseif>` and multiple clause conditions to create tighter (and better performing) code. Save Listing 9.8 as `guess3.cfm`.

Listing 9.8 guess3.cfm

```
<!---
Name:        guess3.cfm
Author:      Ben Forta (ben@forta.com)
Description: if statement demonstration
Created:     01/01/2010
--->

<html>
<head>
 <title>Guess the Number - 3</title>
</head>

<body>

<!--- Pick a random number --->
<cfset RandomNumber=RandRange(1, 10)>

<!--- Check if number was passed --->
<cfif IsDefined("URL.guess")
      AND (RandomNumber IS URL.guess)>
 <!--- It matched --->
 <cfoutput>
 You got it, I picked #RandomNumber#! Good job!
 </cfoutput>
<cfelseif IsDefined("URL.guess")
          AND (RandomNumber IS NOT URL.guess)>
 <!--- Did not match --->
 <cfoutput>
 Sorry, I picked #RandomNumber#! Try again!
 </cfoutput>
<cfelse>
 <!--- No guess specified, give instructions --->
 You did not guess a number.<BR>
 To guess a number, reload this page adding
 <B>?guess=n</B> (where n is the guess, for
```

Listing 9.8 (CONTINUED)

```
example, ?guess=5). Number should be between
 1 and 10.
</cfif>

</body>
</html>
```

Again, the code starts with the random number generation. Then this `<cfif>` statement is used:

```
<cfif IsDefined("URL.guess")
      AND (RandomNumber IS URL.guess)>
```

As explained earlier, AND requires that both conditions be TRUE. Therefore, the first message is displayed only if URL.guess exists and if the numbers match. The second condition is in a `<cfelseif>` statement:

```
<cfelseif IsDefined("URL.guess")
          AND (RandomNumber IS NOT URL.guess)>
```

Here too, IsDefined() is used to check that URL.guess exists. The second condition is TRUE only when the numbers don't match, in which case the second message is displayed.

NOTE

Notice that the `<cfif>` and `<cfelseif>` statements in Listing 9.8 are split over two lines. ColdFusion ignores white space (including line breaks), so code can be spread over as many lines as needed, and shorter lines of code (as used here) can be easier to read.

The `<cfelse>` here is evaluated only if `<cfif>` and `<cfelseif>` are both not evaluated, in which case it would be clear that URL.guess was not defined.

The same result occurs, but this time without nesting.

CAUTION

As a rule, don't nest unless you really have to. Although nesting is legal within your code, nested code tends to be easier to make mistakes in, harder to debug, and slower to execute.

Take a look at this line of code again:

```
<cfif IsDefined("URL.guess")
      AND (RandomNumber IS URL.guess)>
```

You might be wondering why an error would not be generated if URL.guess did not exist. After all, if the IsDefined() returns FALSE, shouldn't the next condition cause an error because URL.guess is being referred to?

The answer is no, because ColdFusion supports *short-circuit evaluation*. This means that conditions that don't affect a result are never evaluated. In an AND condition, if the first condition returns FALSE, then the result will always be FALSE, regardless of whether the second condition returns TRUE or FALSE. Similarly, in an OR condition, if the first condition is TRUE, the result will always be TRUE, regardless of whether the second condition is TRUE or FALSE. With short-circuit evaluation, conditions that don't affect the final result aren't executed, to save processing time. So in the previous example, if IsDefined("URL.guess") returns FALSE, RandomNumber IS URL.guess is never even evaluated.

Let's finish this game application with one last revision. Listing 9.9 should be saved as file guess4.cfm.

Listing 9.9 guess4.cfm

```
<!---
Name:        guess4.cfm
Author:      Ben Forta (ben@forta.com)
Description: if statement demonstration
Created:     01/01/2010
--->

<html>
<head>
 <title>Guess the Number - 4</title>
</head>

<body>

<!--- Set range --->
<cfset GuessLow=1>
<cfset GuessHigh=10>

<!--- Pick a random number --->
<cfset RandomNumber=RandRange(GuessLow, GuessHigh)>
<!--- Was a guess specified? --->
<cfset HaveGuess=IsDefined("URL.guess")>

<!--- If specified, did it match? --->
<cfset Match=(HaveGuess)
        AND (RandomNumber IS URL.guess)>

<!--- Feedback --->
<cfoutput>
<cfif Match>
 <!--- It matched --->
 You got it, I picked #RandomNumber#! Good job!
<cfelseif HaveGuess>
 <!--- Did not match --->
 Sorry, I picked #RandomNumber#! Try again!
<cfelse>
 <!--- No guess specified, give instructions --->
 You did not guess a number.<BR>
 To guess a number, reload this page adding
 <B>?guess=n</B> (where n is the guess, for
 example, ?guess=5). Number should be between
 #GuessLow# and #GuessHigh#.
</cfif>
</cfoutput>

</body>
</html>
```

Quite a few changes were made in Listing 9.9. First, the range high and low values are now variables, defined as follows:

```
<!--- Set range --->
<cfset GuessLow=1>
<cfset GuessHigh=10>
```

By saving these to variables, changing the range (perhaps to allow numbers 1–20) will be easier. These variables are passed to the RandRange() function and are used in the final output (when instructions are given if no guess was specified) so that the allowed range is included in the instructions.

Next, the simple assignment <cfset HaveGuess=IsDefined("URL.guess")> sets variable HaveGuess to either TRUE (if guess was specified) or FALSE. The next assignment sets a variable named Match to TRUE if the numbers match (and guess was specified) or to FALSE. In other words, two simple <cfset> statements contain all the necessary intelligence and decision making, and because the results are saved to variables, using this information is very easy indeed.

This makes the display code much cleaner. <cfif Match> displays the first message if the correct guess was provided. <cfelseif HaveGuess> is executed only if the <cfif> failed, which must mean the guess was wrong. In addition, the <cfelse> displays the instructions (with the correct range included automatically).

It doesn't get much cleaner than that.

NOTE

Listing 9.9 demonstrates a coding practice whereby logic (or intelligence) and presentation are separated. This is a practice that should be adopted whenever possible, as the resulting code will be both cleaner and more reusable.

Switch Statements

All the conditional processing used thus far has involved <cfif> statements. But as I stated at the beginning of this chapter, ColdFusion also supports another form of conditional processing: *switch statements*.

The best way to understand switch statements is to see them used. Listing 9.10 should be saved as file switch.cfm.

When you have executed Listing 9.10, you'll notice that it does exactly what Listing 9.5 (file if5.cfm) does. The code here is very different, however.

Listing 9.10 switch.cfm

```
<!---
Name:         switch.cfm
Author:       Ben Forta (ben@forta.com)
Description:  Demonstrate use of <cfswitch> and <cfcase>
Created:      01/01/2010
--->

<html>
<head>
```

Listing 9.10 (CONTINUED)

```
<title>Switch</title>
</head>

<body>

<!--- Get day of week --->
<cfset dow=DayOfWeek(Now())>

<!--- Let the user know --->
<cfswitch expression="#dow#">

  <!--- Is it Sunday? --->
  <cfcase value="1">
  It is the weekend! But make the most of it, tomorrow it's back to work.
  </cfcase>

  <!--- Is it Saturday? --->
  <cfcase value="7">
  It is the weekend! And even better, tomorrow is the weekend too!
  </cfcase>

  <!--- If code reaches here it's not the weekend --->
  <cfdefaultcase>
  No, it's not the weekend yet, sorry!
  </cfdefaultcase>
</cfswitch>

</body>
</html>
```

First the day of the week is saved to variable dow (as it was earlier), but that variable is then passed to a <cfswitch> statement:

```
<cfswitch expression="#dow#">
```

<cfswitch> takes an expression to evaluate; here, the value in dow is used. The expression is a string, so number signs are needed around dow. Otherwise, the text dow will be evaluated instead of the value of that variable.

<cfswitch> statements include <cfcase> statements, which each match a specific value that expression could return. The first <cfcase> is executed if expression is 1 (Sunday) because 1 is specified as the value in <cfcase value="1">. Similarly, the second <cfcase> is executed if expression is 7 (Saturday). Whichever <cfcase> matches the expression is the one that is processed, and in this example, the text between the <cfcase> and </cfcase> tags is displayed.

If no <cfcase> matches the expression, the optional <cfdefaultcase> block is executed. <cfdefaultcase> is similar to <cfelse> in a <cfif> statement.

As I said, the end result is exactly the same as in the example using <cfif>. So, why would you use <cfswitch> over <cfif>? For two reasons:

- <cfswitch> usually executes more quickly than <cfif>.

- <cfswitch> code tends to be neater and more manageable.

You can't always use <cfswitch>, however. Unlike <cfif>, <cfswitch> can be used only if all conditions are checking against the same expression. In other words, when the conditions are all the same, and only the values being compared against differ. If you need to check a set of entirely different conditions, <cfswitch> would not be an option, which is why you couldn't use it in the game example.

TIP

Although the example here uses <cfswitch> to display text, that is not all this tag can do. In fact, just about any code you can imagine can be placed between <cfcase> and </cfcase>. <cfcase> tags are evaluated in order, so it makes sense to place the values that you expect to match more often before those that will match much less often. Doing so can improve application performance slightly because ColdFusion won't have to evaluate values unnecessarily. This is also true of sets of <cfif> and <cfelseif> statements: Conditions that are expected to match more frequently should be moved higher up the list.

Using Looping

Loops are another fundamental language element supported by most development platforms. Loops do just that—they loop. Loops provide a mechanism with which to repeat tasks, and Cold-Fusion supports several types of loops, all via the <cfloop> tag:

- Index loops, used to repeat a set number of times
- Conditional loops, used to repeat until a specified condition becomes FALSE
- Query loops, used to iterate through database query results
- List loops, used to iterate through a specified list
- Collection loops, used to loop through structures
- File loops, used to loop through the lines in a file

You won't use all these loop types here, but to acquaint you with <cfloop>, let's look at a few examples.

The Index Loop

One of the most frequently used loops is the index loop, used to loop a set number of times (from a specified value to another specified value). To learn about this loop, you'll generate a simple list (see Figure 9.8). Type the code in Listing 9.11, and save it in 9 as loop1.cfm.

Figure 9.8

Loops can build lists and other display elements automatically.

Listing 9.11 loop1.cfm

```
<!---
Name:        loop1.cfm
Author:      Ben Forta (ben@forta.com)
Description: Demonstrate use of <cfloop from to>
Created:     01/01/2010
--->

<html>
<head>
 <title>Loop 1</title>
</head>

<body>

<!--- Start list --->
<ul>

<!--- loop from 1 to 10 --->
<cfloop from="1" to="10" index="i">
 <!--- Write item --->
 <cfoutput><li>Item #i#</li></cfoutput>
</cfloop>

<!--- end list --->
</ul>

</body>
</html>
```

<cfloop> is used to create a block of code to be executed over and over. The code in Listing 9.11 creates a simple loop that displays a list of numbers in an HTML unordered list from 1 to 10. The HTML unordered list is started before the <cfloop> (you wouldn't want to start it in the loop, because you'd be starting a new list on each iteration) and ends after the </cfloop>. The loop itself is created using the following code:

```
<cfloop from="1" to="10" index="i">
```

In an index loop the from and to values must be specified and the code between <cfloop> and </cfloop> is repeated that many times. Here, from="1" and to="10", so the loop repeats 10 times. Within the loop itself, a variable named in the index attribute contains the current increment, so i will be 1 the first time around, 2 the second time, and so on.

Within the loop, the value of i is displayed in a list item using the following code:

```
<cfoutput><li>Item #i#</li></cfoutput>
```

The first time around, when i is 1, the generated output will be

```
<li>Item 1</li>
```

and on the second loop it will be

```
<li>Item 2</li>
```

and so on.

TIP

Want to loop backwards? You can. Use the `step` attribute to specify how to count from the `from` value to the `to` value. `step="-1"` makes the count go backward, one number at a time.

The List Loop

List loops are designed to make working with ColdFusion lists simple and error-free. Whether it is lists created by form submissions, manual lists, lists derived from database queries (regardless of the origin), any list (with any delimiter) can be iterated over using `<cfloop>`.

➜   For an introduction to lists, see Chapter 8.

The following example uses a list created in Chapter 8 and loops through the list displaying one element at a time (see Figure 9.9). Save Listing 9.12 as `loop2.cfm`.

Figure 9.9

Any lists, with any delimiter, can be iterated using `<cfloop>`.

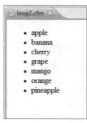

Listing 9.12   `loop2.cfm`

```
<!---
Name:        loop2.cfm
Author:      Ben Forta (ben@forta.com)
Description: Demonstrate use of <cfloop list>
Created:     01/01/2010
--->

<html>
<head>
 <title>Loop 2</title>
</head>

<body>

<!--- Create list --->
<cfset fruit="apple,banana,cherry,grape,mango,orange,pineapple">

<!--- Start list --->
<ul>

<!--- Loop through list --->
<cfloop list="#fruit#" index="i">
 <!--- Write item --->
 <cfoutput><li>#i#</li></cfoutput>
</cfloop>
```

Listing 9.12 (CONTINUED)

```
<!--- end list --->
</ul>

</body>
</html>
```

`<cfset>` is used to create the list—a comma-delimited list of fruit. `<cfloop>` takes the list to be processed in the `list` attribute, and because `list` accepts a string, number signs must be used around the variable name `fruit`.

`<cfloop>` repeats the loop once for every element in the list. In addition, within the loop, it makes the current element available in the variable specified in the `index` attribute—in this example, `i`. So, `i` is `apple` on the first iteration, `banana` on the second iteration, and so on.

NOTE

Lists also can be looped over using index loops. `from="1" to="#ListLen(fruit)#"` sets the `to` and `from` properly. Within the loop, `ListGetAt()` can be used to obtain the element.

Nested Loops

Like the `<cfif>` and `<cfswitch>` statements, loops can be nested. Nesting loops lets you create extremely powerful code, as long as you are very careful in constructing the loops. Listing 9.13 contains a practical example of nested loops, using three loops to display a table of Web browser–safe colors (seen in Figure 9.10). Save the code as `loop3.cfm`.

Figure 9.10

Displaying the Web browser–safe color palette requires the use of three nested loops.

Listing 9.13 `loop3.cfm`

```
<!---
Name:        loop3.cfm
Author:      Ben Forta (ben@forta.com)
Description: Demonstrate use of nested loops
Created:     01/01/2010
--->

<html>
<head>
 <title>Loop 3</title>
</head>

<body>

<!--- Hex value list --->
<cfset hex="00,33,66,99,CC,FF">

<!--- Create table --->
<table>

<!--- Start RR loop --->
<cfloop index="red" list="#hex#">
 <!--- Start GG loop --->
 <cfloop index="green" list="#hex#">
  <tr>
  <!--- Start BB loop --->
  <cfloop index="blue" list="#hex#">
   <!--- Build RGB value --->
   <cfset rgb=red&green&blue>
   <!--- And display it --->
   <cfoutput>
   <td bgcolor="###rgb#" width="100" align="center">#rgb#</td>
   </cfoutput>
  </cfloop>
  </tr>
 </cfloop>
</cfloop>

</table>

</body>
</html>
```

Listing 9.13 warrants explanation. Colors in Web pages are expressed as RGB values (as in red, green, blue). The idea is that by adjusting the amount of red, green, and blue within a color, every possible color can be created. RGB values are specified using hexadecimal notation. Don't panic if you have forgotten base-n arithmetic—it's quite simple, actually. The amount of color is specified as a number, from 0 (none) to 255 (all). But instead of 0–255, the hexadecimal equivalents (00–FF) are used. So, pure red is all red and no green or blue, or FF0000; yellow is all red and green and no blue, or FFFF00.

Still confused? Execute the code and you'll see a complete list of colors and the RGB value for each.

To list all the colors, the code must loop through all possible combinations—list all shades of red, and within each shade of red list each shade of green, and within each shade of green list each shade of blue. In the innermost loop, a variable named rgb is created as follows:

```
<cfset rgb=red&green&blue>
```

On the very first iteration red, green, and blue are all 00, so rgb is 000000. On the next iteration red and green are still 00, but blue is 33, so rgb is 000033. By the time all the loops have been processed, a total of 216 colors have been generated (6 to the power of 3 for you mathematicians out there, because each color has six possible shades as defined in variable hex).

The exact mechanics of RGB value generation aren't important here. The key point is that loops can be nested quite easily and within each loop the counters and variables created at an outer loop are visible and usable.

Reusing Code

All developers write—or should write—code with reuse in mind. There are many reasons why this is a good idea:

- **Saving time.** If it's written once, don't write it again.

- **Easier maintenance.** Make a change in one place and any code that uses it gets that change automatically.

- **Easier debugging.** Fewer copies exist out there that will need to be fixed.

- **Group development.** Developers can share code more easily.

Most of the code reuse in this book involves ColdFusion code, but to demonstrate basic reuse, let's look at a simple example.

Orange Whip Studios is building a Web site, slowly. Figure 9.11 shows a Home page (still being worked on), and Figure 9.12 shows a Contact page (also being worked on).

Figure 9.11

The Home page contains basic logos and branding.

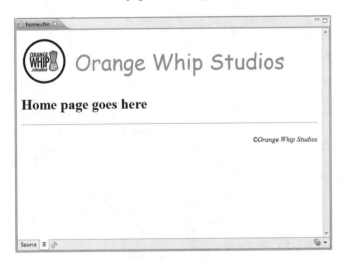

Figure 9.12

The Contact page contains the same elements as the Home page.

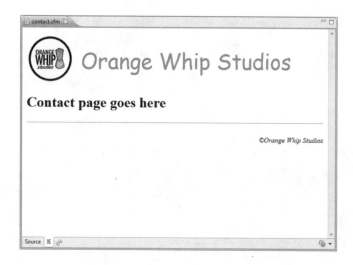

The pages have a lot in common—both have the same header, the same logo, and the same copyright notice. If you were writing plain HTML, you'd have no choice but to copy all the code that creates those page components into every page you were creating.

But you're using ColdFusion, and ColdFusion makes code reuse incredibly simple. The CFML `<cfinclude>` tag is used to include one page in another. `<cfinclude>` specifies the name of a file to include. At runtime, when ColdFusion encounters a `<cfinclude>` tag, it reads the contents of the specified file and processes it as if it were part of the same file.

To demonstrate this, look at Listings 9.14 and 9.15. The former is `ows_header.cfm`, and the latter is `ows_footer.cfm`. Between the two files, all the formatting for the Orange Whip Studios pages is present.

Listing 9.14   `ows_header.cfm`

```
<!---
Name:        ows_header.cfm
Author:      Ben Forta (ben@forta.com)
Description: <cfinclude> header
Created:     01/01/2010
--->

<html>
<head>
 <title>Orange Whip Studios</title>
</head>

<body>

<!--- header --->
<table width="100%">
<tr>
<td>
 <img src="../images/logo_c.gif"
```

Listing 9.14 (CONTINUED)

```
        width="101"
        height="101"
        alt=""
        border="0">
</td>
<td>
 <font face="Comic Sans MS" size="7" color="#ff8000">Orange Whip Studios</font>
</td>
</tr>
</table>
<p>
```

Listing 9.15 ows_footer.cfm

```
<!---
Name:        ows_footer.cfm
Author:      Ben Forta (ben@forta.com)
Description: <cfinclude> footer
Created:     01/01/2010
--->

<p>
<hr>
<p align="right">
<i>&copy;Orange Whip Studios</i>
</p>

</body>
</html>
```

Now that the page header and footer have been created, <cfinclude> can be used to include them in the pages. Listing 9.16 is home.cfm, and Listing 9.17 is contact.cfm.

Listing 9.16 home.cfm

```
<!---
Name:        home.cfm
Author:      Ben Forta (ben@forta.com)
Description: Demonstrate use of <cfinclude>
Created:     01/01/2010
--->

<!--- Include page header --->
<cfinclude template="ows_header.cfm">

<h1>Home page goes here</h1>

<!--- Include page footer --->
<cfinclude template="ows_footer.cfm">
```

Listing 9.17 contact.cfm

```
<!---
Name:         contact.cfm
Author:       Ben Forta (ben@forta.com)
```

Listing 9.17   (CONTINUED)

```
Description: Demonstrate use of <cfinclude>
Created:     01/01/2010s
--->

<!--- Include page header --->
<cfinclude template="ows_header.cfm">

<h1>Contact page goes here</h1>

<!--- Include page footer --->
<cfinclude template="ows_footer.cfm">
```

As you can see, very little code exists in Listings 9.16 and 9.17. Each listing contains two <cfinclude> statements: The first includes file ows_header.cfm (Listing 9.14), and the second includes file ows_ footer.cfm (Listing 9.15). ColdFusion includes those two files and generates the output seen previously in Figures 9.11 and 9.12. The content that is unique to each page can be placed between the two <cfinclude> tags.

To see the real value of this approach, modify ows_header.cfm (change colors, text, or anything else) and then reload home.cfm and contact.cfm to see your changes automatically applied to both.

→   We'll revisit this subject in detail in Chapter 11, "The Basics of Structured Development."

Revisiting Variables

Another important tag is <cfparam>. You won't use this tag here, but in preparation for the next chapters, I'll explain what this tag is and how it is used.

Earlier in this chapter, you used a function named IsDefined(), which is used to check whether a variable exists. You used IsDefined() to simply check for a variable's existence, but what if you wanted to create a variable with a default value if it did not exist? You could do something similar to this:

```
<cfif NOT IsDefined("FirstName")>
 <cfset FirstName="Ben">
</cfif>
```

Why would you want to do this? Well, as a rule, you should not include data validation code in the middle of your core code. This is bad practice for several reasons, the most important of which are that it helps create unreliable code, makes debugging difficult, and makes code reuse very difficult. So, best practices dictate that all variable validation occur before your core code. If required variables are missing, throw an error, redirect the user to another page, or do something else. If optional variables are missing, define them and assign default values. Either way, by the time you get to your core code, you should have no need for variable checking of any kind. It should all have been done already.

And thus the type of code I just showed you.

`<cfparam>` has several uses, but the most common use is simply a way to shortcut the previous code. Look at the following:

```
<cfparam name="FirstName" default="Ben">
```

When ColdFusion processes this line, it checks to see whether a variable named `FirstName` exists. If it does, the tag is ignored and processing continues. If, however, the variable doesn't exist, it will be created right then and there and assigned the value specified in `default`. So by using `<cfparam>`, you can ensure that after that tag has been processed, one way or another the variable referred to exists. And that makes writing clean code that much easier.

TIP

You can use `<CFPARAM>` to check for (and create) variables in specific scopes, including **URL** and **FORM**. This can greatly simplify the processing of passed values, as you will see in the coming chapters.

CHAPTER 10

Creating Data-Driven Pages

Accessing Databases

In the past few chapters, you created and executed ColdFusion templates. You worked with different variable types, conditional processing, code reuse, and more.

But this chapter is where it starts to get really interesting. Now it's time to learn how to connect to databases to create complete dynamic and data-driven pages.

NOTE

The examples in this chapter, and indeed all the chapters that follow, use the data in the ows data sources and database. These must be present before continuing. And I'll remind you just this once, all the files created in this chapter need to go in a directory named 10 under the application root (the ows directory under the Web root).

For your first application, you will create a page that lists all movies in the Films table.

Static Web Pages

Before you create your first data-driven ColdFusion template, let's look at how *not* to create this page.

Listing 10.1 contains the HTML code for the movie list Web page. The HTML code is relatively simple; it contains header information and then a list of movies, one per line, separated by line breaks (the HTML <br> tag).

Listing 10.1 `movies.htm`—HTML Code for Movie List

```
<html>
<head>
 <title>Orange Whip Studios - Movie List</title>
</head>

<body>
```

Listing 10.1 (CONTINUED)

```html
<h1>Movie List</h1>

Being Unbearably Light<br>
Charlie's Devils<br>
Closet Encounters of the Odd Kind<br>
Folded Laundry, Concealed Ticket<br>
Forrest Trump<br>
Four Bar-Mitzvahs and a Circumcision<br>
Geriatric Park<br>
Gladly Ate Her<br>
Ground Hog Day<br>
Hannah and Her Blisters<br>
Harry's Pottery<br>
It's a Wonderful Wife<br>
Kramer vs. George<br>
Mission Improbable<br>
Nightmare on Overwhelmed Street<br>
Raiders of the Lost Aardvark<br>
Silence of the Clams<br>
Starlet Wars<br>
Strangers on a Stain<br>
The Funeral Planner<br>
The Sixth Nonsense<br>
Use Your ColdFusion II<br>
West End Story<br>

</body>
</html>
```

Figure 10.1 shows the output this code listing generates.

Figure 10.1

You can create the movie list page as a static HTML file.

Dynamic Web Pages

Why is a static HTML file not the way to create the Web page? What would you have to do when a new movie is created, or when a movie is dropped? What would you do if a movie title or tag line changed?

You could directly modify the HTML code to reflect these changes, but you already have all this information in a database. Why would you want to have to enter it all again? You'd run the risk of making mistakes—information being misspelled, entries out of order, and possibly missing movies altogether. As the number of movies in the list grows, so will the potential for errors. In addition, visitors will be looking at inaccurate information during the period between updating the table and updating the Web page.

A much easier and more reliable solution is to have the Web page display the contents of your Films table. This way, any table changes are immediately available to all viewers. The Web page would be dynamically built based on the contents of the Films table.

To create your first data-driven ColdFusion template, enter the code as it appears in Listing 10.2 and save it in the 10 directory as movies1.cfm. (Don't worry if the ColdFusion code doesn't make much sense yet; I will explain it in detail in just a moment.)

Listing 10.2   movies1.cfm—The Basic Movie List

```
<!---
Name:        movies1.cfm
Author:      Ben Forta (ben@forta.com)
Description: First data-driven Web page
Created:     01/01/2010
--->

<!--- Get movie list from database --->
<cfquery name="movies" datasource="ows">
SELECT MovieTitle
FROM Films
ORDER BY MovieTitle
</cfquery>

<!--- Create HTML page --->
<html>
<head>
 <title>Orange Whip Studios - Movie List</title>
</head>

<body>

<h1>Movie List</h1>

<!--- Display movie list --->
<cfoutput query="movies">
#MovieTitle#<br>
</cfoutput>

</body>
</html>
```

Now run this page in ColdFusion Builder, or run it in your browser as

```
http://localhost:8500/ows/10/movies1.cfm
```

TIP

As a reminder, the port number (**8500** in the above URL) is only needed if you are using the integrated HTTP server. If you are using ColdFusion with an external HTTP server, then don't specify the port.

The results will be identical to Figure 10.1.

Understanding Data-Driven Templates

As you can see, there is no difference at all (other than the file extension in the URL) between the static page and the dynamic page. If you look at the HTML source just generated, you'll see that aside from a lot of extra white space, the dynamically generated code is exactly the same as the static code you entered in Listing 10.1 and nothing like the (much shorter) dynamic code you entered in Listing 10.2.

How did the code in Listing 10.2 become the HTML source code that generated Figure 10.1? Let's review the code listing carefully.

The `<cfquery>` Tag

Listing 10.2 starts off with a comment block (as should all the code you write). Then comes a ColdFusion tag called `<cfquery>`, which submits a SQL statement to a specified data source. The SQL statement is usually a SQL SELECT statement, but it could also be an INSERT, an UPDATE, a DELETE, a stored procedure call, or any other SQL statement.

→ See Chapter 6, "Introducing SQL," for an overview of data sources, SQL, and SQL statements.

The `<cfquery>` tag has several attributes, or parameters, that are passed to it when used. The `<cfquery>` in Listing 10.2 uses only two attributes:

- `name`: This attribute is used to name the query and any returned data.

- `datasource`: This attribute contains the name of the data source to be used.

The query `name` you specified is `movies`. This name will be used later when you process the results generated by the query.

CAUTION

Don't use reserved words (words that have special meaning to ColdFusion) as your query name. For example, don't name a query URL, as URL is a reserved prefix.

NOTE

Query names passed to `<cfquery>` need not be unique to each query within your page. If you do reuse query names, subsequent `<cfquery>` calls will overwrite the results retrieved by the earlier query.

You specified `ows` for the `datasource` attribute, which is the name of the data source created earlier. The `datasource` attribute is required; without it, ColdFusion would not know which database to execute the SQL statement against.

TIP

As of ColdFusion 9, `datasource` can be defined in the Application.cfc file instead of in each `<cfquery>` tag. Application. cfc is introduced in Chapter 18, "Introducing the Web Application Framework."

The SQL statement to be executed is specified between the `<cfquery>` and `</cfquery>` tags. The following SQL statement was used, which retrieves all movie titles sorted alphabetically:

```
SELECT MovieTitle
FROM Films
ORDER BY MovieTitle
```

TIP

The SQL statement in Listing 10.2 is broken up over many lines to make the code more readable. Although it's perfectly legal to write a long SQL statement that is wider than the width of your editor, these generally should be broken up over as many lines as needed.

ColdFusion pays no attention to the actual text between the `<cfquery>` and `</cfquery>` tags (unless you include CFML tags or functions, which we'll get to later in this chapter). Whatever is between those tags is sent to the data source for processing.

When ColdFusion encounters a `<cfquery>` tag, it creates a query request and submits it to the specified data source. The results, if any, are stored in a temporary buffer and are identified by the name specified in the `name` attribute. All this happens before ColdFusion processes the next line in the template.

NOTE

You'll recall that ColdFusion tags (including the `<cfquery>` tag) are never sent to the Web server for transmission to the browser. Unlike HTML tags, which are browser instructions, CFML tags are ColdFusion instructions.

NOTE

ColdFusion doesn't validate the SQL code you specify. If syntax errors exist in the SQL code, ColdFusion won't let you know because that's not its job. The data source will return error messages if appropriate, and ColdFusion will display those to you. But it's the data source (and the database or database driver) that returns those error messages, not ColdFusion.

It's important to note that, at this point, no data has been displayed. `<cfquery>` retrieves data from a database table, but it doesn't display that data. Actually, it does nothing at all with the data—that's your job. All it does is execute a specified SQL statement when the `</cfquery>` tag is reached. `<cfquery>` has no impact on generated content at all, and retrieved data is never sent to the client (unless you send it).

The next lines in the template are standard HTML tags, headers, title, and headings. Because these aren't ColdFusion tags, they are sent to the Web server and then on to the client browser.

Using `<cfoutput>` to Display `<cfquery>` Data

Next, the query results are displayed, one row per line. To loop through the query results, the `<cfoutput>` tag is used.

`<cfoutput>` is the same ColdFusion output tag you used earlier (in Chapter 8, "The Basics of CFML"). This time, however, you use it to create a code block that is used to output the results of a `<cfquery>`. For ColdFusion to know which query results to output, the query name is passed to `<cfoutput>` in the query attribute. The name provided is the same that was assigned to the `<cfquery>` tag's name attribute. In this case, the name is movies.

CAUTION

The query `name` passed to `<cfquery>` must be a valid (existing) query; otherwise, ColdFusion will generate an error.

The code between `<cfoutput query="movies">` and `</cfoutput>` is the output code block. Cold-Fusion uses this code once for every row retrieved. Because 23 rows are currently in the Films table, the `<cfoutput>` code is looped through 23 times. And any HTML or CFML tags within that block are repeated as well—once for each row.

NOTE

So what is the minimum number of times a `<cfoutput>` code block will be processed? It depends on whether you are using the `query` attribute. Without a `query`, the code block is processed once. With a `query` block, it's processed once if a single row exists in the query, and not at all if the query returned no results.

TIP

You'll notice that I put the SQL query at the very top of the page instead of right where it was needed (in the middle of the output). This is the recommended way to write your code—queries should be organized at the top of the page, all together. This will help you write cleaner code and will also simplify any testing and debugging if (or rather, when) the need arises.

Using Table Columns

As explained in Chapter 8, ColdFusion uses # to delimit expressions and variables. ColdFusion expressions also can be columns retrieved by a `<cfquery>`. Whatever column name is specified is used; ColdFusion replaces the column name with the column's actual value. When ColdFusion processed the output block, it replaced #MovieTitle# with the contents of the MovieTitle column that was retrieved in the movies query. Each time the output code block is used, that row's MovieTitle value is inserted into the HTML code.

ColdFusion-generated content can be treated as any other content in an HTML document; any of the HTML formatting tags can be applied to them. In this example, the query results must be separated by a line break (the `<br>` tag).

Look at the following line of code:

```
#MovieTitle#<br>
```

That first row retrieved is movie *Being Unbearably Light*, so when processing the first row the above code will generate the following:

```
Being Unbearably Light<br>
```

The output of Listing 10.2 is dynamically generated—each time the page is refreshed, the database query is executed and the output is generated.

NOTE

Want to prove this for yourself? Open the database and make a change to any of the movie titles and then refresh the Web page—you'll see that the output will reflect the changes as soon as they are made.

If you are thinking that constantly rereading the database tables seems unnecessary and likely to affect performance, you're right. Chapter 27, "Improving Performance," in *Adobe ColdFusion 9 Web Application Construction Kit, Volume 2: Application Development*, teaches tips and techniques to optimize the performance of data-driven sites.

The Dynamic Advantage

To see the real power of data-driven pages, take a look at Listing 10.3. This is the same code as in Listing 10.2, but a column has been added to the SQL statement (retrieving `PitchText` as well now) and the output has been modified so that it displays both the `MovieTitle` and `PitchText` columns. Save this file as `movies2.cfm` (you can edit `movies1.cfm` and use the Save As option (in the File menu) to save it as `movies2.cfm`, if you find that easier). Now run the page in ColdFusion Builder or run it in your browser as follows:

```
http://localhost:8500/ows/10/movies2.cfm
```

TIP

Again, drop the port if not using the internal HTTP server.

Figure 10.2 shows the output generated by the revised code.

Figure 10.2

Data-driven pages are easy to modify because only the template needs changing, not every single row.

Listing 10.3   `movies2.cfm`—The Extended Movie List

```
<!---
Name:        movies2.cfm
Author:      Ben Forta (ben@forta.com)
Description: Retrieving multiple database columns
Created:     01/01/2010
--->

<!--- Get movie list from database --->
<cfquery name="movies" datasource="ows">
SELECT MovieTitle, PitchText
```

Listing 10.3 (CONTINUED)

```
FROM Films
ORDER BY MovieTitle
</cfquery>

<!--- Create HTML page --->
<html>
<head>
 <title>Orange Whip Studios - Movie List</title>
</head>

<body>

<h1>Movie List</h1>

<!--- Display movie list --->
<cfoutput query="movies">
<p><strong>#MovieTitle#</strong><br>
#PitchText#</p>
</cfoutput>

</body>
</html>
```

As you can see, two table columns are now used, each delimited by number signs. The MovieTitle is displayed in bold (using `<strong>` and `</strong>` tags) and is followed by a line break; on the next line PitchText is displayed followed by a paragraph break. So for the first row displayed, the previous code becomes

```
<p><strong>#MovieTitle#</strong><br>
#PitchText#</p>
```

Compare that to what you'd have had to change in movies.htm to update a static page to look like Figure 10.2, and you'll start to appreciate the dynamic page advantage.

Excited? You should be. Welcome to ColdFusion and the wonderful world of dynamic data-driven Web pages!

Displaying Database Query Results

Listings 10.2 and 10.3 displayed data in simple line-by-line outputs. But that's not all you can do with ColdFusion—in fact, there is no type of output that *can't* be generated with it. ColdFusion has absolutely nothing to do with formatting and generating output; as long as you can write what you want (in HTML, JavaScript, Flash, DHTML, Ajax, or any other client technology), Cold-Fusion generates the output dynamically.

To better understand this, let's look at some alternative output options.

Displaying Data Using Lists

HTML features support for two list types—ordered lists (in which each list item is automatically numbered) and unordered lists (in which list items are preceded by bullets). Creating HTML lists is very simple:

1. Start the list with `<ul>` (for an unordered list) or `<ol>` (for an ordered list).

2. End the list with a matching end tag (`</ul>` or `</ol>`).

3. Between the list's start and end tags, specify the list members (called *list items*) between `<li>` and `</li>` tags.

   For example, the following is a simple bulleted (unordered) list containing three names:

```
<ul
 <li>Ben Forta</li>
 <li>Charlie Arehart</li>
 <li>Ray Camden</li>
</UL>
```

   The numbered (ordered) equivalent of this list would be:

```
<ol
 <li>Ben Forta</li>
 <li>Charlie Arehart</li>
 <li>Ray Camden</li>
</ol>
```

So how would you display the movie list in an unordered list? Listing 10.4 contains the code, which you should save as `movies3.cfm`. Execute the code in your browser (or in ColdFusion Builder, if you prefer); the output should look like Figure 10.3.

Figure 10.3

HTML unordered lists provide a simple way to display data-driven output.

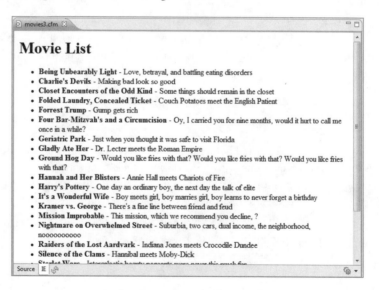

Listing 10.4 `movies3.cfm`—The Movie List in an Unordered List

```
<!---
Name:        movies3.cfm
Author:      Ben Forta (ben@forta.com)
Description: Data-driven HTML list
Created:     01/01/2010
--->
```

Listing 10.4 (CONTINUED)

```
<!--- Get movie list from database --->
<cfquery name="movies" datasource="ows">
SELECT MovieTitle, PitchText
FROM Films
ORDER BY MovieTitle
</cfquery>

<!--- Create HTML page --->
<html>
<head>
 <title>Orange Whip Studios - Movie List</title>
</head>

<body>

<h1>Movie List</h1>

<!--- Display movie list --->
<ul>
 <cfoutput query="movies">
  <li><strong>#MovieTitle#</strong> - #PitchText#</li>
 </cfoutput>
</ul>

</body>
</html>
```

Let's review Listing 10.4 together. It should look familiar because it's essentially the same code as Listing 10.3 (`movies2.cfm`), only the actual data output has changed. The new output code is:

```
<ul>
 <cfoutput query="movies">
  <li><strong>#MovieTitle#</strong> - #PitchText#</li>
 </cfoutput>
</ul>
```

As you can see, the list is started before the `<cfoutput>` tag, and it's ended after the `</cfoutput>` tag. This is important—everything within the output block is repeated once for every row retrieved. Therefore, if the list was started inside the output block, 23 lists would be generated, with each containing a single movie, instead of a single list containing 23 movies. Only the data to be repeated should be placed inside the output block.

The output code itself is simple. For the first row, the code

```
<li><strong>#MovieTitle#</strong> - #PitchText#</li>
```

becomes

```
<li><strong>Being Unbearably Light</strong>
 - Love, betrayal, and battling eating disorders</li>
```

which is a valid list item with the movie title in bold (using `<strong>` and `</strong>`) followed by the tag line.

NOTE

As you can see, changing output formatting affects (or should affect) only an isolated portion of your code. As such, many developers first test whether their code works using simple output (line breaks or lists) before they write complex user interfaces. This can make development much easier (debugging core code and the user interface at the same time is no fun).

CAUTION

Be careful when placing code within an output block. Only code that is to be repeated for each row should be placed between `<cfoutput>` and `</cfoutput>`. Any other code should go outside the tags.

Displaying Data Using Tables

Another important way to display data is using tables. HTML tables enable you to create grids that can contain text, graphics, and more. Tables help facilitate a more controlled page layout, helping you place content side by side, in columns, wrapped around images, and more.

Creating tables involves three sets of tags:

- `<table>` and `</table>`: Used to create the table

- `<tr>` and `</tr>`: Used to create rows in the table

- `<td>` and `</td>`: Used to insert cells within a table row (`<th>` and `</th>` also can be used for header cells—essentially data cells formatted a little differently, usually centered and in bold)

So a simple table with a header row, two columns, and three rows of data (as seen in Figure 10.4) might look like this:

```
<table>
 <tr>
  <th>First Name</th>
  <th>Last Name</th>
 </tr>
 <tr>
  <td>Ben</td>
  <td>Forta</td>
 </tr>
 <tr>
  <td>Charlie</td>
  <td>Arehart</td>
 </tr>
 <tr>
  <td>Ray</td>
  <td>Camden</td>
 </tr>
</table>
```

Figure 10.4

HTML tables are constructed using tags to create the table, rows, and individual cells.

First Name	Last Name
Ben	Forta
Charlie	Arehart
Ray	Camden

With that brief intro to HTML tables, let's modify the movie listing to display the list in an HTML table. Listing 10.5 contains a modified version of the code (again, you can use Save As to create a copy of the previous version for editing). Save the file as movies4.cfm, and then execute it to display an output similar to that shown in Figure 10.5.

Figure 10.5

Tables provide a convenient mechanism for displaying data in a grid-like format.

Listing 10.5 movies4.cfm—The Movie List in an HTML Table

```
<!---
Name:        movies4.cfm
Author:      Ben Forta (ben@forta.com)
Description: Data-driven HTML table
Created:     01/02/2010
--->

<!--- Get movie list from database --->
<cfquery name="movies" datasource="ows">
SELECT MovieTitle, PitchText
FROM Films
ORDER BY MovieTitle
</cfquery>

<!--- Create HTML page --->
<html>
<head>
 <title>Orange Whip Studios - Movie List</title>
</head>

<body>

<h1>Movie List</h1>

<!--- Display movie list --->
<table border="1">
 <cfoutput query="movies">
 <tr>
  <td>#MovieTitle#</td>
```

Listing 10.5 (CONTINUED)

```
      <td>#PitchText#</td>
    </tr>
  </cfoutput>
</table>

</body>
</html>
```

Once again, the code in Listing 10.5 is similar to the previous examples, and once again, it's only the output block that has changed.

The table is created using the code `<table border="1">`—a table with a border. The `<table>` and `</table>` tags are placed *outside* the output block (you want a single table, not a table for each row).

The table needs a new table row for each row in the query. So the `<tr>` and `</tr>` tags are within the output loop, and within them are two cells (containing `MovieTitle` and `PitchText`).

As you can see in Figure 10.5, this code creates a single table with as many rows as there are query rows (23 in this example).

TIP

Viewing the source code generated by ColdFusion is useful when debugging template problems. When you view the source, you are looking at the complete output as it was sent to your browser. If you ever need to ascertain why a Web page doesn't look the way you intended it to look, a good place to start is comparing your template with the source code it generated.

You'll probably find yourself using tables extensively. To ensure that dynamic HTML table creation is properly understood, another example is in order.

This time the table will contain two rows for each query row. The first will contain two cells— one for the title and tag line and one for the release date. The second row will contain the movie summary (and because the summary can be lengthy, its cell spans both columns). The output generated can be seen in Figure 10.6.

Figure 10.6

For greater control, HTML tables can contain cells that span two or more columns (and rows).

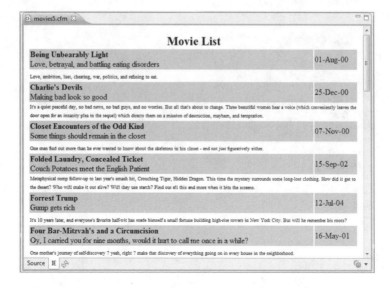

Listing 10.6 contains the revised code; this time save the file as movies5.cfm and execute it in your browser.

Listing 10.6   movies5.cfm—The Movie List in an HTML Table

```
<!---
Name:        movies5.cfm
Author:      Ben Forta (ben@forta.com)
Description: Data-driven HTML table
Created:     01/01/2010
--->

<!--- Get movie list from database --->
<cfquery name="movies" datasource="ows">
SELECT MovieTitle, PitchText,
       Summary, DateInTheaters
FROM Films
ORDER BY MovieTitle
</cfquery>

<!--- Create HTML page --->
<html>
<head>
 <title>Orange Whip Studios - Movie List</title>
</head>

<body>

<!--- Start table --->
<table>
 <tr>
  <th colspan="2">
   <h2>Movie List</h2>
  </th>
 </tr>
 <!--- loop through movies --->
 <cfoutput query="movies">
  <tr bgcolor="##cccccc">
   <td>
    <strong>#MovieTitle#</strong>
    <br>
    #PitchText#
   </td>
   <td>
    #DateFormat(DateInTheaters)#
   </td>
  </tr>
  <tr>
   <td colspan="2">
    #Summary#
   </td>
  </tr>
 </cfoutput>
 <!--- End of movie loop --->
</table>

</body>
</html>
```

A few changes have been made in Listing 10.6. First, the `<cfquery>` SELECT statement has been modified to retrieve two additional columns—Summary contains the movie summary, and DateInTheaters contains the movie's public release date.

In addition, the following HTML code has been added *before* the `<cfoutput>` tag:

```
<tr>
  <th colspan="2">
   <font size="+2">Movie List</font>
  </th>
</tr>
```

This creates a header cell (header contents usually are centered and displayed in bold) containing the text Movie List as a table title. Because the table is two columns wide, the title must span both columns, so the optional attribute colspan="2" is specified.

The output block itself creates two rows (two sets of `<tr>` and `</tr>` tags) per movie. The first contains two cells—one with the MovieTitle and PitchText (with a line break between them) and the other with the release date formatted for display using the DateFormat() function. The second row contains a single cell spanning both columns and displaying Summary.

➡ The DateFormat() function was introduced in Chapter 8.

As seen in Figure 10.6, the table row containing the title and tag line has a colored background. To set the background color of a table row (or a specific table cell, or even the entire table for that matter) the bgcolor attribute is used, and the color is specified using known named (like red and green) or RGB values in hexadecimal notation as follows:

```
<tr bgcolor="#cccccc">
```

NOTE

For simplicity, this example uses hard-coded table values. In general, hard coding is not a preferred practice. As a general rule, you should use CSS to control colors and fonts and the like. While CSS is beyond the scope of this chapter, I do suggest that you take the time to learn and understand this important Web browser technology.

Hexadecimal values are preceded by a #, the same character used to delimit ColdFusion expressions. If the above code were used in our `<cfoutput>` block, ColdFusion would have generated an error message complaining about a missing closing # (it would think that cccccc was an expression needing a closing #). As such, our table code escapes the # as follows:

```
<tr bgcolor="##cccccc">
```

➡ Escaping # was covered in Chapter 8.

TIP

Pay close attention to which code you place within and without the `<cfoutput>` block. Misplacing a `<tr>` or `</td>` tag could result in a badly formatted HTML table, and some browsers might opt to not even display that table.

As you can see, as long as you know the basic HTML syntax and know what needs to be repeated for each database row and what doesn't, creating dynamic data-driven output is quick and painless.

TIP

ColdFusion features a tag named `<cftable>` that can be used to automate the entire process of creating data-driven HTML tables. Although this tag works, I recommend against using it. HTML tables aren't difficult to learn and create, and doing so is well worth the effort because you'll find that you have far more control over the exact format and output.

CAUTION

I know I've said it several times already, but because this is one of the most common beginners' mistakes (and a very aggravating one to debug at that), I'll say it one last time: When creating dynamic output, pay special attention to what needs to be repeated and what does not. Anything that needs to be displayed once per row (either before or after the row) must go in the output block; anything else must not.

Using Result Variables

So far, you have displayed data retrieved using database queries. But sometimes you'll need access to data about queries (and not just data within queries). For example, if you wanted to display the number of movies retrieved, where would you get that count from?

To simplify this type of operation, ColdFusion can return special variables with every query using the optional RESULT structure. Table 10.1 lists these variables, and as you can see, RecordCount can provide the number of rows retrieved.

Table 10.1   Query RESULT Variables

VARIABLE	DESCRIPTION
Cached	Flag indicating whether or not returned query is a cached copy
ColumnList	Names of columns in query results (comma-delimited list)
ExecutionTime	Query execution time (in milliseconds)
RecordCount	Number of rows in a query
SQL	The SQL statement as submitted for processing

To demonstrate using these special variables, create the file `movies6.cfm`, as shown in Listing 10.7. This code, which is based on `movies5.cfm`, generates the output seen in Figure 10.7. Save the code, and execute it in your browser.

Listing 10.7   `movies6.cfm`—Using Query Variables

```
<!---
Name:        movies6.cfm
Author:      Ben Forta (ben@forta.com)
Description: Using query variables
Created:     01/01/2010
--->

<!--- Get movie list from database --->
<cfquery name="movies" datasource="ows" result="result">
SELECT MovieTitle, PitchText,
       Summary, DateInTheaters
FROM Films
```

Figure 10.7

RecordCount can be accessed to obtain the number of rows in a query.

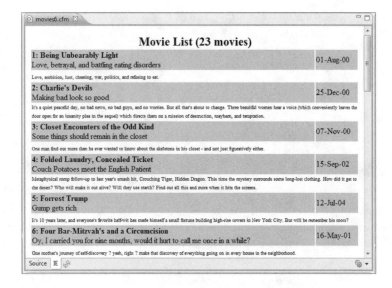

Listing 10.7 (CONTINUED)

```
ORDER BY MovieTitle
</cfquery>

<!--- Create HTML page --->
<html>
<head>
 <title>Orange Whip Studios - Movie List</title>
</head>

<body>

<!--- Start table --->
<table>
 <tr>
  <th colspan="2">
   <h2>
   <cfoutput>
   Movie List (#result.RecordCount# movies)
   </cfoutput>
   </h2>
  </th>
 </tr>
 <!--- loop through movies --->
 <cfoutput query="movies">
  <tr bgcolor="##cccccc">
   <td>
    <strong>#CurrentRow#: #MovieTitle#</strong>
    <br>
    #PitchText#
   </td>
   <td>
    #DateFormat(DateInTheaters)#
```

Listing 10.7 (CONTINUED)

```
     </td>
    </tr>
    <tr>
     <td colspan="2">
      #Summary#
     </td>
    </tr>
   </cfoutput>
   <!--- End of movie loop --->
  </table>

  </body>
  </html>
```

So what changed here? Only three modifications were made to this code. First, the `<cfquery>` RESULT attribute was specified so that, when processed, the structure named `result` would be created containing the query execution results. In addition, the title (above the output block) now reads as follows:

```
Movie List (#result.RecordCount# movies)
```

`#result.RecordCount#` returns the number of rows retrieved—in this case, 23. Like any other expression, the text `result.RecordCount` must be enclosed within number signs and must be between `<cfoutput>` and `</cfoutput>` tags. But unlike many other expressions, here the prefix `result` is required. Why? Because this code isn't referring to a column in a named query. Rather, `RecordCount` is a member of a structure named `result`, and so the fully qualified variable name must be specified.

TIP

Here the query name prefix is required because the query was not specified in the `<cfoutput>` loop. Within an output loop, the query name isn't required, but it can be used to prevent ambiguity (for example, if there were variables with the same names as table columns).

Here you use `RecordCount` purely for display purposes. But as you will see later in this chapter, it can be used in other ways, too (for example, checking to see whether a query returned any data at all).

The other line of code that changed is the movie title display, which now has `#CurrentRow#:` in front of it. `CurrentRow` is another special variable, but this time it's in `<cfoutput>` instead of `<cfquery>`. Within an output loop, `CurrentRow` keeps a tally of the iterations—it contains 1 when the first row is processed, 2 when the second row is processed, and so on. In this example, it's used to number the movies (as seen in Figure 10.7).

`CurrentRow` can also be used it to implement fancy formatting, for example, alternating the background color for every other row (a *green paper* effect). Listing 10.8 is `movies7.cfm`, a modified version of `movies4.cfm` (I used that older version as it's simpler and looks better for this example). Background color, as previously seen, is set using the `bgcolor` attribute, but unlike in the previous example, here the colors are being set dynamically and programmatically.

The big change in Listing 10.8 is the `<cfif>` statement right inside the `<cfoutput>` loop. As you will recall, `<cfif>` is used to evaluate if statements (conditions), and here the following `<cfif>` statement is used:

```
<cfif CurrentRow MOD 2 IS 1>
```

➡ The `<cfif>` statement was introduced in Chapter 9, "Programming with CFML."

Listing 10.8 `movies7.cfm`—Implementing Alternating Colors

```
<!---
Name:        movies7.cfm
Author:      Ben Forta (ben@forta.com)
Description: Implementing alternating colors
Created:     01/01/2010
--->

<!--- Get movie list from database --->
<cfquery name="movies" datasource="ows">
SELECT MovieTitle, PitchText
FROM Films
ORDER BY MovieTitle
</cfquery>
<!--- Create HTML page --->
<html>
<head>
 <title>Orange Whip Studios - Movie List</title>
</head>

<body>

<h1>Movie List</h1>

<!--- Display movie list --->
<table>
 <cfoutput query="movies">
  <!--- What color should this row be? --->
   <cfif CurrentRow MOD 2 IS 1>
    <cfset bgcolor="MediumSeaGreen">
   <cfelse>
    <cfset bgcolor="White">
   </cfif>
  <tr bgcolor="#bgcolor#">
   <td>#MovieTitle#</td>
   <td>#PitchText#</td>
  </tr>
 </cfoutput>
</table>

</body>
</html>
```

CurrentRow contains the current loop counter as previously explained. MOD is an arithmetic operator that returns the reminder of an equation, and so testing for MOD 2 is a way to check for odd or even numbers (divide a number by 2, if the remainder is 1 the number is odd otherwise the number is even). So checking MOD 2 IS 1 is effectively checking that *the number is odd*.

Within the <cfif> statement one of two <cfset> tags will be called; if the CurrentRow is odd then the first is called (setting a variable named bgcolor to MediumSeaGreen), and if even then the second is called (setting bgcolor to white). Once the </cfif> is reached a variable named bgcolor will exist and will contain a color (MediumSeaGreen or white, depending on whether CurrentRow is odd or even). As the <cfif> code is within the <cfoutput> block it's processed once for every row, and so bgcolor is reset on each row.

→ See Chapter 8 for an introduction to the <cfset> tag.

Then bgcolor is then passed to the <tr> tag's bgcolor attribute so that on odd rows the <tr> tag becomes:

```
<tr bgcolor=">
```

and on even rows it becomes:

```
<tr bgcolor="White">
```

TIP

You'll notice that I named the variable in Listing 10.8 bgcolor, the same as the HTML attribute with which it was used. This isn't required (you may name variables as you wish) but doing so makes the code clearer as the variable's use is then blatantly obvious.

NOTE

The value in CurrentRow isn't the row's unique ID (primary key). In fact, the number has nothing to do with the table data at all. It's merely a loop counter and should never be relied on as anything else.

Grouping Result Output

Before a new level of complexity is introduced, let's review how ColdFusion processes queries.

In ColdFusion, data queries are created using the <cfquery> tag. <cfquery> performs a SQL operation and retrieves results if any exist. Results are stored temporarily by ColdFusion and remain only for the duration of the processing of the template that contained the query.

The <cfoutput> tag is used to output query results. <cfoutput> takes a query name as an attribute and then loops through all the rows that were retrieved by the query. The code block between <cfoutput> and </cfoutput> is repeated once for each and every row retrieved.

All the examples created until now displayed results in a single list or single table.

What would you do if you wanted to process the results in subsets? For example, suppose you wanted to list movies by rating. You could change the SQL statement in the <cfquery> to retrieve the rating ID and set the sort order to be RatingID and then by MovieTitle.

This would retrieve the data in the correct order, but how would you display it? If you used <cfoutput> as you have until now, every row created by the <cfoutput> block would have to be the same. If one had the rating displayed, all would have to because every row that is processed is processed with the same block of code.

Look at Figure 10.8. As you can see, the screen contains nested lists. The top-level list contains the rating IDs, and within each rating ID is a second list containing all the movies with that rating. How would you create an output like this?

Figure 10.8

Grouping provides a means with which to display data grouped into logical sets.

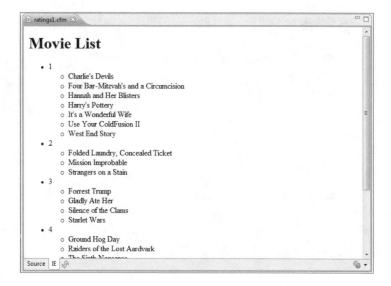

Listing 10.9 contains the code for a new page; save this as `ratings1.cfm` and execute it in your browser.

Listing 10.9   `ratings1.cfm`—Grouping Query Output

```
<!---
Name:        ratings1.cfm
Author:      Ben Forta (ben@forta.com)
Description: Query output grouping
Created:     01/01/2010
--->

<!--- Get movie list from database --->
<cfquery name="movies" datasource="ows">
SELECT MovieTitle, RatingID
FROM Films
ORDER BY RatingID, MovieTitle
</cfquery>

<!--- Create HTML page --->
<html>
<head>
 <title>Orange Whip Studios - Movie List</title>
</head>
```

Listing 10.9 (CONTINUED)

```
<body>

<h1>Movie List</h1>

<!--- Display movie list --->
<ul>
 <!--- Loop through ratings --->
 <cfoutput query="movies" group="RatingID">
  <li>#RatingID#</li>
  <ul>
   <!--- For each rating, list movies --->
   <cfoutput>
    <li>#MovieTitle#</li>
   </cfoutput>
  </ul>
 </cfoutput>
</ul>

</body>
</html>
```

Listing 10.9 starts with the comment block, followed by a `<cfquery>` that retrieves all the movies (title and rating only) sorted by `RatingID` and `MovieTitle` (by `RatingID` and within each `RatingID` by `MovieTitle`).

The display section of the code starts by creating an unordered list—this is the outer list, which contains the ratings.

Then, `<cfoutput>` is used again to create an output block, but this time the `group` attribute has been added. `group="RatingID"` tells the output block to loop through the outer loop only when `RatingID` changes. In other words, the outer loop is processed once per group value. So in this example, it's processed once per `RatingID` value—regardless of the number of movies with that `RatingID`.

Then the `RatingID` is displayed, and a second unordered list is started—this is for the inner list within each `RatingID`.

Next, comes a second `<cfoutput>` block that displays the `MovieTitle`. No query is specified here; ColdFusion doesn't need one. Why? Because `group` is being used, ColdFusion knows which query is being used and loops through the inner `<cfoutput>` only as long as `RatingID` doesn't change.

As soon as `RatingID` changes, the inner `<cfoutput>` loop stops and the inner list is terminated with a `</ul>`.

This repeats until all rows have been processed, at which time the outer `<cfoutput>` terminates and the final `</ul>` is generated.

So how many times is each `<cfoutput>` processed? The movie list contains 23 rows with a total of 6 ratings. So the outer loop is processed 6 times, and the inner loop is processed 23 times. This outer list contains 6 items (each `RatingID` value), and each item contains a sub-list containing the movies with that `RatingID`.

NOTE

For grouping to work, groups must be created in the exact same order as the sort order (the **ORDER BY** clause) in the SQL statement itself.

Listing 10.10 contains a modified version of Listing 10.9, this time displaying the results in an HTML table (as seen in Figure 10.9). Save Listing 10.10 as `ratings2.cfm`, and then execute it in your browser.

Figure 10.9

Grouped data can be used in lists, tables, and any other form of data presentation.

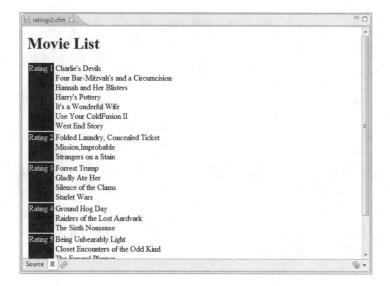

Listing 10.10 `ratings2.cfm`—Grouping Query Output

```
<!---
Name:        ratings2.cfm
Author:      Ben Forta (ben@forta.com)
Description: Query output grouping
Created:     01/01/2010
--->

<!--- Get movie list from database --->
<cfquery name="movies" datasource="ows">
SELECT MovieTitle, RatingID
FROM Films
ORDER BY RatingID, MovieTitle
</cfquery>
<!--- Create HTML page --->
<html>
<head>
 <title>Orange Whip Studios - Movie List</title>
</head>

<body>

<h1>Movie List</h1>
```

Listing 10.10 (CONTINUED)

```
<!--- Display movie list --->
<table>
 <!--- Loop through ratings --->
 <cfoutput query="movies" group="RatingID">
  <tr valign="top">
   <td bgcolor="##000000">
     <font color="##FFFFFF">Rating #RatingID#</font>
   </td>
   <td>
    <!--- For each rating, list movies --->
    <cfoutput>
     #MovieTitle#<br>
    </cfoutput>
   </td>
  </tr>
 </cfoutput>
</table>

</body>
</html>
```

The only thing that has changed in Listing 10.10 is the output code. Again, the `<cfoutput>` tags are nested—the outer loops through `RatingID` and the inner loops through the movies.

The HTML table is created before any looping occurs (you want only one table). Then, for each `RatingID` a new table row is created containing two cells. The left cell contains the `RatingID`, and the right cell contains the movies.

To do this, the inner `<cfoutput>` loop is used in that right cell (between the `<TD>` and `</td>` tags) so that, for each `RatingID` listed on the left, all the appropriate movies are listed on the right.

TIP

A single level of grouping is used here, but there is no limit to the number of levels in which data can be grouped. To group multiple levels (groups within groups), you simply need an additional `<cfoutput>` per group (and of course, the SQL statement must sort the data appropriately).

Using Data Drill-Down

Now that you've learned almost everything you need to know about the `<cfoutput>` tag, let's put it all together in a complete application.

Data drill-down is a popular form of user interface within Web applications because it enables the progressive and gradual selection of desired data. Data drill-down applications usually are made up of three levels of interface:

- A search screen

- A results screen (displaying the results of any searches)

- A details screen (displaying the details for any row selected in the results screen)

You won't create the search screen here (forms are introduced in the next chapter), but you will create the latter two screens. Your application will display a list of movies (similar to the screens created earlier in this chapter) and will allow visitors to click any movie to see detailed information about it.

Introducing Dynamic SQL

You've used lots of <cfquery> tags thus far, and each of them has contained hard-coded SQL—SQL that you typed and that stays the same (the results may differ if the data in the database changes, but the SQL itself always stays the same). But SQL passed to ColdFusion need not be static and hard-coded; the real power of <cfquery> is seen when SQL is constructed dynamically.

To demonstrate what we mean, Listing 10.11 contains the code for a new file named dynamicsql. cfm. Save the code and execute it to see a screen like the one shown in Figure 10.10.

Figure 10.10

The <cfquery> result structure contains the final (post–dynamic processing) SQL and additional information.

Dump Returned Query (NAME)

query					
RESULTSET	query				
			FILMID	MOVIETITLE	PITCHTEXT
		1	1	Being Unbearably Light	Love, betrayal, and battling eating disorders
CACHED	false				
EXECUTIONTIME	1				
SQL	SELECT FilmID, MovieTitle, PitchText FROM Films WHERE FilmID=1				

Dump Returned Result (RESULT)

struct	
CACHED	false
COLUMNLIST	FILMID,MOVIETITLE,PITCHTEXT
EXECUTIONTIME	1
RECORDCOUNT	1
SQL	SELECT FilmID, MovieTitle, PitchText FROM Films WHERE FilmID=1

Listing 10.11   dynamicsql.cfm—Dynamic SQL Demonstration

```
<!---
Name:        dynamicsql.cfm
Author:      Ben Forta (ben@forta.com)
Description: Dynamic SQL demonstration
Created:     01/01/2010
--->

<!--- Create FilmID variable --->
<cfset FilmID=1>

<!--- Get a movie from database --->
<cfquery name="movie"
         datasource="ows"
         result="results">
SELECT FilmID, MovieTitle, PitchText
FROM Films
```

Listing 10.11 (CONTINUED)

```
WHERE FilmID=#FilmID#
</cfquery>

<h1>Dump Returned Query (NAME)</h1>
<cfdump var="#movie#">
<h1>Dump Returned Result (RESULT)</h1>
<cfdump var="#results#">
```

Listing 10.11 starts by creating a variable as follows:

```
<cfset FilmID=1>
```

Next comes a <cfquery> tag containing the following SQL:

```
SELECT FilmID, MovieTitle, PitchText
FROM Films
WHERE FilmID=#FilmID#
```

The WHERE clause specifies the row to be retrieved, and would usually be an actual value. For example, to retrieve the movie with a FilmID of 1 you would use this SQL:

```
SELECT FilmID, MovieTitle, PitchText
FROM Films
WHERE FilmID=1
```

→ See Chapter 6, "Introducing SQL," for a detailed explanation of the SELECT statement and its WHERE clause.

And this is exactly what the code in Listing 10.11 does. #FilmID# is a ColdFusion expression, and so ColdFusion will process it, returning the value of FilmID which is 1 (as set in the <cfset> earlier).

In other words, the SQL used here is dynamic in that the actual SQL statement itself can change (in this example based on the value of FilmID). If you wanted to retrieve a different movie you could simply update FilmID so that it contained a different value.

The last block of code contains two <cfdump> tags:

```
<h1>Display Data</h1>
<cfdump var="#movie#">
<h1>Display cfquery Results</h1>
<cfdump var="#results#">
```

The former simply dumps the returned query (the data contained in the movie variable). The latter dumps the results structure, exposing a field named SQL that contains the SQL used, and additional information (including the same query variables listed in Table 10.1 earlier in this chapter).

As seen previously, the use of result is always optional, but if needed it can expose useful information about tag execution.

NOTE

The result structure may contain additional members, depending on the <cfquery> attributes used.

Implementing Data Drill-Down Interfaces

Now that you've seen how dynamic SQL is used, let's return to data drill-down pages. The first screen you need to create is the details page—the one that will be displayed when a movie is selected. Figure 10.11 shows the details for one movie.

Figure 10.11

In data drill-down applications, the details page displays all of the details for a specific record.

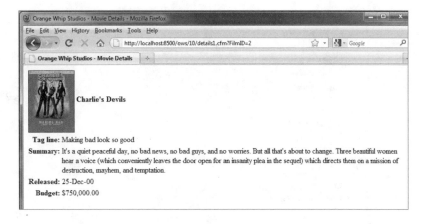

Listing 10.12 contains the code for the file `details1.cfm`. You'll not be able to run this page as is in ColdFusion Builder (you'll learn why in a moment). So save the code and then execute it in your browser with this URL:

```
http://localhost:8500/ows/10/details1.cfm?FilmID=2
```

You should see a screen like the one in Figure 10.11.

Listing 10.12 `details1.cfm`—Data Drill-Down Details

```
<!---
Name:        details1.cfm
Author:      Ben Forta (ben@forta.com)
Description: Data drill-down details
Created:     01/01/2010
--->

<!--- Get a movie from database --->
<cfquery name="movie" datasource="ows">
SELECT FilmID, MovieTitle,
       PitchText, Summary,
       DateInTheaters, AmountBudgeted
FROM Films
WHERE FilmID=#URL.FilmID#
</cfquery>

<!--- Create HTML page --->
<html>
<head>
 <title>Orange Whip Studios - Movie Details</title>
</head>
```

Listing 10.12 (CONTINUED)

```
<body>

<!--- Display movie details --->
<cfoutput query="movie">

<table>
 <tr>
  <td colspan="2">
   <img src="../images/f#filmid#.gif"
        alt="#movietitle#"
        align="middle">
   <strong>#MovieTitle#</strong>
  </td>
 </tr>
 <tr valign="top">
  <th align="right">Tag line:</th>
  <td>#PitchText#</td>
 </tr>
 <tr valign="top">
  <th align="right">Summary:</th>
  <td>#Summary#</td>
 </tr>
 <tr valign="top">
  <th align="right">Released:</th>
  <td>#DateFormat(DateInTheaters)#</td>
 </tr>
 <tr valign="top">
  <th align="right">Budget:</th>
  <td>#DollarFormat(AmountBudgeted)#</td>
 </tr>
</table>

</cfoutput>

</body>
</html>
```

There are several important things to point out in Listing 10.12. Let's start with the SQL statement:

```
SELECT FilmID, MovieTitle,
       PitchText, Summary,
       DateInTheaters, AmountBudgeted
FROM Films
WHERE FilmID=#URL.FilmID#
```

The WHERE clause here is used to select a specific movie by its primary key (FilmID). But instead of comparing it to a real number, a ColdFusion variable is used—#URL.FilmID#. This is dynamic SQL, similar to the example in Listing 10.11 above. When ColdFusion encounters #URL.FilmID#, it replaces that expression with whatever the value of the URL parameter FilmID is. So if the URL parameter FilmID had a value of 2, the generated SQL would look like this:

```
SELECT FilmID, MovieTitle,
       PitchText, Summary,
       DateInTheaters, AmountBudgeted
FROM Films
WHERE FilmID=2
```

This is why I had you append ?FilmID=2 to the URL when you executed this page. Without a FilmID parameter, this code would have failed, but we'll get to that in a moment.

The beauty of this technique is that it allows the same details page to be used for an unlimited number of database records—each FilmID specified generates a different page. If FilmID were 10, the SQL statement would have a WHERE clause of FilmID=10, and so on.

→ URL variables were briefly introduced in Chapter 9.

The rest of the code in Listing 10.12 is self-explanatory. The details are displayed in an HTML table with the title spanning two columns. Dates are formatted using the DateFormat() function, and monetary amounts are formatted using the DollarFormat() function (which, as its name suggests, formats numbers as dollar amounts).

NOTE

Support for other currencies is also available via the locale functions.

One interesting line of code, though, is the <img> tag (used to display the movie poster image):

```
<img src="../images/f#filmid#.gif"
     alt="#movietitle#"
     align="middle">
```

Binary data, like images, can be stored in databases just like any other data, but accessing these images requires special processing that is beyond the scope of this chapter. And so in this application images are stored in a directory and named using the primary key values. Therefore, in this example, the image for FilmID 2 is f2.gif, and that image is stored in the images directory under the application root. By using #FilmID# in the file name, images can be referred to dynamically. In this example, for FilmID 2 the <img> tag becomes

```
<img src="../images/f2.gif"
     alt="Charlie's Devils"
     align="middle">
```

Try executing Listing 10.12 again, but this time don't pass the FilmID parameter (or just run the code in ColdFusion Builder). What happens when you execute the code? You probably received an error message similar to the one in Figure 10.12 telling you that you were referring to a variable that doesn't exist. You can't use URL.FilmID in your SQL statement if no URL parameter named FilmID exists. This is why you could not run the code as is in ColdFusion Builder, because you would not have had a way to pass URL.FilmID as a parameter.

The solution (which you looked at briefly in Chapter 9) is to check that the variable exists before using it. Listing 10.13 contains an updated version of the code; save it as details2.cfm and execute it. What happens now if no FilmID is specified?

Figure 10.12

Do not refer to a variable that does not exist; if you do, an error message will be generated.

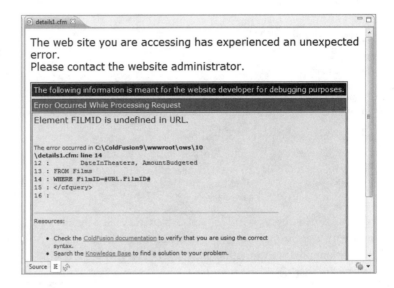

Listing 10.13 details2.cfm—Data Drill-Down Details

```
<!---
Name:        details2.cfm
Author:      Ben Forta (ben@forta.com)
Description: Data drill-down details
             with basic validation
Created:     07/01/07
--->

<!--- Make sure FilmID was passed --->
<cfif not IsDefined("URL.filmid")>
 <!--- it wasn't, send to movie list --->
 <cflocation url="movies6.cfm">
</cfif>

<!--- Get a movie from database --->
<cfquery name="movie" datasource="ows">
SELECT FilmID, MovieTitle,
       PitchText, Summary,
       DateInTheaters, AmountBudgeted
FROM Films
WHERE FilmID=#URL.FilmID#
</cfquery>

<!--- Create HTML page --->
<html>
<head>
<title>Orange Whip Studios - Movie Details</title>
</head>

<body>

<!--- Display movie details --->
```

Listing 10.13 (CONTINUED)

```
<cfoutput query="movie">

<table>
 <tr>
  <td colspan="2">
   <img src="../images/f#filmid#.gif"
        alt="#movietitle#"
        align="middle">
   <strong>#MovieTitle#</strong>
  </td>
 </tr>
 <tr valign="top">
  <th align="right">Tag line:</th>
  <td>#PitchText#</td>
 </tr>
 <tr valign="top">
  <th align="right">Summary:</th>
  <td>#Summary#</td>
 </tr>
 <tr valign="top">
  <th align="right">Released:</th>
  <td>#DateFormat(DateInTheaters)#</td>
 </tr>
 <tr valign="top">
  <th align="right">Budget:</th>
  <td>#DollarFormat(AmountBudgeted)#</td>
 </tr>
</table>

</cfoutput>

</body>
</html>
```

The only thing that has changed in Listing 10.13 is the inclusion of the following code *before* the
<CFQUERY> tag:

```
<!--- Make sure FilmID was passed --->
<cfif not IsDefined("URL.filmid")>
 <!--- it wasn't, send to movie list --->
 <cflocation url="movies6.cfm">
</cfif>
```

If FilmID was not passed, users should never have gotten to this page. You could simply display
an error message, but instead, why not send them where they need to go? <cflocation> is a Cold-
Fusion tag that redirects users to other pages (or even other sites). So the <cfif> statement checks
to see whether URL.FilmID exists (using the IsDefined() function). If it does not, the user is sent to
the movies6.cfm page automatically. Now the SQL code won't execute without a FilmID because if
no FilmID exists, the <cfquery> tag is never even reached.

→   The IsDefined() function was introduced in Chapter 9.

So far so good, but you're not there yet. Two other possible trouble spots still exist. Try executing the following URL:

```
http://localhost:8500/ows/10/details2.cfm?FilmID=1
```

1 is a valid FilmID, so the movie details are displayed. But FilmID 1 doesn't have a movie image, which means the <img> tag is pointing to a nonexistent image, causing a browser error.

In addition, try this URL:

```
http://localhost:8500/ows/10/details2.cfm?FilmID=1000
```

No movie with a FilmID of 1000 exists, so no movie is displayed, but no error message is displayed either.

Neither of these problems is critical, but they should be addressed anyway. Listing 10.14 contains a final version of the details page; save this file as details3.cfm.

Listing 10.14 details3.cfm—Data Drill-Down Details

```
<!---
Name:        details3.cfm
Author:      Ben Forta (ben@forta.com)
Description: Data drill-down details
             with complete validation
Created:     01/01/2010
--->

<!--- Movie list page --->
<cfset list_page="movies8.cfm">

<!--- Make sure FilmID was passed --->
<cfif not IsDefined("URL.filmid")>
 <!--- it wasn't, send to movie list --->
 <cflocation url="#list_page#">
</cfif>

<!--- Get a movie from database --->
<cfquery name="movie" datasource="ows" result="result">
SELECT FilmID, MovieTitle,
       PitchText, Summary,
       DateInTheaters, AmountBudgeted
FROM Films
WHERE FilmID=#URL.FilmID#
</cfquery>

<!--- Make sure have a movie --->
<cfif result.RecordCount IS 0>
 <!--- It wasn't, send to movie list --->
 <cflocation url="#list_page#">
</cfif>

<!--- Build image paths --->
<cfset image_src="../images/f#movie.FilmID#.gif">
<cfset image_path=ExpandPath(image_src)>

<!--- Create HTML page --->
```

Listing 10.14 (CONTINUED)

```
<html>
<head>
 <title>Orange Whip Studios - Movie Details</title>
</head>

<body>

<!--- Display movie details --->
<cfoutput query="movie">

<table>
 <tr>
  <td colspan="2">
   <!--- Check of image file exists --->
   <cfif FileExists(image_path)>
    <!--- If it does, display it --->
    <img src="#image_src#"
        alt="#movietitle#"
        align="middle">
   </cfif>
   <strong>#MovieTitle#</strong>
  </td>
 </tr>
 <tr valign="top">
  <th align="right">Tag line:</th>
  <td>#PitchText#</td>
 </tr>
 <tr valign="top">
  <th align="right">Summary:</th>
  <td>#Summary#</td>
 </tr>
 <tr valign="top">
  <th align="right">Released:</th>
  <td>#DateFormat(DateInTheaters)#</td>
 </tr>
 <tr valign="top">
  <th align="right">Budget:</th>
  <td>#DollarFormat(AmountBudgeted)#</td>
 </tr>
</table>

<p>

<!--- Link back to movie list --->
 [<a href="#list_page#">Movie list</a>]

</cfoutput>

</body>
</html>
```

A lot has changed here, so let's walk through the code together.

The first line of code is a <cfset> statement that sets a variable named list_page to movies8.cfm. You'll see why this was done in a moment.

Next comes the check for the URL parameter FilmID. If it's not present, <cflocation> is used to redirect the user to the page referred to in variable list_page (the movie list, same as before).

Then comes the query itself—same as before; no changes there.

After the query comes a new <cfif> statement that checks to see whether result.RecordCount IS 0. You will recall that RecordCount lets you know how many rows were retrieved by a query, so if RecordCount IS 0, you know that no rows were retrieved. The only way this could happen is if an invalid FilmID were specified, in which case <cflocation> would be used to send the user back to the movie list page—one problem solved. (Earlier I said that I'd show you an alternative use for RecordCount; well, I just did.)

Next comes a set of two <cfset> statements:

```
<!--- Build image paths --->
<cfset image_src="../images/f#movie.FilmID#.gif">
<cfset image_path=ExpandPath(image_src)>
```

The goal here is to check that the movie image exists before the <img> tag is used to insert it. ColdFusion provides a function named FileExists() that can be used to check for the existence of files, but there is a catch.

Images always have at least two paths by which they are referred—the actual path on disk and the URL (usually a relative URL). So in this example, the image for FilmID 2 would have a path on disk that might look similar to c:coldfusion8wwwrootowsimagesf2.gif and a URL that might look similar to ../images/f2.gif. Usually, you care about only the URL—the actual physical location of a file isn't important within the browser. But to check for a file's existence, you do need the actual path (that is what you must pass to FileExists()). And the code you used to build the path (using #FilmID# in the SRC) was a relative path. Enter the two <cfset> statements. The first simply creates a variable named image_src that contains the dynamically generated relative file name (in the case of FilmID 2, it would be ../images/f2.gif), the same technique used in the <img> tag in the previous versions of this code. The second uses a ColdFusion function named ExpandPath() that converts relative paths to complete physical paths (here saving that path to image_path).

At this point, no determination has been made as to whether to display the image. All you have done is created two variables, each containing a path—one physical, suitable for using with FileExists(), and one relative, suitable for use in an <img> tag.

Next comes the details display, which is the same as it was before, except now the <img> tag is enclosed within a <cfif> statement that checks whether FileExists(image_path). If the image exists, FileExists() returns TRUE and the <img> tag is inserted using image_src as the SRC. If FileExists() returns FALSE (meaning the movie had no image), the <img> tag isn't generated—problem number two solved.

NOTE

Of course, the two variables image_path and image_src aren't actually necessary, and the code would have worked if the processing was all done inline. But the approach used here is cleaner, more intuitive, and easier to read, and it will help you write better code.

At the very bottom of the page is a new link that enables users to get back to the movie list page. This link also uses the `list_page` variable. And by now, I hope the reason that a variable for the movie link URL is used is blatantly obvious. The code now has three locations that refer to the movie list file. Had they all been hard-coded, making changes would involve more work and would be more error-prone (the likelihood of you missing one occurrence grows with the number of occurrences). By using a variable, all that needs to change is the variable assignment at the top of the page—the rest all works as is.

The last thing to do is to update the movie-listing page so it contains links to the new `details3.cfm` page. Listing 10.15 contains the revised movie listing code (based on `movies6.cfm`). Save it as `movies8.cfm` and then run it to see the finished page complete with usable links.

Listing 10.15 `movies8.cfm`—Data Drill-Down Results Page

```
<!---
Name:        movies8.cfm
Author:      Ben Forta (ben@forta.com)
Description: Data drill-down
Created:     01/01/2010
--->

<!--- Get movie list from database --->
<cfquery name="movies" datasource="ows" result="result">
SELECT FilmID, MovieTitle, PitchText,
       Summary, DateInTheaters
FROM Films
ORDER BY MovieTitle
</cfquery>

<!--- Create HTML page --->
<html>
<head>
 <title>Orange Whip Studios - Movie List</title>
</head>
<body>

<!--- Start table --->
<table>
 <tr>
  <th colspan="2">
   <font size="+2">
   <cfoutput>
   Movie List (#result.RecordCount# movies)
   </cfoutput>
   </font>
  </th>
 </tr>
 <!--- loop through movies --->
 <cfoutput query="movies">
  <tr bgcolor="##cccccc">
   <td>
    <strong>
    #CurrentRow#:
    <a href="details3.cfm?FilmID=#URLEncodedFormat(Trim(FilmID))#">#MovieTitle#</a>
```

Listing 10.15 (CONTINUED)

```
    </strong>
    <br>
    #PitchText#
   </td>
   <td>
    #DateFormat(DateInTheaters)#
   </td>
  </tr>
  <tr>
   <td colspan="2">
    <font size="-2">#Summary#</font>
   </td>
  </tr>
 </cfoutput>
 <!--- End of movie loop --->
 </table>

</body>
</html>
```

Just two changes have been made in Listing 10.15. The SELECT statement in the <cfquery> now also retrieves the FilmID column—you need that to pass to the details page. (You will recall that the details page needs the FilmID passed as a URL parameter.)

The display of MovieTitle has been changed to read

```
<a href="details3.cfm?FilmID=#URLEncodedFormat(Trim(FilmID))#">
#MovieTitle#</a>
```

The HTML <a href> tag is used to create links to other pages. The text between the <a> and </a> tags is clickable, and when it's clicked, the user is taken to the URL specified in the href attribute. So the tag <a href="details3.cfm">Click here</a> displays the text Click here, which, if clicked, takes the user to page details3.cfm.

But you need FilmID to be passed to the details page, so for FilmID 1 the href needed would read

```
<a href="details3.cfm?FilmID=1">Being Unbearably Light</a>
```

And for FilmID 2 it would have to be

```
<a href="details3.cfm?FilmID=2">Charlie's Devils</a>
```

These links are created using the FilmID column so that the URL parameter FilmID is correctly populated with the appropriate value for each movie. As ColdFusion loops through the movies, it creates a link for each one of them. The links all point to the same page—details3.cfm. The only thing that differs is the value passed to the FilmID parameter, and this value is then used in details3.cfm to display the correct movie. So for the movie with FilmID of 1, the URL correctly becomes

```
<a href="details3.cfm?FilmID=1">Being Unbearably Light</a>
```

Try it out; you should be able to click any movie to see the details and then click the link at the bottom of the details page to get back.

Pretty impressive for just two files containing fewer than 150 lines of ColdFusion code (including all HTML and comments).

NOTE

You probably noticed that when constructing URLs for an `href`, we used two functions, `Trim()` and `URLEncodedFormat()`, instead of just referring to the column directly.

`Trim()` was used to get rid of any extra spaces (if any existed). URLs have size limitations, and care should be taken to not waste URL space.

The `URLEncodedFormat()` function is even more important. As you already know, `?` is used to separate the URL from any parameters passed to it, `=` is used to assign parameter values, and `&` is used to separate parameters. Of course, this means that these characters can't be used within URL parameter values; many others can't be used, either (spaces, periods, and so on).

So how are these values passed? They're passed using a special format in which characters are replaced by a set of numbers that represent them. On the receiving end, the numbers can be converted back to the original characters (and ColdFusion does this for you automatically).

The `URLEncodedFormat()` function takes a string and returns a version of it that is URL safe.

When you populate a URL from a variable (any variable, including a database column), you run the risk that the values used might contain these illegal characters—characters that need to be converted. Therefore, you always should use `URLEncodedFormat()` (as was done in the previous example) so that if any invalid characters exist, they will be converted automatically and transparently. (Even in this chapter's example, in which you know `FilmID` contains only numbers that are safe, it still pays to encode the values in case someone changes something someday.)

Securing Dynamic SQL Statements

As you've just seen, the ability to create SQL statements dynamically using variables and more provides ColdFusion developers with incredible power and flexibility. But this power is not without risk, and before concluding this chapter, we need to look at the very real danger of SQL injection attacks.

Consider the following dynamic ColdFusion query, an example from earlier in this chapter:

```
<!--- Get a movie from database --->
<cfquery name="movie" datasource="ows" result="result">
SELECT FilmID, MovieTitle,
       PitchText, Summary,
       DateInTheaters, AmountBudgeted
FROM Films
WHERE FilmID=#URL.FilmID#
</cfquery>
```

Here a WHERE clause is being populated dynamically using a URL parameter. This type of code is common and popular, and you'll be using this technique continuously as you build Web applications. If the URL were

```
http://mydomain/path/file.cfm?FilmID=100
```

the resulting SQL statement would be

```
SELECT FilmID, MovieTitle,
       PitchText, Summary,
       DateInTheaters, AmountBudgeted
FROM Films
WHERE FilmID=100
```

But what if someone tampered with that URL so that it read

```
http://mydomain/path/file.cfm?FilmID=100;DELETE+Films
```

Now the resulting SQL would be

```
SELECT FilmID, MovieTitle,
       PitchText, Summary,
       DateInTheaters, AmountBudgeted
FROM Films
WHERE FilmID=100;
DELETE Films
```

And depending on the database being used, you could end up executing two statements: first SELECT, and then DELETE Films (which would promptly delete all data from the Films table).

Scared? You should be. SQL statements are not just used for queries. They are also used by most databases to create and drop tables, create user logins, change passwords, set security levels, manage scheduled events, even create and drop entire databases, as well as to implement whatever features your database supports that are be accessible this way.

This type of attack, deliberately manipulating URLs and more to maliciously change generated SQL, is known as a SQL injection attack. And hackers are always looking for signs that dynamic SQL is being generated so as to launch these attacks. This is a very real and dangerous threat. Indeed, SQL injection attacks are among the most common forms of attacks on Web sites.

NOTE

Before we go further, I must point out that this is not a ColdFusion vulnerability. In fact, it is not even a bug or a hole. This is truly a feature: many DBMSs do indeed allow queries to contain more than a single operation, and this is legal and by design.

In addition, the risk discussed here is one that all Web application developers needs to be cognizant of, whether they are using ColdFusion, PHP, ASP.NET, Java, or anything else.

So how can you protect your application?

Checking All Received Variables

First, you should always be checking parameters before passing them to your database. As a rule, never, ever pass client-supplied data (URL parameters, form fields, or even cookies) to your database unchecked. Attacks aside, it is flat-out unsafe to ever assume that data submitted by a client can be used as is.

Thus, you could be using code like this:

```
<cfparam name="URL.FilmID" type="integer">
```

You can add this line before your SQL statements. Actually, you should add a line like this before you even use any passed variables, first thing on your page. And this single line of code will lock out most SQL injection attacks by ensuring that expected values are what they should be.

NOTE

How? SQL injection (within ColdFusion applications) is primarily an issue in nontext fields (in numeric fields, for example). If a text value is tampered with, you'll end up with tampered text, but that text will all be part of the core string (within quotation marks) passed as a value, and it will therefore not be executed as separate statements. Numbers, on the other hand, are not enclosed in quotation marks, and so extraneous text can be tampered with to create an additional SQL statement. And <cfparam> can protect you.

Of course, you may want more control, in which case you could use code like this:

```
<cfif IsDefined("URL.FilmID")
and not IsNumeric(URL.FilmID)>
... throw an error or something ...
</cfif>
```

By checking that received values are of the expected type, you'll ensure the safety of your application.

TIP

Another benefit of defining all variables at the top of each page using <cfparam> tags is that you can use these tags to create variables with default values. This approach allows you to keep all variable validation and initialization in a single place, which keeps the rest of your code much cleaner.

Using <cfqueryparam>

The <cfqueryparam> tag can optionally be used within <cfquery> tags. It is primarily used for variable binding, which is beyond the scope of this chapter. But it has another important use that is very relevant to this discussion.

As an additional line of defense against SQL injection attacks, you could use <cfqueryparam>, as seen here:

```
<cfquery name="movie" datasource="ows" result="result">
SELECT FilmID, MovieTitle,
       PitchText, Summary,
       DateInTheaters, AmountBudgeted
FROM Films
WHERE FilmID=<cfqueryparam value="#URL.FilmID#"
                           cfsqltype="CF_SQL_INTEGER">
</cfquery>
```

If the previous tampered-with URL were passed to the this query, the value would be rejected, and an error would be thrown. The cfsqltype code performs data-type validation checks, and values that do not match the type are rejected. That's it—only integers are allowed, and malicious, tampered-with URL parameters are not integers.

TIP

Using <cfqueryparam> can also improve SQL query execution time and thus your application performance.

Securing Against SQL Injection Attacks

SQL injection attacks have been around for as long as dynamic SQL itself, and unfortunately, many sites get hacked using the methods just described.

ColdFusion has made it incredibly easy to protect yourself against such attacks. Be it by using `<cfparam>` or `<cfqueryparam>` or your own conditional processing, it's simple to protect yourself, and your responsibility to do so.

- Use `<cfqueryparam>` for every single variable in every single `<cfquery>` statement.

- Use `<cfparam>` at the top of every page to initialize and validate each and every variable.

My personal recommendation is that you do both.

Debugging Dynamic Database Queries

Before we finish this chapter, there is something you should be aware of. Look at the following code:

```
<!--- Get a movie from database --->
<cfquery name="movie" datasource="ows">
SELECT FilmID, MovieTitle,
       PitchText, Summary,
       DateInTheaters, AmountBudgeted
FROM Films
WHERE FilmID=#URL.FilmID#
</cfquery>
```

As you now know, this code builds a dynamic SQL statement—the expression `#URL.FilmID#` is replaced by the contents of that variable to construct a complete SQL SELECT statement at runtime.

This particular example is a simple one; a single expression is used in a simple WHERE clause. But as the complexity of the expressions (or the number of them) increases, so does the chance that you'll introduce problems in your SQL. And to find these problems, you'll need to know exactly what SQL was generated by ColdFusion—taking into account all dynamic processing.

I already showed you one way to obtain the dynamically generated SQL (using the optional `<cfquery>` result attribute). But here is another option.

In Chapter 2, "Accessing the ColdFusion Administrator," I mentioned the debugging screens (and told you that we'd use them in this chapter). The debugging screens can be used to append debug output to the bottom of generated pages, as seen in Figure 10.13.

As you can see, the appended output contains database query information (including the SQL, number of rows retrieved, and execution time), page execution time, passed parameters, CGI variables, and much more.

To try this for yourself, see Chapter 2 for instructions on turning on debug output. Once enabled, execute any page in your browser and the debug output will be appended automatically.

Figure 10.13

Dynamic SQL information is displayed along with the standard ColdFusion debugging output.

TIP

Most ColdFusion developers find that the tags you have learned thus far, `<cfquery>`, `<cfoutput>`, `<cfset>`, `<cfif>`, and `<cflocation>`, account for almost all the CFML code they ever write. As such, it's highly recommended that you try every example in this chapter before proceeding.

CHAPTER 11

The Basics of Structured Development

You have now seen just how easy dynamic page development is using ColdFusion. Combining SQL queries (even dynamically created queries) and output code is the key to building just about any Web-based applications.

We still have much to cover, but before going any further I'd like to take a little detour to revisit dynamic page generation and consider structured development.

Understanding Structured Development

The best way to understand structured development—what it does and the problems it solves—is to look at an example. Listing 11.1 should be familiar; it's the first data-driven example we looked at in Chapter 10, "Creating Data-Driven Pages."

Listing 11.1   movies1.cfm—The Basic Movie List

```
<!---
Name:        movies1.cfm
Author:      Ben Forta (ben@forta.com)
Description: First data-driven Web page
Created:     01/01/2010
--->

<!--- Get movie list from database --->
<cfquery name="movies" datasource="ows">
SELECT MovieTitle
FROM Films
ORDER BY MovieTitle
</cfquery>

<!--- Create HTML page --->
<html>
<head>
```

Listing 11.1 (CONTINUED)

```
    <title>Orange Whip Studios - Movie List</title>
    </head>

    <body>

    <h1>Movie List</h1>

    <!--- Display movie list --->
    <cfoutput query="movies">
    #MovieTitle#<br>
    </cfoutput>

    </body>
    </html>
```

As explained in Chapter 10, this code first retrieves data from a database, then loops through the returned results, outputting one movie at a time. #MovieTitle# in the <cfoutput> loop refers to the MovieTitle column in the Films database table, the column retrieved in the <cfquery> tag.

Simple, right? Maybe not. As innocent as Listing 11.1 looks, the makings of a developer's nightmare lurk in its depths. Let me explain.

Consider what would happen if the database table changed. Maybe you had to rename a column; or maybe you were rethinking your table layout and needed to split a table into multiple tables; or maybe your field name was Movie Title (with a space, which will work in some databases, but is a really bad practice) and you needed to change it to a legal name; or…

You get the idea. If the table field name changed, any and all SQL that referred to that field would have to change too. As we saw in Chapter 10, when you build applications you end up with references to database tables in a lot of different files very quickly. If a table changes, each file that referred to that table would need to change. Failure to do so would generate errors because the SQL would be invalid.

"No problem," you think. "A quick find-and-replace will locate all those queries." And you may be right; locating every <cfquery> in your application isn't that difficult. ColdFusion Builder—and just about any editor out there—will allow searching across multiple files and folders.

But that won't be enough. Why? Because if MovieTitle were changed you'd need to update your SQL and any CFML code that refers to that column. That #MovieTitle# in the <cfoutput> block would need updating too.

"Okay," you think, "I can do a search for #MovieTitle# as well, and do another find-and-replace." But that won't work, because you'd also need to find code like this:

```
    <cfoutput>#UCase(MovieTitle)#</cfoutput>
```

and this:

```
    <cfset display="Title: " & MovieTitle>
```

and more.

Single-Tier Applications

The problem with the code in Listing 11.1 (and indeed, all of the code written in the previous chapter) is that the presentation code is closely tied to the data access code. Developers refer to this type of application as being *single tiered*. Basically there is one layer or tier to the application, and it contains everything from database code to application logic.

➡ The processing of the guessing game in Chapter 9, "Programming with CFML," is an example of application logic.

For simple applications, this may not be a problem. But as applications grow in complexity and size, so does the likelihood of something breaking later when you least expect it. Too many applications have been broken by simple changes in one part of an application that had unforeseen implications elsewhere.

And the problem isn't just the risk of something breaking. Take a look at the SQL code used in the various <cfquery> tags in the listing in Chapter 10. You'll notice that they are all similar and many are exactly the same, copied from file to file. That isn't efficient use of code. If you were to tweak a query—perhaps to improve performance—you'd need to do so for lots of queries. If you were to make security-related changes to your queries you'd need to do those all over the place too, and more.

➡ The security issues to be aware of when using <cfquery> and dynamically constructed SQL were explained in Chapter 10, "Creating Data-Driven Pages."

So we have two different but related problems: presentation and content are too closely coupled; and code is repeated multiple times in multiple files.

Fortunately, there is a single solution to both problems.

Multi-Tier Applications

As we said, a single-tiered application is just that, with everything thrown into a single tier. A *multi-tiered* application (or an *n-tier* application) is an application that is broken into different layers, each responsible for just part of the complete application.

This may sound complex, but it needn't be. Consider the code in Listing 11.1 (and all of the data-driven code in Chapter 10). That code could be broken up as follows:

- Data is stored in the database.

- All database access queries are stored in a special file. This file does no data presentation (it doesn't generate HTML, for example) and all database access is via this file.

- All presentation (the HTML and <cfoutput> blocks) goes in another file. This file doesn't contain any database interaction; rather, it relies on the previous file for that.

Breaking applications into tiers forces developers to think about data and application logic differently than presentation, and this is a good thing. Consider the following:

- If you made changes to a back-end database, only code in the data access layer would need to change; presentation code would not.

- As the same data access code can be used by multiple presentation files, any changes made once will be applied to all uses of that code.

- You're free to change the presentation at will, be it colors, tables, adding alternative client technologies (like Macromedia Flash), or more. These changes are presentation-tier changes, so the database access code will remain as is.

I know this sounds a little abstract, but bear with me. It will all make sense in a moment. The key is a special type of file called a ColdFusion Component.

Introducing ColdFusion Components

Like the ColdFusion templates you have already seen, ColdFusion Components are ColdFusion files that you create and use. Both are plain text files and both contain CFML code, but that's where the similarities end.

- ColdFusion templates have no fixed format, and can contain all sorts of tags in any order. ColdFusion Components have a very strict and rigid format.

- ColdFusion templates are processed starting at the top of the file and working downward. ColdFusion Components have one or more starting and ending points, essentially different blocks of functionality within a single file.

- ColdFusion templates have a `.cfm` extension. ColdFusion Components have a `.cfc` extension.

- ColdFusion templates are designed to be invoked by a user (in a browser). ColdFusion Components are generally invoked by other code (and not by end users directly).

NOTE

If you have experience with object-oriented development and are familiar with the concept of objects, much of this will be familiar. ColdFusion Components are a form of object, essentially providing the basics of object functionality without the pain associated with so many object-oriented languages. If you have no idea what an object is, don't let that scare you. In true form, ColdFusion makes this all as simple as CFML.

You will be using ColdFusion Components (CFCs for short) extensively throughout the rest of this book. In this chapter we will revisit examples from the previous chapter, this time using CFCs.

As already explained, CFCs are plain text files, so they can be created using any editor, including ColdFusion Builder. However, ColdFusion Builder comes with sophisticated built-in support for creating and using CFCs, and we'll use these features shortly.

NOTE

Developers use the term *refactor* to describe the process of taking applications and restructuring them to make them more reusable and more efficient.

Creating Your First CFC

To create ColdFusion Components, you need to learn some important new CFML tags.

All the files created in this chapter need to go in a directory named 11 under the application root (the ows directory under the Web root).

The first thing you need to create a ColdFusion Component is a new file, so create a file named intro.cfc in the 11 folder. Delete any automatically generated content, and make sure that the file is empty.

The <cfcomponent> Tag

ColdFusion Components are defined using a tag named <cfcomponent>. (Intuitive, eh?) All of the code that makes up the CFC must be placed in between <cfcomponent> and </cfcomponent> tags (Listing 11.2). Nothing may be placed before the opening <cfcomponent> or after the closing </cfcomponent>.

Listing 11.2 intro.cfc—Introduction CFC Step 1

```
<!--- This is the introductory CFC --->
<cfcomponent>

</cfcomponent>
```

Once you have typed in this code, save your new file as intro.cfc. You have just created a Cold-Fusion Component. It does absolutely nothing at this point, but it's a ColdFusion Component nonetheless.

TIP

I just stated that nothing can be before the opening <cfcomponent> or after the closing </cfcomponent>, but as you can see in Listing 11.2 that isn't entirely accurate. No code may be outside of those tags, but comments are indeed allowed (and should be used).

The <cffunction> Tag

ColdFusion Components usually contain one or more *functions* (often called *methods*; the two terms are effectively interchangeable). A function is simply a block of code that performs an operation, and usually returns results. Each function is defined using a tag named <cffunction> and terminated with the matching closing tag </cffunction>.

<cffunction> takes a series of attributes, but only two are really important:

- name is the name of the function (it must be unique within the CFC; the same method name may be used in two different CFCs but not twice in the same CFC).

- returntype is the type of the results that will be returned (string, date, array, query, etc.).

Listing 11.3 is intro.cfc again, but this time we've introduced three functions.

Listing 11.3 `intro.cfc`—Introduction CFC Step 2

```
<!--- This is the introductory CFC --->
<cfcomponent>

<!--- Get today's date --->
<cffunction name="today" returntype="date">

</cffunction>

<!--- Get tomorrow's date --->
<cffunction name="tomorrow" returntype="date">

</cffunction>

<!--- Get yesterday's date --->
<cffunction name="yesterday" returntype="date">

</cffunction>

</cfcomponent>
```

As you can see, each function is defined with a pair of `<cffunction>` tags. The functions in Listing 11.3 have no content yet. If there were content—and there will be shortly—it would go in between those tags. Each function is uniquely named, and each function has its return data type specified. In this example all three functions return a `date`, today's date, tomorrow's date, and yesterday's date, respectively.

TIP

The `returntype` attribute may be omitted, but you should get into the habit of always defining the return type. This provides greater error checking and will ensure safer function use.

The `<cfreturn>` Tag

When a ColdFusion Component is used, the name of the function to be executed is specified. Any code in that function is processed, and a result is returned back to the calling code. To return data, a `<cfreturn>` tag is used. Listing 11.4 is a modified version of the previous listing, this time with `<cfreturn>` tags included in the body.

Listing 11.4 `intro.cfc`—Introduction CFC Step 3

```
<!--- This is the introductory CFC --->
<cfcomponent>

<!--- Get today's date --->
<cffunction name="today" returntype="date">
  <cfreturn Now()>
</cffunction>

<!--- Get tomorrow's date --->
<cffunction name="tomorrow" returntype="date">
  <cfreturn DateAdd("d", 1, Now())>
</cffunction>
```

Listing 11.4 (CONTINUED)

```
<!--- Get yesterday's date --->
<cffunction name="yesterday" returntype="date">
   <cfreturn DateAdd("d", -1, Now())>
</cffunction>

</cfcomponent>
```

Usually CFC functions contain lots of processing and then a result is returned by `<cfreturn>`. But that need not be the case, as seen here. These three functions have single-line bodies, expressions being calculated right within `<cfreturn>` tags. The `today` function returns `Now()`, `tomorrow` uses `DateAdd()` to add 1 day to `Now()`. `yesterday` adds -1 day to `Now()`, essentially subtracting a day from today's date.

→   The `Now()` function was introduced in Chapter 8, "The Basics of CFML."

Of course, performing calculations in the returned expression is optional, and the code

```
<!--- Get tomorrow's date --->
<cffunction name="tomorrow" returntype="date">
   <cfreturn DateAdd("d", 1, Now())>
</cffunction>
```

could have been written as

```
<!--- Get tomorrow's date --->
<cffunction name="tomorrow" returntype="date">
   <cfset var result=DateAdd("d", 1, Now())>
   <cfreturn result>
</cffunction>
```

This latter form is what most CFC functions tend to look like.

TIP

Every CFC function should have one—and only one—`<cfreturn>` tag. Avoid the bad practice of having multiple `<cfreturn>` tags in a single function.

TIP

Technically, functions need not return a result, but best practices dictate that every CFC function return something, even if it is a simple true/false flag.

The `<cfargument>` Tag

The functions defined thus far are simple ones, in that they accept no data and return a result. But many of the functions that you'll create will need to accept data. For example, if you were creating a CFC function that returned movie details, you'd need to pass the desired movie ID to the function.

In CFC lingo, passed data are called *arguments* and the tag that is used to define arguments is the `<cfargument>` tag. If used, `<cfargument>` must be the very first code within a `<cffunction>`, and multiple `<cfargument>` tags may be used if needed.

TIP

You may sometimes see the word parameter used too. Parameters and arguments are one and the same.

The following code snippet demonstrates the use of `<cfargument>`:

```
<cfargument name="radius" type="numeric" required="yes">
```

This code (which would go into a `<cffunction>`) defines an argument named `radius` that is required and must be a `numeric` value. `type` and `required` are both optional, and if not specified then any type will be accepted, as would no value at all.

To demonstrate the use of arguments, here is a complete function:

```
<!--- Perform geometric calculations --->
<cffunction name="geometry" returntype="struct">
    <!--- Need a radius --->
    <cfargument name="radius" type="numeric" required="yes">
    <!--- Define result variable --->
    <cfset var result=StructNew()>
    <!--- Save radius --->
    <cfset result.radius=radius>
    <!--- First circle --->
    <cfset result.circle=StructNew()>
    <!--- Calculate circle circumference --->
    <cfset result.circle.circumference=2*Pi()*radius>
    <!--- Calculate circle area --->
    <cfset result.circle.area=Pi()*(radius^2)>
    <!--- Now sphere --->
    <cfset result.sphere=StructNew()>
    <!--- Calculate sphere volume --->
    <cfset result.sphere.volume=(4/3)*Pi()*(radius^3)>
    <!--- Calculate sphere surface area --->
    <cfset result.sphere.surface=4*result.circle.area>
    <!--- Return it --->
    <cfreturn result>
</cffunction>
```

The `geometry` function performs a series of geometric calculations. Provide it with a `radius` value and it will return a structure containing two structures. The first is named `circle` and contains the calculated circumference and area of a circle of the specified `radius`. The second is named `sphere` and contains the calculated surface area and volume of a sphere of the specified `radius`.

If all that sounds like something from a long-forgotten math class, don't worry. The point isn't the geometry itself, but the fact that these calculations can be buried within a CFC function. (That, and the fact that I really do love math.)

As before, the function is named using the `<cffunction>` name attribute, and this time `returntype="struct"` (a structure). The `<cfargument>` tag accepts a required `numeric` value as the `radius`.

The code then uses the following code to define a structure named `result` that will contain the values to be returned:

```
<!--- Define result variable --->
<cfset var result=StructNew()>
```

➜   Structures and the `StructNew()` function were introduced in Chapter 8.

The rest of the code defines two nested structures, and then uses <cfset> tags to perform the actual calculations (saving the results of the calculations into the result structure). The last line of code returns the structure with a <cfreturn> tag.

NOTE

You may have noticed that the <cfset> used to create the result structure included the word var. We'll explain this in later chapters. For now, suffice to say that all local variables within CFC functions should be defined using var as seen here.

Listing 11.5 contains the final complete intro.cfc.

Listing 11.5 intro.cfc—Introduction CFC Step 4

```
<!--- This is the introductory CFC --->
<cfcomponent>

<!--- Get today's date --->
<cffunction name="today" returntype="date">
   <cfreturn Now()>
</cffunction>

<!--- Get tomorrow's date --->
<cffunction name="tomorrow" returntype="date">
   <cfreturn DateAdd("d", 1, Now())>
</cffunction>

<!--- Get yesterday's date --->
<cffunction name="yesterday" returntype="date">
   <cfreturn DateAdd("d", -1, Now())>
</cffunction>

<!--- Perform geometric calculations --->
<cffunction name="geometry" returntype="struct">
   <!--- Need a radius --->
   <cfargument name="radius" type="numeric" required="yes">
   <!--- Define result variable --->
   <cfset var result=StructNew()>
   <!--- Save radius --->
   <cfset result.radius=radius>
   <!--- First circle --->
   <cfset result.circle=StructNew()>
   <!--- Calculate circle circumference --->
   <cfset result.circle.circumference=2*Pi()*radius>
   <!--- Calculate circle area --->
   <cfset result.circle.area=Pi()*(radius^2)>
   <!--- Now sphere --->
   <cfset result.sphere=StructNew()>
   <!--- Calculate sphere volume --->
   <cfset result.sphere.volume=(4/3)*Pi()*(radius^3)>
   <!--- Calculate sphere surface area --->
   <cfset result.sphere.surface=4*result.circle.area>
   <!--- Return it --->
   <cfreturn result>
</cffunction>

</cfcomponent>
```

You now have a complete ColdFusion Component containing four methods. Great—but how do you actually use your new creation?

Using ColdFusion Components

ColdFusion Components are used by other ColdFusion code, although rather than used, CFCs are said to be *invoked*. A special tag is used to invoke ColdFusion Components, and not surprisingly the tag is named <cfinvoke>. To invoke a ColdFusion Component you'll need to specify several things:

- The name of the CFC to be used.

- The name of the method to be invoked (CFCs may contain multiple methods).

- The name of a variable that should contain any returned data.

- In addition, if the CFC method being invoked accepts arguments, those arguments are to be provided.

Listing 11.6 is a simple file named testcfc.cfm. As its name suggests, it tests the CFC file you just created.

Listing 11.6 testcfc.cfm—CFC Tester Step 1

```
<!---
Name:        testcfc.cfm
Author:      Ben Forta (ben@forta.com)
Description: Quick CFC test
Created:     01/01/2010
--->

<!--- Title --->
<h1>Testing intro.cfc</h1>

<!--- Get today's date --->
<cfinvoke component="intro"
          method="today"
          returnvariable="todayRet">

<!--- Output --->
<cfoutput>
Today is #DateFormat(todayRet)#<br>
</cfoutput>
```

Let's take a quick look at this code. The <cfinvoke> needs to know the name of the component to be used, and component="intro" tells ColdFusion to find a file named intro.cfc in the current folder. As already seen, CFCs can contain multiple functions, so ColdFusion needs to know which method in the CFC to invoke. method="today" tells ColdFusion to find the function named today and invoke it. today returns a value (today's date), and so returnvariable="todayRet" tells Cold-Fusion to save whatever today returns in a variable named todayRet.

NOTE

If the variable name specified in returnvariable doesn't exist, it will be created. If it does exist it will be overwritten.

When ColdFusion processes the <cfinvoke> tag, it locates and opens the intro.cfc file, finds the today function, executes it, and saves the result in a variable named todayRet. The code then displays that value using a simple <cfoutput> block.

If you were to run testcfc.cfm you would see a result like the one in Figure 11.1.

Figure 11.1

CFC processing is hidden from ColdFusion-generated output.

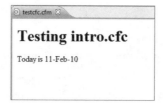

NOTE

Be sure to run the .cfm file and not the .cfc file or the results won't be what you expect.

Pretty simple, right? Well, it gets even simpler when using ColdFusion Builder.

Using ColdFusion Builder CFC Support

You have seen how to use <cfinvoke> to invoke a ColdFusion Component method. You'll now learn how to invoke a CFC method without writing any code at all. Here are the steps:

1. Locate the ColdFusion Builder Services Browser tab (it should be in the panel beneath the actual editor window).

2. Expand the localhost option to display a list of all known ColdFusion Components, ordered by the folder they are in. By default, every CFC known to ColdFusion is shown.

3. You should see a folder named ows.11 listed; ows.11 is folder 11 within folder ows (dot notation is used in folder path names).

4. Once you have located the folder, click the arrow to its left to display the Cold-Fusion Components within it (there'll be just one named ows.11.intro, the file created previously).

5. Click the arrow next to ows.11.intro to display the methods it contains, as shown in Figure 11.2.

Figure 11.2

The ColdFusion Builder Services Browser tab provides easy access to ColdFusion Components and their methods.

6. ColdFusion Builder lists all CFC methods, along with their return type and any arguments.

7. Make sure that file `testcfc.cfm` is open in ColdFusion Builder. Click the line after the existing `<cfinvoke>` code and before the `<cfoutput>` block (that's where we want the new code inserted), and then right-click the `tomorrow()` method on the Services Browser tab and choose Insert CFInvoke.

8. ColdFusion Builder will generate a complete `<cfinvoke>` tag for you, specifying the correct `component` and `method` values and defining a `returnvariable` value. In the code, rename `returnvariable` to `tomorrowRet`.

9. Add the following code to the `<cfoutput>` block (after the existing line of code):

```
Tomorrow is #DateFormat(tomorrowRet)#<br>
```

The `testcfc.cfm` file should now look like Listing 11.7.

Listing 11.7 `testcfc.cfm`—CFC Tester Step 2

```
<!---
Name:        testcfc.cfm
Author:      Ben Forta (ben@forta.com)
Description: Quick CFC test
Created:     01/01/2010
--->

<!--- Title --->
<h1>Testing intro.cfc</h1>

<!--- Get today's date --->
<cfinvoke component="intro"
          method="today"
          returnvariable="todayRet">
<!--- Get tomorrow's date --->
<cfinvoke
 component="ows.11.intro"
 method="tomorrow"
 returnvariable="tomorrowRet">
</cfinvoke>

<!--- Output --->
<cfoutput>
Today is #DateFormat(todayRet)#<br>
Tomorrow is #DateFormat(tomorrowRet)#<br>
</cfoutput>
```

Run `testcfc.cfm`. You should see a page like the one in Figure 11.3.

Figure 11.3

Be sure to test ColdFusion Component invocations by executing test code.

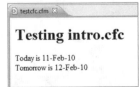

Testing intro.cfc

Today is 11-Feb-10
Tomorrow is 12-Feb-10

You'll notice that ColdFusion Builder generated a closing `</cfinvoke>` tag. This was not needed in our simple invocation, but it does no harm being there either.

NOTE

The CFC path generated by ColdFusion Builder is the full path (starting from the Web root). This is only required when accessing a component in another directory, but does no harm here. You can change `component="ows.11.intro"` to `component="intro"` if you like.

The ColdFusion Component method you just used is a simple one. It accepts no arguments and returns a simple value. Let's try this again, but now using a more complicated method, the `geometry` method. Here are the steps:

1. Locate the `ows.11.geometry` method on the Services Browser tab.

2. Select the `geometry` method and insert a `CFInvoke` call (you can place it the very end of the page).

   ColdFusion Builder generates a `<cfinvoke>` that looks like this:

   ```
   <cfinvoke
    component="ows.11.intro"
    method="geometry"
    returnvariable="intro">
      <cfinvokeargument name="radius" value=""/>
   </cfinvoke>
   ```

   `<cfinvokeargument>` is used within `<cfinvoke>` tags to pass arguments to invoked methods. As the `geometry` method requires that an argument (the `radius`) be passed to it, Cold-Fusion Builder generates a `<cfinvokeargument>` tag. The argument `name` is automatically set by ColdFusion Builder (`name="radius"`), but you need to specify the `value`.

3. Replace the empty `value=""` with an actual value, a number of your choice (any positive number, for example, `10`).

4. Change the `returnVariable` value to `geometryRet`.

5. The geometry method returns a structure, and the simplest way to see the results is to use `<cfdump>`, so add the following after the `</cfinvoke>` tag:

   ```
   <!--- Display it --->
   <cfdump var="#geometryRet#">
   ```

6. The final test code should look like Listing 11.8. Run the page. You should see output that looks like that in Figure 11.4.

Listing 11.8   `testcfc.cfm`—CFC Tester Step 3

```
<!---
Name:        testcfc.cfm
Author:      Ben Forta (ben@forta.com)
Description: Quick CFC test
Created:     01/01/2010
--->
```

Listing 11.8 (CONTINUED)

```
<!--- Title --->
<h1>Testing intro.cfc</h1>

<!--- Get today's date --->
<cfinvoke component="intro"
          method="today"
          returnvariable="todayRet">
<!--- Get tomorrow's date --->
<cfinvoke
    component="ows.11.intro"
    method="tomorrow"
    returnVariable="tomorrowRet" >
</cfinvoke>

<!--- Output --->
<cfoutput>
Today is #DateFormat(todayRet)#<br/>
Tomorrow is #DateFormat(tomorrowRet)#<br/>
</cfoutput>

<!--- Geometry test --->
<cfinvoke
    component="ows.11.intro"
    method="geometry"
    returnVariable="geometryRet" >
    <cfinvokeargument name="radius" value="10" />
</cfinvoke>

<!--- Display it --->
<cfdump var="#geometryRet#">
```

Figure 11.4

Use <cfdump> to quickly display complex data types.

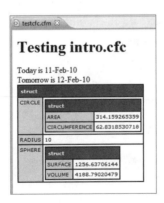

Before we go any further, let's take another look at the invocation of the geometry method. This is the code generated by ColdFusion Builder:

```
<cfinvoke
  component="ows.11.intro"
  method="geometry"
```

```
    returnvariable="intro">
      <cfinvokeargument name="radius" value=""/>
    </cfinvoke>
```

`<cfinvoke>` takes the name of the component, the method, and the name of the `returnvariable`, as it did previously. The `radius` that must be passed to `geometry` is passed using a `<cfinvokeargument>` tag that takes a `name` (the argument name) and a `value` (the value for that argument). If multiple arguments were needed, then multiple `<cfinvokeargument>` tags could be used.

NOTE

You can now see why ColdFusion Builder inserted a closing `</cfinvoke>` tag, as this is needed when nested `<cfinvokeargument>` tags are used.

There is another way to pass arguments to a CFC method, without using `<cfinvokeargument>`. Take a look at this code snippet:

```
<cfinvoke
  component="ows.11.intro"
  method="geometry"
  radius="10"
  returnvariable="geometryRet">
```

This code is functionally identical to the previous snippet, but it doesn't use `<cfinvokeargument>`. Instead, it simply passes the argument as a `name=value` pair, in this case `radius="10"`. You are free to use either syntax.

TIP

Many developers find the `name=value` syntax better suited for simple methods without lots of arguments, and the `<cfinvokeargument>` better suited for more complex methods with lots of arguments (and possibly optional arguments).

As you have seen, ColdFusion Builder makes using existing ColdFusion Components very easy. Over time you will likely accumulate quite a collection of ColdFusion Components, and being able to simply select and invoke them is very handy.

Using a CFC for Database Access

In Chapter 10 we created an application that listed all Orange Whip Studios movies, and allowed them to be clicked on to display more details. The final versions of those files (`movies8.cfm` and `details3.cfm` in the `10` folder) each contain `<cfquery>` tags, and refer to query columns in `<cfoutput>` blocks.

We'll now revisit that application, this time moving the database interaction out of the two `.cfm` files and into a new file named `movies.cfc`. But instead of creating `movies.cfc` from scratch, we'll use ColdFusion Builder to complete much the layout for us. Here are the steps:

1. Click the `11` folder in the Navigator panel.

2. Right-click the `11` folder and choose New > ColdFusion Component to display the New ColdFusion Component screen as shown in Figure 11.5.

3. You'll be prompted for component details. In the Component Name field, type `movies` (without the `.cfc` extension). You can ignore all the other fields for now.

Figure 11.5

ColdFusion Builder can walk you through creating CFCs.

4. Now you need to define the methods needed. Click Next to display the Component Properties and Functions screen.

5. The `movies.cfc` file will need two methods: one to list all movies and one to return movie details. Click the Add Function button to display the New Function screen (as seen in Figure 11.6). Set the name to `List` and choose `query` as the return type. You can ignore the attributes for now. Click OK.

Figure 11.6

CFC functions are defined on the New Function screen.

6. Click Add Function to add the second method. Set the name to `GetDetails` and choose query as the return type Then click OK.

You should now see your two defined functions, as shown in Figure 11.7.

Figure 11.7

Each CFC function must be uniquely named.

7. The `List` method needs no arguments (it simply returns all movies), but `GetDetails` requires that a movie ID be passed as an argument. Arguments are defined on the New Function Argument screen, so click the `GetDetails` function and then click Add Argument to display that screen (shown in Figure 11.8).

Figure 11.8

Method arguments are defined on the New Function Argument screen.

8. Set the name to `FilmID` and the type to `Numeric` and check the `Required` check box. Then click OK.

9. Click the Finish button, and ColdFusion Builder will generate a ColdFusion Component shell named `movies.cfc` in the 11 folder.

The generated ColdFusion Components isn't complete, because ColdFusion Builder can't know what you intend to do within the CFC methods. But ColdFusion Builder was able to create the following basic layout, allowing you to fill in the missing pieces:

```
<cfcomponent>
    <cffunction name="GetDetals" access="package" returntype="query">
        <cfargument name="FilmID" type="numeric" required="true" />
    </cffunction>
    <cffunction name="List" access="package" returntype="query">
    </cffunction>
</cfcomponent>
```

You now need to insert a query into each of the methods. The List method query should be

```
<!--- Define local variables --->
<cfset var movies="">

<!--- Get movie list from database --->
<cfquery name="movies" datasource="ows">
SELECT FilmID, MovieTitle, PitchText,
       Summary, DateInTheaters
FROM Films
ORDER BY MovieTitle
</cfquery>
```

and the GetDetails method query should be

```
<!--- Define local variables --->
<cfset var movie="">

<!--- Get a movie from database --->
<cfquery name="movie" datasource="ows">
SELECT FilmID, MovieTitle,
       PitchText, Summary,
       DateInTheaters, AmountBudgeted
FROM Films
WHERE FilmID=#ARGUMENTS.FilmID#
</cfquery>
```

These queries are the same as the ones used in Chapter 10, with the exception of the WHERE clause in the second query, which has been changed from

```
WHERE FilmID=#URL.FilmID#
```

to

```
WHERE FilmID=#ARGUMENTS.FilmID#
```

as the FilmID is now a CFC method argument instead of a URL parameter.

TIP

Feel free to copy and paste the `<cfquery>` tags from movies8.cfm and details3.cfm in the 10 folder.

Now that each method contains its query, edit the `<cfreturn>` tag in each so that the query is returned. Listing 11.9 contains what your final edited movies.cfc should look like.

Listing 11.9   `movies.cfc`—Movie Data-Abstraction Component

```
<cfcomponent>

<cffunction name="List" access="public"
            returnType="query" output="false">

    <!--- Define local variables --->
    <cfset var movies="">

    <!--- Get movie list from database --->
    <cfquery name="movies" datasource="ows">
    SELECT FilmID, MovieTitle, PitchText,
           Summary, DateInTheaters
    FROM Films
    ORDER BY MovieTitle
    </cfquery>

    <cfreturn movies>
</cffunction>

<cffunction name="GetDetails" access="public"
            returnType="query" output="false">
    <cfargument name="FilmID" type="numeric" required="true">

    <!--- Define local variables --->
    <cfset var movies="">

    <!--- Get a movie from database --->
    <cfquery name="movie" datasource="ows">
    SELECT FilmID, MovieTitle,
           PitchText, Summary,
           DateInTheaters, AmountBudgeted
    FROM Films
    WHERE FilmID=#ARGUMENTS.FilmID#
    </cfquery>

    <cfreturn movie>
</cffunction>

</cfcomponent>
```

The code in Listing 11.9 should be quite familiar by now. It contains two methods, `List` and `GetDetails`. `List` executes a query to obtain all movies and returns that `movies` query. `GetDetails` accepts `FilmID` as an argument, then uses `<cfquery>` to retrieve that movie, then returns that `movie` query. Both methods populate local variables, the query results generated by `FilmID`, so those variables are first defined using `<cfset>` and the `FilmID` keyword (as mentioned previously).

Now that you have `movies.cfc` complete, you need the `.cfm` pages that will invoke the CFC methods. Listing 11.10 contains `movies.cfm` (which is based on `10/movies8.cfm`) and Listing 11.11 contains `details.cfm` (which is based on `10/details3.cfm`).

TIP

To save time and typing, feel free to start by copying from the two aforementioned files in the `10` folder.

Listing 11.10 `movies.cfm`—CFC-Driven Movie List

```
<!---
Name:        movies.cfm
Author:      Ben Forta (ben@forta.com)
Description: CFC driven data drill-down
Created:     01/01/2010
--->

<!--- Get movie list --->
<cfinvoke
 component="movies"
 method="List"
 returnvariable="movies">

<!--- Create HTML page --->
<html>
<head>
 <title>Orange Whip Studios - Movie List</title>
</head>

<body>

<!--- Start table --->
<table>
 <tr>
  <th colspan="2">
   <font size="+2">
   <cfoutput>
   Movie List (#Movies.RecordCount# movies)
   </cfoutput>
   </font>
  </th>
 </tr>
 <!--- loop through movies --->
 <cfoutput query="movies">
  <tr bgcolor="##cccccc">
   <td>
    <strong>
    #CurrentRow#:<a href="details.cfm?FilmID=
       #URLEncodedFormat(Trim(FilmID))#">#MovieTitle#</a>
    </strong>
    <br>
    #PitchText#
   </td>
   <td>
    #DateFormat(DateInTheaters)#
   </td>
  </tr>
  <tr>
   <td colspan="2">
    <font size="-2">#Summary#</font>
   </td>
  </tr>
 </cfoutput>
 <!--- End of movie loop --->
</table>

</body>
</html>
```

Listing 11.11 details.cfm—CFC-Driven Movie Details

```
<!---
Name:        details.cfm
Author:      Ben Forta (ben@forta.com)
Description: CFC driven data drill-down details
             with complete validation
Created:     01/01/2010
--->

<!--- Movie list page --->
<cfset list_page="movies.cfm">

<!--- Make sure FilmID was passed --->
<cfif not IsDefined("URL.filmid")>
 <!--- it wasn't, send to movie list --->
 <cflocation url="#list_page#">
</cfif>

<!--- Get movie details --->
<cfinvoke
 component="movies"
 method="GetDetails"
 returnvariable="movie"
 FilmID="#URL.filmid#">

<!--- Make sure have a movie --->
<cfif movie.RecordCount IS 0>
 <!--- It wasn't, send to movie list --->
 <cflocation url="#list_page#">
</cfif>

<!--- Build image paths --->
<cfset image_src="../images/f#movie.FilmID#.gif">
<cfset image_path=ExpandPath(image_src)>

<!--- Create HTML page --->
<html>
<head>
 <title>Orange Whip Studios - Movie Details</title>
</head>

<body>

<!--- Display movie details --->
<cfoutput query="movie">

<table>
 <tr>
  <td colspan="2">
   <!--- Check of image file exists --->
   <cfif FileExists(image_path)>
    <!--- If it does, display it --->
    <img src="../images/f#filmid#.gif"
       alt="#movietitle#"
       align="middle">
   </cfif>
   <b>#MovieTitle#</b>
```

Listing 11.11   (CONTINUED)

```
     </td>
    </tr>
    <tr valign="top">
     <th align="right">Tag line:</th>
     <td>#PitchText#</td>
    </tr>
    <tr valign="top">
     <th align="right">Summary:</th>
     <td>#Summary#</td>
    </tr>
    <tr valign="top">
     <th align="right">Released:</th>
     <td>#DateFormat(DateInTheaters)#</td>
    </tr>
    <tr valign="top">
     <th align="right">Budget:</th>
     <td>#DollarFormat(AmountBudgeted)#</td>
    </tr>
   </table>

   <p>

   <!--- Link back to movie list --->
   [<a href="#list_page#">Movie list</a>]

   </cfoutput>

   </body>
   </html>
```

I'm not going to walk through all of Listings 11.10 and 11.11, as most of that code was explained in detail in Chapter 10. However, notice that in both listings the <cfquery> tags have been removed and replaced with <cfinvoke> tags. The <cfinvoke> in Listing 11.10 passes no arguments and receives a query as a result (which I named movies to match the original name so as to not have to change any other code). The <cfinvoke> in Listing 11.11 passes URL.FilmID as an argument to GetDetails (previously it had been used in a <cfquery> directly).

Run movies.cfm. The code should execute exactly as it did in Chapter 10, but this time you are running a multi-tiered application, one that will be much easier to manage and maintain in the future.

Now that we are done, let's consider the solution. Have we actually solved any problems? Haven't we merely moved the problem from one file to another? To go back to our original concern—the fact that data access code and presentation code were too closely tied—isn't that still the case? If a table column name changed, wouldn't presentation code still break?

Actually, we've made life much better. True, all we did was move the SQL from one file to another, but in doing so we reduced the number of times SQL statements occur, and also divorced the presentation code from the data access code. If a table column name did change, all you'd need to do is modify the method that accesses the data. The methods could still return the column names you expected previously (perhaps using SQL aliases, or by building queries manually), so while you'd need to update the relevant CFC methods, you should not need to update anything else at all. This is definitely a major improvement.

More On Using ColdFusion Components

You've now had firsthand experience with ColdFusion Components, and you'll be using them extensively as you work through this book. ColdFusion Components make it easy to tier applications, and this results in

- Cleaner code

- More reusable code

- More maintainable code (code that is less prone to breakage when changes are made)

But before closing this chapter, there are a few additional points about ColdFusion Components worth mentioning.

Where to Save CFCs

The ColdFusion Components created in this chapter (and indeed, throughout this book) are stored within the work folder. This is ideal when learning ColdFusion, but in practice this isn't what you'd want to do.

Most developers create a specific cfc folder (or several of them) and store all common ColdFusion Components in them. This will make it easier to locate and maintain them. As you have seen, Cold-Fusion Builder automatically accommodates for path considerations when generating <cfinvoke> tags.

Unit Testing

One important benefit of ColdFusion Components not mentioned thus far is testing. As you build applications you'll want to test your work regularly. And the larger and more complex an application becomes, the harder testing becomes. This is even more problematic when code gets in the way. For example, if you were testing the SQL in a <cfquery> you wouldn't want HTML layout issues to unnecessarily complicate the testing.

Breaking code into tiers greatly simplifies testing. Once you've written your ColdFusion Component you can (and should) create a simple test page, one that doesn't have complex display code and simply invokes methods and dumps their output—much like we did in the geometry example earlier in this chapter. Experienced developers typically have simple test front-ends for each Cold-Fusion Component they create. This practice is highly recommended.

Documenting ColdFusion Components

As your ColdFusion Component collection grows, so will the uses you find for them. So will the number of developers who will want to take advantage of them, assuming you're working with other developers. As such, it is really important to document your ColdFusion Components, explaining what they do, what each method does, and what you expect passed to any arguments.

Documenting ColdFusion Components is so important that self-documenting features are built right into the tags used to create them. Each of the CFC tags used in this chapter, <cfcomponent>,

<cffunction>, and <cfargument>, take an optional attribute named hint. As you can see in Listing 11.12, the hint attribute has been used to add little snippets of documentation to our movies.cfc file.

Listing 11.12 movies.cfc—Providing CFC Hints

```
<!--- Movie component --->
<cfcomponent hint="Movie database abstraction">

 <!--- List method --->
 <cffunction name="List" access="public"
             returnType="query" output="false"
             hint="List all movies">

  <!--- Define local variables --->
  <cfset var movies="">

  <!--- Get movie list from database --->
  <cfquery name="movies" datasource="ows">
  SELECT FilmID, MovieTitle, PitchText,
         Summary, DateInTheaters
  FROM Films
  ORDER BY MovieTitle
  </cfquery>
  <cfreturn movies>
 </cffunction>

 <!--- GetDetails method --->
 <cffunction name="GetDetails" access="public"
             returnType="query" output="false"
             hint="Get movie details for a specific movie">
 <cfargument name="FilmID" type="numeric"
             required="true" hint="Film ID">

  <!--- Define local variables --->
  <cfset var movie="">

  <!--- Get a movie from database --->
  <cfquery name="movie" datasource="ows">
  SELECT FilmID, MovieTitle,
         PitchText, Summary,
         DateInTheaters, AmountBudgeted
  FROM Films
  WHERE FilmID=#ARGUMENTS.FilmID#
  </cfquery>
  <cfreturn movie>
 </cffunction>

</cfcomponent>
```

So what do these hints do? They have absolutely no impact on the actual processing of the Cold-Fusion Components. Rather, they are used by ColdFusion to generate documentation on the fly, as seen in Figure 11.9.

Figure 11.9

ColdFusion auto-generates ColdFusion Component documentation using the information gleaned from the tags used to create it.

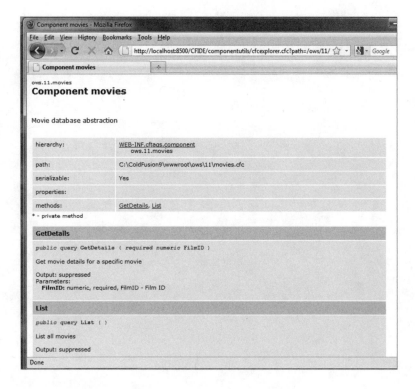

Earlier in this chapter I told you not to run the .cfc directly, and said that if you did, the result might not be what you'd expect. Well, the result is actually documentation, like the example shown in Figure 11.9. To access this documentation you can

- Specify the URL to the .cfc in your browser.

- Browse the .cfc in ColdFusion Builder.

NOTE

When you browse CFC documentation you may be asked for your ColdFusion Administrator's password.

You can type hints manually, if you like. In addition, the Create Component wizard used earlier in this chapter allows hint text to be provided while building the CFC. However you decide to do it, providing hint text is highly recommended.

ColdFusion Forms

Using Forms

In Chapter 10, "Creating Data-Driven Pages," you learned how to create ColdFusion templates that dynamically display data retrieved from databases. The Films table has just 23 rows, so the data fit easily in a Web browser window and required only minimal scrolling.

What do you do if you have hundreds or thousands of rows? Displaying all that data in one long list is impractical. Scrolling through lists of movies to find the one you want just doesn't work well. The solution is to enable users to search for what they want by specifying what they are looking for. You can allow them to enter a title, an actor's name, or part of the tag line. You can then display only the movies that meet the search criteria.

To accomplish this, you need to do two things. First, you must create your search form using the HTML <form> tags. Second, you must create a template that builds SQL SELECT statements dynamically based on the data collected and submitted by the form.

➡ See Chapter 6, "Introducing SQL," for an explanation of the SELECT statement.

Creating Forms

Before you can create a search form, you need to learn how ColdFusion interacts with HTML forms. Listing 12.1 contains the code for a sample form that prompts for a first and last name. Create this template, then save it in a new folder named 12 (under the application root) as form1.cfm.

TIP

As a reminder, the files created in this chapter are in directory 12, so use that in your URLs too.

Listing 12.1 form1.cfm—HTML Forms

```
<!---
Name:        form1.cfm
Author:      Ben Forta (ben@forta.com)
Description: Introduction to forms
Created:     01/01/2010
--->

<html>
<head>
 <title>Learning ColdFusion Forms 1</title>
</head>

<body>

<!--- Movie search form --->
<form action="form1_action.cfm" method="POST">

Please enter the movie name and then click
<strong>Process</strong>.
<p>
Movie:
<input type="text" name="MovieTitle">
<br>
<input type="submit" value="Process">
</p>
</form>

</body>
</html>
```

Execute this code to display the form, as shown in Figure 12.1.

Figure 12.1

You can use HTML forms to collect data to be submitted to ColdFusion.

This form is simple, with a single-data entry field and a submit button, but it helps clearly demonstrate how forms are used to submit data to ColdFusion.

Using HTML Form Tags

You create HTML forms by using the <form> tag. <form> usually takes two parameters passed as tag attributes. The action attribute specifies the name of the script or program that the Web server should execute in response to the form's submission. To submit a form to ColdFusion, you specify the name of the ColdFusion template that will process the form. The following example specifies that the template form1_action.cfm should process the submitted form:

```
action="form1_action.cfm"
```

The `method` attribute specifies how data is sent back to the Web server. As a rule, all ColdFusion forms should be submitted as type `post`.

CAUTION

The default submission type is not `post`; it is usually `get`. If you omit the `method="post"` attribute from your form tag, you run the risk of losing form data, particularly in long forms or forms with `textarea` controls.

Your form has only a single data entry field: `<input type="text" name="MovieTitle">`. This is a simple text field. The `name` attribute in the `<input>` tag specifies the name of the field, and ColdFusion uses this name to refer to the field when it is processed.

Each field in a form is usually given a unique name. If two fields have the same name, both sets of values are returned to be processed and are separated by a comma. You usually want to be able to validate and manipulate each field individually, so each field should have its own name. The notable exceptions are the check box and radio button input types, which we'll describe shortly.

The last item in the form is an `<input>` of type `submit`. The submit `<input>` type creates a button that, when clicked, submits the form contents to the Web server for processing. Almost every form has a submit button (or a graphic image that acts like a submit button). The `value` attribute specifies the text to display within the button, so `<input type="submit" value="Process">` creates a submit button with the text `Process` in it.

TIP

When you're using an `input` type of submit, you should always specify button text by using the `value` attribute. If you don't, the default text `Submit Query` (or something similar) is displayed, which is likely to confuse your users.

Form Submission Error Messages

If you enter a movie title into the field and submit the form right now, you will receive a ColdFusion error message like the one in Figure 12.2. This error says that file `form1_action.cfm` can't be found.

Figure 12.2

ColdFusion returns an error message when it can't process your request.

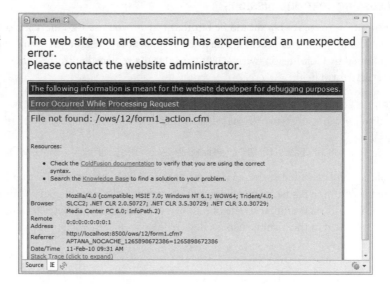

This error message is perfectly valid, of course. You submitted a form to be passed to ColdFusion and processed it with a template, but you haven't created that template yet. So your next task is to create a template to process the form submission.

Processing Form Submissions

To demonstrate how to process returned forms, you must create a simple template that echoes the movie title you entered. The template is shown in Listing 12.2.

Listing 12.2 `form1_action.cfm`—Processing Form Fields

```
<!---
Name:        form1_action.cfm
Author:      Ben Forta (ben@forta.com)
Description: Introduction to forms
Created:     01/01/2010
--->

<html>
<head>
 <title>Learning ColdFusion Forms 1</title>
</head>

<body>

<!--- Display search text --->
<cfoutput>
<strong>Movie title:</strong> #FORM.MovieTitle#
</cfoutput>

</body>
</html>
```

Processing Text Submissions

By now the `<cfoutput>` tag should be familiar to you; you use it to mark a block of code that Cold-Fusion should parse and process. The line `<strong>Movie title:</strong> #FORM.MovieTitle#` is processed by ColdFusion, with `#FORM.MovieTitle#` replaced with the value you entered in the `MovieTitle` form field.

NOTE

Use of the prefix FORM is optional. Using it prevents ambiguity and improves performance, but it also makes the code less reusable.

➔   See Chapter 8, "The Basics of CFML," for a detailed discussion of the ColdFusion `<cfoutput>` tag.

Create a template called `form1_action.cfm` that contains the code in Listing 12.2 and save it. Then resubmit your movie's name by clicking the form's submit button again. This time you should see a browser display similar to the one shown in Figure 12.3. Whatever name you enter in the `MovieTitle` field in the form is displayed.

Figure 12.3

Submitted form fields
can be displayed
simply by referring to
the field name.

As you can see, FORM fields are used in ColdFusion like any other variable type.

Processing Check Boxes and Radio Buttons

Other input types you will frequently use are check boxes and radio buttons:

- **Check boxes** are used to select options that have one of two states: on or off, yes or no, and true or false. To ask a visitor whether they want to be added to a mailing list, for example, you would create a check box field. If the user selects the box, their name is added to the mailing list; if the user doesn't select the box, their name is not added.

- **Radio buttons** are used to select one of at least two mutually exclusive options. You can implement a field prompting for payment type with options such as Cash, Check, Credit card, or P.O.

The code example in Listing 12.3 creates a form that uses both option buttons and check box fields.

Listing 12.3 `form2.cfm`—Using Check Boxes and Radio Buttons

```
<!---
Name:        form2.cfm
Author:      Ben Forta (ben@forta.com)
Description: Introduction to forms
Created:     01/01/2010
--->

<html>

<head>
 <title>Learning ColdFusion Forms 2</title>
</head>

<body>

<!--- Payment and mailing list form --->
<form action="form2_action.cfm" method="POST">

Please fill in this form and then click <strong>Process</strong>.
<p>
<!--- Payment type radio buttons --->
Payment type:<br>
<input type="radio" name="PaymentType" value="Cash">Cash<br>
<input type="radio" name="PaymentType" value="Check">Check<br>
<input type="radio" name="PaymentType" value="Credit card">Credit card<br>
<input type="radio" name="PaymentType" value="P.O.">P.O.
</p>
<p>
```

Listing 12.3 (CONTINUED)

```
<!--- Mailing list checkbox --->
Would you like to be added to our mailing list?
<input type="checkbox" name="MailingList" value="Yes">
</p>
<p>
<input type="submit" value="Process">
</p>
</form>

</body>

</html>
```

Figure 12.4 shows how this form appears in your browser.

Figure 12.4

You can use input types of option buttons and check boxes to facilitate the selection of options.

Before you create `form2_action.cfm` to process this form, you should note a couple of important points. First, look at the four lines of code that make up the Payment Type radio button selection:

```
<input type="radio" name="PaymentType" value="Cash">Cash<br>
<input type="radio" name="PaymentType" value="Check">Check<br>
<input type="radio" name="PaymentType" value="Credit card">Credit card<br>
<input type="radio" name="PaymentType" value="P.O.">P.O.
```

Each one contains the exact same name attribute—name="PaymentType". The four <input> fields have the same name so your browser knows they are part of the same set. If each radio button had a separate name, the browser wouldn't know that these buttons are mutually exclusive and thus would allow the selection of more than one button.

Another important point: Unlike <input> type text, radio buttons don't prompt the user for any textual input. Therefore, you must use the value attribute for the browser to associate a particular value with each radio button. The code value="Cash" instructs the browser to return the value Cash in the PaymentType field if that radio button is selected.

Now that you understand radio button and check box fields, you're ready to create a template to process them. Create a template called form2_action.cfm using the template code in Listing 12.4.

Listing 12.4 `form2_action.cfm`—Processing Option Buttons and Check Boxes

```
<!---
Name:        form2_action.cfm
Author:      Ben Forta (ben@forta.com)
Description: Introduction to forms
Created:     01/01/2010
--->

<html>

<head>
 <title>Learning ColdFusion Forms 2</title>
</head>

<body>

<!--- Display feedback to user --->
<cfoutput>
<!--- Payment type --->
Hello,<br>
You selected <strong>#FORM.PaymentType#</strong> as your payment type.<br>

<!--- Mailing list --->
<cfif MailingList IS "Yes">
 You will be added to our mailing list.
<cfelse>
 You will not be added to our mailing list.
</cfif>

</cfoutput>

</body>

</html>
```

The form processing code in Listing 12.4 displays the payment type the user selects. The field `PaymentType` is fully qualified with the `FORM` field type to prevent name collisions.

When the check box is selected, the value specified in the `value` attribute is returned; in this case, the value is `Yes`. If the `value` attribute is omitted, the default value of `on` is returned.

➡ See Chapter 9, "Programming with CFML," for details on using the `<CFIF>` tag.

Now, execute `form2.cfm` in your browser, select a payment option, and select the mailing list check box. Click the Process button. Your browser display should look like Figure 12.5.

Figure 12.5

You can use Cold-Fusion templates to process user-selected options.

form2.cfm

Hello,
You selected **Credit card** as your payment type.
You will be added to our mailing list.

That worked exactly as intended, so now get ready to complicate things a little. Reload template `form2.cfm` and submit it without selecting a payment type or by leaving the `MailingList` check box unselected. ColdFusion generates an error message, as shown in Figure 12.6. As you can see, the field you don't select generates an `element is undefined` error.

Figure 12.6

Option buttons or check boxes that are submitted with no value generate a ColdFusion error.

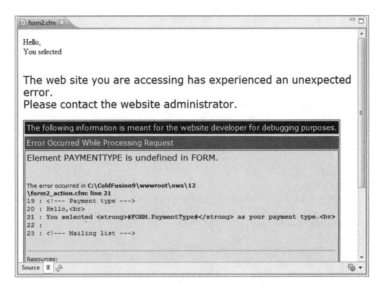

Check the code in Listing 12.3 to verify that the form fields do in fact exist. Why does ColdFusion report that the form field doesn't exist? That is one of the quirks of HTML forms. If you select a check box, the `on` value is submitted; but, *nothing* is submitted if you don't select the check box—not even an empty field. The same is true of radio buttons: If you make no selection, the field isn't submitted at all. (This behavior is the exact opposite of the text `<input>` type, which returns empty fields as opposed to no field.)

How do you work around this limitation? You could modify your form processing script to check which fields exist by using the `#IsDefined()#` function and, if the field exists, process it.

But the simpler solution is to prevent the browser from omitting fields that aren't selected. You can modify the radio button field so that one radio button is pre-selected. This way, users will have to make a selection or use the pre-selected option. To pre-select a radio button, just add the attribute `checked` to it.

Check boxes are trickier because by their nature they must be able to be turned off. Check boxes are used for on/off states, and, when the check box is off, there is no value to submit. The solution here is to set a default value in the `action` template. As you have already learned, this can be done easily using the `<cfparam>` tag. Look at this code:

```
<cfparam NAME="FORM.MailingList" default="No">
```

When ColdFusion encounters this line, it checks to see whether a variable named `FORM.MailingList` exists. If it does, processing continues. If it doesn't exist, ColdFusion creates the variable and sets the value to whatever is specified in the default attribute. The key here is that either way—whether the variable exists or not—the variable does exist after the <cfparam> tag is processed. It is therefore safe to refer to that variable further down the template code.

The updated form is shown in Listing 12.5. The first option button in the PaymentType field is modified to read <input type="radio" name="PaymentType" value="Cash" checked>. The checked attribute ensures that a button is checked. The MailingList check box has a value of Yes when it is checked, and the <cfparam> in the action page ensures that if MailingList is not checked, the value automatically is set to No.

Listing 12.5 form3.cfm—Pre-selecting Form Field Values

```
<!---
Name:        form3.cfm
Author:      Ben Forta (ben@forta.com)
Description: Introduction to forms
Created:     01/01/2010
--->

<html>

<head>
 <title>Learning ColdFusion Forms 3</title>
</head>

<body>
<!--- Payment and mailing list form --->
<form action="form3_action.cfm" method="POST">

Please fill in this form and then click <strong>Process</strong>.
<p>
<!--- Payment type radio buttons --->
Payment type:<br>
<input type="radio" name="PaymentType" value="Cash" CHECKED>Cash<br>
<input type="radio" name="PaymentType" value="Check">Check<br>
<input type="radio" name="PaymentType" value="Credit card">Credit card<br>
<input type="radio" name="PaymentType" value="P.O.">P.O.
</p>
<p>
<!--- Mailing list checkbox --->
Would you like to be added to our mailing list?
<input type="checkbox" name="MailingList" value="Yes">
</p>
<p>
<input type="submit" value="Process">
</p>

</form>

</body>

</html>
```

Create and save this template as form3.cfm. Then create a new file named form3_action.cfm containing the code in form2_action.cfm, and add the following code to the top of the page (right below the comments):

```
<!--- Initialize variables --->
<cfparam name="MailingList" default="No">
```

Try using it and experiment with the two fields. You'll find that this form is reliable and robust, and it doesn't generate ColdFusion error messages, no matter which options are selected (or not).

Processing List Boxes

Another field type you will frequently use is the *list box*. Using list boxes is an efficient way to enable users to select one or more options. If a list box is created to accept only a single selection, you can be guaranteed that a value is always returned. If you don't set one of the options to be preselected, the first one in the list is selected. An option always has to be selected.

List boxes that allow multiple selections also allow no selections at all. If you use a multiple-selection list box, you once again have to find a way to ensure that ColdFusion doesn't generate variable is undefined errors.

Listing 12.6 contains the same data-entry form you just created, but it replaces the option buttons with a list box. Save this template as form4.cfm, and then test it with your browser.

Listing 12.6 form4.cfm—Using a <select> List Box for Options

```
<!---
Name:          form4.cfm
Author:        Ben Forta (ben@forta.com)
Description:   Introduction to forms
Created:       01/01/2010
--->

<html>

<head>
 <title>Learning ColdFusion Forms 4</title>
</head>

<body>

<!--- Payment and mailing list form --->
<form action="form3_action.cfm" method="POST">

Please fill in this form and then click <strong>Process</strong>.
<p>
<!--- Payment type select list --->
Payment type:<br>
<select name="PaymentType">
 <option value="Cash">Cash</option>
 <option value="Check">Check</option>
 <option value="Credit card">Credit card</option>
 <option value="P.O.">P.O.</option>
</select>
```

Listing 12.6 (CONTINUED)

```
</p>
<p>
<!--- Mailing list checkbox --->
Would you like to be added to our mailing list?
<input type="checkbox" name="MailingList" value="Yes">
</p>
<p>
<input type="submit" value="Process">
</p>
</form>

</body>

</html>
```

For this particular form, the browser display shown in Figure 12.7 is probably a better user interface. The choice of whether to use radio buttons or list boxes is yours, and no hard and fast rules exist as to when to use one versus the other. The following guidelines, however, might help you determine which to use:

- If you need to allow the selection of multiple items or of no items at all, use a list box.

- List boxes take up less screen space. With a list box, 100 options take up no more precious real estate than a single option.

- Radio buttons present all the options to the users without requiring mouse clicks. (Statistically, users more often select options that are readily visible.)

Figure 12.7

You can use HTML list boxes to select one or more options.

Processing Text Areas

Text area fields are boxes in which the users can enter free-form text. When you create a text area field, you specify the number of rows and columns of screen space it should occupy. This area, however, doesn't restrict the amount of text users can enter. The field scrolls both horizontally and vertically to enable the users to enter more text.

Listing 12.7 creates an HTML form with a text area field for user comments. The field's width is specified as a number of characters that can be typed on a single line; the height is the number of lines that are displayed without scrolling.

TIP

The `<textarea>` `cols` attribute is specified as a number of characters that can fit on a single line. This setting is dependent on the font in which the text is displayed, and the font is browser specific. Be sure you test any `<textarea>` fields in more than one browser because a field that fits nicely in one might not fit at all in another.

Listing 12.7   form5.cfm—Using a `<textarea>` Field

```
<!---
Name:        form5.cfm
Author:      Ben Forta (ben@forta.com)
Description: Introduction to forms
Created:     01/01/2010
--->

<html>

<head>
 <title>Learning ColdFusion Forms 5</title>
</head>

<body>

<!--- Comments form --->
<form action="form5_action.cfm" method="POST">
Please enter your comments in the box provided, and then click <strong>Send</
strong>.
<p>
<textarea name="Comments" rows="6" cols="40"></textarea>
</p>
<p>
<input type="submit" value="Send">
</p>
</form>

</body>

</html>
```

Listing 12.8 contains ColdFusion code that displays the contents of a `<textarea>` field.

Listing 12.8   form5_action.cfm—Processing `<textarea>` Fields

```
<!---
Name:        form5_action.cfm
Author:      Ben Forta (ben@forta.com)
Description: Introduction to forms
Created:     01/01/2010
--->

<html>

<head>
 <title>Learning ColdFusion Forms 5</title>
</head>
```

Listing 12.8 (CONTINUED)

```
<body>

<!--- Display feedback to user --->
<cfoutput>

Thank you for your comments. You entered:
<p>
<strong>#FORM.comments#</strong>
</p>
</cfoutput>

</body>

</html>
```

Figure 12.8 shows the `<textarea>` field you created, and Figure 12.9 shows how ColdFusion displays the field.

Figure 12.8

The HTML `<textarea>` field is a means by which you can accept free-form text input from users.

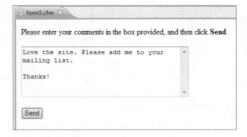

Figure 12.9

Without ColdFusion output functions, `<textarea>` fields are not displayed with line breaks preserved.

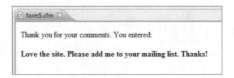

Try entering line breaks (by pressing Enter [Windows] or Return [Mac]) in the text field and then submit it. What happens to the line breaks? Line break characters are considered white-space characters (just like spaces) by your browser, and all white space is ignored by browsers.

```
WHITE SPACE IS IGNORED
```

is displayed no differently than

```
WHITE SPACE        IS        IGNORED
```

The only way to display line breaks is to replace the line break with an HTML paragraph tag: `<p>`. You therefore have to parse through the entire field text and insert both opening `<p>` tags and closing `</p>` tags wherever necessary. Fortunately, ColdFusion makes this task a simple one. The ColdFusion `#ParagraphFormat()#` function automatically replaces every double line break with a

<p> tag. (Single line breaks aren't replaced because ColdFusion has no way of knowing whether the next line is a new paragraph or part of the current one.)

> **NOTE**
>
> The ColdFusion `Replace()` and `ReplaceList()` functions can be used instead of `ParagraphFormat()` to have greater control over the paragraph formatting.

The code in Listing 12.9 contains the same comments form as the one in Listing 12.7, with two differences. First, default field text is provided. Unlike other `<input>` types, `<textarea>` default text is specified between `<textarea>` and `</textarea>` tags—not in a `value` attribute. Second, you use the `wrap` attribute to wrap text entered into the field automatically. `wrap="virtual"` instructs the browser to wrap to the next line automatically, just as most word processors and editors do.

Listing 12.9 `form6.cfm`—The HTML `<textarea>` Field

```
<!---
Name:        form6.cfm
Author:      Ben Forta (ben@forta.com)
Description: Introduction to forms
Created:     01/01/2010
--->

<html>

<head>
 <title>Learning ColdFusion Forms 6</title>
</head>

<body>

<!--- Comments form --->
<form action="form6_action.cfm" method="POST">

Please enter your comments in the box provided, and then click <strong>Send</strong>.
<p>
<textarea name="Comments" rows="6" cols="40" wrap="virtual">
Enter your comments here ...
</textarea>
</p>
<p>
<input type="submit" value="Send">
</p>
</form>

</body>

</html>
```

Listing 12.10 shows the template to display the user-supplied comments. The Comments field code is changed to `#ParagraphFormat(FORM.Comments)#`, ensuring that multiple line breaks are maintained and displayed correctly, as shown in Figure 12.10.

Figure 12.10

You should use the ColdFusion `ParagraphFormat()` function to display `<textarea>` fields with their line breaks preserved.

Listing 12.10 form6_action.cfm—Using `ParagraphFormat`

```
<!---
Name:        form6_action.cfm
Author:      Ben Forta (ben@forta.com)
Description: Introduction to forms
Created:     01/01/2010
--->

<html>

<head>
 <title>Learning ColdFusion Forms 6</title>
</head>

<body>

<!--- Display feedback to user --->
<cfoutput>

Thank you for your comments. You entered:
<p>
<strong>#ParagraphFormat(FORM.comments)#</strong>

</cfoutput>

</body>

</html>
```

Processing Buttons

The HTML forms specification supports only two types of buttons. Almost all forms, including all the forms you create in this chapter, have a *submit* button. Submit, as its name implies, instructs the browser to submit the form fields to a Web server.

TIP

Most newer browsers actually do not require a submit button at all, and force a submit if the Enter (Windows) or Return (Mac) key is pressed.

The second supported button type is reset. *Reset* clears all form entries and restores default values if any existed. Any text entered into `<input type="text">` or `<textarea>` fields is cleared, as are any check box, list box, and option button selections. Many forms have reset buttons, but you never need more than one.

TIP

Usability experts frown upon using reset buttons, as many people accidentally click them when they mean to submit.

On the other hand, you might want more than one submit button. For example, if you're using a form to modify a record, you could have two submit buttons: one for Update and one for Delete. (Of course, you also could use two forms to accomplish this task.) If you create multiple submit buttons, you must name the button with the name attribute and be sure to assign a different value attribute for each. The code in Listing 12.11 contains a reset button and two submit buttons.

Listing 12.11 form7.cfm—Template with a Reset

```
<!---
Name:        form7.cfm
Author:      Ben Forta (ben@forta.com)
Description: Introduction to forms
Created:     01/01/2010
--->

<html>

<head>
 <title>Learning ColdFusion Forms 7</title>
</head>

<body>

<!--- Update/delete form --->
<form action="form7_action.cfm" method="POST">

<p>

Movie:
<input type="text" name="MovieTitle">
</p>

<p>
<!--- Submit buttons --->
<input type="submit" name="Operation" value="Update">
<input type="submit" name="Operation" value="Delete">
<!--- Reset button --->
<input type="reset" value="Clear">
</p>
</form>

</body>

</html>
```

The result of this code is shown in Figure 12.11.

Figure 12.11

When you're using multiple submit buttons, you must assign a different value to each button.

When you name submit buttons, you treat them as any other form field. Listing 12.12 demonstrates how to determine which submit button was clicked. The code `<cfif FORM.Operation IS "Update">` checks whether the Update button was clicked, and `<cfelseif FORM.Operation IS "Delete">` checks whether Delete was clicked, but only if Update was not clicked.

Listing 12.12   `form7_action.cfm`—Multiple Submit Button Processing

```
<!---
Name:        form7_action.cfm
Author:      Ben Forta (ben@forta.com)
Description: Introduction to forms
Created:     01/01/2010
--->

<html>
<head>
 <title>Learning ColdFusion Forms 7</title>
</head>

<body>

<!--- User feedback --->
<cfoutput>

<cfif FORM.Operation IS "Update">
 <!--- Update button clicked --->
 You opted to <strong>update</strong> #MovieTitle#
<cfelseif FORM.Operation IS "Delete">
 <!--- Delete button clicked --->
 You opted to <strong>delete</strong> #MovieTitle#
</cfif>

</cfoutput>

</body>

</html>
```

Creating Dynamic SQL Statements

NOTE

This section uses `<cfquery>` tags for data access, and the example here should use ColdFusion Components as was described in the preceding chapter. However, to keep the examples simpler I will violate the rules I just taught you. I guess I'm saying that every rule has exceptions.

Now that you're familiar with forms and how ColdFusion processes them, you can return to creating a movie search screen. The first screen enables visitors to search for a movie by title. Because this requires text input, you will need an <input> field of type text. The field name can be anything you want, but using the same name as the table column to which you're comparing the value is generally a good idea.

TIP

When you're creating search screens, you can give your form fields any descriptive name you want. When first starting to build ColdFusion applications, however, you may want to make sure that the field names match the table column names, to make matching HTML form fields and SQL easier.

The code in Listing 12.13 contains a simple HTML form not unlike the test forms you created earlier in this chapter. The form contains a single text field called MovieTitle and a submit button.

Listing 12.13   search1.cfm—Code Listing for Movie Search Screen

```
<!---
Name:        search1.cfm
Author:      Ben Forta (ben@forta.com)
Description: Creating search screens
Created:     01/01/2010
--->

<html>

<head>
 <title>Orange Whip Studios - Movies</title>
</head>

<body>

<!--- Page header --->
<cfinclude template="header.cfm">

<!--- Search form --->
<form action="results1.cfm" method="POST">

<table align="center" border="1">
 <tr>
  <td>
  Movie:
  </td>
  <td>
  <input type="text" name="MovieTitle">
  </td>
 </tr>
 <tr>
  <td colspan="2" align="center">
  <input type="submit" value="Search">
  </td>
 </tr>
</table>
```

Listing 12.13 (CONTINUED)

```
</form>

</body>

</html>
```

Save this form as `search1.cfm`, then execute it to display a screen like the one in Figure 12.12.

Figure 12.12

The movie search screen enables users to search by movie title.

Listing 12.13 starts off with a comment block, followed by the standard HTML headers and `<body>` tag. Then a `<cfinclude>` tag is used to include a common header, file `header.cfm` (which puts the logo and title at the top of the page).

➡ See Chapter 9 for information on using the `<cfinclude>` tag.

The form itself is placed inside an HTML table. This is a very popular technique that can be used to better control form field placement. The form contains a single field, `MovieTitle`, and a submit button.

The `<form>` action attribute specifies which ColdFusion template should be used to process this search. The code `action="results1.cfm"` instructs ColdFusion to use the template `results1.cfm`, which is shown in Listing 12.14. Create this template and save it as `results1.cfm`.

Listing 12.14   `results1.cfm`—Passed Form Field in a SQL WHERE Clause

```
<!---
Name:        results1.cfm
Author:      Ben Forta (ben@forta.com)
Description: Creating search screens
Created:     01/01/2010
--->
```

Listing 12.14 (CONTINUED)

```
<!--- Get movie list from database --->
<cfquery name="movies" datasource="ows">
SELECT MovieTitle, PitchText,
       Summary, DateInTheaters
FROM Films
WHERE MovieTitle LIKE '%#FORM.MovieTitle#%'
ORDER BY MovieTitle
</cfquery>

<!--- Create HTML page --->
<html>
<head>
 <title>Orange Whip Studios - Movies</title>
</head>

<body>

<!--- Page header --->
<cfinclude template="header.cfm">

<!--- Display movie list --->
<table>
 <tr>
  <th colspan="2">
   <cfoutput>
   <font size="+3">Movie List (#Movies.RecordCount# movies)</font>
   </cfoutput>
  </th>
 </tr>
 <cfoutput query="movies">
  <tr>
   <td>
   <font size="+2"><strong>#CurrentRow#: #MovieTitle#</strong></font><br>
   <font size="+1"><em>#PitchText#</em></font>
   </td>
   <td>Released: #DateFormat(DateInTheaters)#</td>
  </tr>
  <tr>
   <td colspan="2">#Summary#</td>
  </tr>
 </cfoutput>
</table>

</body>
</html>
```

The code in Listing 12.14 is based on the movie lists created in the last chapter, so most of the code should be very familiar. The only big change here is in the <cfquery> tag.

The WHERE clause in Listing 12.14 contains a ColdFusion field rather than a static value. You will recall that when ColdFusion parses templates, it replaces field names with the values contained within the field. So, look at the following WHERE clause:

```
WHERE MovieTitle LIKE '%#FORM.MovieTitle#%'
```

#FORM.MovieTitle# is replaced with whatever was entered in the MovieTitle form field. If the word Her was entered then the WHERE clause becomes

```
WHERE MovieTitle LIKE '%Her%'
```

which will find all movies with the text her anywhere in the MovieTitle. If you search for all movies containing C, the code WHERE MovieTitle LIKE '%#FORM.MovieTitle#%' would become WHERE MovieTitle LIKE '%C%', and so on. You can do this with any clauses, not just the LIKE operator.

NOTE

If no search text is specified at all, the clause becomes WHERE MovieTitle LIKE '%%'—a wildcard search that finds all records.

→   See Chapter 10 for an introduction to the <CFQUERY> tag.

→   See Chapter 6 for an explanation of the LIKE operator.

You use a LIKE clause to enable users to enter partial text. The clause WHERE MovieTitle = 'Her' finds only movies with a title of her; movies with her in the name along with other text are not retrieved. Using a wildcard, as in WHERE MovieTitle LIKE '%Her%', enables users to also search on partial names.

Try experimenting with different search strings. The sample output should look like the output shown in Figure 12.13. Depending on the search criteria you specify, you'll see different search results, of course.

Figure 12.13

By building WHERE clauses dynamically, you can create different search conditions on the fly.

To complete the application, try copying the movie detail page (created in Chapter 10) and modify results1.cfm so that it enables the drill-down of the displayed search results. You'll then have a complete drill-down application.

Building Truly Dynamic Statements

No sooner do you roll out your movie search screen at Orange Whip Studios, but you immediately find yourself inundated with requests. "Searching by title is great, but what about searching by tag line or rating?" your users ask. Now that you have introduced the ability to search for data, your users want to be able to search on several fields.

Adding fields to your search screen is simple enough. Add two fields: one for tag line and one for rating. The code for the updated search screen is shown in Listing 12.15.

Listing 12.15 search2.cfm—Movie Search Screen

```
<!---
Name:        search2.cfm
Author:      Ben Forta (ben@forta.com)
Description: Creating search screens
Created:     01/01/2010
--->

<html>

<head>
 <title>Orange Whip Studios - Movies</title>
</head>

<body>

<!--- Page header --->
<cfinclude template="header.cfm">

<!--- Search form --->
<form action="results2.cfm" method="POST">

<table align="center" border="1">
 <tr>
  <td>
  Movie:
  </td>
  <td>
  <input type="text" name="MovieTitle">
  </td>
 </tr>
 <tr>
  <td>
  Tag line:
  </td>
  <td>
  <input type="text" name="PitchText">
  </td>
 </tr>
 <tr>
  <td>
  Rating:
  </td>
  <td>
```

Listing 12.15 (CONTINUED)

```
    <input type="text" name="RatingID"> (1-6)
    </td>
   </tr>
   <tr>
    <td colspan="2" align="center">
    <input type="submit" value="Search">
    </td>
   </tr>
  </table>

  </form>

  </body>

  </html>
```

This form lets users specify text in one of three fields, as shown in Figure 12.14.

Figure 12.14

The movie search screen now allows searching by three fields.

You must create a search template before you can actually perform a search. The complete search code is shown in Listing 12.16; save this file as `results2.cfm`.

Listing 12.16 `results2.cfm`—Building SQL Statements Dynamically

```
<!---
Name:        results2.cfm
Author:      Ben Forta (ben@forta.com)
Description: Creating search screens
Created:     01/01/2010
--->

<!--- Get movie list from database --->
<cfquery name="movies" datasource="ows">
```

Listing 12.16 (CONTINUED)

```
SELECT MovieTitle, PitchText, Summary, DateInTheaters
FROM Films
<!--- Search by movie title --->
<cfif FORM.MovieTitle IS NOT "">
 WHERE MovieTitle LIKE '%#FORM.MovieTitle#%'
</cfif>
<!--- Search by tag line --->
<cfif FORM.PitchText IS NOT "">
 WHERE PitchText LIKE '%#FORM.PitchText#%'
</cfif>
<!--- Search by rating --->
<cfif FORM.RatingID IS NOT "">
 WHERE RatingID = #FORM.RatingID#
</cfif>
ORDER BY MovieTitle
</cfquery>

<!--- Create HTML page --->
<html>
<head>
 <title>Orange Whip Studios - Movies</title>
</head>

<body>

<!--- Page header --->
<cfinclude template="header.cfm">

<!--- Display movie list --->
<table>
<tr>
 <cfoutput>
 <th colspan="2">
 <font size="+3">Movie List (#Movies.RecordCount# movies)</font>
 </TH>
 </cfoutput>
</tr>
<cfoutput query="movies">
<tr>
 <td>
 <font size="+2"><strong>#CurrentRow#: #MovieTitle#</strong></font><br>
 <font size="+1"><em>#PitchText#</em></font>
 </td>
 <td>Released: #DateFormat(DateInTheaters)#</td>
</tr>
<tr>
 <td colspan="2">#Summary#</td>
</tr>
</cfoutput>
</table>

</body>
</html>
```

Understanding Dynamic SQL

Before you actually perform a search, take a closer look at the template in Listing 12.16. The `<cfquery>` tag is similar to the one you used in the previous search template, but in this one the SQL SELECT statement in the SQL attribute is incomplete. It doesn't specify a WHERE clause with which to perform a search, nor does it specify a search order. No WHERE clause is specified because the search screen has to support not one, but four search types, as follows:

- If none of the three search fields is specified, no WHERE clause should be used, so that all movies can be retrieved.

- If a movie title is specified, the WHERE clause must filter data to find only movies containing the specified title text. For example, if the is specified as the search text, the WHERE clause has to be WHERE MovieTitle LIKE '%the%'.

- If tag-line text is specified, the WHERE clause needs to filter data to find only movies containing the specified text. For example, if bad is specified as the search text, the WHERE clause must be WHERE PitchText LIKE '%bad%'.

- If you're searching by rating and specify 2 as the search text, a WHERE clause of WHERE RatingID = 2 is necessary.

How can a single search template handle all these search conditions? The answer is dynamic SQL.

When you're creating dynamic SQL statements, you break the statement into separate common SQL and specific SQL. The common SQL is the part of the SQL statement you always want. The sample SQL statement has two common parts:

```
SELECT MovieTitle, PitchText, Summary, DateInTheaters
FROM Films
```

and

```
ORDER BY MovieTitle
```

The common text is all the SQL statement you need if no search criteria are provided. If, however, search text is specified, the number of possible WHERE clauses is endless.

Take another look at Listing 12.16 to understand the process of creating dynamic SQL statements. The code `<cfif FORM.MovieTitle IS NOT "">` checks to see that the MovieTitle form field isn't empty. This condition fails if no text is entered into the MovieTitle field in the search form, in which case any code until the `</CFIF>` is ignored.

➡ See Chapter 9 for details on using `<CFIF>`.

If a value does appear in the MovieTitle field, the code WHERE MovieTitle LIKE '#FORM.Movie Title#%' is processed and appended to the SQL statement. #FORM.MovieTitle# is a field and is replaced with whatever text is entered in the MovieTitle field. If the is specified as the text for which to search, this statement translates to `WHERE MovieTitle LIKE '%the%'`. This text is appended to the previous SQL statement, which now becomes the following:

```
SELECT MovieTitle, PitchText, Summary, DateInTheaters
FROM Films
WHERE MovieTitle LIKE '%the%'
```

All you need now is the `ORDER BY` clause. Even though `ORDER BY` is fixed and doesn't change with different searches, it must be built dynamically because the `ORDER BY` clause must come after the `WHERE` clause, if one exists. After ColdFusion processes the code `ORDER BY MovieTitle`, the finished SQL statement reads as follows:

```
SELECT MovieTitle, PitchText, Summary, DateInTheaters
FROM Films
WHERE MovieTitle LIKE '%the%'
ORDER BY MovieTitle
```

NOTE

You may not use double quotation marks in a SQL statement. When ColdFusion encounters a double quotation mark, it thinks it has reached the end of the SQL statement. It then generates an error message because extra text appears where ColdFusion thinks there should be none. To include text strings with the SQL statement, use only single quotation marks.

Similarly, if a `RatingID` is specified (for example, the value 2) as the search text, the complete SQL statement reads as follows:

```
SELECT MovieTitle, PitchText, Summary, DateInTheaters
FROM Films
WHERE RatingID = 2
ORDER BY MovieTitle
```

The code `<cfif FORM.MovieTitle IS NOT "">` evaluates to `FALSE` because `FORM.MovieTitle` is actually empty; ColdFusion therefore checks the next condition, which is also `FALSE`, and so on. Because `RatingID` was specified, the third `<CFIF>` condition is `TRUE` and the previous `SELECT` statement is generated.

NOTE

You may have noticed that there are single quotation marks around `FORM.MovieTitle` and `FORM.PitchText` but not `FORM.RatingID`. Why? Because `MovieTitle` and `PitchText` have text data types in the database table, whereas `RatingID` is numeric. SQL is not `typeless`, and it will require that you specify quotes where needed to create strings if that is what is expected.

So, one template is capable of generating four different sets of SQL `SELECT` statements, of which the values can be dynamic. Try performing various searches, but for now, use only one form field at a time.

Concatenating SQL Clauses

Now try entering text in two search fields, or all three of them. What happens? You probably generated an error like the one in Figure 12.15.

Figure 12.15

Dynamic SQL must be generated carefully to avoid building invalid SQL.

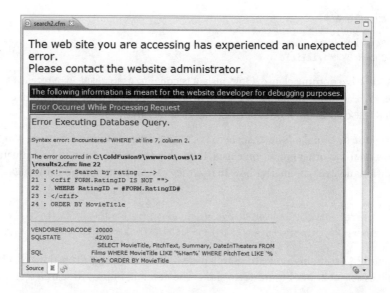

Why did this happen? Well, suppose `the` was specified as the `MovieTitle` and `2` as the `RatingID`. Walk through the `<cfif>` statements to work out what the generated SQL would look like. The first condition will be TRUE, the second will be FALSE, and the third will be TRUE. The SELECT statement would therefore look like this:

```
SELECT MovieTitle, PitchText, Summary, DateInTheaters
FROM Films
WHERE MovieTitle LIKE '%the%'
WHERE RatingID = 2
ORDER BY MovieTitle
```

Obviously, this is not a valid SELECT statement—only one WHERE clause is allowed. The correct syntax for this statement is

```
SELECT MovieTitle, PitchText, Summary, DateInTheaters
FROM Films
WHERE MovieTitle LIKE '%the%'
 AND RatingID = 2
ORDER BY MovieTitle
```

So how would you generate this code? You couldn't hard-code any condition with a WHERE or an AND, because you wouldn't know whether it was the first clause. The MovieTitle clause, if used, will always be the first, but it might not always be used.

One obvious solution (which I suggest you avoid at all costs) is to use embedded `<cfif>` statements to intelligently include WHERE or AND as necessary. However, this type of code is very complex and error prone.

A better solution would be to never need WHERE at all—only use AND. How can you do this? Look at the following SQL statement:

```
SELECT MovieTitle, PitchText, Summary, DateInTheaters
FROM Films
```

```
WHERE 0=0
 AND MovieTitle LIKE '%the%'
 AND RatingID = 2
ORDER BY MovieTitle
```

`WHERE 0=0` is a dummy clause. Obviously 0 is equal to 0, so `WHERE 0=0` retrieves every row in the table. For each row the database checks to see whether 0 is 0, which of course it always is. This is a legal `WHERE` clause, but it does nothing because it is always `TRUE`.

So why use it? Simple. Now that there is a `WHERE` clause, you can safely use `AND` for every dynamic condition. If no other condition exists, then only the `WHERE 0=0` will be evaluated. But if additional conditions do exist, no matter how many, they can all be appended using `AND`.

NOTE

There is nothing magical about `WHERE 0=0`. You can use any condition that will always be `TRUE`: `WHERE 'A'='A'`, `WHERE primary key = primary key` (using the table's primary key), and just about anything else you want.

Listing 12.17 contains a revised search page (this time using a drop-down list box for the rating); save it as `search3.cfm`. Figure 12.16 shows the new and improved search screen.

Figure 12.16

Drop-down list boxes are well suited for selections of one of a set of finite options.

Listing 12.18 contains the revised results page; save it as `results3.cfm`.

Listing 12.17 `search3.cfm`—Revised Movie Search Screen

```
<!---
Name:        search3.cfm
Author:      Ben Forta (ben@forta.com)
Description: Creating search screens
Created:     01/01/2010
--->

<html>
```

Listing 12.17 (CONTINUED)

```
  <head>
   <title>Orange Whip Studios - Movies</title>
  </head>

  <body>

  <!--- Page header --->
  <cfinclude template="header.cfm">

  <!--- Search form --->
  <form action="results3.cfm" method="POST">

  <table align="center" border="1">
   <tr>
    <td>
    Movie:
    </td>
    <td>
    <input type="text" name="MovieTitle">
    </td>
   </tr>
   <tr>
    <td>
    Tag line:
    </td>
    <td>
    <input type="text" name="PitchText">
    </td>
   </tr>
   <tr>
    <td>
    Rating:
    </td>
    <td>
     <select name="RatingID">
      <option value=""></option>
      <option value="1">General</option>
      <option value="2">Kids</option>
      <option value="3">Accompanied Minors</option>
      <option value="4">Teens</option>
      <option value="5">Adults</option>
      <option value="6">Mature Audiences</option>
     </select>
    </td>
   </tr>
   <tr>
    <td colspan="2" align="center">
    <input type="submit" value="Search">
    </td>
   </tr>
  </table>

  </form>

  </body>

  </html>
```

The only change in Listing 12.17 is the drop-down list box for the RatingID. Manually entering 1 to 6 isn't intuitive, and is highly error prone. For finite lists such as this drop-down list, boxes are a better option. This doesn't change the form field processing, though. Either way, RatingID is sent to the action page, shown in Listing 12.18.

Listing 12.18 results3.cfm—Concatenating SQL Clauses

```
<!---
Name:        results3.cfm
Author:      Ben Forta (ben@forta.com)
Description: Creating search screens
Created:     01/01/2010
--->

<!--- Get movie list from database --->
<cfquery name="movies" datasource="ows">
SELECT MovieTitle, PitchText, Summary, DateInTheaters
FROM Films
WHERE 0=0
<!--- Search by movie title --->
<cfif FORM.MovieTitle IS NOT "">
 AND MovieTitle LIKE '%#FORM.MovieTitle#%'
</cfif>
<!--- Search by tag line --->
<cfif FORM.PitchText IS NOT "">
 AND PitchText LIKE '%#FORM.PitchText#%'
</cfif>
<!--- Search by rating --->
<cfif FORM.RatingID IS NOT "">
 AND RatingID = #FORM.RatingID#
</cfif>
ORDER BY MovieTitle
</cfquery>

<!--- Create HTML page --->
<html>
<head>
 <title>Orange Whip Studios - Movies</title>
</head>

<body>
<!--- Page header --->
<cfinclude template="header.cfm">

<!--- Display movie list --->
<table>
 <tr>
  <th colspan="2">
   <cfoutput>
   <font size="+3">Movie List (#Movies.RecordCount# movies)</font>
   </cfoutput>
  </th>
 </tr>
 <cfoutput query="movies">
  <tr>
   <td>
```

Listing 12.18 (CONTINUED)

```
      <font size="+2"><strong>#CurrentRow#: #MovieTitle#</strong></font><br>
      <font size="+1"><em>#PitchText#</em></font>
    </td>
    <td>Released: #DateFormat(DateInTheaters)#</td>
  </tr>
  <tr>
    <td colspan="2">#Summary#</td>
  </tr>
</cfoutput>
</table>

</body>
</html>
```

The `<cfquery>` in Listing 12.18 now contains a dummy clause and then three optional AND clauses, each within a `<cfif>` statement. So what will this do?

- If no form fields are filled in, only the dummy WHERE clause will be used.

- If any single form field is filled in, the WHERE clause will contain the dummy and a single real clause appended using AND.

- If any two form fields are filled in, the WHERE clause will have three clauses, one dummy and two real.

- If all three clauses are filled in, the WHERE clause will contain four clauses, one dummy and three real.

In other words, a single template can now generate eight different combinations of WHERE clauses, and each can have an unlimited number of values. All that in less than 20 lines of code—it doesn't get much more powerful than that.

After you create the template, use your browser to perform various combinations of searches. You'll find that this new search template is both powerful and flexible. Indeed, this technique for creating truly dynamic SQL SELECT statements will likely be the basis for some sophisticated database interaction in real-world applications.

TIP

Debugging dynamic SQL statement creation can be tricky, and troubleshooting requires that you know exactly what SQL your ColdFusion code created. To do this, use the techniques described in Chapter 10 (debug output and obtaining a `result` from `<cfquery>`).

Creating Dynamic Search Screens

There is one final improvement to be made to your application. The list of ratings used in the search form has been hard-coded (refer to Listing 12.17). Remember that you're creating data-driven applications. Everything in your application should be data-driven. You don't want to have to manually enter data, not even in list boxes. Rather, you want the list box to be driven by the data in the `FilmsRatings` table. This way, you can acquire changes automatically when ratings are added or when a rating name changes.

Listing 12.19 is identical to Listing 12.17, with the exception of the addition of a new `<cfquery>` and a `<cfoutput>` block to process its contents.

Listing 12.19   search4.cfm—Data-Driven Forms

```
<!---
Name:        search4.cfm
Author:      Ben Forta (ben@forta.com)
Description: Creating search screens
Created:     01/01/2010
--->

<!--- Get ratings --->
<cfquery datasource="ows" name="ratings">
SELECT RatingID, Rating
FROM FilmsRatings
ORDER BY RatingID
</cfquery>

<html>

<head>
 <title>Orange Whip Studios - Movies</title>
</head>

<body>

<!--- Page header --->
<cfinclude template="header.cfm">

<!--- Search form --->
<form action="results3.cfm" method="POST">

<table align="center" border="1">
 <tr>
  <td>
  Movie:
  </td>
  <td>
  <input type="text" name="MovieTitle">
  </td>
 </tr>
 <tr>
  <td>
  Tag line:
  </td>
  <td>
  <input type="text" name="PitchText">
  </td>
 </tr>
 <tr>
  <td>
  Rating:
```

Listing 12.19 (CONTINUED)

```
      </td>
      <td>
      <select name="RatingID">
       <option value=""></option>
       <cfoutput query="ratings">
        <option value="#RatingID#">#Rating#</option>
       </cfoutput>
      </select>
      </td>
     </tr>
     <tr>
      <td colspan="2" align="center">
      <input type="submit" value="Search">
      </td>
     </tr>
    </table>

    </form>

    </body>

    </html>
```

The code in Listing 12.19 demonstrates a data-driven form. The `<cfquery>` at the top of the template should be familiar to you by now. It creates a result set called `ratings`, which contains the ID and name of each rating in the database.

The drop-down list box also has been changed. The `<select>` tag creates the list box, and it is terminated with the `</select>` tag, as before. The individual entries in the list box are specified with the `<option>` tag, but here that tag is within a `<cfoutput>` block. This block is executed once for each row retrieved by the `<cfquery>`, creating an `<OPTION>` entry for each one.

As it loops through the `ratings` result set, the `<cfquery>` block creates the individual options, using the `RatingID` field as the `value` and `Rating` as the description. So when ColdFusion processes `RatingID 1 (General)`, the code generated is

```
<option value="1">General</option>
```

The end result is exactly the same as the screen shown previously in Figure 12.16, but this time it is populated by a database query (instead of being hard-coded).

Also notice that a blank `<option>` line is included in the list box. Remember that list boxes always must have a selection, so if you want to allow your users to not select any option, you need to give them a *no option* option (the blank option).

And there you have it: dynamic data-driven forms used to perform dynamic data-driven searches using dynamic data-driven SQL.

CHAPTER **13**

Form Data Validation

Understanding Form Validation

HTML forms are used to collect data from users by using several field types. Forms are used for data entry, as front-end search engines, for filling out orders, for signing guest books, for providing user names and passwords to secure applications, and much more. Although forms have become one of the most important features in HTML, these forms provide almost no data validation tools.

This becomes a real problem when developing Web-based applications. As a developer, you need to be able to control what data users can enter into what fields. Without that, your programs will constantly be breaking due to mismatched or unanticipated data. And thus far, you have used forms only as search front ends—when forms are used to insert or update database tables (as you'll see in Chapter 14, "Using Forms to Add or Change Data"), this becomes even more critical.

Thankfully, ColdFusion provides a complete and robust set of tools with which to implement form data validation, both client-side and server-side.

Since its inception, HTML has always provided Web page developers with a variety of ways to format and display data. With each revision to the HTML specification, additional data display mechanisms have been made available. As a result, HTML is a powerful data-publishing tool.

Although its data presentation options continue to improve, HTML's data collection capabilities leave much to be desired. In fact, they have barely changed at all since the language's very early days. Although there is hope for a change in HTML 5, at the time this book is being written, the most widely used browsers do not support the enhanced form options. Therefore, we have to work with the form options available to the widely used browsers.

HTML data collection is performed using forms. HTML forms support the following field types:

- Free-form text fields
- Select box (or drop-down list boxes)
- Radio buttons
- Check boxes
- Multi-line text boxes
- Password (hidden input) boxes

→ See Chapter 12, "ColdFusion Forms," for more information about HTML forms and using them with ColdFusion.

So what's wrong with this list? Actually, nothing. These field types are all the standard fields you would expect to be available to you in any development language. What is wrong, however, is that these fields have extremely limited capabilities. There are two primary limitations:

- Inability to mark fields as required
- Inability to define data types or filters, for example, to only accepting digits, a ZIP code, an e-mail address, or a phone number

What this means is that there is no simple way to tell HTML to disallow form submission if certain fields are left empty. Similarly, HTML can't be instructed to accept only certain values or types of data in specific fields.

HTML itself has exactly one validation option, the maxlength attribute, which can be used to specify the maximum number of characters that can be entered in a text field. That's it—no other validation options are available.

To work around these limitations, HTML developers have typically adopted two forms of validation options:

- Server-side validation
- Client-side validation

Comparing Server-Side and Client-Side Validation

Server-side validation involves checking for required fields or invalid values after a form has been submitted. The script on the server first validates the form and then continues processing only if all validation requirements are met. Typically, an error message is sent back to the user's browser if validation fails; the user then goes back to the page, makes the corrections, and resubmits the form. Of course, the form submission must be validated again upon resubmission, and the process must be repeated if the validation fails again.

Client-side scripting lets the developer embed instructions to the browser within the HTML code. Because HTML itself provides no mechanism for doing this, developers have resorted to using scripting languages, such as JavaScript, which is supported by just about every browser. These interpreted languages support basic data manipulation and user feedback and are thus well suited for form validation. To validate a form, the page author would create a function to be executed as soon as a Submit button is clicked. This function would perform any necessary validation right inside of the browser, and allow the submission to proceed only if the validation check was successful. The advantage of this approach is that the user doesn't have to submit a form to find out an error occurred in it. Notification of any errors occurs prior to form submission.

Pros and Cons of Each Option

Neither of these options is perfect, and they are thus often used together, complementing each other. Table 13.1 lists the pros and cons of each option.

Table 13.1   The Pros and Cons of Client and Server Form Validation

VALIDATION TYPE	PROS	CONS
Server-side	Very safe, will always work, regardless of the browser used and any browser settings	Not very user-friendly, user must submit form before validation occurs; any errors require resubmission
Client-side	More user-friendly, users prefer knowing what is wrong before form submission	Less safe, not supported by some older browsers; can be disabled, scripting languages have a lengthy learning curve

From a user's perspective, client-side validation is preferable. Obviously, users want to know what's wrong with the data they entered *before* they submit the form for processing. From a developer's perspective, however, server-side validation is simpler to code, guaranteed to always work regardless of the browser used, and less likely to fall victim to browser incompatibilities.

TIP

Form field validation should never be considered optional, and you should get in the habit of always using some type of validation in each and every form you create. Failure to do so will inevitably cause errors and broken applications later.

Using Server-Side Validation

As mentioned earlier, server-side validation involves adding code to your application that performs form field validation after the form is submitted. In ColdFusion this usually is achieved with a series of <cfif> statements that check each field's value and data types. If any validation steps fail, processing can be terminated with the <cfabort> function, or the user can be redirected to another page (maybe the form itself) using <cflocation>.

Using Manual Server-Side Validation

The code shown in Listing 13.1 is a simple login prompt used to gain access to an intranet site. The file (which you should save as login1.cfm in a new directory named 13) prompts for a user ID and password. HTML's only validation rule, maxlength, is used in both form fields to restrict the number of characters that can be entered. The form itself is shown in Figure 13.1.

Figure 13.1

HTML forms support basic field types, such as text and password boxes.

Listing 13.1 login1.cfm—Simple Login Screen

```
<!---
Name:        login1.cfm
Author:      Ben Forta (ben@forta.com)
Description: Basic server-side validation
Created:     01/01/2010
--->

<html>

<head>
  <title>Orange Whip Studios - Intranet</title>
</head>

<body>

<!--- Page header --->
<cfinclude template="header.cfm">

<!--- Login form --->
<form action="process1.cfm" method="post">

<table align="center" bgcolor="orange">
  <tr>
    <td align="right">
      ID:
    </td>
    <td>
      <input type="text"
             name="LoginID"
             maxlength="5">
    </td>
  </tr>
```

Listing 13.1   (CONTINUED)

```
    <tr>
      <td align="right">
        Password:
      </td>
      <td>
        <input type="password"
               name="LoginPassword"
               maxlength="20">
      </td>
    </tr>
    <tr>
      <td colspan="2" align="center">
        <input type="submit" value="Login">
      </td>
    </tr>
  </table>

</form>

</body>

</html>
```

This particular form gets submitted to a template named process1.cfm (specified in the action attribute). That template is responsible for validating the user input and processing the login only if all the validation rules passed. The validation rules necessary here are

- Login ID is required.

- Login ID must be numeric.

- Login password is required.

To perform this validation, three <cfif> statements are used, as shown in Listing 13.2.

Listing 13.2   process1.cfm—Basic Server-Side Login Validation Code

```
<!---
Name:        process1.cfm
Author:      Ben Forta (ben@forta.com)
Description: Basic server-side validation
Created:     01/01/2010
--->

<html>

<head>
  <title>Orange Whip Studios - Intranet</title>
</head>

<body>

<!--- Page header --->
<cfinclude template="header.cfm">
```

Listing 13.2 (CONTINUED)

```
<!--- Make sure LoginID is not empty --->
<cfif Len(Trim(LoginID)) IS 0>
 <h1>ERROR! ID can't be left blank!</h1>
 <cfabort>
</cfif>

<!--- Make sure LoginID is a number --->
<cfif IsNumeric(LoginID) IS "No">
 <h1>ERROR! Invalid ID specified!</h1>
 <cfabort>
</cfif>

<!--- Make sure LoginPassword is not empty --->
<cfif Len(Trim(LoginPassword)) IS 0>
 <h1>ERROR! Password can't be left blank!</h1>
 <cfabort>
</cfif>

<p align="center">
<h1>Intranet</h1>
</p>

Intranet would go here.

</body>

</html>
```

The first <cfif> checks the length of LoginID after trimming it with the Trim() function. The Trim() function is necessary to trap space characters that are technically valid characters in a text field but are not valid here. If the Len() function returns 0, an error message is displayed, and the <cfabort> statement halts further processing.

TIP

Checking the length of the trimmed string (to determine whether it's empty) is functionally the same as doing a comparison against an empty string, like this:

```
<cfif Trim(LoginID) IS "">
```

The reason I used Len() to get the string length (instead of comparing it to "") is that numeric comparisons are generally processed more quickly than string comparisons. For even greater performance, I could have eliminated the comparison value and used the following:

```
<cfif not Len(Trim(LoginID))>
```

The second <cfif> statement checks the data type. The IsNumeric() function returns TRUE if the passed value was numeric (contained only digits, for example) or FALSE if not. Once again, if the <cfif> check fails, an error is displayed and <cfabort> halts further processing, as shown in Figure 13.2. The third <cfif> checks that a password was specified (and that that the field was not left blank).

Figure 13.2

<cfif> statements can be used to perform validation checks and then display error messages if the checks fail.

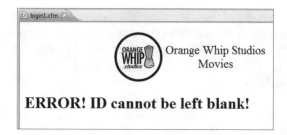

This form of validation is the most powerful and flexible of all the validation options available to you. There's no limit to the number of <cfif> statements you can use, and there's no limit to the number of functions or tags you can use within them. You can even perform database operations (perhaps to check that a password matches) and use the results in comparisons.

TIP

The <cfif> statements can be combined using **AND** and **OR** operators if necessary. For example, the first two <cfif> statements shown in Listing 13.2 could be combined to read

```
<cfif (Len(Trim(LoginID)) IS 0) OR (NOT IsNumeric(LoginID))>
```

Of course, there is a downside to all of this. Managing and maintaining all of those <cfif> statements can get tedious and complex, especially since most of your forms will likely contain more than just two controls, as ours did here.

Using <cfparam> Server-Side Validation

One solution to the proliferation of <cfif> statements in Listing 13.2 is to use the <cfparam> tag (first introduced in Chapter 9, "Programming with CFML"). The <cfparam> tag has two distinct functions:

- Providing default values for variables
- Performing field value validation

The difference is whether or not a default is provided. Look at this example:

```
<cfparam name="LoginID">
```

No default value is provided, and so LoginID is required, and if not present an error will be thrown.

By contrast, this next example has a default value:

```
<cfparam name="color" default="red">
```

In this example color isn't required, and if not present, the default value of red will be used.

<cfparam> also supports one additional attribute, a type, as seen in this example:

```
<cfparam name="LoginID" type="integer">
```

In this example LoginID is required (because no default is specified). In addition, it must be an integer (a number), and if it's something other than an integer an error will be thrown. Cold-Fusion supports a complete range of validation types, as listed in Table 13.2.

Table 13.2 Supported Validation Types

TYPE	DESCRIPTION
any	Allows any value
array	A ColdFusion array
binary	A binary value
	booleatrue (yes, true, or any non-zero number) or false (no, false, or 0)
creditcard	A 13- or 16-digit credit card number that matches the MOD10 algorithm
date	A date and time value (same as time)
email	A well-formatted e-mail address
eurodate	A date value in dd/mm/yy format
float	A numeric value (same as numeric)
guid	A UUID in the form xxxxxxxx-xxxx-xxxx-xxxx-xxxxxxxxxxxx
integer	An integer value
numeric	A numeric value (same as float)
query	A ColdFusion query
range	A range of numbers (range must be specified)
regex	A regular expression pattern (same as regular_expression)
regular_expression	A regular expression pattern (same as regex)
social_security_number	A US format social security number (same as ssn)
ss	A US format Social Security number (same as social_security_number)
string	A string of one or more characters
struct	A ColdFusion structure
telephone	A US format phone number
time	A date and time value (same as date)
url	A file, ftp, http, https, mailto, or news URL
usdate	A date value in mm/dd/yy format
uuid	A ColdFusion UUID in the form xxxxxxxx-xxxx-xxxx-xxxxxxxxxxxxxxx
variablename	A string that meets ColdFusion variable naming rules
xml	An XML object or string
zipcode	A US 5- or 5+4-digit ZIP code

Listing 13.3 is an updated version of Listing 13.2, this time replacing the `<cfif>` statements with `<cfparam>` tags.

Listing 13.3   `process2.cfm`—`<cfparam>` Server-Side Validation

```
<!---
Name:        process2.cfm
Author:      Ben Forta (ben@forta.com)
Description: <cfparam> server-side validation
Created:     01/01/2010
--->

<!--- Form field validation --->
<cfparam name="FORM.LoginID" type="integer">
<cfparam name="FORM.LoginPassword">

<html>

<head>
  <title>Orange Whip Studios - Intranet</title>
</head>

<body>

<!--- Page header --->
<cfinclude template="header.cfm">
<p align="center">
<h1>Intranet</h1>
</p>

Intranet would go here.

</body>

</html>
```

The code in Listing 13.3 is much cleaner and simpler than the code in Listing 13.2, yet it accomplishes the same thing. To test this code, modify `login1.cfm` and change the `<form>` tag so that `action="process2.cfm"`. Try submitting the form with errors and you'll see a screen like the one shown in Figure 13.3.

As you can see, there's a trade-off here. `<cfparam>` makes validation much simpler, but you lose control over formatting and presentation. `<cfif>` statements are a lot more work, but you retain total control over ColdFusion processing.

NOTE

The screen shown in Figure 13.3 is the default ColdFusion error screen. This screen can be changed using the `<cferror>` tag, which will be introduced in Chapter 18, "Introducing the Web Application Framework."

There is, however, a downside with both forms of server-side validation. If you were to add or rename a field, for example, you'd have to remember to update the destination page (the page to which the fields get submitted, as specified in the `<form>` `action` attribute), as well as the form itself. As your forms grow in complexity, so does the likelihood of your forms and their validation rules getting out of sync.

Figure 13.3

When using embedded form field validation, ColdFusion automatically displays an error message listing which checks failed.

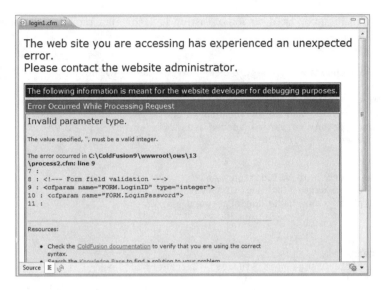

Using Automatic Server-Side Validation

Server-side validation is the safest and most secure form of form field validation, but it can also become a maintenance nightmare. ColdFusion to the rescue!

ColdFusion enables developers to embed basic form validation instructions within an HTML form. These instructions are embedded as hidden form fields. They get sent to the user's browser along with the rest of the form fields, but they aren't displayed to the user. When the user submits the form back to the Web server, however, those hidden fields are submitted too—and ColdFusion can then use them to perform automatic field validation.

These hidden form fields serve as validation rules, and ColdFusion can generate them for you automatically. It does this via some new tags, `<cfform>` and `<cfinput>`. But first, an explanation.

As you have already seen, `<form>`, `<input>`, and related tags are used by browsers to display HTML forms. ColdFusion doesn't process `<form>` or `<input>` tags when it sees them in your code (as it did in Listing 13.1). It simply passes them down to the browser. ColdFusion only processes CFML tags (or expressions without blocks to be processed), not HTML tags.

`<cfform>` is ColdFusion's version of `<form>`, and `<cfinput>` is ColdFusion's version of `<input>`. The tags can be used interchangeably, and the code

```
<form action="process.cfm" method="post">
 <input type="text" name="search">
 <input type="submit">
</form>
```

is functionally identical to

```
<cfform action="process.cfm" method="post">
 <cfinput type="text" name="search">
```

```
    <cfinput type="submit" name="submit">
</cfform>
```

When ColdFusion processes the `<cfform>` tag it simply generates the HTML `<form>` tag, and when it processes `<cfinput>` it generates `<input>`. So why bother doing this? Because these tags essentially intercept the form generation, allowing ColdFusion to insert other code as needed, such as validation code. For example, look at the following code snippet:

```
<cfinput type="password"
         name="LoginPassword"
         maxlength="20"
         required="yes"
         message="Password is required!"
         validateAt="onServer">
```

This tag accepts a password, just like the `<input>` seen in Listing 13.1. But unlike the tag in that listing, here a `<cfinput>` tag is used. And once `<input>` has been replaced with `<cfinput>`, additional attributes (that are instructions to ColdFusion) may be introduced. `required="yes"` tells Cold-Fusion that the `password` field is required, `message` contains the error message to be displayed if validation fails, and `validateAt="onServer"` instructs ColdFusion to validate the page on the server after form submission. When ColdFusion processes this tag it generates an `<input>` tag (because Web browsers would have no idea what `<cfinput>` was anyway), along with other code that it writes for you, hidden form fields that contain validation rules that ColdFusion can process upon form submission.

CAUTION

The `<cfinput>` tag must be used within `<cfform>` tags; you can't use `<cfinput>` with `<form>`. Doing so will throw an error.

Listing 13.4 contains an updated login screen, this time containing `<cfform>` and `<cfinput>` tags providing validation rules.

Listing 13.4 `login2.cfm`—Embedded Server-Side Validation Rules

```
<!---
Name:        login2.cfm
Author:      Ben Forta (ben@forta.com)
Description: Form field validation demo
Created:     01/01/2010
--->

<html>

<head>
  <title>Orange Whip Studios - Intranet</title>
</head>

<body>

<!--- Page header --->
<cfinclude template="header.cfm">

<!--- Login form --->
<cfform action="process2.cfm">
```

Listing 13.4 (CONTINUED)

```
<table align="center" bgcolor="orange">
  <tr>
    <td align="right">
      ID:
    </td>
    <td>
      <cfinput type="text"
               name="LoginID"
               maxlength="5"
               required="yes"
               message="A valid numeric ID is required!"
               validate="integer"
               validateAt="onServer">
    </td>
  </tr>
  <tr>
    <td align="right">
      Password:
    </td>
    <td>
      <cfinput type="password"
               name="LoginPassword"
               maxlength="20"
               required="yes"
               message="Password is required!"
               validateAt="onServer">
    </td>
  </tr>
  <tr>
    <td colspan="2" align="center">
      <cfinput type="submit"
               name="submit"
               value="Login">
    </td>
  </tr>
</table>

</cfform>

</body>

</html>
```

NOTE

When using `<cfinput>` every form field must have a name, even `type="button"`.

If you were to run this code, it would look exactly as it did before (Figure 13.1). That's because ColdFusion generated the same HTML form code as we did before. So where is the difference? Do a View Source, and you'll see that the form generated by ColdFusion looks like this:

```
<html>

<head><script type="text/javascript" src="/CFIDE/scripts/cfform.js"></script>
<script type="text/javascript" src="/CFIDE/scripts/masks.js"></script>
```

```
    <title>Orange Whip Studios - Intranet</title>

<script type="text/javascript">/* <![CDATA[ */
    if (window.ColdFusion) ColdFusion.required['LoginID']=true;
/* ]]> */</script>

<script type="text/javascript">/* <![CDATA[ */
    if (window.ColdFusion) ColdFusion.required['LoginPassword']=true;
/* ]]> */</script>
<script type="text/javascript">
<!--
    _CF_checkCFForm_1 = function(_CF_this)
    {
        //reset on submit
        _CF_error_exists = false;
        _CF_error_messages = new Array();
        _CF_error_fields = new Object();
        _CF_FirstErrorField = null;


        //display error messages and return success
        if( _CF_error_exists )
        {
            if( _CF_error_messages.length > 0 )
            {
                // show alert() message
                _CF_onErrorAlert(_CF_error_messages);
                // set focus to first form error, if the field supports js focus().
                if( _CF_this[_CF_FirstErrorField].type == "text" )
                { _CF_this[_CF_FirstErrorField].focus(); }

            }
            return false;
        }else {
            return true;
        }
    }
//-->
</script>
</head>

<body>




<table align="center">
 <tr>
  <td><img src="../images/logo_c.gif" alt="Orange Whip Studios"></td>
  <td align="center"><font size="+2">Orange Whip Studios<br>Movies</font></td>
 </tr>
</table>


<form name="CFForm_1" id="CFForm_1" action="process2.cfm" method="post"
onsubmit="return _CF_checkCFForm_1(this)">
```

```
<table align="center" bgcolor="orange">
  <tr>
    <td align="right">
      ID:
    </td>
    <td>
      <input name="LoginID" id="LoginID"  type="text" maxlength="5"  />
    </td>
  </tr>
  <tr>
    <td align="right">
      Password:
    </td>
    <td>
      <input name="LoginPassword" id="LoginPassword"  type="password" maxlength="20"
/>
    </td>
  </tr>
  <tr>
    <td colspan="2" align="center">
      <input name="submit" id="submit"  type="submit" value="Login" />
    </td>
  </tr>
</table>

<input type='hidden' name='LoginID_CFFORMINTEGER' value='A valid numeric ID is
required!'>
<input type='hidden' name='LoginID_CFFORMREQUIRED' value='A valid numeric ID is
required!'>
<input type='hidden' name='LoginPassword_CFFORMREQUIRED' value='Password is
required!'>
</form>


</body>

</html>
```

There is no <cfform> in this code, no <cfinput>, and no closing </cfform>. ColdFusion generated the standard HTML form tags, and also made some other changes:

- Listing 13.4 had no method specified, but <cfform> knew to automatically set method="post".

- <cfform>, <cfinput>, and </cfform> were replaced with <form>, <input>, and </form> respectively.

- Three hidden fields were added to the form; these contain the validation rules that ColdFusion will use when processing the form submission.

- Other changes were made too, but those relate to client-side validation, which we'll get to shortly.

Run login2.cfm and submit the form with missing or invalid values. You'll see an error screen like the one shown in Figure 13.4.

Figure 13.4

Validation errors caught by embedded server-side validation throw a friendlier error message screen.

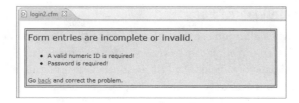

> **NOTE**
>
> The screen shown in Figure 13.4 is the default validation error screen. This screen too can be changed using the `<cferror>` tag.

As you can see, the ColdFusion validation rules are simple and effective. And because the validation rules are embedded into the form itself, your forms and their rules are less likely to get out of sync.

> **NOTE**
>
> The validation rules seen here were generated by ColdFusion automatically. If needed, you can embed the hidden validation rules yourself, although you'll seldom have to. In previous versions of ColdFusion this was necessary, as no automatic generation existed.

Of course, when validation errors occur the user will still have to go back to the form to make any corrections. The benefits of embedded validation rules are really only for developers. Embedded validation does nothing to improve the user experience—for that you need client-side validation.

Using Client-Side Validation

The biggest drawback in using server-side validation is that the validation occurs after form submission. This means that if any validation rules fail, the user must go back to the form, make the corrections, and resubmit it to the server. To make matters worse, some browsers lose the data in the form fields when the Back button is clicked, forcing the user to reenter all the data.

Obviously, this hardly creates a user-friendly interface. Too many good Web sites have lost visitors because their forms were aggravating to work with.

Fortunately, an alternative is available: client-side validation.

Understanding Client-Side Validation

To perform client-side validation, you add a series of browser instructions to your Web page. The browser interprets these instructions and executes them right on the user's computer (i.e., on the client side) before the form ever gets submitted to the server.

To validate a form, you write a script that will trap the form submission and allow it to proceed only if a series of validation checks have passed. If any checks fail, you would display an error message and prevent the form from being submitted.

Of course, to do this, you'd have to learn JavaScript.

Client-Side Validation Via `<cfform>`

You've already seen how ColdFusion can dramatically simplify server-side validation by automatically generating code for you. Well, it can do the same for client-side validation, generating the JavaScript needed to validate form fields. And the best part is that you already know the tags you need to make this work: they are `<cfform>` and `<cfinput>`.

Listing 13.5 contains `login3.cfm`, a slightly modified version of `login2.cfm`. Make that very slightly modified. Can you even see the change?

Listing 13.5   `login3.cfm`—Client-Side Validation Rules

```
<!---
Name:        login3.cfm
Author:      Ben Forta (ben@forta.com)
Description: Form field validation demo
Created:     01/01/2010
--->

<html>

<head>
  <title>Orange Whip Studios - Intranet</title>
</head>

<body>

<!--- Page header --->
<cfinclude template="header.cfm">

<!--- Login form --->
<cfform action="process2.cfm">

<table align="center" bgcolor="orange">
  <tr>
    <td align="right">
      ID:
    </td>
    <td>
      <cfinput type="text"
               name="LoginID"
               maxlength="5"
               required="yes"
               message="A valid numeric ID is required!"
               validate="integer"
               validateAt="onSubmit">
    </td>
  </tr>
  <tr>
    <td align="right">
      Password:
    </td>
    <td>
      <cfinput type="password"
               name="LoginPassword"
               maxlength="20"
```

Listing 13.5 (CONTINUED)

```
                required="yes"
                message="Password is required!"
                validateAt="onSubmit">
      </td>
    </tr>
    <tr>
      <td colspan="2" align="center">
        <cfinput type="submit"
                 name="submit"
                 value="Login">
      </td>
    </tr>
  </table>

</cfform>

</body>

</html>
```

Listings 13.4 and 13.5 are almost identical. The only change is the `validateAt` attribute in the two `<cfinput>` tags, which has been changed from

```
validateAt="onServer"
```

to

```
validateAt="onSubmit"
```

`onServer` tells ColdFusion to generate validation code that will be processed on the server (as seen previously). `onSubmit` tells ColdFusion to generate code that will be processed by the browser when the form is about to be submitted. `validateAt="onSubmit"` generates JavaScript code, which it embeds into your form (in the much the same way as it embedded hidden form fields for server-side validation).

Run `login3.cfm`; the form should look exactly as it did before. But now if you generate an error you'll see a pop-up window right in your browser, as seen in Figure 13.5.

Figure 13.5

Client-side validation error messages are displayed in a browser pop-up box.

Using client-side validation, the form was never submitted, because it failed the validation test. onSubmit validation essentially traps the form submission, and only allows it to continue if it passes all validation tests. This is obviously a far friendlier user experience; if users see a pop-up message like the one in Figure 13.5 they will be able to make corrections and resubmit the form.

NOTE

The pop-up error box is a standard browser dialog that varies from browser to browser, and there is no way to change what it looks like. The only thing you can change are the actual error messages themselves.

It is worth noting that a lot is going on under the hood to make all this work, and ColdFusion has successfully shielded you from it. But do a View Source and you'll see that the generated code has gotten quite lengthy and complex:

```html
<html>

<head><script type="text/javascript" src="/CFIDE/scripts/cfform.js"></script>
<script type="text/javascript" src="/CFIDE/scripts/masks.js"></script>

  <title>Orange Whip Studios - Intranet</title>

<script type="text/javascript">/* <![CDATA[ */
    if (window.ColdFusion) ColdFusion.required['LoginID']=true;
/* ]]> */</script>

<script type="text/javascript">/* <![CDATA[ */
    if (window.ColdFusion) ColdFusion.required['LoginPassword']=true;
/* ]]> */</script>
<script type="text/javascript">
<!--
    _CF_checkCFForm_1 = function(_CF_this)
    {
        //reset on submit
        _CF_error_exists = false;
        _CF_error_messages = new Array();
        _CF_error_fields = new Object();
        _CF_FirstErrorField = null;

        //form element LoginID required check
        if( _CF_hasValue(_CF_this['LoginID'], "TEXT", false ) )
        {
            //form element LoginID 'INTEGER' validation checks
            if (!_CF_checkinteger(_CF_this['LoginID'].value, true))
            {
                _CF_onError(_CF_this, "LoginID", _CF_this['LoginID'].value, "A valid
numeric ID is required!");
                _CF_error_exists = true;
            }

        }else {
            _CF_onError(_CF_this, "LoginID", _CF_this['LoginID'].value, "A valid
numeric ID is required!");
            _CF_error_exists = true;
        }

        //form element LoginPassword required check
```

```
                if( !_CF_hasValue(_CF_this['LoginPassword'], "PASSWORD", false ) )
                {
                    _CF_onError(_CF_this, "LoginPassword", _CF_this['LoginPassword'].value,
"Password is required!");
                    _CF_error_exists = true;
                }


                //display error messages and return success
                if( _CF_error_exists )
                {
                    if( _CF_error_messages.length > 0 )
                    {
                        // show alert() message
                        _CF_onErrorAlert(_CF_error_messages);
                        // set focus to first form error, if the field supports js focus().
                        if( _CF_this[_CF_FirstErrorField].type == "text" )
                        { _CF_this[_CF_FirstErrorField].focus(); }

                    }
                    return false;
                }else {
                    return true;
                }
            }
//-->
</script>
</head>

<body>




<table align="center">
 <tr>
  <td><img src="../images/logo_c.gif" alt="Orange Whip Studios"></td>
  <td align="center"><font size="+2">Orange Whip Studios<br>Movies</font></td>
 </tr>
</table>


<form name="CFForm_1" id="CFForm_1" action="process2.cfm" method="post"
onsubmit="return _CF_checkCFForm_1(this)">

<table align="center" bgcolor="orange">
  <tr>
    <td align="right">
      ID:
    </td>
    <td>
      <input name="LoginID" id="LoginID"  type="text" maxlength="5"  />
    </td>
  </tr>
  <tr>
    <td align="right">
      Password:
```

```
        </td>
        <td>
          <input name="LoginPassword" id="LoginPassword"  type="password" maxlength="20"
/>
        </td>
    </tr>
    <tr>
      <td colspan="2" align="center">
        <input name="submit" id="submit"  type="submit" value="Login" />
      </td>
    </tr>
  </table>

</form>


</body>

</html>
```

That's a lot of code, and most of it is the JavaScript needed to validate form fields.

So what can client-side validation check for? The exact same checks that server-side validation does. Use `required="yes"` to make a form field required, and use `validate=` specifying any of the types listed in Table 13.2 previously. The same validation options are supported by both server-side and client-side validation; all you have to do is decide which you want and specify `validateAt="onServer"` or `validateAt="onSubmit"`.

NOTE

There is actually a third option supported by `validateAt`. To force client-side validation as soon as the user leaves the form field (either by clicking on another field or by tabbing between fields) specify `validateAt="onBlur"`. But use this option sparingly, as this type of validation can annoy your users.

TIP

If `validateAt` is not specified, the default of `validateAt="onSubmit"` will be used.

One of the validation types warrants special mention. `validate="range"` checks that a number is within a specified range, which means that you must provide the range of allowed values. This is done using the `range` attribute, as follows:

```
<cfinput type="text"
         name="age"
         validate="range"
         range="1,100">
```

This code snippet will allow numbers from 1 to 100. You may also specify just a minimum (and no maximum) by only providing one number in the range, as follows:

```
<cfinput type="text"
         name="age"
         validate="range"
         range="18">
```

This code will only allow 18 or higher. To specify a maximum but no minimum, just provide the second number, like this:

```
<cfinput type="text"
         name="age"
         validate="range"
         range=",17">
```

This code will only allow 17 or lower.

NOTE

The actual JavaScript validation code is in a file named `cfform.js` in the `cfide/scripts` directory beneath the Web root. This file is included dynamically using a `<script>` tag whenever any validation is used.

Extending `<cfinput>` Validation Options

You can't add your own validation types to `<cfinput>`, but you can extend the validation by providing *regular expressions*. A regular expression is a search pattern used to match strings. Full coverage of regular expressions is beyond the scope of this book, but here is an example to help explain the concept.

NOTE

Interested in learning more about regular expressions? You may want to get a copy of *Teach Yourself Regular Expressions in 10 Minutes* (Sams, ISBN 0672325667).

Colors used in Web pages are often specified as RGB values (colors specified in amounts of red, green, and blue). RGB values are six characters long—three sets of two hexadecimal values (00 to FF). To obtain a set of RGB values in a form you could use three `<cfinput>` tags like this:

```
Red:
<cfinput type="text"
         name="color_r"
         validate="regex"
         pattern="[A-Fa-f0-9]{ 2,} "
         message="RGB value must be 00-FF"
         size="2"
         maxlength="2">
<br>
Green:
<cfinput type="text"
         name="color_g"
         validate="regex"
         pattern="[A-Fa-f0-9]{ 2,} "
         message="RGB value must be 00-FF"
         size="2"
         maxlength="2">
<br>
Blue:
<cfinput type="text"
         name="color_b"
         validate="regex"
         pattern="[A-Fa-f0-9]{ 2,} "
         message="RGB value must be 00-FF"
```

```
            size="2"
            maxlength="2">
   <br>
```

`validate="regex"` specifies that regular expressions are to be used for validation. The regular expression itself is passed to the `pattern` attribute. `[A-Fa-f0-9]` matches a single character of `A` through `F` (upper- or lowercase) or `0` through `9`. The `{ 2,}` instructs the browser to only accept a minimum of `2` instances of the previous expression. That coupled with `maxlength="2"` provides the exact validation rule needed to accept RGB values.

As you can see, with minimal work you can write regular expressions to validate all sorts of things.

Specifying an Input Mask

We're not quite done yet. Client-side validation provides users with a far better experience than does server-side validation. But let's take this one step further.

All the validation thus far checks for errors after a user inputs data into a form field. Which begs the question, why let users type incorrect data into form fields in the first place? If a form field requires specific data (like `LoginID` in the forms above, which required a numeric ID), let's prevent the user from typing anything else.

As simple as that suggestion sounds, controlling user input at that level is rather complex, and requires some very sophisticated scripting. Fortunately, you don't have to write that validation code either. The `<cfinput>` tag supports an additional attribute named `mask` that accepts an input filter mask. A filter is a string made up of characters that identify what is allowed for each character entered. For example, `9` is used to allow only digits (`0` through `9`). So the following `mask` would only allow two digits and nothing else:

```
   mask="99"
```

Table 13.3 lists the mask characters supported by `<cfinput mask=>`.

Table 13.3 Supported Mask Characters

CHARACTER	ALLOWS
A	A through Z (upper- or lowercase)
9	Any digit
X	A through Z (upper- or lowercase) and any digit
?	Any character
	Any other character inserts that actual character into the input text

So, for a US ZIP code you could use the following mask:

```
   mask="99999-9999"
```

And this mask could work for Canadian postal codes:

```
   mask="A9A 9A9"
```

And to mask a US Social Security number you could use

```
mask="999-99-9999"
```

Of course, masking and validation may be combined, as seen in Listing 13.6, an update to our login page.

Listing 13.6 login4.cfm—Login Screen with Client-Side Validation Rules and Masking

```
<!---
Name:        login4.cfm
Author:      Ben Forta (ben@forta.com)
Description: Form field validation demo
Created:     01/01/2010
--->

<html>

<head>
  <title>Orange Whip Studios - Intranet</title>
</head>

<body>

<!--- Page header --->
<cfinclude template="header.cfm">

<!--- Login form --->
<cfform action="process2.cfm">

<table align="center" bgcolor="orange">
  <tr>
    <td align="right">
      ID:
    </td>
    <td>
      <cfinput type="text"
               name="LoginID"
               maxlength="5"
               required="yes"
               mask="99999"
               message="A valid numeric ID is required!"
               validate="integer"
               validateAt="onSubmit">
    </td>
  </tr>
  <tr>
    <td align="right">
      Password:
    </td>
    <td>
      <cfinput type="password"
               name="LoginPassword"
               maxlength="20"
               required="yes"
               message="Password is required!"
               validateAt="onSubmit">
```

Listing 13.6 (CONTINUED)

```
        </td>
      </tr>
      <tr>
        <td colspan="2" align="center">
          <cfinput type="submit"
                      name="submit"
                      value="Login">
        </td>
      </tr>
    </table>

  </cfform>

  </body>

  </html>
```

Run this new login form. It will look just like the previous login screens, but see what happens when you try to type an alphabetical character into the LoginID field. And all it took was one more <cfinput> attribute.

Validation on the Server and Client

You've seen <cfinput> used to validate on the server and on the client. So far we used one or the other, but it need not be an either/or proposition. In fact, <cfinput> supports the use of multiple validation types at once. All you need to do is specify the types delimited by commas.

So, to validate the UserID field using masks, client-side validation, and server-side validation, you could do the following:

```
<cfinput type="text"
          name="LoginID"
          maxlength="5"
          required="yes"
          mask="99999"
          message="A valid numeric ID is required!"
          validate="integer"
          validateAt="onSubmit,onServer">
```

Preventing Multiple Form Submissions

I want to share one last <cfinput> goodie with you. All Web application developers face the problem of dealing with multiple form submissions. For example, a user fills in a form, clicks the Submit button, and then gets impatient and submits it again and again and again.

If your form was a front end to database searches, this would result in multiple searches being performed. And while this won't negatively impact your data, it will definitely slow the application. This becomes an even bigger issue when forms are used to insert data into database tables (as will be seen in the next chapter). Multiple form submissions then are a real problem, as users could inadvertently insert multiple rows to your table.

Once again, `<cfinput>` comes to the rescue with a special `validate` option that only applies to form buttons. `validate="SubmitOnce"` generates JavaScript code that prevents multiple form submissions. For example, to not allow our login form to be submitted multiple times, the button could be changed to

```
<cfinput type="submit"
        name="submit"
        value="Login"
        validate="SubmitOnce">
```

Clean and simple, thanks to `<cfinput>`.

Putting It All Together

Before you run off and plug `<cfform>` and `<cfinput>` into all your templates, there are some other details that you should know:

- **Not all browsers support JavaScript.** Most newer ones do, but there still are older ones out there. Even if a user's browser supports JavaScript, the user may choose to disable it. Browsers that don't support or that disable JavaScript will generally ignore it, enabling your forms to be submitted without being validated if only client-side validation is used.

- **You should combine the use of JavaScript validation with server-side validation.** These will never fail validation if the browser does support JavaScript, and if the browser doesn't, at least you have some form of validation.

- **Don't rely solely on automatically generated server-side validation (via embedded hidden fields).** Clever hackers could quite easily remove those hidden fields and submit your form without server-side validation.

- **The JavaScript code can be quite lengthy.** This will slightly increase the size of your Web page and thus the time it takes to download it from your Web server.

- **Mix and match validation types.** Use `<cfinput>` to generate multiple validation types; the more validation you do, the safer your applications will be.

- **Manual server-side validation is your last defense.** Regardless of the validation options used, it's safest to always use manual server-side tests (either using `<cfparam>` or `<cfif>` statements). If you are using `<cfinput>`, users will never get caught by those tests, so you may not need to even worry about prettying up the error messages. But for that mischievous user who just wants to find a way in, manual server-side validation is your last defense.

14

Using Forms to Add or Change Data

Adding Data with ColdFusion

Now that you learned all about forms and form data validation in the previous two chapters, it's time to combine the two so as to be able to add and update database table data.

➔ See Chapter 12, "ColdFusion Forms," to learn about HTML forms and how to use them within your ColdFusion applications.

➔ See Chapter 13, "Form Data Validation," for coverage of form field validation techniques and options.

When you created the movie search forms in Chapter 12, you had to create two templates for each search. One creates the user search screen that contains the search form, and the other performs the actual search using the ColdFusion <cfquery> tag. ColdFusion developers usually refer to these as the <form> and action pages, because one contains the form and the other is the file specified as the <form> action.

Breaking an operation into more than one template is typical of ColdFusion, as well as all Web-based data interaction. As explained in Chapter 1, "Introducing ColdFusion," a browser's connection to a Web server is made and broken as necessary. An HTTP connection is made to a Web server whenever a Web page is retrieved. That connection is broken as soon as that page is retrieved. Any subsequent pages are retrieved with a new connection that is used just to retrieve that page.

There is no real way to keep a connection alive for the duration of a complete process—when searching for data, for example. Therefore, the process must be broken up into steps, and, as shown in Chapter 12, each step typically is a separate template.

Adding data via your Web browser is no different. You generally need at least two templates to perform the insertion. One displays the form you use to collect the data; the other processes the data and inserts the record.

Adding data to a table involves the following steps:

1. Display a form to collect the data. The names of any input fields should match the names of the columns in the destination table.

2. Submit the form to ColdFusion for processing. ColdFusion adds the row via the data source using a SQL statement.

Creating an Add Record Form

Forms used to add data are no different from the forms you created to search for data. As seen in Listing 14.1, the form is created using form tags, with a form control for each row table column to be inserted. Save this file as insert1.cfm (in the 14 directory under ows). You'll be able to execute the page to display the form, but don't submit it yet (you have yet to create the action page).

Listing 14.1 insert1.cfm—New Movie Form

```
<!---
Name:        insert1.cfm
Author:      Ben Forta (ben@forta.com)
Description: Table row insertion demo
Created:     01/01/2010
--->

<!--- Get ratings --->
<cfquery datasource="ows" name="ratings">
SELECT RatingID, Rating
FROM FilmsRatings
ORDER BY RatingID
</cfquery>

<!--- Page header --->
<cfinclude template="header.cfm">

<!--- New movie form --->
<form action="insert2.cfm" method="post">

<table align="center" bgcolor="orange">
 <tr>
  <th colspan="2">
   <font size="+1">Add a Movie</font>
  </th>
 </tr>
 <tr>
  <td>
   Movie:
  </td>
  <td>
   <input type="Text"
          name="MovieTitle"
          size="50"
          maxlength="100">
  </td>
 </tr>
```

Listing 14.1 (CONTINUED)

```
<tr>
 <td>
  Tag line:
 </td>
 <td>
  <input type="Text"
         name="PitchText"
         size="50"
         maxlength="100">
 </td>
</tr>
<tr>
 <td>
  Rating:
 </td>
 <td>
  <!--- Ratings list --->
  <select name="RatingID">
   <cfoutput query="ratings">
    <option value="#RatingID#">#Rating#</option>
   </cfoutput>
  </select>
 </td>
</tr>
<tr>
 <td>
  Summary:
 </td>
 <td>
  <textarea name="summary"
            cols="40"
            rows="5"
            wrap="virtual"></textarea>
 </td>
</tr>
<tr>
 <td>
  Budget:
 </td>
 <td>
  <input type="Text"
         name="AmountBudgeted"
         size="10"
         maxlength="10">
 </td>
</tr>
<tr>
 <td>
  Release Date:
 </td>
 <td>
  <input type="Text"
         name="DateInTheaters"
         size="10"
         maxlength="10">
 </td>
```

Listing 14.1 (CONTINUED)

```
    </tr>
    <tr>
     <td>
      Image File:
     </td>
     <td>
      <input type="Text"
             name="ImageName"
             size="20"
             maxlength="50">
     </td>
    </tr>
    <tr>
     <td colspan="2" align="center">
      <input type="submit" value="Insert">
     </td>
      </tr>
   </table>

   </form>

   <!--- Page footer --->
   <cfinclude template="footer.cfm">
```

NOTE

Listing 14.1 contains a form not unlike the forms created in Chapters 12 and 13. This form uses form techniques and validation options described in both of those chapters; refer to them if necessary.

The file insert1.cfm—and indeed all the files in this chapter—includes common header and footer files (header.cfm and footer.cfm, respectively). These files contain the HTML page layout code, including any logos. They are included in each file (using <cfinclude> tags) to facilitate code reuse (and to keep code listings shorter and more manageable). Listings 14.2 and 14.3 contain the code for these two files.

➔ The <cfinclude> tag and code reuse were introduced in Chapter 9, "Programming with CFML."

Listing 14.2 header.cfm—Movie Form Page Header

```
   <!---
   Name:        header.cfm
   Author:      Ben Forta (ben@forta.com)
   Description: Page header
   Created:     01/01/2010
   --->

   <html>

   <head>
    <title>Orange Whip Studios - Intranet</title>
   </head>

   <body>
   <table align="center">
```

Listing 14.2 (CONTINUED)

```
 <tr>
  <td>
   <img src="../images/logo_c.gif" alt="Orange Whip Studios">
  </td>
  <td align="center">
   <font size="+2">Orange Whip Studios<br>Movie Maintenance</font>
  </td>
 </tr>
</table>
```

Listing 14.3 footer.cfm—Movie Form Page Footer

```
<!---
Name:        footer.cfm
Author:      Ben Forta (ben@forta.com)
Description: Page footer
Created:     01/01/2010
--->

</body>

</html>
```

The `<form>` action attribute specifies the name of the template to be used to process the insertion; in this case it's `insert2.cfm`.

Each `<input>` (or `<cfinput>`, if used) field has a field name specified in the `name` attribute. These names correspond to the names of the appropriate columns in the `Films` table.

TIP

ColdFusion Builder users can take advantage of the built-in drag-and-drop features when using table and column names within code. Simply open RDS Dataview, expand the data source, and then expand the Tables item to display the list of tables within the data source. You can then drag the table name into your source code. Similarly, expanding the table name displays a list of the fields within that table, and you can also drag those fields into your source code.

You also specified the `size` and `maxlength` attributes in each of the text fields. `size` is used to specify the size of the text box within the browser window. Without the `size` attribute, the browser uses its default size, which varies from one browser to the next.

The `size` attribute does not restrict the number of characters that can be entered into the field. `size="50"` creates a text field that occupies the space of 50 characters, but the text scrolls within the field if you enter more than 50 characters. To restrict the number of characters that can be entered, you must use the `maxlength` attribute. `maxlength="100"` instructs the browser to allow no more than 100 characters in the field.

The `size` attribute primarily is used for aesthetics and the control of screen appearance. `maxlength` is used to ensure that only data that can be handled is entered into a field. Without `maxlength`, users could enter more data than would fit in a field, and that data would be truncated upon database insertion (or might even generate database errors).

NOTE

You should always use both the `size` and `maxlength` attributes for maximum control over form appearance and data entry. Without them, the browser will use its defaults—and there are no rules governing what these defaults should be.

The `RatingID` field is a drop-down list box populated with a `<cfquery>`.

The Add a Movie form is shown in Figure 14.1.

Figure 14.1

HTML forms can be used as a front end for data insertion.

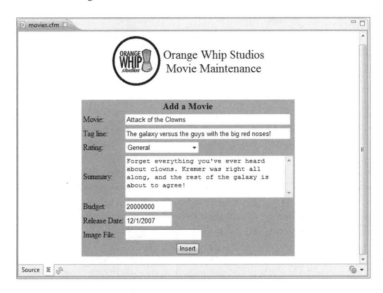

Processing Additions

The next thing you need is a template to process the actual data insertion—the ACTION page mentioned earlier. In this page use the SQL INSERT statement to add the new row to the Films table.

➡ See Chapter 7, "SQL Data Manipulation," for an explanation of the INSERT statement.

As shown in Listing 14.4, the `<cfquery>` tag can be used to pass any SQL statement—not just SELECT statements. The SQL statement here is INSERT, which adds a row to the Films table and sets the values in seven columns to the form values passed by the browser.

Listing 14.4 insert2.cfm—Adding Data with the SQL INSERT Statement

```
<!---
Name:        insert2.cfm
Author:      Ben Forta (ben@forta.com)
Description: Table row insertion demo
Created:     01/01/2010
--->
<!--- Insert movie --->
<cfquery datasource="ows">
INSERT INTO Films(MovieTitle,
                  PitchText,
```

Listing 14.4 (CONTINUED)

```
                    AmountBudgeted,
                    RatingID,
                    Summary,
                    ImageName,
                    DateInTheaters)
    VALUES('#Trim(FORM.MovieTitle)#',
           '#Trim(FORM.PitchText)#',
           #FORM.AmountBudgeted#,
           #FORM.RatingID#,
           '#Trim(FORM.Summary)#',
           '#Trim(FORM.ImageName)#',
           #CreateODBCDate(FORM.DateInTheaters)#)
    </cfquery>

    <!--- Page header --->
    <cfinclude template="header.cfm">

    <!--- Feedback --->
    <cfoutput>
    <h1>New movie '#FORM.MovieTitle#' added</h1>
    </cfoutput>

    <!--- Page footer --->
    <cfinclude template="footer.cfm">
```

Listing 14.4 is pretty self-explanatory. The <cfquery> tag performs the actual INSERT operation. The list of columns into which values are to be assigned is specified, as is the matching VALUES list (these two lists must match exactly, both the columns and their order).

Each of the values used is from a FORM field, but some differences do exist in how the fields are used:

- All string fields have their values enclosed within single quotation marks.

- The two numeric fields (AmountBudgeted and RatingID) have no single quotation marks around them.

- The date field (DateInTheaters) is formatted as a date using the CreateODBCDate() function.

It's important to remember that SQL is not typeless, so it's your job to use quotation marks where necessary to explicitly type variables.

TIP

ColdFusion is very good at handling dates, and can correctly process dates in all sorts of formats. But occasionally a date may be specified in a format that ColdFusion can't parse properly. In that case, it will be your responsibility to format the date so Cold-Fusion understands it. You can do this using the DateFormat() function or the ODBC date function CreateODBCDate() (or the CreateODBCTime() and CreateODBCDateTime() functions). Even though ColdFusion uses JDBC database drivers, the ODBC format generated by the ODBC functions is understood by ColdFusion and will be processed correctly. Listing 14.4 demonstrates the use of the CreateODBCDate() function.

NOTE

Notice that the `<cfquery>` in Listing 14.4 has no `name` attribute. `name` is an optional attribute and is necessary only if you need to manipulate the data returned by `<cfquery>`. Because the operation here is an `INSERT`, no data is returned; the `name` attribute is therefore unnecessary.

Save Listing 14.4 as `insert2.cfm`, and then try submitting a new movie using the form in `insert1.cfm`. You should see a screen similar to the one shown in Figure 14.2.

Figure 14.2

Data can be added via ColdFusion using the SQL `INSERT` statement.

Orange Whip Studios
Movie Maintenance

New movie 'Attack of the Clowns' added

NOTE

You can verify that the movie was added by browsing the table using any of the search templates you created in Chapter 12.

Introducing `<cfinsert>`

The example in Listing 14.4 demonstrates how to add data to a table using the standard SQL `INSERT` command. This works very well if you have to provide data for only a few columns, and if those columns are always provided. If the number of columns can vary, using SQL `INSERT` gets rather complicated.

For example, assume you have two or more data-entry forms for similar data. One might collect a minimal number of fields, whereas another collects a more complete record. How would you create a SQL `INSERT` statement to handle both sets of data?

You could create two separate templates, with a different SQL `INSERT` statement in each, but that's a poor solution. You should always try to avoid having more than one template perform a given operation. That way, you don't run the risk of future changes and revisions being applied incorrectly. If a table or column name changes, for example, you won't have to worry about forgetting one of the templates that references the changed column.

TIP

As a rule, never create more than one template to perform a specific operation. This helps prevent introducing errors into your templates when updates or revisions are made. You're almost always better off creating one template with conditional code than creating two separate templates.

Another solution is to use dynamic SQL. You could write a basic `INSERT` statement and then gradually construct a complete statement by using a series of `<cfif>` statements.

This is a workable solution, but not a very efficient one. The conditional SQL `INSERT` code is far more complex than conditional SQL `SELECT`. The `INSERT` statement requires that both the list of columns and the values be dynamic. In addition, the INSERT syntax requires that you separate all column names and values by commas. This means that every column name and value must be followed by a comma except the last one in the list. Your conditional SQL has to accommodate these syntactical requirements when the statement is constructed.

A better solution is to use <cfinsert>, which is a special ColdFusion tag that hides the complexity of building dynamic SQL INSERT statements. <cfinsert> takes the following parameters as attributes:

- datasource—The name of the data source that contains the table to which the data is to be inserted.

- tablename—The name of the destination table.

- formfields—An optional comma-separated list of fields to be inserted. If this attribute isn't provided, all the fields in the submitted form are used.

Look at the following ColdFusion tag:

```
<cfinsert datasource="ows" tablename="FILMS">
```

This code does exactly the same thing as the <cfquery> tag in Listing 14.4. When ColdFusion processes a <cfinsert> tag, it builds a dynamic SQL INSERT statement under the hood. If a formfields attribute is provided, the specified field names are used. No formfields attribute was specified in this example, so ColdFusion automatically uses the form fields that were submitted, building the list of columns and the values dynamically. <cfinsert> even automatically handles the inclusion of single quotation marks where necessary.

CAUTION

When you use Apache Derby, table names passed to <cfinsert> must be uppercase.

While we are it, the form created in insert1.cfm did not perform any data validation, which could cause database errors to be thrown (try inserting text in a numeric field and see what happens).

Listing 14.5 contains a revised form (a modified version of insert1.cfm); save this file as insert3. cfm. Listing 14.6 contains a revised action page (a modified version of insert2.cfm); save this file as insert4.cfm.

Listing 14.5 insert3.cfm—Using <cfform> for Field Validation

```
<!---
Name:        insert3.cfm
Author:      Ben Forta (ben@forta.com)
Description: Table row insertion demo
Created:     01/01/2010
--->
<!--- Get ratings --->
<cfquery datasource="ows" name="ratings">
SELECT RatingID, Rating
FROM FilmsRatings
ORDER BY RatingID
</cfquery>
```

Listing 14.5 (CONTINUED)

```
<!--- Page header --->
<cfinclude template="header.cfm">

<!--- New movie form --->
<cfform action="insert4.cfm">

<table align="center" bgcolor="orange">
 <tr>
  <th colspan="2">
   <font size="+1">Add a Movie</font>
  </th>
 </tr>
 <tr>
  <td>
   Movie:
  </td>
  <td>
   <cfinput type="Text"
            name="MovieTitle"
            message="MOVIE TITLE is required!"
            required="Yes"
            validateAt="onSubmit,onServer"
            size="50"
            maxlength="100">
  </td>
 </tr>
 <tr>
  <td>
   Tag line:
  </td>
  <td>
   <cfinput type="Text"
            name="PitchText"
            message="TAG LINE is required!"
            required="Yes"
            validateAt="onSubmit,onServer"
            size="50"
            maxlength="100">
  </td>
 </tr>
 <tr>
  <td>
   Rating:
  </td>
  <td>
   <!--- Ratings list --->
   <select name="RatingID">
    <cfoutput query="ratings">
     <option value="#RatingID#">#Rating#</option>
    </cfoutput>
   </select>
  </td>
 </tr>
 <tr>
  <td>
```

Listing 14.5 (CONTINUED)

```
       Summary:
     </td>
     <td>
      <textarea name="summary"
                cols="40"
                rows="5"
                wrap="virtual"></textarea>
     </td>
    </tr>
    <tr>
     <td>
      Budget:
     </td>
     <td>
      <cfinput type="Text"
               name="AmountBudgeted"
               message="BUDGET must be a valid numeric amount!"
               required="NO"
               validate="integer"
               validateAt="onSubmit,onServer"
               size="10"
               maxlength="10">
     </td>
    </tr>
    <tr>
     <td>
      Release Date:
     </td>
     <td>
      <cfinput type="Text"
               name="DateInTheaters"
               message="RELEASE DATE must be a valid date!"
               required="NO"
               validate="date"
               validateAt="onSubmit,onServer"
               size="10"
               maxlength="10">
     </td>
    </tr>
    <tr>
     <td>
      Image File:
     </td>
     <td>
      <cfinput type="Text"
               name="ImageName"
               required="NO"
               size="20"
               maxlength="50">
     </td>
    </tr>
    <tr>
     <td colspan="2" align="center">
      <input type="submit" value="Insert">
     </td>
      </tr>
```

Listing 14.5 (CONTINUED)

```
</table>

</cfform>

<!--- Page footer --->
<cfinclude template="footer.cfm">
```

Listing 14.6 is the same form used previously, except that `<input>` has been replaced with `<cfinput>` so as to validate submitted data, and form field validation has been included, using the techniques described in Chapter 13.

Listing 14.6 insert4.cfm—Adding Data with the `<cfinsert>` Tag

```
<!---
Name:        insert4.cfm
Author:      Ben Forta (ben@forta.com)
Description: Table row insertion demo
Created:     01/01/2010
--->

<!--- Insert movie --->
<cfinsert datasource="ows" tablename="FILMS">

<!--- Page header --->
<cfinclude template="header.cfm">

<!--- Feedback --->
<cfoutput>
<h1>New movie '#FORM.MovieTitle#' added</h1>
</cfoutput>

<!--- Page footer --->
<cfinclude template="footer.cfm">
```

Try adding a movie with these new templates. You'll see that the database inserting code in Listing 14.6 does exactly the same thing as the code in Listing 14.4, but with a much simpler syntax and interface.

Controlling `<cfinsert>` Form Fields

`<cfinsert>` instructs ColdFusion to build SQL INSERT statements dynamically. ColdFusion automatically uses all submitted form fields when building this statement.

Sometimes you might want ColdFusion to not include certain fields. For example, you might have hidden fields in your form that aren't table columns, such as the hidden field shown in Listing 14.7. That field might be there as part of a security system you have implemented; it isn't a column in the table. If you try to pass this field to `<cfinsert>`, ColdFusion passes the hidden Login field as a column to the database. Obviously, this generates an database error, because no Login column exists in the Films table.

Listing 14.7 insert5.cfm—Movie Addition Form with Hidden Login Field

```
<!---
Name:        insert5.cfm
Author:      Ben Forta (ben@forta.com)
Description: Table row insertion demo
Created:     01/01/2010
--->

<!--- Get ratings --->
<cfquery datasource="ows" name="ratings">
SELECT RatingID, Rating
FROM FilmsRatings
ORDER BY RatingID
</cfquery>

<!--- Page header --->
<cfinclude template="header.cfm">

<!--- New movie form --->
<cfform action="insert6.cfm">

<!--- Login field --->
<cfinput type="hidden"
         name="Login"
         value="Ben">

<table align="center" bgcolor="orange">
 <tr>
  <th colspan="2">
   <font size="+1">Add a Movie</font>
  </th>
 </tr>
 <tr>
  <td>
   Movie:
  </td>
  <td>
   <cfinput type="Text"
            name="MovieTitle"
            message="MOVIE TITLE is required!"
            required="Yes"
            validateAt="onSubmit,onServer"
            size="50"
            maxlength="100">
  </td>
 </tr>
 <tr>
  <td>
   Tag line:
  </td>
  <td>
   <cfinput type="Text"
            name="PitchText"
            message="TAG LINE is required!"
            required="Yes"
            validateAt="onSubmit,onServer"
            size="50"
```

Listing 14.7 (CONTINUED)

```
                  maxlength="100">
   </td>
 </tr>
 <tr>
  <td>
   Rating:
  </td>
  <td>
   <!--- Ratings list --->
   <select name="RatingID">
    <cfoutput query="ratings">
     <option value="#RatingID#">#Rating#</option>
    </cfoutput>
   </select>
  </td>
 </tr>
 <tr>
  <td>
   Summary:
  </td>
  <td>
   <textarea name="summary"
             cols="40"
             rows="5"
             wrap="virtual"></textarea>
  </td>
 </tr>
 <tr>
  <td>
   Budget:
  </td>
  <td>
   <cfinput type="Text"
            name="AmountBudgeted"
            message="BUDGET must be a valid numeric amount!"
            required="NO"
            validate="integer"
            validateAt="onSubmit,onServer"
            size="10"
            maxlength="10">
  </td>
 </tr>
 <tr>
  <td>
   Release Date:
  </td>
  <td>
   <cfinput type="Text"
            name="DateInTheaters"
            message="RELEASE DATE must be a valid date!"
            required="NO"
            validate="date"
            validateAt="onSubmit,onServer"
            size="10"
            maxlength="10">
```

Listing 14.7   (CONTINUED)

```
      </td>
    </tr>
    <tr>
     <td>
      Image File:
     </td>
     <td>
      <cfinput type="Text"
               name="ImageName"
               required="NO"
               size="20"
               maxlength="50">
     </td>
    </tr>
    <tr>
     <td colspan="2" align="center">
      <input type="submit" value="Insert">
     </td>
      </tr>
  </table>

</cfform>

<!--- Page footer --->
<cfinclude template="footer.cfm">
```

To solve this problem, you must use the formfields attribute. formfields instructs ColdFusion to process only form fields that are in the list. Any other fields are ignored.

It's important to note that formfields isn't used to specify which fields ColdFusion should process. Rather, it specifies which fields should *not* be processed. The difference is subtle. Not all fields listed in the formfields value need be present. They are processed *if* they are present; if they aren't present, they aren't processed (so no error will be generated). Any fields not listed in the formfields list are ignored.

Listing 14.8 contains an updated data insertion template. The <cfinsert> tag now has a formfields attribute, so now ColdFusion knows to ignore the hidden Login field.

Listing 14.8   insert6.cfm—Using the <cfinsert> formfields Attribute

```
<!---
Name:        insert6.cfm
Author:      Ben Forta (ben@forta.com)
Description: Table row insertion demo
Created:     01/01/2010
--->

<!--- Insert movie --->
<cfinsert datasource="ows"
          tablename="FILMS"
          formfields="MovieTitle,
                      PitchText,
                      AmountBudgeted,
                      RatingID,
```

Listing 14.8 (CONTINUED)

```
                    Summary,
                    ImageName,
                    DateInTheaters">

<!--- Page header --->
<cfinclude template="header.cfm">

<!--- Feedback --->
<cfoutput>
<h1>New movie '#FORM.MovieTitle#' added</h1>
</cfoutput>

<!--- Page footer --->
<cfinclude template="footer.cfm">
```

Collecting Data for More Than One INSERT

Here's another situation where `<cfinsert>` formfields can be used: when a form collects data that needs to be added to more than one table. You can create a template that has two or more `<cfinsert>` statements by using formfields.

As long as each `<cfinsert>` statement has a formfields attribute that specifies which fields are to be used with each INSERT, ColdFusion correctly executes each `<cfinsert>` with its appropriate fields.

`<cfinsert>` Versus SQL INSERT

Adding data to tables using the ColdFusion `<cfinsert>` tag is simpler and helps prevent the creation of multiple similar templates.

So why would you ever *not* use `<cfinsert>`? Is there ever a reason to use SQL INSERT instead of `<cfinsert>`?

The truth is that both are needed. `<cfinsert>` can be used only for simple data insertion to a single table. If you want to insert the results of a SELECT statement, you can't use `<cfinsert>`. And you can't use `<cfinsert>` if you want to insert values other than FORM fields—variables or URL parameters, for example.

These guidelines will help you decide when to use which method:

- For simple operations (single table and no complex processing), use `<cfinsert>` to add data.

- If you find that you need to add specific form fields—and not all that were submitted— use the `<cfinsert>` tag with the formfields attribute.

- If `<cfinsert>` can't be used because you need a complex INSERT statement or are using fields that aren't form fields, use SQL INSERT.

TIP

I have seen many documents and articles attempt to dissuade the use of `<cfinsert>` (and `<cfupdate>` discussed below), primarily because of the limitations already mentioned. In my opinion there is nothing wrong with using these tags at all, recognizing their limitations of course. In fact, I'd even argue that their use is preferable as they are dynamic (if the form changes they may not need changing) and are type aware (they handle type conversions automatically). So don't let the naysayers get you down. CFML is all about making your development life easier, so if these tags make coding easier, use them.

Updating Data with ColdFusion

Updating data with ColdFusion is similar to inserting data. You generally need two templates to update a row—a data-entry form template and a data update one. The big difference between a form used for data addition and one used for data modification is that the latter needs to be populated with existing values.

Building a Data Update Form

Populating an HTML form is a simple process. First, you must retrieve the row to be updated from the table. You do this with a standard `<cfquery>`; the retrieved values are then passed as attributes to the HTML form.

Listing 14.9 contains the code for `update1.cfm`, a template that updates a movie. Save it as `update1.cfm`, and then execute it. Be sure to append the `FilmID`—for example, `?FilmID=13`—as a URL parameter. Your screen should look like Figure 14.3.

Figure 14.3

When you use forms to update data, the form fields usually need to be populated with existing values.

Listing 14.9   `update1.cfm`—Movie Update Form

```
<!---
Name:        update1.cfm
Author:      Ben Forta (ben@forta.com)
Description: Table row update demo
Created:     01/01/2010
```

Listing 14.9   (CONTINUED)

```
--->

<!--- Check that FilmID was provided --->
<cfif NOT IsDefined("URL.FilmID")>
 <h1>You did not specify the FilmID</h1>
 <cfabort>
</cfif>

<!--- Get the film record --->
<cfquery datasource="ows" name="film">
SELECT FilmID, MovieTitle, PitchText,
    AmountBudgeted, RatingID,
    Summary, ImageName, DateInTheaters
FROM Films
WHERE FilmID=#URL.FilmID#
</cfquery>

<!--- Get ratings --->
<cfquery datasource="ows" name="ratings">
SELECT RatingID, Rating
FROM FilmsRatings
ORDER BY RatingID
</cfquery>

<!--- Page header --->
<cfinclude template="header.cfm">

<!--- Update movie form --->
<cfform action="update2.cfm">

<!--- Embed primary key as a hidden field --->
<cfoutput>
<input type="hidden" name="FilmID" value="#Film.FilmID#">
</cfoutput>

<table align="center" bgcolor="orange">
 <tr>
  <th colspan="2">
   <font size="+1">Update a Movie</font>
  </th>
 </tr>
 <tr>
  <td>
   Movie:
  </td>
  <td>
   <cfinput type="Text"
            name="MovieTitle"
            value="#Trim(film.MovieTitle)#"
            message="MOVIE TITLE is required!"
            required="Yes"
            validateAt="onSubmit,onServer"
            size="50"
            maxlength="100">
  </td>
 </tr>
```

Listing 14.9 (CONTINUED)

```
<tr>
 <td>
 Tag line:
 </td>
 <td>
  <cfinput type="Text"
           name="PitchText"
           value="#Trim(film.PitchText)#"
           message="TAG LINE is required!"
           required="Yes"
           validateAt="onSubmit,onServer"
           size="50"
           maxlength="100">
 </td>
</tr>
<tr>
 <td>
 Rating:
 </td>
 <td>
  <!--- Ratings list --->
  <select name="RatingID">
   <cfoutput query="ratings">
    <option value="#RatingID#"
            <cfif ratings.RatingID IS film.RatingID>
            selected
            </cfif>>#Rating#
    </option>
   </cfoutput>
  </select>
 </td>
</tr>
<tr>
 <td>
 Summary:
 </td>
 <td>
  <cfoutput>
  <textarea name="summary"
            cols="40"
            rows="5"
            wrap="virtual">#Trim(Film.Summary)#</textarea>
  </cfoutput>
 </td>
</tr>
<tr>
 <td>
 Budget:
 </td>
 <td>
  <cfinput type="Text"
           name="AmountBudgeted"
           value="#Int(film.AmountBudgeted)#"
           message="BUDGET must be a valid numeric amount!"
           required="NO"
           validate="integer"
```

Listing 14.9 (CONTINUED)

```
                    validateAt="onSubmit,onServer"
                    size="10"
                    maxlength="10">
       </td>
      </tr>
      <tr>
       <td>
        Release Date:
       </td>
       <td>
        <cfinput type="Text"
                 name="DateInTheaters"
                 value="#DateFormat(film.DateInTheaters, "MM/DD/YYYY")#"
                 message="RELEASE DATE must be a valid date!"
                 required="NO"
                 validate="date"
                 validateAt="onSubmit,onServer"
                 size="10"
                 maxlength="10">
       </td>
      </tr>
      <tr>
       <td>
        Image File:
       </td>
       <td>
        <cfinput type="Text"
                 name="ImageName"
                 value="#Trim(film.ImageName)#"
                 required="NO"
                 size="20"
                 maxlength="50">
       </td>
      </tr>
      <tr>
       <td colspan="2" align="center">
        <input type="submit" value="Update">
       </td>
      </tr>
     </table>

    </cfform>

    <!--- Page footer --->
    <cfinclude template="footer.cfm">
```

There is a lot to look at in Listing 14.9. And don't submit the form yet; you have yet to create the action page.

To populate a form with data to be updated, you must first retrieve that row from the table. Therefore, you must specify a FilmID to use this template. Without it, ColdFusion wouldn't know which row to retrieve. To ensure that the FilmID is passed, the first thing you do is check for the existence of the FilmID parameter. The following code returns TRUE only if FilmID was not passed, in which case an error message is sent back to the user and template processing is halted with the `<cfabort>` tag:

```
<CFIF NOT IsDefined("URL.FilmID")>
```

Without the `<cfabort>` tag, ColdFusion continues processing the template. An error message is generated when the `<cfquery>` statement is processed because the WHERE clause WHERE FilmID = #URL.FilmID# references a nonexistent field.

The first `<cfquery>` tag retrieves the row to be edited, and the passed URL is used in the WHERE clause to retrieve the appropriate row. The second `<cfquery>` retrieves the list of ratings for the `<select>` control. To populate the data-entry fields, the current field value is passed to the `<input>` (or `<cfinput>`) value attribute. Whatever is passed to value is displayed in the field, so value="#Film.MovieTitle#" displays the MovieTitle table column.

NOTE

The query name is necessary here as a prefix because it isn't being used within a `<cfoutput>` associated with a query. `<cfinput>` is a ColdFusion tag, so you can pass variables and columns to it without needing to use `<cfoutput>`. If you were using `<input>` instead of `<cfinput>`, the `<input>` tags would need to be within a `<cfoutput>` block. This is another benefit of using `<cfinput>` instead of `<input>`: `<cfinput>` makes populating form fields with dynamic data much easier.

To ensure that no blank spaces exist after the retrieved value, the fields are trimmed with the ColdFusion Trim() function before they are displayed. Why would you do this? Some databases, such as Microsoft SQL Server, pad some text fields with spaces so they take up the full column width in the table. The MovieTitle field is a 255-character-wide column, so a movie title could have a lot of spaces after it. The extra space can be very annoying when you try to edit the field. To append text to a field, you'd first have to backspace or delete all those extra characters.

NOTE

When populating forms with table column values, you should always trim the field first. Unlike standard browser output, spaces in form fields aren't ignored. Removing them allows easier editing. The ColdFusion Trim() function removes spaces at the beginning and end of the value. If you want to trim only trailing spaces, you could use the RTrim() function instead.

Dates and numbers are also formatted specially. By default, dates are displayed in a rather unusable format (and a format that won't be accepted upon form submission). Therefore, DateFormat() is used to format the date in a usable format.

The AmountBudgeted column allows numbers with decimal points; to display the number within the trailing decimal point and zeros, the Int() function can be used to round the number to an integer. You also could have used NumberFormat() for more precise number formatting.

One hidden field exists in the FORM. The following code creates a hidden field called FilmID, which contains the ID of the movie being updated:

```
<input type="hidden" name="FilmID" value="#Film.FilmID#">
```

This hidden field must be present. Without it, ColdFusion has no idea which row you were updating when the form was actually submitted. Also, because it is an `<input>` field (not `<cfinput>`), it must be enclosed within `<cfoutput>` tags.

Remember that HTTP sessions are created and broken as necessary, and every session stands on its own two feet. ColdFusion might retrieve a specific row of data for you in one session, but it doesn't know that in the next session. Therefore, when you update a row, you must specify the primary key so ColdFusion knows which row to update. Hidden fields are one way of doing this because they are sent to the browser as part of the form, but are never displayed and thus can't be edited. However, they are still form fields, and they are submitted along with all other form fields intact upon form submission.

Processing Updates

As with adding data, there are two ways to update rows in a table. The code in Listing 14.10 demonstrates a row update using the SQL UPDATE statement.

→   See Chapter 6, "Introducing SQL," for an explanation of the UPDATE statement.

Listing 14.10   update2.cfm—Updating a Table with SQL UPDATE

```
<!---
Name:        update2.cfm
Author:      Ben Forta (ben@forta.com)
Description: Table row update demo
Created:     01/01/2010
--->

<!--- Update movie --->
<cfquery datasource="ows">
UPDATE Films
SET MovieTitle='#Trim(FORM.MovieTitle)#',
    PitchText='#Trim(FORM.PitchText)#',
    AmountBudgeted=#FORM.AmountBudgeted#,
    RatingID=#FORM.RatingID#,
    Summary='#Trim(FORM.Summary)#',
    ImageName='#Trim(FORM.ImageName)#',
    DateInTheaters=#CreateODBCDate(FORM.DateInTheaters)#
WHERE FilmID=#FORM.FilmID#
</cfquery>

<!--- Page header --->
<cfinclude template="header.cfm">

<!--- Feedback --->
<cfoutput>
<h1>Movie '#FORM.MovieTitle#' updated</h1>
</cfoutput>

<!--- Page footer --->
<cfinclude template="footer.cfm">
```

This SQL statement updates the seven specified rows for the movie whose ID is the passed FORM.FilmID.

To test this update template, try executing template update1.cfm with different FilmID values (passed as URL parameters), and then submit your changes.

Introducing <cfupdate>

As you saw earlier in regards to inserting data, hard-coded SQL statements are neither flexible nor easy to maintain. ColdFusion provides a simpler way to update rows in database tables.

The <cfupdate> tag is similar to the <cfinsert> tag discussed earlier in this chapter. <cfupdate> requires just two attributes—the data source and the name of the table to update—and supports an optional formfields too.

- datasource—The name of the data source that contains the table to which the data is to be updated.

- tablename—The name of the destination table.

- formfields—An optional comma-separated list of fields to be updated. If this attribute isn't provided, all the fields in the submitted form are used.

When using <cfupdate>, ColdFusion automatically locates the row you want to update by looking at the table to ascertain its primary key. All you have to do is ensure that the primary key value is passed, as you did in Listing 14.9 using a hidden field.

The code in Listing 14.11 performs the same update as that in Listing 14.10, but it uses the <cfupdate> tag rather than the SQL UPDATE tag. Obviously, this code is more readable, reusable, and accommodating of form-field changes you might make in the future.

Listing 14.11   update3.cfm—Updating Data with the <cfupdate> Tag

```
<!---
Name:         update3.cfm
Author:       Ben Forta (ben@forta.com)
Description:  Table row update demo
Created:      01/01/2010
--->

<!--- Update movie --->
<cfupdate datasource="ows" tablename="FILMS">

<!--- Page header --->
<cfinclude template="header.cfm">

<!--- Feedback --->
<cfoutput>
<h1>Movie '#FORM.MovieTitle#' updated</h1>
</cfoutput>

<!--- Page footer --->
<cfinclude template="footer.cfm">
```

To use this code, you must change the <form> action attribute in update1.cfm so that it points to update3.cfm. Make this change, and try updating several movies.

`<cfupdate>` Versus SQL UPDATE

As with adding data, the choice to use `<cfupdate>` or SQL UPDATE is yours. The following guidelines as to when to use each option are similar as well:

- Whenever appropriate, use `<cfupdate>` to update data.

- If you find you need to update specific form fields—not all that were submitted—use the `<cfupdate>` tag with the `formfields` attribute.

- If `<cfupdate>` can't be used because you need a complex UPDATE statement or you are using fields that aren't form fields, use SQL UPDATE.

- If you ever need to update multiple (or all) rows in a table, you must use SQL UPDATE.

Deleting Data with ColdFusion

ColdFusion is very efficient at adding and updating data, but not at deleting it. DELETE is always a dangerous operation, and the ColdFusion developers didn't want to make it too easy to delete data by mistake.

To delete data in a ColdFusion template, you must use the SQL DELETE statement, as shown in Listing 14.12. The code first checks to ensure that a FilmID was passed; if the URL.FilmID field isn't present, the statement terminates. If a FilmID is passed, a `<cfquery>` is used to pass a SQL DELETE statement to the data source.

➔ See Chapter 6 for an explanation of the DELETE statement.

Listing 14.12 delete1.cfm—Deleting Table Data with SQL DELETE

```
<!---
Name:        delete1.cfm
Author:      Ben Forta (ben@forta.com)
Description: Table row delete demo
Created:     01/01/2010
--->

<!--- Check that FilmID was provided --->
<cfif NOT IsDefined("FilmID")>
 <h1>You did not specify the FilmID</h1>
<cfabort>
</cfif>

<!--- Delete a movie --->
<cfquery datasource="ows">
DELETE FROM Films
WHERE FilmID=#FilmID#
</cfquery>
```

Listing 14.12 (CONTINUED)

```
<!--- Page header --->
<cfinclude template="header.cfm">

<!--- Feedback --->
<h1>Movie deleted</h1>

<!--- Page footer --->
<cfinclude template="footer.cfm">
```

No `<cfdelete>` tag exists in ColdFusion. The only way to delete rows is to use a SQL DELETE.

NOTE

You will not be able to delete rows in the `Films` table that have related rows in other tables.

Reusing Forms

You can now add to as well as update and delete from your `Films` table. But what if you need to change the form? What if you needed to add a field, or change validation, or update colors? Any changes that need to be made to the Add form also must be made to the Update form.

With all the effort you have gone to in the past few chapters to prevent any duplication of effort, this seems counterproductive.

Indeed it is.

The big difference between an Add and an Update form is whether the fields are prefilled to show current values. Using ColdFusion conditional expressions, you can create a single form that can be used for both adding and updating data.

To do this, all you need is a way to conditionally include the `value` attribute in `<input>`. After all, look at the following two `<input>` statements:

```
<input type="text" name="MovieTitle">
<input type="text" name="MovieTitle" value="#MovieTitle#">
```

The first `<input>` is used for new data; there is no prefilled `value`. The second is for editing, and thus the field is populated with an initial `value`.

Therefore, it wouldn't be hard to create `<input>` fields with `<cfif>` statements embedded in them, conditionally including the `value`. Look at the following code:

```
<input type="text" name="MovieTitle"
 <cfif IsDefined("URL.FilmID")>
 value="#MovieTitle#"
 </CFIF>
>
```

This `<input>` field includes the `value` attribute only if the `FilmID` was passed (meaning that this is an edit operation as opposed to an add operation). Using this technique, a single form field can be used for both adds and edits.

This is perfectly valid code, and this technique is quite popular. The only problem with it is that the code can get very difficult to read. All those embedded <cfif> statements, one for every row, make the code quite complex. There is a better solution.

value can be an empty string, the attribute value="" is perfectly legal and valid. So why not *always* use value, but conditionally populate it? The best way to demonstrate this is to try it, so Listing 14.13 contains the code for edit1.cfm—a new dual-purpose form.

Listing 14.13   edit1.cfm—Combination Insert and Update Form

```
<!---
Name:        edit1.cfm
Author:      Ben Forta (ben@forta.com)
Description: Dual purpose form demo
Created:     01/01/2010
--->

<!--- Check that FilmID was provided --->
<!--- If yes, edit, else add --->
<cfset EditMode=IsDefined("URL.FilmID")>

<!--- If edit mode then get row to edit --->
<cfif EditMode>
 <!--- Get the film record --->
 <cfquery datasource="ows" name="film">
 SELECT FilmID, MovieTitle, PitchText,
        AmountBudgeted, RatingID,
        Summary, ImageName, DateInTheaters
 FROM Films
 WHERE FilmID=#URL.FilmID#
 </cfquery>

 <!--- Save to variables --->
 <cfset MovieTitle=Trim(film.MovieTitle)>
 <cfset PitchText=Trim(film.PitchText)>
 <cfset AmountBudgeted=Int(film.AmountBudgeted)>
 <cfset RatingID=film.RatingID>
 <cfset Summary=Trim(film.Summary)>
 <cfset ImageName=Trim(film.ImageName)>
 <cfset DateInTheaters=DateFormat(film.DateInTheaters, "MM/DD/YYYY")>

 <!--- Form text --->
 <cfset FormTitle="Update a Movie">
 <cfset ButtonText="Update">

<cfelse>

 <!--- Save to variables --->
 <cfset MovieTitle="">
 <cfset PitchText="">
 <cfset AmountBudgeted="">
 <cfset RatingID="">
 <cfset Summary="">
 <cfset ImageName="">
 <cfset DateInTheaters="">
```

Listing 14.13 (CONTINUED)

```
<!--- Form text --->
<cfset FormTitle="Add a Movie">
<cfset ButtonText="Insert">

</cfif>

<!--- Get ratings --->
<cfquery datasource="ows" name="ratings">
SELECT RatingID, Rating
FROM FilmsRatings
ORDER BY RatingID
</cfquery>

<!--- Page header --->
<cfinclude template="header.cfm">

<!--- Add/update movie form --->
<cfform action="edit2.cfm">

<cfif EditMode>
 <!--- Embed primary key as a hidden field --->
<cfinput type="hidden" name="FilmID"
           value="#Film.FilmID#">
</cfif>

<table align="center" bgcolor="orange">
 <tr>
  <th colspan="2">
   <cfoutput>
   <font size="+1">#FormTitle#</font>
   </cfoutput>
  </th>
 </tr>
 <tr>
  <td>
   Movie:
  </td>
  <td>
   <cfinput type="Text"
            name="MovieTitle"
            value="#MovieTitle#"
            message="MOVIE TITLE is required!"
            required="Yes"
            validateAt="onSubmit,onServer"
            size="50"
            maxlength="100">
  </td>
 </tr>
<tr>
  <td>
   Tag line:
  </td>
  <td>
   <cfinput type="Text"
            name="PitchText"
            value="#PitchText#"
```

Listing 14.13   (CONTINUED)

```
                     message="TAG LINE is required!"
                     required="Yes"
                     validateAt="onSubmit,onServer"
                     size="50"
                     maxlength="100">
    </td>
  </tr>
  <tr>
  <td>
    Rating:
  </td>
  <td>
    <!--- Ratings list --->
    <select name="RatingID">
     <cfoutput query="ratings">
      <option value="#RatingID#"
       <cfif ratings.RatingID IS VARIABLES.RatingID>
        selected
       </cfif>>
       #Rating#</option>
     </cfoutput>
    </select>
  </td>
  </tr>
  <tr>
  <td>
    Summary:
  </td>
  <td>
    <cfoutput>
    <textarea name="summary"
              cols="40"
              rows="5"
              wrap="virtual">#Summary#</textarea>
    </cfoutput>
  </td>
  </tr>
  <tr>
  <td>
    Budget:
  </td>
  <td>
    <cfinput type="Text"
             name="AmountBudgeted"
             value="#AmountBudgeted#"
             message="BUDGET must be a valid numeric amount!"
             required="NO"
             validate="integer"
             validateAt="onSubmit,onServer"
             size="10"
             maxlength="10">
  </td>
  </tr>
  <tr>
  <td>
    Release Date:
```

Listing 14.13 (CONTINUED)

```
    </td>
    <td>
     <cfinput type="Text"
              name="DateInTheaters"
              value="#DateInTheaters#"
              message="RELEASE DATE must be a valid date!"
              required="NO"
              validate="date"
              validateAt="onSubmit,onServer"
              size="10"
              maxlength="10">
    </td>
   </tr>
   <tr>
    <td>
     Image File:
    </td>
    <td>
     <cfinput type="Text"
              name="ImageName"
              value="#ImageName#"
              required="NO"
              size="20"
              maxlength="50">
    </td>
   </tr>
   <tr>
    <td colspan="2" align="center">
     <cfoutput>
     <input type="submit" value="#ButtonText#">
     </cfoutput>
    </td>
   </tr>
</table>

</cfform>

<!--- Page footer --->
<cfinclude template="footer.cfm">
```

The code first determines whether the form will be used for an Add or an Update. How can it know this? The difference between how the two are called is in the URL—whether FilmID is passed. The code <cfset EditMode=IsDefined("URL.FilmID")> created a variable named EditMode, which will be TRUE if URL.FilmID exists and FALSE if not. This variable can now be used as necessary throughout the page.

Next comes a <cfif> statement. If editing (EditMode is TRUE) then a <cfquery> is used to retrieve the current values. The fields retrieved by that <cfquery> are saved in local variables using multiple <cfset> tags. No <cfquery> is used if it is an insert operation, but <cfset> is used to create empty variables.

By the time the `</cfif>` has been reached, a set of variables has been created. They'll either contain values (from the `Films` table) or be empty. Either way, they're usable as `value` attributes in `<input>` and `<cfinput>` tags.

Look at the `<cfinput>` fields themselves. You'll notice that no conditional code exists within them, as it did before. Instead, every `<input>` tag has a `value` attribute, regardless of whether this is an insert or an update. The value in the `value` attribute is a ColdFusion variable—a variable that is set at the top of the template, not a database field.

The rest of the code in the template uses these variables, without needing any conditional processing. Even the page title and submit button text can be initialized in variables this way, so `<cfif>` tags aren't necessary for them, either.

The primary key, embedded as a hidden field, is necessary only if a movie is being edited, so the code to embed that field is enclosed within a `<cfif>` statement:

```
<cfif EditMode>
 <!--- Embed primary key as a hidden field --->
<cfinput type="hidden" name="FilmID"
        value="#Film.FilmID#">
</cfif>
```

Even the form header at the top of the page and the text of the submit button are populated using variables. This way, the `<form>` is completely reusable:

```
<INPUT TYPE="submit" VALUE="#ButtonText#">
```

This form is submitted to the same `action` page regardless of whether data is being added or updated. Therefore, the `action` page also must support both additions and updates. Listing 14.14 contains the new action template, edit2.cfm.

Listing 14.14   edit2.cfm—Combination Insert and Update Page

```
<!---
Name:       edit2.cfm
Author:     Ben Forta (ben@forta.com)
Description: Dual purpose form demo
Created:    01/01/2010
--->

<!--- Insert or update? --->
<cfset EditMode=IsDefined("FORM.FilmID")>

<cfif EditMode>
 <!--- Update movie --->
 <cfupdate datasource="ows" tablename="FILMS">
 <cfset action="updated">
<cfelse>
 <!--- Add movie --->
<cfinsert datasource="ows" tablename="FILMS">
 <cfset action="added">
</cfif>

<!--- Page header --->
```

Listing 14.14 (CONTINUED)

```
<cfinclude template="header.cfm">

<!--- Feedback --->
<cfoutput>
<h1>Movie #FORM.MovieTitle# #action#</h1>
</cfoutput>

<!--- Page footer --->
<cfinclude template="footer.cfm">
```

This code also first determines the `EditMode`, this time by checking for a `FORM` field named `FilmID` (the hidden form field). If `EditMode` is `TRUE`, a `<cfupdate>` is used to update the row; otherwise, a `<cfinsert>` is used to insert it. The same `<cfif>` statement also is used to set a variable that is used later in the page when providing user feedback.

It's clean, simple, and reusable.

Creating a Complete Application

Now that you've created add, modify, and delete templates, let's put them all together and create a finished application—and this time, one that is constructed properly, using a CFC for database access.

The following templates are a combination of all you have learned in this and previous chapters.

Listing 14.15 is the ColdFusion Component that provides all database access (to get, add, update, and delete movies).

→ ColdFusion Components were introduced in Chapter 11, "The Basics of Structured Development."

Listing 14.15 `movies.cfc`—Movie Database Access

```
<!---
Name:        movies.cfc
Author:      Ben Forta (ben@forta.com)
Description: Movie database access component
Created:     01/01/2010
--->

<cfcomponent hint="OWS movie database access">

 <!--- Set the datsources --->
 <cfset ds="ows">


 <!--- Get movie list --->
 <cffunction name="list"
             returntype="query"
             hint="List all movies">

  <cfquery datasource="#ds#"
           name="movies">
```

Listing 14.15 (CONTINUED)

```
      SELECT FilmID, MovieTitle
      FROM Films
      ORDER BY MovieTitle
      </cfquery>
      <cfreturn movies>

   </cffunction>


   <!--- Get details for a movie --->
   <cffunction name="get"
               returntype="query"
               hint="Get movie details">
    <cfargument name="FilmID"
                type="numeric"
                required="yes"
                hint="Movie ID">

    <cfquery datasource="#ds#"
             name="movie">
    SELECT FilmID, MovieTitle,
           PitchText, AmountBudgeted,
           RatingID, Summary,
           ImageName, DateInTheaters
    FROM Films
    WHERE FilmID=#ARGUMENTS.FilmID#
    </cfquery>
    <cfreturn movie>

   </cffunction>


   <!--- Add a movie --->
   <cffunction name="add"
               returntype="boolean"
               hint="Add a movie">

    <!--- Method arguments --->
    <cfargument name="MovieTitle"
                type="string"
                required="yes"
                hint="Movie title">
    <cfargument name="PitchText"
                type="string"
                required="yes"
                hint="Movie tag line">
    <cfargument name="AmountBudgeted"
                type="numeric"
                required="yes"
                hint="Projected movie budget">
    <cfargument name="RatingID"
                type="numeric"
                required="yes"
                hint="Movie rating ID">
    <cfargument name="Summary"
                type="string"
```

Listing 14.15 (CONTINUED)

```
                required="yes"
                hint="Movie summary">
    <cfargument name="DateInTheaters"
                type="date"
                required="yes"
                hint="Movie release date">
    <cfargument name="ImageName"
                type="string"
                required="no"
                default=""
                hint="Movie image file name">

    <!--- Insert movie --->
    <cfquery datasource="#ds#">
    INSERT INTO Films(MovieTitle,
                      PitchText,
                      AmountBudgeted,
                      RatingID,
                      Summary,
                      ImageName,
                      DateInTheaters)
    VALUES('#Trim(ARGUMENTS.MovieTitle)#',
           '#Trim(ARGUMENTS.PitchText)#',
           #ARGUMENTS.AmountBudgeted#,
           #ARGUMENTS.RatingID#,
           '#Trim(ARGUMENTS.Summary)#',
           '#Trim(ARGUMENTS.ImageName)#',
           #CreateODBCDate(ARGUMENTS.DateInTheaters)#)
    </cfquery>
    <cfreturn true>

</cffunction>


<!--- Update a movie --->
<cffunction name="update"
            returntype="boolean"
            hint="Update a movie">
    <!--- Method arguments --->
    <cfargument name="FilmID"
                type="numeric"
                required="yes"
                hint="Movie ID">
    <cfargument name="MovieTitle"
                type="string"
                required="yes"
                hint="Movie title">
    <cfargument name="PitchText"
                type="string"
                required="yes"
                hint="Movie tag line">
    <cfargument name="AmountBudgeted"
                type="numeric"
                required="yes"
                hint="Projected movie budget">
    <cfargument name="RatingID"
```

Listing 14.15   (CONTINUED)

```
                type="numeric"
                required="yes"
                hint="Movie rating ID">
<cfargument name="Summary"
            type="string"
            required="yes"
            hint="Movie summary">
<cfargument name="DateInTheaters"
            type="date"
            required="yes"
            hint="Movie release date">
<cfargument name="ImageName"
            type="string"
            required="no"
            default=""
            hint="Movie image file name">

<!--- Update movie --->
<cfquery datasource="#ds#">
UPDATE Films
SET MovieTitle='#Trim(ARGUMENTS.MovieTitle)#',
    PitchText='#Trim(ARGUMENTS.PitchText)#',
    AmountBudgeted=#ARGUMENTS.AmountBudgeted#,
    RatingID=#ARGUMENTS.RatingID#,
    Summary='#Trim(ARGUMENTS.Summary)#',
    ImageName='#Trim(ARGUMENTS.ImageName)#',
    DateInTheaters=#CreateODBCDate(ARGUMENTS.DateInTheaters)#
WHERE FilmID=#ARGUMENTS.FilmID#
</cfquery>
<cfreturn true>

</cffunction>


<!--- Delete a movie --->
<cffunction name="delete"
            returntype="boolean"
            hint="Delete a movie">
  <cfargument name="FilmID"
              type="numeric"
              required="yes"
              hint="Movie ID">

  <cfquery datasource="#ds#">
  DELETE FROM Films
  WHERE FilmID=#ARGUMENTS.FilmID#
  </cfquery>
  <cfreturn true>

</cffunction>


<!--- Get movie ratings --->
<cffunction name="getRatings"
            returntype="query"
```

Listing 14.15 (CONTINUED)

```
                    hint="Get movie ratings list">

    <!--- Get ratings --->
    <cfquery datasource="#ds#"
             name="ratings">
    SELECT RatingID, Rating
    FROM FilmsRatings
    ORDER BY RatingID
    </cfquery>
    <cfreturn ratings>

  </cffunction>


  </cfcomponent>
```

movies.cfc contains six methods: list lists all movies, get gets a specific movie, getRatings returns a list of all possible ratings, and add, update, and delete add, update, and delete movies respectively.

NOTE

Notice that the value passed to all **datasource** attributes in Listing 14.15 is a variable (which is set at the top of the page) so as to not hard-code the value multiple times.

Listing 14.16 is the main movie maintenance page. It displays the movies returned from the Cold-Fusion Component and provides links to edit and delete them (using the data drill-down techniques discussed in previous chapters); it also has a link to add a new movie. The administration page is shown in Figure 14.4.

Figure 14.4

The movie administration page is used to add, edit, and delete movies.

Listing 14.16 movies.cfm—Movie List Maintenance Page

```
<!---
Name:        movies.cfm
Author:      Ben Forta (ben@forta.com)
Description: Movie maintenance application
Created:     01/01/2010
--->

<!--- Get all movies --->
<cfinvoke component="movies"
          method="list"
          returnvariable="movies">

<!--- Page header --->
<cfinclude template="header.cfm">

<table align="center" bgcolor="orange">

 <!--- Loop through movies --->
<cfoutput query="movies">
  <tr>
   <!--- Movie name --->
   <td><strong>#MovieTitle#</strong></td>
   <!--- Edit link --->
   <td>
    [<a href="movie_edit.cfm?FilmID=#FilmID#">Edit</a>]
   </td>
   <!--- Delete link --->
   <td>
    [<a href="movie_delete.cfm?FilmID=#FilmID#">Delete</a>]
   </td>
  </tr>
</cfoutput>

 <tr>
  <td></td>
  <!--- Add movie link --->
  <td colspan="2" align="center">
   [<a href="movie_edit.cfm">Add</a>]
  </td>
 </tr>

</table>

<!--- Page footer --->
<cfinclude template="footer.cfm">
```

Listing 14.15 uses a <cfinvoke> to obtain the movie list, then provides two links for each movie: an edit link (that links to movie_edit.cfm passing the FilmID) and a delete link (movie_delete.cfm, also passing the FilmID). The add link at the bottom of the page also points to movie_edit.cfm but doesn't pass a FilmID (so the form will be used as an add form).

→ Dynamic links and data drill-down were covered in Chapter 12.

Listing 14.17 is essentially the same reusable add and update form you created earlier, but with another useful shortcut.

Listing 14.17 `movie_edit.cfm`—Movie Add and Update Form

```
<!---
Name:        movie_edit.cfm
Author:      Ben Forta (ben@forta.com)
Description: Dual purpose movie edit form
Created:     01/01/2010
--->

<!--- Check that FilmID was provided --->
<!--- If yes, edit, else add --->
<cfset EditMode=IsDefined("URL.FilmID")>

<!--- If edit mode then get row to edit --->
<cfif EditMode>

 <!--- Get the film record --->
 <cfinvoke component="movies"
           method="get"
           filmid="#URL.FilmID#"
           returnvariable="film">

 <!--- Save to variables --->
 <cfset MovieTitle=Trim(film.MovieTitle)>
 <cfset PitchText=Trim(film.PitchText)>
 <cfset AmountBudgeted=Int(film.AmountBudgeted)>
 <cfset RatingID=film.RatingID>
 <cfset Summary=Trim(film.Summary)>
 <cfset ImageName=Trim(film.ImageName)>
 <cfset DateInTheaters=DateFormat(film.DateInTheaters, "MM/DD/YYYY")>

 <!--- Form text --->
 <cfset FormTitle="Update a Movie">
 <cfset ButtonText="Update">

<cfelse>

 <!--- Save to variables --->
 <cfset MovieTitle="">
 <cfset PitchText="">
 <cfset AmountBudgeted="">
 <cfset RatingID="">
 <cfset Summary="">
 <cfset ImageName="">
 <cfset DateInTheaters="">

 <!--- Form text --->
 <cfset FormTitle="Add a Movie">
 <cfset ButtonText="Insert">

</cfif>

<!--- Get ratings --->
 <cfinvoke component="movies"
```

Listing 14.17 (CONTINUED)

```
            method="getRatings"
            returnvariable="ratings">

<!--- Page header --->
<cfinclude template="header.cfm">

<!--- Add/update movie form --->
<cfform action="movie_process.cfm">

<cfif EditMode>
 <!--- Embed primary key as a hidden field --->
 <cfoutput>
 <input type="hidden" name="FilmID" value="#Film.FilmID#">
 </cfoutput>
</cfif>

<table align="center" bgcolor="orange">
 <tr>
  <th colspan="2">
   <cfoutput>
   <font size="+1">#FormTitle#</font>
   </cfoutput>
  </th>
 </tr>
 <tr>
  <td>
   Movie:
  </td>
  <td>
   <cfinput type="Text"
            name="MovieTitle"
            value="#MovieTitle#"
            message="MOVIE TITLE is required!"
            required="Yes"
            validateAt="onSubmit,onServer"
            size="50"
            maxlength="100">
  </td>
 </tr>
 <tr>
  <td>
   Tag line:
  </td>
  <td>
   <cfinput type="Text"
            name="PitchText"
            value="#PitchText#"
            message="TAG LINE is required!"
            required="Yes"
            validateAt="onSubmit,onServer"
            size="50"
            maxlength="100">
  </td>
 </tr>
 <tr>
  <td>
```

Listing 14.17 (CONTINUED)

```
    Rating:
    </td>
    <td>
     <!--- Ratings list --->
     <cfselect name="RatingID"
               query="ratings"
               value="RatingID"
               display="Rating"
               selected="#VARIABLES.RatingID#">
     </cfselect>
    </td>
   </tr>
   <tr>
    <td>
    Summary:
    </td>
    <td>
     <cfoutput>
     <textarea name="summary"
               cols="40"
               rows="5"
               wrap="virtual">#Summary#</textarea>
     </cfoutput>
    </td>
   </tr>
   <tr>
    <td>
    Budget:
    </td>
    <td>
     <cfinput type="Text"
              name="AmountBudgeted"
              value="#AmountBudgeted#"
              message="BUDGET must be a valid numeric amount!"
              required="NO"
              validate="integer"
              validateAt="onSubmit,onServer"
              size="10"
              maxlength="10">
    </td>
   </tr>
   <tr>
    <td>
    Release Date:
    </td>
    <td>
     <cfinput type="Text"
              name="DateInTheaters"
              value="#DateInTheaters#"
              message="RELEASE DATE must be a valid date!"
              required="NO"
              validate="date"
              validateAt="onSubmit,onServer"
              size="10"
              maxlength="10">
    </td>
```

Listing 14.17 (CONTINUED)

```
   </tr>
   <tr>
    <td>
     Image File:
    </td>
    <td>
     <cfinput type="Text"
                name="ImageName"
                value="#ImageName#"
                required="NO"
                size="20"
                maxlength="50">
    </td>
   </tr>
   <tr>
    <td colspan="2" align="center">
     <cfoutput>
     <input type="submit" value="#ButtonText#">
     </cfoutput>
    </td>
   </tr>
  </table>

 </cfform>

 <!--- Page footer --->
 <cfinclude template="footer.cfm">
```

There are only three changes in Listing 14.17. All <cfquery> tags have been removed and replaced by <cfinvoke> tags (obtaining the data from movies.cfc). The action has been changed to point to a new file—movie_process.cfm. In addition, look at the RatingID field. It uses a new tag named <cfselect>. This tag, which can be used only within <cfform> and </cfform> tags, simplifies the creation of dynamic data-driven <select> controls. The code

```
<cfselect name="RatingID"
           query="ratings"
           value="RatingID"
           display="Rating"
           selected="#VARIABLES.RatingID#">
</cfselect>
```

is functionally the same as

```
<select name="RatingID">
 <cfoutput query="ratings">
  <option value="#RatingID#"
   <cfif ratings.RatingID IS VARIABLES.RatingID>
    selected
   </cfif>>
   #Rating#</option>
 </cfoutput>
</select>
```

Obviously, using <cfselect> is much cleaner and simpler. It creates a <select> control named RatingID that is populated with the ratings query, using the RatingID column as the value and displaying the Rating column. Whatever value is in the variable RatingID will be used to pre-select the selected option in the control.

Listing 14.18 calls the appropriate movies.cfc methods to add or update movies.

Listing 14.18 movie_process.cfm—Movie Insert and Update

```
<!---
Name:        movie_process.cfm
Author:      Ben Forta (ben@forta.com)
Description: Process edit page
Created:     01/01/2010
--->

<!--- Edit or update? --->
<cfif IsDefined("FORM.FilmID")>
 <cfset method="update">
<cfelse>
 <cfset method="add">
</cfif>

<!--- Do it --->
<cfinvoke component="movies"
          method="#method#">
 <!--- FilmID only if update method --->
 <cfif IsDefined("FORM.FilmID")>
  <cfinvokeargument name="FilmID"
                    value="#FORM.FilmID#">
 </cfif>
 <cfinvokeargument name="MovieTitle"
                   value="#Trim(FORM.MovieTitle)#">
 <cfinvokeargument name="PitchText"
                   value="#Trim(FORM.PitchText)#">
 <cfinvokeargument name="AmountBudgeted"
                   value="#Int(FORM.AmountBudgeted)#">
 <cfinvokeargument name="RatingID"
                   value="#Int(FORM.RatingID)#">
 <cfinvokeargument name="Summary"
                   value="#Trim(FORM.Summary)#">
 <cfinvokeargument name="ImageName"
                   value="#Trim(FORM.ImageName)#">
 <cfinvokeargument name="DateInTheaters"
                   value="#DateFormat(FORM.DateInTheaters)#">
</cfinvoke>

<!--- When done go back to movie list --->
<cflocation url="movies.cfm">
```

Listing 14.18 uses a <cfif> statement to determine which method to invoke (add or update). It then uses a <cfinvoke> tag set containing a <cfinvokeargument> for each argument.

TIP

<cfinvokeargument> tags may be included conditionally, as is the case here for the FilmID argument. This is an advantage of <cfinvokeargument> syntax over name=value syntax.

Listing 14.19 simply invokes the CFC `delete` method to delete a movie. The code in Listings 14.18 and 14.19 provide no user feedback at all. Instead, they return to the administration screen using the `<cflocation>` tag as soon as they finish processing the database changes. `<cflocation>` is used to switch from the current template being processed to any other URL, including another ColdFusion template. The following sample code instructs ColdFusion to switch to the `movies.cfm` template:

```
<cflocation URL="movies.cfm">
```

This way, the updated movie list is displayed, ready for further processing, as soon as any change is completed.

TIP

This example could be further enhanced by not making the action page determine which CFC method to invoke. Instead, you could have a single update method that (based on passed arguments) creates or updates a row as needed. This approach would be preferable.

Listing 14.19 `movie_delete.cfm`—Movie Delete Processing

```
<!---
Name:        movie_delete.cfm
Author:      Ben Forta (ben@forta.com)
Description: Delete a movie
Created:     01/01/2010
--->

<!--- Check that FilmID was provided --->
<cfif NOT IsDefined("FilmID")>
 <h1>You did not specify the FilmID</h1>
 <cfabort>
</cfif>

<!--- Delete a movie --->
<cfinvoke component="movies"
          method="delete"
          filmid="#URL.FilmID#">

<!--- When done go back to movie list --->
<cflocation url="movies.cfm">
```

And there you have it: a complete *n*-tier application featuring data display, edit and delete using data-drill down, and reusable data-driven add and edit forms—all in under 300 lines of code, including comments. Extremely powerful, and not complicated at all.

Beyond HTML Forms: ColdFusion-Powered Ajax

You've used HTML forms extensively in the past few chapters, and forms will undoubtedly play an important role in all of the applications you build. HTML forms are easy to create and work with, but they are also very limited and not overly capable.

For example, HTML form controls lack commonly needed controls such as date choosers and data grids. They lack any real form field validation, as discussed previously. They also are also essentially bound to the page request model of the Web: every change requires a roundtrip back to the server and a subsequent page refresh.

HTML forms leave much to be desired, and Web developers have acquired something of a love-hate relationship with forms, appreciating their simplicity but despising the lack of functionality that this simplicity causes.

To get around these problems and limitations, ColdFusion has constantly sought new and innovative technologies to include with the product for you to use. From Java applets to Adobe Flash controls to XForms abstractions, as new options become available, ColdFusion tries to take advantage of them.

ColdFusion 8 and 9 continue this pattern with powerful new HTML controls and with simplified Ajax support. This chapter explores these new options.

NOTE

Coverage of XForms and Adobe Flash forms are beyond the scope of this book and are thus not discussed in this chapter.

Using the Extended Controls

An example provides the best introduction to ColdFusion's extended form controls. In Chapter 14, "Using Forms to Add or Change Data," you created a series of forms to allow users to insert and update movie data in the `Films` table. One of those fields was a date field that required users to enter a valid movie release date.

Asking users to enter dates is always asking for trouble. Some users will enter digits for months and others will spell out or abbreviate months, some users will enter two-digit years and others will enter four-digit years, some users will enter hyphens as separators and others will use slashes—you get the idea. Rather than asking the user to enter a date manually, you really need a date control: a pop-up calendar that lets users browse months and click desired dates. But, as already noted, there is no date control in HTML forms.

Fortunately, there is one in `<cfform>`, and it does exactly what we want. To create a date field, all you need to do is use `<cfinput>` and change `type` to `type="datefield"`—it's that simple.

Listing 15.1 is an updated insert form (based on the one created in Chapter 14); Figure 15.1 shows the new form.

Figure 15.1

ColdFusion offers enhanced form controls, including a rich text editor and a date field.

Listing 15.1 insert1.cfm—New Movie Form

```
<!---
Name:        insert1.cfm
Author:      Ben Forta (ben@forta.com)
Description: Advanced HTML controls
Created:     01/01/2010
--->

<!--- Get ratings --->
```

Listing 15.1 (CONTINUED)

```coldfusion
<cfquery datasource="ows" name="ratings">
SELECT RatingID, Rating
FROM FilmsRatings
ORDER BY RatingID
</cfquery>

<!--- Page header --->
<cfinclude template="header.cfm">

<!--- New movie form --->
<cfform action="insert2.cfm">

<table align="center" bgcolor="orange">
 <tr>
  <th colspan="2">
   <font size="+1">Add a Movie</font>
  </th>
 </tr>
 <tr>
  <td>
   Movie:
  </td>
  <td>
   <cfinput type="Text"
            name="MovieTitle"
            message="MOVIE TITLE is required!"
            required="Yes"
            validateAt="onSubmit,onServer"
            size="50"
            maxlength="100">
  </td>
 </tr>
 <tr>
  <td>
   Tag line:
  </td>
  <td>
   <cfinput type="Text"
            name="PitchText"
            message="TAG LINE is required!"
            required="Yes"
            validateAt="onSubmit,onServer"
            size="50"
            maxlength="100">
  </td>
 </tr>
 <tr>
  <td>
   Rating:
  </td>
  <td>
   <!--- Ratings list --->
   <cfselect name="RatingID"
             query="ratings"
             display="Rating"
             value="RatingID" />
```

Listing 15.1 (CONTINUED)

```
     </td>
    </tr>
    <tr>
     <td>
      Summary:
     </td>
     <td>
      <cftextarea name="summary"
                  richtext="true"
                  toolbar="Basic"
                  height="150"
                  wrap="virtual" />
     </td>
    </tr>
    <tr>
     <td>
      Budget:
     </td>
     <td>
      <cfinput type="Text"
               name="AmountBudgeted"
               message="BUDGET must be a valid numeric amount!"
               required="NO"
               validate="integer"
               validateAt="onSubmit,onServer"
               size="10"
               maxlength="10">
     </td>
    </tr>
    <tr>
     <td>
      Release Date:
     </td>
     <td>
      <cfinput type="DateField"
               name="DateInTheaters"
               message="RELEASE DATE must be a valid date!"
               required="NO"
               validate="date"
               validateAt="onSubmit,onServer"
               size="10"
               maxlength="10">
     </td>
    </tr>
    <tr>
     <td>
      Image File:
     </td>
     <td>
      <cfinput type="Text"
               name="ImageName"
               required="NO"
               size="20"
               maxlength="50">
     </td>
    </tr>
```

Listing 15.1 (CONTINUED)

```
  <tr>
   <td colspan="2" align="center">
    <input type="submit" value="Insert">
   </td>
    </tr>
  </table>

</cfform>

<!--- Page footer --->
<cfinclude template="footer.cfm">
```

Most of Listing 15.1 should be self-explanatory by now. A `<cfquery>` is used to retrieve ratings to be used in a subsequent `<cfselect>` control, and `<cfform>` is used to create the actual form. The `DateInTheaters` field is now of type `type="datefield"`, which creates the nice pop-up date field seen in Figure 15.1.

I also stuck another goodie in the code without telling you. The `<cftextarea>` box is no longer a simple text control; it is now an actual editor that lets you highlight text to make it bold, and so on. To use this feature, all you need to do is add `richtext="true"` to the `<cftextarea>` tag.

The real beauty of these controls is that they work as-is—no plug-ins are needed, and they have no special browser requirements. All current browsers on all major operating systems are supported.

NOTE

The rich text control is highly configurable, providing full control over the toolbars and buttons as well as the color schemes (via skins). In this example, the `Basic` toolbar was used. The other built-in toolbar is `Default`, and it contains several rows of buttons (far more than we need here). You can also create custom toolbars if necessary. Consult the ColdFusion documentation for information on creating and modifying toolbars.

ColdFusion Extended Form Controls

You've seen examples of two of ColdFusion's extended form controls. But what other control types are supported? Table 15.1 lists the form controls along with their CFML syntax and usage notes (and notes those that support Ajax use, which will be described later in this chapter).

Table 15.1 Extended Forms Controls

CONTROL	SYNTAX	NOTES
Auto Suggest	`<cfinput type="text" autosuggest="">`	Supports simple and Ajax use
Button	`<cfinput type="button">`	Functions just like HTML `<input type="button">`
Check Box	`<cfinput type="checkbox">`	Functions just like HTML `<input type="checkbox">`
Data Grid	`<cfgrid>`	Supports simple and Ajax use
Date Field	`<cfinput type="datefield">`	Not supported in HTML

Table 15.1 (CONTINUED)

CONTROL	SYNTAX	NOTES
Hidden	`<cfinput type="hidden">`	Functions just like HTML `<input type="hidden">`
Password	`<cfinput type="password">`	Functions just like HTML `<input type="password">`
Select	`<cfselect>`	Supports simple and Ajax use
Submit	`<cfinput type="submit">`	Functions just like HTML `<input type="submit">`
Text	`<cfinput type="text">`	Functions just like HTML `<input type="text">`
Textarea	`<cftextarea>`	Functions just like HTML `<textarea>`
Tree	`<cftree>`	Supports simple and Ajax use
Rich Text	`<cftextarea richtext="true">`	

You've already seen examples of the date field and rich text editor; let's look at a few more controls.

The `<cfgrid>` control is used to create data grids: two-dimensional spreadsheet–type views of data as shown in Figure 15.2.

Figure 15.2

ColdFusion's data grid makes it easy to display multiple rows in a scrollable grid.

Listing 15.2 contains the code that created the grid shown in Figure 15.2.

Listing 15.2 `grid1.cfm`—Basic Data Grid

```
<!---
Name:       grid1.cfm
Author:     Ben Forta (ben@forta.com)
```

Listing 15.2 (CONTINUED)

```
Description: Basic data grid
Created:      01/01/2010
--->

<!--- Get movies --->
<cfinvoke component="movies"
          method="list"
          returnvariable="movies">

<!--- Page header --->
<cfinclude template="header.cfm">

<!--- Display grid --->
<cfform>
<cfgrid name="movieGrid"
        width="400"
        format="html"
        query="movies" />
</cfform>

<!--- Page footer --->
<cfinclude template="footer.cfm">
```

Listing 15.2 invokes the list method in movies.cfc to obtain a list of movies. It then creates a data grid using <cfgrid>, passing the query to it.

Listing 15.3 is the list method used to populate the grid.

Listing 15.3 List Method

```
<!--- Get movie list --->
 <cffunction name="list"
             returntype="query"
             hint="List all movies">

  <!--- Create local variables --->
  <cfset var movies="">

  <cfquery datasource="#ds#"
           name="movies">
  SELECT FilmID, MovieTitle, Summary, Rating
  FROM Films, FilmsRatings
  WHERE Films.RatingID=FilmsRatings.RatingID
  ORDER BY MovieTitle
  </cfquery>
  <cfreturn movies>

 </cffunction>
```

This is all it takes to populate a data grid. Data in the grid can be sorted by clicking column headers (click once to sort in ascending order and click again to sort in descending order), and columns can be resized and moved as needed.

By default, `<cfgrid>` displays all of the columns in the passed query, using the column names as the grid headers. This behavior can be changed by using the `<cfgridcolumn>` tag, as seen in Listing 15.4, which creates an updated data grid.

Listing 15.4 `grid2.cfm`—Controlling the Data Grid Display

```
<!---
Name:        grid2.cfm
Author:      Ben Forta (ben@forta.com)
Description: Controlling data grid display
Created:     01/01/2010
--->

<!--- Get movies --->
<cfinvoke component="movies"
          method="list"
          returnvariable="movies">

<!--- Page header --->
<cfinclude template="header.cfm">

<!--- Display grid --->
<cfform>
<cfgrid name="movieGrid"
        width="600"
        format="html"
        query="movies">
   <cfgridcolumn name="FilmID"
                 display="no">
   <cfgridcolumn name="MovieTitle"
                 header="Title"
                 width="200">
   <cfgridcolumn name="Rating"
                 header="Rating"
                 width="100">
   <cfgridcolumn name="Summary"
                 header="Summary"
                 width="400">
</cfgrid>
</cfform>

<!--- Page footer --->
<cfinclude template="footer.cfm">
```

The updated listing explicitly prevents the `FilmID` column from being displayed and then provides alternate headers and widths for the other three columns.

TIP

The `<cfgridcolumn>` attribute also can be used to control the order in which grid columns appear.

NOTE

Additional `<cfgridcolumn>` attributes enable control of fonts, colors, and much more.

Another useful control, one that does not exist in HTML itself, is the auto-suggest control. This is actually less a control and more a change to the way that text input controls usually work.

Imagine that you have a form that prompts the user to enter an address. There are lots of possible options for the `City` field, but if you have lots of city names already stored in your database tables, you can assist the user by providing a drop-down list of suggestions (which the user can select or just ignore). This type of control is called an auto-suggest control, and it usually pops up only if the user pauses, giving you the opportunity to suggest text options.

There is no auto-suggest control in HTML. Creating an auto-suggest control requires writing some pretty sophisticated JavaScript—unless you are using ColdFusion, that is, in which case you don't have to write any JavaScript at all.

To turn `<cfinput type="text">` into an auto-suggest control, all you need to do is provide the suggestions. For example, the following code creates an auto-suggest control:

```
<cfinput type="text"
         name="fruit"
         autosuggest="apple,banana,lemon,lime,mango,orange,pear">
```

If you were to save and run this code, you would see a regular text input control. But if you typed the letter *L* and paused, you'd see a pop-up box containing the two options that begin with the letter *L*.

Of course, the list need not be hard-coded. Listing 15.5 contains a complete auto-suggest example that creates the screen shown in Figure 15.3.

Figure 15.3

Auto-suggest lists can be hard-coded and populated programmatically.

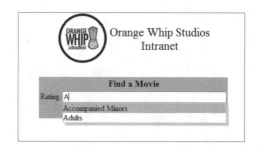

Listing 15.5 `autosuggest1.cfm`—Basic Auto-Suggest

```
<!---
Name:        autosuggest1.cfm
Author:      Ben Forta (ben@forta.com)
Description: Basic auto-suggest
Created:     01/01/2010
--->

<!--- Get ratings --->
<cfquery datasource="ows" name="ratings">
SELECT Rating
FROM FilmsRatings
ORDER BY Rating
</cfquery>
<!--- Convert to list --->
```

Listing 15.5 (CONTINUED)

```
<cfset list=ValueList(ratings.Rating)>

<!--- Page header --->
<cfinclude template="header.cfm">

<!--- Search form --->
<cfform>

<table align="center" bgcolor="orange">
 <tr>
  <th colspan="2">
   <font size="+1">Find a Movie</font>
  </th>
 </tr>
 <tr>
  <td>
   Rating:
  </td>
  <td>
   <cfinput type="Text"
            name="Rating"
            autosuggest="#list#"
            size="50"
            maxlength="100">
  </td>
 </tr>
 <tr>
  <td colspan="2" align="center">
   <input type="submit" value="Search">
  </td>
  </tr>
</table>

</cfform>

<!--- Page footer --->
<cfinclude template="footer.cfm">
```

The code in Listing 15.5 gets a list of ratings using `<cfquery>`. Auto-suggest values need to be passed as a comma-delimited list, and so a list is constructed using the `ValueList()` function, which takes the name of a query column and returns a comma-delimited list of all of the values in that column. That list is then passed to `<cfinput>` as `autosuggest="#list#"`.

NOTE

All of the controls discussed here use JavaScript internally and require that JavaScript be enabled in the browser. If you view the source code on the generated page, you'll see the JavaScript that is included and generated.

Working with Ajax

All of the controls used thus far have embedded data (queries, lists, and so on) inside of the controls themselves. That works in many situations, but consider the following scenarios.

What if your auto-suggest values are being populated by a table that contains thousands of entries? You don't want to load all of these entries into a list in the control itself. For starters, that will increase the page size significantly and seriously affect performance, but also, you don't want to show your user that many options. What you really want is no data at all in the auto-suggest control; when the user types some text and pauses, you want your application to send that text to ColdFusion, which then returns the relevant auto-suggest entries. And of course, you want this process to work without refreshing the page.

Or suppose that the data grid we created previously displayed all of the movies at once. This is fine here, because our table contains only 23 movies. But what if the database table had hundreds or even thousands of entries? You wouldn't want them all displayed at once. Instead, you to show a page of data at a time, allowing users to scroll back and forth as needed. And of course, this process too would have to work without refreshing the page.

Is this doable?

The answer is yes, and this is where Ajax comes into play. Ajax (which stands for Asynchronous JavaScript and XML) is not a product or a technology. Actually, it's not any single thing you can point to. Rather, it is a technique that combines DHTML and JavaScript with the capability of Web browsers to make asynchronous HTTP calls.

If that sounds obscure, don't worry. What it simply means is that JavaScript (the scripting language supported by just about every Web browser) has the capability to issue Web page requests under programmatic control—requests that don't actually update or refresh the screen. By coupling that capability with some clever JavaScript and DHTML, you can make Web browsers do some very interesting things, including addressing the scenarios just mentioned.

→ Ajax, and indeed ColdFusion's Ajax support, cannot be covered fully in one introductory chapter. In this chapter, you learn the basics; for more information, see Chapter 30, "Advanced ColdFusion-Powered Ajax," in *Adobe ColdFusion 9 Web Application Construction Kit, Volume 2: Application Development.*

Chapter 11, "The Basics of Structured Development," introduced ColdFusion Components (which we have been using ever since). Well, ColdFusion Components are the key to the way that ColdFusion's Ajax controls work. As just explained, Ajax controls make calls back to the server as needed, and in ColdFusion those calls are to CFCs.

Let's revisit the auto-suggest example, this time using an Ajax auto-suggest control. First we'll look at the CFC method needed to power the control. Listing 15.6 shows the code.

Listing 15.6 `lookupMovie` Method

```
<!--- Lookup used for auto suggest --->
<cffunction name="lookupMovie"
            access="remote"
            returntype="string"
            hint="Lookup method for Ajax auto-suggest">
  <cfargument name="search"
              type="any"
              required="false"
              default="">
```

Listing 15.6 (CONTINUED)

```
<!--- Define variables --->
<cfset var data="">

<!--- Do search --->
<cfquery datasource="#ds#" name="data">
SELECT MovieTitle
FROM Films
WHERE UCase(MovieTitle) LIKE UCase('#ARGUMENTS.search#%')
ORDER BY MovieTitle
</cfquery>

<!--- And return it --->
<cfreturn ValueList(data.MovieTitle)>
</cffunction>
```

Most of the code in Listing 15.6 is code you have seen before, but there are some very important points to note here. First, the method contains an attribute of access="remote". Usually, CFC methods can be invoked only by other ColdFusion code running on the same server, but a CFC method that needs to be invoked by a Web browser (as is the case with Ajax controls) needs to be explicitly granted that right, and that is what access="remote" does.

NOTE

Any CFC methods that include access="remote" can be invoked remotely, even by other users. Be very careful with the methods you expose, and pay attention to CFC security (discussed in Chapter 24, "Creating Advanced ColdFusion Components," in Volume 2).

The lookupMovie method accepts an argument—the string the user has entered thus far—uses that text in <cfquery>, and then returns a comma-delimited list containing the matches (the format required by the auto-suggest control).

Now let's look at the client-side code that uses a <cfinput> control that uses the lookupMovie method. Listing 15.7 contains the code, and the result is shown in Figure 15.4.

Figure 15.4

Ajax-powered auto-suggest controls retrieve their suggestions by making calls back to ColdFusion.

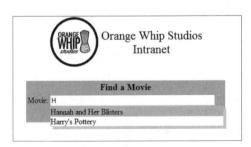

Listing 15.7 autosuggest2.cfm—Ajax Auto-Suggest

```
<!---
Name:        autosuggest2.cfm
Author:      Ben Forta (ben@forta.com)
Description: Ajax auto-suggest
Created:     01/01/2010
```

Listing 15.7 (CONTINUED)

```
--->

<!--- Page header --->
<cfinclude template="header.cfm">

<!--- Search form --->
<cfform>

<table align="center" bgcolor="orange">
 <tr>
  <th colspan="2">
   <font size="+1">Find a Movie</font>
  </th>
 </tr>
 <tr>
  <td>
   Movie:
  </td>
  <td>
   <cfinput type="Text"
            name="MovieTitle"
            autosuggest="cfc:movies.lookupMovie({cfautosuggestvalue})"
            size="50"
            maxlength="100">
  </td>
 </tr>
 <tr>
  <td colspan="2" align="center">
   <input type="submit" value="Search">
  </td>
  </tr>
</table>

</cfform>

<!--- Page footer --->
<cfinclude template="footer.cfm">
```

The first thing you'll notice about Listing 15.7 is that it contains no database query and no <cfinvoke> to invoke a CFC method. Instead, we've added this line to the <cfinput> control:

```
autosuggest="cfc:movies.lookupMovie({cfautosuggestvalue})"
```

Unlike the example in Listing 15.5, autosuggest does not contain a list. Rather, it points to a CFC, in this case a CFC named movies (in the current folder), and a method named lookupMovie (the method in Listing 15.6). The lookupMovie method expects a string to be passed to it, the text that the user has typed thus far. Rather than requiring you to write JavaScript to extract that value, Cold-Fusion allows you to refer to a special client-side variable named cfautosuggestvalue, which will automatically be replaced by the actual value entered by the user when the CFC method is invoked. The cfautosuggestvalue variable is enclosed within curly braces ({ and }), which ColdFusion uses to delimit expressions within client-side code (in much the same way as server-side code uses # to delimit expressions).

NOTE

A full path is not needed when pointing to a CFC in the current folder. To point to a CFC in another folder, a fully qualified path is needed.

Save the code and give it a try. Each time you type text and pause, an asynchronous call is made to the CFC method, data is retrieved and returned, and suggestions are made.

You've now created an Ajax-powered control without having to worry about what Ajax actually is and without having to write a single line of JavaScript.

And that's why we love ColdFusion!

Let's look at another, more complex example: a data grid that must handle any amount of data, supporting paging as needed.

Again, the solution has two parts: the CFC that actually accesses the data, and the client-side code that is bound to it. Let's look at the CFC method first; Listing 15.8 shows the code.

Listing 15.8 `lookupMovie` Method

```
<!--- Browse movies --->
 <cffunction name="browse"
             access="remote"
             returntype="struct"
             hint="Browse method for Ajax grid">
   <cfargument name="page"
               type="numeric"
               required="yes">
   <cfargument name="pageSize"
               type="numeric"
               required="yes">
   <cfargument name="gridsortcolumn"
               type="string"
               required="no"
               default="">
   <cfargument name="gridsortdir"
               type="string"
               required="no"
               default="">

   <!--- Local variables --->
   <cfset var movies="">

   <cfquery datasource="#ds#"
            name="movies">
   SELECT FilmID, MovieTitle, Summary, Rating
   FROM Films, FilmsRatings
   WHERE Films.RatingID=FilmsRatings.RatingID
    <cfif ARGUMENTS.gridsortcolumn NEQ ""
        and ARGUMENTS.gridsortdir NEQ "">
      ORDER BY #ARGUMENTS.gridsortcolumn# #ARGUMENTS.gridsortdir#
    </cfif>
   </cfquery>

   <!--- And return it as a grid structure --->
```

Listing 15.8 (CONTINUED)

```
        <cfreturn QueryConvertForGrid(movies,
                                      ARGUMENTS.page,
                                      ARGUMENTS.pageSize)>
    </cffunction>
```

Listing 15.8 contains a method named browse that is used to browse through rows in a table. The browse method returns data, one page at a time, and so it has to know the page that is requested as well as the number of rows per page. That way, if there are 10 rows per page and page 3 is requested, browse will know to return rows 21 to 30, and so on. These values must be passed by the client with each request, and indeed they are the first two arguments in this method. In addition, as mentioned previously, users can sort data grid contents by clicking column headers, and so the current sort column and direction are also passed by the client (if the user sorted data).

The method then uses <cfquery> to retrieve the data, optionally appending a SQL ORDER BY clause if the user sorted data.

Finally, the ColdFusion QueryConvertForGrid() function extracts the data for the desired page and formats it as needed by <cfgrid>, and the results are returned.

The client-side code creates the <cfgrid> control that uses the browse method. Listing 15.9 contains the code, and the result is shown in Figure 15.5.

Figure 15.5

An Ajax-powered data grid supports record paging as well as on-demand sorting.

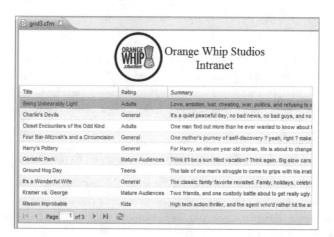

Listing 15.9 grid3.cfm—Ajax Data Grid

```
<!---
Name:        grid3.cfm
Author:      Ben Forta (ben@forta.com)
Description: Ajax data grid
Created:     01/01/2010
--->

<!--- Page header --->
<cfinclude template="header.cfm">
```

Listing 15.9 (CONTINUED)

```
<!--- Display grid --->
<cfform>
<cfgrid name="movieGrid"
        width="600"
        format="html"
        pagesize="10"
        striperows="yes"
        bind="cfc:movies.browse({cfgridpage},
                                {cfgridpagesize},
                                {cfgridsortcolumn},
                                {cfgridsortdirection})">
    <cfgridcolumn name="FilmID"
                  display="no">
    <cfgridcolumn name="MovieTitle"
                  header="Title"
                  width="200">
    <cfgridcolumn name="Rating"
                  header="Rating"
                  width="100">
    <cfgridcolumn name="Summary"
                  header="Summary"
                  width="400">
</cfgrid>
</cfform>

<!--- Page footer --->
<cfinclude template="footer.cfm">
```

This `<cfgrid>` control is similar to the one in Listing 15.4. The big change is that the `query` attribute (which passes an actual query) has been replaced by a new `bind` attribute. The `bind` attribute points to a CFC method, using the same syntax as in the auto-suggest example previously. As already explained, the CFC method expects up to four arguments (the first two, current page and size, are required, and the last two, sort column and direction, are optional). Again, ColdFusion provides special variables that can be used in place of actual values: `{cfgridpage}` is replaced by the current page, `{cfgridpagesize}` is replaced by the value passed to the `pagesize` attribute, and so on.

All you need to do is save and run the code. To display the first page of data, JavaScript in the Web browser invokes the CFC method, obtaining the first set of rows. Then, as you browse from page to page or as you sort and resort data, that CFC method is called asynchronously, in the background, and the grid is updated.

NOTE

The `<cfgrid>` control supports data editing too, but that function is not covered in this chapter.

Using Bindings

You have already seen examples of bindings: The Ajax-powered auto-suggest control and data grids both used bindings to refer to ColdFusion Component methods on the server.

Bindings can also be used on the client side, allowing one control to refer to, and interact with, other controls. Let's look at some basic examples.

➜ For full coverage of ColdFusion Ajax bindings, refer to Chapter 30.

We'll start with yet another data grid, but one with an interesting twist. As shown in Figure 15.6, this new data grid has a `<textarea>` box alongside it, so that when a movie is selected in the grid, the detailed summary is displayed in the box on the right. This type of user interface obviously requires interaction between controls, and thus it requires bindings.

Figure 15.6

Bindings allow controls to interact with other controls.

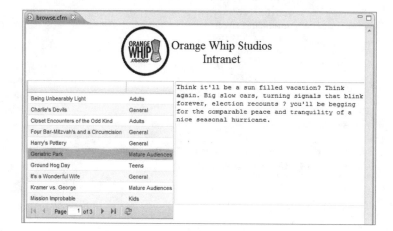

The CFC method that powers this new data grid is the same as the one used previously, so we won't revisit it here. But the client-side code, shown in Listing 15.10, warrants a closer look.

Listing 15.10 browse.cfm—Ajax Data Grid

```
<!---
Name:        browse.cfm
Author:      Ben Forta (ben@forta.com)
Description: Demonstrate using bindings
Created:     01/01/2010
--->

<!--- Page header --->
<cfinclude template="header.cfm">

<!--- Display --->
<cfform>

<table>
<tr valign="top">

<!--- The grid --->
<td>
<cfgrid name="movieGrid"
        width="300"
        format="html"
```

Listing 15.10 (CONTINUED)

```
                pagesize="10"
                striperows="yes"
                bind="cfc:movies.browse({cfgridpage},
                                        {cfgridpagesize},
                                        {cfgridsortcolumn},
                                        {cfgridsortdirection})">
        <cfgridcolumn name="FilmID"
                      display="no">
        <cfgridcolumn name="MovieTitle"
                      header="Title"
                      width="200">
        <cfgridcolumn name="Rating"
                      header="Rating"
                      width="100">
        <cfgridcolumn name="Summary"
                      display="no">
    </cfgrid>
    </td>

    <!--- Summary box --->
    <td>
    <cftextarea name="summary" rows="15"  cols="50"
                bind="{movieGrid.summary}" />
    </td>

    </tr>
    </table>
    </cfform>

    <!--- Page footer --->
    <cfinclude template="footer.cfm">
```

Aside from some table tags and control sizing, most of Listing 15.8 is used unchanged. The big change is the following code:

```
<cftextarea name="summary" rows="15"  cols="50"
            bind="{movieGrid.summary}" />
```

Here, a `<cftextarea>` area is created and named, and its size specified. Then `bind` is used to connect `<cftextarea>` to `movieGrid.summary` (the summary column in `movieGrid`, the data grid). This way, whenever the selection in the `movieGrid` data grid changes, the value in `<cftextarea>` is updated automatically.

Let's look at one final example: a more complex use of bindings. We've used `<select>` controls several times, and those controls have typically been populated with data retrieved from a database.

But what if you want multiple related `<select>` controls? What if you want a `<select>` control that lists all of the movie ratings and then another `<select>` control that lists the movies for whatever rating was selected in the first control? Obviously this scenario requires a way to make calls to ColdFusion to obtain the ratings initially and then a way to obtain a new list of movies whenever the rating changes. An example of the desired results is shown in Figure 15.7. How can we achieve these results?

Figure 15.7

Bindings can be used to trigger asynchronous calls to ColdFusion as needed.

Well, if you have not figured it out yourself, the answer is to use bindings and Ajax-type asynchronous calls to ColdFusion Components.

We need two methods for this example: one to populate each of the `<select>` controls. Let's look at the CFC methods, shown in Listing 15.11, first.

Listing 15.11 `getRatings` and `getFilms` Methods

```
<!--- Get array of ratings types --->
<cffunction name="getRatings"
            access="remote"
            returnType="query"
            hint="Get ratings for Ajax SELECT">
  <!--- Define variables --->
  <cfset var data="">

  <!--- Get data --->
  <cfquery name="data" datasource="#ds#">
  SELECT RatingID, Trim(Rating) AS Rating   FROM FilmsRatings
  ORDER BY Rating
  </cfquery>

  <!--- And return it --->
  <cfreturn data>
</cffunction>


<!--- Get films by rating --->
<cffunction name="getFilms"
            access="remote"
            returnType="query"
            hint="Get films by rating for Ajax SELECT">
  <cfargument name="RatingID"
              type="numeric"
              required="true">

  <!--- Define variables --->
  <cfset var data="">

  <!--- Get data --->
  <cfquery name="data" datasource="#ds#">
  SELECT FilmID, Trim(MovieTitle) AS MovieTitle   FROM Films
  WHERE RatingID = #ARGUMENTS.RatingID#
```

Listing 15.11 (CONTINUED)

```
    ORDER BY MovieTitle
  </cfquery>


  <!--- And return it --->
  <cfreturn data>
</cffunction>
```

As before, both methods return queries, and both are access="remote". The getRatings method does not need to accept any arguments; it simply obtains the list of ratings. The getFilms method accepts a single argument, RatingID, and then retrieves just the movies that match that rating, which are then returned. The SQL statements in both methods use a SQL Trim() function to get rid of any trailing spaces (as these could distort the display within Ajax controls).

Simple enough. But what about the client side? The code is in Listing 15.12.

Listing 15.12 selects.cfm—Related SELECT Controls

```
<!---
Name:        selects.cfm
Author:      Ben Forta (ben@forta.com)
Description: Related SELECT controls
Created:     01/01/2010
--->

<!--- Page header --->
<cfinclude template="header.cfm">

<!--- Search form --->
<cfform>

<table align="center" bgcolor="orange">
 <tr>
  <th colspan="2">
   <font size="+1">Find a Movie</font>
  </th>
 </tr>
 <tr>
  <td>
   Rating:<br>
   <cfselect name="RatingID"
             bind="cfc:movies.getRatings()"
             display="Rating"
             value="RatingID"
             bindonload="true" />
  </td>
  <td>
   Movie:<br>
   <cfselect name="FilmID"
             bind="cfc:movies.getFilms({RatingID})"
             display="MovieTitle"
             value="FilmID" />
  </td>
 </tr>
```

Listing 15.12 (CONTINUED)

```
  <tr>
   <td colspan="2" align="center">
    <input type="submit" value="Search">
   </td>
    </tr>
</table>

</cfform>


<!--- Page footer --->
<cfinclude template="footer.cfm">
```

The code in Listing 15.12 contains two <cfselect> controls, both of which have a bind attribute connecting them to our two CFC methods. But there are two important differences between the controls.

The first <cfselect> control, RatingID, is simply bound to the getRatings method, and no arguments are passed (none are needed). However, getRatings would never be called because no event would force that call (unlike with the data grid used previously, which automatically requests the first page, <cfselect> bindings occur when something triggers them). This is why bindonload="true" is added; it tells the JavaScript code to trigger a server call as soon as the control is loaded, and that way the first <cfselect> control is automatically populated and ready for use. As the asynchronous server call returns a query, display and value are used to specify the columns to be used for the generated <option> tags.

The second <cfselect> control, FilmID, is bound to the getFilms method, which requires that a RatingID argument be passed to it. Thus, {RatingID} (the name of the first <cfselect> control) is passed as an argument to getFilms, and {RatingID} is replaced by the actual RatingID value when the call is made. This way, whenever the value in RatingID (the first <cfselect> control) changes, the binding on the second <cfselect> control is fired, and the list is updated—clean and simple.

And there you have it: extensions to HTML form controls that you can use as needed, and simple yet powerful Ajax functionality when that is called for.

Graphing, Printing, and Reporting

Many ColdFusion applications involve some type of data reporting. If you're building an online store, for instance, you'll want to generate printable invoices or create a series of report-style pages that show the number of products sold per month. If you're building a community site, you might create a page that shows how many people log on during which parts of the day, or run a report of daily usage. Or, if you're building a Web site for a movie studio (ahem), you might create reports that show the expenses to date for each film, and which films are in danger of going over budget.

It'd be easy to imagine how each of these pages would turn out, if you could only use the skills you have already learned in this book. The pages would be easy to create with various uses of the `<cfquery>` and `<cfoutput>` tags, and they could be packed with useful information. You might even come up with some really attractive, creative uses of HTML tables to make the information easier to digest.

As the saying goes, a picture is often as good as a thousand words—or a thousand totals or subtotals. ColdFusion provides exciting and revolutionary features that let you dynamically create charts and graphs, printable documents, and complete reports that can be used to report on whatever data you want.

Generating Graphs

We'll start with an overview of the charting features included in ColdFusion. ColdFusion comes with a series of tags that will allow you to

- Create many different types of graphs, including pie charts, bar graphs, line graphs, and scatter charts.

- Format your graphs options that control fonts, colors, labels, and more.

- Display the graphs on any ColdFusion page as JPEG images, PNG images, or interactive Flash charts.

- Allow users to drill down on data shown in your charts. For instance, you could have people click the wedges in a pie chart, revealing the data represented in that wedge.

- Combine several different charts, displaying them together on the page. For instance, you might create a scatter chart that shows individual purchases over time, and then add a line chart on top of it that shows users' average spending.

- Save the charts to the server's drive for later use.

Building Simple Charts

Now that you have an idea of what you can do with ColdFusion's charting features, let's get started with some basic examples. Most of the time, you will create charts with just two CFML tags, `<cfchart>` and `<cfchartseries>`.

Introducing `<cfchart>` and `<cfchartseries>`

To display a chart on a ColdFusion page, you use the `<cfchart>` tag. This tag controls the height, width, and formatting of your chart, but it doesn't display anything. Within the `<cfchart>` tag, you use the `<cfchartseries>` tag, which determines the type of chart (like bar or pie) and the actual data to show on the chart.

NOTE

Actually, you will occasionally want to place multiple `<cfchartseries>` tags within a `<cfchart>` tag. See "Combining Multiple Chart Series" later in this chapter.

Table 16.1 shows the most important attributes for the `<cfchart>` tag, and Table 16.2 shows the most important attributes for `<cfchartseries>`.

Table 16.1 Basic `<cfchart>` Tag Syntax

ATTRIBUTE	DESCRIPTION
chartwidth	Optional. The width of the chart, in pixels. The default is 320.
chartheight	Optional. The height of the chart, in pixels. The default is 240.
xaxistitle	Optional. The text to display along the chart's x-axis.
yaxistitle	Optional. The text to display along the chart's y-axis.
url	Optional. The URL of a page to send the user to when various sections of the chart are clicked. You can pass variables in the URL so you know what part of the chart the user clicked. See "Drilling Down from Charts" later in this chapter.
format	Optional. The type of image format in which the chart should be created. The valid choices are flash (the default), jpg, and png.
seriesplacement	Optional. For charts that have more than one data series, you can use this attribute—cluster, stacked, percent, or default—to control how the series are combined visually. Use cluster if the data series represent related pieces of information that should be presented next to one another, rather than added together visually. Use stacked or percent if the data series represent values that should be added up to a single whole value for each item you're plotting. See "Combining Multiple Chart Series" later in this chapter.

NOTE

Because these tags have a large number of attributes (more than 40 in all), we are introducing only the most important attributes in these tables. Others are introduced later in this chapter.

Table 16.2 Basic <cfchartseries> Syntax

ATTRIBUTE	DESCRIPTION
type	Required. The type of chart to create. Usually, you will set this to either bar, line, area, or pie. Other chart types are cone, curve, cylinder, scatter, step, and pyramid. The ColdFusion documentation includes some nice pictures of these more unusual types of graphs.
query	Optional. The name of a query that contains data to chart. If you don't provide a query attribute, you will need to provide <cfchartdata> tags to tell ColdFusion the data to display in the chart.
valuecolum	Required if a query is provided. The name of the column that contains the actual value (the number to represent graphically) for each data point on the chart.
itemcolum	Required if a query is provided. The name of the column that contains labels for each data point on the chart.

NOTE

In this chapter, you will often see the term data point. Data points are the actual pieces of data that are displayed on a chart. If you're creating a pie chart, the data points are the slices of the pie. In a bar chart, the data points are the bars. In a line or scatter chart, the data points are the individual points that have been plotted on the graph.

NOTE

You don't have to have a query object to create a chart. You can also create data points manually using the <cfchartdata> tag. See "Plotting Individual Points with <cfchartdata>" later in this chapter.

Creating Your First Chart

Listing 16.1 shows how to use <cfchart> and <cfchartseries> to create a simple bar chart. The resulting chart is shown in Figure 16.1. As you can see, it doesn't take much code to produce a reasonably helpful bar chart. Anyone can glance at this chart and instantly understand which films cost more than the average, and by how much.

Listing 16.1 Chart1.cfm—Creating a Simple Bar Chart from Query Data

```
<!---
Name:        Chart1.cfm
Author:      Ben Forta
Description: Basic bar chart
Created:     01/01/2010
--->

<!--- Get information from the database --->
<cfinvoke component="ChartData"
          method="GetBudgetData"
```

Listing 16.1 (CONTINUED)

```
            returnvariable="ChartQuery"
            maxrows="10">

<html>
<head>
<title>Chart: Film Budgets</title>
</head>

<body>
<h2>Chart: Film Budgets</h2>

<!--- This defines the size and appearance of the chart --->
<cfchart chartwidth="750"
         chartheight="500"
         yaxistitle="Budget">

  <!--- within the chart --->
  <cfchartseries type="bar"
                 query="chartquery"
                 valuecolumn="amountbudgeted"
                 itemcolumn="movietitle">

</cfchart>

</body>
</html>
```

Figure 16.1

It's easy to create simple charts with <cfchart> and <cfchartdata>.

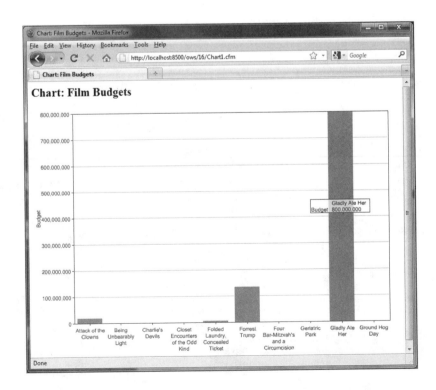

First, an ordinary <cfinvoke> tag is used to select invoke a CFC method that returns film and budget information from the database. Then a <cfchart> tag is used to establish the size of the chart, and to specify that the word Budget appear along the y-axis (that is, at the bottom of the chart). Finally, within the <cfchart> block, a <cfchartseries> tag is used to create a bar chart. ColdFusion is instructed to chart the information in the ChartQuery record set, plotting the data in the AmountBudgeted column and using the MovieTitle column to provide a label for each piece of information.

NOTE

For this example and the next few listings, we are using maxrows="10" (passed to the <cfquery> tag) to limit the number of films displayed in the chart to ten. This keeps the pictures of the graphs simple while you're learning how to use the charting tags. Just eliminate the maxrows attribute to see all films displayed in the chart.

The charts created here are Adobe Flash charts, as that is the default chart format generated by ColdFusion. Charts may also be generated as static images (in JPEG and PNG formats), although static charts aren't as functional or feature rich.

TIP

Data is presented in the chart in the order in which it's retrieved from the database. To change the order, just sort the query differently using the appropriate SQL ORDER BY clause.

Changing the Chart Type

The first chart we created was a bar chart. It's easy to change your code so that it displays a different kind of graph. Just change the type attribute of the <cfchartseries> tag. Figure 16.2 shows the pie chart created by the Chart2.cfm, the code for which is shown in Listing 16.2. The differences are that type="Pie" is used in the <cfchartseries> tag.

Listing 16.2 Chart2.cfm—Creating a Simple Pie Chart from Query Data

```
<!---
Name:        Chart2.cfm
Author:      Ben Forta
Description: Basic pie chart
Created:     01/01/2010
--->

<!--- Get information from the database --->
<cfinvoke component="ChartData"
          method="GetBudgetData"
          returnvariable="ChartQuery"
          maxrows="10">

<html>
<head>
<title>Chart: Film Budgets</title>
</head>

<body>
<h2>Chart: Film Budgets</h2>
```

Listing 16.2 (CONTINUED)

```
<!--- This defines the size and appearance of the chart --->
<cfchart chartwidth="750"
         chartheight="500"
         yaxistitle="Budget">

<!--- within the chart --->
 <cfchartseries type="pie"
                query="chartquery"
                valuecolumn="amountbudgeted"
                itemcolumn="movietitle">

</cfchart>

</body>
</html>
```

Figure 16.2

Changing the chart type is simply a matter of changing the type attribute.

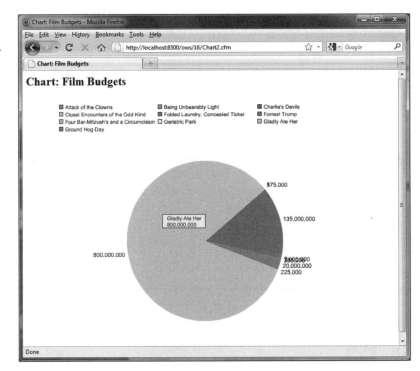

Formatting Your Charts

Now that you understand the basics of how to produce simple charts, let's learn some formatting options to make your charts look better and more closely meet your users' needs. In general, your goal should be to make the charts as easy on the eyes as possible—it helps people concentrate on the data.

Adding Depth with 3D Charts

One of the easiest ways to make a basic chart look more sophisticated is to give it a 3D look. Table 16.3 shows the `<cfchart>` options available for adding a 3D effect to your charts. Get out the red-and-blue glasses!

NOTE

Whether the 3D effect makes a chart easier to read depends on the situation. It tends to look nice in simple creations, especially bar charts with relatively few data points. Once a chart displays many data points, the 3D effect becomes distracting.

NOTE

The `xoffset` and `yoffset` attributes have no discernible effect on pie charts. You can make a pie chart display with a 3D appearance using `show3d="Yes"`, but you can't control the offsets.

Listing 16.3 shows how to produce a 3D graph by adding these attributes to the code from Listing 16.1. The `xoffset` and `yoffset` have been tweaked to make the bars look like they are being viewed from the top a bit more than from the side. The results are shown in Figure 16.3.

Figure 16.3

Add 3D chart effects to better display chart details.

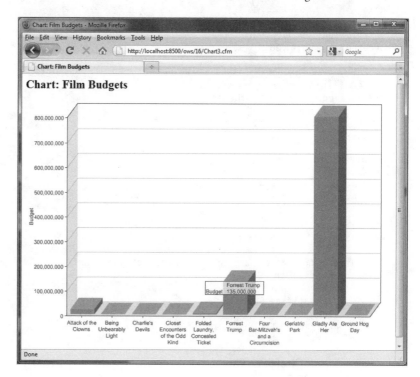

Table 16.3 `<cfchart>` Options for a 3D Effect

ATTRIBUTE	DESCRIPTION
show3d	Whether to show the chart with a 3D effect. The default is No.
xoffset	The amount that the chart should be rotated on the x-axis. In other words, this controls to what extent the chart appears to be viewed from the side. You can use a value anywhere from -1 to 1, but in general you will want to experiment with low, positive numbers (between .01 and .3) for best results. A value of 0 means no 3D effect horizontally. The default is .1.
yoffset	Similarly, the amount that the chart should be turned around its y-axis. This controls the extent the chart seems to be viewed from the top. Again, you will probably want to experiment with low, positive numbers (between .01 and .3) for best results. A value of 0 means no 3D effect vertically. The default is .1.

Listing 16.3 `Chart3.cfm`—Adding a 3D Appearance

```
<!---
Name:        Chart3.cfm
Author:      Ben Forta
Description: 3D bar chart
Created:     01/01/2010
--->

<!--- Get information from the database --->
<cfinvoke component="ChartData"
          method="GetBudgetData"
          returnvariable="ChartQuery"
          maxrows="10">

<html>
<head>
<title>Chart: Film Budgets</title>
</head>

<body>
<h2>Chart: Film Budgets</h2>

<!--- This defines the size and appearance of the chart --->
<cfchart chartwidth="750"
         chartheight="500"
         yaxistitle="Budget"
         show3d="yes"
         xoffset=".03"
         yoffset=".06">

  <!--- within the chart --->
  <cfchartseries type="bar"
                 query="chartquery"
                 valuecolumn="amountbudgeted"
                 itemcolumn="movietitle">

</cfchart>

</body>
</html>
```

Controlling Fonts and Colors

ColdFusion provides a number of formatting attributes that you can use to control fonts, colors, and borders. Some of the attributes are applied at the `<cfchart>` level and others at the `<cfchartseries>` level. The full list of attributes and their values is too long to include here, so please refer to the ColdFusion documentation.

NOTE

All of the attributes that control color can accept Web-style hexadecimal color values, such as `FFFFFF` for white or `0000FF` for blue. In addition, any of the following named colors can be used: `Aqua`, `Black`, `Blue`, `Fuchsia`, `Gray`, `Green`, `Lime`, `Maroon`, `Navy`, `Olive`, `Purple`, `Red`, `Silver`, `Teal`, `White`, and `Yellow`.

Listing 16.4 and Figure 16.4 show how some of the formatting attributes can be combined to improve the appearance of the bar charts you have seen so far.

Figure 16.4

The ColdFusion charting tags provide extensive control over chart formatting.

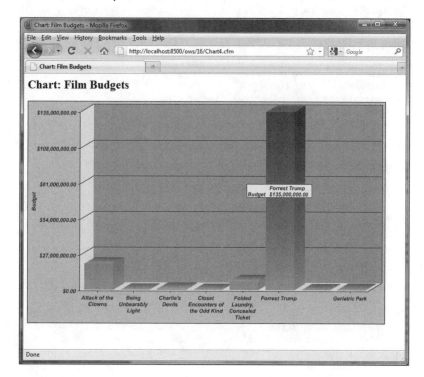

Controlling Grid Lines and Axis Labels

One of the most important aspects of nearly any chart are the numbers and labels that surround the actual graphic on the x- and y-axes. The graphic itself is what lends the chart its ability to convey a message visually, but it's the numbers surrounding the graphic that give it a context. ColdFusion provides you with a number of options for controlling the *scale* of each axis (that is, the distance between the highest and lowest values that could be plotted on the chart), and for controlling how many different numbers are actually displayed along the axes.

NOTE

You can't adjust the scale in such a way that it would obscure or chop off any of the actual data being shown in the chart. If your `scalefrom` value is higher than the lowest data point on the graph, ColdFusion will use the data point's value instead. For instance, if the lowest budget being plotted in one of the budget chart examples is $34,000 and you provide `scalefrom="50000"`, Cold-Fusion will start the scale at $34,000. The inverse is also true; if you provide a `scaleto` value that is lower than the highest data point, that point's value will be used instead.

Listing 16.4 shows how formatting, axis, and grid line options can be added to a chart to give it more appeal, and the axis labels have been formatted as currency (Figure 16.4). You can't see the colors in this book, but different shades of light blue have been used for the data background and the overall chart background. The text is in a dark navy type, and the bars of the chart themselves have a green gradient. Also note that the number of grid lines (that is, the number of numbered tick marks along the horizontal axis) has been set to 6 with the `gridlines` attribute. This means that there will be five tick marks (in addition to the first one), evenly distributed across the range.

Listing 16.4 `Chart4.cfm`—Add Formatting, Grid Line, and Axis Options

```
<!---
Name:        Chart4.cfm
Author:      Ben Forta
Description: Extensive chart formatting
Created:     01/01/2010
--->

<!--- Get information from the database --->
<cfinvoke component="ChartData"
          method="GetBudgetData"
          returnvariable="ChartQuery"
          maxrows="10">

<html>
<head>
<title>Chart: Film Budgets</title>
</head>

<body>
<h2>Chart: Film Budgets</h2>

<!--- This defines the size and appearance of the chart --->
<cfchart chartwidth="750"
         chartheight="450"
         yaxistitle="Budget"
         <!--- 3D appearance --->
         show3d="yes"
         xoffset=".04"
         yoffset=".04"
         <!--- Fonts and colors --->
         showborder="yes"
         foregroundcolor="003366"
         backgroundcolor="99dddd"
         databackgroundcolor="66bbbb"
         tipbgcolor="ffff99"
         fontsize="11"
         fontbold="yes"
```

Listing 16.4 (CONTINUED)

```
                fontitalic="yes"
                <!--- gridlines and axis labels --->
                scalefrom="0"
                scaleto="1500000"
                gridlines="6"
                showygridlines="yes"
                labelformat="currency">

        <!--- within the chart --->
        <cfchartseries type="bar"
                    seriescolor="green"
                    serieslabel="Budget Details:"
                    query="chartquery"
                    valuecolumn="amountbudgeted"
                    itemcolumn="movietitle"
                    paintstyle="light">

    </cfchart>

    </body>
    </html>
```

NOTE

When providing hexadecimal color values, the traditional number sign (#) is optional. If you provide it, though, you must escape the # by doubling it, so ColdFusion doesn't think you're trying to reference a variable. In other words, you could provide `backgroundcolor="99DDDD"` or `backgroundcolor="##99DDDD"` as you prefer, but not `backgroundcolor="#99DDDD"`.

Using Multiple Data Series

Now that you've been introduced to the basic principles involved in creating and formatting charts, we'd like to explain some of the more advanced aspects of ColdFusion charting support. In the next section, you will learn how to combine several chart types into a single graph. Then you will learn how to create charts that users can click, so they can drill down on information presented in the graph.

Combining Multiple Chart Series

So far, all the charts you've seen have contained only one `<cfchartseries>` tag. This makes sense, considering that the charts have presented only one set of information at a time. But it's also possible to create charts that represent more than one set of information, simply by adding additional `<cfchartseries>` tags within the `<cfchart>` block. The additional `<cfchartseries>` tags can each display different columns from the same query, or they can display information from different queries or data sources altogether.

The bar chart examples so far all show the budget for each film. It might be helpful to show not only the budget for each film but also the actual expenses to date, so that a glance at the chart will reveal which films are over budget and by how much.

Figure 16.5 shows just such a chart. There are now two bars for each film, clustered in pairs. One bar shows the budget for the film and the other shows the actual expenses for the film to date, as recorded in the Expenses table. Listing 16.5 shows the code used to produce this chart.

Figure 16.5

Multiple data series can be used in a single chart.

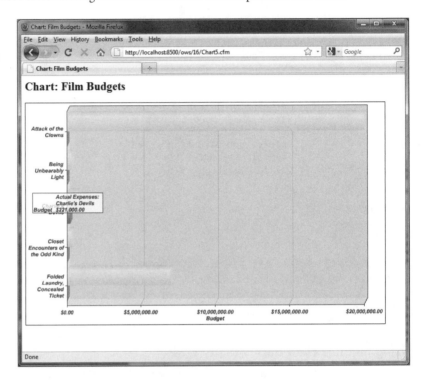

Listing 16.5 Chart5.cfm—Plotting Two Related Sets of Data

```
<!---
Name:        Chart5.cfm
Author:      Ben Forta
Description: Using multiple data series
Created:     01/01/2010
--->

<!--- Get information from the database --->
<cfinvoke component="ChartData"
          method="GetExpenses"
          returnvariable="ChartQuery"
          maxrows="5">

<html>
<head>
<title>Chart: Film Budgets</title>
</head>

<body>
<h2>Chart: Film Budgets</h2>
```

Listing 16.5 (CONTINUED)

```
<!--- This defines the size and appearance of the chart --->
<cfchart chartwidth="750"
         chartheight="450"
         yaxistitle="Budget"
         seriesplacement="cluster"
          <!--- 3D appearance --->
         show3d="yes"
         xoffset=".01"
         yoffset=".03"
         <!--- Fonts and colors --->
         showborder="yes"
         databackgroundcolor="dddddd"
         fontbold="yes"
         fontitalic="yes"
         <!--- gridlines and axis labels --->
         scaleto="800000"
         gridlines="5"
         showxgridlines="yes"
         showygridlines="no"
         labelformat="currency">

<!--- Budget chart --->
<cfchartseries type="horizontalbar"
               seriescolor="99ff99"
               serieslabel="Amount Budgeted:"
               query="chartquery"
               valuecolumn="amountbudgeted"
               itemcolumn="movietitle">

<!--- Expenses chart --->
<cfchartseries type="horizontalbar"
               seriescolor="ff4444"
               serieslabel="Actual Expenses:"
               query="chartquery"
               valuecolumn="expensetotal"
               itemcolumn="movietitle"
               paintstyle="light">

</cfchart>

</body>
</html>
```

Nearly any time you have multiple columns of information in the same query, you can display them using code similar to that used in this listing. The unspoken assumption is that the data in the first row of the AmountBudgeted and ExpenseTotal columns are related to the same real-world item. In this case, that real-world item is the first film.

Combining Series of Different Types

You're free to use different type values (line, bar, area, scatter, and so on) for each <cfchartseries> tag in the same chart. For instance, you might want to modify Listing 16.5 so that one series uses area and the other line. Line graphs are generally used to represent a single concept that changes over time, rather than blocks of individual data like film budgets, but in this particular case the result is rather effective. You're invited to experiment with different combinations of bar charts to see the various possibilities for yourself.

NOTE

You can't combine pie charts with other types of charts. Any `<cfchartseries>` tags that try to mix pie charts with other types will be ignored.

You can also experiment with the `seriesplacement` attribute to tell ColdFusion to change the way your chart series are combined. For instance, you can use `seriesplacement="stacked"` to have the bars shown stacked (as seen in Figure 16.6).

Figure 16.6

Multiple data series can be used in a single chart.

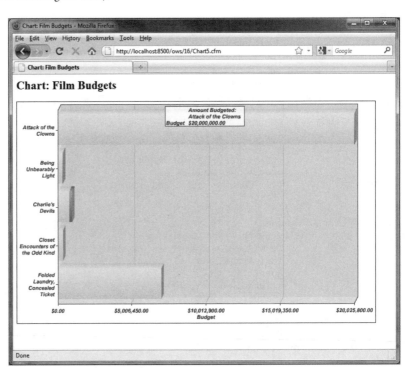

Drilling Down from Charts

The `<cfchart>` tag supports a URL attribute that you can use to create *clickable* charts, where the user can click the various data points in the chart to link to a different page. Of course, the page you bring users to when they click the chart is up to you. Generally, the idea is to allow users to zoom in or drill down on the data point they clicked.

For instance, if a chart displays information about film expenses, as in the examples above, then clicking one of the expense bars might display an HTML table that lists the actual expense records. Or it might bring up a second chart, this one a pie chart that shows the distribution of the individual expenses for that particular film. In either case, your clickable chart can be thought of as a navigation element, not unlike a toolbar or a set of HTML links. It's a way for users to explore your data visually.

Creating a Clickable Chart

To create a clickable chart, simply add a URL attribute to the `<cfchart>` tag. When the user clicks one of the data points in the chart (the slices of a pie chart, the bars in a bar chart, the points in a line graph, and so on), they will be sent to the URL you specify. So, if you want the browser to navigate to a ColdFusion page called `FilmExpenseDetail.cfm` when a chart is clicked, you would use `url="FilmExpenseDetail.cfm"`. You can use any type of relative or absolute URL that is acceptable to use in a normal HTML link.

For the detail page to be dynamic, however, it will need to know which data point the user clicked. To make this possible, ColdFusion lets you pass the actual data that the user is clicking as URL variables. To do so, include any of the special values shown in Table 16.4 in the `url` attribute. ColdFusion will create a dynamic URL for each data point by replacing these special values with the actual data for that data point.

Table 16.4 Special Values for Passing in `<cfchart>` URLs

VARIABLE	DESCRIPTION
`$value$`	The value of the selected row (that is, the value in the `valuecolumn` attribute of the `<cfchartseries>` tag for the data point that was clicked). This is typically the value that you're most interested in passing in the URL.
`$itemlabel$`	The label of the selected row (that is, the value in the `itemcolumn` for the data point that was clicked).
`$serieslabel$`	The series label (that is, the value of the `serieslabel` attribute of the `<cfchartseries>` tag). It's usually only necessary to include this value in the URL if you have multiple `<cfchartseries>` tags in your chart; this value becomes the way that the target page knows which series the user clicked.

For instance, consider the following `<cfchart>` tag:

```
<cfchart url="FilmExpenseDetail.cfm?MovieTitle=$itemlabel$">
```

When the user clicks the slices in this pie chart, the title of the film they clicked on will be passed to the `FilmExpenseDetail.cfm` page as a URL parameter named `MovieTitle`. Within `FilmExpenseDetail.cfm`, the value will be available as `URL.MovieTitle`, which can be used just like any other variable in the URL scope.

Listing 16.6 shows how the URL attribute can be used to create a clickable chart. This listing creates a pie chart that breaks down the overall budget for Orange Whip Studios by film. When users click a slice of the pie, they are presented with the detail page shown in Figure 16.7. You'll see the code for the detail page in a moment.

Figure 16.7

Graph details can be
displayed using chart
drill-down functions.

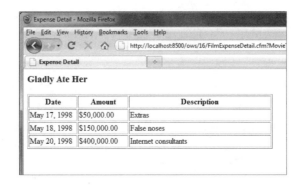

Listing 16.6   Chart6.cfm—Creating Chart with Drill-Down Functionality

```
<!---
Name:          Chart6.cfm
Author:        Ben Forta
Description:   Display a pie chart with drill-down support
Created:       01/01/2010
--->

<!--- Get information from the database --->
<cfinvoke component="ChartData"
          method="GetExpenses"
          returnvariable="ChartQuery"
          maxrows="10">

<html>
<head>
<title>Chart: Film Budgets</title>
</head>

<body>
<h2>Chart: Film Budgets</h2>

<!--- This defines the size and appearance of the chart --->
<cfchart chartwidth="550"
         chartheight="300"
         pieslicestyle="solid"
         show3d="yes"
         yoffset=".9"
         url="FilmExpenseDetail.cfm?MovieTitle=$ITEMLABEL$">

   <!--- Within the chart --->
   <cfchartseries type="pie"
                  query="chartquery"
                  valuecolumn="amountbudgeted"
                  itemcolumn="movietitle">

</cfchart>

</body>
</html>
```

Creating the Detail Page

Creating the detail page shown in Figure 16.7 is relatively straightforward. Just use the URL parameters passed by the URL attribute of the `<cfchart>` in Listing 16.6 to query the database for the appropriate Expense records. The records can then be displayed using normal `<cfoutput>` and HTML table tags.

There is one bit of unpleasantness to deal with, though. Unfortunately, `<cfchart>` doesn't provide a straightforward way to pass a unique identifier in URLs generated by `<cfchart>`. The only things you can pass are the actual label and value of the data point displayed on the graph (with the special `$ITEMLABEL$` and `$VALUE$` values, respectively).

So, for the example at hand (see Listing 16.7), the only pieces of information that can be passed to the `FilmExpenseDetail.cfm` page are the film's title and budget, since those are the only values that the chart is aware of. Ordinarily, it would be far preferable to pass the `FilmID` in the URL, thereby eliminating any problems that would come up if there were two films with the same title. Since this isn't currently possible in ColdFusion, the film will have to be identified by its title (and budget) alone.

NOTE

Keep this limitation in mind when creating drill-down applications with `<cfchart>`. If a data point can't be safely and uniquely identified by the combination of the label and value displayed in the graph, you probably won't be able to implement drill-down.

Listing 16.7 `FilmExpenseDetail.cfm`—Detail Page Displayed on Drill-Down

```
<!---
Name:        FilmExpenseDetail.cfm
Author:      Ben Forta
Description: Movie drill-down
Created:     01/01/2010
--->

<!--- These URL parameters will be passed by the chart --->
<cfparam name="URL.MovieTitle" type="string">

<!--- Get information from the database --->
<cfinvoke component="ChartData"
          method="GetFilmID"
          returnvariable="FilmID"
          movietitle="#URL.MovieTitle#">

<!--- Show an error message if we could not determine the FilmID --->
<cfif FilmID IS -1>
  <cfthrow message="Could not retrieve film information."
           detail="Unknown movie title provided.">
</cfif>

<!--- Now that we know the FilmID, we can select the --->
<!--- corresponding expense records from the database --->
<cfinvoke component="ChartData"
          method="GetExpenseDetails"
          returnvariable="ExpenseQuery"
          filmid="#FilmID#">
```

Listing 16.7 (CONTINUED)

```html
<html>
<head>
<title>Expense Detail</title>
</head>

<body>

<cfoutput>
 <!--- page heading --->
 <h3>#URL.MovieTitle#</h3>

 <!--- html table for expense display --->
 <table border="1" width="500">
  <tr>
   <th width="100">Date</th>
   <th width="100">Amount</th>
   <th width="300">Description</th>
  </tr>

  <!--- for each expense in the query... --->
  <cfloop query="expensequery">
   <tr>
    <td>#LSDateFormat(ExpenseDate)#</td>
    <td>#LSCurrencyFormat(ExpenseAmount)#</td>
    <td>#Description#</td>
   </tr>
  </cfloop>

 </table>
</cfoutput>

</body>
</html>
```

The purpose of the method invocation is to determine the FilmID that corresponds to the MovieTitle parameter passed to the page (from the chart in Listing 16.6). As a precautionary measure, the Budget parameter is also included in the query criteria. This means that if two films happen to have the same title, they can still be correctly identified as long as their budgets are different. For the rest of the page, FilmID holds the ID number for the film and can be used to retrieve any related information from the database.

NOTE

If no films are retrieved from the database (or if more than one is retrieved), an error message is displayed with the <cfthrow> tag.

Drilling Down to Another Chart

You may want to drill down to a different chart that shows a different view or subset of the data, rather just drilling down to a simple HTML page. The second chart page, in turn, could drill down to another page, and so on. You could use any of the drill-down techniques discussed in this section to put together such a multilayered data-navigation interface.

Plotting Individual Points with `<cfchartdata>`

The most common way to provide the actual data to a `<cfchartseries>` tag is to specify a QUERY attribute, then tell ColdFusion which columns of the query to look in by specifying `itemcolumn` and `valuecolumn` attributes. All of the examples you've seen so far in this chapter have supplied their data in this way.

It's also possible to omit the `query`, `itemcolumn`, and `valuecolumn` attributes and instead plot the data points individually using the `<cfchartdata>` tag, nested within your `<cfchartseries>`. The `<cfchartdata>` approach can come in handy if you want to permanently hard-code certain data points onto your charts, if you need to format your data in a special way, or if you come across a situation where you can't extract the desired data from a query in a completely straightforward manner.

Table 16.5 shows the syntax for the `<cfchartdata>` tag.

Table 16.5   `<cfchartdata>` Syntax

ATTRIBUTE	DESCRIPTION
item	The item associated with the data point you're plotting, such as a film title, a category of purchases, or a period of time—in other words, the information you would normally supply to the `itemcolumn` attribute of the `<cfchartseries>` tag.
value	The value of the data point (a number). This is what you would normally supply to the `valuecolumn` attribute of `<cfchartseries>`.

For instance, if you have a query called `ChartQuery` with two columns, `ExpenseDate` and `Expense Amount`, and you wanted to make sure the date was formatted to your liking when it was displayed on the chart, you could use

```
<cfchartseries type="line">
 <cfloop query="ChartQuery">
  <cfchartdata item="#DateFormat(ExpenseDate, 'm/d/yy')#"
               value="#ExpenseAmount#">
 </cfloop>
</cfchartseries>
```

instead of

```
<cfchartseries type="line"
               query="ChartQuery"
               valuecolumn="ExpenseAmount"
               itemcolumn="ExpenseDate">
```

This technique is also useful when creating charts based on data that are not query based. Using `<cfchartdata>` you can pass any data to a chart.

Using Charts with Flash Remoting

It's possible to use the `name` attribute to capture the binary content of a chart and then make it available to the Adobe Flash Player via Flash Remoting. This capability allows you to create a

Flash movie that displays dynamically generated charts on the fly, perhaps as a part of a sophisticated data-entry or reporting interface, all without reloading the page to display an updated or changed chart. This topic is beyond the scope of this book.

Creating Printable Pages

It's long been a hassle to easily generate printable content from within Web pages, and this is a source of serious aggravation for Web application developers (all developers, not just ColdFusion developers). Considering that a very significant chunk of Web application development tends to be data reporting and presentation type applications, this is a big problem.

The truth is, Web browsers just don't print Web pages properly, so developers have had to resort to complex and painful workarounds to put content in a printable format.

ColdFusion solves this problem simply with the `<cfdocument>` family of tags.

Using the `<cfdocument>` Tag

We'll start with a really simple example. Listing 16.8 contains simple text wrapped within a pair of `<cfdocument>` tags. The generated output is seen in Figure 16.8.

Figure 16.8

Adobe PDF format is the most commonly used printable document format on the Web.

Listing 16.8   `Print1.cfm`—Basic PDF Generation

```
<!---
Name:        Print1.cfm
Author:      Ben Forta
Description: Simple printable output
Created:     01/01/2010
--->

<cfdocument format="pdf">
Hello world!
</cfdocument>
```

The code in Listing 16.8 couldn't be simpler. By wrapping text in between <cfdocument> and </cfdocument> tags, content between those tags is converted into a PDF file on the fly, and embedded in the page.

Of course, you're not limited to static text; you can use dynamic CFML within the document content, too. Listing 16.9 uses a mixture of HTML, CFML, and dynamic data to create a printable report (seen in Figure 16.9).

Figure 16.9

Printable output may contain HTML, CFML, and more.

Listing 16.9 `Print2.cfm`—Data-Driven Document Generation

```
<!---
Name:        Print2.cfm
Author:      Ben Forta
Description: Data driven printable output
Created:     01/01/2010
--->

<!--- Get budget data --->
<cfinvoke component="ChartData"
          method="GetBudgetData"
          returnvariable="BudgetData">

<!--- Generate document --->
<cfdocument format="pdf">

<!--- Header --->
<table align="center">
 <tr>
<td>
 <img src="../images/logo_c.gif"
      alt="Orange Whip Studios">
</td>
<td align="center">
<font size="+2">Orange Whip Studios<br>Movies</font>
</td>
 </tr>
</table>

<!--- Title --->
<div align="center">
<h2>Budget Data</h2>
</div>

<!--- Details --->
<table>
 <tr>
  <th>Movie</th>
  <th>Budget</th>
 </tr>
 <cfoutput query="BudgetData">
  <tr>
   <td><strong>#MovieTitle#</strong></td>
   <td>#LSCurrencyFormat(AmountBudgeted)#</td>
  </tr>
 </cfoutput>
</table>

</cfdocument>
```

What Is Supported by `<cfdocument>`?

You'll notice that the code in Listing 16.9 uses a mixture of HTML (including tags like `<font>`, which generally should be avoided), an image, tables, CFML expressions, and more. The `<cfdocument>` tag supports all of the following:

- HTML 4
- XML 1
- DOM level 1 and 2
- CSS1 and CSS2

In other words, `<cfdocument>` should be more than able to convert all sorts of pages into printable PDF.

Creating Printable Versions of Pages

You will likely often need to create printable versions of existing pages. It would be tempting to try and simply conditionally include `<cfdocument>` tags in existing pages, but unfortunately that won't work: ColdFusion won't parse the page correctly because it thinks your tags aren't properly paired.

The solution to this problem is to create a wrapper page, one that defines the printable document and includes the original page. Listing 16.10 is a modified version of a page we created in Chapter 11, "The Basics of Structured Development"; it simply displays movie details. The modified page is seen in Figure 16.10.

Figure 16.10

It's often convenient to provide links to printable versions of pages.

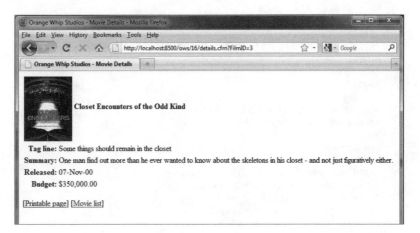

Listing 16.10 `details.cfm`—Movie Details Page

```
<!---
Name:        details.cfm
Author:      Ben Forta (ben@forta.com)
Description: CFC driven data drill-down details
             with complete validation
```

Listing 16.10   (CONTINUED)

```
Created:     01/01/2010
--->

<!--- Movie list page --->
<cfset list_page="movies.cfm">

<!--- Make sure FilmID was passed --->
<cfif not IsDefined("URL.filmid")>
 <!--- it wasn't, send to movie list --->
 <cflocation url="#list_page#">
</cfif>

<!--- Get movie details --->
<cfinvoke
 component="ows.11.movies"
 method="GetDetails"
 returnvariable="movie"
 FilmID="#URL.filmid#">

<!--- Make sure we have a movie --->
<cfif movie.RecordCount IS 0>
 <!--- It wasn't, send to movie list --->
 <cflocation url="#list_page#">
</cfif>

<!--- Build image paths --->
<cfset image_src="../images/f#movie.FilmID#.gif">
<cfset image_path=ExpandPath(image_src)>

<!--- Create HTML page --->
<html>
<head>
 <title>Orange Whip Studios - Movie Details</title>
</head>

<body>

<!--- Display movie details --->
<cfoutput query="movie">

<table>
 <tr>
  <td colspan="2">
   <!--- Check if image file exists --->
   <cfif FileExists(image_path)>
    <!--- If it does, display it --->
    <img src="../images/f#filmid#.gif"
        alt="#movietitle#"
        align="middle">
   </cfif>
   <b>#MovieTitle#</b>
  </td>
 </tr>
```

Listing 16.10 (CONTINUED)

```
   <tr valign="top">
    <th align="right">Tag line:</th>
    <td>#PitchText#</td>
   </tr>
   <tr valign="top">
    <th align="right">Summary:</th>
    <td>#Summary#</td>
   </tr>
   <tr valign="top">
    <th align="right">Released:</th>
    <td>#DateFormat(DateInTheaters)#</td>
   </tr>
   <tr valign="top">
    <th align="right">Budget:</th>
    <td>#DollarFormat(AmountBudgeted)#</td>
   </tr>
  </table>

 <p>

 <!--- Links --->
 [<a href="detailsprint.cfm?FilmID=#URL.FilmID#">Printable page</a>]
 [<a href="#list_page#">Movie list</a>]

 </cfoutput>

 </body>
 </html>
```

The big change to this page is a line added to the links section at the bottom. A new link to a Printable page has been created; when clicked, it opens detailsprint.cfm, passing the FilmID to that page. The code for that page is remarkably simple, as seen in Listing 16.11.

Listing 16.11 detailsprint.cfm—Printable Movie Details Page

```
 <!---
 Name:        detailsprint.cfm
 Author:      Ben Forta (ben@forta.com)
 Description: Printable version of details page
 Created:     01/01/2010
 --->

 <cfdocument format="pdf">
 <cfinclude template="details.cfm">
 </cfdocument>
```

Listing 16.11 creates a document using <cfdocument> tags, and includes the existing details page to generate the printable output seen in Figure 16.11.

Figure 16.11

Generated documents may contain page headers and footers.

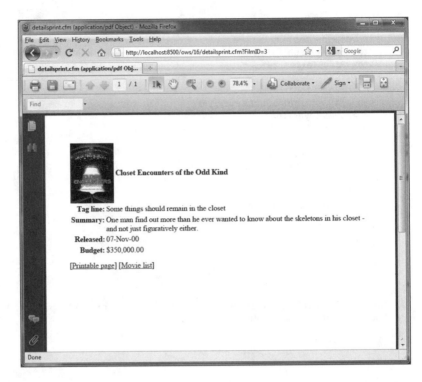

NOTE

The links in `details.cfm` work in the generated printable output.

In addition to the format attribute used here, `<cfdocument>` supports a whole series of attributes to give you greater control over printed output.

Saving Generated Output

`<cfdocument>` embeds generated output in your Web page. You may opt to save the generated files to disk instead of serving them in real time. Reasons to do this include

- Caching, so as to not have to regenerate pages unnecessarily
- Emailing generated content
- Generating pages that can be served statically

To save generated output, simply provide a file name in the `filename` attribute.

Controlling Output Using the `<cfdocumentitem>` Tag

`<cfdocumentitem>` is used within a `<cfdocument>` tag set to embed additional items. `<cfdocument item>` requires that a type be specified. Table 16.6 lists the supported types.

Table 16.6 `<cfdocumentitem>` Types

TYPE	DESCRIPTION
footer	Page footer.
header	Page header.
pagebreak	Embed a page break; this type takes no body.

NOTE

Page breaks are calculated automatically by ColdFusion. Use `<cfdocumentitem type="pagebreak">` to embed manual breaks.

Listing 16.12 is a revised printable movie listing, with more options specified.

Listing 16.12 `Print3.cfm`—Printable Output with Additional Items

```
<!---
Name:        Print3.cfm
Author:      Ben Forta
Description: Printable output with additional options
Created:     01/01/2010
--->

<!--- Get budget data --->
<cfinvoke component="ChartData"
          method="GetBudgetData"
          returnvariable="BudgetData">

<!--- Generate document --->
<cfdocument format="pdf">

<!--- Header --->
<cfdocumentitem type="header">
OWS Budget Report
</cfdocumentitem>
<!--- Footer --->
<cfdocumentitem type="footer">
<p align="center">
<cfoutput>
#CFDOCUMENT.currentpagenumber# of #CFDOCUMENT.totalpagecount#
</cfoutput>
</p>
</cfdocumentitem>


<!--- Header --->
<table align="center">
 <tr>
  <td><img src="../images/logo_c.gif" alt="Orange Whip Studios"></td>
  <td align="center"><font size="+2">Orange Whip Studios<br>Movies</font></td>
 </tr>
</table>

<!--- Title --->
```

Listing 16.12   (CONTINUED)

```
<div align="center">
<h2>Budget Data</h2>
</div>

<!--- Page break --->
<cfdocumentitem type="pagebreak" />

<!--- Details --->
<table>
 <tr>
  <th>Movie</th>
  <th>Budget</th>
 </tr>
 <cfoutput query="BudgetData">
  <tr>
   <td><strong>#MovieTitle#</strong></td>
   <td>#LSCurrencyFormat(AmountBudgeted)#</td>
  </tr>
 </cfoutput>
</table>

</cfdocument>
```

Listing 16.12 warrants some explanation. The <cfdocument> content now contains the following code:

```
<!--- Header --->
<cfdocumentitem type="header">
OWS Budget Report
</cfdocumentitem>
```

This code defines a page header, text that will be placed at the top of each page. A footer is also defined as follows:

```
<!--- Footer --->
<cfdocumentitem type="footer">
<p align="center">
<cfoutput>
#CFDOCUMENT.currentpagenumber# of #CFDOCUMENT.totalpagecount#
</cfoutput>
</p>
</cfdocumentitem>
```

This page footer contains two special variables. Within a <cfdocument> tag, a special scope exists named CFDOCUMENT. It contains two variables, as listed in Table 16.7. These variables may be used in headers and footers, as used in this example.

Table 16.7   CFDOCUMENT Scope Variables

TYPE	DESCRIPTION
currentpagenumber	Current page number
totalpagecount	Total number of generated pages

In addition, the code in Listing 16.12 embeds a manual page break using this code:

```
<!--- Page break --->
<cfdocumentitem type="pagebreak" />
```

`<cfdocumentitem>` must always have an end tag, even when no body is specified. The trailing / is a shortcut that you can use. In other words, the above tag is functionally identical to

```
<!--- Page break --->
<cfdocumentitem type="pagebreak"></cfdocumentitem>
```

Defining Sections with `<cfdocumentsection>`

As you have seen, you have a lot of control over generated pages using the `<cfdocument>` and `<cfdocumentitem>` tags. But sometimes you may want different options in different parts of the same document. For example, you may want a title page to have different margins than other pages. Or you may want different headers and footers in different parts of the document.

To do this, you use `<cfdocumentsection>` tags. A `<cfdocument>` tag pair may contain one or more sections, each defined using `<cfdocumentsection>` tags. Within each section you can specify alternate margins, and can use `<cfdocumentitem>` tags to specify headers and footers for each section.

NOTE

When using `<cfdocumentsection>`, all content must be in sections. ColdFusion ignores any content outside of sections.

Generating Reports

`<cfdocument>` is designed to create printable versions of Web pages. These Web pages may be reports (many will be), and may involve such features as

- Banded reports

- Calculated totals and sums

- Repeating and non-repeating regions

- Embedded charts

Understanding the ColdFusion Report Builder

While these reports can indeed be created manually, there is a better way, using the ColdFusion Report Builder. The ColdFusion Report Builder is a stand-alone program used to define ColdFusion Report templates. It can be run on its own, and also directly from within Dreamweaver by double-clicking on a report file.

NOTE

At this time, the ColdFusion Report Builder is a Windows-only utility. But reports created using the Report Builder can be processed by ColdFusion on any platform, and reports can be viewed on any platform.

The ColdFusion Report Builder creates and edits a special ColdFusion file with a .cfr extension. Unlike .cfm and .cfc files, .cfr files can't be edited with a text editor; the ColdFusion Report Builder must be used. .cfr files are report templates that may be used as is, or invoked from CFML code as needed (as we'll explain below).

To launch the Report Builder, select ColdFusion Report Builder from the Windows Adobe > ColdFusion 9 program group.

Using the Setup Wizard

The first time the ColdFusion Report Builder is run, a setup wizard will be launched (as seen in Figure 16.12). This wizard configures the Report Builder so it's ready for use.

Figure 16.12

The ColdFusion Report Builder setup wizard configures the Report Builder for use.

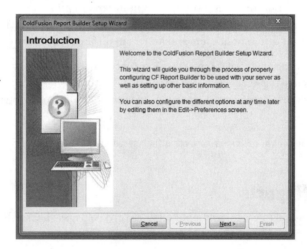

Click the Next button to provide basic information pertaining to measurement units. Once you have made your selections, click Next and you will be asked to specify how the Report Builder should connect to ColdFusion (as seen in Figure 16.13).

Figure 16.13

The Report Builder needs to know how to connect to ColdFusion.

The ColdFusion Report Builder uses RDS to connect to ColdFusion, and you will be prompted for the server name and login information (as seen in Figure 16.14).

Figure 16.14

RDS login information must be provided to gain access to full Report Builder functionality.

NOTE

You can use the ColdFusion Report Builder without RDS, but you won't be able to use the Query Builder, Chart Wizard, and some other functionality.

Once you have completed the wizard, you'll be ready to start building reports.

NOTE

You can rerun the setup wizard at any time by selecting File > New in the Report Builder, and then selecting the Server Setup Wizard option.

Introducing the ColdFusion Report Builder

The ColdFusion Report Builder screen looks a lot like other report writing tools that you may have used. The screen, seen in Figure 16.15, contains several sections you should be aware of:

- The large open space in the middle of the Report Builder is where reports are defined and edited.

- The toolbox on the left contains buttons to insert images, fields, subreports, and more into reports, as well as buttons used to manage element alignment.

- On the top of the screen are toolbars for file opening, editing, fonts, etc.

- The Properties panel at the upper right displays the properties for any report item, and allows for quick property editing.

- The Fields and Parameters panel on the lower right is used to access query columns, calculated fields, and input parameters.

Figure 16.15

The Report Builder interface is used to define and edit ColdFusion reports.

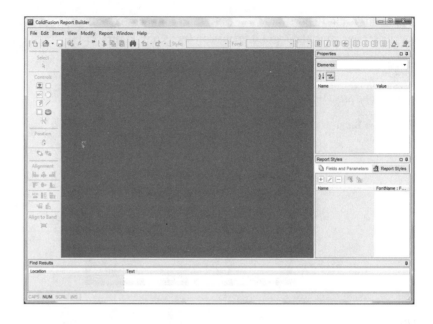

The ColdFusion Report Builder allows for multiple .cfr files to be open at once if needed.

Using the Report Wizard

The simplest way to create a report, and indeed the fastest way to learn the Report Builder, is to use the Report Creation Wizard. We'll start by creating a report of movie expenses. Here are the steps to follow:

1. Select File > New (or click the New button) to display the ColdFusion Report Builder Gallery dialog (seen in Figure 16.16).

Figure 16.16

The ColdFusion Report Builder Gallery is used to create new blank reports or to launch the report wizard.

2. Select Report Creation Wizard, and click OK to launch the wizard. First we need the query columns to be used in the report. You may click Add to add the query columns manually, Import to import a query from an existing report, or Query Builder to launch

the Query Builder (seen in Figure 16.17). We'll use the Query Builder, so click that button.

3. The SQL Query Builder has two modes, Figure 16.17 shows the SQL Query Builder interactive mode; you can also click the Advanced check box to enter the SQL manually. We'll use the SQL Query Builder mode. On the left you'll see a list of available data sources; expand the ows data source and then expand Tables to display the available tables.

Figure 16.17

The SQL Query Builder simplifies the process of generating report SQL statements.

NOTE

You won't see available data sources if RDS isn't used.

4. Drag the Films and Expenses tables into the SQL Query Builder (as seen in Figure 16.18). Notice how the SQL statement changes to reflect the table selections.

5. The Report Builder will attempt to figure out table relationships automatically, as it did here (seen in Figure 16.18). If necessary, you can also join tables manually. For example, to join the Films and Expenses tables, select the FilmID column in one of the tables and drag it to the FilmID column in there. A link will indicate that the tables are joined.

NOTE

To change the join type, right-click on the box in the line that links the tables.

6. Double-click on the MovieTitle column in Films to select that column.

7. Double-click on the ExpenseDate, Description, and ExpenseAmount columns in Expenses (in that order) to select those three columns.

Figure 16.18

The SQL Query Builder shows SQL changes as selections are made.

8. The report needs to be sorted by MovieTitle and then by ExpenseDate, so click on the Sort Type column for MovieTitle and select Ascending, then do the same for ExpenseDate (as seen in Figure 16.19).

Figure 16.19

SQL ORDER BY clauses can be created by selecting the desired sort type and sequence.

9. Now that the SQL selection is complete, test it by clicking the Test Query button. The query results will be displayed in a pop-up window.

10. Close the query results window, and click Save to save the query (and columns) into the wizard (Figure 16.20).

Figure 16.20

The SQL Query Builder inserts selected columns back into the wizard.

11. Click Next, and the wizard will prompt you for any report grouping (used to create report bands). We want the report grouped by movie, so double-click MoveTitle to move it to the Group by Fields column. Then click Next.

12. You will then be prompted for a report layout, page orientation, and paper size. Select Left Aligned, and then click Next.

TIP

As you click on any report layout, a sample preview shows you what it will look like.

13. You will then be prompted for the report style. Default should be used for all reports except subreports (reports embedded in other reports). You can also specify whether or not to generate totals for numeric fields, as well as the number of columns desired. Leave all the values as is, and click Next.

14. To select a color theme to use, pick one of the colors, then click Next.

15. The final wizard screen prompts for a title, headers, and footers. Enter Move Expenses as the title, and click Finish to generate your report.

16. When the wizard ends, your new report will be displayed in the Report Builder (as seen in Figure 16.21).

17. The report has a title already, but it has a generic CompanyName at the top. CompanyName is static text, and it can be edited by simply double-clicking on the text to display the Edit Label Text dialog box (see Figure 16.22). Change the text to Orange Whip Studios and click OK.

Figure 16.21

The wizard generates
a complete report
and displays it in the
Report Builder.

Figure 16.22

Static text can be
edited by double-
clicking on it.

18. Save your new report (select File > Save, or click the Save button), name it `expenses.cfr`,
and save it in the `/ows/16` folder.

19. The final step is to preview the report, to make sure that it's working as intended. Click
the Preview button (the one with a globe with a lightning bolt through it), or press F12.
A preview (in FlashPaper format, by default) will be displayed (as seen in Figure 16.23).

Notice that the query fields and calculated fields in the Fields and Parameters panel have been
populated with the information provided to the wizard. You can edit these if needed.

Here is a very important item: The report displays expense dates, but these are not formatted
properly. Double-click the `query.EXPENSEDATE` field and you'll see a screen like the one in Figure 16.24. This is the Expression Builder, and it can be used to embed any CFML expressions
into your report. If you want to convert text to uppercase, access special variables, or perform any
special processing, you can do so using CFML expressions. For now, change `query.EXPENSEDATE` so
that it reads `DateFormat(query.EXPENSEDATE)`. Do the same for `query.EXPENSEAMOUNT`, changing it
to `DollarFormat(query.EXPENSEAMOUNT)`, and then click OK. Now the date and amount will be formatted properly. This is one of ColdFusion Report Builder's most powerful features.

Figure 16.23

Preview your reports using the integrated preview feature.

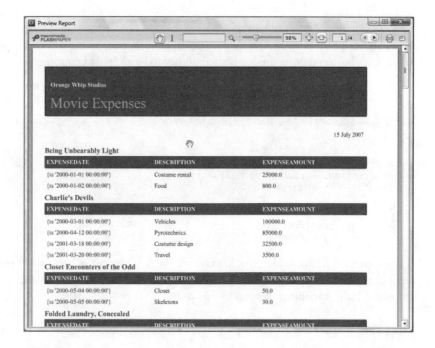

Figure 16.24

Use Query Fields to edit database query fields, and Calculated Fields to define calculated fields for your report.

TIP

You can zoom in on the report you're working on by clicking the x1, x2, and x4 buttons above each report.

Running Your Reports

To run your report, invoke the full URL to it from within your browser. The report will be displayed, exactly as it was when previewed in the ColdFusion Report Builder.

Invoking Reports from Within ColdFusion Code

Being able to run reports in browsers is useful, but other reporting tools can do that, too. What makes ColdFusion reports unique is their ability to be altered at runtime.

Look at Listing 16.13. It uses a tag named `<cfreport>` to embed a report into a `.cfm` file.

Listing 16.13 Report1.cfm—Basic Report Invocation

```
<!---
Name:        Report1.cfm
Author:      Ben Forta
Description: Invoke a ColdFusion report
Created:     01/01/2010
--->

<cfreport template="Expenses.cfr"
          format="PDF" />
```

If you were to run this code, it would generate the same report as before, but now you're generating it in your own CFML instead of it's being generated automatically. Why is this of value? Look at Listing 16.14, a modified version of this code.

Listing 16.14 Report2.cfm—Passing a Query to a Report

```
<!---
Name:        Report2.cfm
Author:      Ben Forta
Description: Invoke a ColdFusion report
Created:     01/01/2010
--->

<cfquery name="Expenses" datasource="ows">
SELECT    Films.MovieTitle, Expenses.ExpenseDate,
          Expenses.Description,
          Expenses.ExpenseAmount
FROM      Films, Expenses
WHERE     Expenses.FilmID = Films.FilmID
ORDER BY  Films.MovieTitle, expenses.expensedate
</cfquery>

<cfreport template="Expenses.cfr"
          query="Expenses"
          format="PDF" />
```

Listing 16.14 uses `<cfquery>` to create a database query, and then passes that query to the `<cfreport>` tag overriding the query within the report. This query is exactly the same as the one used within the report, but now that you can see how queries can be created and passed to reports, you can start to see this feature's power. After all, you already know how to dynamically create queries; using that knowledge, you can create a form that prompts for the information to be included in the report, allowing you to create truly dynamic reports.

Let's look at an example. Listing 16.15 is a simple form; it allows for the selection of a movie or specifying all movies.

Listing 16.15 ReportForm1.cfm—Report Front End

```
<!---
Name:        ReportForm1.cfm
Author:      Ben Forta
Description: Report form front end
Created:     01/01/2010
--->

<!--- Get movie list --->
<cfquery datasource="ows" name="movies">
SELECT FilmID, MovieTitle
FROM Films
ORDER BY MovieTitle
</cfquery>


<html>

<head>
<title>Orange Whip Studios Expenses Report</title>
</head>

<body>

<cfform action="Report3.cfm">
Select movie:
<cfselect name="FilmID"
          query="movies"
          display="MovieTitle"
          value="FilmID"
          queryPosition="below">
 <option value="">--- ALL ---</option>
</cfselect>
<br>
<cfinput name="sbmt"
         type="submit"
         value="Report">
</cfform>

</body>

</html>
```

The form in Listing 16.15 prompts for a movie, and passes FilmID to Report3.cfm, shown in Listing 16.16.

Listing 16.16 Report3.cfm—Dynamic Report

```
<!---
Name:        Report3.cfm
Author:      Ben Forta
Description: Invoke a ColdFusion report
Created:     01/01/2010
--->

<cfparam name="FilmID" default="">
```

Listing 16.16 (CONTINUED)

```
<cfquery name="Expenses" datasource="ows">
SELECT    Films.MovieTitle, Expenses.ExpenseDate,
          Expenses.Description,
          Expenses.ExpenseAmount
FROM      Films, Expenses
WHERE     Expenses.FilmID = Films.FilmID
<cfif FilmID NEQ "">
 AND Films.FilmID = #FilmID#
</cfif>
ORDER BY  Films.MovieTitle, expenses.expensedate
</cfquery>

<cfreport template="Expenses.cfr"
          query="Expenses"
          format="PDF" />
```

Listing 16.16 is the same as Listing 16.14, but this time the `<cfquery>` is being created dynamically, so the query can select either all expenses or just expenses for a specific movie. The same `<cfreport>` tag is used, but now the report can display expenses for all movies, or just a single movie.

This functionality is so important that the ColdFusion Report Builder can actually automatically create calling CFML code for you. To try this, return to the ColdFusion Query Builder (with the expenses.cfr report open), and click on the Code Snippet button (the one with tags on it). You will see a screen that contains calling CFML code, either a single .cfm file (Figure 16.25) or a .cfc and a .cfm file. (Figure 16.26). You can select the code style using the radio buttons at the bottom of the page, and then click Save to save the generated ColdFusion code ready for you to use (and modify, if needed).

Figure 16.25

The Report Builder can generate calling CFML code.

Figure 16.26

The Report Builder can also generate a `.cfc` file containing the query and a `.cfm` file invoking that query and calling the report.

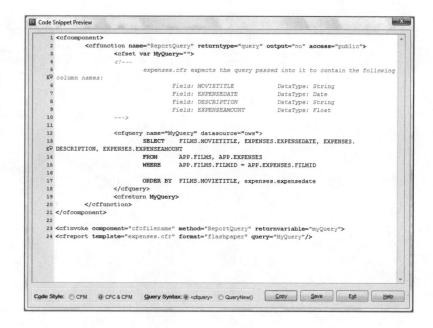

And a Whole Lot More, Too

We've only scratched the surface. The ColdFusion Report Builder is a powerful tool that in truth is deserving of far more space than can be devoted here. But it is also an easy-to-use tool, and one that you are encouraged to experiment with. Some features worth paying attention to are

- The various properties available when clicking on different report sections and elements

- The Chart button, which launches a Chart Wizard used to embed charts within reports (actually, the Wizard generates `<cfchart>` tags, the same tags used earlier in this chapter)

- The Subreport button, used to embed one report inside of another

- The Print When property that can be used to conditionally include or exclude parts of reports

- Input parameters, used to pass `name=value` pairs to reports at runtime

- Text Styles, which allow styles to be used for formatting

CHAPTER 17

Debugging and Troubleshooting

Troubleshooting ColdFusion Applications

As with any development tool, sooner or later you're going to find yourself debugging or trouble-shooting a ColdFusion application problem. Many elements have to work seamlessly for a ColdFusion application to function correctly. The key to isolating and correcting problems is an understanding of such things as ColdFusion, data sources, SQL syntax, URL syntax, and your Web server—and more important, how these all work with each other.

If the prospect of debugging application errors sounds daunting, don't panic. ColdFusion has powerful built-in debugging and error-reporting features. These capabilities, coupled with logical and systematic evaluation of trouble spots, will let you diagnose and correct all sorts of problems.

This chapter teaches you how to use the ColdFusion debugging tools and introduces techniques that will help you quickly locate the source of a problem. More importantly, because an ounce of prevention is worth a pound of cure, we introduce guidelines and techniques that help prevent common errors from occurring in the first place.

NOTE

This chapter does not discuss the ColdFusion 9 interactive step debugger. See Chapter 45, "Using the Debugger," online, for more information about this powerful new tool for understanding and debugging ColdFusion applications. The chapter also does not focus on ColdFusion server configuration problems; this topic is beyond the introductory scope of Volume 1.

Understanding What Can Go Wrong

As an application developer, sooner or later you are going to have to diagnose, or *debug*, a ColdFusion application problem. Because ColdFusion relies on so many other software components to work its magic, there are a lot of places where things can go wrong.

This chapter makes the following assumptions:

- You are familiar with basic ColdFusion concepts.

- You understand how ColdFusion uses data sources for all database interaction.

- You are familiar with basic SQL syntax and use.

- You know how to use the ColdFusion Administrator.

- You are comfortable using Adobe ColdFusion Builder.

If you aren't familiar with any of these topics, I strongly recommend you read the chapters about them before proceeding.

→ See Chapter 1, "Introducing ColdFusion," for more information on how ColdFusion works and how all the pieces fit together to create a complete application.

→ See Chapter 2, "Accessing the ColdFusion Administrator," to learn how to enable debugging output using the ColdFusion Administrator.

→ See Chapter 5, "Reviewing the Databases," for a detailed explanation of databases, tables, rows, columns, keys, and other database-related terms.

→ See Chapter 6, "Introducing SQL," for more information about data sources and how ColdFusion uses them for all database interaction.

Almost all ColdFusion programming errors fall into one of the following categories:

- Web server configuration problems

- Database errors

- SQL statement syntax or logic errors

- CFML and HTML syntax errors

- Other common page processing problems

Let's look at each of these potential problem areas.

Debugging Web Server Configuration Problems

You should almost never encounter problems caused by Web server misconfiguration during routine, day-to-day operations. These types of problems almost always occur either during the initial ColdFusion setup or while testing ColdFusion for the first time. After ColdFusion is installed and configured correctly, it will generally stay that way.

The only exception to this is the possibility of an error telling you that ColdFusion isn't running. Obviously, ColdFusion must be running to process templates. Steps to verify that the server is running, and to start it if it isn't, differ based on your operating system:

- If you're running ColdFusion under Microsoft Windows, you should run the Services applet. It will show whether the service is running and will enable you to start it if it isn't.

- If you're running ColdFusion under Linux, Solaris, or Mac OS, use the ps command (or ps -ef|grep cfusion) to list running processes to see whether ColdFusion is running.

TIP

Windows services can be started automatically every time the system is restarted. The service Startup option must be set to Automatic for a service to start automatically. This setting is turned on by the ColdFusion installation procedure and typically should be left on at all times. If the service doesn't automatically start, check these options.

TIP

If your operating system features a mechanism by which to automatically start services or daemons upon system restart, use it.

One other situation worth noting is when you are prompted to save a file every time you request a ColdFusion page. If this is the case, one of two things is happening:

- ColdFusion isn't installed correctly on the Web server.

- You are accessing URLs locally (using the browser File > Open option) instead of via the Web server.

Debugging Database Errors

Many kinds of errors can occur in database processing stemming from problems in the way that either ColdFusion or the database server is configured.

ColdFusion relies on database drivers (JDBC) for all its database interaction. You will receive database driver error messages when ColdFusion can't communicate with the appropriate driver or when the driver can't communicate with the database.

Database driver error messages are usually generated by the driver, not by ColdFusion, with ColdFusion displaying whatever error message it has received from the database driver. Unfortunately these error messages are often cryptic or even misleading.

Database driver error messages vary from driver to driver, so it would be pointless to list all the possible error messages here. Instead, we will look at the more common symptoms and how to fix the problems that cause them.

TIP

You can use the ColdFusion Administrator to verify that a data source is correctly configured.

Receiving the Data Source Not Found Error Message

ColdFusion communicates with databases via database drivers. If the database driver reports that the database could not be found, check the following:

- Make sure you have created the data source.

- Verify that the data source name is spelled correctly. Data source names are not case sensitive, so you don't have to worry about that.

Receiving Login or Permission Errors When Trying to Access a Data Source

Database systems typically require you to log on to a database before you can access it. When setting up a data source, you generally must specify the login name and password the driver should use to gain access (whether you're working in the ColdFusion Administrator or using the `<cfquery>` tag's `UserName` and `Password` attributes).

If you create the data source in the ColdFusion Administrator, your settings will be verified when you submit the form to add the data source. Any problems will cause an error message to appear. If you specify the login credentials in the `<cfquery>` tag, any such errors will be displayed in a run-time error when the page is executed.

The following steps will help you locate the source of this problem:

- Verify that the login name and password are spelled correctly. (You won't be able to see the password in the ColdFusion Administrator—only asterisks are displayed in the password field.)

- On some database systems, passwords are case sensitive. Be sure that you haven't left the Caps Lock key on by mistake.

- Verify that the name and password you are using does indeed have access to the database to which you are trying to connect. You can do this using a client application that came with your database system.

- Verify that the login being used actually has rights to the specific tables and views you are using and to the specific statements (`SELECT`, `INSERT`, and so on). Many DBMSs enable administrators to grant or deny users rights to specific objects and specific operations on specific objects.

TIP

When you're testing security- and rights-related problems, be sure you test using the same login and password as the ones used in the data source definition.

Receiving Table Name Error Messages

After verifying that the data source name is correct, you still may get errors because of the table name. Some database servers, such as Microsoft SQL Server, are case sensitive with regard to table names. In addition, in some cases you must provide a fully qualified table name. You can do this in two ways:

- Explicitly provide the fully qualified table name whenever it is passed to a SQL statement. Fully qualified table names are usually made up of three parts, separated by periods. The first is the name of the schema or database containing the table; the second is the owner name (possibly `dbo`); and the third is the actual table name itself.

- Some database drivers, such as the Microsoft SQL Server driver, let you specify a default database name to be used if none is explicitly provided. If this option is set, its value is used whenever a fully qualified name isn't provided.

TIP

If your database driver lets you specify a default database name, use that feature. You can then write fewer and simpler hard-coded SQL statements.

Debugging SQL Statement or Logic Errors

Debugging SQL statements is one of the two types of troubleshooting you may spend much of your debugging time doing (the other is debugging ColdFusion syntax errors, which we'll get to next). You will find yourself debugging SQL statements if you run into either of these situations:

- ColdFusion reports SQL syntax errors. Figure 17.1, for example, is an error caused by misspelling a table name in a SQL statement. If you see only partial debug output, as shown in Figure 17.2, access the ColdFusion Administrator and turn on the Enable Robust Exception Information option on the Debug Output Settings screen. (While this setting is very helpful in development, it is generally inappropriate to enable this setting in production environments, in which sharing the details for errors can expose sensitive information about your files, databases, and other configuration details.)

- No syntax errors are reported, but the specified SQL statement didn't achieve the expected results.

Obviously, a prerequisite to debugging SQL statements is a good working knowledge of the SQL language. I'm assuming you are already familiar with the basic SQL statements and are comfortable using them.

Figure 17.1

ColdFusion displays SQL error messages as reported by the database driver.

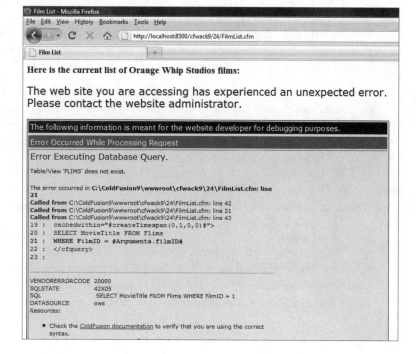

Figure 17.2

During development, be sure that Enable Robust Exception Information is turned on in the ColdFusion Administrator, or you won't see complete debug output.

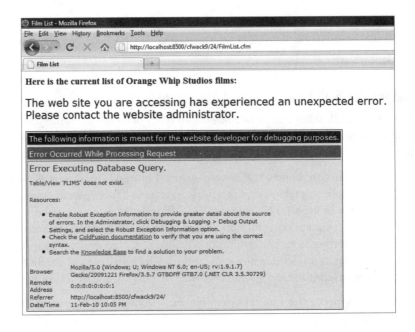

→ See Chapter 7, "SQL Data Manipulation," for information about basic SQL statements and examples of their uses.

The keys to successfully debugging SQL statements are as follows:

- **Isolate the problem.** Debugging SQL statements inside ColdFusion templates can be tricky, especially when creating dynamic SQL statements. See the section "Viewing Dynamically Generated SQL" later in this chapter for help on viewing the SQL generated at runtime. Try executing the same statement from within another database client, replacing dynamic parameters with fixed values if appropriate.

- The big difference between ColdFusion SQL statements and statements entered in any other database client is the use of ColdFusion variables. If you are using ColdFusion variables in your statement, verify that you are enclosing them in quotation marks when necessary (if the column expects a string value). If a number is expected, the variable must *not* be enclosed in quotation marks.

NOTE

Many databases do not support double quotation marks, but instead expect single quotation marks.

- **Look at the bigger picture.** Dynamic SQL statements are one of ColdFusion's most powerful features, but this power comes at a price. When you create a dynamic SQL statement, you are effectively relinquishing direct control over the statement itself and are allowing it to be changed based on other conditions. This means that the code for a single ColdFusion query can be used to generate an infinite number of queries.

Because some of these queries might work and others might not, debugging dynamic SQL requires that you be able to determine exactly what the dynamically created SQL statement looks like. Again, ColdFusion makes this an easy task, as you will see later in this chapter in the section "Viewing Dynamically Generated SQL."

- Break complex SQL statements into smaller, simpler statements. If you are debugging a query that contains subqueries, verify that the subqueries properly work independently of the outer query.

CAUTION

Be careful not to omit number signs (#) around the variable names in your SQL code. Consider the following SQL statement:

```
DELETE Actors
WHERE ActorID=ActorID
```

The code is supposed to delete a specific actor: the one whose ID is specified in `ActorID`. But because the number signs were omitted, instead of passing the actor ID, the name of the actor ID column is passed. The result? Every row in the `Actors` table is deleted instead of just the one—all because of missing number signs.

Here is an even more correct statement, also including the number signs:

```
DELETE Actors
WHERE ActorID=<cfqueryparam value="#url.stateid#" cfsqltype="CF_SQL_NUMERIC">
```

This statement ensures that only numeric values are passed to the SQL statement.

Incidentally, this `WHERE` clause illustrates why you should always test `WHERE` clauses in a `SELECT` statement before using them in a `DELETE` or `UPDATE` statement.

Whenever a SQL syntax error occurs, ColdFusion displays the SQL statement it submitted (if you selected Enable Robust Exception Information in the Administrator debug output settings). The fully constructed statement is displayed if your SQL statement was constructed dynamically. The variable name values are displayed.

NOTE

If you ever encounter strange database driver error messages about mismatched data types or incorrect numbers of parameters, check to see if you have mistyped any table or column names and that you have single quotation marks where necessary. More often than not, that is what causes that error.

TIP

If you're using ColdFusion Builder, you can completely avoid typos in table and column names by using the RDS Dataview drag-and-drop support. Open RDS Dataview (Window > Show View > RDS Dataview) and select (or configure) your server, select the desired data source, and expand the tables to find the table and column you need. You can then click the table or column name and drag it to the editor window, where it will be inserted when you release the mouse key.

Viewing Dynamically Generated SQL

As discussed earlier in this chapter, a common challenge in debugging SQL problems in ColdFusion is identifying the SQL statement generated dynamically within a `<cfquery>` tag, because any valid

CFML can be used to create any valid SQL. Fortunately, there are several solutions, some new in recent releases.

Perhaps the most traditional approach is to use the ColdFusion debugging information, which can be enabled in the ColdFusion Administrator. The Debug Output Settings page contains a check box labeled Database Activity, and during development, you can enable this option to display the full SQL statement and data source name (and with the Enable Robust Exception Information option, this information is displayed in any database-related error messages). The debugging output options are discussed further in the section "ColdFusion Debugging Output Options" later in this chapter.

NOTE

Newer options have become available since ColdFusion MX 7, and these can be of particular value when you cannot enable debugging. ColdFusion MX 7 added a new Result attribute for `<cfquery>` (and other tags), which enables you to name a variable whose value will be a structure containing metadata about the tag after its execution. In the case of a `<cfquery>` tag, one of the resulting keys is SQL, which holds the dynamically generated SQL.

ColdFusion 8 also added, on the data source definition screen (under Advanced Settings), a Log Activity option, which you can use to name a log file to which ColdFusion will write the details of all database calls for that data source.

Debugging CFML and HTML Syntax Errors

Debugging of syntax errors, whether in CFML or HTML, is another type of troubleshooting you'll find yourself doing. Thankfully, CFML syntax errors are among the easiest bugs to find.

ColdFusion syntax errors are usually one of the following:

- Mismatched number signs (#) or quotation marks
- Mismatched begin and end tags; a `<cfif>` without a matching `</cfif>`, for example
- Incorrectly nested tags
- A tag with a missing or incorrectly spelled attribute
- Missing quotation marks around tag attributes
- Incorrect use of tags

If any of these errors occur, ColdFusion generates a descriptive error message, as shown in Figure 17.3. The error message lists the problematic code (and a few lines before and after it) and identifies exactly what the problem is.

CAUTION

If your template contains HTML forms, frames, or tables, you might have trouble viewing generated error messages. If an error occurs in the middle of a table, for example, that table will never be terminated, and there's no way to know how the browser will attempt to render the partial table. If the table isn't rendered and displayed properly, you won't see the error message.

Figure 17.3

ColdFusion generates descriptive error messages when syntax errors occur.

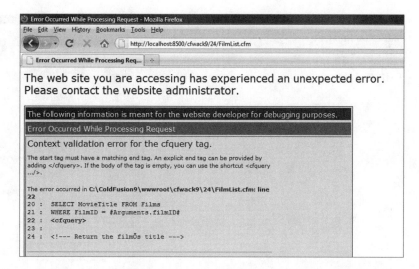

TIP

If you think an error has occurred but no error message is displayed, you can view the source in the browser. The generated source will contain any error messages that were included in the Web page but not displayed.

One of the most common CFML or HTML errors is missing or mismatched tags. Indenting your code, as shown in the following, is a good way to ensure that all tags are correctly matched:

```
<cfif some condition here>
 <cfoutput>
  Output code here
  <cfif another condition>
   Some other output code here
  </cfif>
 </cfoutput>
<cfelse>
 Some action here
</cfif>
```

ColdFusion Builder users can take advantage of the available features designed to help avoid common tag mismatching problems. For instance, as you type code, the editor automatically checks for coding syntax errors and reports them with a red X to the left of the line in error. If you roll the mouse over that red X, a pop-up message offers more details. Figure 17.4 shows the error message for the same closing `cfquery` tag without the needed slash shown in Figure 17.3.

→ For more information about ColdFusion Builder, see Chapter 3, "Introducing ColdFusion Builder."

Figure 17.4

ColdFusion Builder offers built-in error checking as you type CFML (and other) code.

Debugging Other Common Page Processing Problems

Besides syntactical problems, which can be detected and resolved with the help of ColdFusion Builder, several problems can occur that are more typically logical errors, ranging from problems with variables to problems with the way that HTML is processed in the browser or that browser input is processed in CFML.

Inspecting CFML Variable Contents During Processing

Sometimes problems throw no errors at all when you run the template. This can occur when your code is syntactically valid, but a logic problem exists somewhere. Aside from using the interactive debugger (which is discussed in Chapter 45), the primary way to locate this type of bug is to inspect variable contents during processing. Several ways to do this are available:

- Embed variable display code as necessary in your page, dumping the contents of variables to the screen (or to HTML comments you can view using View Source in your browser).

- The `<cfdump>` tag (introduced in Chapter 8, "The Basics of CFML") can display the contents of any variable, even complex variables, and can be used to aid debugging when necessary (and as of ColdFusion 8, this dump output can be directed to a log file or the ColdFusion console).

- The `<cflog>` tag can display the contents of any variable, writing its output to a log file.

- The `<cftrace>` tag can display the contents of any variable, and its operation can be enabled and disabled via the Administrator, as discussed later in this chapter, in the section "Using Tracing."

- By displaying variable contents, you usually can determine what sort of processing is being performed by various code blocks at any point during page processing.

TIP

You can use `<cfabort>` anywhere in the middle of your template to force ColdFusion to halt further processing. You can move the `<cfabort>` tag farther down the template as you verify that lines of code work.

TIP

During development, when you find yourself alternating between needing debugging information and not needing it, you can enclose debug code in `<cfif IsDebugMode()>` and `</cfif>`. This way, your debug output will be processed only if debugging output is enabled in the ColdFusion Administrator.

Debugging Code When Images Aren't Displayed

If image files (and other files) aren't displayed when you reference them from HTML you generate within ColdFusion, the problem may be path related. If you're using relative paths (and you generally should be), be sure that the path being sent to the browser is valid. Having too many or too few periods and slashes in the path is a common problem.

TIP

Most browsers let you check image paths (constructing full URLs from relative paths in your code) by right-clicking (Windows) or Control-clicking (Mac) the image and viewing the properties.

Debugging Code When URL Variables Aren't Processed

Chapter 10, "Creating Data-Driven Pages," discusses how to pass data on URLs. Parameters you pass on a URL may not be processed by ColdFusion, even though you see them present in the URL. URLs and URL parameters can be finicky, so abide by the following rules:

- URLs can have only one question mark character in them. The question mark separates the URL itself from the query string (the URL parameters).

- Each additional URL parameter must be separated by an ampersand (&).

- URLs should not contain spaces or other special characters. Older browsers may stop processing the URL at the space or special character. If you are generating URLs dynamically based on table column data, be sure to trim any spaces from those values. If you must use spaces, replace them with plus signs. You can use the ColdFusion `URLEncodedFormat()` function to convert text to URL-safe text.

TIP

ColdFusion debug output, discussed in the following section, lists all URL parameters passed to your page. This is an invaluable debugging tool.

Debugging Form Problems

Chapter 12, "ColdFusion Forms," introduced the use of forms for processing user input. A number of problems can occur when processing forms.

For instance, submitting a form with the wrong method can cause an error. Web browsers submit data to Web servers in either of two ways, with GET or POST, and the submission method is specified in the <form> or <cfform> method attribute. As a rule, forms should always be submitted to Cold-Fusion using the POST method, but note that the default method for <form> is GET, so if you omit or misspell method="POST", ColdFusion may be incapable of processing your form correctly.

You may occasionally get a variable is undefined error message when referring to form fields in the action template. A common problem is the absence of form variables for radio buttons, check boxes, and list boxes if they aren't selected by the user. It's important to remember this when referring to form fields in an action template. If you refer to a check box without first checking for its existence, an error will occur.

The solution is always to check for the existence of any form fields (or for variables that may not exist) before using them, by using the isdefined function. Alternatively, you can use the <CFPARAM> tag to assign default values to variables, thereby ensuring that they always exist. (This discussion also applies to the detection and handling of undefined URL variables.)

How can you check which form fields were actually submitted and what their values are? Enable ColdFusion debugging (as explained shortly); then any time you submit a form, its action page will contain a debugging output section that will describe the submitted form fields. This is shown in Figure 17.5. A variable named FORM.FIELDNAMES contains a comma-delimited list of all the submitted fields, and the Form Fields section lists all the submitted fields and their values. You can also dump the contents of the FORM scope from within code using <cfdump var="#form#">, which may be useful if debugging output is not enabled.

Figure 17.5

ColdFusion displays form-specific debugging information if debugging is enabled.

Besides the problem of a form field perhaps not existing, you may have situations in which the fields exist but the corresponding form variables in CFML don't match what you expect. Here are some other problems to watch for in your form definition:

- Be sure all form fields have names (used to create a variable in ColdFusion).

- Be sure related check boxes or radio buttons have the same name (unless using Flash Forms, in which case check boxes must be uniquely named).

- Be sure form field names are specified within double quotation marks.

- Be sure form field names have no spaces or other special characters in them.

- Be sure that all quotation marks around attribute values match.

ColdFusion Debugging Output Options

Previous sections of this chapter have discussed the use of ColdFusion debugging output. This section discusses the debugging output options, which are enabled or disabled via the ColdFusion Administrator, as explained in Chapter 2, in the section "Enabling Debugging."

TIP

You can restrict the display of debugging information to specific IP addresses. If you enable debugging, you should use this feature to prevent debugging screens from being displayed to your site's visitors.

CAUTION

At a minimum, the local host IP address (**127.0.0.1**) should be specified. If no IP address is in the list, debugging information will be sent to anyone who browses any ColdFusion page.

TIP

A long-time problem for ColdFusion developers has been getting their administrators to let them access the Administrator so that they can change options such as those discussed in this section. As of ColdFusion 8, an administrator can define username and password combinations to permit individuals to access the Administrator. Using this capability plus the Sandbox Security feature (in ColdFusion Enterprise), debugging can be restricted further, to one or more applications on a server. See Chapter 55, "Creating Server Sandboxes," in *Adobe ColdFusion 9 Web Application Construction Kit Volume 3: Advanced Application Development,* for more information about the new per-user admin configuration and sandbox security.

ColdFusion supports two debugging modes. They both provide the same basic functionality, but with different interfaces.

Classic Debugging

The *classic* debugging interface appends debugging information to the end of any generated Web pages, as shown in Figure 17.6. The advantage of this format is that it doesn't use any complex client-side technology, so it's safer to use on a wide variety of browsers.

To select this option, which is the default upon installation, select `classic.cfm` as the debug format in the ColdFusion Administrator.

Figure 17.6

ColdFusion can append debugging information to any generated Web page.

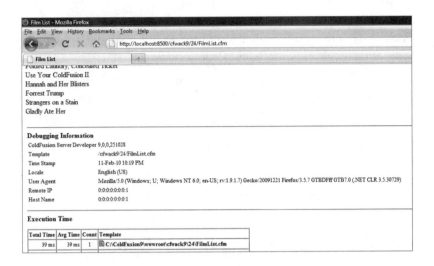

NOTE
This is known as the classic format because it's the format supported in ColdFusion since the very first versions of the product.

Dockable Debugging

ColdFusion also features a powerful DHTML-based debugging interface. As seen in Figure 17.7, debug information is displayed in a tree control in a separate pop-up window, or docked to the output itself (by clicking the Docked Debug Pane link, shown at the bottom of Figure 17.7). The advantage of this dockable format (aside from a much cleaner and easier-to-use interface) is that the debug output doesn't interfere with the page itself.

To select this option, select `dockable.cfm` as the debug format in the ColdFusion Administrator.

Using Debugging Options

Regardless of how the debugging information is accessed (through any of the options just listed) you'll have access to the same information:

- Execution time, so you can locate poorly performing code

- Database activity, so you can determine exactly what was passed to the database drivers (after any dynamic processing), what was returned, and how long this processing took

- Tracing information (explained below)

- Variables and their values

As you move from page to page within your application, the debug output will provide insight into what's actually going on within your code.

NOTE
The exact information displayed in debug output is managed by options in the ColdFusion Administrator, discussed in Chapter 2.

Figure 17.7

ColdFusion debug output can be displayed in a pop-up DHTML-based window.

CAUTION
While this debugging information is valuable, it does incur some overhead, even noticeable in development for some complex applications. It is especially recommended that you disable it in a production environment. Though a Debugging IP Addresses option is available (offered as the next link in the Administrator navigational toolbar), that feature simply controls who sees the debugging output; the overhead is still incurred on each page execution by all users.

Using Tracing

The ColdFusion Administrator debugging output contains a wealth of information, but you may on occasion also want to generate your own debug output. For example, you may want to

- Check the values of variables within a loop.

- Determine which code path or branch (perhaps in a series of `<cfif>` statements) is being followed.

- Inspect SESSION or other variables.

- Check for the presence of expected URL parameters or FORM fields.

- Display the number of rows retrieved by a query.

- Check the timing of a block of code.

This kind of information is useful in debugging logic problems—those annoying situations where code is valid syntactically, but some logic flaw (or unexpected situation) is preventing it from functioning as expected.

We previously discussed the `<cfdump>` tag, which by default displays its output in the generated output of the page. If you instead want to insert your own information within the automated debug output, you can use the `<cftrace>` tag, which embeds trace information on the page. The `<cftrace>` tag takes a series of attributes (all optional) that let you dump variable contents, display text (dynamic or static), abort processing, and more.

The simplest use of `<cftrace>` is to place a pair of the tags around a block of code; the generated output will then report the amount of time required to get to each trace and the difference in the amount of time between this operation and each subsequent one. Figure 17.8 shows the result of placing a pair of `<cftrace>` tags around a `cfoutput` loop. Note that the generated trace output is included with the standard debug output (if that option is enabled in the ColdFusion Administrator; see the Tracing Information option on the Debug Output Settings page).

Figure 17.8

Trace output (generated using `<CFTRACE>`) is included with debug output.

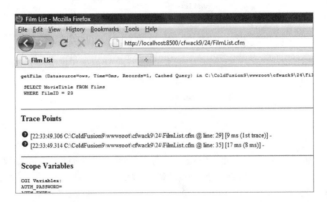

You can also use `<cftrace>` to display additional diagnostic data, using the `text` attribute. Simply embed such `<cftrace>` tags at strategic locations in your code. For example, if you're trying to figure out why variables are being set to specific values, use `<cftrace>` statements at the top of the page, before and after any statements that could set variable values (or that could call code that may set variable values).

To output simple text use, the following `<cftrace>` syntax:

```
<cftrace text="Just before the cfinclude">
```

To display variable values, you could use the following:

```
<cftrace text="firstname at top of page" var="firstname">
```

Note that the `<cftrace>` tag writes its output both to the debugging output and to a `cftrace.log` file (in the ColdFusion logs directory). You can also cause it to display its output at the point where the tag is executed, using the `Inline="yes"` attribute.

Also note that tracing can be enabled and disabled on the Debug Output Settings page of the ColdFusion Administrator, so that you can leave the tags in your source code even in production. They will not generate any output or use any resources if the tracing information option in the Administrator is disabled.

Additional `<cftrace>` attributes allow for message categorization and prioritization, but the two examples here are usually all you need. By embedding `<cftrace>` blocks in your code you'll get a clear and systematic view into what happened, when, and why.

Code Timing

Another challenge in solving problems with ColdFusion code entails understanding how long some tag or section of code takes to execute. Fortunately, ColdFusion offers several tools to help identify code timing:

- `GetTickCount()`
- `<cftrace>`
- `<cftimer>`
- `cfquery.executiontime`
- `Result` attribute
- Server monitor profiling feature

One of the oldest ways to identify code timing is to use the `getTickcount()` function, which returns a number of milliseconds since a point in the past. This function can be used to compare the count of milliseconds at one point to the count at a later point.

However, it can be simpler to use a similar, built-in feature of the `<cftrace>` tag. When this tag executes, it displays the elapsed time since a previous `<cftrace>` tag was executed. You can surround a code block you want to time with `<cftrace>` tags.

ColdFusion also has a tag devoted to code timing: `<cftimer>`. You wrap it around code to be timed, and it offers additional features that are different from (and some the same as) `<cftrace>`.

If you want to know how long a given `<cfquery>` tag took to execute, note that the available variable, `cfquery.executiontime`, holds the number of milliseconds. That shows the value for the last query executed, but as of ColdFusion 7, you can use the available `Result` attribute on any query, returning a structure that includes an `executiontime` value with the same timing information for that specific query (and disabling `cfquery.executiontime`).

Finally, the ColdFusion Enterprise server monitor includes profiling functionality that can show the time taken to execute each tag in an application. The server monitor is discussed in Chapter 47, "Monitoring System Performance," in Volume 3.

Using the ColdFusion Log Files

ColdFusion logs all warnings and errors to log files, which aids you and Adobe Technical Support in troubleshooting problems. ColdFusion log files are created when the ColdFusion service starts. You can delete these log files if they get too large, or move them to another directory for processing. If you do move or delete the log files, ColdFusion creates new ones automatically.

Most of the ColdFusion log files are plain-text, comma-delimited files. You can import these files into a database or spreadsheet application of your choice for analysis.

The ColdFusion Administrator Log Files page lists available log files (see Figure 17.9) and includes a sophisticated log file viewer that enables you to browse (see Figure 17.10), search, and analyze log file data as necessary.

Figure 17.9

The ColdFusion Administrator lists all available log files.

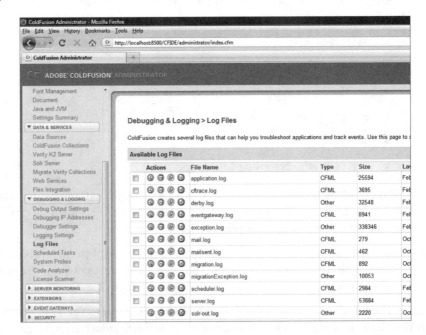

Figure 17.10

The Log Viewer supports browsing through log file entries.

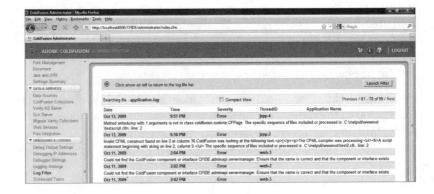

More sophisticated analysis filtering is supported (see Figure 17.11), allowing you to include or exclude filter conditions to locate exactly the logged messages you need. This is particularly useful on very busy systems, where multiple requests could be logging messages at the same time. Being able to filter by thread ID and time ranges helps find logging needles in the log file haystack.

Figure 17.11

Use the Log Viewer Filter window to search for specific log file entries.

Additionally, ColdFusion Builder adds a ColdFusion Tailview log viewer that permits access to and display of the log files from within the editor.

ColdFusion creates several log files. Some of the important ones are

- `application.log`: Contains generated CFML errors, syntax errors, and other runtime error conditions and messages.

- `cftrace.log`: Contains entries made using the `<cftrace>` tag.

- `eventgateway.log`: Contains errors and status messages related to the Event Gateway engine.

- `exception.log`: Contains Java exceptions thrown when errors occur.

- `flash.log`: Contains errors generated during Flash generation.

- `mail.log`: Contains errors generated while sending mail.

- `server.log`: Contains information about ColdFusion itself, including server stop and start times.

In addition to the standard log files, certain logs can be enabled based on ColdFusion Administrator settings (such as `mailsent.log` and `scheduler.log`), and specific operations (such as restoring an archive) can create their own log files.

As a rule, you should monitor and browse log files regularly, as these often contain the first indication of problems occurring. For added convenience, the log file viewer in the ColdFusion Administrator allows filtering, sorting, downloading for further analysis and archiving.

TIP

Some errors are browser related. If you're having a hard time reproducing reported error messages, try to determine which version of which browser the user was running and on which platform. You may have run into browser bugs (some versions of popular browsers are very buggy). To help you find these problems, the log files list any identification information provided by a browser, along with the error message.

ColdFusion offers still more logs, which many miss since they are not listed on the ColdFusion Administrator Log Files page. Sometimes called the runtime or JRun logs, these can often provide vital additional information, especially regarding problems with ColdFusion itself.

While the logs discussed previously in this section typically are found in the [coldfusion]\logs directory, these other logs typically are found in the [coldfusion]\runtime\logs directory. They may have names like coldfusion-out.log and coldfusion-event.log. (In the Multiserver form of ColdFusion deployment, these logs are instead found in the [jrun4]\logs directory.)

Preventing Problems

As mentioned earlier, the best approach to troubleshooting ColdFusion problems (and indeed any development problems) is to prevent them from occurring in the first place.

Bugs are inevitable. As the size of an application grows, so does the likelihood of a bug being introduced. As an application developer, you need to have two goals in mind:

- Develop bug-free code.

- In the event that your code isn't bug-free, make sure it's easy to debug.

As an application developer myself, I know that these are lofty goals. The reality is that application development almost always takes longer than planned, and sacrifices have to be made if release dates are to be met. Code quality is usually the first thing that gets sacrificed.

Sooner or later these sacrifices will come back to haunt you. Then come the long debugging sessions, rapid code fixes, software upgrades, and possibly even data conversion. Then, because the rapidly patched code often introduces bugs of its own, the whole cycle starts again.

Although there is no surefire way of preventing all bugs, some guidelines and coding practices can both help prevent many of them and make finding them easier when they do occur. Here are my 10 Commandments of ColdFusion Development:

1. **Plan Before You Code.** We've all done it, and probably more than once. ColdFusion makes it so easy to start coding that you're often tempted to start projects by firing up an editor and creating CFM files. That's a bad thing indeed. Nothing is more harmful to your development efforts than failing to plan properly. You should be spending more time planning than coding—and I don't mean planning your IPO and subsequent retirement. Planning involves thinking through every aspect of your application, from database design to UI considerations, from resource management to schedules and deliverables, and from feature lists with implementation details to language and presentation. You'd never build a house without detailed blueprints (well, you might try, but you'd never get the necessary permits to start work), and building an application is no different. I'm constantly amazed by the number of applications I'm asked to look at that have no supporting documentation. And these aren't just from small development shops; I'm talking about some of the largest and most respected corporations. Scalability problems? I wouldn't doubt it. I'd actually be amazed if such an application ever did scale. You can't

expect scalability from an application that grew in spite of its developers. Nor can you expect it to be bug free, manageable, or delivered on time. Yes, I know that detailed planning takes time, time none of us have. But in the long run you'll come out ahead.

2. **Organize Your Application.** An extension of planning your application is organizing it (along with any other applications). Applications are made up of lots of little bits and pieces, and keeping them organized is imperative. This includes directory structures and determining where common files should go, moving images to their own directory (or server), breaking long files into smaller, more manageable (and more reusable) ones (including CFCs), and even ensuring consistent organization among different applications. Going back to the prior commandment, Plan Before You Code, all organization should be documented in detail as part of that plan. You should also consider using ColdFusion frameworks such as Fusebox, *Model-Glue*, and *Mach-II* to help you structure your applications, especially if you work in a large team or have multiple developers performing maintenance on a project over time.

3. **Set Coding Standards.** This is an interesting one, and one I get asked about often. Adobe hasn't published formal recommendations on coding standards, nor in my opinion should they. Adobe's job is to create killer tools and products for developers, and our job is to use them however works best for us. I don't believe that a single set of coding standards would work for all developers. At the same time, I don't believe any developer should be writing code that doesn't adhere to some standard—any standard. Coding standards include everything from file-naming and directory-naming conventions to variable-naming conventions, to code organization and ordering within your source, to error handling, to componentization, and much more. For example, if all variables that contain dates begin with `dt`, then references to a variable named `dtOrderDate` become self-explanatory. The purpose of coding standards is to ensure some level of consistency in your code. Whether it's to allow other developers to understand and work with your code, or simply so that you'll know what you did (and why) six months down the line, coding standards provide a mechanism to create code that describes and explains itself. There is no right or wrong coding standard, as long as one is used. However, you can use the ColdFusion MX Coding Guidelines, created for internal Adobe use but available publicly (`http://livedocs.adobe.com/wtg/public/coding_standards/contents.html`), as a starting point. Note that these guidelines have not been updated since ColdFusion 7.

4. **Comment Your Code.** This is an obvious one, but apparently few of us have the time to pay attention to the obvious. So, I'll say it once again: All code must be commented. (For the record, I'd fire an employee on the spot for turning in code that wasn't commented; that's how serious an offense I believe this one to be.) Every source code file needs a descriptive header listing a description, the author information, the creation date, a chronological list of changes, any dependencies and assumptions, and any other relevant information. In addition, every conditional statement, every loop, every set of variable assignments, and every include or component reference must be commented with a simple statement explaining what is being done and why. It's a pain, I know. But

the next time you (or anyone else) have to work with the code, you'll appreciate the effort immeasurably. And you might even be able to safely make code changes without breaking things in the process.

5. **Never Make Changes on a Live Server.** This is another obvious one, but one worth stating anyway. All development and testing should occur on servers established for just that purpose. Yes, this means you'll need additional hardware, but the cost of a new box is nothing compared to the cost of bringing down your application because that little change wasn't as little as you expected. And ColdFusion is available free for development, so each developer can have his or her own copy. Write your code, test it, debug it as necessary, deploy it to a testing server, test it some more, and test it some more, and then finally deploy it to your live production server. And don't repeat this process too often. Again, don't edit the code directly on the production server. Instead of uploading even slightly changed versions of your application every day, collect the changes, test them some more, and deploy them monthly, or weekly, or whenever works best for you. The key here is that your production server is sacred; don't touch it at all unless you have to—and the less frequently, the better. Nothing is ever as minor and as isolated as it seems, and there is no change worth crashing a server over.

6. **Functionality First, Then Features.** This is yet another obvious one, and a common beginner's mistake. Yes, writing fancy code or using DHTML menu-generation code (or Ajax or Flash Forms features) is far more fun than writing or using data-entry validation routines (especially server side), but validation routines are typically far more important to the success and reliability of your application. Concentrate on creating a complete working application; then pretty it up as necessary. Do so and increase the chance that you'll finish on schedule for a change. The final result might not be as cool as you'd like, but there is something to be said for an application that actually works, even an uncool one. Furthermore, (as explained in the next commandment) debugging logic problems is difficult when the code is cluttered with fancy formatting and features.

7. **Build and Test Incrementally.** Testing and debugging complete applications is difficult. The bigger an application is, the more components are used, and the more developers working on a project, the harder debugging and testing is. When you develop core components of your application, test them. Write little test routines, create stubs to return hard-coded values, or use smoke-and-mirrors as necessary, but however you do it, do it. Every component you write must have its own test utility. Various CFML unit testing frameworks, such as CFUnit (`http://cfunit.sourceforge.net/`) and CFC-Unit (`http://www.cfcunit.org/cfcunit/`) are available. Feel free to use these if they help, or create your own. Obviously, you'll have to test your complete application when you're finished and some problems won't come to light until then, but the more you can test code blocks in isolation, the better.

8. **Never Reinvent the Wheel, and Plan Not To.** This is one I have written about extensively. Write code with reuse in mind, and reuse code whenever possible. When designing your code, put in the extra time up front to ensure it isn't hard-coded or highly task

specific unless it absolutely has to be. The benefits? Being able to reuse existing code shortens your development time. You stand a far greater chance of creating bug-free code when you use components that have already been used and tested. Plus, if you do make subsequent fixes and corrections, all code that uses the improved components benefit. This has a lot of benefits and no downside whatsoever.

9. **Use All the Tools at Your Disposal, Not Just ColdFusion.** ColdFusion applications usually aren't stand-alone entities. They rely on database servers, mail servers, etc. In addition, ColdFusion can leverage Web Services, Java, Flex, Ajax, Flash Remoting, Live-Cycle Data Services, COM, .NET, CORBA, C/C++ code, and more. Use these tools, as many as necessary, and always try to select the best one for a specific job. The best ColdFusion applications aren't the ones written purely in ColdFusion; they are the ones that leverage the best technologies for the job, all held together by ColdFusion.

10. **Implement Version Control and Source Code Tracking.** Source code will change, and changes are dangerous. As your applications grow, so does the need for tracking changes and source code control. Select a version control package that works for you, and use it. Key features to look for are the ability to lock files (so no one else edits a file while you edit it—if that does happen, someone's changes will be lost) or merge concurrent changes, the ability to view change history (what changed, by whom, and when), the ability to roll back complete applications (so that when the latest upgrade bombs you can easily roll back an entire application to a prior known state), the ability to create and check file dependencies (so you'll know what other code is affected by changes you make), and reporting. In addition, if you can integrate the product with ColdFusion Builder, that's even better. The bottom line: I don't care which product you use, just use one.

TIP

Until you implement a version-control mechanism, at least use the ColdFusion Builder Local History feature. You can right-click a file in the Navigator (project) view (or right-click in the editor while viewing a file opened from a project) and choose Compare With > Local History. This feature lets you see previous revisions of the file, though only up to a limit of days and amounts set in Window > Preferences > General > Workspace > Local History.

➡ Chapter 11, "The Basics of Structured Development," teaches the basics of code reuse and how to create your own components.

PART 3

Building ColdFusion Applications

Introducing the Web Application Framework

ColdFusion provides a small but very important set of features for building sophisticated Web applications. The features have to do with making all your ColdFusion templates for a particular site or project behave as if they were related to one another—that is, to make them behave as a single application. These features are referred to collectively as the Web application framework.

The Web application framework is designed to help you with the following:

- **Consistent look and feel.** The application framework enables you to easily include a consistent header or footer at the top and bottom of every page in your application. It also lets you apply the same look and feel to user error messages. You can also use it to keep things like fonts and headings consistent from page to page.

- **Sharing variables between pages.** So far, the variables you have worked with in this book all "die" when each page request has been processed. The Web application framework gives you a variety of ways to maintain the values of variables between page requests. The variables can be maintained on a per-user, per-session, or application-wide basis.

- **Before and after processing.** The application framework gives you an easy way to execute custom code you want just *before* each page request. A common use for this capability is to provide password security for your application. You can also execute custom code just *after* the request. Along with executing code before and after a request, you can execute code when the application starts and when it expires. This lets you specify application-wide variables when it starts up, and doing cleanup once the application expires.

- **Handling errors.** In a perfect world, developers would never make mistakes, but for those of us who live in this world, mistakes happen. The application framework provides a simple way to handle errors. It also handles requests for missing ColdFusion templates.

Considered together, it's the Web application framework that really lets you present a Web experience to your users. Without these features, your individual templates would always stand on their own, acting as little mini-programs. The framework is the force that binds your templates together.

Using `Application.cfc`

To get started with the Web application framework, you first must create a special file called `Application.cfc`. In most respects, this file is just an ordinary ColdFusion component. (Components are discussed in depth in Chapter 24, "Creating Advanced ColdFusion Components," in *Adobe ColdFusion 9 Web Application Construction Kit, Volume 2: Application Development*.) Only two things make `Application.cfc` special:

- The code in your `Application.cfc` file will be automatically executed just before any of the pages in your application.

- You can't visit an `Application.cfc` page directly. If you attempt to visit an `Application.cfc` page with a browser, you will receive an error message from ColdFusion.

The `Application.cfc` file is sometimes referred to as the application component. It might not sound all that special so far, but you will find that the two special properties actually go a long way toward making your applications more cohesive and easier to develop.

NOTE

On Unix/Linux systems, file names are case sensitive. The `Application.cfc` file must be spelled exactly as shown here, using a capital A. Even if you are doing your development with Windows systems in mind, pay attention to the case so ColdFusion will be capable of finding the file if you decide to move your application to a Linux or Unix server later.

NOTE

Previous versions of ColdFusion used another file, `Application.cfm`, to enable the application framework. This still works in the current version of ColdFusion. However, the use of `Application.cfc` is now recommended instead of `Application.cfm`.

Placement of `Application.cfc`

As we said, the code in your `Application.cfc` file is automatically executed just before each of the pages that make up your application. You might be wondering how exactly ColdFusion does this. How will it know which files make up your application and which ones don't?

The answer is quite simple: Whenever a user visits a `.cfm` page, ColdFusion looks to see whether a file named `Application.cfc` exists in the same directory as the requested page. If so, ColdFusion automatically executes it. Later on, you'll see exactly which methods of the CFC are executed.

If no `Application.cfc` exists in the same folder as the requested page, ColdFusion looks in that folder's parent folder. If no `Application.cfc` file exists there, it looks in *that* parent's folder, and so on, until there are no more parent folders to look in.

NOTE

This behavior can be modified on the ColdFusion Administrator's Server Settings page.

All this means is that you should do something you were probably already going to do anyway, namely, put all the ColdFusion templates for a particular application within a single folder, somewhere within your Web server's document root. Let's call that directory your application folder. Within the application folder, you can organize your ColdFusion templates any way you choose, using any number of subfolders, sub-subfolders, and so on. If you put an Application.cfc file in the application folder, it will be executed when any the application's templates are run. It's that simple.

For instance, consider the fictional folder structure shown in Figure 18.1. Here, the application folder is the folder named MyApp, which is sitting within the Web server's document root. Some basic Web pages are located in there, such as the company's Home page (Index.cfm), a How To Contact Us page (ContactUs.cfm), and a Company Info page (CompanyInfo.cfm). There is also a SiteHeader.cfm template there, which we intend to include at the top of each page.

Figure 18.1

The Application.cfc file gets included before any of your application's templates.

Because a file called Application.cfc also exists in this folder, it's automatically included every time a user visits Index.cfm or ContactUs.cfm. It's also included whenever a user visits any of the ColdFusion templates stored in the Intranet or Store folders, or any of the subfolders of the Intranet folder. No matter how deep the subfolder structure gets, the Application.cfc file in the MyApp folder will be automatically included.

NOTE

Don't worry about re-creating this folder structure yourself. None of the code examples for this chapter rely on it. We're just trying to clarify where your Application.cfc template might go in a real-world application.

Application.cfc **Structure**

As you will learn in Chapter 24, a ColdFusion Component is a collection of methods and data. You can think of it as a package of information (the data) and things you can do with the information (the methods). The Application.cfc file lets you do just that—create both data and methods. However, some methods are special. For example, if you create a method called onRequestStart, the method will execute before each and every page request. Table 18.1 lists these methods and how they work. Later in the chapter we will demonstrate how these work.

Table 18.1 Application.cfc Methods

METHOD	PURPOSE
onApplicationStart	Run when the application begins. This will run the first time a user executes a page inside the application. This method can be used to initialize application variables.

Table 18.1 (CONTINUED)

METHOD	PURPOSE
onApplicationEnd	Executed when the application ends. All applications have a timeout, defined either by the application itself or the default application timeout value specified in the ColdFusion Administrator. An application times out when no one requests a file. You can use this method to record the status of application variables to a database, log to a file, or even send an email notifying you that the application has timed out.
onRequestStart	Executed before each page request. This could be used to specify Request scoped variables needed for pages in the application, check security credentials, or perform other checks that need to happen on every page request.
onRequestEnd	Executed before each page request. This could be used to specify Request scoped variables needed for pages in the application, check security credentials, or perform other checks that need to happen on every page request.
onRequest	Executed immediately after onRequestStart. Can be used to filter requests and modify the result.
onCFCRequest	Executed for CFC access via HTTP only.
onSessionStart	Executed when a user's session starts. Sessions are covered in Chapter 19, "Working with Sessions."
onSessionEnd	Executed when a user's session ends.
onError	Executed when an error occurs. This will be covered in greater depth later in the chapter.
onMissingTemplate	Executed when a request for a ColdFusion template is made and that template does not exist.

In our examples for this chapter, we will focus mainly on the onApplicationStart, onRequestStart, onError, and onMissingTemplate methods. Chapter 19 will cover onSessionStart and onSessionEnd.

A Basic Application.cfc Template

Take a look at Listing 18.1, a simple Application.cfc file. This example makes use of the onRequestStart method. Because the <cfset> tag is executed before each page request, the companyName variable can be referred to within any of the application's ColdFusion templates. For instance, the value of the companyName variable will always be Orange Whip Studios.

If you save this listing, be sure to save it as Application.cfc, not Application1.cfc.

Listing 18.1 Application1.cfc—A Simple Application Template

```
<!---
 Filename: Application.cfc (The "Application Component")
 Created by: Raymond Camden (ray@camdenfamily.com)
 Purpose: Sets "constant" variables and includes consistent header
--->
```

Listing 18.1 (CONTINUED)

```
<cfcomponent output="false">

  <cffunction name="onRequestStart" returnType="boolean" output="true">
    <!--- Any variables set here can be used by all our pages --->

    <cfset request.companyName = "Orange Whip Studios">

    <!--- Display our Site Header at top of every page --->
    <cfinclude template="SiteHeader.cfm">

    <cfreturn true>
  </cffunction>

</cfcomponent>
```

As you will learn in Chapter 24, all components begin and end with the `<cfcomponent>` tag. This component only uses one method, `onRequestStart`. This method will execute before each request. The method begins by defining two `request` scope variables, `dataSource` and `companyName`.

In addition, the `<cfinclude>` tag in Listing 18.1 ensures that the company's standard page header will be shown at the top of each page. Listing 18.2 shows the `SiteHeader.cfm` template itself. Note that it can use the `CompanyName` variable that gets set by `Application.cfc`.

If this were your application, you would no longer have to put that `<cfinclude>` tag at the top of the `Index.cfm` or `CompanyInfo.cfm` pages (see Figure 18.1), and you wouldn't have to remember to include it in any new templates. ColdFusion would now be taking care of that for you.

Listing 18.2 `SiteHeader.cfm`—Simple Header Included on Each Page

```
<!---
 Filename: SiteHeader.cfm
 Created by: Nate Weiss (NMW)
 Please Note Included in every page by Application.cfc
--->

<html>
<head>
<title><cfoutput>#request.companyName#</cfoutput></title>
<style>
.header {
  font-size: 18px;
  font-family: sans-serif;
}
.footer {
  font-size: 10px;
  color: silver;
  font-family: sans-serif;
}
body {
  font-family: sans-serif;
}
.error {
  color: gray;
}
```

Listing 18.2 (CONTINUED)

```
</style>
</head>

<body>

<!--- Company Logo --->
<img src="../images/logo_c.gif" width="101" height="101" alt=""
    align="absmiddle" border="0">
<cfoutput><span class="header">#request.companyName#</span></cfoutput>
<br clear="left">
```

Using onRequestEnd()

The Web application framework also reserves the special OnRequestEnd method, which is executed automatically at the end of every page request, rather than at the beginning. Listing 18.3 is a modification of Listing 18.1. This time our Application.cfc includes an onRequestEnd method. It has just one line of code, a simple <cfinclude> tag to include the SiteFooter.cfm template at the bottom of every page. Listing 18.4 shows the SiteFooter.cfm file itself, which displays a copyright notice. The net effect is that the copyright notice is displayed at the bottom of every page in the application.

Of course, there are other ways to get this effect. You could forget about this OnRequestEnd() business and just put the <cfinclude> tag at the bottom of every page in your application. But that might be tedious, and you might occasionally forget to do it. Or, you could just put the copyright notice in the OnRequestEnd method and get rid of the SiteFooter.cfm file altogether. That would be fine, but leaving them in separate files keeps things more manageable if the footer becomes more complicated in the future.

If you save Listing 18.3, be sure to save it as Application.cfc, not Application2.cfc.

Listing 18.3 Application2.cfc—Including a Site Footer at the Bottom of Every Page

```
<!---
 Filename: Application.cfc (The "Application Component")
 Created by: Raymond Camden (ray@camdenfamily.com)
 Purpose: Sets "constant" variables and includes consistent header
--->

<cfcomponent output="false">

  <cffunction name="onRequestStart" returnType="boolean" output="true">
    <!--- Any variables set here can be used by all our pages --->
<cfset request.companyName = "Orange Whip Studios">

    <!--- Display our Site Header at top of every page --->
    <cfinclude template="SiteHeader.cfm">

    <cfreturn true>
  </cffunction>

  <cffunction name="onRequestEnd" returnType="void" output="true">
```

Listing 18.3 (CONTINUED)

```
        <!--- Display our Site Footer at bottom of every page --->
        <cfinclude template="SiteFooter.cfm">

    </cffunction>

</cfcomponent>
```

Listing 18.4 `SiteFooter.cfm`—Simple Footer That Gets Included by `OnRequestEnd()`

```
<!---
 Filename: SiteFooter.cfm
 Created by: Nate Weiss (NMW)
 Please Note Included in every page by OnRequestEnd.cfm
--->

<!--- Display copyright notice at bottom of every page --->
<cfoutput>
  <p class="footer">
  (c) #year(now())# #request.companyName#. All rights reserved.
  </p></cfoutput>

</body>
</html>
```

NOTE

The expression `#year(now())#` is a simple way to display the current year. You also could use `#dateFormat(now(),"yyyy")#` to get the same effect.

TIP

While `Application.cfc` makes it easy to automatically add headers or footers (or both!) to your site, it is typically not recommended for such purposes. As you can imagine, there may be times when you *don't* want a footer on a page. In those cases, you would have to manually add a clause to prevent the footer. As time goes on, that code may get more and more complex. In general, best practices recommend using either `<cfinclude>` or custom tags for layout purposes.

Listing 18.5 provides preliminary code for Orange Whip Studio's home page. As you can see, it's just a simple message that welcomes the user to the site. Of course, in practice, this is where you would provide links to all the interesting parts of the application. The point of this template is to demonstrate that the site header and footer are now going to be automatically included at the top and bottom of all ordinary ColdFusion templates in this folder (or its subfolders). Note that this template is also able to use the `REQUEST.companyName` variable that was set in the `Application.cfc` file.

If you save this file, be sure to save it as `Index.cfm`, not `Index1.cfm`.

Listing 18.5 `Index1.cfm`—A Basic Home Page for Orange Whip Studios

```
<!---
 Filename: Index.cfm
 Created by: Nate Weiss (NMW)
 Please Note Header and Footer are automatically provided
--->

<cfoutput>
```

Listing 18.5 (CONTINUED)

```
<blockquote>
<p>Hello, and welcome to the home of
#REQUEST.companyName# on the web! We certainly
hope you enjoy your visit. We take pride in
producing movies that are almost as good
as the ones they are copied from. We've
been doing it for years. On this site, you'll
be able to find out about all our classic films
from the golden age of Orange Whip Studios,
as well as our latest and greatest new releases.
Have fun!
</blockquote>
</cfoutput>
```

Using Application Variables

So far in this chapter, you have seen how ColdFusion's Web application framework features help you maintain a consistent look and feel throughout your application. You've also seen how easy it is to set up "before and after" processing with the special Application.cfc component and the onRequestStart and onRequestEnd methods. In other words, your pages are starting to look and behave cohesively.

Next, you will learn how your application's templates can start sharing variables between page requests. Basically, this is the part where your application gets a piece of the server's memory in which to store values. This is where it gets a brain.

What Are Application Variables?

Pretend it's Oscar season. Orange Whip Studios feels that all of its films are contenders. Tensions are high, and the president wants a new "Featured Movie" box on the studio's home page to help create more "buzz" than its bitter rival, Miramax. The featured movie should be different each time the home page is viewed, shamelessly rotating through all of the studio's movies. It's your job to get this project done, pronto.

Hmmm. You could retrieve all the movies from the database for each page request and somehow pick one at random, but that wouldn't guarantee that the same movie wouldn't get picked three or four times in a row. What you want is some way to remember your current spot in the list of movies, so they all get shown evenly, in order. You consider making a table to remember which movies have been shown and then deleting all rows from the table when it's time to rotate through them again, but that seems like overkill. You wish there was some kind of variable that would persist between page requests, instead of dying at the bottom of each page like the ColdFusion variables you're used to.

Well, that's exactly what application variables are for. Instead of a variable called lastMovieID, you could set a variable called application.lastMovieID. After you set this variable value to 5, say, it remains set at 5 until you change it again (or until the server is restarted). In essence, application variables let you set aside a little piece of ColdFusion's memory that your application can use for its own purposes.

When to Use Application Variables

Generally, you can use application variables whenever you need a variable to be shared among all pages and all visitors to your application. The variable is kept in ColdFusion's memory, and any page in your application can access or change its value. If some code on one of your pages changes the value of an application variable, the next hit to any of your application's pages will reflect the new value.

NOTE

This means you should not use application variables if you want a separate copy of the variable to exist for each visitor to your site. In other words, application variables shouldn't be used for anything personalized, because they don't distinguish between your site's visitors.

→ Chapter 19 explains how to create variables that are maintained separately for each visitor.

Consider application variables for

- Rotating banner ads evenly, so that all ads get shown the same number of times

- Keeping counters of various types of events, such as the number of people currently online or the number of hits since the server was started

- Maintaining some type of information that changes only occasionally or perhaps doesn't change at all, but can take time to compute or retrieve; your site's title and root URL are examples

Do *not* use application variables for per-user tasks, such as these:

- Maintaining a shopping cart

- Remembering a user's email address or username from visit to visit

- Keeping a history of the pages a user has visited while he has been on your site

Using the `Application.cfc` Component

We've already discussed the special purpose of the `Application.cfc` file. What we didn't mention was that by including an `Application.cfc` file, you automatically enable the use of Application variables. Application variables are one type of persistent variable; you will learn about two other types—client and session variables—in Chapter 19.

So far, the example `Application.cfc` files we have shown have only demonstrated methods. Components can also contain data. There are two main scopes in a component used to store data: `VARIABLES` and `THIS`. Earlier we mentioned that components can use any method names you want. But in the `Application.cfc` component, some method names were special. The same applies to the `THIS` scope. By setting particular values in the `THIS` scope you can control how the application behaves. For now we will focus on just three of those values, demonstrated in Table 18.2.

Table 18.2 THIS Scope Values Relevant to Application Variables

ATTRIBUTE	DESCRIPTION
name	A name for your application. The name can be anything you want, up to 64 characters long. ColdFusion uses this name internally to store and look up your application variables for you. It should be unique by server.
applicationTimeout	Optional. How long you want your application variables to live in the server's memory. If you don't provide this value, it defaults to whatever is set up in the Memory Variables page of the ColdFusion Administrator. See the section "Application Variable Timeouts," later in this chapter. The maximum value can't be higher than the maximum value specified in the Memory Variables page of the ColdFusion Administrator.
datasource	Optional. Almost every ColdFusion application makes use of the database, and along with that the <cfquery> tag. Because this tag is used so often, ColdFusion 9 added the capability to set a default data source for all queries within one application.

NOTE

ColdFusion maintains your application variables based on the THIS scopes NAME value. Therefore, it's important that no other applications on the same ColdFusion server use the same NAME. If they do, ColdFusion will consider them to be the same application and will share the variables among all the combined pages. Changing a variable in one also changes it in the other, and so on. It's conceivable to find yourself in a situation where this is actually what you want (if for some reason all the pages in your application simply can't be nested within a single folder); otherwise, make sure that each Application.cfc's THIS scope gets its own NAME.

Using Application Variables

Now that application variables have been enabled, using them is quite simple. Basically, you create or set an application variable the same way you would set a normal variable, generally using the <cfset> tag. The only difference is the presence of the word APPLICATION, followed by a dot. For instance, the following line would set the APPLICATION.ourHitCount variable to 0. The variable would then be available to all pages in the application and would hold the value of 0 until it was changed:

```
<cfset APPLICATION.ourHitCount = 0>
```

You can use application variables in any of the same places you would use ordinary ones. For instance, the following code adds one to an application variable and then outputs the new value, rounded to the nearest thousandth:

```
<cfset APPLICATION.ourHitCount = APPLICATION.ourHitCount + 1>
<cfoutput>#round(APPLICATION.ourHitCount / 1000)># thousand</cfoutput>
```

You also can use application variables with ColdFusion tags, such as <cfif>, <cfparam>, and <cfoutput>. See Chapter 8, "The Basics of ColdFusion," and Chapter 9, "Programming with CFML," if you want to review the use of variables in general.

Initializing Application Variables

Application variables are persistent. That simply means that once you create them, they stick around. Because of this, there is no reason to set them on every request. Once you create an Application variable, you don't need to create it. Once simple way to handle that would be with the isDefined() function.

```
<cfif not isDefined("application.foo")>
  <cfset application.foo = "bar">
</cfif>
```

This code will check to see if the variable application.foo exists. If it doesn't, it will create it. However, the Application.cfc component provides an even easier way to do this. One of the special methods mention in Table 18.1 is the onApplicationStart() method. This method will execute only when the application starts. Conversely, there is also an onApplicationEnd() method. This could be used to do a variety of things. Listing 18.6 shows a newer version of the Application.cfc worked on earlier.

If you save this file, be sure to save it as Application.cfc, not Application3.cfc.

Listing 18.6 Application3.cfc—Using onApplicationStart and onApplicationEnd

```
<!---
 Filename: Application.cfc (The "Application Component")
 Created by: Raymond Camden (ray@camdenfamily.com)
 Purpose: Sets "constant" variables and includes consistent header
--->

<cfcomponent output="false">

  <cfset this.name = "ows18">
  <cfset this.dataSource = "ows">

  <cffunction name="onApplicationStart" returnType="boolean" output="false">
    <!--- When did the application start? --->
    <cfset application.appStarted = now()>

    <cfreturn true>
  </cffunction>

  <cffunction name="onApplicationEnd" returnType="void" output="false">
    <cfargument name="appScope" required="true">

    <!--- Log how many minutes the application stayed alive --->
    <cflog file="#this.name#" text=
"App ended after #dateDiff('n',arguments.appScope.appStarted,now())# minutes.">

  </cffunction>

  <cffunction name="onRequestStart" returnType="boolean" output="true">
    <!--- Any variables set here can be used by all our pages --->
<cfset request.companyName = "Orange Whip Studios">

    <!--- Display our Site Header at top of every page --->
    <cfinclude template="SiteHeader.cfm">
```

Listing 18.6 (CONTINUED)

```
      <cfreturn true>
    </cffunction>

    <cffunction name="onRequestEnd" returnType="void" output="true">

    <!--- Display our Site Footer at bottom of every page --->
    <cfinclude template="SiteFooter.cfm">

    </cffunction>

</cfcomponent>
```

There's a lot of new code here, so let's tackle it bit by bit. The first new line is

```
    <cfset this.name = "ows18>
```

This line uses the THIS scope to name the application. Remember, every name for your application should be unique. If you use the same name for multiple Application.cfc files, they will essentially act as the same application. Notice that this line of code is outside any method. This line will be run when the Application.cfc file is loaded by ColdFusion.

In the same block you will find this line:

```
    <cfset this.dataSource = "ows">
```

As described earlier, this code sets a default data source for all queries and other database-driven tags within the application.

The next set of new code is the onApplicationStart method. This method really does only one thing: it creates a variable called APPLICATION.appStarted initialized with the current time. The idea is to simply store the time the application started. ColdFusion automatically calls this method when the application is first started by a user. You don't have to do anything special to enable this function—ColdFusion handles it for you.

Next we have the onApplicationEnd method. This method will fire when the application ends. Normally the only way to execute ColdFusion code automatically is with the ColdFusion Scheduler. Outside of that, ColdFusion code only executes when someone requests a file. The onApplicationEnd method (as well as the onSessionEnd method) runs without anyone actually requesting a ColdFusion document.

Because this method is triggered when the application ends and not by a user request , you can't output anything from this method. Even if you did, no one could see it! What you can do is clean up the application. This can include logging information to a database or file, firing off an email, or doing any number of things that would make sense when an application ends. Let's examine the method line by line. The first line is

```
    <cfargument name="appScope" required="true">
```

This simply defines an argument sent to the method. In our case, the ColdFusion server automatically sends a copy of the APPLICATION scope (all the data you stored in it) to the onApplicationEnd method. This is important. You can't access the APPLICATION scope they way you can normally. Instead, you have to use the copy passed in the method. The next line will show an example of this:

```
<cflog file="#this.name#" text=
"App ended after #dateDiff('n',arguments.appScope.appStarted,now())# minutes.">
```

The <cflog> tag simply logs information to a file. We are only using two of the attributes in this line. The file attribute simply tells <cflog> what name to use for the file. When providing a file name, you don't add the ".log" to the name; <cflog> will do that for you. In our code, we use the value of the Application's name. Recall that we set the name using the THIS scope earlier in the component. The text attribute defines what is sent to the file. If you remember, we stored the time the application loaded in a variable called application.appStarted. As we said above, we can't access the APPLICATION scope in the onApplicationEnd method. Instead, we have to use the copy passed in. We called this argument appScope, so we can access our original value as arguments. appScope.appStarted. We use the dateDiff function to return the number of minutes between when the application started and the current time. This lets us log the total time the application was running before it timed out.

The rest of the file simply duplicates the onRequestStart and onRequestEnd methods we described earlier.

Putting Application Variables to Work

Application variables can make it relatively easy to get the little featured movie widget up and running. Again, the idea is for a callout-style box, which cycles through each of Orange Whip Studio's films, to display on the site's home page. The box should change each time the page is accessed, rotating evenly through all the movies.

Listing 18.7 shows one simple way to get this done, using application variables. Note that the template is broken into two separate parts. The first half is the interesting part, in which an application variable called MovieList is used to rotate the featured movie correctly. The second half simply outputs the name and description to the page.

Listing 18.7 FeaturedMovie.cfm—Using Application Variables to Track Content Rotation

```
<!---
 Filename: FeaturedMovie.cfm
 Created by: Nate Weiss (NMW)
 Purpose: Displays a single movie on the page, on a rotating basis
 Please Note Application variables must be enabled
--->

<!--- List of movies to show (list starts out empty) --->
<cfparam name="application.movieList" type="string" default="">

<!--- If this is the first time we're running this, --->
<!--- Or we have run out of movies to rotate through --->
<cfif listLen(application.movieList) eq 0>
 <!--- Get all current FilmIDs from the database --->
 <cfquery name="getFilmIDs">
 SELECT FilmID FROM Films
```

Listing 18.7 (CONTINUED)

```
 ORDER BY MovieTitle
 </cfquery>

 <!--- Turn FilmIDs into a simple comma-separated list --->
 <cfset application.movieList = valueList(getFilmIDs.FilmID)>
 </cfif>

 <!--- Pick the first movie in the list to show right now --->
 <cfset thisMovieID = listFirst(application.MovieList)>
 <!--- Re-save the list, as all movies *except* the first --->
 <cfset application.movieList = listRest(application.movieList)>
 <!--- Now that we have chosen the film to "Feature", --->
 <!--- Get all important info about it from database. --->
 <cfquery name="GetFilm">
  SELECT
  MovieTitle, Summary, Rating,
  AmountBudgeted, DateInTheaters
  FROM Films f, FilmsRatings r
  WHERE FilmID = #thisMovieID#
  AND f.RatingID = r.RatingID
 </cfquery>

 <!--- Now Display Our Featured Movie --->
 <cfoutput>
  <!--- Define formatting for our "feature" display --->
  <style type="text/css">
  TH.fm { background:RoyalBlue;color:white;text-align:left;
  font-family:sans-serif;font-size:10px}
  TD.fm { background:LightSteelBlue;
  font-family:sans-serif;font-size:12px}
  </style>

  <!--- Show info about featured movie in HTML Table --->
  <table width="150" align="right" border="0" cellspacing="0">
  <tr><th class="fm">
  Featured Film
  </th></tr>
  <!--- Movie Title, Summary, Rating --->
  <tr><td class="fm">
  <b>#getFilm.MovieTitle#</b><br>
  #getFilm.Summary#<br>
  <p align="right">Rated: #getFilm.Rating#</p>
  </td></tr>
  <!--- Cost (rounded to millions), release date --->
  <tr><th class="fm">
  Production Cost $#round(getFilm.AmountBudgeted / 1000000)# Million<br>
  In Theaters #dateFormat(getFilm.DateInTheaters, "mmmm d")#<br>
  </th></tr>
  </table>
  <br clear="all">
 </cfoutput>
```

As you can see, the top half of the template is pretty simple. The idea is to use an application variable called movieList to hold a list of available movies. If 20 movies are in the database, the list holds 20 movie IDs at first. The first time the home page is visited, the first movie is featured and then removed from the list, leaving 19 movies in the list. The next time, the second movie is featured (leaving 18), and so on until all the movies have been featured. Then the process begins again.

Looking at the code line by line, you can see how this actually happens.

The `<cfparam>` tag is used to set the `application.movieList` variable to an empty string if it doesn't exist already. Because the variable will essentially live forever once set, this line has an effect only the first time this template runs (until the server is restarted). This line could be moved to the `onApplicationStart` method of the `Application.cfc` file. We are keeping it here to make it a bit simpler to see what is going on with this template.

The `<cfif>` tag is used to test whether the `movieList` variable is currently empty. It is empty if this is the first time the template has run or if all the available movies have been featured in rotation already. If the list is empty, it is filled with the list of current movie IDs. Getting the current list is a simple two-step process of querying the database and then using the `valueList` function to create the list from the query results.

The `listFirst()` function is used to get the first movie's ID from the list. The value is placed in the `thisMovieID` variable. This is the movie to feature on the page.

Finally, the `listRest()` function is used to chop off the first movie ID from the `APPLICATION.movieList` variable. The variable now holds one fewer movie. Eventually, its length will dwindle to zero, in which case the `<cfif>` tag will again test whether the `movieList` variable is currently empty, repeating the cycle.

Now that the movie to be featured has been picked (it's in the `thisMovieID` variable), actually displaying the movie's name and other information is straightforward. The `<cfquery>` in the second half of Listing 18.7 selects the necessary information from the database, and then a simple HTML table is used to display the movie in a nicely formatted box.

At this point, Listing 18.7 can be visited on its own, but it was really meant to show the featured movie on Orange Whip's home page. Simply include the template using the `<cfinclude>` tag, as shown in Listing 18.8.

Figure 18.2 shows the results.

Figure 18.2

Application variables enable the featured movie to be rotated evenly among all page requests.

Listing 18.8   `Index2.cfm`—Including the Featured Movie in the Company's Home Page

```
<!---
 Filename: Index.cfm
 Created by: Nate Weiss (NMW)
 Please Note Header and Footer are automatically provided
--->

<cfoutput>
 <p>Hello, and welcome to the home of
 #request.companyName# on the web! We certainly
 hope you enjoy your visit. We take pride in
 producing movies that are almost as good
 as the ones they are copied from. We've
 been doing it for years. On this site, you'll
 be able to find out about all our classic films
 from the golden age of Orange Whip Studios,
 as well as our latest and greatest new releases.
 Have fun!<br>
</cfoutput>

<!--- Show a "Featured Movie" --->
<cfinclude template="FeaturedMovie.cfm">
```

Customizing the Look of Error Messages

The Web application framework provides a simple way to customize the look of error messages that can occur while users are accessing your pages. As you know, error messages might appear because of syntax problems in your code, because of database connection problems, or just because users have left out one or more required fields while filling out a form.

The application framework lets you customize any of these error messages. You can even hide them from the user's view entirely if you want. This enables you to maintain a consistent look and feel throughout your application, even when those dreaded error messages occur. You even have multiple ways to handle exceptions. We will cover both, dealing with the simplest solution first.

Introducing the `<cferror>` Tag

You use the `<cferror>` tag to specify how error messages should be displayed. Customizing the error messages that appear throughout your application is generally a two-step process:

1. First, you create an *error display template*, which displays the error message along with whatever graphics or other formatting you consider appropriate.

2. Next, you include a `<cferror>` tag that tells ColdFusion to display errors using the error display template you just created. In general, you place the `<cferror>` tag in your `Application.cfc` file.

Table 18.3 shows the attributes supported by the `<cferror>` tag.

The next two sections discuss how to customize the error messages displayed for *exception errors* (syntax errors, database errors, and so on) and *validation errors* (when the user fails to fill out a form correctly).

Table 18.3 `<cferror>` Tag Attributes

ATTRIBUTE	DESCRIPTION
type	The type of error you want to catch and display using your customized error display template. The allowable values are `Request`, `Validation`, and `Exception`. The `Validation` type is no longer recommended for use and will not be covered. If you don't supply this attribute, it is assumed to be `Request`, but it's best to always supply it.
template	Required. The relative path and file name of your customized error display template. You specify the file name in the same way as you would specify an include file with the `<cfinclude>` tag.
mailto	Optional. An email address for a site administrator that the user could use to send some type of notification that the error occurred. The only purpose of this attribute is to pass an appropriate email address to your error display template. It doesn't actually send any email messages on its own.
exception	Optional. The specific exception that you want to catch and display using your customized error display template. The default value is `Any`, which is appropriate for most circumstances. See Chapter 44, "Error Handling," online, for a discussion of the other values you can supply here.

Request Versus Exception Error Templates

If you want to customize the way error messages are displayed, you first must create an error display template. This template is displayed to the user whenever a page request can't be completed because of some type of uncaught error condition.

ColdFusion actually allows you to create two types of error display templates:

- **Request error display templates.** The simplest way to show a customized error message. You can include whatever images or formatting you want so that the error matches your site's look and feel. However, CFML tags, such as `<cfoutput>`, `<cfset>`, or `<cfinclude>`, are not allowed. CFML functions and variables also are not allowed. Request error templates provide a last-resort way to handle errors. They normally are run after an exception error template fails.

- **Exception error display templates.** These are more flexible. You can use whatever CFML tags you want. For instance, you might want to have ColdFusion automatically send an email to the webmaster when certain types of errors occur. The main caveat is that ColdFusion can't display such a template for certain serious errors.

In general, the best practice is to create one template of each type. Then the exception template is displayed most often, unless the error is so serious that ColdFusion can't safely continue interpreting

CFML tags, in which case the request template is displayed. The request template also kicks in if the exception template *itself* causes an error or can't be found.

NOTE

If you don't care about being able to use CFML tags in these error display templates, you can just create the request template and skip creating the exception one.

NOTE

For those history buffs out there, the request type of error display template is a holdover from earlier versions of ColdFusion. At one time, you could never respond intelligently to any type of error. Thankfully, those days are over.

Creating a Customized Request Error Page

To create the request display template, do the following:

1. Create a new ColdFusion template called `ErrorRequest.cfm`, located in the same directory as your `Application.cfc` file. Include whatever images or formatting you want, using whatever `<img>` or other tags you would normally. Remember to *not* put any CFML tags in this template.

2. Include the special `error.diagnostics` variable wherever you want the actual error message to appear, if you want it to appear at all. Contrary to what you are used to, the variable does not have to be between `<cfoutput>` tags.

3. If you want, you can include the special `error.mailTo` variable to display the email address of your site's webmaster or some other appropriate person. You also can use any of the other variables shown in Table 18.4.

4. Include a `<cferror>` tag in your `Application.cfc` file, with the `type` attribute set to `Request` and the `template` attribute set to `ErrorRequest.cfm`. This is what associates your error display template with your application.

Table 18.4 Special `error` Variables Available in an Error Display Template

ATTRIBUTE	DESCRIPTION
`error.browser`	The browser that was used when the error occurred as reported by the browser itself. This is the same value that is normally available to you as the `#cgi.http_user_agent#` variable, which generally includes the browser version number and operating system.
`error.dateTime`	The date and time the error occurred, in the form MM/DD/YY HH:MM:SS. You can use the `dateFormat()` function to format the date differently in an exception template, but not in a request template.
`error.diagnostics`	The actual error message. In general, this is the most important thing to include (or not to include) in an error display template. Please note that the exact text of this message can be affected by the settings currently enabled in the Debugging Settings page of the ColdFusion Administrator. See Chapter 17, "Debugging and Troubleshooting," for details.

Table 18.4 (CONTINUED)

ATTRIBUTE	DESCRIPTION
error.generatedContent	The actual HTML that had been generated by the requested ColdFusion template (and any included templates, and so on) up until the moment that the error occurred. You could use this to display the part of the page that had been successfully generated.
error.HTTPReferer	The page the user was coming from when the error occurred, assuming that the user got to the problem page via a link or form submission. This value is reported by the browser and can sometimes be blank (especially if the user visited the page directly by typing its URL). Note the incorrect spelling of the word referrer.
error.mailTo	An email address, presumably for a site administrator or webmaster, as provided to the `<cferror>` tag. See the following examples to learn how this actually should be used.
error.queryString	The query string provided to the template in which the error occurred. In other words, everything after the ? sign in the page's URL. This is the same value that is normally available to you as the `#cgi.query_string#` variable.
error.remoteAddress	The IP address of the user's machine. This is the same value that is normally available to you as the `#cgi.remote_addr#` variable.
error.template	File name of the ColdFusion template (`.cfm` file) in which the error occurred.

Listing 18.9 is a good example of a request error display template. Note that no `<cfoutput>` or other CFML tags are present. Also note that the only variables used are the special `error` variables mentioned previously.

Listing 18.9 `ErrorRequest.cfm`—Customizing the Display of Error Messages

```
<!---
 Filename: ErrorRequest.cfm
 Created by: Nate Weiss (NMW)
 Please Note Included via <cferror> in Application.cfc
--->

<html>
<head><title>Error</title></head>
<body>

<!--- Display sarcastic message to poor user --->
<h2>Who Knew?</h2>
<p>We are very sorry, but a technical problem prevents us from
showing you what you are looking for. Unfortunately, these things
happen from time to time, even though we have only the most
top-notch people on our technical staff. Perhaps all of
our programmers need a raise, or more vacation time. As always,
there is also the very real possibility that SPACE ALIENS
(or our rivals at Miramax Studios) have sabotaged our website.
<p>That said, we will naturally try to correct this problem
as soon as we possibly can. Please try again shortly.
```

Listing 18.9 (CONTINUED)

```
<!--- Provide "mailto" link so user can send email --->
<p>If you want, you can
<a href="mailto:#error.mailTo#">send the webmaster an email</a>.
<p>Thank you.<br>

<!--- Maybe the company logo will make them feel better --->
<img src="../images/logo_b.gif" width="73" height="73" alt="" border="0">

<!--- Display the actual error message --->
<blockquote>
<hr><span class="error">#error.diagnostics#</span></blockquote>

</body>
</html>
```

→ ColdFusion also provides the `<cftry>` and `<cfcatch>` tags, which enable you to trap specific errors and respond to or recover from them as appropriate. For details, see Chapter 45, "Using the Debugger," online.

Listing 18.10 shows how to use the `<cferror>` tag in your `Application.cfc` file. Note that the email address webmaster@orangewhipstudios.com is being provided as the tag's mailTo attribute, which means that the webmaster's email address will be inserted in place of the error.mailTo reference in Listing 18.9. Figure 18.3 shows how an error message would now be shown if you were to make a coding error in one of your templates.

Figure 18.3

Customized error pages help maintain your application's look and feel.

We are very sorry, but a technical problem prevents us from showing you what you are looking for. Unfortunately, these things happen from time to time, even though we have only the most top-notch people on our technical staff. Perhaps all of our programmers need a raise, or more vacation time. As always, there is also the very real possibility that SPACE ALIENS (or our rivals at Miramax Studios) have sabotaged our website.

That said, we will naturally try to correct this problem as soon as we possibly can. Please try again shortly.

If you want, you can send the webmaster an email.

Thank you.

Variable X is undefined.
The error occurred on line 17.

To test this listing, save it as `Application.cfc`, not `Application4.cfc`.

Listing 18.10 `Application4.cfc`—Use of the `<cferror>` Tag in `Application.cfc`

```
<!---
 Filename: Application.cfc (The "Application Component")
 Created by: Raymond Camden (ray@camdenfamily.com)
 Purpose: Sets "constant" variables and includes consistent header
--->

<cfcomponent output="false">
```

Listing 18.10 (CONTINUED)

```
        <cfset this.name = "ows18">
        <cfset this.dataSource = "ows">
        <cferror type="Request" template="ErrorRequest.cfm"
                 mailto="webmaster@orangewhipstudios.com">

        <cffunction name="onApplicationStart" returnType="boolean" output="false">
          <!--- When did the application start? --->
          <cfset application.appStarted = now()>

          <cfreturn true>
        </cffunction>

        <cffunction name="onApplicationEnd" returnType="void" output="false">
          <cfargument name="appScope" required="true">

          <!--- Log how many minutes the application stayed alive --->
          <cflog file="#this.name#" text=
"App ended after #dateDiff('n',arguments.appScope.appStarted,now())# minutes.">

        </cffunction>

        <cffunction name="onRequestStart" returnType="boolean" output="true">
          <!--- Any variables set here can be used by all our pages --->
  <cfset request.companyName = "Orange Whip Studios">

          <!--- Display our Site Header at top of every page --->
          <cfinclude template="SiteHeader.cfm">

          <cfreturn true>
        </cffunction>

        <cffunction name="onRequestEnd" returnType="void" output="true">

          <!--- Display our Site Footer at bottom of every page --->
          <cfinclude template="SiteFooter.cfm">

        </cffunction>

     </cfcomponent>
```

Additional `error` Variables

In Listing 18.9, you saw how the `error.diagnostics` variable can be used to show the user which specific error actually occurred. A number of additional variables can be used in the same way. You will see several of these used in Listing 18.11 in the next section.

NOTE

Note that the `error.generatedContent` variable is not available in request error display templates.

TIP

These are the only variables you can use in request error display templates. You can use all types of ColdFusion variables in exception error display templates, discussed next.

Creating a Customized Exception Error Page

You have seen how to create a request error display template, in which you are prevented from using any CFML tags or functions. Now you can create an exception error template, in which you *can* use whatever CFML tags and functions you want.

For instance, Listing 18.11 is similar to Listing 18.10, but it doesn't display the error.diagnostics message to the user. This means that the user won't know which type of error actually occurred. After all, your users might not care about the specifics, and you might not want them to see the actual error message in the first place. In addition, instead of allowing the user to send an email message to the webmaster, this template has ColdFusion send an email message to the webmaster automatically, via the <cfmail> tag.

Now all you have to do is add a second <cferror> tag to your Application.cfc file, this time specifying type="Exception" and template="ErrorException.cfm". You should put this <cferror> tag right after the first one, so the first one can execute if some problem occurs with your exception error display template. Since this modification is so simple, it won't be listed in the chapter. It is available at the book Web site with the name Application5.cfc.

Listing 18.11 ErrorException.cfm—Sending an Email When an Error Occurs

```
<!---
 Filename: ErrorException.cfm
 Created by: Nate Weiss (NMW)
 Please Note Included via <cferror> in Application.cfc
--->

<html>
<head><title>Error</title></head>
<body>

<!--- Display sarcastic message to poor user --->
<h2>Who Knew?</h2>
<p>We are very sorry, but a technical problem prevents us from
showing you what you are looking for. Unfortunately, these things
happen from time to time, even though we have only the most
top-notch people on our technical staff. Perhaps all of
our programmers need a raise, or more vacation time. As always,
there is also the very real possibility that SPACE ALIENS
(or our rivals at Miramax Studios) have sabotaged our website.<br>
<p>That said, we will naturally try to correct this problem
as soon as we possibly can. Please try again shortly.
Thank you.<br>

<!--- Maybe the company logo will make them feel better --->
<img src="../images/logo_b.gif" width="73" height="73" alt="" border="0">

<!--- Send an email message to site administrator --->
<!--- (or whatever address provided to <cferror>) --->
<cfif error.mailTo neq "">
 <cfmail to="#error.mailTo#" from="errorsender@orangewhipstudios.com"
 subject="Error on Page #error.Template#">
 Error Date/Time: #error.dateTime#
 User's Browser: #error.browser#
```

Listing 18.11 (CONTINUED)

```
URL Parameters: #error.queryString#
Previous Page: #error.HTTPReferer#
------------------------------------
#error.diagnostics#
</cfmail>
</cfif>
```

NOTE

Because sending automated error emails is a great way to show how exception templates can be used, the `<cfmail>` tag has been introduced a bit ahead of time here. Its use in Listing 18.11 should be self-explanatory: The ColdFusion server sends a simple email message to the webmaster. The email will contain the error message, date, browser version, and so on because of the `error` variables referred to between the opening and closing `<cfmail>` tags.

→ See Chapter 20, "Interacting with Email," for details.

→ The webmaster could also look in ColdFusion's logs to see any errors that might be occurring throughout the application. See Chapter 17 for details.

Using the `OnError` Method

As we discussed earlier in the chapter, the `Application.cfc` contains a set of special methods that are executed depending on certain situations. We demonstrated how the `onApplicationStart` and `onApplicationEnd` methods are executed automatically based on the life of the ColdFusion application. One more special method is the `onError` method. As you can probably guess, this method is called whenever an exception occurs. Unlike the `<cferror>` tag, which is tied to a specific error type or exception, the `onError` method will fire on *any* error.

So how can you use this method? The method could do many of the things demonstrated in the listings we've already covered. You can mail the error to the administrator, or log the error to a file or database. You can even display a message to the user, but remember that the `onError` method will be run for any error. So for example, if your `onApplicationEnd` method throws an error, the `onError` method will run. The output won't be displayed, obviously, since no one is there to actually see it.

Another option to consider when using the `onError` method is to use it to handle the non-visual portions of the error (emailing the administrator, logging, etc.), and use the `<cfthrow>` tag to let your `<cferror>` tags take over. The `<cfthrow>` tag is discussed in Chapter 44. Think of the `onError` method as simply taking care of the error temporarily, and then passing it back to ColdFusion. If you have already created your request, exception, and validation templates, this approach lets you continue using those templates, while adding a bit of extra functionality to your application. Listing 18.12 demonstrates the latest version of our `Application.cfc` file, this time with an `onError` method. If you save this template, be sure to save it as `Application.cfc`, not `Application5.cfc`.

Listing 18.12 `Application5.cfc`—Working with `onError`

```
<!---
    Filename: Application.cfc (The "Application Component")
    Created by: Raymond Camden (ray@camdenfamily.com)
```

Listing 18.12 (CONTINUED)

```
    Purpose: Sets "constant" variables and includes consistent header
--->

<cfcomponent output="false">

  <cfset this.name = "ows18">
  <cfset this.dataSource = "ows">

  <cferror type="Request" template="ErrorRequest.cfm"
          mailto="webmaster@orangewhipstudios.com">
  <cferror type="Exception" template="ErrorException.cfm"
          mailto="webmaster@orangewhipstudios.com">

  <cffunction name="onApplicationStart" returnType="boolean" output="false">
    <!--- When did the application start? --->
    <cfset application.appStarted = now()>

    <cfreturn true>
  </cffunction>

  <cffunction name="onApplicationEnd" returnType="void" output="false">
    <cfargument name="appScope" required="true">

    <!--- Log how many minutes the application stayed alive --->
    <cflog file="#this.name#" text=
"App ended after #dateDiff('n',arguments.appScope.appStarted,now())# minutes.">

  </cffunction>

  <cffunction name="onRequestStart" returnType="boolean" output="true">
    <!--- Any variables set here can be used by all our pages --->
<cfset request.companyName = "Orange Whip Studios">

    <!--- Display our Site Header at top of every page --->
    <cfinclude template="SiteHeader.cfm">

    <cfreturn true>
  </cffunction>

  <cffunction name="onRequestEnd" returnType="void" output="true">

<!--- Display our Site Footer at bottom of every page --->
<cfinclude template="SiteFooter.cfm">

  </cffunction>

  <cffunction name="onError" returnType="void" output="false">
    <cfargument name="exception" required="true">
    <cfargument name="eventName" type="string" required="true">

    <!--- Use the cflog tag to record info on the error --->
    <cfif arguments.eventName is "">
      <cflog file="#this.name#" type="error"
              text="#arguments.exception.message#">
    <cfelse>
      <cflog file="#this.name#" type="error"
```

Listing 18.12 (CONTINUED)

```
      text="Error in Method [#arguments.eventName#] #arguments.exception.message#">
        </cfif>

        <!--- Let the <cferror> tags do their job. --->
        <cfthrow object="#arguments.exception#">

    </cffunction>

  </cfcomponent>
```

The only thing new in this template is the onError method at the end, so we'll focus on that portion. The onError method is automatically passed two arguments. The first is the exception itself. This is just like the ERROR structure discussed earlier. It has the same values and we can use it to email, log to a file, or anything else. The second argument passed to the method is the name of the event that was running when the exception occurred. This argument will only have a value when the error occurs within the Application.cfc file itself. So for example, if the onApplicationStart method threw an error, that method name would be passed to the onError method. The onError method in Listing 18.12 checks to see if an eventName argument has a value. If it doesn't, it simply logs the error. Note that it uses the same file value as the onApplicationEnd's <cflog> tag. The value passed to the log is just the exception message. If the eventName argument wasn't blank, the text passed to the log is modified slightly to contain the event name as well. Lastly, we use the <cfthrow> tag to pass the error back out again from the onError method. Don't worry too much about this tag now; it's covered in Chapter 44. Just consider the onError method here as being part of a "chain" of code blocks that will handle the error.

→   ColdFusion also provides the <cftry> and <cfcatch> tags, which allow you to trap specific errors and respond to or recover from them as appropriate. See Chapter 44 for details.

Handling Missing Templates

ColdFusion 8 added the capability to handle requests for ColdFusion files that do not exist. In the past, handling these requests was problematic and required updating of the Web server settings. Now you can simply add another method to your Application.cfc file to handle these missing templates.

Note, though, that this support for missing templates helps only with requests for missing Cold-Fusion files. If a user requests dharma.html (notice that the extension is html, not cfm), then ColdFusion can't help you; instead, the 404 handler of your Web server will handle the request.

Using onMissingTemplate

The new method that we'll be adding to our Application.cfc file is the onMissingTemplate function. This method is passed one argument: the name of the script that was requested. Listing 18.13 shows the latest version of the Application.cfc file. Be sure to save this file as Application.cfc, not Application6.cfc.

Listing 18.13 `Application6.cfc`—Working with onMissingTemplate

```
<!---
 Filename: Application.cfc (The "Application Component")
 Created by: Raymond Camden (ray@camdenfamily.com)
 Purpose: Sets "constant" variables and includes consistent header
--->

<cfcomponent output="false">

  <cfset this.name = "ows18">
  <cfset this.dataSource = "ows">

  <cferror type="Request" template="ErrorRequest.cfm"
           mailto="webmaster@orangewhipstudios.com">
  <cferror type="Exception" template="ErrorException.cfm"
           mailto="webmaster@orangewhipstudios.com">

  <cffunction name="onApplicationStart" returnType="boolean" output="false">
    <!--- When did the application start? --->
    <cfset application.appStarted = now()>

    <cfreturn true>
  </cffunction>

  <cffunction name="onApplicationEnd" returnType="void" output="false">
    <cfargument name="appScope" required="true">

    <!--- Log how many minutes the application stayed alive --->
    <cflog file="#this.name#" text=
"App ended after #dateDiff('n',arguments.appScope.appStarted,now())# minutes.">

  </cffunction>

  <cffunction name="onRequestStart" returnType="boolean" output="true">
    <!--- Any variables set here can be used by all our pages --->
<cfset request.companyName = "Orange Whip Studios">

    <!--- Display our Site Header at top of every page --->
    <cfinclude template="SiteHeader.cfm">

    <cfreturn true>
  </cffunction>

  <cffunction name="onRequestEnd" returnType="void" output="true">

    <!--- Display our Site Footer at bottom of every page --->
    <cfinclude template="SiteFooter.cfm">

  </cffunction>

  <cffunction name="onError" returnType="void" output="false">
    <cfargument name="exception" required="true">
    <cfargument name="eventName" type="string" required="true">

    <!--- Use the cflog tag to record info on the error --->
    <cfif arguments.eventName is "">
      <cflog file="#this.name#" type="error"
```

Listing 18.13 (CONTINUED)

```
                  text="#arguments.exception.message#">
    <cfelse>
      <cflog file="#this.name#" type="error"
 text="Error in Method [#arguments.eventName#] #arguments.exception.message#">
    </cfif>

    <!--- Let the <cferror> tags do their job. --->
    <cfthrow object="#arguments.exception#">

  </cffunction>


  <cffunction name="onMissingTemplate" returnType="boolean" output="false">
    <cfargument name="targetpage" type="string" required="true">

    <!--- log it --->
    <cflog file="#this.name#" text="Missing Template: #arguments.targetpage#">
    <cflocation url="404.cfm?missingtemplate=#urlEncodedFormat(arguments.targetpage)#"
addToken="false">

  </cffunction>

  </cfcomponent>
```

Let's focus on the new code in this document: the onMissingTemplate method. As stated earlier, this method takes one argument: the name of the template being requested. So if you requested jedi.cfm and that file did not exist, that is the value that would be passed to the function. The complete path is passed as well as the name, so you would really end up with something like this: /ows/c18/dharma.cfm. We do two things in the method. First we log the fact that a missing-template event occurred. This is important because if you commonly see people loading a file that does not exist, you may want to add the file anyway. Second, we send the user to a file named 404.cfm. We pass the template as a URL variable. 404.cfm will display a nice error message for the user. You can see this in Listing 18.14.

Listing 18.14 404.cfm—Handling Missing Templates

```
<!--- Filename: 404.cfm
  Created by: Raymond Camden (ray@camdenfamily.com)
  Purpose: Display a message about a missing file.
--->

<cfparam name="url.missingtemplate" default="">

<cfoutput>
<p>
Sorry, we could not load #url.missingtemplate#. Please try our <a href="index.
cfm">home page</a> instead.
</p>
</cfoutput>
```

This file doesn't do very much. It first ensures that the URL variable, missingtemplate, has a default value. It then tells the user that the requested file didn't exist and kindly provides a link back to the home page.

Special Considerations

In some circumstances, ColdFusion will notice if you request a subdirectory that does not contain an index page. An index page is any file that the Web server recognizes as a file to run in a folder if no particular file name is specified. If no such file exists, the Web server may respond with a list of files. Typically, though, this is not done because it presents a security risk. If you do want this behavior, then you need to specify a new THIS scope variable named welcomeFileList. This variable consists of a list of files that match the index files specified by your Web server. It tells ColdFusion when it should and should not run onMissingTemplate for a subdirectory. However, this scenario applies only to the embedded JRun Web server. It does not apply to common Web servers such as Apache or IIS.

Using Locks to Protect Against Race Conditions

ColdFusion is a *multithreaded* application, meaning that the server can process more than one page request at a time. Generally speaking, this is a wonderful feature. Because the server can in effect do more than one thing at a time, it can tend to two or three (or 50) simultaneous visitors to your application.

But as wonderful as multithreading is, it also means that you need to think carefully about situations where more than one person is accessing a particular page at the same time. Unless you take steps to prevent it, the two page requests can be reading or changing the same application variable at the very same moment. If you are using application variables to track any type of data that changes over time, and the integrity of the data is critical to your application (such as any type of counter, total, or statistic), you must tell ColdFusion what to do when two page requests are trying to execute the same "shared data-changing" code at the same time.

NOTE

> This isn't something that only ColdFusion programmers face. In one fashion or another, you'll run into these issues in any multi-threaded programming environment. ColdFusion just makes the issue really easy to deal with.

Of course, ColdFusion provides solutions to help you deal with concurrent page requests quite easily. One possible solution is the <cflock> tag. You can use the <cflock> tag to mark the areas of your code that set, change, access, or display application variables. The <cflock> tag ensures that those potentially problematic parts of your code don't execute at the same time as other potentially problematic parts. As you will learn in this section, your locking instructions will cause one page to wait a moment while the other does its work, thus avoiding any potential problems. In other words, you keep your code thread-safe yourself.

NOTE

> If you use the onApplicationStart method, you don't need to use any <cflock> tags. All application variables created there are entirely thread-safe. The same applies for onSessionStart.

What Is a Race Condition?

It's time to pause for just a moment of theory. You need to understand the concept of a race condition and how such conditions can occur in your ColdFusion applications. Simply put, a race condition is any situation where two different page requests can change the same information at the very same moment in time. In many situations, race conditions can lead to undesired results. In other situations, you may not care about them at all.

NOTE

We seriously recommend taking a few moments to really visualize and understand this stuff, especially if you are going to be using application variables to hold values that change over time (especially values that increment numerically as your application does its work).

Here's an example that should make this really easy to understand. Imagine an application variable called `application.HitCount`. The purpose of this variable is to track the number of individual page views that an application has responded to since the ColdFusion server was started. Simple code like the following is used in the `onRequestStart` method to advance the counter by one every time a user visits a page:

```
<cfset application.hitCount = application.hitCount + 1>
```

So far, so good. The code seems to do what it's supposed to. Every time a page is viewed, the variable's value is increased by one. You can output it at any time to display the current number of hits. No problem.

But what happens if two people visit a page at the same time? We know that ColdFusion doesn't process the pages one after another; it processes them at the very same time. Keeping that in mind, consider what ColdFusion has to do to execute the `<cfset>` tag shown above. Three basic mini-steps are required to complete it:

1. ColdFusion gets the current value of `application.hitCount`.

2. It adds one to the value.

3. Finally, it sets the `application.hitCount` to the new, incremented value.

The big problem is that another page request may have changed the value of the variable between steps 1 and 2, or between steps 2 and 3. Just for fun, let's say the hit count variable is currently holding a value of 100. Now two users, Bob and Jane, both type in your application's URL at the same time. For whatever reason, Jane's request gets to the server a split moment after Bob's. Bob's request performs the first mini-step (getting the value of 100). Now, while Bob's request is performing the second mini-step (the addition), Jane's request is doing its first step: finding out what ColdFusion has for the current value of the application variable (uh-oh, still 100). While Bob's request performs the *third* mini-step (updating the counter to 101), Jane's request is still doing its *second* step (adding one to 100). Jane's request now finishes its third step, which sets the application variable to, you guessed it, 101. That is, when both requests are finished, the hit count has only increased by one, even though two requests have come through since hit number 100. A bit of information has been lost.

Granted, for a simple hit counter like this, a teensy bit of information loss probably isn't all that important. You may not care that the hit count is off by one or two every once in a while. But what if the application variable in question was something more like `application.totalSalesToDate`? If a similar kind of "mistake" occurred in something like a sales total, you might have a real problem on your hands.

NOTE

Again, it is important to note that this isn't a problem specific to ColdFusion. It's a simple, logical problem that would present itself in almost any real-world situation where several different "people" (here, the people are Web users) are trying to look at or change the same information at the same time.

NOTE

By definition, the chances of a race condition problem actually occurring in an application will increase as the number of people using the application increases. That is, these kinds of problems tend to be "stealth" problems that are difficult to catch until an application is battle-tested.

The solution is to use <cflock> tags to make sure that two requests don't execute the <cfset> tag (or whatever problematic code) at the same exact moment. For example, <cflock> tags would cause Jane's request to wait for Bob's request to be finished with that <cfset> before it started working on the <cfset> itself.

<cflock> **Tag Syntax**

Now that you know what race conditions are and how they can lead to unpredictable results, it's time to learn how to use locking to avoid them. We'll get into the nuances shortly, but the basic idea is to place opening and closing <cflock> tags around any part of your code that changes application variables (or session variables, which are discussed in the next chapter) or any other type of information that might be shared or changed by concurrent page requests. Table 18.5 takes a closer look at the tag's syntax.

Table 18.5   <cflock> Tag Syntax

ATTRIBUTE	DESCRIPTION
type	Optional. The type, or strength, of the lock. Allowable values are Exclusive and ReadOnly. You should use Exclusive to indicate blocks of code that change the values of shared variables. Use ReadOnly to indicate blocks of code that aren't going to be changing any shared values, but that always need to be reading or outputting the most recent version of the information. If you don't provide a type, the default of Exclusive is assumed.
scope	The type of persistent variables you are using between the <cflock> tags. Allowable values are Application, Session, Request, and Server. You would use a <cflock> with scope="Application" around any code that uses application variables. You would set this value to Session around code that uses session variables, which are discussed in the next chapter. If the code must be locked on a per-request basis, use the Request value. The use of server variables is not discussed in this book and is generally discouraged.

Table 18.5 (CONTINUED)

ATTRIBUTE	DESCRIPTION
name	Optional. You can provide a name attribute instead of scope to get finer-grained control over your locks. This is discussed in the "Using Named Locks Instead of scope" section, later in this chapter. You must always provide a name or a scope, but you can't provide both.
timeout	Required. The length of time, in seconds, that ColdFusion will wait to obtain the lock. If another visitor's request has a similar `<cflock>` on it, ColdFusion will wait for this many seconds for the locked part of the other request to finish before proceeding. Generally, 10 is a sensible value to use here.
throwOnTimeout	Optional. The default is Yes, which means an error message will be displayed if ColdFusion can't obtain the lock within the timeout period you specified. (You can catch this error using `<cfcatch>` to deal with the situation differently. See Chapter 44 for details.)

Using Exclusive Locks

As Table 18.5 shows, there are two types of locks: Exclusive and ReadOnly. Let's start off simple, and talk about `<cflock>` tags of type="Exclusive". If you want, you can solve your race condition problems using only Exclusive locks.

Exclusive locks work like this. When your template gets to an opening `<cflock>` tag in your code, it requests the corresponding lock from the server. There is only one available lock for each scope (Application, Session, Request, or Server), which is why it's called "exclusive." Once this Exclusive lock has been bestowed upon your template, it stays there until the closing `</cflock>` tag in your code, at which point the lock is released and returned to the server. While your template has the lock (that is, while the code between the `<cflock>` tags is running), all other templates that want an application-level lock must wait in line. ColdFusion pauses the other templates (right at their opening `<cflock>` tags) until your template releases the lock.

The code shown in Listing 18.15 shows how to place Exclusive locks in your code. This listing is similar to the previous version of the Featured Movie template (Listing 18.7). The only important difference is the pair of `<cflock>` tags at the top of the code. Note that the `<cflock>` tags surround the entire portion of the template that is capable of changing the current value of the APPLICATION. movieList variable.

Listing 18.15 FeaturedMovie2.cfm—Using Exclusive Locks to Safely Update Application Data

```
<!---
  Filename: FeaturedMovie2.cfm
  Created by: Nate Weiss (NMW)
  Purpose: Displays a single movie on the page, on a rotating basis
  Please Note Application variables must be enabled
--->

<!--- Need to lock when accessing shared data --->
<cflock scope="application" type="Exclusive" timeout="10">
```

Listing 18.15 (CONTINUED)

```coldfusion
      <!--- List of movies to show (list starts out empty) --->
      <cfparam name="application.movieList" type="string" default="">

      <!--- If this is the first time we're running this, --->
      <!--- Or we have run out of movies to rotate through --->
      <cfif listLen(application.movieList) eq 0>
        <!--- Get all current FilmIDs from the database --->
                <cfquery name="getFilmIDs">
                SELECT FilmID FROM Films
                ORDER BY MovieTitle
                </cfquery>

                <!--- Turn FilmIDs into a simple comma-separated list --->
                <cfset application.movieList = valueList(getFilmIDs.FilmID)>
      </cfif>

      <!--- Pick the first movie in the list to show right now --->
      <cfset thisMovieID = listFirst(application.movieList, 1)>
      <!--- Re-save the list, as all movies *except* the first --->
      <cfset application.movieList = listRest(application.movieList, 1)>
    </cflock>


    <!--- Now that we have chosen the film to "Feature", --->
    <!--- Get all important info about it from database. --->
    <cfquery name="GetFilm">
     SELECT
     MovieTitle, Summary, Rating,
     AmountBudgeted, DateInTheaters
     FROM Films f, FilmsRatings r
     WHERE FilmID = #thisMovieID#
     AND f.RatingID = r.RatingID
    </cfquery>

    <!--- Now Display Our Featured Movie --->
    <cfoutput>
            <!--- Define formatting for our "feature" display --->
            <style type="text/css">
            TH.fm { background:RoyalBlue;color:white;text-align:left;
            font-family:sans-serif;font-size:10px}
            TD.fm { background:LightSteelBlue;
            font-family:sans-serif;font-size:12px}
            </style>

            <!--- Show info about featured movie in HTML Table --->
            <table width="150" align="right" border="0" cellspacing="0">
            <tr><th class="fm">
            Featured Film
            </th></tr>
            <!--- Movie Title, Summary, Rating --->
            <tr><td class="fm">
            <b>#getFilm.MovieTitle#</b><br>
            #getFilm.Summary#<br>
            <p align="right">Rated: #getFilm.Rating#</p>
            </td></tr>
            <!--- Cost (rounded to millions), release date --->
```

Listing 18.15 (CONTINUED)

```
                    <tr><th class="fm">
                    Production Cost $#round(getFilm.AmountBudgeted / 1000000)# Million<br>
                    In Theaters #dateFormat(getFilm.DateInTheaters, "mmmm d")#<br>
                    </th></tr>
                    </table>
                    <br clear="all">
            </cfoutput>
```

The purpose of the `<cflock>` tag in Listing 18.15 is to ensure that only one instance of the block is ever allowed to occur at the very same moment in time. For example, consider what happens if two different users request the page within a moment of each other. If by chance the second page request gets to the start of the block before the first one has exited it, the second request will be forced to wait until the first instance of the block has completed its work. This guarantees that funny race condition behavior doesn't take place (like one of the movies getting skipped or shown twice).

TIP

If it helps, think of locks as being like hall passes back in grade school. If you wanted to go to the bathroom, you needed to get a pass from the teacher. Nobody else was allowed to go to the bathroom until you came back and returned the pass. This was to protect the students (and the bathroom) from becoming, um, corrupted, right?

Using `ReadOnly` Locks

Okay, you've seen how `Exclusive` locks work. They simply make sure that no two blocks of the same `scope` are allowed to execute at once. If two requests need the same lock at the same time, the first one blocks the second one. But in some situations this can be overkill, and lead to more waiting around than is really necessary.

ColdFusion also provides `ReadOnly` locks, which are less extreme. `ReadOnly` locks don't block each other. They only get blocked by `Exclusive` locks. In plain English, a `ReadOnly` lock means, "If the variables in this block are being changed somewhere else, wait until the changes are finished before running this block." Use a `ReadOnly` lock if you have some code that definitely needs to read the correct, current value of an application variable, but isn't going to change it at all. Then just double-check that all code that *does* change the variable is between `Exclusive` locks. This way, you are guaranteed to always be reading or displaying the correct, most current value of the variable, but without the unwanted side effect of forcing other page requests to wait in line.

Do this whenever you are going to be reading the value of a variable a lot, but changing its value only occasionally.

NOTE

In other words, `ReadOnly` locks don't have any effect on their own. They only have an effect when some other page request has an `Exclusive` lock.

To demonstrate how much sense this all makes, let's adapt the featured movie example a bit. So far, the featured movie has rotated with every page request. What if you still wanted the movies to rotate evenly and in order, but instead of rotating with every page request, you want the movie to change once every five minutes (or ten minutes, or once an hour)?

Here is an adapted version of the featured movie template that gets this job done (see Listing 18.16). The code is a bit more complicated than the last version. For the moment, don't worry about the code itself. Just note that the portion of the code that makes changes in the APPLICATION scope is in an Exclusive lock. The portion of the code that grabs the current feature movie from the APPLICATION scope (which is also really short and quick) is inside a ReadOnly lock.

Listing 18.16 FeaturedMovie3.cfm—Using Exclusive and ReadOnly Locks

```
<!---
Filename: FeaturedMovie3.cfm
Created by: Nate Weiss (NMW)
Purpose: Displays a single movie on the page, on a rotating basis
Please Note Application variables must be enabled
--->

<!--- We want to obtain an exclusive lock if this --->
<!--- is the first time this template has executed, --->
<!--- or the time for this featured movie has expired --->
<cfif (not isDefined("APPLICATION.movieRotation"))
 or (dateCompare(APPLICATION.movieRotation.currentUntil, now()) eq -1)>

  <!--- Make sure all requests wait for this block --->
  <!--- to finish before displaying the featured movie --->
  <cflock scope="APPLICATION" type="Exclusive" timeout="10">

      <!--- If this is the first time the template has executed... --->
      <cfif not isDefined("APPLICATION.movieRotation")>

            <!--- Get all current FilmIDs from the database --->
            <cfquery name="GetFilmIDs" datasource="#REQUEST.dataSource#">
            SELECT FilmID FROM Films
            ORDER BY MovieTitle
            </cfquery>

            <!--- Create structure for rotating featured movies --->
            <cfset st = structNew()>
            <cfset st.movieList = valueList(getFilmIDs.FilmID)>
            <cfset st.currentPos = 1>

            <!--- Place structure into APPLICATION scope --->
            <cfset APPLICATION.movieRotation = st>

    <!--- ...otherwise, the time for the featured movie has expired --->
    <cfelse>
      <!--- Shorthand name for structure in application scope --->
      <cfset st = APPLICATION.movieRotation>

      <!--- If we haven't gotten to the last movie yet --->
      <cfif st.currentPos lt listLen(st.movieList)>
        <cfset st.currentPos = st.currentPos + 1>
      <!--- if already at last movie, start over at beginning --->
      <cfelse>
        <cfset st.currentPos = 1>
      </cfif>

    </cfif>
```

Listing 18.16 (CONTINUED)

```
    <!--- In any case, choose the movie at the current position in list --->
    <cfset st.currentMovie = listGetAt(st.movieList, st.currentPos)>
    <!--- This featured movie should "expire" a short time from now --->
    <cfset st.currentUntil = dateAdd("s", 5, now())>
    </cflock>

</cfif>

<!--- Use a ReadOnly lock to grab current movie from application scope... --->
<!--- If the exclusive block above is currently executing in another thread, --->
<!--- then ColdFusion will 'wait' before executing the code in this block. --->
<cflock scope="APPLICATION" type="ReadOnly" timeout="10">
  <cfset thisMovieID = APPLICATION.movieRotation.currentMovie>
</cflock>


<!--- Now that we have chosen the film to "Feature", --->
<!--- Get all important info about it from database. --->
<cfquery name="GetFilm" datasource="#REQUEST.dataSource#">
 SELECT
 MovieTitle, Summary, Rating,
 AmountBudgeted, DateInTheaters
 FROM Films f, FilmsRatings r
WHERE FilmID =
 <cfqueryparam cfsqltype="cf_sql_integer" value="#thisMovieID#">
 AND f.RatingID = r.RatingID
</cfquery>

<!--- Now Display Our Featured Movie --->
<cfoutput>
 <!--- Define formatting for our "feature" display --->
 <style type="text/css">
 TH.fm { background:RoyalBlue;color:white;text-align:left;
 font-family:sans-serif;font-size:10px}
 TD.fm { background:LightSteelBlue;
 font-family:sans-serif;font-size:12px}
 </style>

 <!--- Show info about featured movie in HTML Table --->
 <table width="150" align="right" border="0" cellspacing="0">
 <tr><th class="fm">
 Featured Film
 </th></tr>
 <!--- Movie Title, Summary, Rating --->
 <tr><td class="fm">
 <b>#getFilm.MovieTitle#</b><br>
 #getFilm.Summary#<br>
 <p align="right">Rated: #getFilm.Rating#</p>
 </td></tr>
 <!--- Cost (rounded to millions), release date --->
 <tr><th class="fm">
 Production Cost $#round(val(getFilm.AmountBudgeted) / 1000000)# Million<br>
 In Theaters #dateFormat(getFilm.DateInTheaters, "mmmm d")#<br>
 </th></tr>
 </table>
 <br clear="all">
</cfoutput>
```

The first thing this template does is check whether changes need to be made in the APPLICATION scope. Changes will be made if the template hasn't been run before, or if it's time to rotate the featured movie. (Remember, the rotation is now based on time.) If changes are called for, an Exclusive lock is opened. Within the lock, if the template hasn't been run before, a list of movies is retrieved from the database and stored as a value called movieList, just as before. In addition, a value called currentPos is set to 1 (to indicate the first movie). This value will increase as the movies are cycled through. Execution then proceeds to the bottom of the <cflock> block, where the current movie id is plucked from the list, and a value called currentUntil is set to a moment in time a few seconds in the future.

On the other hand, if the lock was opened because the currentUntil value has passed (we're still inside the Exclusive lock block), then it's time to pick the next movie from the list. As long as the end of the list hasn't already been reached, the only thing required is to advance currentPos by one. If the last movie *has* already been reached, the currentPos is reset to the beginning of the list.

NOTE

At any rate, the entire Exclusive lock block at the top of the template executes only once in a while, when the movie needs to change. If you are rotating movies every 10 minutes and have a fair number of visitors, the lock is needed only in the vast minority of page requests.

Underneath, a second <cflock> block of type="ReadOnly" uses a <cfset> to read the current featured movie from the APPLICATION scope into a local variable. The ReadOnly lock ensures that if the featured movie is currently being changed in some other page request, the <cfset> will wait until the change is complete. Since the change occurs only once in a while, the page is usually able to execute without having to wait at all.

TIP

Think of ReadOnly locks as a way of optimizing the performance of code that needs some kind of locking to remain correct. For instance, this template could have been written using only Exclusive locks, and doing so would have made sure that the results were always correct (no race conditions). The introduction of the ReadOnly lock is a way of making sure that the locks have as little impact on performance as possible.

NOTE

You'll encounter the notion of explicitly locking potentially concurrent actions in database products as well. Conceptually, database products use the SQL keywords BEGIN TRANSACTION and COMMIT TRANSACTION in a way that's analogous to ColdFusion's interpretation of beginning and ending <cflock> tags.

Using Named Locks Instead of SCOPE

You've seen why locks are sometimes needed to avoid race conditions. You've seen the simplest way to implement them—with Exclusive locks. You've seen how to avoid potential bottlenecks by using a mix of Exclusive and ReadOnly locks. Hopefully, you've noticed a pattern emerging: If you're worried about race conditions, your goal should be to protect your data with <cflock>, but to do so in the least obtrusive way possible. That is, you want your code to be "smart" about when page requests wait for each other.

So far, all of the <cflock> tags in this chapter have been *scoped locks*. Each has used a scope= "Application" attribute to say, "This lock should block or be blocked by all other locks in the application." As you have seen, scoped locks are really simple to implement once you "get" the conceptual issue at hand. The problem with scoped locks is that they often end up locking too much.

There's no problem when you're using only application variables to represent a single concept. For instance, the various versions of the Featured Movie template track a few different variables, but they are all related to the same concept of a featured movie that rotates over time.

Consider what happens, though, if you need to add a rotating Featured Actor widget to your application. Such a widget would be similar to the featured movie but it would rotate at a different rate or according to some other logic. Just for the heck of it, pretend there's also a Featured Director widget, plus a couple of hit counters that also maintain data at the application level, and so on. Assume for the moment that these various widgets appear on different pages, rather than all on the same page.

Using the techniques you've learned so far, whenever one of these mini-applications needs to change the data it keeps in the APPLICATION scope, it will use a <cflock> with scope="Application" to protect itself against race conditions. The problem is that the scope="Application" lock is not only going to block or be blocked by instances of that same widget in other page requests. It's going to block or be blocked by all locks in the entire application. If all of your widgets are only touching their own application variables, this approach is overkill. If the Featured Actor widget doesn't touch the same variables that the featured movie widget uses, then there's no possibility of a race condition. Therefore, allowing reads and writes by the two widgets to block one another is a waste of time, but scope="Application" doesn't know that.

ColdFusion gives you further control over this kind of problem by supporting named locks. To add named locks to your code, you use a name attribute in your <cflock> tags, instead of a scope attribute. Named lock blocks will only block or wait for other lock blocks that have the same name.

For instance, instead of using a scoped lock, like this:

```
<cflock
  scope="Application"
  type="Exclusive"
  timeout="10">
```

you could use a named lock, like this:

```
<cflock
  name="OrangeWhipMovieRotation"
  type="Exclusive"
  timeout="10">
```

This way, you can feel comfortable manipulating the variables used by the featured movie widget, knowing that the Exclusive lock you've asked for will affect only those pieces of code that are also dealing with the same variables. Page requests that need to display the Featured Movie or Featured Director widget won't be blocked needlessly.

The name of the lock is considered globally for the entire server, not just for your application, so you need to make sure that the name of the lock isn't used in other applications. The easiest way to do this is to always incorporate the application's name (or something similar) as a part of the lock name. That's why the `<cflock>` tag shown above includes `OrangeWhip` at the start of the `name` attribute. Another way to get the same effect would be to use the automatic `APPLICATION.applicationName` variable as a part of the `name`, like so:

```
<cflock
  name="#APPLICATION.applicationName#MovieRotation"
  type="Exclusive"
  timeout="10">
```

The Web site for this book includes a `FeaturedMovie4.cfm` template, which is almost the same as `FeaturedMovie3.cfm`, shown in Listing 18.16. The only difference is that it uses `name= "OrangeWhipMovieRotation"` (as shown above) instead of `scope="Application"` in each of the `<cflock>` tags.

NOTE

So it turns out that the `scope="Application"` attribute is really just a shortcut. Its effect is equivalent to writing a named lock that uses the name of your application (or some other identifier that is unique to your application) as the `name`.

Nested Locks and Deadlocks

It's usually okay to nest named locks within one another, as long as the `name` for each lock block is different. However, if they aren't nested in the same order in all parts of your code, it's possible that your application will encounter deadlocks while it runs. Deadlocks are situations where it's impossible for two page requests to move forward because they are each requesting a lock that the other already has. Consider a template with an `Exclusive` lock named `LockA`, with another `<cflock>` named `LockB` nested within it. Now consider another template, which nests `LockA` within `LockB`. If both templates execute at the same time, the first page request might be granted an `Exclusive` lock for `LockA`, and the second could get an `Exclusive` lock for `LockB`. Now neither template can move forward. Both locks will time out and throw errors. This is deadlock.

Entire books have been written about various ways to solve this kind of puzzle; there's no way we can tell you how to handle every possible situation. Our advice is this: If you need to nest named locks, go ahead as long as they will be nested in the same combination and order in all of your templates. If the combination or order needs to be different in different places, use scoped locks instead. The overhead and aggravation you might encounter in trying to manage and debug potential deadlocks isn't worth the added cost introduced by the `scope` shorthand.

Don't confuse this discussion (nesting locks with different names) with nesting locks that have the same `name` or `scope`. In general, you should never nest `<cflock>` tags that have the same `scope` or `name`. A `ReadOnly` lock that is nested within an `Exclusive` lock with the same `scope` or `name` has no additional benefit (it's always safe to read if you already have an `Exclusive` lock). And if the `Exclusive` lock is nested within a `ReadOnly` lock, then the `Exclusive` lock can never be obtained (because it needs to wait for all `ReadOnly` locks to end first), and thus will always time out and throw an error.

Application Variable Timeouts

By default, application variables are kept on the server almost indefinitely. They die only if two whole days pass without any visits to any of the application's pages. After two days of inactivity, ColdFusion considers the APPLICATION scope to have expired, and the onApplicationEnd method of the Application.cfc file is called, if it exists. Whether or not this method exists, all associated application variables are flushed from its memory.

If one of your applications uses a large number of application variables but is used very rarely, you could consider decreasing the amount of time that the APPLICATION scope takes to expire. Doing so would let ColdFusion reuse the memory taken up by the application variables. In practice, there might be few situations in which this flexibility is useful, but you should still know what your options are if you want to think about ways to tweak the way your applications behave.

Two ways are available to adjust the application timeout period from its two-day default value. You can use the ColdFusion Administrator or the applicationTimeout value of the THIS scope in the Application.cfc file.

Adjusting Timeouts Using APPLICATIONTIMEOUT

The Application.CFC THIS scope takes an optional applicationTimeout value. You can use this to explicitly specify how long an unused APPLICATION scope will remain in memory before it expires.

The applicationTimeout value expects a ColdFusion *time span* value, which is a special type of numeric information used to describe a period of time in terms of days, hours, minutes, and seconds. All this means is that you must specify the application timeout using the createTimeSpan() function, which takes four numeric arguments to represent the desired number of days, hours, minutes, and seconds, respectively.

For instance, to specify that an application should time out after two hours of inactivity, you would use code such as this:

```
<cfset this.applicationTimeout="#createTimeSpan(0,2,0,0)#">
```

NOTE

If you don't specify an applicationTimeout attribute, the Default Timeout value in the Variables page of the ColdFusion Administrator is used. See the next section, "Adjusting Timeouts Using the ColdFusion Administrator," for details.

NOTE

If you specify an applicationTimeout that exceeds the Maximum Timeout value in the Variables page of the ColdFusion Administrator, the Maximum Timeout in the Administrator is used instead. See the next section for details.

Don't forget that you can now execute code when the application times out. Listing 18.6 demonstrated a simple use of the onApplicationEnd method.

Adjusting Timeouts Using the ColdFusion Administrator

To adjust the amount of time that each application's APPLICATION scope should live before it expires, follow these steps:

1. Navigate to the Memory Variables page of the ColdFusion Administrator.

2. Under Default Timeout, fill in the days, hours, minutes, and seconds fields for application variables.

3. If you want, you also can adjust the Maximum Timeout for application variables here. If any developers attempt to use a longer timeout with the applicationTimeout value in the Application.cfc THIS scope, this value will be used instead (no error message is displayed).

4. Click Submit Changes.

Using onRequest()

So far we have seen examples of how you can run code before and after a page request, as well as during the startup and end of the application. Another way to modify the behavior of your pages is with the onRequest method. This method is executed after the onRequestStart method, and before the onRequestEnd method. It takes one argument, the template currently being executed. If you don't actually include the template, using <cfinclude>, then your page won't show up.

This method has some drawbacks. The method tends to "leak" variables into the template itself. If all of this sounds confusing, don't worry. Typically you won't need to use the onRequest method. If you simply want to wrap a page with a header and footer, for example, you can just use onRequestStart and onRequestEnd.

With that in mind, let's look at a simple example of where the onRequest method can be helpful. You may have seen some Web sites that have "Print" versions of their articles. These are versions of the article that normally have much reduced HTML. This is easy to build to do with advanced style sheets, or dynamically with ColdFusion, but what if you have old content, or pages, that weren't built to support a Print version? We can use the onRequest method to handle this situation. Listing 18.17 shows a modified version of our latest Application.cfc file. Since we are only modifying two methods and adding the onRequest method, we only list them below. The book Web site has the entire file.

Listing 18.17 Application7.cfc—Using onRequest

```
<cffunction name="onRequestStart" returnType="boolean" output="true">
  <!--- Any variables set here can be used by all our pages --->
<cfset request.companyName = "Orange Whip Studios">

  <!--- Display our Site Header at top of every page --->
  <cfif not isDefined("url.print")>
    <cfinclude template="SiteHeader.cfm">
  </cfif>

  <cfreturn true>
```

Listing 18.17   (CONTINUED)

```
    </cffunction>

    <cffunction name="onRequestEnd" returnType="void" output="true">

      <!--- Display our Site Footer at bottom of every page --->
      <cfif not isDefined("url.print")>
        <cfinclude template="SiteFooter.cfm">
      </cfif>

    </cffunction>

    <cffunction name="onRequest" returnType="void" outout="true">
      <cfargument name="targetPage" type="string" required="true">
      <cfset var content = "">

      <cfif not isDefined("url.print")>
        <cfinclude template="#arguments.targetPage#">
      <cfelse>
        <!--- Show the Print version --->
        <!--- First we let the file run and save the result --->
        <cfsavecontent variable="content">
          <cfinclude template="#arguments.targetPage#">
        </cfsavecontent>

        <!--- Remove HTML --->
        <cfset content = reReplace(content,"<.*?>","","all")>
        <cfoutput><pre>#content#</pre></cfoutput>

      </cfif>
    </cffunction>
```

Let's start with the onRequestStart and onRequestEnd methods. Both of these methods are the same as in the earlier version, except now they check for the existence of a URL variable print. If the variable exists, these methods don't include the header and footer. Now let's look at the onRequest method. This method takes one argument, the file name of the template being executed. You must include this template or it will never show up. Once again we check for the existence of the URL variable print. If it doesn't exist, we simply include the file.

The interesting part comes up when the variable *does* exist. First, we <cfinclude> the template, but wrap it with the <cfsavecontent> tag. This runs the template and saves all the content into a variable, in this case, content. Next, we use a regular expression (discussed in Chapter 39, "Using Regular Expressions," in Volume 2) to remove the HTML. Don't worry too much about this code—just know that it will remove all the HTML and leave the text behind. Lastly, we output the result wrapped in <pre> tags. The net result is that HTML that looks like so:

```
<h1>Welcome to our Site</h1>
Thanks for <b>visiting!</b>.
```

will be rendered like so:

```
Welcome to our Site
Thanks for visiting!
```

Now a Print version of your site can be generated by just adding a print=1 to the current URL.

Handling Server Startup

ColdFusion 9 adds support for a new feature, `Server.cfc`, that allows you to specify a special component that will be run when the server starts. This feature is enabled on the ColdFusion Administrator settings page. You must first enable the feature, and then you must specify which component will contain the code to be run upon server startup. By default, this is a component called `Server` within your Web root.

When enabled, ColdFusion will execute one method, `onServerStart`, when your server starts. Because the server is in the midst of starting, you can't use `CFHTTP` to hit another `.cfm` file on the server, but you can do other things. The following code creates a simple component that both logs and sends an email when the server starts:

```
<cfcomponent>
    <cffunction name="onServerStart">
        <cflog file="myserver" text="Server starting up!">
        <cfmail to="you@yourdomain.com" from=you@yourdomain.com
        subject="Server Started">
The ColdFusion Server just started up.
        </cfmail>
    </cffunction>
</cfcomponent>
```

To actually enable this functionality, first go to your ColdFusion Administrator, Settings page and click the Component with `onServerStart()` Method check box. In the box next to this, specify `ows.18.Server` as the path to the component. This tells ColdFusion where to look for the component. Last, restart your ColdFusion server. After the server has started, you can check both the log file and the email to confirm that ColdFusion ran the component. Remember that the ColdFusion Administrator provides a log viewer as well as a way to view undelivered email. The `Server.cfc` component cannot prevent the server from starting. If you need functionality like that, consider using `Server.cfc` to set a `server` scope variable that other applications can check when they start.

CHAPTER **19**

Working with Sessions

In Chapter 18, "Introducing the Web Application Framework," you learned about application variables, which live in your ColdFusion server's memory between page requests. You also learned that application variables are shared between all pages in your application. There are plenty of uses for application variables, but because they aren't maintained separately for each user, they don't go far in helping you create a personalized site experience.

This chapter continues the discussion of the Web application framework, focusing on the features that let you track variables on a per-user basis. This opens up all kinds of opportunities for keeping track of what each user needs, wants, has seen, or is interacting with. And in true ColdFusion style, it's all very easy to learn and use.

Addressing the Web's Statelessness

The basic building blocks of the Web—TCP/IP, HTTP, and HTML—don't directly address any notion of a "session" on the Web. Users don't log in to the Web, nor do they ever log out. So without some additional work, each page visit stands alone, in its own context. Content is requested by the browser, the server responds, and that's the end of it. No connection is maintained, and the server isn't notified when the user leaves the site altogether.

Out of the box, HTTP and HTML don't even provide a way to know who the users are or where they are. As a user moves from page to page in your site—perhaps interacting with things along the way—there's no way to track their progress or choices along the way. As far as each page request is concerned, there's only the current moment, with no future and no past. The Web is thus said to be "stateless" because it doesn't provide any built-in infrastructure to track the *state* (or status or condition) of what a user is doing.

What does the Web's statelessness mean to you as a Web developer? It means that without some type of server-side mechanism to simulate the notion of a session, you would have no way to remember that a user has put something into a shopping cart, say, or to remember the fact that the user has logged in to your site. The Web itself provides no short-term memory for remembering the contents of shopping carts and other types of choices users make during a visit. You need something to provide that short-term memory for you. That's exactly what you will learn about in this chapter.

The Problem of Maintaining State

The fact that HTTP and HTML are stateless is no accident. A main reason the Web is so wildly popular is the fact that it is so simple. It probably wouldn't have gotten so big so fast if a whole infrastructure needed to be in place for logging in and out of each Web server, or if it assumed that you needed to maintain a constant connection to a server to keep your current session open.

The simplicity of the sessionless approach also enables the tremendous scalability that benefits Web applications and the Web as a whole. It's what makes Web applications so thin and lightweight and what allows Web servers to serve so many people simultaneously. So the Web's statelessness is by design, and most people should be glad that it is.

Except for us Web developers. Our lives would probably be a lot easier if some kind of universal user ID existed, issued by, um, the United Nations or something. That couldn't be faked. And that could identify who the user was, no matter what computer they were sitting at. Until that happens, we need another way to track a user's movements as they move through our own little pieces of the Web.

Solutions Provided by ColdFusion

Expanding on the Web application framework—which already sets aside part of the server's brain to deal with each application—ColdFusion provides three types of variables that help you maintain the state of a user's visit from page to page and between visits.

Similar to application variables (which you learned about in the last chapter), all three of these are persistent variables because they stay alive between page requests. However, they are different from application variables because they are maintained separately for each browser that visits your site. It's almost as if ColdFusion had a tiny little part of its memory set aside for each visitor.

Cookies

Cookies are a simple mechanism for asking a browser to remember something, such as a user's favorite color or perhaps some type of ID number. The information is stored in the client machine's memory (or on one of its drives). You can store only a small amount of information using cookies, and users generally have a way to turn off cookies in their browsers' settings. Cookies have gotten a lot of bad press in the past few years, so many users turn them off at the browser level.

NOTE

Cookies aren't a ColdFusion feature per se, but a browser/Web server feature. ColdFusion just makes it easy to work with them.

Client Variables

Client variables are like cookies, except that the information is stored on the server, rather than on the client machine. The values are physically stored in the server's Windows Registry or in a database. Client variables are designed to hold semi-permanent data, such as preferences that should live for weeks or months between a user's visits.

Session Variables

Similar to client variables, *session variables* are stored on the server. However, instead of being stored physically, they are simply maintained in the server's RAM. Session variables are designed to hold temporary data, such as items in a shopping cart or steps in some type of wizard-style data-entry mechanism that takes the user several pages to complete.

Choosing Which Type of Variables to Use

With three types of per-visitor variables from which to choose, developers sometimes have a hard time figuring the best type to use for a particular task. We recommend that you look through this whole chapter before you start using any of them in your own application. However, in the future, you might want to refresh your memory about which type to use. Table 19.1 lists the major pros and cons of cookies, client variables, and session variables.

Table 19.1 Pros and Cons of Cookies, Client Variables, and Session Variables

VARIABLE TYPE	PROS	CONS
COOKIE	Not ColdFusion specific, so are familiar to most developers.	Simple values only (no arrays, structures or queries).
		Can persist for same visit only, or until a specific date/time. Limited storage capacity. User can turn them off. Have a bad reputation.
CLIENT	Much larger storage capacity. Values never leave the server. Persist between server restarts. Cookies not needed to retain values during single visit. Stored in server's registry or in any SQL database.	Can persist for months. Cookies required to remember values between visits. Simple values only (no arrays, structures, and so on), but see the discussion of `serializeJSON` in "Storing Complex Data Types in Client Variables" later in this chapter.
SESSION	High performance; stored in ColdFusion server's RAM only. Complex values allowed (arrays, structures, and so on). Can be used without cookies.	Values do not persist between server restarts.

Using Cookies to Remember Preferences

Cookies are simple variables that can be stored on a client machine. Basically, the server asks the browser to remember a variable with such-and-such a name and such-and-such a value. The browser returns the variable to the server as it requests successive pages from that same server. In other words, after the server sets the value on the browser, the browser continues to remind the server about it as the user moves from page to page. The net effect is that each site essentially has a small portion of the browser's memory in which to store little bits of information.

Introducing the `COOKIE` Scope

Cookies aren't something specific to ColdFusion. Any server-side scripting programming environment can set them, and they can even be set by client-side languages such as JavaScript. Depending on the language, the actual code necessary to set or retrieve a cookie varies a bit, of course. The best implementations keep coders from having to understand the details of the actual communication between the browser and server. It's best if the coder can just concentrate on the task at hand.

In ColdFusion, the notion of cookies is exposed to you via the simple, elegant `COOKIE` scope. Similar to the `APPLICATION` scope you learned about in the previous chapter, the `COOKIE` scope is automatically maintained by ColdFusion. Setting a variable within the `COOKIE` scope instructs the browser to remember the cookie. Referring to a variable within the `COOKIE` scope returns the value of the cookie on the browser's machine.

For instance, the following line asks the user's browser to remember a cookie variable called `MyMessage`. The value of the cookie is `"Hello, World!"`:

```
<cfset cookie.myMessage = "Hello, World!">
```

From that point on, you could output the value of `#cookie.myMessage#` in your CFML code, between `<cfoutput>` tags. The `"Hello, World"` message would be output in place of the variable.

A Simple Cookie Exercise

This simple exercise will illustrate what happens when you use cookies. First, temporarily change your browser's preferences so that you will receive notice whenever a cookie is being set.

To be notified when a cookie is set on your browser, follow these guidelines:

- If you are using Firefox, choose Tools and then Options. On the Privacy tab in the Cookie section, change Keep Until to Ask Me Every Time.

- If you are using Internet Explorer (version 5 or later), select Internet Options from the Tools menu, and then select the Security tab. Make sure the appropriate zone is selected; then select Custom Level and check the Prompt options for both Allow Cookies That Are Stored on Your Computer and Allow Per-Session Cookies.

- If you are using some other browser or version, the steps you take might be slightly different, but you should have a way to turn on some type of notification when cookies are set.

Now use your browser to visit the `CookieSet.cfm` template shown in Listing 19.1. You should see a prompt asking if you want to accept the cookie. The prompt might look different depending on browser and version, but it generally will show you the name and value of the cookie being set. (Note that you can even refuse to allow the cookie to be set.) Go ahead and let the browser store the cookie by clicking OK.

If you now visit the `CookieShow.cfm` template shown in Listing 19.2, you will see the message you `started your visit at:`, followed by the exact time you visited the code in Listing 19.1. Click your browser's Reload button a few times, so you can see that the value doesn't change. The value persists between page requests. If you go back to Listing 19.1, the cookie will be reset to a new value.

Close your browser, reopen it, and visit the `CookieShow.cfm` template again. You will see an error message from ColdFusion, telling you that the `COOKIE.TimeVisitStart` variable doesn't exist. By default, cookies expire when the browser is closed. Therefore, the variable is no longer passed to the server with each page request and is unknown to ColdFusion.

Listing 19.1 `CookieSet.cfm`—Setting a Cookie

```
<!---
 Filename: CookieSet.cfm
 Created by: Nate Weiss (NMW)
 Purpose: Sets a cookie to remember time of this page request
--->

<html>
<head><title>Cookie Demonstration</title></head>
<body>

<!--- Set a cookie to remember the time right now --->
<cfset cookie.TimeVisitStart = timeFormat(now(), "h:mm:ss tt")>

The cookie has been set.

</body>
</html>
```

Listing 19.2 `CookieShow.cfm`—Displaying a Cookie's Value

```
<!---
 Filename: CookieShow.cfm
 Created by: Nate Weiss (NMW)
 Please Note Displays the value of the TimeVisitStart cookie,
 which gets set by CookieSet.cfm
--->

<html>
<head><title>Cookie Demonstration</title></head>
<body>

<cfoutput>
 You started your visit at:
 #cookie.TimeVisitStart#<br>
</cfoutput>

</body>
</html>
```

Using Cookies

You can easily build on the last example to make it more useful in the real world. For instance, you wouldn't want the Time Started value to be reset every time the user visited the first page; you probably want the value to be recorded only the first time. So it would make sense to first test for the cookie's existence and only set the cookie if it doesn't already exist. It would also make sense to remember the full date/time value of the user's first visit, rather than just the time.

So, instead of

```
<cfset cookie.TimeVisitStart = timeFormat(now(), "h:mm:ss tt")>
```

you could use

```
<cfif not isDefined("cookie.VisitStart")>
 <cfset cookie.VisitStart = now()>
</cfif>
```

In fact, the `isDefined` test and the `<cfset>` tag can be replaced with a single `<cfparam>` tag:

```
<cfparam name="cookie.VisitStart" type="date" default="#now()#">
```

This `<cfparam>` tag can be placed in your `Application.cfc` file so it is encountered before each page request is processed. You can now be assured that ColdFusion will set the cookie the first time the user hits your application, no matter what page the user starts on, and that you will never get a `parameter doesn't exist` error message, because the cookie is guaranteed to always be defined. As discussed previously, the cookie will be reset if the user closes and reopens the browser.

➔ If you need a quick reminder on the difference between `<cfset>` and `<cfparam>`, see Chapter 8, "The Basics of CFML," and Chapter 9, "Programming with CFML."

You could then output the time elapsed in your application by outputting the difference between the cookie's value and the current time. You could put this code wherever you wanted in your application, perhaps as part of some type of header or footer message. For instance, the following code would display the number of minutes that the user has been using the application:

```
<cfoutput>
 Minutes Elapsed: #dateDiff("n", cookie.VisitStart, now())#
</cfoutput>
```

The next two listings bring these lines together. Listing 19.3 is an `Application.cfc` file that includes the `<cfparam>` tag shown previously. Listing 19.4 is a file called `ShowTimeElapsed.cfm`, which can be used to display the elapsed time in any of the current application's pages by using `<cfinclude>`. You also can visit Listing 19.4 on its own—Figure 19.1 shows how the results would look.

Figure 19.1

Cookies can be used to track users, preferences, or, in this case, elapsed times.

Minutes Elapsed: 1:01

Be sure to save Listing 19.3 as `Application.cfc`, not `Application1.cfc`.

Listing 19.3 `Application1.cfc`—Defining a Cookie Variable in `Application.cfc`

```
<!---
Filename: Application.cfc
Created by: Raymond Camden (ray@camdenfamily.com)
Handles application events.
--->

<cfcomponent output="false">

  <cffunction name="onRequestStart" output="false" returnType="boolean">
    <cfparam name="cookie.VisitStart" type="date" default="#now()#">
    <cfreturn true>
  </cffunction>

</cfcomponent>
```

Listing 19.4 `ShowTimeElapsed.cfm`—Performing Calculations Based on Cookies

```
<!---
Filename: ShowTimeElapsed.cfm
Created by: Nate Weiss (NMW)
Please Note Can be <cfincluded> in any page in your application
--->

<!--- Find number of seconds passed since visit started --->
<!--- (difference between cookie value and current time) --->
<cfset secsSinceStart = dateDiff("s", cookie.VisitStart, now())>
<!--- Break it down into numbers of minutes and seconds --->
<cfset minutesElapsed = int(secsSinceStart / 60)>
<cfset secondsElapsed = secsSinceStart MOD 60>

<!--- Display the minutes/seconds elapsed --->
<cfoutput>
Minutes Elapsed:
#minutesElapsed#:#numberFormat(secondsElapsed, "00")#
</cfoutput>
```

NOTE

What is the meaning of `output="false"` and `returnType="boolean"` in the methods in Listing 19.3? These are optional arguments that help define how CFC methods run. By using `output=false`, we limit the white space generated by the methods. Using `returnType=boolean` simply means that the method returns true or false. Again, these are optional attributes, but it's good practice to use them.

Because `cookie.VisitStart` is always a ColdFusion date/time value, getting the raw number of seconds since the visit started is easy—you use the `dateDiff` function. If the difference in seconds between the cookie value and the present moment (the value returned by the `now` function) is 206, you know that 206 seconds have passed since the cookie was set.

Because most people are more comfortable seeing time expressed in minutes and seconds, Listing 19.4 does some simple math on the raw number of seconds elapsed. First, it calculates the number of whole minutes that have elapsed, by dividing `SecsSinceStart` by 60 and rounding down to the nearest integer. Next, it calculates the number of seconds to display after the number of minutes by finding the modulus (which is the remainder left when SecsSinceStart is divided by 60).

Gaining More Control with `<cfcookie>`

You already have learned how to set cookies using the `<cfset>` tag and the special COOKIE scope (Listings 19.1 to 19.3). Using that technique, setting cookies is as simple as setting normal variables. However, sometimes you will want more control over how cookies get set.

Introducing the `<cfcookie>` Tag

To provide you with that additional control, ColdFusion provides the `<cfcookie>` tag, which is an alternative syntax for setting cookie variables. Once set, you can access or display the cookies as you have learned so far, by referring to them in the special cookie scope.

Table 19.2 introduces the attributes available when using `<cfcookie>`.

Table 19.2 `<cfcookie>` Tag Syntax

ATTRIBUTE	PURPOSE
name	Required. The name of the cookie variable. If you use NAME="VisitStart", the cookie will thereafter become known as cookie.VisitStart.
value	Optional. The value of the cookie. To set the cookie's value to the current date and time, use VALUE="#now()#".
expires	Optional. When the cookie should expire. You can provide any of the following: ■ A specific expiration date (such as 3/18/2002) or a date/time value. ■ The number of days you want the cookie to exist before expiring, such as 10 or 90. ■ The word never, which is a shortcut for setting the expiration date far into the future, so it effectively never expires. ■ The word now, which is a shortcut for setting the expiration date in the recent past, so it is already considered expired. This is how you delete a cookie. If you don't specify an expires attribute, the cookie will do what it does normally, which is to expire when the user closes the browser. See "Controlling Cookie Expiration," on the next page.
domain	Optional. You can use this attribute to share the cookie with other servers within your own Internet domain. By default, the cookie is visible only to the server that set it. See "Controlling the Way Cookies Are Shared," on the next page.
path	Optional. You can use this attribute to specify which pages on your server should be able to use this cookie. By default, the cookie can be accessed by all pages on the server once set. See "Controlling the Way Cookies Are Shared," on the next page.
secure	Optional. You can use this attribute to specify whether the cookie should be sent back to the server if a secure connection is being used. The default is No. See "Controlling the Way Cookies Are Shared," on the next page.

Controlling Cookie Expiration

The most common reason for using `<cfcookie>` instead of a simple `<cfset>` is to control how long the cookie will exist before it expires. For instance, looking back at the `Application.cfc` file shown in Listing 19.3, what if you didn't want the Elapsed Time counter to start over each time the user closed the browser?

Say you wanted the elapsed time to keep counting for up to a week. You would replace the `<cfparam>` line in Listing 19.3 with the following:

```
<!--- If no "VisitStart" cookie exists, create it --->
<cfif not isDefined("cookie.VisitStart")>
 <cfcookie
 name="VisitStart"
 value="#now()#"
 expires="7">
</cfif>
```

Controlling the Way Cookies Are Shared

Netscape's original cookie specification defines three additional concepts that haven't been discussed yet. All three have to do with giving you more granular control over which pages your cookies are visible to:

- **A domain can be specified as each cookie is set.** The basic idea is that a cookie should always be visible only to the server that set the cookie originally. This is to protect users' privacy. However, if a company is running several Web servers, it is considered fair that a cookie set on one server be visible to the others. Specifying a domain for a cookie makes the cookies visible to all servers within that domain. An example of this could be a server named `www.foo.com` that wants to share a cookie with the server `store.foo.com`, which is in the same domain. By default, cookies work for only a specific domain.

- **A path can be specified as each cookie is set.** This enables you to control whether the cookie should be visible to the entire Web server (or Web servers), or just part. For instance, if a cookie will be used only by the pages within the `ows` folder in the Web server's root, it might make sense for the browser to not return the cookie to any other pages, even those on the same server. The path could be set to `/ows`, which would ensure that the cookie is visible only to the pages within the ows folder. This way, two applications on the same server can each set cookies with the same name without overwriting one another, as long as the applications use different paths when setting the cookies.

- **A cookie can be marked as secure.** This means that it should be returned to the server only when a secure connection is being used (that is, if the page's URL starts with `https://` instead of `http://`). If the browser is asked to visit an ordinary (nonsecure) page on the server, the cookie isn't sent and thus isn't visible to the server. This doesn't mean that the cookie will be stored on the user's computer in a more secure fashion; it just means that it won't be transmitted back to the server unless SSL encryption is being used.

As a ColdFusion developer, you have access to these three concepts by way of the domain, path, and secure attributes of the `<cfcookie>` tag. As Table 19.2 showed, all three attributes are optional.

Let's say you have three servers, named one.orangewhip.com, two.orangewhip.com, and three. orangewhip.com. To set a cookie that would be shared among the three servers, take the portion of the domain names they share, including the first dot. The following code would set a cookie visible to all three servers (and any other servers whose host names end in .orangewhip.com):

```
<!--- Share cookie over our whole domain --->
<cfcookie
name="VisitStart"
value="#now()#"
domain=".orangewhip.com">
```

The next example uses the path attribute to share the cookie among all pages that have a /ows at the beginning of the path portion of their URLs (the part after the host name). For instance, the following would set a cookie that would be visible to a page with a path of /ows/Home.cfm and /ows/ store/checkout.cfm, but not /owintra/login.cfm:

```
<!--- Only share cookie within ows folder --->
<cfcookie
name="VisitStart"
value="#now()#"
path="/ows">
```

Finally, this last example uses the secure attribute to tell the browser to make the cookie visible only to pages that are at secure (https://) URLs. In addition, the cookie will expire in 30 days and will be shared among the servers in the orangewhip.com domain, but only within the /ows portion of each server:

```
<!--- This cookie is shared but confidential --->
<cfcookie
name="VisitStart"
value="#Now()#"
expires="30"
domain=".orangewhip.com"
path="/ows"
secure="Yes">
```

NOTE

You can specify that you want to share cookies only within a particular subdomain. For instance, `domain=".intranet. orangewhip.com"` shares the cookie within all servers that have `.intranet.orangewhip.com` at the end of their host names. However, there must always be a leading dot at the beginning of the `domain` attribute.

You can't share cookies based on IP addresses. To share cookies between servers, the servers must have Internet domain names.

The `domain` attribute is commonly misunderstood. Sometimes people assume that you can use it to specify other domains to share the cookies with. But `domain` can be used only to specify whether to share the cookies with other servers in the same domain.

Sharing Cookies with Other Applications

Because cookies aren't a ColdFusion-specific feature, cookies set with, say, Active Server Pages are visible in ColdFusion's COOKIE scope, and cookies set with `<cfcookie>` are visible to other applications, such as PHP, ASP.NET, or JavaServer Pages. The browser doesn't know which language is powering which pages. All it cares about is whether the requirements for the domain, path, security, and expiration have been met. If so, it makes the cookie available to the server.

TIP

If you find that cookies set in another language aren't visible to ColdFusion, the problem might be the path part of the cookie. For instance, whereas ColdFusion sets the path to / by default so that the cookie is visible to all pages on the server, JavaScript sets the path to match that of the current page by default. Try setting the path part of the cookie to / so that it will behave more like one set with ColdFusion. The syntax to do this varies from language to language.

Cookie Limitations

There are some pretty serious restrictions on what you can store in cookies, mostly established by the original specification:

- **Only simple strings can be stored.** Because dates and numbers can be expressed as strings, you can store them as cookies. But no ColdFusion-specific data types, such as arrays and structures, can be specified as the value for a cookie.

- **A maximum of 20 cookies can be set within any one domain.** This prevents cookies from eventually taking up a lot of hard drive space. Browsers might or might not choose to enforce this limit.

- **A cookie can be only 4 KB long.** The name of the cookie is considered part of its length.

- **The browser isn't obligated to store more than 300 cookies.** (That is 300 total, counting all cookies set by all the world's servers.) The browser can delete the least recently used cookie when the 300-cookie limit has been reached. That said, many modern browsers choose not to enforce this limit.

Using Client Variables

Client variables are similar to cookies, except that they are stored on the server, rather than on the client (browser) machine. In many situations, you can use the two almost interchangeably. You're already familiar with cookies, so learning how to use client variables will be a snap. Instead of using the `cookie` prefix before a variable name, you simply use the `client` prefix.

Okay, there's a little bit more to it than that, but not much.

NOTE

Before you can use the `client` prefix, you must enable ColdFusion's Client Management feature. See the section "Enabling Client Variables," later in this chapter.

NOTE

It's worth noting that client variables can also be configured so that they are stored on the browser machine, if you take special steps in the ColdFusion Administrator. They then become essentially equivalent to cookies. See the section "Adjusting How Client Variables Are Stored," later in this chapter.

How Do Client Variables Work?

Client variables work like this:

1. The first time a particular user visits your site, ColdFusion generates a unique ID number to identify the user's browser.

2. ColdFusion sets this ID number as a cookie called CFID on the user's browser. From that point on, the browser identifies itself to ColdFusion by presenting this ID.

3. When you set a client variable in your code, ColdFusion stores the value for you on the server side, without sending anything to the browser machine. It stores the CFID number along with the variable, to keep them associated internally.

4. Later, when you access or output the variable, ColdFusion simply retrieves the value based on the variable name and the CFID number.

For the most part, this process is hidden to you as a developer. You simply use the CLIENT scope prefix in your code; ColdFusion takes care of the rest. Also note that a second cookie, CFTOKEN, is also sent by the server. This helps secure data because the browser must supply the correct token along with the ID value.

Enabling Client Variables

Before you can use client variables in your code, you must enable them using an Application.cfc file. In the last chapter, you learned how to use this file to enable application variables. You can modify the behavior of the application using THIS scope variables. Table 19.3 lists values relevant to client variables.

Table 19.3   Additional Application.cfc THIS Scope Values Relevant to Client Variables

ATTRIBUTE	DESCRIPTION
name	Optional. A name for your application. For more information about the NAME attribute, see the section "Using Application Variables" in Chapter 18.
clientManagement	Yes or No. Setting this value to Yes enables client variables for the application.
clientStorage	Optional. You can set this attribute to the word Registry, which means the actual client variables will be stored in the Registry (on Windows servers). You can also provide a data source name, which will cause the variables to be stored in a database. If you omit this attribute, it defaults to Registry unless you have changed the default in the ColdFusion Administrator. For details, see "Adjusting How Client Variables Are Stored," later. Another option is Cookie, which tells ColdFusion to store the client variables as cookies on the user's browser.

Table 19.3 (CONTINUED)

ATTRIBUTE	DESCRIPTION
setClientCookies	Optional. The default is Yes, which allows ColdFusion to automatically set the CFID cookie on each browser, which it uses to track client variables properly for each browser. You can set this value to No if you don't want the cookies to be set. But if you do so, you will need to do a bit of extra work. For details, see "Adjusting How Client Variables Are Stored," later.
setDomainCookies	Optional. The default is No, which tells ColdFusion to set the CFID cookie so that it is visible only to the current server. If you have several ColdFusion servers operating in a cluster together, you can set this to Yes to share client variables between all your ColdFusion servers. For details, see "Adjusting How Client Variables Are Stored," later.

For now, just concentrate on the clientManagement attribute (the others are discussed later). Listing 19.5 shows how easy it is to enable client variables for your application. After you save this code in the Application.cfc file for your application, you can start using client variables. (Be sure to save Listing 19.5 as Application.cfc, not Application2.cfc.)

NOTE

If you attempt to use client variables without enabling them first, an error message will be displayed.

Listing 19.5 Application2.cfc—Enabling Client Variables in Application.cfc

```
<!---
 Filename: Application.cfc
 Created by: Raymond Camden (ray@camdenfamily.com)
 Handles application events.
--->

<cfcomponent output="false">

  <cfset this.name="OrangeWhipSite">
  <cfset this.clientManagement=true>
  <cfset this.dataSource="ows">

</cfcomponent>
```

Using Client Variables

Client variables are ideal for storing things like user preferences, recent form entries, and other types of values that you don't want to force your users to provide over and over again.

Remembering Values for Next Time

Consider a typical search form, in which the user types what they are looking for and then submits the form to see the search results. It might be nice if the form could remember what the user's last search was.

The code in Listing 19.6 lets it do just that. The basic idea is that the form's search criteria field will already be filled in, using the value of a variable called SearchPreFill. The value of this variable is set at the top of the page and will be set to the last search the user ran, if available. If no last search information exists (if this is the first time the user has used this page), it will be blank.

Listing 19.6 SearchForm1.cfm—Using Client Variables to Remember the User's Last Search

```
<!---
Filename: SearchForm1.cfm
Created by: Nate Weiss (NMW)
Please Note Maintains "last" search via Client variables
--->

<!--- Determine value for "Search Prefill" feature --->
<!--- When user submits form, save search criteria in client variable --->
<cfif isDefined("form.searchCriteria")>
 <cfset client.lastSearch = form.searchCriteria>
 <cfset searchPreFill = form.searchCriteria>

<!--- If not submitting yet, get prior search word (if possible) --->
<cfelseif isDefined("client.lastSearch")>
 <CFSET searchPreFill = client.lastSearch>

<!--- If no prior search criteria exist, just show empty string --->
<cfelse>
 <cfset searchPreFill = "">
</cfif>


<html>
<head><title>Search Orange Whip</title></head>
<body>
 <h2>Search Orange Whip</h2>

 <!--- Simple search form, which submits back to this page --->
 <cfoutput>
 <form action="#cgi.script_name#" method="post">

 <!--- "Search Criteria" field --->
 Search For:
<input name="SearchCriteria" value="#searchPreFill#">
  <!--- Submit button --->
 <input type="submit" value="Search"><br>

 </form>
 </cfoutput>


 </body>
 </html>
```

The first part of this template (the <cfif> part) does most of the work because it's in charge of setting the searchPreFill variable that provides the "last search" memory for the user. There are three different conditions to deal with. If the user currently is submitting the form to run the search, their search criteria should be saved in a client variable called client.lastSearch.

If the user isn't currently submitting the form but has run a search in the past, their last search criteria should be retrieved from the `lastSearch` client variable. If no last search is available, the `isDefined("client.lastSearch")` test will fail, and `searchPreFill` should just be set to an empty string.

The rest of the code is an ordinary form. Note, though, that the value of the `searchPreFill` variable is passed to the `<input>` tag, which presents the user with the search field.

If you visit this page in your browser for the first time, the search field will be blank. To test the use of client variables, type a word or two to search for and submit the form. Of course, no actual search takes place because no database code yet exists in the example, but the form should correctly remember the search criteria you typed. You can close the browser and reopen it, and the value should still be there.

NOTE

Assuming that you haven't changed anything in the ColdFusion Administrator to the contrary, the value of `client`. `LastSearch` will continue to be remembered until the user is away from the site for 90 days.

Using Several Client Variables Together

No limit is set on the number of client variables you can use. Listing 19.7 builds on the search form from Listing 19.6, this time allowing the user to specify the number of records the search should return. A second client variable, called `lastMaxRows`, remembers the value, using the same simple `<cfif>` logic shown in the previous listing.

Listing 19.7   `SearchForm2.cfm`—Using Client Variables to Remember Search Preferences

```
<!---
 Filename: SearchForm2.cfm
 Created by: Nate Weiss (NMW)
 Please Note Maintains "last" search via Client variables
--->

<!---
  When user submits form, save search criteria in Client variable
--->
<cfif isDefined("form.searchCriteria")>
 <cfset client.lastSearch = form.searchCriteria>
 <cfset client.lastMaxRows = form.searchMaxRows>
<!--- if not submitting yet, get prior search word (if possible) --->
<cfelseif isDefined("client.lastSearch") and
          isDefined("client.lastMaxRows")>
 <cfset searchCriteria = client.lastSearch>
 <cfset searchMaxRows = client.lastMaxRows>
<!--- if no prior search criteria exists, just show empty string --->
<cfelse>
 <cfset searchCriteria = "">
 <cfset searchMaxRows = 10>
</cfif>

<html>
<head><title>Search Orange Whip</title></head>
```

Listing 19.7 (CONTINUED)

```
<body>

<h2>Search Orange Whip</h2>

<!--- Simple search form, which submits back to this page --->
<cfoutput>
<form action="#cgi.script_name#" method="post">

<!--- "Search Criteria" field --->
Search For:
<input name="SearchCriteria" value="#searchCriteria#">

<!--- "Max Matches" field --->
<i>show up to
<input name="SearchMaxRows" value="#searchMaxRows#" size="2">
matches</i><br>

<!--- Submit button --->
<input type="Submit" value="Search"><br>

</form>
</cfoutput>

<!--- If we have something to search for, do it now --->
<cfif searchCriteria neq "">
  <!--- Get matching film entries from database --->
  <cfquery name="getMatches">
  SELECT FilmID, MovieTitle, Summary
  FROM Films
  WHERE MovieTitle LIKE
  <cfqueryparam cfsqltype="cf_sql_varchar" value="%#SearchCriteria#%">
  OR Summary LIKE
  <cfqueryparam cfsqltype="cf_sql_varchar" value="%#SearchCriteria#%">
  ORDER BY MovieTitle
  </cfquery>

  <!--- Show number of matches --->
  <cfoutput>
  <hr><i>#getMatches.recordCount# records found for
  "#searchCriteria#"</i><br>
  </cfoutput>

  <!--- Show matches, up to maximum number of rows --->
  <cfoutput query="getMatches" maxrows="#searchMaxRows#">
  <p><b>#MovieTitle#</b><br>
  #Summary#<br>
  </cfoutput>
</cfif>

</body>
</html>
```

Next, the actual search is performed, using simple LIKE code in a <cfquery> tag. When the results are output, the user's maximum records preference is provided to the <cfoutput> tag's maxrows attribute. Any rows beyond the preferred maximum aren't shown. (If you want to brush up on the `<cfquery>` and `<cfoutput>` code used here, see Chapter 10, "Creating Data-Driven Pages.")

Not only does this version of the template remember the user's last search criteria, but it also actually reruns the user's last query before they even submit the form. This means the user's last search results will be redisplayed each time they visit the page, making the search results appear to be persistent.

You easily could change this behavior by changing the second `<cfif>` test to `isDefined("form. SearchCriteria")`. The last search would still appear prefilled in the search form, but the search itself wouldn't be rerun until the user clicked the Search button. Use client variables in whatever way makes sense for your application.

TIP

To improve performance, you could add a `cachedwithin` or `cachedafter` attribute to the `<cfquery>` tag, which enables ColdFusion to deliver any repeat searches directly from the server's RAM memory. For details, see Chapter 27, "Improving Performance," in *Adobe ColdFusion 9 Web Application Construction Kit, Volume 2: Application Development*.

Deleting Client Variables

Once set, client variables are stored semi-permanently: they're deleted only if a user's browser doesn't return to your site for 90 days. In the next section, you learn how to adjust the number of days that the variables are kept, but sometimes you will need to delete a client variable programmatically.

NOTE

It's important to understand that a client doesn't have its own expiration date. Client variables don't expire individually; the whole client record is what expires. So, it's not that a client variable is deleted 90 days after it is set. Rather, the client variable (and all other client variables assigned to the user's machine) is deleted after the user lets 90 days pass before revisiting any pages in the application. For more information about tweaking the expiration system, see "Adjusting How Long Client Variables Are Kept," in the next section.

ColdFusion provides a `deleteClientVariable()` function, which enables you to delete individual client variables by name. The function takes one argument: the name of the client variable you want to delete (the name isn't case sensitive). Another handy housekeeping feature is that `getClientVariablesList()` function, which returns a comma-separated list of the client-variable names that have been set for the current browser.

Listing 19.8 shows how these two functions can be used together to delete all client variables that have been set for a user's browser. You could use code such as this on a start-over type of page, or if the user has chosen to log out of a special area.

Listing 19.8 `DeleteClientVars.cfm`— Deleting Client Variables Set for the Current Browser

```
<!---
 Filename: DeleteClientVars.cfm
 Created by: Nate Weiss (NMW)
 Purpose: Deletes all client variables associated with browser
--->
```

Listing 19.8 (CONTINUED)

```
<html>
<head><title>Clearing Your Preferences</title></head>
<body>

<h2>Clearing Your Preferences</h2>

<!--- For each client-variable set for this browser... --->
<cfloop list="#getClientVariablesList()#" index="thisVarName">
 <!--- Go ahead and delete the client variable! --->
 <cfset deleteClientVariable(thisVarName)>

 <cfoutput>#thisVarName# deleted.<br></cfoutput>
</cfloop>

<p>Your preferences have been cleared.</p>

</body>
</html>
```

Along with `deleteClientVariable()`, you can also treat the `CLIENT` scope like a structure. So for example, you can remove the client variable name using `structDelete(CLIENT,"name")`.

Adjusting How Client Variables Are Stored

Out of the box, ColdFusion stores client variables in the server's Registry and will delete all client variables for any visitors who don't return to your site for 90 or more days. You can, of course, tweak these behaviors to suit your needs. This section discusses the client-variable storage options available.

Adjusting How Long Client Variables Are Kept

Normally, client variables are maintained on what amounts to a permanent basis for users who visit your site at least once every 90 days. If a user actually lets 90 days pass without visiting your site (for shame!), all of their client variables are purged by ColdFusion. This helps keep the client-variable store from becoming ridiculously large.

To adjust this value from the default of 90 days, do the following:

1. Open the ColdFusion Administrator.

2. Navigate to the Client Variables page.

3. Under Storage Name, click the Registry link.

4. Change the Purge Data for Clients That Remain Unvisited For value to the number of days you want; then click Submit Changes.

NOTE

Remember, there isn't a separate timeout for each client variable. The only time client variables are automatically purged is if the client browser hasn't visited the server at all for 90 days (or whatever the purge-data setting has been set to).

Storing Client Variables in a Database

ColdFusion can store your client variables in a database instead of in the Registry. This will appeal to people who don't like the idea of the Registry being used for storage, or who find that they must make the Registry very large to accommodate the number of client variables they need to maintain. The ability to store client variables in a SQL database is particularly important if you are running several servers in a cluster. You can have all the servers in the cluster keep your application's client variables in the same database, thereby giving you a way to keep variables persistent between pages without worrying about what will happen if the user ends up at a different server in the cluster on their next visit. See the section "Sharing Client Variables Between Servers," later.

NOTE

When using the term Registry, we are referring to the Windows Registry, assuming that ColdFusion Server is installed on a Windows machine. On other platforms, ColdFusion ships with a simple Registry replacement for storage of client variables. Linux and Unix users can still use the default client storage mechanism of the Registry. However, the Registry replacement isn't a high-performance beast, and isn't recommended for applications that get a lot of traffic.

NOTE

Although the Registry provides a quick and simple way to use client variables, using it is almost never recommended for a live Web site.

To store your client variables in a database, follow these steps:

1. Create a new database to hold the client variables. You don't need to create any tables in the database; ColdFusion will do that on its own. If you want, you can use an existing database, but we recommend that you use a fresh, dedicated database for storing client variables.

2. Use the ColdFusion Administrator to create a new data source for your new database. See Chapter 6, "Introducing SQL," for details.

3. Navigate to the Client Variables page of the ColdFusion Administrator.

4. Select your new data source from the drop-down list, then click the Add button. The page for adding to or editing the client store appears, as shown in Figure 19.2.

5. Adjust the Purge Data for Clients That Remain Unvisited For value as desired. This value was described in "Adjusting How Long Client Variables Are Kept," above. As the page in the Administrator notes, if you are using the client variable database in a cluster situation, this option should be enabled for only one server in the cluster. If you aren't using a cluster, you should keep this option enabled.

6. Check the Disable Global Client Variable Updates check box unless you are particularly interested in the accuracy of the `hitcount` and `lastvisit` properties. In general, we recommend that you check this option, because it can greatly lessen the strain on the database. The only side effect is that client variables will be purged based on the last time a client variable was set or changed, rather than the last time the user visited your site.

Figure 19.2

You can have ColdFusion store your application's client variables in a database, rather than in the Registry.

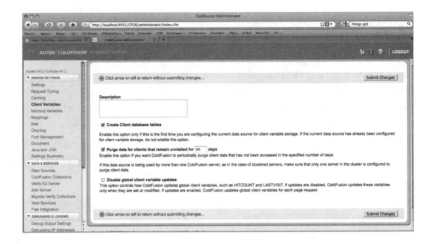

7. Leave the Create Client Database Tables option checked, unless you have already gone through that process for this database in the past.

8. Click the Submit Changes button.

You now can supply the new data source name to the `clientStorage` value in the `This` scope from the `Application.cfc` file (refer to Table 19.3). All of your application's client variables now will be stored in the database instead of in the Registry.

TIP

If you go back to the Client Variables page of the ColdFusion Administrator and change the Default Storage Mechanism for Client Sessions value to the data source you just created, it will be used for all applications that don't specify a `clientStorage` attribute (refer to Table 19.3).

Sharing Client Variables Between Servers

As explained at the beginning of this section, ColdFusion tracks each browser by setting its own client-tracking cookie called `CFID`. Normally, it sets this cookie so that it is sent back only to the server that set it. If you have three ColdFusion servers, each visitor will be given a different `CFID` number for each server, which in turn means that client variables will be maintained separately for each server.

In many situations, especially if you are operating several servers in a cluster, you will want client variables to be shared between the servers, so that a `CLIENT.lastSearch` variable set by one server will be visible to the others.

To share client variables between servers, do the following:

1. Have ColdFusion store your application's client variables in a database, rather than in the Registry. Be sure to do this on all servers in question. For instructions, see the section "Storing Client Variables in a Database," above.

2. Add a `setDomainCookies="Yes"` attribute to your application's `THIS` scope in the `Application.cfc` file. This causes ColdFusion to set the `CFID` cookie in such a way that it will be shared among all servers in the same Internet domain. This is the rough equivalent of using the `DOMAIN` attribute in a `<cfcookie>` tag.

Now you can use client variables in your code as you normally would. No matter which server a user visits, ColdFusion will store all client variables in the common database you set up.

NOTE

For cookies to be shared between servers, they all must be members of the same top-level Internet domain (for instance, `orangewhip.com`).

TIP

For more information about using client variables in a clustered environment, see Chapter 50, "Managing Session State in Clusters," in *Adobe ColdFusion 9 Web Application Construction Kit, Volume 3: Advanced Application Development*.

Storing Client Variables as Cookies

Somewhat paradoxically, you can tell ColdFusion to store your application's client variables in cookies on the user's machine, rather than on the server side. You do this by setting the `clientStorage` value in the `THIS` scope from the `Application.cfc` file to `Cookie`. This basically lets you continue using the `client` prefix even if you want the variables to essentially be stored as cookies.

This might be useful, for instance, in situations where you are selling your code as a third-party application and want your licensees to have the option of using a server-side or client-side data store. Unfortunately, the size limitations for cookies will apply (see the section "Cookie Limitations," above). This is a somewhat esoteric subject, so it isn't discussed in full here. Please consult the ColdFusion documentation for more information about this feature.

NOTE

The cookie-storage mechanism for client variables can be useful in a clustered environment or a site that gets an extremely large number of discrete visitors.

Using Client Variables Without Requiring Cookies

Above, you learned that ColdFusion maintains the association between a browser and its client variables by storing a `CFID` cookie on the browser machine. That would seem to imply that client variables won't work if a browser doesn't support cookies or has had them disabled. Don't worry; all isn't completely lost.

Actually, ColdFusion normally sets two cookies with which to track client variables: the `cfid` value already mentioned and a randomly generated `cftoken` value. Think of `cfid` and `cftoken` as being similar to a username and password, respectively. Only if the `cfid` and `cftoken` are both valid will ColdFusion be capable of successfully looking up the appropriate client variables. If the browser doesn't provide the values, for whatever reason (perhaps because the user has configured the browser not to use cookies or because a firewall between the user and your server is stripping cookies out of each page request), ColdFusion won't be able to look up the browser's client variables. In fact, it will be forced to consider the browser to be a new, first-time visitor, and it will generate a new cfid and cftoken for the browser—which, of course, means that all client variables that might have been set during previous page visits will be lost.

You can still use client variables without requiring cookies, but it takes a bit more work. Basically, you need to make the cfid and cftoken available to ColdFusion yourself, by passing the values manually in the URL to every single page in your application.

So, if you want your client variables to work for browsers that don't (or won't) support cookies, you must include the cfid and cftoken as URL parameters. So, a link such as

```
<a href="MyPage.cfm">Click Here</a>
```

would be changed to the following, which would need to be placed between <cfoutput> tags:

```
<a href="MyPage.cfm?CFID=#client.cfid#&CFTOKEN=#client.cftoken#">Click Here</a>
```

ColdFusion provides a shortcut property you can use to make this task less tedious. Instead of providing the cfid and cftoken in the URL, you can just pass the special CLIENT.urlToken property, which always holds the current cfid and cftoken name/value pairs together in one string, including the & and = signs. This means the previous line of code can be shortened to the following, which would still need to be placed between <cfoutput> tags:

```
<a href="MyPage.cfm?#client.urlToken#">Click Here</a>
```

You must be sure to pass CLIENT.urlToken in every URL, not just in links. For instance, if you are using a <form> (or <cfform>) tag, you must pass the token value in the form's action, such as this:

```
<form action="MyPage.cfm?#client.urlToken#" method="Post">
```

If you are using frames, you must pass the token value in the src attribute, such as this:

```
<frame src="MyPage.cfm?#client.urlToken#">
```

And so on. Basically, you must look through your code and ensure that whenever you see one of your .cfm templates in a URL of any type, you correctly pass the token value.

ColdFusion provides yet another shortcut as well. The URLSessionFormat function will actually detect whether the current browser can accept cookies. You pass a URL, and ColdFusion will return either the URL as is (if the browser accepts cookies) or the URL with the token information. If you use this function, the form tag becomes

```
<form action="#URLSessionFormat("MyPage.cfm")" method="Post">
```

NOTE

Remember that the URLSessionFormat value must always be placed between <cfoutput> tags, unless the URL is being passed as an attribute to a CFML tag (any tag that starts with CF, such as <cfform>).

TIP
If users bookmark one of your pages, the `cfid` and `cftoken` information should be part of the bookmarked URL, so that their client variables aren't lost even if their browsers don't support cookies. However, if they just type your site's URL into their browsers directly, it's unlikely that they will include the `cfid` and `cftoken`. ColdFusion will be forced to consider them as new visitors, which in turn means that the prior visit's client variables will be lost. ColdFusion will eventually purge the lost session (see the section "Adjusting How Long Client Variables Are Kept," earlier in this chapter).

NOTE
In addition to the `cfid`, `cftoken`, and `urlToken` properties mentioned here, several other automatically maintained properties of the `CLIENT` scope are available, including `hitCout`, `lastVisit`, and `timeCreated`.

Storing Complex Data Types in Client Variables

As mentioned earlier, you can store only simple values (strings, numbers, dates, and Boolean values) in the `CLIENT` scope. If you attempt to store one of ColdFusion's complex data types (structures, arrays, queries, and object references) as a client variable, you get an error message.

You can, however, use the `serializeJSON()` function to transform a complex value into a JSON string. In this serialized form, the value can be stored as a client variable. Later, when you want to use the variable, you can use the `deserializeJSON()` function to transform it from a string back into its complex form.

Using Session Variables

We have already has covered a lot of ground in this chapter. You have learned about cookies and client variables and how they can be used to make an application aware of its individual users and what they are doing. ColdFusion's Web application framework provides one more type of persistent variable to discuss: session variables.

What Are Session Variables?

Session variables are similar to client variables in that they are stored on the server rather than in the browser's memory. Unlike client variables, however, session variables persist only for a user's current session. Later you'll learn exactly how a session is defined, but for now, think of it as synonymous with a user's visit to your site. So session variables should be seen as per-visit variables, whereas client variables are per-user variables intended to persist between each user's visits.

Session variables aren't stored physically in a database or the server's Registry. Instead, they are stored in the server's RAM. This makes sense, considering that they are intended to persist for only a short time. Also, because ColdFusion doesn't need to physically store and retrieve the variables, you can expect session variables to work a bit more quickly than client variables.

Enabling Session Variables

As with client variables, you must enable session variables using an `Application.cfc` file before you can use them in your code. Table 19.4 lists the additional `THIS` scope values relevant to session variables. In general, all you need to do is specify a `name` and then set `sessionManagement="Yes"`.

Table 19.4 Additional `Application.cfc` `THIS` Scope Values Relevant to Session Variables

ATTRIBUTE	PURPOSE
`name`	A name for your application.
`sessionManagement`	Yes or No. Set to Yes to enable the use of session variables. If you attempt to use session variables in your code without setting this attribute to Yes, an error message will be displayed when the code is executed.
`sessionTimeout`	Optional. How long you want your session variables to live in the server's memory. If you don't provide this value, it defaults to whatever is set up in the Variables page of the ColdFusion Administrator. See the section "When Does a Session End?" later. The ColdFusion Administrator specifies a maximum setting for session timeouts. If you specify a value higher than the maximum set in the Administrator, the value specified in the Administrator will be used instead.

For example, to enable session management, you might use something such as this in your `Application.cfc` file:

```
<!--- Name application and enable Session and Application variables --->
<cfset this.name="OrangeWhipSite">
<cfset this.sessionManagement="Yes">
<cfset this.dataSource="ows">
```

NOTE

Session variables can be disabled globally (for the entire server) in the ColdFusion Administrator. If the Enable Session Variables option on the Memory Variables page of the Administrator is not checked, you will not be able to use session variables, regardless of what you set the `sessionManagement` attribute to.

The Web site for this book includes an `Application3.cfc` template, which enables session management. It is identical to the `Application2.cfc` template used earlier to enable client variables (Listing 19.5), except that `sessionManagement` is set to `Yes`, rather than to `clientManagement`.

Using Session Variables

After you have enabled session variables using `sessionMangement`, you can start using them in your code. ColdFusion provides a special `SESSION` variable scope, which works similarly to the `CLIENT` and `COOKIE` scopes you are already familiar with. You can set and use session variables simply by using the `session` prefix in front of a variable's name.

For instance, instead of the `client.lastSearch` used in the `SearchForm.cfm` examples above, you could call the variable `session.lastSearch`. The examples would still work in essentially the same way. The only difference in behavior would be that the memory interval of each user's last search would be short (until the end of the session), rather than long (90 days, by default).

For something such as search results, the shorter memory provided by using session variables might feel more intuitive for the user. That is, a user might expect the search page to remember their last search phrase during the same visit, but they might be surprised—or irritated—if it remembered search criteria from weeks or months in the past.

You will often find yourself using session and client variables together in the same application. Generally, things that should be remembered for only the current visit belong in session variables, whereas things that should be remembered between visits should be kept in client variables.

Using Session Variables for Multiple-Page Data Entry

Session variables can be especially handy for data-entry processes that require the user to fill out a number of pages. Let's say you have been asked to put together a data-entry interface for Orange Whip Studios' intranet. The idea is for your users to be able to add new film records to the studio's database. A number of pieces of information will need to be supplied by the user (title, director, actors, and so on).

The most obvious solution would be to just create one long, complex form. However, suppose further that you have been specifically asked not to do this because it might confuse the interns the company hires to do its data-entry tasks.

After carefully considering your options, you decide to present the data-entry screens in a familiar wizard format, with Next and Back buttons the users can use to navigate between steps. However, it's important that nothing actually be entered into the database until the user has finished all the steps. This means the wizard must remember everything the user has entered, even though they may be moving freely back and forth between steps.

Hmm. You could pass everything from step to step as hidden form fields, but that sounds like a lot of work, and it feels wrong to put the burden of remembering all that data on the client. You'd like to keep the information on the server side. You could create some type of temporary tables in your database, and keep updating the temporary values until the user is finished, but that also sounds like a lot of work. Plus, how would you keep the values separate for each user? And what if the user abandons the wizard partway through?

The answer, of course, is to use session variables, which are perfect for this type of situation. You only need to track the information for a short time, so session variables are appropriate. Also, session variables aren't kept permanently on the server, so you won't be storing any excess data if the user doesn't finish the wizard.

Maintaining Structures in the SESSION Scope

The following code snippet creates a new structure called session.movWiz. It contains several pieces of information, most of which start out blank (set to an empty string). Because the variable is in the SESSION scope, a separate version of the structure is kept for each user, but only for the user's current visit. The stepNum value is in charge of tracking which step of the data-entry wizard each user is currently on:

```
<cfif not isDefined("session.movWiz")>
  <!--- If structure is undefined, create/initialize it --->
```

```
<cfset session.movWiz = structNew()>
<!--- Represents current wizard step; start at one --->
< cfset session.movWiz.stepNum = 1>
<!--- We will collect these from user; start blank --->
<cfset session.movWiz.movieTitle = "">
<cfset session.movWiz.pitchText = "">
<cfset session.movWiz.directorID = "">
<cfset session.movWiz.ratingID = "">
<cfset session.movWiz.actorIDs = "">
<cfset session.novWiz.starActorID = "">
</cfif>
```

Updating the values in the session.movWiz structure is simple enough. Assume for the moment that the wizard contains Back and Next buttons named goBack and goNext, respectively. The following snippet would increment the stepNum part of the structure by 1 when the user clicks the Next button, and decrement it by 1 if the user clicks Back:

```
<!--- If user clicked Back button, go back a step --->
<cfif isDefined("form.goBack")>
 <cfset session.movWiz.stepNum = session.movWiz.stepNum - 1>
<!--- If user clicked Next button, go forward one --->
<cfelseif isDefined("form.goNext")>
 <cfset session.MovWiz.stepNum = session.movWiz.stepNum + 1>
</cfif>
```

The other values in the movWiz structure can be accessed and updated in a similar way. For instance, to present the user with a text-entry field for the new movie's title, you could use something such as this:

```
<cfinput
name="MovieTitle"
value="#session.movWiz.movieTitle#">
```

The input field will be prefilled with the current value of the movieTitle part of the movWiz structure. If the previous snippet was in a form and submitted to the server, the value the user typed could be saved back into the movWiz structure using the following line:

```
<cfset session.movWiz.movieTitle = form.movieTitle>
```

Putting It All Together

The code in Listing 19.9 combines all the previous snippets into a simple, intuitive wizard interface that users will find familiar and easy to use. The listing is a bit longer than usual, but each part is easy to understand.

The idea here is to create a self-submitting form page that changes depending on which step of the wizard the user is on. The first time the user comes to the page, they see Step 1 of the wizard. They submit the form, which calls the template again, they see Step 2, and so on.

This data-entry wizard will collect information from the user in five steps, as follows:

1. The film's title, a one-line description, and the rating, which eventually will be placed in the Films table

2. The film's director (the user can list only one), which is inserted in the `FilmsDirectors` table

3. The actors in the movie (the user can list any number), which will be inserted in the `FilmsActors` table

4. Which of the film's actors gets top billing, which sets the `IsStarringRole` column of the `FilmsActors` table to true

5. A final confirmation screen, with a Finish button

The following examples use variables in the SESSION scope without locking the accesses by way of the `<cflock>` tag. While extremely unlikely, it is theoretically possible that simultaneous visits to this template *from the same browser* could cause the wizard to collect information in an inconsistent manner. See the section "Locking Revisited," later in this chapter.

Listing 19.9 `NewMovieWizard.cfm`— Using Session Variables to Guide through a Multistep Process

```
<!---
 Filename: NewMovieWizard.cfm
 Created by: Nate Weiss (NMW)
 Please Note Session variables must be enabled
--->

<!--- Total Number of Steps in the Wizard --->
<cfset numberOfSteps = 5>

<!--- The session.movWiz structure holds users' entries --->
<!--- as they move through wizard. Make sure it exists! --->
<cfif not isDefined("session.movWiz")>
 <!--- If structure undefined, create/initialize it --->
 <cfset session.movWiz = structNew()>
 <!--- Represents current wizard step; start at one --->
 <cfset session.movWiz.stepNum = 1>
 <!--- We will collect these from user; start blank --->
 <cfset session.movWiz.movieTitle = "">
 <cfset session.movWiz.pitchText = "">
 <cfset session.movWiz.directorID = "">
 <cfset session.movWiz.ratingID = "">
 <cfset session.movWiz.actorIDs = "">
 <cfset session.movWiz.starActorID = "">
</cfif>


<!--- If user just submitted MovieTitle, remember it --->
<!--- Do same for the DirectorID, Actors, and so on. --->
<cfif isDefined("form.movieTitle")>
 <cfset session.movWiz.movieTitle = form.movieTitle>
 <cfset session.movWiz.pitchText = form.pitchText>
 <cfset session.movWiz.ratingID = form.ratingID>
<cfelseif isDefined("form.directorID")>
 <cfset session.movWiz.directorID = form.directorID>
<cfelseif isDefined("form.actorID")>
 <cfset session.movWiz.actorIDs = form.actorID>
<cfelseif isDefined("form.starActorID")>
```

Listing 19.9 (CONTINUED)

```
     <cfset session.movWiz.starActorID = form.starActorID>
   </cfif>


   <!--- If user clicked "Back" button, go back a step --->
   <cfif isDefined("form.goBack")>
    <cfset session.movWiz.stepNum = url.stepNum - 1>
   <!--- If user clicked "Next" button, go forward one --->
   <cfelseif isDefined("form.goNext")>
    <cfset session.movWiz.stepNum = url.stepNum + 1>
   <!--- If user clicked "Finished" button, we're done --->
   <cfelseif isDefined("form.goDone")>
    <cflocation url="NewMovieCommit.cfm">
   </cfif>


   <html>
   <head><title>New Movie Wizard</title></head>
   <body>

   <!--- Show title and current step --->
   <cfoutput>
    <b>New Movie Wizard</b><br>
    Step #session.movWiz.StepNum# of #NumberOfSteps#<br>
   </cfoutput>


   <!--- Data Entry Form, which submits back to itself --->
   <cfform
    action="NewMovieWizard.cfm?StepNum=#session.movWiz.stepNum#"
    method="POST">

    <!--- Display the appropriate wizard step --->
    <cfswitch expression="#session.movWiz.stepNum#">
    <!--- Step One: Movie Title --->
    <cfcase value="1">
    <!--- Get potential film ratings from database --->
    <cfquery name="getRatings" datasource="ows">
    SELECT RatingID, Rating
    FROM FilmsRatings
    ORDER BY RatingID
    </cfquery>

    <!--- Show text entry field for title --->
    What is the title of the movie?<br>
    <cfinput
    name="MovieTitle"
    SIZE="50"
    VALUE="#session.movWiz.MovieTitle#">

    <!--- Show text entry field for short description --->
    <p>What is the "pitch" or "one-liner" for the movie?<br>
    <cfinput
    name="pitchText"
    size="50"
    value="#session.movWiz.pitchText#">
```

Listing 19.9 (CONTINUED)

```
<!--- Series of radio buttons for movie rating --->
<p>Please select the rating:<br>
<cfloop query="getRatings">
<!--- Re-select this rating if it was previously selected --->
<cfset isChecked = ratingID EQ session.movWiz.ratingID>
<!--- Display radio button --->
<cfinput
type="radio"
name="ratingID"
checked="#isChecked#"
value="#ratingID#"><cfoutput>#rating#<br></cfoutput>
</cfloop>
</cfcase>


<!--- Step Two: Pick Director --->
<cfcase value="2">
<!--- Get list of directors from database --->
<cfquery name="getDirectors">
SELECT DirectorID, FirstName || ' ' || LastName As FullName
FROM Directors
ORDER BY LastName
</cfquery>


<!--- Show all Directors in SELECT list --->
<!--- Pre-select if user has chosen one --->
Who will be directing the movie?<br>
<cfselect
size="#getDirectors.recordCount#"
query="getDirectors"
name="directorID"
display="fullName"
value="directorID"
selected="#session.movWiz.directorID#"/>
</cfcase>


<!--- Step Three: Pick Actors --->
<cfcase value="3">
<!--- get list of actors from database --->
<cfquery name="getActors" datasource="ows">
SELECT * FROM Actors
ORDER BY NameLast
</cfquery>


What actors will be in the movie?<br>
<!--- For each actor, display checkbox --->
<cfloop query="GetActors">
<!--- Should checkbox be pre-checked? --->
<cfset isChecked = listFind(session.movWiz.actorIDs, actorID)>
<!--- Checkbox itself --->
<cfinput
type="checkbox"
name="actorID"
value="#actorID#"
checked="#isChecked#">
<!--- Actor name --->
<cfoutput>#nameFirst# #nameLast#</cfoutput><br>
</cfloop>
```

Listing 19.9   (CONTINUED)

```
</cfcase>

<!--- Step Four: Who is the star? --->
<cfcase value="4">
<cfif session.movWiz.actorIDs EQ "">
Please go back to the last step and choose at least one
actor or actress to be in the movie.
<cfelse>
<!--- Get actors who are in the film --->
<cfquery name="getActors" DATASOURCE="ows">
SELECT * FROM Actors
WHERE ActorID IN (#session.movWiz.ActorIDs#)
ORDER BY NameLast
</cfquery>

Which one of the actors will get top billing?<br>
<!--- For each actor, display radio button --->
<cfloop query="getActors">
<!--- Should radio be pre-checked? --->
<cfset isChecked = session.movWiz.starActorID EQ actorID>
<!--- Radio button itself --->
<cfinput
type="radio"
name="starActorID"
value="#actorID#"
checked="#isChecked#">
<!--- Actor name --->
<cfoutput>#nameFirst# #nameLast#</cfoutput><br>
</cfloop>
</cfif>
</cfcase>

<!--- Step Five: Final Confirmation --->
<cfcase value="5">
You have successfully finished the New Movie Wizard.<br>
Click the Finish button to add the movie to the database.<br>
Click Back if you need to change anything.<br>
</cfcase>
</cfswitch>


<p>
<!--- Show Back button, unless at first step --->
<cfif session.movWiz.stepNum GT 1>
<input type="submit" name="goBack" value="&lt;&lt; Back">
</cfif>
<!--- Show Next button, unless at last step --->
<!--- If at last step, show "Finish" button --->
<cfif session.movWiz.stepNum lt numberOfSteps>
<input type="submit" name="goNext" value="Next &gt;&gt;">
<cfelse>
<input type="submit" name="goDone" value="Finish">
</cfif>
</cfform>


</body>
</html>
```

NOTE

To help keep this code as clear as possible, Listing 19.9 doesn't prevent the user from leaving various form fields blank. Data validation could be added using the techniques introduced in Chapter 13, "Form Data Validation."

First, a variable called `numberOfSteps` is defined, set to `5`. This keeps the `5` from needing to be hard-coded throughout the rest of the template. Next, the `SESSION.movWiz` structure is defined, using the syntax shown in the first code snippet that appeared before this listing. The structure contains a default value for each piece of information that will be collected from the user.

Next, a `<cfif>` / `<cfelseif>` block is used to determine whether the step the user just completed contains a form element named `movieTitle`. If so, the corresponding value in the `SESSION.movWiz` structure is updated with the form's value, thus remembering the user's entry for later. The other possible form fields are also tested for this block of code in the same manner.

Next, the code checks to see whether a form field named `goBack` was submitted. If so, it means the user clicked the Back button in the wizard interface (see Figure 19.3). Therefore, the `stepNum` value in the `movWiz` structure should be decremented by 1, effectively moving the user back a step. An equivalent test is performed for fields named `goNext` and `goFinish`. If the user clicks `goFinish`, they are redirected to another template called `NewMovieCommit.cfm`, which actually takes care of inserting the records in the database.

Figure 19.3

Session variables are perfect for creating wizard-style interfaces.

The rest of the code displays the correct form to the user, depending on which step they are on. If it's step 1, the first `cfcase` tag kicks in, displaying form fields for the movie's title and short description. Each of the form fields is prefilled with the current value of the corresponding value from `SESSION.movWiz`. That means the fields will be blank when the user begins, but if they later click the Back button to return to the first step, they will see the value that they previously entered. That is, a session variable is being used to maintain the state of the various steps of the wizard.

The other `<cfcase>` sections are similar to the first. Each presents form fields to the user (check boxes, radio buttons, and so on), always prefilled or preselected with the current values from `session.movWiz`. As the user clicks Next or Back to submit the values for a particular step, their entries are stored in the `session.movWiz` structure by the code near the top of the template.

The last bit of code simply decides whether to show Next, Back, and Finish buttons for each step of the wizard. As would be expected, the Finish button is shown only on the last step, the Next button for all steps except the last, and the Back button for all steps except the first.

Deleting Session Variables

Like the CLIENT scope, session values are treated like a struct. This means the structDelete() function can be used to delete session values.

For instance, to delete the session.movWiz variable, you could use the following line:

```
<cfset structDelete(session, "movWiz")>
```

Listing 19.10 is the NewMovieCommit.cfm template, which is called when the user clicks the Finish button on the last step of the New Movie Wizard (refer to Listing 19.9). Most of this listing is made up of ordinary <cfquery> code, simply inserting the values from the session.MovWiz structure into the correct tables in the database.

After all of the records are inserted, the movWiz variable is removed from the session structure, using the syntax shown previously. At that point, the user can be directed back to the NewMovieWizard.cfm template, where they can enter information for another movie. The wizard code will see that the movWiz structure no longer exists for the user, and therefore will create a new structure, with blank initial values for the movie title and other information.

Listing 19.10 NewMovieCommit.cfm—Deleting Unnecessary Session Variables

```
<!---
Filename: NewMovieCommit.cfm
Created by: Nate Weiss (NMW)
Purpose: Inserts new movie and associated records into
database. Gets called by NewMovieWizard.cfm
--->


<!--- Insert film record --->
<cfquery result="r">
   INSERT INTO Films(
   MovieTitle,
   PitchText,
   RatingID)
   VALUES (
   <cfqueryparam cfsqltype="cf_sql_varchar"
    value="#SESSION.MovWiz.MovieTitle#">,
    <cfqueryparam cfsqltype="cf_sql_varchar"
   value="#SESSION.MovWiz.PitchText#">,
    <cfqueryparam cfsqltype="cf_sql_integer"
    value="#SESSION.MovWiz.RatingID#"> )
   </cfquery>
   <!--- when using the result attribute, you can get the ID of
   the last inserted record. --->
   <cfset newId = r.generatedKey>

<!--- Insert director record --->
<cfquery >
```

Listing 19.10   (CONTINUED)

```
    INSERT INTO FilmsDirectors(FilmID, DirectorID, Salary)
    VALUES (<cfqueryparam cfsqltype="cf_sql_integer" value="#newID#">,
    <cfqueryparam cfsqltype="cf_sql_integer" value="#session.MovWiz.DirectorID#">,
    0)
</cfquery>

<!--- Insert actor records --->
<cfloop list="#session.movWiz.actorIDs#" index="thisActor">
 <cfset isStar = thisActor eq session.movWiz.starActorId?1:0>
 <cfquery datasource="ows">
 INSERT INTO FilmsActors(FilmID, ActorID, Salary, IsStarringRole)
 VALUES (<cfqueryparam cfsqltype="cf_sql_integer" value="#newID#">,
  <cfqueryparam cfsqltype="cf_sql_integer" value="#thisActor#">,
  0,
  <cfqueryparam cfsqltype="cf_sql_bit" value="#isStar#">)
 </cfquery>
</cfloop>

<!--- Remove MovWiz variable from SESSION structure --->
<!--- User will be started over on return to wizard --->
<cfset structDelete(session, "movWiz")>

<!--- Display message to user --->
<html>
<head><title>Movie Added</title></head>
<body>
 <h2>Movie Added</h2>
 <p>The movie has been added to the database.</p>

 <!--- Link to go through the wizard again --->
 <p><a href="NewMovieWizard.cfm">Enter Another Movie</a></p>

</body>
</html>
```

NOTE

When we insert the movie into the database, we use the result struct to get the ID of the last inserted record.

One interesting thing about the wizard metaphor is that users expect wizards to adapt themselves based on the choices they make along the way. For instance, the last step of this wizard (in which the user indicates which of the movie's stars gets top billing) looks different depending on the previous step (in which the user lists any number of stars in the movie). You also could decide to skip certain steps based on the film's budget, add more steps if the director and actors have worked together before, and so on. This would be relatively hard to do if you were collecting all the information in one long form.

As you can see in Listing 19.10, this version of the wizard doesn't collect salary information to be inserted into the FilmsActors and FilmsDirectors tables. Nor does it perform any data validation. For instance, the user can leave the movie title field blank without getting an error message.

When Does a Session End?

Developers often wonder when exactly a session ends. The simple answer is that by default, Cold-Fusion's Session Management feature is based on time. A particular session is considered to be expired if more than 20 minutes pass without another request from the same client. At that point, the SESSION scope associated with that browser is freed from the server's memory.

That said, ColdFusion provides a few options that you can use to subtly change the definition of a session, and to control more precisely when a particular session ends.

J2EE Session Variables and ColdFusion

ColdFusion includes an option that allows you to use J2EE session variables. This new option is different from the "classic" ColdFusion implementation of session variables, which have been available in previous versions.

The traditional implementation uses ColdFusion-specific cfid and cftoken cookies to identify the client (that is, the browser). Whenever a client visits pages in your application within a certain period of time, those page requests are considered to be part of the same session. By default, this time period is 20 minutes. If more than 20 minutes pass without another page request from the client, the session "times out" and the session information is discarded from the server's memory. If the user closes the browser and then reopens it and visits your page again, the same session will still be in effect. That is, ColdFusion's classic strategy is to uniquely identify the machine, then define the concept of "session" solely in terms of time.

The J2EE session variables option causes ColdFusion to define a session somewhat differently. Instead of using cfid and cftoken cookies, which persist between sessions, to track the user's machine, it uses a different cookie, called jSessionID. This cookie isn't persistent, and thus expires when a user closes the browser. Therefore, if the user reopens their browser and visits your page again, it is an entirely new session.

To enable the J2EE session variables feature, select the Use J2EE Session Variables check box on the ColdFusion Administrator's Memory Variables page.

Once you enable this option, sessions will expire whenever the user closes their browser, or when the session timeout period elapses between requests (whichever comes first).

> **NOTE**
>
> The use of the jSessionID cookie is part of the Java J2EE specification. Using J2EE session variables makes it easy to share session variables with other J2EE code that may be working alongside your ColdFusion templates, such as Java Servlets, Enterprise JavaBeans, JSPs, and so on. In other words, telling ColdFusion to use J2EE session variables is a great way to integrate your ColdFusion code with other J2EE technologies so they can all behave as a single application. The assumption here is that the closing of a browser should be interpreted as a desire to end a session. J2EE sessions are also more secure, which is another good reason to use them!

Default Behavior

Again, by default, a session doesn't automatically end when the user closes the browser. You can see this yourself by visiting one of the session examples discussed in this book, such as the New Movie Wizard (refer to Listing 19.9). Fill out the wizard partway, then close your browser. Now reopen it. Nothing has happened to your session's copy of the SESSION scope, so you still are on the same step of the wizard that you were before you closed your browser. As far as ColdFusion is concerned, you just reloaded the page.

Adjusting the Session Timeout Period

You can adjust the session timeout period for your session variables by following the same basic steps you take to adjust the timeout period for application variables. That is, you can adjust the default timeout of 20 minutes using the ColdFusion Administrator, or you can use the sessionTimeout attribute in the THIS scope defined in your Application.cfc file to set a specific session timeout for your application.

➡ For specific instructions, see the section "Application Variable Timeouts" in Chapter 18.

Expiring a Session Programmatically

If you want a session in your code to expire, there are a few ways to handle it. In the past, you could use the <cfapplication> tag with a sessionTimeout value of 0 seconds. A more appropriate way, however, would be to simply remove the session values by hand using the structDelete() function. For instance, if you wanted to give your users some type of log-out link, you could use structDelete() to remove the session variables you set to mark a user as being logged on.

Ending the Session When the Browser Closes

The simplest way to make session variables expire when the user closes their browser is by telling ColdFusion to use J2EE session variables, as explained earlier in the "J2EE Session Variables and ColdFusion" section. When in this mode, the ColdFusion server sets a nonpersistent cookie to track the session (as opposed to the traditional session-variable mode, in which persistent cookies are set). Thus, when the browser is closed, the session-tracking cookie is lost, which means that a new session will be created if the user reopens their browser and comes back to your application.

Assuming that you aren't using J2EE session variables, one option is to set the setClientCookies attribute in the THIS scope in your Application.cfc file to No, which means that the cfid and cftoken cookies ColdFusion normally uses to track each browser's session (and client) variables will not be maintained as persistent cookies on each client machine. If you aren't using client variables, or don't need your client variables to persist after the user closes their browser, this can be a viable option.

If you do decide to set setClientCookie="No", you must manually pass the cfid and cftoken in the URL for every page request, as if the user's browser did not support cookies at all. See the section "Using Client Variables Without Requiring Cookies," earlier in this chapter, for specific instructions.

If you want to use `setClientCookie="No"` but don't want to pass the `cfid` and `cftoken` in every URL, you could set the `cfid` and `cftoken` on your own, as nonpersistent cookies. This means the values would be stored as cookies on the user's browser, but the cookies would expire when the user closes their browser. The most straightforward way to get this effect is to use two `<cfset>` tags in your `Application.cfc`'s `onSessionStart` method, as follows:

```
<!--- Preserve Session/Client variables only until browser closes --->
<cfset Cookie.cfid = session.cfid>
<cfset Cookie.cftoken = session.cftoken>
```

This technique essentially causes ColdFusion to lose all memory of the client machine when the user closes their browser. When the user returns next time, no `cfid` will be presented to the server, and ColdFusion will be forced to issue a new `cfid` value, effectively abandoning any session and client variables that were associated with the browser in the past. The expiration behavior will be very similar to that of J2EE session variables.

NOTE

Please note that by setting the `cfid` and `cftoken` cookies yourself in this way, you will lose all session and client variables for your application when the user closes their browser. If you are using both client and session variables, and want the client variables to persist between sessions but the session variables to expire when the user closes their browser, then you should use either the technique shown next or J2EE session variables as discussed earlier.

A completely different technique is to set your own nonpersistent cookie, perhaps called `cookie.browserOpen`. If a user closes the browser, the cookie no longer exists. Therefore, you can use the cookie's nonexistence as a cue for the session to expire programmatically, as discussed in the previous section.

Unfortunately, there is a downside to this technique. If the browser doesn't support cookies or has had them disabled, the session will expire with every page request. However, as long as you know that cookies will be supported (for instance, in an intranet application), it will serve you well.

Using Session Variables Without Requiring Cookies

Unless you take special steps, the browser must accept a cookie or two in order for session variables to work correctly in ColdFusion. If your application needs to work even with browsers that don't (or won't) accept cookies, you need to pass the value of the special `session.URLToken` variable in each URL, just as you need to pass `client.urlToken` to allow client variables to work without using cookies. This will ensure that the appropriate `cfid`, `cftoken`, or `jSessionID` values are available for each page request, even if the browser can't provide the value as a cookie. See "Using Client Variables Without Requiring Cookies," earlier in this chapter, for specific instructions. As before, you can use the `URLSessionFormat` to put the `URLToken` value in the URL for you.

TIP

If you are using both client and session variables in your application, you can just pass either `session.urlToken` or `client.urlToken`. You don't need to worry about passing both values in the URL. If you do pass them both, that's fine too.

Other Examples of Session Variables

A number of our other examples use session variables. You might want to skim through the code listings outlined here to see some other uses for session variables:

- In Chapter 20, "Interacting with Email," session variables are used to help users check their email messages from a ColdFusion template.

- In Chapter 21, "Securing Your Applications," session variables are used to track the logged-in status of users.

Working with onSessionStart and onSessionEnd

Earlier in the chapter, we talked about how session variables can be enabled in the Application.cfc file and how handy they are for tracking information about your users. Another feature you may find handy is the ability to run code at both the beginning and end of a session. There are many ways this can be useful. Let's say that you want to note when a user first enters your system. You can do this easily with this code:

```
<cfset session.entered = now()>
```

This line of code is simple enough. However, you want to run it only once. You could use the isDefined function to check whether the variable exists, but an even easier approach is to use the onSessionStart method of the Application.cfc file. This is a special method run only at the beginning of a user's session. Conversely, it may be handy to notice when a user's session ends. In the past, doing this was (mostly) impossible in ColdFusion. But now that we have the powerful features provided by the Application.cfc file, we can handle scenarios like this. The onSessionEnd method is fired whenever a user's session times out. One simple use of this feature is to log to a text file. Because we are noting when a user first enters the system, we can log the total time the user is on the system. Listing 19.11 presents an example of this. Be sure to save the file as Application.cfc.

Listing 19.11 Application4.cfc—Supporting Session Events

```
<!---
  Filename: Application.cfc
  Created by: Raymond Camden (ray@camdenfamily.com)
  Handles application events.
--->

<cfcomponent output="false">

  <cfset this.name="OrangeWhipSite_c20">
  <cfset this.sessionManagement=true>
  <cfset this.sessiontimeout = createtimespan(0,0,0,10)>

  <cffunction name="onSessionStart" returnType="void">
    <cfset session.created = now()>
  </cffunction>

  <cffunction name="onSessionEnd" returnType="void">
```

Listing 19.11 (CONTINUED)

```
        <cfargument name="theSession" type="struct" required="true">
        <cfset var duration = dateDiff("s",arguments.theSession.created,now())>
        <cflog file="#this.name#" text="Session lasted for #duration# seconds.">
    </cffunction>

</cfcomponent>
```

Let's take a look at the two methods in this component. The onSessionStart method simply sets the created variable to the current time. The onSessionEnd method is going to use this variable. First note that inside the onSessionEnd method, you can't access the SESSION scope directly. Instead, the SESSION scope is passed as an argument to the method. We create a variable to store the number of seconds that the session was alive and then log this information to a text file. You may have noticed the dramatically short sessiontimeout value. This value was shortened so that this scenario would be easier to test. You don't have to log only to a file. You can also store the results in a database. This log would provide a handy way to see how long users stick around on your Web site.

Locking Revisited

Like application variables, session variables are kept in the server's RAM. This means that the same types of race condition problems can occur if session variables are being read and accessed by two different page requests at the same time. (See the section "Using Locks to Protect Against Race Conditions" in Chapter 18.)

→   If you haven't yet read "Using Locks to Protect Against Race Conditions" in Chapter 18, please take a look at that section before you continue.

Sessions and the `<cflock>` Tag

Just as it's possible to run into race conditions with application variables, it's also possible for race conditions to crop up when using session variables. In general, it's much less likely that race conditions will occur at the session level than at the application level, as there is usually only one page request coming from each session at any given time. Even though it's unlikely in the grand scheme of things, it still is quite possible that more than one request could be processed from a session at the same time. Here are some examples:

- Pages that use frames can allow a browser to make more than one page request at the same time. If, say, a frame set contains three individual frame pages, most browsers will issue all three follow-up requests at once.

- Pages that use Ajax provide another example of a possible race condition. Multiple Ajax requests can be fired from one page. All these requests may end up running at the same time.

- If for whatever reason (perhaps network congestion or a heavy load on your ColdFusion server) a particular page is taking a long time to come up, many users tend to click their browser's Reload or Refresh button a few times. Or they might submit a form multiple times. In either case, it's quite possible that a second or third request might get to the server before the first request does.

In other words, although race conditions are probably less likely to occur with session variables than they are with application variables, it is still possible to encounter them. Therefore, if the nature of your session variables is such that concurrent access would be a bad thing, you need to use the <cflock> tag. In general, you will use <cflock> just as it was shown in Chapter 18, except you use scope="Session" instead of scope="Application".

Remember, though, that in *most* cases you don't need to care about locking. For example, most session variables are set once (when you log in, for example) and read many times. There is no need to lock these session variables, even if your site uses frames or cfcontent.

NOTE

Locks of SCOPE="Session" will affect only those locks that have been issued to the same session, which is of course what you want. In plain English, a <cflock> with scope="Session" means "don't let other page requests from this session interfere with the code in this block."

Interacting with Email

ColdFusion's main purpose is to create dynamic, data-driven Web pages. But it also provides a set of email-related tags that let you send email messages that are just as dynamic and data-driven as your Web pages. You can also write ColdFusion templates that check and retrieve email messages, and even respond to them automatically.

NOTE

`<cfmail>` sends standard, Internet-style email messages using the Simple Mail Transport Protocol (SMTP). SMTP isn't explained in detail in this book; for now, all you need to know about SMTP is that it's the standard for sending email on the Internet. Virtually all email programs, such as Thunderbird, Outlook, Apple Mail, and so on send standard SMTP mail. The exceptions are proprietary messaging systems, such as Lotus Notes or older Microsoft Mail (MAPI-style) clients. If you want to learn more about the underpinnings of the SMTP protocol, visit the World Wide Web Consortium's Web site at www.wc3.org.

Introducing the `<cfmail>` Tag

You can use the `<cfmail>` tag to send email messages from your ColdFusion templates. After the server is set up correctly, you can use `<cfmail>` to send email messages to anyone with a standard Internet-style email address. As far as the receiver is concerned, the email messages you send with `<cfmail>` are just like messages sent via a normal email sending program.

Table 20.1 shows the key attributes for the `<cfmail>` tag. These are the attributes you will use most often. For clarity, they are presented here in a separate table. You have almost certainly sent email messages before, so you will immediately understand what most of these attributes do.

NOTE

Some additional `<cfmail>` attributes are introduced later in this chapter (see Table 20.2 in the "Sending Data-Driven Mail" section and Table 20.4 in the "Overriding the Default Mail Server Settings" section).

Table 20.1 Key `<cfmail>` Attributes for Sending Email Messages

ATTRIBUTE	PURPOSE
subject	Required. The subject of the email message.
from	Required. The email address that should be used to send the message. This is the address the message will be from when it's received. The address must be a standard Internet-style email address (see the section "Using Friendly Email Addresses," later in this chapter).
to	Required. The address or addresses to send the message to. To specify multiple addresses, separate them with commas. Each must be a standard Internet-style email address (see the section "Using Friendly Email Addresses").
cc	Optional. Address or addresses to send a carbon copy of the message to. This is the equivalent of using the CC feature when sending mail with a normal email program. To specify multiple addresses, separate them with commas. Each must be a standard Internet-style email address (see the section "Using Friendly Email Addresses").
bcc	Optional. Address or addresses to send a blind carbon copy of the message to. Equivalent to using the BCC feature when sending mail with a normal email program. To specify multiple addresses, separate them with commas. Each must be a standard Internet-style email address (see the section "Using Friendly Email Addresses").
replyTo	Optional. Specifies the address replies will be sent to.
failTo	Optional. Specifies an address where failure notifications can be sent.
type	Optional. Text or HTML. Text is the default, which means that the message will be sent as a normal, plain-text message. HTML means that HTML tags within the message will be interpreted as HTML, so you can specify fonts and include images in the email message. See "Sending HTML-Formatted Mail," later in this chapter.
wrapText	Optional. If specified, the text in your email will automatically wrap according to the number passed in. A typical value for wrapText is 72. The default value is to not wrap text.
mailerID	Optional. Can be used to specify the X-Mailer header that is sent with the email message. The X-Mailer header is meant to identify which software program was used to send the message. This header is generally never seen by the recipient of the message but can be important to systems in between, such as firewalls. Using the mailerID, you can make it appear as if your message is being sent by a different piece of software. If you find that your outgoing messages are being filtered out when sent to certain users, try using a mailerID that matches another mail client (such as Outlook Express or some other popular, end-user mail client).
mimeAttach	Optional. A document on the server's drive that should be included in the mail message as an attachment. This is an older way to specify attachments, maintained for backward compatibility. It's now recommended that you use the `<cfmailparam>` tag to specify attachments. For details, see "Adding Attachments," later in this chapter.
charset	Optional. This specifies the character encoding that will be used in the email. It defaults to the value set in the ColdFusion Administrator.

Table 20.1 (CONTINUED)

ATTRIBUTE	PURPOSE
spoolEnable	Optional. Controls whether the email message should be sent right away, before ColdFusion begins processing the rest of the template. The default value is Yes, which means that the message is created and placed in a queue. The actual sending will take place as soon as possible, but not necessarily before the page request has been completed. If you use spoolEnable="No", the message will be sent right away; ColdFusion won't proceed beyond the <cfmail> tag until the sending has been completed. In other words, No forces the mail sending to be a synchronous process; Yes (the default) lets it be an asynchronous process.
priority	Optional. Determines the priority of the email. This attribute can be either a number from 1 to 5, with 1 representing the most important priority, or a string value from the following list: highest (or urgent), high, normal, low (or non-urgent).
sign, keystore, keystorepassword, keyalias, keypassword, remove	Optional. Provides support for digitally signing email. This attribute is beyond the scope of this chapter but keep it in mind in case you need to sign email sent by ColdFusion.
useSSL, useTLS	Optional. Specifies whether to use Secure Sockets Layer or Transport Level Security, respectively.

Specifying a Mail Server in the Administrator

Before you can actually use the <cfmail> tag to send email messages, you need to specify a mail server. You can specify the mail server in the <cfmail> tag, in the Application.cfc file, or in the ColdFusion Administrator. If specified in the Administrator, then this mail server will be used by default if no other method is specified.

To set up ColdFusion to send email, follow these steps:

1. If you don't know it already, find out the host name or IP address for the SMTP mail server ColdFusion should use to send messages. Usually, this is the same server your normal email client program (Outlook Express, Eudora, and so on) uses to send your own mail, so you typically can find the host name or IP address somewhere in your mail client's Settings or Preferences. Often, the host name starts with something such as mail or smtp, as in mail.orangewhipstudios.com. For testing, you can use localhost as the server name. As long as you don't really have a mail server running on your local machine, this server name allows you to send mail and test your email setup locally.

2. Open the ColdFusion Administrator and navigate to the Mail page, as shown in Figure 20.1.

3. Provide the mail server's host name or IP address in the Mail Server field.

4. Check the Verify Mail Server Connection option. Obviously, if you are using localhost as the server, then you would **not** check this option.

Figure 20.1

Before messages can be sent, ColdFusion needs to know which mail server to use.

```
Server Settings > Mail

Mail Server Settings


Mail Server       [                    ]
Specifies the server for sending SMTP mail messages. You can specify an Internet address (for examp
User name         [                    ]
Password          [                    ]
If your mail server requires authentication, you can specify a user name and password to use.
```

5. If your mail server operates on a port other than the usual port number 25, provide the port number in the Server Port field. (This usually isn't necessary.)

6. Save your changes by clicking the Submit Changes button.

→ For more information about the other Mail Server options shown in Figure 20.1, see Chapter 25, "ColdFusion Server Configuration," in *Adobe ColdFusion 9 Web Application Construction Kit, Volume 2: Application Development.*

Sending Email Messages

Sending an email message via a ColdFusion template is easy. Simply code a pair of opening and closing `<cfmail>` tags, and provide the `to`, `from`, and `subject` attributes as appropriate. Between the tags, type the actual message that should be sent to the recipient.

Of course, you can use ColdFusion variables and functions between the `<cfmail>` tags to build the message dynamically, using the # sign syntax you're used to. You don't need to place `<cfoutput>` tags within (or outside) the `<cfmail>` tags; your # variables and expressions will be evaluated as if there were a `<cfoutput>` tag in effect.

TIP

As you look through the examples in this chapter, you will find that the `<cfmail>` tag is basically a specially modified `<cfoutput>` tag. It has similar behavior (variables and expressions are evaluated) and attributes (`group`, `maxrows`, and so on, as listed in Table 20.2).

Sending a Simple Message

Listing 20.1 shows how easy it is to use the `<cfmail>` tag to send a message. The idea behind this template is to provide a simple form for people working in Orange Whip Studios' personnel department. Rather than having to open their normal email client programs, they can just use this Web page. It displays a simple form for the user to type a message and specify a recipient. When the form is submitted, the message is sent.

Listing 20.1 `PersonnelMail1.cfm`—Sending Email with ColdFusion

```
<!---
 Filename: PersonnelMail1.cfm
 Author: Nate Weiss (NMW)
 Purpose: A simple form for sending email
--->
```

Listing 20.1 (CONTINUED)

```
<html>
<head>
 <title>Personnel Office Mailer</title>
 <!--- Apply simple CSS formatting to <th> cells --->
 <style>
 th { background:blue;color:white;text-align:right}
 </style>
</head>
<body>

<h2>Personnel Office Mailer</h2>

<!--- If the user is submitting the Form... --->
<cfif isDefined("form.subject")>

  <!--- We do not want ColdFusion to suppress whitespace here --->
  <cfprocessingdirective suppressWhitespace="No">

<!--- Send the mail message, based on form input --->
<cfmail
 subject="#form.subject#"
 from="personnel@orangewhipstudios.com"
 to="#form.toAddress#"
 bcc="personneldirector@orangewhipstudios.com"
>This is a message from the Personnel Office:
#form.messageBody#

If you have any questions about this message, please
write back or call us at extension 352. Thanks!</cfmail>

  </cfprocessingdirective>

 <!--- Display "success" message to user --->
 <p>The email message was sent.<br>

<!--- Otherwise, display the form to user... --->
<cfelse>
 <!--- Provide simple form for recipient and message --->
 <cfform action="#cgi.script_name#" method="post">

 <table cellPadding="2" cellSpacing="2">
 <!--- Table row: Input for Email Address --->
 <tr>
 <th>EMail Address:</th>
 <td>
 <cfinput type="text" name="toAddress" required="yes" size="40"
 message="You must provide an email address.">
 </td>
 </tr>

 <!--- Table row: Input for E-mail Subject --->
 <tr>
 <th>Subject:</th>
 <td>
 <cfinput type="text" name="subject" required="yes" size="40"
 message="You must provide a subject for the email.">
```

Listing 20.1 (CONTINUED)

```
</td>
</tr>

<!--- Table row: Input for actual Message Text --->
<tr>
<th>Your Message:</th>
<td>
<cftextarea name="messageBody" cols="30" rows="5" wrap="hard"
required="yes" message="You must provide a message body." />
</td>
</tr>

<!--- Table row: Submit button to send message --->
<tr>
<td> </td>
<td>
<cfinput type="submit" name="submit" value="Send Message Now">
</td>
</tr>
</table>
</cfform>
</cfif>

</body>
</html>
```

There are two parts to this listing, divided by the large <cfif>/<cfelse> block. When the page is first visited, the second part of the template runs, which displays the form shown in Figure 20.2.

Figure 20.2

Creating a Web-based mail-sending mechanism for your users is easy.

Personnel Office Mailer

EMail Address:

Subject:

Your Message:

Send Message Now

When the form is submitted, the first part of the template kicks in, which actually sends the email message with the <cfmail> tag. The message's subject line and "to" address are specified by the appropriate form values, and the content of the message itself is constructed by combining the #form.messageBody# variable with some static text. Additionally, each message sent by this template is also sent to the personnel director as a blind carbon copy, via the bcc attribute.

Around the <cfmail> tag, the <cfprocessingdirective> tag is used to turn off ColdFusion's default white-space-suppression behavior. This is needed in this template because the <cfmail> tag that follows is written to output the exact text of the email message, which includes newline and other white space characters that should be included literally in the actual email message. Without the <cfprocessingdirective> tag, ColdFusion would see the newline characters within the <cfoutput> tags as evil white space, deserving to be ruthlessly suppressed.

→   For more information about white-space suppression and the <cfprocessingdirective> tag, see the "Controlling White Space" section in Chapter 27, "Improving Performance," in Volume 2.

NOTE

There is a reason why the opening and closing <cfmail> tags are not indented in this listing. If they were, the spaces or tabs used to do the indenting would show up in the actual email message. You will need to make some exceptions to your usual indenting practices when using <cfmail>. The exception would be when using type="HTML", as discussed in the "Sending HTML-Formatted Mail" section, because white space isn't significant in HTML.

Using Friendly Email Addresses

The email address provided to the to, from, cc, and bcc attributes can be specified as just the email address itself (such as rcamden@orangewhipstudios.com), or as a combination of the address and the address's friendly name. The friendly name is usually the person's real-life first and last names.

To specify a friendly name along with an email address, place the friendly name between double quotation marks, followed by the actual email address between angle brackets. So, instead of

```
rcamden@orangewhipstudios.com
```

you would provide

```
"Raymond Camden" <rcamden@orangewhipstudios.com>
```

To provide such an address to the from, to, cc, or bcc attribute of the <cfmail> tag, you must double up each double quotation mark shown above, assuming that you are already using double quotation marks around the whole attribute value. So, you might end up with something such as the following:

```
<cfmail
  subject="Dinner Plans"
  from="""Raymond Camden"" <rcamden@orangewhipstudios.com>"
  to="""Belinda Foxile"" <bfoxile@orangewhipstudios.com>">
```

If you find the use of the doubled-up double quotation marks confusing, you could surround the from and to attributes with single quotation marks instead of double quotation marks, which would allow you to provide the double-quotation characters around the friendly name normally, like so:

```
<cfmail
  subject="Dinner Plans"
  from='"Raymond Camden" <rcamden@orangewhipstudios.com>'
  to='"Belinda Foxile" <bfoxile@orangewhipstudios.com>'>
```

Now, when the message is sent, the "to" and "from" addresses shown in the recipient's email program can be shown with each person's real-life name along with their email address. How the friendly name and email address are actually presented to the user is up to the email client software.

The version of the `PersonnelMail.cfm` template shown in Listing 20.2 is nearly the same as the one from Listing 20.1, except that this version collects the recipient's friendly name in addition to their email address. Additionally, this version uses a bit of JavaScript to attempt to pre-fill the email address field based on the friendly name. When the user changes the value in the `FirstName` or `LastName` field, the `ToAddress` field is filled in with the first letter of the first name, plus the whole last name.

NOTE

There isn't space to go through the JavaScript code used in this template in detail. It's provided to give you an idea of one place where JavaScript can be useful. Consult a JavaScript reference or online tutorial for details. One good place to look is the JavaScript section of the Reference tab of the Code panel in Dreamweaver.

Limiting Input

This version of the form makes it impossible to send messages to anyone outside of Orange Whip Studios, by simply hard-coding the `@orangewhipstudios.com` part of the email address into the `<cfmail>` tag itself. Also, it forces users to select from a short list of subject lines, rather than typing their own subjects, as shown in Figure 20.3.

Figure 20.3

Web-based forms can make sending email almost foolproof.

In a real-world application, you probably would make different choices about what exactly to allow users to do. The point is that by limiting the amount of input required, you can make it simpler for users to send consistent email messages, thus increasing the value of your application. This can be a lot of what differentiates Web pages that send mail from ordinary email programs, which can be more complex for users to learn.

Listing 20.2 `PersonnelMail2.cfm`—Providing Friendly Names Along with Email Addresses

```
<!---
 Filename: PersonnelMail2.cfm
 Author: Nate Weiss (NMW)
 Purpose: A simple form for sending email
--->

<html>
<head>
 <title>Personnel Office Mailer</title>
```

Listing 20.2 (CONTINUED)

```
<!--- Apply simple CSS formatting to <th> cells --->
<style>
th { background:blue;color:white;
font-family:sans-serif;font-size:12px;
text-align:right;padding:5px;}
</style>

<!--- Function to guess email based on first/last name --->
<script language="javaScript">
function guessEmail() {
 var guess;

  with (document.mailForm) {
   guess = firstName.value.substr(0,1) + lastName.value;
   toAddress.value = guess.toLowerCase();
   } ;
 } ;
</script>
</head>

<!--- Put cursor in FirstName field when page loads --->
<body <cfif not isDefined("form.subject")>
 onLoad="document.mailForm.firstName.focus()"
 </cfif>
>

<!--- If the user is submitting the form... --->
<cfif isDefined("form.subject")>
 <cfset recipEmail = listFirst(form.toAddress, "@") & "@orangewhipstudios.com">

 <!--- We do not want ColdFusion to suppress whitespace here --->
 <cfprocessingdirective suppressWhitespace="no">

 <!--- Send the mail message, based on form input --->
 <cfmail
 subject="#form.subject#"
 from="""Personnel Office"" <personnel@orangewhipstudios.com>"
 to="""#form.firstName# #form.lastName#"" <#recipEmail#>"
 bcc="personneldirector@orangewhipstudios.com"
>This is a message from the Personnel Office:

#uCase(form.subject)#

#form.messageBody#

If you have any questions about this message, please
write back or call us at extension 352. Thanks!</cfmail>

 </cfprocessingdirective>

 <!--- Display "success" message to user --->
 <p>The email message was sent.<br>
```

Listing 20.2 (CONTINUED)

```
<!--- Otherwise, display the form to user... --->
<cfelse>
 <!--- Provide simple form for recipient and message --->
 <cfform action="#cgi.script_name#" name="mailForm" method="post">

  <table cellPadding="2" cellSpacing="2">
  <!--- Table row: Input for Recipient's Name --->
  <tr>
  <th>Recipient's Name:</th>
  <td>
  <cfinput type="text" name="firstName" required="yes" size="15"
  message="You must provide a first name."
  onChange="guessEmail()">

  <cfinput type="text" name="lastName" required="yes" size="20"
  message="You must provide a first name."
  onChange="guessEmail()">
  </td>
  </tr>

  <!--- Table row: Input for EMail Address --->
  <tr>
  <th>EMail Address:</th>
  <td>
  <cfinput type="text" name="toAddress" required="yes" size="20"
  message="You must provide the recipient's email.">@orangewhipstudios.com
  </td>
  </tr>

  <!--- Table row: Input for EMail Subject --->
  <tr>
  <th>Subject:</th>
  <td>
  <cfselect name="subject">
  <option>Sorry, but you have been fired.
  <option>Congratulations! You got a raise!
  <option>Just FYI, you have hit the glass ceiling.
  <option>The company dress code, Capri Pants, and you
  <option>All your Ben Forta are belong to us.
  </cfselect>
  </td>
  </tr>

  <!--- Table row: Input for actual Message Text --->
  <tr>
  <th>Your Message:</th>
  <td>
  <cftextarea name="messageBody" cols="30" rows="5" wrap="hard"
  required="yes" message="You must provide a message body." />
  </td>
  </tr>

  <!--- Table row: Submit button to send message --->
  <tr>
  <td> </td>
```

Listing 20.2 (CONTINUED)

```
<td>
<cfinput type="submit" name="submit" value="Send Message Now">
</td>
</tr>
</table>
</cfform>
</cfif>

</body>
</html>
```

Checking Your Work

If you aren't using a real mail server, how can you check the email sent from ColdFusion? If you used `localhost` as your mail server and a real mail server doesn't exist, ColdFusion will simply leave the mail messages in a special folder. This folder typically is called Undeliver and is found under the Mail folder directly beneath the location where ColdFusion was installed. Each mail message will be created as a text file ending in a .cfmail extension. If you want, you can open the messages with a text editor. The ColdFusion Administrator provides an even slicker way. On the Mail settings page, click the View Undelivered Mail button. This takes you to a simple interface to browse all the undelivered messages. You can view them, delete them, and send them back to the mail spool in case you set up a real mail server. Figure 20.4 shows an example.

Figure 20.4

The ColdFusion Administrator provides a simple way to check the results of email generated by ColdFusion.

Sending Data-Driven Mail

In the last section, you saw that `<cfmail>` can be thought of as an extended version of the `<cfoutput>` tag because ColdFusion variables and expressions are evaluated without the need for an explicit `<cfoutput>` within the `<cfmail>`. The similarity between the two tags doesn't end there. They also share attributes specific to the notion of looping over query records. This capability enables you to send data-driven email messages using nearly the same syntax and techniques that you use to output data-driven HTML code.

Table 20.2 shows the `<cfmail>` attributes relevant to sending data-driven mail. Each of these attributes behaves the same way as the corresponding attributes for `<cfoutput>`. Instead of causing HTML output to be repeated for each row in a query, these attributes have to do with repeating email message content for each row in a query.

Table 20.2   Additional `<cfmail>` Attributes for Sending Data-Driven Email Messages

ATTRIBUTE	PURPOSE
query	Optional. A query to use for sending data-driven email. Very similar to the QUERY attribute of the `<cfoutput>` tag.
startRow	Optional. A number that indicates which row of the query to consider when sending data-driven email. The default is to start at the first row. Equivalent to the startRow attribute of the `<cfoutput>` tag.
maxRows	Optional. A maximum number of query rows to consider when sending data-driven email. Equivalent to the maxRows attribute of the `<cfoutput>` tag.
group	Optional. A column name from the query that indicates groups of records. Additional output or processing can occur when each new group is encountered. You can indicate nested groups by providing a comma-separated list of column names. Equivalent to the group attribute of the `<cfoutput>` tag.
groupCaseSensitive	Optional. Whether to consider text case when determining when a new group of records has been encountered in the column(s) indicated by group. Equivalent to the groupCaseSensitive attribute of the `<cfoutput>` tag.

NOTE

You may be thinking that a few of these additional attributes aren't really necessary. In today's ColdFusion, you usually can achieve the same results using a `<cfloop>` tag around a `<cfmail>` tag to send out multiple messages or using `<cfloop>` within `<cfmail>` to include queried information in the message itself. However, the `<cfmail>` tag appeared in CFML before the `<cfloop>` tag existed, which is one reason why these attributes exist today.

Including Query Data in Messages

By adding a query attribute to the `<cfmail>` tag, you can easily include query data in the email messages your application sends. Adding the query attribute to `<cfmail>` is similar to adding query to a `<cfoutput>` tag—the content inside the tags will repeat for each row of the query.

Additionally, if you add a group attribute, you can nest a pair of `<cfoutput>` tags within the `<cfmail>` tag. If you do, the inner `<cfoutput>` block is repeated for every record from the query, and everything outside the `<cfoutput>` block is output only when the value in the group column changes. This is just like the group behavior of the `<cfoutput>` tag itself.

→   See Chapter 10, "Creating Data-Driven Pages," for more information about grouping query results.

Listing 20.3 shows how the `<cfmail>` tag can be used with the query and group attributes to send data-driven email messages. This example creates a CFML custom tag called `<cf_SendOrderConfirmation>`, which takes one attribute called orderID, like this:

```
<!--- Send Confirmation E-Mail, via Custom Tag --->
<cf_SendOrderConfirmation
 orderID="3">
```

The idea is for the tag to compose an order-confirmation type of email message for the person who placed the order, detailing the items they purchased and when. If you've ever bought something online, you probably received such a confirmation email immediately after placing your order.

NOTE

You should save this listing as a file called **SendOrderConfirmation.cfm**, either in the special **CustomTags** folder or in the same folder as the other examples from this chapter.

➜ See Chapter 23, "Creating Custom Tags," in Volume 2, for information about the **CustomTags** folder and CFML custom tags in general.

Listing 20.3 SendOrderConfirmation1.cfm—Sending a Data-Driven Email Message

```
<!---
 Filename: SendOrderConfirmation1.cfm
 Author: Nate Weiss (NMW)
 Purpose: Sends an email message to the person who placed an order
--->

<!--- Tag attributes --->
<cfparam name="attributes.orderID" type="numeric">

<!--- Retrieve order information from database --->
<cfquery name="getOrder">
 SELECT
 c.ContactID, c.FirstName, c.LastName, c.Email,
 o.OrderDate, o.ShipAddress, o.ShipCity,
 o.ShipState, o.ShipZip, o.ShipCountry,
 oi.OrderQty, oi.ItemPrice,
 m.MerchName,
 f.MovieTitle
 FROM
 Contacts c,
 MerchandiseOrders o,
 MerchandiseOrdersItems oi,
 Merchandise m,
 Films f
 WHERE
 o.OrderID =
 <cfqueryparam cfsqltype="cf_sql_integer" value="#attributes.orderID#">
 AND c.ContactID = o.ContactID
 AND m.MerchID = oi.ItemID
 AND o.OrderID = oi.OrderID
 AND f.FilmID = m.FilmID
 ORDER BY
 m.MerchName
</cfquery>

<!--- Re-Query the GetOrders query to find total $ spent --->
<!--- The DBTYPE="Query" invokes CF's "Query Of Queries" --->
<cfquery dbtype="query" name="getTotal">
 SELECT SUM(ItemPrice * OrderQty) AS OrderTotal
 FROM GetOrder
```

Listing 20.3 (CONTINUED)

```
</cfquery>

<!--- We do not want ColdFusion to suppress whitespace here --->
<cfprocessingdirective suppressWhitespace="no">

<!--- Send email to the user --->
<!--- Because of the GROUP attribute, the inner <CFOUTPUT> --->
<!--- block will be repeated for each item in the order --->
<cfmail query="getOrder" group="ContactID" groupCasesensitive="no"
 startrow="1" subject="Thanks for your order (Order number #ATTRIBUTES.orderID#)"
 to="""#FirstName# #LastName#"" <#Email#>"
 from="""Orange Whip Online Store"" <orders@orangewhipstudios.com>"
>Thank you for ordering from Orange Whip Studios.
Here are the details of your order, which will ship shortly.
Please save or print this email for your records.

Order Number: #attributes.orderID#
Items Ordered: #recordCount#
Date of Order: #dateFormat(OrderDate, "dddd, mmmm d, yyyy")#
 #timeFormat(OrderDate)#


----------------------------------------------------
<cfoutput>
#currentRow#. #MerchName#
 (in commemoration of the film "#MovieTitle#")
 Price: #LSCurrencyFormat(ItemPrice)#
 Qty: #OrderQty#
</cfoutput>
----------------------------------------------------
Order Total: #lsCurrencyFormat(getTotal.OrderTotal)#

This order will be shipped to:
#FirstName# #LastName#
#ShipAddress#
#ShipCity#
#ShipState# #ShipZip# #ShipCountry#

If you have any questions, please write back to us at
orders@orangewhipstudios.com, or just reply to this email.
</cfmail>

</cfprocessingdirective>
```

This listing first needs to retrieve all the relevant information about the order from the database, including the orderer's name and shipping address; the name, price, and quantity of each item ordered; and the title of the movie that goes along with each item. This is all obtained using a single query called getOrder, which is long but fairly straightforward.

The getOrders query returns one row for each item that was ordered in the specified orderID. Because there is, by definition, only one row for each orderID and only one ContactID for each order, the columns from the MerchandiseOrders and Contacts tables (marked with the o and c aliases in the query) will have the same values for each row. Therefore, the query can be thought of as being grouped by the `ContactID` column (or any of the other columns from the `MerchandiseOrders` or `Contacts` tables).

Next, ColdFusion's query of queries feature is used to get the grand total of the order, which is simply the sum of each price times the quantity ordered. This query returns just one row (because there is no `GROUP BY` clause) and just one column (called `OrderTotal`), which means that the total can be output at any time by referring to `getTotal.OrderTotal`.

You could forgo the `getTotal` query and just add the prices by looping over the `getOrders` query. However, getting the total via the query of queries feature is a quick and convenient way to obtain the total, using familiar SQL-style syntax.

NOTE

In general, you should use the `<cfprocessingdirective>` tag with `suppressWhitespace="No"` whenever you send data-driven email. The exception would be if you were using `type="HTML"` in the `<cfmail>` tag, in which case you should leave the suppression-suppression options alone. See the section "Sending HTML-Formatted Mail," later in the chapter, for details.

Now the `<cfmail>` tag is used to actually send the confirmation message. Because the `query` attribute is set to the `getOrder` query, the columns in that query can be freely referred to in the `to` attribute and the body of the email message itself. Columns specific to each item ordered are referred to within the `<cfoutput>` block. Columns specific to the order in general are referred to outside the `<cfoutput>` block, which will be repeated only once because there is only one group of records as defined by the `group` attribute (that is, all the query records have the same `ContactID` value).

Sending Bulk Messages

You can easily use ColdFusion to send messages to an entire mailing list. Simply execute a query that returns the email addresses of all the people the message should be sent to, then refer to the email column of the query in the `<cfmail>` tag's to attribute.

Listing 20.4 shows how easy sending a message to a mailing list is. This listing is similar to the Personnel Office Mailer templates from earlier (refer to Listings 20.1 and 20.2). It enables the user (presumably someone within Orange Whip Studios' public relations department) to type a message that will be sent to everyone on the studio's mailing list.

Listing 20.4 `SendBulkEmail.cfm`—Sending a Message to Everyone on a Mailing List

```
<!---
 Filename: SendBulkEmail.cfm
 Author: Nate Weiss (NMW)
 Purpose: Creates form for sending email to everyone on the mailing list
--->

<html>
<head>
 <title>Mailing List</title>
 <!--- Apply simple CSS formatting to <TH> cells --->
```

Listing 20.4 (CONTINUED)

```
<style>
th { background:blue;color:white;
font-family:sans-serif;font-size:12px;
text-align:right;padding:5px;}
</style>
</head>

<body>

<!--- Page Title --->
<h2>Send Message To Mailing List</h2>

<!--- If the user is submitting the form... --->
<cfif isDefined("form.subject")>
 <!--- Retrieve "mailing list" records from database --->
 <cfquery name="getList">
 SELECT FirstName, LastName, EMail
 FROM Contacts
 WHERE MailingList = 1
 </cfquery>

 <!--- Send the mail message, based on form input --->
 <cfmail query="getList" subject="#form.subject#"
 from="""Orange Whip Studios"" <mailings@orangewhipstudios.com>"
 to="""#FirstName# #LastName#"" <#EMail#>"
 bcc="personneldirector@orangewhipstudios.com"
>#FORM.messageBody#
</cfmail>

 <!--- Display "success" message to user --->
 <p>The email message was sent.<br>

<!--- Otherwise, display the form to user... --->
<cfelse>
 <!--- Provide simple form for recipient and message --->
 <cfform action="#cgi.script_name#" name="mailForm" method="POST">

 <table cellPadding="2" cellSpacing="2">
 <!--- Table row: Input for email Subject --->
 <tr>
 <th>Subject:</th>
 <td>
 <cfinput type="text" name="subject" required="yes" size="40"
 message="You must provide a subject for the email.">
 </td>
 </tr>

 <!--- Table row: Input for actual Message Text --->
 <tr>
 <th>Your Message:</th>
 <td>
 <cftextarea name="messageBody" cols="30" rows="5" wrap="hard"
 required="yes" message="You must provide a message body." />
 </td>
 </tr>
```

Listing 20.4 (CONTINUED)

```
<!--- Table row: Submit button to send message --->
<tr>
<td> </td>
<td>
<cfinput type="submit" name="submit" value="Send Message Now">
</td>
</tr>
</table>
</cfform>
</cfif>

</body>
</html>
```

Like Listings 20.1 and 20.2, this listing presents a simple form to the user, in which a subject and message can be typed. When the form is submitted, the <cfif> block at the top of the template is executed.

The getList query retrieves the name and email address for each person in the Contacts table who has consented to be on the mailing list (that is, where the Boolean MailingList column is set to 1, which represents true or yes). Then, the <cfmail> tag is used to send the message to each user. Because of the query="getList" attribute, <cfmail> executes once for each row in the query.

Note that the query isn't using the datasource attribute. This attribute is specified in the Application.cfc file. We will be creating this file later in the chapter, but you should copy this file into the same folder as SendBulkEmail.cfm before testing.

Sending HTML-Formatted Mail

As noted in Table 20.1, you can set the optional type attribute of the <cfmail> tag to HTML, which enables you to use ordinary HTML tags to add formatting, images, and other media elements to your mail messages.

The following rules apply:

- The recipient's email client program must be HTML enabled. Most modern email clients, such as Outlook Express or Thunderbird, know how to display the contents of email messages as HTML. However, if the message is read in a program that isn't HTML enabled, the user will see the message literally, including the actual HTML tags.

- The mail message should be a well-formed HTML document, including opening and closing <html>, <head>, and <body> tags.

- All references to external URLs must be fully qualified, absolute URLs, including the http:// or https://. In particular, this includes the href attribute for links and the src attribute for images.

The version of the <cf_SendOrderConfirmation> tag in Listing 20.5 expands on the previous version (refer to Listing 20.3) by adding a useHTML attribute. If the tag is called with useHTML="Yes", an

HTML-formatted version of the confirmation email is sent, including small pictures of each item that was ordered. If useHTML is No or is omitted, the email is sent as plain text (as in the previous version).

Although this approach is not covered in this chapter, you can use `<cfmailpart>` to send both HTML and plain text messages. This will send two versions of the same email to the client. The downside is that the doubling up makes each mail message that much larger.

Listing 20.5 SendOrderConfirmation2.cfm—Using HTML Tags to Format a Mail Message

```
<!---
Filename: SendOrderConfirmation2.cfm
Author: Nate Weiss (NMW)
Purpose: Sends an email message to the person who placed an order
--->

<!--- Tag attributes --->
<cfparam name="attributes.orderID" type="numeric">
<cfparam name="attributes.useHTML" type="boolean" default="yes">

<!--- Local variables --->
<cfset imgSrcPath = "http://#cgi.http_host#/ows/images">

<!--- Retrieve order information from database --->
<cfquery name="getOrder">
 SELECT
 c.ContactID, c.FirstName, c.LastName, c.Email,
 o.OrderDate, o.ShipAddress, o.ShipCity,
 o.ShipState, o.ShipZip, o.ShipCountry,
 oi.OrderQty, oi.ItemPrice,
 m.MerchName, m.ImageNameSmall,
 f.MovieTitle
 FROM
 Contacts c,
 MerchandiseOrders o,
 MerchandiseOrdersItems oi,
 Merchandise m,
 Films f
 WHERE
 o.OrderID = #attributes.OrderID#
 AND c.ContactID = o.ContactID
 AND m.MerchID = oi.ItemID
 AND o.OrderID = oi.OrderID
 AND f.FilmID = m.FilmID
 ORDER BY
 m.MerchName
</cfquery>

<!--- Display an error message if query returned no records --->
<cfif getOrder.recordCount eq 0>
 <cfthrow message="Failed to obtain order information."
 detail="Either the Order ID was incorrect, or order has no detail records.">
 <!--- Display an error message if email blank or not valid --->
<cfelseif isValid("email", getOwer.email)>
 <cfthrow message="Failed to obtain order information."
```

Listing 20.5 (CONTINUED)

```
detail="Email addresses need to have an @ sign and at least one 'dot'.">
</cfif>

<!--- Query the GetOrders query to find total $$ --->
<cfquery dbtype="query" name="getTotal">
 SELECT SUM(ItemPrice * OrderQty) AS OrderTotal
 FROM GetOrder
</cfquery>


<!--- *** If we are sending HTML-Formatted Email *** --->
<cfif attributes.useHTML>

 <!--- Send Email to the user --->
 <!--- Because of the GROUP attribute, the inner <CFOUTPUT> --->
 <!--- block will be repeated for each item in the order --->
 <cfmail query="getOrder" group="ContactID" groupCasesensitive="No"
 subject="Thanks for your order (Order number #ATTRIBUTES.orderID#)"
 to="""#FirstName# #LastName#"" <#Email#>"
 from="""Orange Whip Online Store"" <orders@orangewhipstudios.com>"
 type="HTML">

 <html>
 <head>
 <style type="text/css">
 body { font-family:sans-serif;font-size:12px;color:navy}
 td { font-size:12px}
 th { font-size:12px;color:white;
 background:navy;text-align:left}
 </style>
 </head>
 <body>

 <h2>Thank you for your Order</h2>

 <p><b>Thank you for ordering from
 <a href="http://www.orangewhipstudios.com">Orange Whip Studios</a>.</b><br>
 Here are the details of your order, which will ship shortly.
 Please save or print this email for your records.<br>

 <p>
 <strong>Order Number:</strong> #ATTRIBUTES.orderID#<br>
 <strong>Items Ordered:</strong> #recordCount#<br>
 <strong>Date of Order:</strong>
 #dateFormat(OrderDate, "dddd, mmmm d, yyyy")#
 #timeFormat(OrderDate)#<br>

 <table>
 <cfoutput>
 <tr valign="top">
 <th colspan="2">
 #MerchName#
 </th>
 </tr>
 <tr>
 <td>
```

Listing 20.5 (CONTINUED)

```
<!--- If there is an image available... --->
<cfif ImageNameSmall neq "">
<img src="#imgSrcPath#/#ImageNameSmall#"
alt="#MerchName#" width="50" height="50" border="0">
</cfif>
</td>
<td>
<em>(in commemoration of the film "#MovieTitle#")</em><br>
<strong>Price:</strong> #lsCurrencyFormat(ItemPrice)#<br>
<strong>Qty:</strong> #OrderQty#<br> <br>
</td>
</tr>
</cfoutput>
</table>

<p>Order Total: #lsCurrencyFormat(getTotal.OrderTotal)#<br>

<p><strong>This order will be shipped to:</strong><br>
#FirstName# #LastName#<br>
#ShipAddress#<br>
#ShipCity#<br>
#ShipState# #ShipZip# #ShipCountry#<br>

<p>If you have any questions, please write back to us at
<a href="orders@orangewhipstudios.com">orders@orangewhipstudios.com</a>,
or just reply to this email.<br>
</body>
</html>
</cfmail>


<!--- *** If we are NOT sending HTML-Formatted Email *** --->
<cfelse>

<!--- We do not want ColdFusion to suppress whitespace here --->
<cfprocessingdirective suppressWhitespace="no">

<!--- Send email to the user --->
<!--- Because of the GROUP attribute, the inner <CFOUTPUT> --->
<!--- block will be repeated for each item in the order --->
<cfmail query="getOrder" group="ContactID" groupCasesensitive="No"
 subject="Thanks for your order (Order number #attributes.OrderID#)"
 to="""#FirstName# #LastName#"" <#Email#>"
 from="""Orange Whip Online Store"" <orders@orangewhipstudios.com>"
>Thank you for ordering from Orange Whip Studios.
Here are the details of your order, which will ship shortly.
Please save or print this email for your records.

Order Number: #attributes.orderID#
Items Ordered: #recordCount#
Date of Order: #dateFormat(OrderDate, "dddd, mmmm d, yyyy")#
 #timeFormat(OrderDate)#


-------------------------------------------------
<cfoutput>
#currentRow#. #MerchName#
```

Listing 20.5 (CONTINUED)

```
    (in commemoration of the film "#MovieTitle#")
    Price: #lsCurrencyFormat(ItemPrice)#
    Qty: #OrderQty#
</cfoutput>
------------------------------------------------------
Order Total: #lsCurrencyFormat(getTotal.OrderTotal)#

This order will be shipped to:
#FirstName# #LastName#
#ShipAddress#
#ShipCity#
#ShipState# #ShipZip# #ShipCountry#

If you have any questions, please write back to us at
orders@orangewhipstudios.com, or just reply to this email.
</cfmail>

</cfprocessingdirective>

</cfif>
```

In most respects, Listing 20.5 is nearly identical to the prior version (refer to Listing 20.3). A simple <cfif> determines whether the tag is being called with useHTML="Yes". If so, <cfmail> is used with type="HTML" to send an HTML-formatted message. If not, a separate <cfmail> tag is used to send a plain-text message. Note that the <cfprocessingdirective> tag is needed only around the plain-text version of the message because HTML isn't sensitive to white space.

As already noted, a fully qualified URL must be provided for images to be correctly displayed in email messages. To make this easier, a variable called imgSrcPath is defined at the top of the template, which will always hold the fully qualified URL path to the ows/images folder. This variable can then be used in the src attribute of any <img> tags within the message. For instance, assuming that you are visiting a copy of ColdFusion server on your local machine, this variable will evaluate to something such as http://localhost/ows/images/.

NOTE

The cgi.http_host variable can be used to refer to the host name of the ColdFusion server. The cgi.server_name also could be used to get the same value.

In addition, Listing 20.5 does two quick checks after the getOrder query to ensure that it makes sense for the rest of the template to continue. If the query fails to return any records, the orderID passed to the tag is assumed to be invalid, and an appropriate error message is displayed. An error message is also displayed if the Email column returned by the query is not a valid email.

The error messages created by the <cfthrow> tags in this example can be caught with the <cfcatch> tag, as discussed in Chapter 44, "Error Handling," online.

NOTE

If the recipient doesn't use an HTML-enabled mail client to read the message, the message will be shown literally, including the actual HTML tags. Therefore, you should send messages of type="HTML" only if you know the recipient is using an HTML-enabled email client program.

Adding Custom Mail Headers

All SMTP email messages contain a number of mail headers, which give Internet mail servers the information necessary to route the message to its destination. Mail headers also provide information used by the email client program to show the message to the user, such as the message date and the sender's email address.

ColdFusion lets you add your own mail headers to mail messages, using the <cfmailparam> tag.

TIP

You can see what these mail headers look like by using an ordinary email client program. For instance, in Apple Mail, select a message and then choose View > Message > Raw Source.

Introducing the <cfmailparam> Tag

ColdFusion provides a tag called <cfmailparam> that can be used to add custom headers to your mail messages. It also can be used to add attachments to your messages, which is discussed in the next section. The <cfmailparam> tag is allowed only between opening and closing <cfmail> tags. Table 20.3 shows which attributes can be provided to <cfmailparam>.

Table 20.3   <cfmailparam> Tag Attributes

ATTRIBUTE	PURPOSE
name	The name of the custom mail header you want to add to the message. You can provide any mail header name you want. (You must provide a name or file attribute, but not both in the same <cfmailparam> tag.)
value	The actual value for the mail header specified by name. The type of string you provide for value will depend on which mail header you are adding to the message. Required if the name attribute is provided.
file	The file name of the document or other file that should be sent as an attachment to the mail message. The file name must include a fully qualified, file-system-style path—for instance a drive letter if ColdFusion is running on a Windows machine. (You must provide a name or file attribute, but not both in the same <cfmailparam> tag.)
type	Describes the MIME media type of the file. This must either be a valid MIME type or one of the following simpler values: text (same as MIME type text/plain), plain (same as MIME type text/plain), or html (same as MIME type text/html).
contentID	Specifies an identifier for the attached file. This is used to identify the file that an img or other tag in the email uses.
disposition	This attribute describes how the file should be attached to the email. There are two possible values, attachment and inline. The default, attachment, means the file is added as attachment. If you specify inline, the file will be included in the message.

Adding Attachments

As noted in Table 20.3, you can also use the <cfmailparam> tag to add a file attachment to a mail message. Simply place a <cfmailparam> tag between the opening and closing <cfmail> tags, specifying the attachment's file name with the file attribute. The file name must be provided as a fully qualified file-system path, including the drive letter and volume name. It can't be expressed as a relative path or URL.

NOTE

The file name you provide for a file value must point to a location on the ColdFusion server's drives (or a location on the local network). It can't refer to a location on the browser machine. ColdFusion has no way to grab a document from the browser's drive. If you want a user to be able to attach a file to a <cfmail> email, you first must have them upload the file to the server. See Chapter 61, "Interacting with the Operating System," in *ColdFusion 9 Web Application Construction Kit, Volume 3: Advanced Application Development*, for details about file uploads.

TIP

The attachment doesn't have to be in your Web server's document root. In fact, you might want to ensure that it's not, if you want people to be able to access it only via email, rather than via the Web.

To add a Word document called BusinessPlan.doc as an attachment, you might include the following <cfmailparam> tag between your opening and closing <cfmail> tags:

```
<!-- Attach business plan document to message --->
<cfmailparam
  file="c:\ OwsMailAttachments\ BusinessPlan.doc">
```

TIP

To add multiple attachments to a message, simply provide multiple <cfmailparam> tags, each specifying one file.

Overriding the Default Mail Server Settings

Earlier in this chapter, you learned about the settings on the Mail/Mail Logging page of the ColdFusion Administrator (refer to Figure 20.1). These settings tell ColdFusion which mail server to communicate with to send the messages that your templates generate. In most situations, you can simply provide these settings once, in the ColdFusion Administrator, and forget about them. ColdFusion will use the settings to send all messages.

However, you might encounter situations in which you want to specify the mail server settings within individual <cfmail> tags. For instance, your company might have two mail servers set up, one for bulk messages and another for ordinary messages. Or you might not have access to the ColdFusion Administrator for some reason, perhaps because your application is sitting on a shared ColdFusion server at an Internet service provider (ISP).

To specify the mail server for a particular <cfmail> tag, add the server attribute, as explained in Table 20.4. You also can provide the port and timeout attributes to completely override all mail server settings from the ColdFusion Administrator.

NOTE

If you need to provide these attributes for your `<cfmail>` tags, consider setting a variable called `APPLICATION.mailServer` in your `Application.cfc` file and then specifying `server="#APPLICATION.mailServer#"` for each `<cfmail>` tag.

Table 20.4   Additional   `<cfmail>` Attributes for Overriding the Mail Server Settings

ATTRIBUTE	PURPOSE
server	Optional. The host name or IP address of the mail server ColdFusion should use to actually send the message. If omitted, this defaults to the Mail Server setting on the Mail/Mail Logging page of the ColdFusion Administrator. If you are using the Enterprise edition of ColdFusion, a list of mail servers can be provided here.
port	Optional. The port number on which the mail server is listening. If omitted, this defaults to the Server Port setting on the Mail/Mail Logging page of the ColdFusion Administrator. The standard port number is 25. Unless your mail server has been set up in a nonstandard way, you should never need to specify the port.
timeout	Optional. The number of seconds ColdFusion should spend trying to connect to the mail server. If omitted, this defaults to the Connection Timeout setting on the Mail/Mail Logging page of the ColdFusion Administrator.
username	Optional. The username to use when connecting to the mail server. If omitted, this defaults to the Username setting on the Mail/Mail Logging page of the ColdFusion Administrator.
password	Optional. The password to use when connecting to the mail server. If omitted, this defaults to the Password setting on the Mail/Mail Logging page of the ColdFusion Administrator.

Along with specifying mail server settings in the `<cfmail>` tag, you can supply server information using Application.cfc. The This scope within Application.cfc recognizes a special setting, smtpserver. A structure containing servername, username, and password can be supplied. If specified, this setting will override the server setting specified in the ColdFusion Administrator, but it will *not* override a server specified in the `<cfmail>` tag.

Retrieving Email with ColdFusion

You have already seen how the `<cfmail>` tag can be used to send mail messages via your Cold-Fusion templates. You can also create ColdFusion templates that receive and process incoming mail messages. What your templates do with the messages is up to you. You might display each message to the user, or you might have ColdFusion periodically monitor the contents of a particular mailbox, responding to each incoming message in some way.

Introducing the `<cfpop>` Tag

To check or receive email messages with ColdFusion, you use the `<cfpop>` tag, providing the username and password for the email mailbox you want ColdFusion to look in. ColdFusion will connect to the appropriate mail server in the same way that your own email client program connects to retrieve your mail for you.

Table 20.5 lists the attributes supported by the `<cfpop>` tag.

NOTE

The `<cfpop>` tag can only be used to check email that is sitting on a mail server that uses the Post Office Protocol (POP, or POP3). POP servers are by far the most popular type of mailbox server, largely because the POP protocol is very simple. Some mail servers use the newer Internet Mail Access Protocol (IMAP, or IMAP4). The `<cfpop>` tag can't be used to retrieve messages from IMAP mailboxes.*Document6*). The `<cfimap>` tag, discussed later in the chapter, should be used instead.

Table 20.5   `<cfpop>` Tag Attributes

ATTRIBUTE	PURPOSE
action	GetHeaderOnly, GetAll, or Delete. Use GetHeaderOnly to quickly retrieve just the basic information (the subject, who it's from, and so on) about messages, without retrieving the messages themselves. Use GetAll to retrieve actual messages, including any attachments (which might take some time). Use Delete to delete a message from the mailbox.
server	Required. The POP server to which ColdFusion should connect. You can provide either a host name, such as pop.orangewhipstudios.com, or an IP address.
username	Required. The username for the POP mailbox ColdFusion should access. This is likely to be case sensitive, depending on the POP server.
password	Required. The password for the POP mailbox ColdFusion should access. This is likely to be case sensitive, depending on the POP server.
name	ColdFusion places information about incoming messages into a query object. You will loop through the records in the query to perform whatever processing you need for each message. Provide a name (such as GetMessages) for the query object here. This attribute is required if the action is GetHeaderOnly or GetAll.
maxrows	Optional. The maximum number of messages that should be retrieved. Because you don't know how many messages might be in the mailbox you are accessing, it's usually a good idea to provide maxrows unless you are providing messagenumber (later in this table).
startRow	Optional. The first message that should be retrieved. If, for instance, you already have processed the first 10 messages currently in the mailbox, you could specify startRow="11" to start at the 11th message.
messageNumber	Optional. If the action is GetHeaderOnly or GetAll, you can use this attribute to specify messages to retrieve from the POP server. If the action is Delete, this is the message or messages you want to delete from the mailbox. In either case, you can provide either a single message number or a comma-separated list of message numbers.

Table 20.5 (CONTINUED)

ATTRIBUTE	PURPOSE
attachmentPath	Optional. If the action is GetAll, you can specify a directory on the server's drive in which ColdFusion should save any attachments. If you don't provide this attribute, the attachments won't be saved.
generateUniqueFilenames	Optional. This attribute should be provided only if you are using the attachmentPath attribute. If Yes, ColdFusion will ensure that two attachments that happen to have the same file name will get unique file names when they are saved on the server's drive. If No (the default), each attachment is saved with its original file name, regardless of whether a file with the same name already exists in the attachmentPath directory.
port	Optional. If the POP server specified in server is listening for requests on a nonstandard port, specify the port number here. The default value is 110, which is the standard port used by most POP servers.
timeout	Optional. This attribute indicates how many seconds ColdFusion should wait for each response from the POP server. The default value is 60.
debug	Optional. If enabled, ColdFusion will log additional information about the cfpop call. This information is logged to either the console or a log file.
uid	Optional. A UUID, or a list of UUIDs, that represents unique IDs for mail messages to be retrieved. This attribute is better than messageNumber because messageNumber may change between requests.

When the <cfpop> tag is used with action="GetHeaderOnly", it will return a query object that contains one row for each message in the specified mailbox. The columns of the query object are shown in Table 20.6.

Table 20.6 Columns Returned by <cfpop> for ACTION="GetHeaderOnly"

COLUMN	EXPLANATION
messageNumber	A number that represents the slot the current message is occupying in the mailbox on the POP server. The first message that arrives in a user's mailbox is message number 1. The next one to arrive is message number 2. When a message is deleted, any message behind the deleted message moves into the deleted message's slot. That is, if the first message is deleted, the second message becomes message number 1. In other words, the messageNumber isn't a unique identifier for the message. It's just a way to refer to the messages currently in the mailbox. It is safer to use uid.

Table 20.6 (CONTINUED)

COLUMN	EXPLANATION
date	The date the message was originally sent. Unfortunately, this date value isn't returned as a native CFML `Date` object. You must use the `ParseDateTime()` function to turn the value into something you can use ColdFusion's date functions with (see Listing 20.6, later in this chapter, for an example).
subject	The subject line of the message.
from	The email address that the message is reported to be from. This address might or might not contain a friendly name for the sender, delimited by quotation marks and angle brackets (see the section "Using Friendly Email Addresses," earlier in this chapter). It's worth noting that there's no guarantee that the `from` address is a real email address that can actually receive replies.
to	The email address to which the message was sent. This address might or might not contain a friendly name for the sender, delimited by quotation marks and angle brackets (see the section "Using Friendly Email Addresses").
cc	The email address or addresses to which the message was CC'd, if any. You can use ColdFusion's list functions to get the individual email addresses. Each address might or might not contain a friendly name for the sender, delimited by quotation marks and angle brackets (see the section "Using Friendly Email Addresses").
replyTo	The address to use when replying to the message, if provided. If the message's sender didn't provide a Reply-To address, the column will contain an empty string, in which case it would be most appropriate for replies to go to the `from` address. This address might or might not contain a friendly name for the sender, delimited by quotation marks and angle brackets (see the section "Using Friendly Email Addresses").
header	The raw, unparsed header section of the message. This usually contains information about how the message was routed to the mail server, along with information about which program was used to send the message, the MIME content type of the message, and so on. You need to know about the header names defined by the SMTP protocol (see the section "Adding Custom Mail Headers" earlier in this chapter) to make use of `header`.
messageid	A unique identifier for the mail message. It is not the same value as that used in the `uid` column.
uid	A unique identifier for the mail message. This can be used to retrieve or delete individual messages. It should be used instead of `messageNumber` because `messageNumber` may change.

If the `<cfpop>` tag is used with `action="GetAll"`, the returned query object will contain all the columns from Table 20.6, plus the columns listed in Table 20.7.

Table 20.7 Additional Columns Returned by `<cfpop>` for `action="GetAll"`

COLUMN	EXPLANATION
body	The actual body of the message, as a simple string. This string usually contains just plain text, but if the message was sent as an HTML-formatted message, it contains HTML tags. You can check for the presence of a `Content-Type` header value of `text/html` to determine whether the message is HTML formatted (see Listing 20.8, later in this chapter, for an example).
attachment	If you provided an `attachmentPath` attribute to the `<cfpop>` tag, this column contains a list of the attachment file names as they were named when originally attached to the message. The list of attachments is separated by tab characters. You can use ColdFusion's list functions to process the list, but you must specify `Chr(9)` (which is the tab character) as the delimiter for each list function, as in `listLen(ATTACHMENTS, Chr(9))`.
attachmentFiles	If you provided an `attachmentPath` attribute to the `<cfpop>` tag, this column contains a list of the attachment file names as they were saved on the ColdFusion server (in the directory specified by `attachmentPath`). You can use the values in this list to delete, show, or move the files after the message has been retrieved. Like the `attachments` column, this list is separated by tab characters.
textBody	If an email contains both a plain-text and an HTML body, this value will contain the plain-text version of the email.
htmlBody	If an email contains both a plain-text and an HTML body, this value will contain the HTML version of the email.

Retrieving the List of Messages

Most uses of the `<cfpop>` tag call for all three of the `action` values it supports. Whether you are using the tag to display messages to your users (such as a Web-based system for checking mail) or an automated agent that responds to incoming email messages on its own, the sequence of events probably involves these steps:

1. Log in to the mail server with `action="GetHeaderOnly"` to get the list of messages currently in the specified mailbox. At this point, you can display or make decisions based on who the message is from, the date, or the subject line.

2. Use `action="GetAll"` to retrieve the full text of individual messages.

3. Use `action="Delete"` to delete messages.

Listing 20.6 is the first of three templates that demonstrate how to use `<cfpop>` by creating a Web-based system for users to check their mail. This template asks the user to log in by providing the information ColdFusion needs to access their email mailbox (username, password, and mail server). It then checks the user's mailbox for messages and displays the From address, date, and subject line for each. The user can click each message's subject to read the full message.

Listing 20.6 `CheckMail.cfm`—The Beginnings of a Simple POP Client

```
<!---
 Filename: CheckMail.cfm
 Author: Nate Weiss (NMW)
 Purpose: Creates a very simple POP client
--->

<html>
<head><title>Check Your Mail</title></head>
<body>

<!--- Simple CSS-based formatting styles --->
<style>
 body { font-family:sans-serif;font-size:12px}
 th { font-size:12px;background:navy;color:white}
 td { font-size:12px;background:lightgrey;color:navy}
</style>

<h2>Check Your Mail</h2>

<!--- If user is logging out, --->
<!--- or if user is submitting a different username/password --->
<cfif isDefined("url.logout") or isDefined("form.popServer")>
 <cfset structDelete(session, "mail")>
</cfif>

<!--- If we don't have a username/password --->
<cfif not isDefined("session.mail")>
 <!--- Show "mail server login" form --->
 <cfinclude template="CheckMailLogin.cfm">
</cfif>

<!--- If we need to contact server for list of messages --->
<!--- (if just logged in, or if clicked "Refresh" link) --->
<cfif not isDefined("session.mail.getMessages") or isDefined("url.refresh")>
 <!--- Flush page output buffer --->
 <cfflush>

 <!--- Contact POP Server and retieve messages --->
 <cfpop action="GetHeaderOnly" name="session.mail.getMessages"
 server="#session.mail.popServer#"
 username="#session.mail.username#" password="#session.mail.password#"
 maxrows="50">
</cfif>


<!--- If no messages were retrieved... --->
<cfif session.mail.getMessages.recordCount eq 0>
 <p>You have no mail messages at this time.<br>

<!--- If messages were retrieved... --->
<cfelse>
 <!--- Display Messages in HTML Table Format --->
 <table border="0" cellSpacing="2" cellSpacing="2" cols="3" width="550">
 <!--- Column Headings for Table --->
 <tr>
```

Listing 20.6 (CONTINUED)

```
<th width="100">Date Sent</th>
<th width="200">From</th>
<th width="200">Subject</th>
</tr>
<!--- Display info about each message in a table row --->
<cfoutput query="session.mail.getMessages">
<!--- Parse Date from the "date" mail header --->
<cfset msgDate = parseDateTime(date,"pop")>
<!--- Let user click on Subject to read full message --->
<cfset linkURL = "CheckMailMsg.cfm?uid=#urlEncodedFormat(uid)#">

<tr valign="baseline">
<!--- Show parsed Date and Time for message--->
<td>
<strong>#dateFormat(msgDate)#</strong><br>
#timeFormat(msgDate)# #ReplyTo#
</td>
<!--- Show "From" address, escaping brackets --->
<td>#htmlEditFormat(From)#</td>
<td><strong><a href="#linkURL#">#Subject#</a></strong></td>
</tr>
</cfoutput>
</table>

</cfif>

<!--- "Refresh" link to get new list of messages --->
<strong><a href="CheckMail.cfm?Refresh=Yes">Refresh Message List</a></strong><br>
<!--- "Log Out" link to discard SESSION.Mail info --->
<a href="CheckMail.cfm?Logout=Yes">Log Out</a><br>

</body>
</html>
```

NOTE

Don't forget to copy the `Application.cfc` file from the downloaded files. The code isn't described until Listing 20.8.

This template maintains a structure in the session scope called `session.mail`. The `SESSION.mail` structure holds information about the current user's POP server, username, and password. It also holds a query object called `getMessages`, which is returned by the `<cfpop>` tag when the user's mailbox is first checked.

At the top of the template, a `<cfif>` test checks to see whether a URL parameter named `logout` has been provided. If so, the `session.mail` structure is deleted from the server's memory, which effectively logs the user out. Later, you will see how this works. The same thing happens if a FORM parameter named `popServer` exists, which indicates that the user is trying to submit a different username and password from the login form. (I'll explain this in a moment.)

Next, a similar `<cfif>` tests checks to see whether the `SESSION.mail` structure exists. If not, the template concludes that the user hasn't logged in yet, so it displays a simple login form by including the `CheckMailLogin.cfm` template. (Since this is a simple form, it will not be shown in the chapter. Copy the file from the location from which you downloaded the chapter code.) In any case, all code after this `<cfif>` test is guaranteed to execute only if the user has logged in. The `session.mail` structure will contain `username`, `password`, and `popServer` values, which can later be passed to all `<cfpop>` tags for the remainder of the session.

The next `<cfif>` test checks to see whether ColdFusion needs to access the user's mailbox to get a list of current messages. ColdFusion should do this whenever `session.mail.getMessages` doesn't exist yet (which means that the user has just logged in), or if the page has been passed a `refresh` parameter in the URL (which means that the user has just clicked the Refresh Message List link). If so, the `<cfpop>` tag is called with `action="GetHeaderOnly"`, which means that ColdFusion should get a list of messages from the mail server (which is usually pretty fast), rather than getting the actual text of each message (which can be quite slow, especially if some of the messages have attachments). Note that the `<cfpop>` tag is provided with the username, password, and POP server name that the user provided when they first logged in (now available in the `session.mail` structure).

NOTE

> Because the `session.mail.getMessages` object is a ColdFusion query, it also contains the automatic `CurrentRow` and `RecordCount` attributes returned by ordinary `<cfquery>` tags.

At this point, the template has retrieved the list of current messages from the user's mailbox, so all that's left to do is to display them to the user. The remainder of Listing 20.6 simply outputs the list of messages in a simple HTML table format, using an ordinary `<cfoutput>` block that loops over the `session.mail.getMessages` query object. Within this loop, the code can refer to the `Date` column of the query object to access a message's date or to the `Subject` column to access the message's subject line. The first time through the loop, these variables refer to the first message retrieved from the user's mailbox. The second time, the variables refer to the second message, and so on.

Just inside the `<cfoutput>` block, a ColdFusion date variable called `msgDate` is created using the `parseDateTime()` function with the optional `POP` attribute. This is necessary because the `Date` column returned by `<cfpop>` doesn't contain native CFML date value, as you might expect. Instead, it contains the date in the special date format required by the mail-sending protocol (SMTP). The `parseDateTime()` function is needed to parse this special date string into a proper CFML `Date` value you can provide to ColdFusion's date functions (such as the `dateFormat()` and `dateAdd()` functions).

NOTE

> Unfortunately, the format used for the date portion of mail messages varies somewhat. The `parseDateTime()` function doesn't properly parse the date string that some incoming messages have. If the function encounters a date that it can't parse correctly, an error message results.

Inside the `<cfoutput>` block, the basic information about the message is output as a table row. The date of the message is shown using the `dateFormat()` and `timeFormat()` functions. The Subject line of the message is presented as a link to the `CheckMailMsg.cfm` template (see Listing 20.7), passing the `UID` for the current message in the URL. Because the `UID` identifies the message, the user can click the subject to view the whole message.

At the bottom of the template, the user is provided with Refresh Message List and Log Out links, which simply reload the listing with either `refresh=Yes` or `logout=Yes` in the URL.

NOTE

Because email addresses can contain angle brackets (see the section "Using Friendly Email Addresses," earlier in this chapter), you should always use the `htmlEditFormat()` function when displaying an email address returned by `<cfpop>` in a Web page. Otherwise, the browser will think the angle brackets are meant to indicate an HTML tag, which means that the email address won't show up visibly on the page (although it will be part of the page's HTML if you view source). Here, `htmlEditFormat()` is used on the `From` column, but you should use it whenever you output the `To`, `CC`, or `ReplyTo` columns as well.

Receiving and Deleting Messages

Listing 20.7 is the `CheckMailMsg.cfm` template the user will be directed to whenever they click the subject line in the list of messages. This template requires that a URL parameter called `UID` be passed to it, which indicates the `uid` of the message the user clicked. In addition, the template can be passed a `Delete` parameter, which indicates that the user wants to delete the specified message.

Listing 20.7 `CheckMailMsg.cfm`—Retrieving the Full Text of an Individual Message

```
<!---
 Filename: CheckMailMsg.cfm
 Author: Nate Weiss (NMW)
 Purpose: Allows the user to view a message on their POP server
--->

<html>
<head><title>Mail Message</title></head>
<body>

<!--- Simple CSS-based formatting styles --->
<style>
 body { font-family:sans-serif;font-size:12px}
 th { font-size:12px;background:navy;color:white}
 td { font-size:12px;background:lightgrey;color:navy}
</style>

<h2>Mail Message</h2>

<!--- A message uid must be passed in the url --->
<cfparam name="url.uid">
<cfparam name="url.delete" type="boolean" default="No">

<!--- If we don't have a username/password --->
<!--- send user to main CheckMail.cfm page --->
<cfif not isDefined("session.mail.getMessages")>
 <cflocation url="CheckMail.cfm">
</cfif>

<!--- find our position in the query --->
<cfset position = listFindNoCase(valueList(session.mail.getMessages.uid), url.uid)>

<!--- If the user is trying to delete the message --->
<cfif url.delete>
```

Listing 20.7 (CONTINUED)

```
<!--- Contact POP Server and delete the message --->
<cfpop action="Delete" uid="#url.uid#"
server="#session.mail.popServer#"
username="#session.mail.username#"
password="#session.mail.password#">

<!--- Send user back to main "Check Mail" page --->
<cflocation url="CheckMail.cfm?refresh=Yes" addToken="false">


<!--- If not deleting, retrieve and show the message --->
<cfelse>
<!--- Contact POP Server and retrieve the message --->
<cfpop action="GetAll" name="GetMsg"
uid="#url.uid#"
server="#session.mail.popServer#"
username="#session.mail.username#"
password="#session.mail.password#">

<cfset msgDate = parseDateTime(getMsg.Date, "pop")>

<!--- If message was not retrieved from POP server --->
<cfif getMsg.recordCount neq 1>
<cfthrow message="Message could not be retrieved."
detail="Perhaps the message has already been deleted.">
</cfif>

<!--- We will provide a link to Delete message --->
<cfset deleteurl = "#cgi.script_name#?uid=#uid#&delete=Yes">

<!--- Display message in a simple table format --->
<table border="0" cellSpacing="0" cellPadding="3">
<cfoutput>
<tr>
<th bgcolor="wheat" align="left" nowrap>
Message #position# of #session.mail.getMessages.recordCount#
</th>
<td align="right" bgcolor="beige">
<!--- Provide "Back" button, if appropriate --->
<cfif position gt 1>
<cfset prevuid = session.mail.getMessages.uid[decrementValue(position)]>
<a href="CheckMailMsg.cfm?uid=#prevuid#">
<img src="../images/browseback.gif"
width="40" height="16" alt="Back" border="0"></a>
</cfif>
<!--- Provide "Next" button, if appropriate --->
<cfif position lt session.mail.getMessages.recordCount>
<cfset nextuid = session.mail.getMessages.uid[incrementValue(position)]>
<a href="CheckMailMsg.cfm?uid=#nextuid#">
<img src="../images/browsenext.gif"
width="40" height="16" alt="Next" border="0"></a>
</cfif>
</td>
</tr>
<tr>
<th align="right">From:</th>
```

Listing 20.7 (CONTINUED)

```
<td>#htmlEditFormat(getMsg.From)#</td>
</tr>
<cfif getMsg.CC neq "">
<tr>
<th align="right">CC:</th>
<td>#htmlEditFormat(getMsg.CC)#</td>
</tr>
</cfif>
<tr>
<th align="right">Date:</th>
<td>#dateFormat(msgDate)# #timeFormat(msgDate)#</td>
</tr>
<tr>
<th align="right">Subject:</th>
<td>#getMsg.Subject#</td>
</tr>
<tr>
<td bgcolor="beige" colspan="2">
<strong>Message:</strong><br>
<cfif len(getMsg.htmlBody)>
#getMsg.htmlBody#
<cfelse>
#htmlCodeFormat(getMsg.textBody)#
</cfif>
  </td>
</tr>
</cfoutput>
</table>

<cfoutput>
<!--- Provide link back to list of messages --->
<strong><a href="CheckMail.cfm">Back To Message List</a></strong><br>
<!--- Provide link to Delete message --->
<a href="#deleteurl#">Delete Message</a><br>
<!--- "Log Out" link to discard session.Mail info --->
<a href="CheckMail.cfm?Logout=Yes">Log Out</a><br>
</cfoutput>
</cfif>

</body>
</html>
```

NOTE

Be sure to save the previous listing as `CheckMailMsg.cfm`, not `CheckMailMsg1.cfm`.

As a sanity check, the user is first sent back to the `CheckMail.cfm` template (refer to Listing 20.6) if the `session.mail.getMessages` query doesn't exist. This would happen if the user's session had timed out or if the user had somehow navigated to the page without logging in first. In any case, sending them back to `CheckMail.cfm` causes the login form to be displayed.

Because we are not using the `messageNumber` value, we need to find what position our mail is in the query. This will let us display a numerical mail number instead of the useful, but ugly, UID value.

By using the listFindNoCase function on the valueList of the UID column, we can determine the position of the UID in the query as a whole.

Next, a <cfif> test is used to see whether delete=Yes was passed in the URL. If so, the message is deleted using the action="Delete" attribute of the <cfpop> tag, specifying the passed URL.uid as the uid to delete. The user is then sent back to CheckMail.cfm with refresh=Yes in the URL, which causes CheckMail.cfm to re-contact the mail server and repopulate the session.mail.getMessages query with the revised list of messages (which should no longer include the deleted message).

If the user isn't deleting the message, the template simply retrieves and displays it in a simple HTML table format. To do so, <cfpop> is called again, this time with action="GetAll" and the messagenumber of the desired message. Then the columns returned by <cfpop> can be displayed, much as they were in Listing 20.6. Because the action was "GetAll", this template could use the BODY and HEADER columns listed previously in Table 20.7. The end result is that the user has a convenient way to view, scroll through, and delete messages.

At the bottom of the template, users are provided with the links to log out or return to the list of messages. They are also provided with a link to delete the current message, which simply reloads the current page with delete=Yes in the URL, causing the Delete logic mentioned previously to execute.

Receiving Attachments

As noted previously in Table 20.5, the <cfpop> tag includes an attachmentPath attribute that, when provided, tells ColdFusion to save any attachments to a message to a folder on the server's drive. Your template can then process the attachments in whatever way is appropriate: move the files to a certain location, parse through them, display them to the user, or whatever your application needs. Only a few minor modifications are needed to add support for attachments. In the downloaded zip file containing all the code for this chapter, the file CheckMailMsg2.cfm contains this new version. The notable changes are shown here:

```
<!--- Store attachments in "Attach" subfolder --->
<cfset attachDir = expandPath("Attach")>
<!--- Set a variable to hold the Tab character --->
<cfset TAB = chr(9)>

<!--- Create the folder if it doesn't already exist --->
<cfif not directoryExists(attachDir)>
 <cfdirectory action="create" directory="#attachDir#">
</cfif>
```

This code block simply looks for and creates a folder called Attach beneath the current directory.

```
<!--- Contact POP Server and retrieve the message --->
 <cfpop action="GetAll" name="GetMsg"
 uid="#url.uid#"
 server="#session.mail.popServer#"
 username="#session.mail.username#"
 password="#session.mail.password#"
 attachmentPath="#attachDir#"
 generateUniqueFilenames="Yes">
```

The <cfpop> tag has been modified to specify the attachment directory created earlier. Also note that we tell <cfpop> to generate unique file names for attachments. If two email messages have attachments with the same name, this instruction ensures that they do not overwrite each other.

```
<!--- If this message has any attachments --->
<cfset numAttachments = listLen(getMsg.Attachments, TAB)>
<cfif numattachments gt 0>
<tr>
<th align="right">Attachments:</th>
<td>
<!--- For each attachment, provide a link --->
<cfloop from="1" to="#numAttachments#" index="i">
<!--- Original filename, as it was attached to message --->
<cfset thisFileOrig = listGetAt(getMsg.Attachments, i, TAB)>
<!--- Full path to file, as it was saved on this server --->
<cfset thisFilePath = listGetAt(getMsg.attachmentFiles, i, TAB)>
<!--- Relative URL to file, so user can click to get it --->
<cfset thisFileURL = "Attach/#getFileFromPath(thisFilePath)#">
<!--- Actual link --->
<a href="#thisFileURL#">#thisFileOrig#</a><br>
</cfloop>
</td>
</tr>
</cfif>
```

Last, within the message detail display, we can check to see whether attachments were associated with the message. By default, ColdFusion creates a tab-delimited list, and this is used to parse and loop over the possible attachments. Each attachment is then listed with a simple link that the user can use to download or view the attachment.

Deleting Attachments After Use

One problem with downloading attachments via <cfpop> is that the attachment files that get placed into attachDir are never deleted. Over time, the directory would fill up with every attachment for every message that was ever displayed by the template. It would be nice to delete the files when the user was finished looking at the message, but because of the stateless nature of the Web, you don't really know when that is. You could delete each user's attachment files when they log out, but the user could close their browser without logging out. Luckily, ColdFusion allows you to run code automatically when a session ends. This is done via the onSessionEnd() method of the Application.cfc file.

Listing 20.8 lists the Application.cfc file for the application.

Listing 20.8 Application.cfc—Deleting Attachment Files Previously Saved by <CFPOP>

```
<!---
 Filename: Application.cfc
 Created by: Raymond Camden (ray@camdenfamily.com)
 Please Note Executes for every page request
--->

<cfcomponent output="false">
```

Listing 20.8   (CONTINUED)

```
<!--- Name the application. --->
<cfset this.name="OrangeWhipSite">
<cfset this.dataSource = "ows">

<!--- Turn on session management. --->
<cfset this.sessionManagement=true>
<cfset this.clientManagement=true>

<cffunction name="onSessionEnd" output="false" returnType="void">
  <!--- Look for attachments to delete --->

  <cfset var attachDir = expandPath("Attach")>
  <cfset var getFiles = "">
  <cfset var thisFile = "">

  <!--- Get a list of all files in the directory --->
  <cfdirectory directory="#attachDir#" name="getFiles">

  <!--- For each file in the directory --->
  <cfloop query="getFiles">
    <!--- If it's a file (rather than a directory) --->
    <cfif getFiles.type neq "Dir">
      <!--- Get full filename of this file --->
      <cfset thisFile = expandPath("Attach\ #getFiles.Name#")>

      <!--- Go ahead and delete the file --->
      <cffile action="delete" file="#thisFile#">
    </cfif>
  </cfloop>

</cffunction>

</cfcomponent>
```

Most of this file simply handles turning on CLIENT and SESSION management. The onSessionEnd()
method is what we are concerned with. This method will fire when the user's session expires. It
uses <cfdirectory> to get all the files in the attachment directory. It then loops over and deletes
each file.

Introducing the <cfimap> Tag

The <cfpop> tag has long been the only means by which ColdFusion could read email. With
ColdFusion 9, you now can use the <cfimap> tag as well. The Internet Message Access Protocol
(IMAP) is widely used as an alternative to POP. IMAP provides some benefits over POP. For
example, IMAP servers can recognize whether a mail message has been read or not. IMAP also
supports server-side folders, which allows multiple clients to organize mail in the same way.

As you can probably guess, the <cfimap> tag has attributes and features similar to the <cfpop> tag.
Table 20.8 lists the attributes supported by the <cfimap> tag.

Table 20.8 `<cfimape>` Tag Attributes

ATTRIBUTE	PURPOSE
action, GetHeaderOnly, GetAll, CreateFolder, DeleteFolder, Open, Close, RenameFolder, ListAllFolders, MarkRead, MoveEmail, or Delete	Use GetHeaderOnly to quickly retrieve just the basic information (the subject, who the message is from, and so on) about messages, without retrieving the messages themselves. Use GetAll to retrieve actual messages, including any attachments (which may take some time to download). Use Delete to delete a message from the mailbox. The various folder actions allow you to manage folders and move email into them. MarkRead marks an email as being read. The open and close options allow you to work with one connected IMAP server over multiple commands. Since the connection isn't re-created, your IMAP actions will run more quickly.
server	Required. The IMAP server to which ColdFusion should connect. You can provide either a host name, such as pop.orangewhipstudios.com, or an IP address.
connection	The variable name of the connection. Used when opening and closing connections and, if passed to other operations will use the existing connection.
folder	Used when getting email or performing folder operations. Defaults to INBOX.
username	Required. The username for the IMAP mailbox that ColdFusion should access. This name is likely to be case sensitive, depending on the POP server.
password	Required. The password for the IMAP mailbox that ColdFusion should access. This password is likely to be case sensitive, depending on the POP server.
name	ColdFusion places information about incoming messages into a query object. You loop through the records in the query to perform whatever processing you need for each message. Provide a name (such as GetMessages) for the query object here. This attribute is required if the action value is GetHeaderOnly or GetAll.
maxrows	Optional. The maximum number of messages that should be retrieved. Because you don't know how many messages are in the mailbox you are accessing, it's usually a good idea to specify maxrows unless you specify messagenumber (later in this table).
startRow	Optional. The first message that should be retrieved. If, for instance, you already have processed the first 10 messages currently in the mailbox, you could specify startRow="11" to start at the 11th message.
messageNumber	Optional. If the action value is GetHeaderOnly or GetAll, you can use this attribute to specify messages to retrieve from the IMAP server. If the action value is Delete, this attribute specifies the message or messages you want to delete from the mailbox. In either case, you can provide either a single message number or a comma-separated list of message numbers.
newFolder	Used to specify the name of the folder used when renaming a folder or moving email into a folder.

Table 20.8 (CONTINUED)

ATTRIBUTE	PURPOSE
recurse	Specifies whether ColdFusion should recurse through subfolders when performing mail actions. Defaults to false.
secure	Specifies whether the connection should be secure. Defaults to false.
attachmentPath	Optional. If the action value is GetAll, you can specify a directory on the server's drive in which ColdFusion should save any attachments. If you don't provide this attribute, the attachments won't be saved.
generateUniqueFilenames	Optional. This attribute should be provided only if you are using the attachmentPath attribute. If Yes is specified, ColdFusion will ensure that two attachments that happen to have the same file name will get unique file names when they are saved on the server's drive. If No (the default) is specified, each attachment is saved with its original file name, regardless of whether a file with the same name already exists in the attachmentPath directory.
port	Optional. If the IMAP server specified in server is listening for requests on a nonstandard port, specify the port number here. The default value is 110, which is the standard port used by most POP servers.
timeout	Optional. Indicates how many seconds ColdFusion should wait for each response from the IMAP server. The default value is 60.
debug	Optional. If this attribute is enabled, ColdFusion will log additional information about the cfpop call. This information is logged to either the console or a log file.
stopOnError	Specifies whether an error on the mail server should throw an error on the ColdFusion server. Defaults to true.
uid	Optional. A UUID, or a list of UUIDs, that represents a unique ID for each mail message to be retrieved. This attribute is better than messageNumber because messageNumber may change between requests.

Much like the <cfpop> tag, <cfimap> with action="GetHeaderOnly" will return a query object that contains one row for each message in the specified mailbox. Table 20.9 lists only columns that are *different* from the query returned by <cfpop>.

Table 20.9 Unique Columns Returned by <cfimap> for ACTION="GetHeaderOnly"

COLUMN	EXPLANATION
size	The size of the message in bytes
lines	The number of lines (in plain text) in the message
rxDate	The date the message was received
sentDate	The date the message was originally sent
answered	A yes/no field signifying whether the message has a reply

Table 20.9 (CONTINUED)

COLUMN	EXPLANATION
deleted	A yes/no field signifying whether the message has been deleted
draft	A yes/no field signifying whether the message is a draft
flagged	A yes/no field signifying whether the message is flagged
recent	A yes/no field signifying whether the message arrived recently
seen	A yes/no field signifying whether the message has been read

The results from the getAll action mimic that of the <cfpop> tag. The results of the ListAllFolders action are listed in Table 20.10.

Table 20.10 Columns Returned by <cfimap> for ACTION="ListAllFolders"

COLUMN	EXPLANATION
fullName	The full path of the folder
name	The name of the folder
new	The number of new messages in the folder
totalMessages	The total number of messages in the folder
unread	The total number of unread messages in the folder

In general, working with IMAP is very similar to working with POP. You can get mail headers, message bodies, attachments, and so on. You can build a Web-based mail client just as easily with <cfimap> as you can with <cfpop>. You can actually build much richer clients, though, because of the additional information returned by IMAP (including message status and folders). Listing 20.9 demonstrates a simple IMAP-based browser.

Listing 20.9 imagebrowser.cfm—Simple IMAP-based mail reader

```
<cfset imapserver = "foo.goo.com">
<cfset username = "cfjedimaster@boyzoid.com">
<cfset password = "zoidrules">

<cfimap server="#imapserver#" username="#username#" password="#password#"
        action="open" connection="imapCon">

<cfimap action="listAllFolders" connection="imapCon" name="folders" recurse="true">

<table border="1">
  <tr>
    <th>Name</th>
    <th>Messages (New)</th>
  </tr>
  <cfoutput query="folders">
    <cfset link = "imapbrowser.cfm?folder=">
    <cfset link &= urlEncodedFormat(fullname)>
    <tr>
```

Listing 20.9   (CONTINUED)

```
            <td><a href="#link#">#fullname#</a></td>
            <td>#totalMessages# (#unread#)</td>
        </tr>
    </cfoutput>
</table>

<cfif isDefined("url.folder")>

    <cfoutput><h2>Messages for #url.folder#</h2></cfoutput>

    <cfimap action="getHeaderOnly" connection="imapCon"
    name="mail" folder="#url.folder#">

    <table border="1">
      <tr>
      <th>From</th>
      <th>Subject</th>
      <th>Sent</th>
      <th>Read</th>
      </tr>

      <cfoutput query="mail">
        <tr>
          <td>#htmlEditFormat(from)#</td>
          <td>#subject#</td>
          <td>#dateFormat(sentdate)# #timeFormat(sentdate)#</td>
          <td>#seen#</td>
        </tr>
      </cfoutput>

    </table>

</cfif>

<cfimap action="close" connection="imapCon">
```

Listing 20.9 begins by setting a few variables that we will use to authenticate the IMAP server. You will need to find your own Exchange server, or other IMAP compatible server, to test this yourself.

Next, we create a connection for the server. This is done using the open action of the <cfimap> tag. Once opened, the connection will be stored in a variable called imapCon, as represented by the connection attribute. By storing this connection in a variable, we can perform other actions without having to reauthenticate with the server.

Now that we have a connection, we can list all the folders available on the server. Most IMAP servers will have similar folders, such as Contacts, Journal, Inbox, and Tasks. These folders are returned as queries. The query is output with a simple HTML table. Note that for each folder, we create a link:

```
            <cfset link = "imapbrowser.cfm?folder=">
            <cfset link &= urlEncodedFormat(fullname)>
```

The link points back to itself and passes the full-name value from the query. Beneath this, we check to see whether that url variable exists. If it does, we then use another <cfimap> call to get all the email for that particular folder. Because we aren't building a full mail browser here, we simply display the header values in another table.

CHAPTER 21

Securing Your Applications

At this point, you have learned how to create interactive, data-driven pages for your users and have started to see how your applications can really come alive using the various persistent scopes (particularly client and session variables) provided by ColdFusion's Web application framework. Now is a good time to learn how to lock down your application pages so they require a user name and password and show only the right information to the right people.

Options for Securing Your Application

This section briefly outlines the topics to consider if you need to secure access to your ColdFusion templates. You can use more than one of these options at the same time if you want.

- SSL encryption

- HTTP basic authentication

- Application-based security

- ColdFusion's `<cflogin>` framework

- ColdFusion Sandbox Security

- Operating System Security

SSL Encryption

Most of today's Web servers allow you to make a connection between the browser and the server more secure by using encryption. After encryption has been enabled, your ColdFusion templates and related files become available at URLs that begin with `https://` instead of `http://`. The HTML code your templates generate is scrambled on its way out of the Web server. Provided that everything has been set up correctly, browsers can unscramble the HTML and use it normally. The framework that makes all of this possible is called the Secure Sockets Layer (SSL).

Browsers generally display a small key or lock icon in their status bar to indicate that a page is encrypted. You probably have encountered many such sites yourself, especially on pages where you are asked to provide a credit card number.

This topic isn't discussed in detail here because encryption is enabled at the Web-server level and doesn't affect the ColdFusion Application Server directly. You don't need to do anything special in your ColdFusion templates for it to work properly. The encryption and decryption are taken care of by your Web server and each user's browser.

You might want to look into turning on your Web server's encryption options for sections of your applications that need to display or collect valuable pieces of information. For instance, most users hesitate to enter a credit card number on a page that isn't secure, so you should think about using encryption during any type of checkout process in your applications.

> **TIP**
>
> If you are working on a company intranet project, you might consider enabling SSL for the entire application, especially if employees will access it from outside your local network.

The steps you take to enable encryption differ depending on which Web server software you are using (Apache, Microsoft IIS, and so on). You will need to consult your Web server's documentation for details. Along the way, you will learn a bit about public and private keys, and you will probably need to buy an annual SSL certificate from a company such as VeriSign. VeriSign's Web site is also a good place to look if you want to find out more about SSL and HTTPS technology in general. Visit the company at `http://www.verisign.com`.

> **TIP**
>
> If you want your code to be capable of detecting whether a page is being accessed with an `https://` URL, you can use one of the variables in the `CGI` scope to make this determination. The variables might have slightly different names from server to server, but they generally start with `HTTPS`. For instance, on a Microsoft IIS server, the value of `CGI.HTTPS` is `on` or `off`, depending on whether the page is being accessed in an encrypted context. Another way to perform the test is by looking at the value of `CGI.SERVER_PORT`; under most circumstances, it will hold a value of `443` if encryption is being used, and a value of `80` if not. We recommend that you turn on the Show Variables debugging option in the ColdFusion Administrator to see which HTTPS-related variables are made available by your Web server software.

HTTP Basic Authentication

Nearly all Web servers provide support for something called HTTP basic authentication. *Basic authentication* is a method for password-protecting your Web documents and images and usually is used to protect static files, such as straight HTML files. However, you can certainly use basic authentication to password-protect your ColdFusion templates. Users will be prompted for their user names and passwords via a dialog box presented by the browser, as shown in Figure 21.1. You won't have control over the look or wording of the dialog box, which varies from browser to browser.

Figure 21.1

Figure 21.1

Basic authentication
prompts the user to
log in using a standard
dialog box.

Basic authentication isn't the focus of this chapter. However, it is a quick, easy way to put a password on a particular folder, individual files, or an entire Web site. It is usually best for situations in which you want to give the same type of access to everyone who has a password. With basic authentication, you don't need to write any ColdFusion code to control which users are allowed to see what. Depending on the Web server software you are using, the user names and passwords for each user might be kept in a text file, an LDAP server, an ODBC database, or some type of proprietary format.

To find out how to enable basic authentication, see your Web server's documentation.

NOTE

One of the shortcomings of HTTP Basic Authentication is that the user's entries for user name and password are sent to the server with every page request, and the password isn't scrambled strongly. Therefore you may want to consider enabling SSL Encryption (discussed in the previous section) when using HTTP Basic Authentication, which will cause all communications between server and browser to be scrambled.

TIP

When basic authentication is used, you should be able to find out which user name was provided by examining either the `#CGI.AUTH_USER#` variable or the `#CGI.REMOTE_USER#` variable. The variable name depends on the Web server software you are using.

NOTE

Microsoft's Web servers and browsers extend the idea of basic authentication by providing a proprietary option called Integrated Windows Authentication (also referred to as NTLM or Challenge/Response Authentication), which enables people to access a Web server using their Windows user names and passwords. For purposes of this section, consider Windows Authentication to be in the same general category as basic authentication. That is, it isn't covered specifically in this book and is enabled at the Web-server level.

Application-Based Security

The term *application-based security* is used here to cover any situation in which you give users an ordinary Web-based form with which to log in. Most often, this means using the same HTML form techniques you already know to present that form to the user, then using a database query to verify that the user name and password they typed was valid.

This method of security gives you the most control over the user experience, such as what the login page looks like, when it is presented, how long users remain logged in, and what they have access to. In other words, by creating a homegrown security or login process, you get to make it work however you need it to. The downside, of course, is that you must do a bit of extra work to figure out exactly what you need and how to get it done. That's what a large portion of this chapter is all about.

ColdFusion's `<cflogin>` Framework

ColdFusion provides a set of tags and functions for creating login pages and generally enforcing rules about which of your application's pages can be used by whom. The tags are `<cflogin>`, `<cfloginuser>`, and `<cflogout>`. For basic Web applications, the framework provides the same kind of user experience as session-based security. The main purpose of the framework is to make it easier to secure more advanced applications that make use of ColdFusion Components and Flash Remoting.

NOTE

For details and examples, see the "Using ColdFusion's `<cflogin>` Framework," later in this chapter.

ColdFusion Sandbox Security

ColdFusion 9 provides a set of features called Sandbox Security (also called Resource Security. Aimed mostly at Internet service providers and hosting companies, the Sandbox Security system in ColdFusion is simpler, while still remaining flexible and powerful. It is now possible to use the ColdFusion Administrator to designate which data sources, CFML tags, and other server resources can be used by which applications. For instance, if a single ColdFusion server is being used by several different developers, they can each feel confident that the others won't be able to access the data in their data sources. Also, if an ISP doesn't want developers to be able to create or read files on the server itself via the `<cffile>` tag (discussed in Chapter 61, "Interacting with the Operating System," in *Adobe ColdFusion 9 Web Application Construction Kit, Volume 3: Advanced Application Development*), it's easy for the ISP to disallow the use of `<cffile>` while still allowing developers to use the rest of CFML's functionality.

NOTE

Because it is designed primarily for ISPs and hosting companies that administer ColdFusion servers, Sandbox Security isn't covered in detail in this book. If you have an interest in what the Sandbox Security system can allow and disallow, please refer to the ColdFusion documentation, the online help for the Sandbox Security page in the ColdFusion Administrator, or our companion volume, *Adobe ColdFusion 9 Web Application Construction Kit, Volume 2: Application Development*.

Operating System Security

Included in ColdFusion is a `<cfntauthenticate>` tag. This allows you to integrate your ColdFusion code directly with the operating system's security (as long as your operating system is Windows). The tag, `<cfntauthenticate>`, allows you to not only check a user name and password against a Windows domain. You can optionally also return the list of groups a user belongs to.

Using ColdFusion to Control Access

The rest of this chapter discusses how to build your own form-based security mechanism. In general, putting such a mechanism in place requires three basic steps:

- Deciding which pages or information should be password-protected

- Creating a login page and verifying the user name and password

- Restricting access to pages or information based on who the user is, either using a homegrown session-based mechanism or with the `<cflogin>` framework

Deciding What to Protect

First, you have to decide exactly what it is you are trying to protect with your security measures. Of course, this step doesn't involve writing any code, but we strongly recommend that you think about this as thoroughly as possible. You should spend some time just working through what type of security measures your applications need and how users will gain access.

Be sure you have answers to these questions:

- Does the whole application need to be secured, or just a portion of it? For company intranets, you usually want to secure the whole application. For Internet sites available to the general public, you usually want to secure only certain sections (Members Only or Registered Users areas, for instance).

- What granularity of access do you need? Some applications need to lock only certain people out of particular folders or pages. Others need to lock people out at a more precise, data-aware level. For instance, if you are creating some type of Manage Your Account page, you aren't trying to keep a registered user out of the page. Instead, you need to ensure that the users see and change only their own account information.

- When should the user be asked for their user name and password? When they first enter your application, or only when they try to get something that requires it? The former might make the security seem more cohesive to the user, whereas the latter might be more user friendly.

We also recommend that you think about how passwords will be maintained, rather than what they will protect:

- Should user names and passwords become invalid after a period of time? For instance, if a user has purchased a 30-day membership to your site, what happens on the 31st day?

- Does the user need the option of voluntarily changing their password? What about their user name?

- Should some users be able to log in only from certain IP addresses? Or during certain times of the day, or days of the week?

- How will user names and passwords be managed? Do you need to implement some form of user groups, such as users in an operating system? Do you need to be able to grant rights to view certain items on a group level? What about on an individual user level?

The answers to these questions will help you create whatever database tables or other validation mechanics will be necessary to implement the security policies you have envisioned. You will learn where and when to refer to any such custom tables as you work through the code examples in this chapter.

Using Session Variables for Authentication

An effective and straightforward method for handling the mechanics of user logins is outlined in the following section. Basically, the strategy is to turn on ColdFusion's session-management features, which you learned about in Chapter 19, "Working with Sessions," and use session variables to track whether each user has logged in. There are many ways to go about this, but it can be as simple as setting a single variable in the SESSION scope after a user logs in.

NOTE

Before you can use the SESSION scope in your applications, you need to enable it using the `Application.cfc` file. See Chapter 19 for details.

Checking and Maintaining Login Status

For instance, assume for the moment that the user has just filled out a user name/password form (more on that later), and you have verified that the user name and password are correct. You could then use a line such as the following to remember that the user is logged in:

```
<cfset session.isLoggedIn = "Yes">
```

As you learned in the last chapter, the isLoggedIn variable is tracked for the rest of the user's visit (until their session times out). From this point forward, if you wanted to ensure that the user was logged in before they were shown something, all you would need to do would be to check for the presence of the variable:

```
<cfif not isDefined("session.isLoggedIn")>
 Sorry, you don't have permission to look at that.
 <cfabort>
</cfif>
```

And with that, you have modest security. Clearly, this isn't final code yet, but that really is the basic idea. A user won't be able to get past the second snippet unless their session has already encountered the first. The rest of the examples in this chapter are just expanded variations on these two code snippets.

So, all you have to do is put these two lines in the correct places. The first line must be wrapped within whatever code validates a user's password (probably by checking in some type of database table), and the second line must be put on whatever pages you need to protect.

Restricting Access to Your Application

Assume for the moment that you want to require your users to log in as soon as they enter your application. You could put a login form on your application's front page or home page, but what if a user doesn't go through that page for whatever reason? For instance, if they use a bookmark or type the URL for some other page, they would bypass your login screen. You must figure out a way to ensure that the user gets prompted for a password on the first page request for each session, regardless of which page they are actually asking for.

A great solution is to use the special `Application.cfc` file set aside by ColdFusion's Web application framework, which you learned about in Chapter 18, "Introducing the Web Application Framework." You will recall that if you create a template called `Application.cfc`, it automatically is included before each page request. This means you could put some code in `Application.cfc` to see whether the `SESSION` scope is holding an `isLoggedIn` value, as discussed previously. If it's not holding a value, the user must be presented with a login form. If it is holding a value, the user has already logged in during the current session.

With that in mind, take a look at the `Application.cfc` file shown in Listing 21.1. Make sure to save this listing as `Application.cfc`, not `Application1.cfc`.

Listing 21.1   `Application1.cfc`—Sending a User to a Login Page

```
<!---
  Filename: Application.cfc
  Created by: Raymond Camden (ray@camdenfamily.com)
  Please Note Executes for every page request
--->

<cfcomponent output="false">

  <!--- Name the application. --->
  <cfset this.name="OrangeWhipSite">
  <!--- Turn on session management. --->
  <cfset this.sessionManagement=true>
  <!--- Default datasource --->
  <cfset this.dataSource="ows">

  <cffunction name="onApplicationStart" output="false" returnType="void">

    <!--- Any variables set here can be used by all our pages --->
    <cfset application.companyName = "Orange Whip Studios">

  </cffunction>

  <cffunction name="onRequestStart" output="false" returnType="void">

    <!--- If user isn't logged in, force them to now --->
    <cfif not isDefined("session.auth.isLoggedIn")>
      <!--- If the user is now submitting "Login" form, --->
      <!--- Include "Login Check" code to validate user --->
      <cfif isDefined("form.UserLogin")>
        <cfinclude template="loginCheck.cfm">
      </cfif>

      <cfinclude template="loginForm.cfm">
      <cfabort>
    </cfif>

  </cffunction>

</cfcomponent>
```

First, the application is named using the THIS scope. Then sessionManagement is turned on. Don't forget that sessions are *not* enabled by default. The first method in the Application.cfc file, onApplicationStart, will run when the application starts up, or when the first user hits the site. One variable is set. It will be used later on in other code listings. The onRequestStart method will run before every request. An isDefined() test is used to check whether the isLoggedIn value is present. If it's not, a <cfinclude> tag is used to include the template called LoginForm.cfm, which presents a login screen to the user. Note that a <cfabort> tag is placed directly after the <cfinclude> so that nothing further is presented.

The net effect is that all pages in your application have now been locked down and will never appear until you create code that sets the SESSION.auth.isLoggedIn value.

> **NOTE**
>
> Soon, you will see how the Auth structure can be used to hold other values relevant to the user's login status. If you don't need to track any additional information along with the login status, you could use a variable named SESSION.IsLoggedIn instead of SESSION.Auth.IsLoggedIn. However, it's not much extra work to add the Auth structure, and it gives you some extra flexibility.

Creating a Login Page

The next step is to create a login page, where the user can enter their user name and password. The code in Listing 21.1 is a simple example. This code still doesn't actually do anything when submitted, but it's helpful to see that most login pages are built with ordinary <form> or <cfform> code. Nearly all login pages are some variation of this skeleton.

Figure 21.2 shows what the form will look like to a user.

Figure 21.2

Users are forced to log in before they can access sensitive information in this application.

> **NOTE**
>
> Use type="password" wherever you ask your users to type a password, as shown in Listing 21.2. That way, as the user types, their password will be masked so that someone looking over their shoulder can't see their password.

Listing 21.2 LoginForm.cfm—A Basic Login Page

```
<!---
  Filename: LoginForm.cfm
  Created by: Nate Weiss (NMW)
  Purpose: Presented whenever a user has not logged in yet
  Please Note Included by Application.cfc
--->

<!--- If the user is now submitting "Login" form, --->
```

Listing 21.2 (CONTINUED)

```
<!--- Include "Login Check" code to validate user --->
<cfif isDefined("form.UserLogin")>
 <cfinclude template="LoginCheck.cfm">
</cfif>



<html>
<head>
 <title>Please Log In</title>
</head>

<!--- Place cursor in "User Name" field when page loads--->
<body onLoad="document.LoginForm.userLogin.focus();">

<!--- Start our Login Form --->
<cfform action="#cgi.script_name#?#cgi.query_string#" name="LoginForm"
method="post">
<!--- Use an HTML table for simple formatting --->
 <table border="0">
 <tr><th colspan="2" bgcolor="silver">Please Log In</th></tr>
 <tr>
 <th>Username:</th>
 <td>

 <!--- Text field for "User Name" --->
 <cfinput
 type="text"
 name="userLogin"
 size="20"
 value=""
 maxlength="100"
 required="Yes"
 message="Please type your Username first.">

 </td>
 </tr><tr>
 <th>Password:</th>
 <td>

 <!--- Text field for Password --->
 <cfinput
 type="password"
 name="userPassword"
 size="12"
 value=""
 maxlength="100"
 required="Yes"
 message="Please type your Password first.">

 <!--- Submit Button that reads "Enter" --->
 <input type="Submit" value="Enter">

 </td>
 </tr>
```

Listing 21.2 (CONTINUED)

```
  </table>

</cfform>

</body>
</html>
```

NOTE

In general, users won't be visiting `LoginForm.cfm` directly. Instead, the code in Listing 21.2 is included by the `<cfif>` test performed in the `Application.cfc` page (Listing 21.1) the first time the user accesses some other page in the application (such as the `OrderHistory.cfm` template shown later in Listing 21.4).

Please note that this form's `action` attribute is set to `#cgi.script_name#`. The special `cgi.script_name` variable always holds the relative URL to the currently executing ColdFusion template. So, for example, if the user is being presented with the login form after requesting a template called `HomePage.cfm`, this form will again request that same page when submitted. In other words, this form always submits back to the URL of the page on which it is appearing. Along with the current script, we also append the current query string, using `cgi.query_string`. This ensures that if the person requested `HomePage.cfm?id=5`, the portion after the question mark, known as the query string, will also be included when we submit the form.

TIP

Using `cgi.script_name` and `cgi.query_string` can come in handy any time your code needs to be capable of reloading or resubmitting the currently executing template.

When the form is actually submitted, the `form.userLogin` value will exist, indicating that the user has typed a user name and password that should be checked for accuracy. As a result, the `<cfinclude>` tag fires, and it includes the password-validation code in the `LoginCheck.cfm` template (see Listing 21.3).

The Text and Password fields on this form use the `required` and `message` client-side validation attributes provided by `<cfinput>` and `<cfform>`. See Chapter 13, "Form Data Validation," if you need to review form field validation techniques.

NOTE

This template's `<body>` tag has JavaScript code in its `onLoad` attribute, which causes the cursor to be placed in the `userLogin` field when the page loads. You must consult a different reference for a full discussion of JavaScript, but you can use this same basic technique to cause any form element to have focus when a page first loads.

TIP

JavaScript is case sensitive, so the `onLoad` code must be capitalized correctly; otherwise, scripting-error messages will pop up in the browser. Of course, you can just leave out the `onLoad` code altogether if you want.

Verifying the Login Name and Password

Listing 21.3 provides simple code for your `LoginCheck.cfm` template. This is the template that will be included when the user attempts to gain access by submitting the login form from Listing 21.2.

The most important line in this template is the `<cfset>` line that sets the `session.auth.isLoggedIn` variable to `Yes`. After this value is set for the session, the `isDefined()` test in the `Application.cfc` file (refer to Listing 21.1) will succeed and the user will be able to view pages normally.

Listing 21.3 `LoginCheck.cfm`—Granting Access

```
<!---
 Filename: LoginCheck.cfm
 Created by: Nate Weiss (NMW)
 Purpose: Validates a user's password entries
 Please Note Included by LoginForm.cfm
--->

<!--- Make sure we have Login name and Password --->
<cfparam name="form.userLogin" type="string">
<cfparam name="form.userPassword" type="string">

<!--- Find record with this Username/Password --->
<!--- If no rows returned, password not valid --->
<cfquery name="getUser">
 SELECT ContactID, FirstName
 FROM Contacts
 WHERE UserLogin =
 <cfqueryparam cfsqltype="cf_sql_varchar" value="#form.UserLogin#">
 AND UserPassword =
 <cfqueryparam cfsqltype="cf_sql_varchar" value="#form.UserPassword#">
</cfquery>

<!--- If the username and password are correct --->
<cfif getUser.recordCount eq 1>
 <!--- Remember user's logged-in status, plus --->
 <!--- ContactID and First Name, in structure --->
 <cfset session.auth = structNew()>
 <cfset session.auth.isLoggedIn = "Yes">
 <cfset session.auth.contactID = getUser.contactID>
 <cfset session.auth.firstName = getUser.firstName>

 <!--- Now that user is logged in, send them --->
 <!--- to whatever page makes sense to start --->
 <cflocation url="#cgi.script_name#?#cgi.query_string#">
</cfif>
```

TIP

The query in this template can be adapted or replaced with any type of database or lookup procedure you need. For instance, rather than looking in a database table, you could query an LDAP server to get the user's first name. Another suggestion would be to make use of encrypted or hashed passwords. This approach ensures that someone who gets access to your database may not be able to access the passwords as well.

First, the two `<cfparam>` tags ensure that the login name and password are indeed available as form fields, which they should be unless a user has somehow been directed to this page in error. Next, a simple `<cfquery>` tag attempts to retrieve a record from the `Contacts` table where the `UserLogin` and `UserPassword` columns match the user name and password that were entered in the login form. If this query returns a record, the user has, by definition, entered a valid user name and password and thus should be considered logged in.

> **TIP**
>
> Note the use of `<cfqueryparam>`. This tag helps prevent cross-site scripting (XSS) attacks. In addition, in most databases it will result in a slight performance boost. This tag is described in more detail in Chapter 10, "Creating Data-Driven Pages."

Assume for the moment that the user name and password are correct. The value of `getUser.recordCount` is therefore 1, so the code inside the `<cfif>` block executes. A new structure called `auth` is created in the `session` scope, and three values are placed within the new structure. The most important of the three is the `isLoggedIn` value, which is used here basically in the same way that was outlined in the original code snippets near the beginning of this chapter.

The user's unique ID number (their `contactID`) is also placed in the `session.auth` structure, as is their first name. The idea here is to populate the `session.auth` structure with whatever information is pertinent to the fact that the user has indeed been authenticated. Therefore, any little bits of information that might be helpful to have later in the user's session can be saved in the `auth` structure now.

> **TIP**
>
> By keeping the `session.auth.FirstName` value, for instance, you will be able to display the user's first name on any page, which will give your application a friendly, personalized feel. And, by keeping the `session.auth.contactID` value, you will be able to run queries against the database based on the user's authenticated ID number.

Finally, the `<cflocation>` tag is used to redirect the user to the current value of `cgi.script_name` and `cgi.query_string`. Because `cgi.script_name` and `cgi.query_string` were also used for the action of the login form, this value will still reflect the page the user was originally looking for, before the login form appeared. The browser will respond by rerequesting the original page with the same query string. This time, the `session.auth.isLoggedIn` test in `Application.cfc` (refer to Listing 21.1) won't `<cfinclude>` the login form, and the user will thus be allowed to see the content they originally were looking for.

> **NOTE**
>
> The underlying assumption here is that no two users can have the same `UserLogin` and `UserPassword`. You must ensure that this rule is enforced in your application. For instance, when a user first chooses (or is assigned) their user name and password, there needs to be a check in place to ensure that nobody else already has them.

You may be wondering how you can now test the login. Multiple users exist in the `Contacts` table, but you can log in with the user name `ben` and password `forta`. Our application currently only has an `Application.cfc` file and two files related to security. The download for this series includes a simple `index.cfm` file that is empty. You can copy that file or simply create a blank `index.cfm` file. If you then try to request it, you should see the security code fire up and load the login form instead.

Personalizing Based on Login

After Listings 21.1 through 21.3 are in place, the `session.auth` structure is guaranteed to exist for all your application's pages. What's more, the user's unique ID and first name will be available as session.auth.contactID and session.auth.firstName, respectively. This makes providing users with personalized pages, such as Manage My Account or My Order History, easy.

Listing 21.4 shows a template called OrderHistory.cfm, which lets a user review the merchandise orders they have placed in the past. Because the authenticated contactID is readily available, doing this in a reasonably secure fashion is easy. In most respects, this is just a data-display template, the likes of which you learned about in Chapter 10. The only new concept here is the notion of using authenticated identification information from the SESSION scope (in this case, the contactID).

Listing 21.4 OrderHistory.cfm—Personalizing Based on Login

```
<!---
 Filename: OrderHistory.cfm
 Created by: Nate Weiss (NMW)
 Purpose: Displays a user's order history
--->

<!--- Retrieve user's orders, based on ContactID --->
<cfquery name="getOrders">
 SELECT OrderID, OrderDate,
 (SELECT Count(*)
 FROM MerchandiseOrdersItems oi
 WHERE oi.OrderID = o.OrderID) AS ItemCount
 FROM MerchandiseOrders o
 WHERE ContactID =
 <cfqueryparam cfsqltype="cf_sql_integer" value="#session.auth.contactID#">
 ORDER BY OrderDate DESC
</cfquery>

<html>
<head>
 <title>Your Order History</title>
</head>
<body>
<!--- Personalized message at top of page--->
<cfoutput>
 <h2>Your Order History</h2>
 <p><strong>Welcome back, #session.auth.firstName#!</strong><br>
 You have placed <strong>#getOrders.recordCount#</strong>
 orders with us to date.</p>
</cfoutput>

<!--- Display orders in a simple HTML table --->
<table border="1" width="300" cellpadding="5" cellspacing="2">
 <!--- Column headers --->
 <tr>
 <th>Date Ordered</th>
 <th>Items</th>
 </tr>

 <!--- Display each order as a table row --->
 <cfoutput query="getOrders">
 <tr>
 <td>
```

Listing 21.4 (CONTINUED)

```
<a href="OrderHistory.cfm?OrderID=#OrderID#">
#dateFormat(orderDate, "mmmm d, yyyy")#
</a>
</td>
<td>
<strong>#itemCount#</strong>
</td>
</tr>
</cfoutput>
</table>

</body>
</html>
```

First, a fairly ordinary `<cfquery>` tag is used to retrieve information about the orders the user has placed. Because the user's authenticated `contactID` is being used in the WHERE clause, you can be certain that you will be retrieving the order information appropriate only for this user.

Next, a personalized message is displayed to the user, including their first name. Then the order records are displayed using an ordinary `<cfoutput query>` block. The order records are displayed in a simple tabular format using simple HTML table formatting. Figure 21.3 shows what the results will look like for the end user.

Figure 21.3

After a user's identifi-cation information is authenticated, providing a per-sonalized experience is easy.

Your Order History

Welcome back, Ben !
You have placed **2** orders with us to date.

Date Ordered	Items
March 5, 2010	2
March 1, 2010	1

Being Careful with Passed Parameters

When you are dealing with sensitive information, such as account or purchase histories, you need to be more careful when passing parameters from page to page. It's easy to let yourself feel that your work is done after you force your users to log in. Of course, forcing them to log in is an important step, but your code still needs to check things internally before it exposes sensitive data.

Recognizing the Problem

Here's a scenario that illustrates a potential vulnerability. After putting together the `OrderHistory` `.cfm` template shown in Listing 21.4, you realize that people will need to be able to see the details of each order, such as the individual items purchased. You decide to allow the user to click in each order's Order Date column to see the details of that order. You decide, sensibly, to turn each order's date into a link that passes the desired order's ID number as a URL parameter.

So, you decide to change this:

```
#dateFormat(orderDate, "mmmm d, yyyy")#
```

to this:

```
<a href="OrderHistory.cfm?OrderID=#OrderID#">
 #dateFormat(OrderDate, "mmmm d, yyyy")#
</a>
```

This is fine. When the user clicks the link, the same template is executed—this time with the desired order number available as URL.OrderID. You just need to add an isDefined() check to see whether the URL parameter exists, and if so, run a second query to obtain the detail records (item name, price, and quantity) for the desired order. After a bit of thought, you come up with the following:

```
<cfif isDefined("url.orderID")>
 <cfquery name="getDetail" >
 SELECT m.MerchName, oi.ItemPrice, oi.OrderQty
 FROM Merchandise m, MerchandiseOrdersItems oi
 WHERE m.MerchID = oi.ItemID
 AND oi.OrderID = <cfqueryparam cfsqltype="cf_sql_integer" value="#url.orderID#">
 </cfquery>
</cfif>
```

The problem with this code is that it doesn't ensure that the order number passed in the URL indeed belongs to the user. After the user notices that the order number is being passed in the URL, they might try to play around with the passed parameters just to, ahem, see what happens. And, indeed, if the user changes the ?orderID=5 part of the URL to, say, ?orderID=10, they will be able to see the details of some other person's order. Depending on what type of application you are building, this kind of vulnerability could be a huge problem.

Checking Passed Parameters

The problem is relatively easy to solve. You just need to ensure that, whenever you retrieve sensitive information based on a url or form parameter, you somehow verify that the parameter is one the user has the right to request. In this case, you must ensure that the url.OrderID value is associated with the user's ID number, session.auth.contactID.

In this application, the easiest policy to enforce is probably ensuring that each query involves the session.auth.contactID value somewhere in its WHERE clause. Therefore, to turn the unsafe query shown previously into a safe one, you would add another subquery or inner join to the query, so the Orders table is directly involved. After the Orders table is involved, the query can include a check against its ContactID column.

A safe version of the snippet shown previously would be the following, which adds a subquery at the end to ensure the OrderID is a legitimate one for the current user:

```
<cfif isDefined("url.orderID")>
 <cfquery name="getDetail" >
 SELECT m.MerchName, oi.ItemPrice, oi.OrderQty
 FROM Merchandise m, MerchandiseOrdersItems oi
 WHERE m.MerchID = oi.ItemID
```

```
  AND oi.OrderID = <cfqueryparam cfsqltype="cf_sql_integer" value="#url.orderID#">
  AND oi.OrderID IN
  (SELECT o.OrderID FROM MerchandiseOrders o
  WHERE o.ContactID = <cfqueryparam cfsqltype="cf_sql_integer"
  value="#session.auth.contactID#">)
  </cfquery>
</cfif>
```

Another way to phrase the query, using an additional join, would be

```
<cfif isDefined("URL.orderID")>
  <cfquery name="getDetail" >
  SELECT
  m.MerchName, m.MerchPrice,
  oi.ItemPrice, oi.OrderQty
  FROM
  (Merchandise m INNER JOIN
  MerchandiseOrdersItems oi
  ON m.MerchID = oi.ItemID) INNER JOIN
  MerchandiseOrders o
  ON o.OrderID = oi.OrderID
  WHERE o.ContactID = <cfqueryparam cfsqltype="cf_sql_integer"
  value="#session.auth.contactID#">
  AND oi.OrderID = <cfqueryparam cfsqltype="cf_sql_integer" value="#url.orderID#">
  </cfquery>
</cfif>
```

With either of these snippets, it doesn't matter if the user alters the orderID in the URL. Because the contactID is now part of the query's WHERE criteria, it will return zero records if the requested orderID isn't consistent with the session's authenticated ContactID. Thus, the user will never be able to view any orders but their own.

Putting It Together and Getting Interactive

The OrderHistory2.cfm template shown in Listing 21.5 builds on the previous version (refer to Listing 21.4) by adding the ability for the user to view details about each order. The code is a bit longer, but there really aren't any big surprises here. The main additions display the detail information. Some formatting has also been applied to make the template look nicer when displayed to the user.

Listing 21.5 OrderHistory2.cfm—Providing Details About Orders

```
<!---
 Filename: OrderHistory2.cfm
 Created by: Nate Weiss (NMW)
 Purpose: Displays a user's order history
--->

<!--- Retrieve user's orders, based on ContactID --->
<cfquery name="getOrders">
 SELECT OrderID, OrderDate,
 (SELECT Count(*)
 FROM MerchandiseOrdersItems oi
 WHERE oi.OrderID = o.OrderID) AS ItemCount
```

Listing 21.5 (CONTINUED)

```
FROM MerchandiseOrders o
WHERE ContactID =
<cfqueryparam cfsqltype="cf_sql_integer" value="#session.auth.contactID#">
ORDER BY OrderDate DESC
</cfquery>

<!--- Determine if a numeric OrderID was passed in URL --->
<cfset showDetail = isDefined("url.orderID") and isNumeric(url.orderID)>

<!--- If an OrderID was passed, get details for the order --->
<!--- Query must check against ContactID for security --->
<cfif showDetail>
 <cfquery name="getDetail">
 SELECT m.MerchName, oi.ItemPrice, oi.OrderQty
 FROM Merchandise m, MerchandiseOrdersItems oi
 WHERE m.MerchID = oi.ItemID
 AND oi.OrderID =
 <cfqueryparam cfsqltype="cf_sql_integer" value="#url.orderid#">
 AND oi.OrderID IN
 (SELECT o.OrderID FROM MerchandiseOrders o
 WHERE o.ContactID =
 <cfqueryparam cfsqltype="cf_sql_integer" value="#session.auth.contactID#">)
 </cfquery>

 <!--- If no Detail records, don't show detail --->
 <!--- User may be trying to "hack" URL parameters --->
 <cfif getDetail.recordCount eq 0>
 <cfset showDetail = False>
 </cfif>
</cfif>


<html>
<head>
 <title>Your Order History</title>

 <!--- Apply some simple CSS style formatting --->
 <style type="text/css">
 BODY { font-family:sans-serif;font-size:12px;color:navy}
 H2 { font-size:20px}
 TH { font-family:sans-serif;font-size:12px;color:white;
 background:MediumBlue;text-align:left}
 TD { font-family:sans-serif;font-size:12px}
 </style>
</head>
<body>

<!--- Personalized message at top of page--->
<cfoutput>
 <h2>Your Order History</h2>
 <p><strong>Welcome back, #session.auth.firstName#!</strong><br>
 You have placed <strong>#getOrders.recordCount#</strong>
 orders with us to date.</p>
</cfoutput>
```

Listing 21.5 (CONTINUED)

```
<!--- Display orders in a simple HTML table --->
<table border="1" width="300" cellpadding="5" cellspacing="2">
 <!--- Column headers --->
 <tr>
 <th>Date Ordered</th>
 <th>Items</th>
 </tr>

 <!--- Display each order as a table row --->
 <cfoutput query="getOrders">
 <!--- Determine whether to show details for this order --->
 <!--- Show Down arrow if expanded, otherwise Right --->
 <cfset isExpanded = showDetail and (getOrders.OrderID eq url.orderID)>
 <cfset arrowIcon = iif(isExpanded, "'ArrowDown.gif'", "'ArrowRight.gif'")>

 <tr>
 <td>
 <!--- Link to show order details, with arrow icon --->
 <a href="OrderHistory2.cfm?OrderID=#orderID#">
 <img src="../images/#arrowIcon#" width="16" height="16" border="0">
 #dateFormat(orderDate, "mmmm d, yyyy")#
 </a>
 </td>
 <td>
 <strong>#itemCount#</strong>
 </td>
 </tr>

 <!--- Show details for this order, if appropriate --->
 <cfif isExpanded>
 <cfset orderTotal = 0>
 <tr>
 <td colspan="2">

 <!--- Show details within nested table --->
 <table width="100%" cellspacing="0" border="0">
 <!--- Nested table's column headers --->
 <tr>
 <th>Item</th><th>Qty</th><th>Price</th>
 </tr>

 <!--- Show each ordered item as a table row --->
 <cfloop query="getDetail">
 <cfset orderTotal = orderTotal + itemPrice>
 <tr>
 <td>#merchName#</td>
 <td>#orderQty#</td>
 <td>#dollarFormat(itemPrice)#</td>
 </tr>
 </cfloop>

 <!--- Last row in nested table for total --->
 <tr>
 <td colspan="2"><b>Total:</b></td>
 <td><strong>#dollarFormat(orderTotal)#</strong></td>
 </tr>
```

Listing 21.5 (CONTINUED)

```
    </table>
    </td>
    </tr>
    </cfif>
    </cfoutput>
  </table>

  </body>
  </html>
```

The first `<cfquery>` is unchanged from Listing 21.4. Next, a Boolean variable called `showDetail` is created. Its value is `true` if a number is passed as `url.orderID`. In that case, the second `<cfquery>` (which was shown in the code snippet before the listing) executes and returns only detail records for the session's `contactID`. The `<cfif>` test after the query resets `showDetail` to `false` if the second query fails to return any records. The remainder of the code can rely on `showDetail` being `true` only if a legitimate `orderID` was passed in the URL.

Two `<cfset>` tags have been added at the top of the main `<cfoutput>` block to determine whether the `orderID` of the order currently being output is the same as the `orderID` passed in the URL. If so, the `isExpanded` variable is set to `true`. Additionally, an `arrowIcon` variable is created, which is used to display an open or closed icon to indicate whether each order record is expanded. If the current order is the one the user has asked for details about, `isExpanded` is `true` and `arrowIcon` is set to show the `ArrowDown.gif` image. If not, the `ArrowRight.gif` image is shown instead. The appropriate arrow is displayed using an `<img>` tag a few lines later.

At the end of the template is a large `<cfif>` block, which causes order details to be shown if `isExpanded` is `true`. If so, an additional row is added to the main HTML table, with a `colspan` of 2 so that the new row has just one cell spanning the `Date Ordered` and `Items` columns. Within the new cell, another, nested `<table>` is added, which shows one row for each record in the `getDetail` query via a `<cfloop>` block. As each detail row is output, the `orderTotal` variable is incremented by the price of each item. Therefore, by the time the `<cfloop>` is finished, `orderTotal` will indeed contain the total amount the customer paid. The total is displayed as the last row of the nested table.

The result is a pleasant-looking interface in which the user can quickly see the details for each order. At first, only the order dates and item counts are displayed (as shown previously in Figure 21.3), with an arrow pointing to the right to indicate that the order isn't expanded. If the user clicks the arrow or the order date, the page is reloaded, now with the arrow pointing down and the order details nested under the date. Figure 21.4 shows the results.

Figure 21.4

With a little bit of caution, you can safely provide an interactive interface for sensitive information.

NOTE

A `<style>` block is included in the `<head>` section of this listing to apply some CSS-based formatting. All type on the page will be shown in a blue, sans serif font (usually Arial or Helvetica, depending on the operating system), except for `<th>` cells, which will be shown with white type on a blue background. Consult a CSS reference for details.

Other Scenarios

This chapter has outlined a practical way to force a user to log in to your application and to show them only the appropriate information. Of course, your actual needs are likely to vary somewhat from what has been discussed here. Here are a couple of other scenarios that are commonly encountered, with suggestions about how to tackle them.

Delaying the Login Until Necessary

The examples in this chapter assume that the entire application needs to be secured and that each user should be forced to log in when they first visit any of your application's pages. If, however, only a few pages need to be secured here and there, you might want to delay the login step until the user actually requests something of a sensitive nature. For instance, it might be that the user doesn't need to log in unless they try to visit pages such as Manage My Account or My Order History. For all other pages, no security measures are necessary.

To get this effect, you could move the `isDefined("session.auth.isLoggedIn")` check from `Application.cfc` (refer to Listing 21.1) to a new template called `ForceUserLogin.cfm`. Then, at the top of any page that requires a password, you could put a `<cfinclude>` tag with a `template="ForceLogin.cfm"` attribute. This is a simple but effective way to enforce application security only where it's needed. Yet another alternative would be to place all pages that need to be secured within one subfolder. You can then use an `Application.cfc` file in that subfolder to protect all the files.

Implementing Different Access Levels

This chapter has focused on the problems of forcing users to log in and using the login information to safely provide sensitive information. Once logged in, each user is treated equally in this chapter's examples. Each user simply has the right to see their own data.

If you are building a complex application that needs to allow certain users to do more than others, you might need to create some type of access right or permission or user level. This need is most commonly encountered in intranet applications, in which executives need to be able to view report pages that most employees cannot see, or in which only certain high-level managers can review the performance files of other employees.

Maybe all you need is to add another column somewhere to tell you which type of user each person is. For the Orange Whip Studios example, this might mean adding a new Yes/No column called `IsPrivileged` to the `Contacts` table. The idea is that if this column is set to true, the user should get access to certain special things that others don't have. Then, in `LoginCheck.cfm` (refer to Listing 21.3), select this new column along with the `ContactID` and `FirstName` columns in the

`<cfquery>`, and add a line that saves the `isPrivileged` value in the `session.auth` structure, such as this:

```
<cfset session.auth.isPrivileged = getUser.IsPrivileged>
```

TIP

For an intranet application, you might use a column called `IsSupervisor` or `IsAdministrator` instead of `IsPrivileged`.

Now, whenever you need to determine whether something that requires special privileges should be shown, you could use a simple `<cfif>` test, such as

```
<cfif session.auth.isPrivileged>
 <a href="SalesData.cfm">Sacred Sales Data</a>
</cfif>
```

Or instead of a simple Yes/No column, you might have a numeric column named `UserLevel` and save it in the `session.auth` structure in `LoginCheck.cfm`. This would give you an easy way to set up various access levels, where 1 might be used for normal employees, 2 for supervisors, 3 for managers, 4 for executives, and 100 for developers. So, if only security level 3 and above should be able to view a page, you could use something similar to this:

```
<cfif session.auth.userLevel lt 3>
 Access denied!
 <cfabort>
</cfif>
```

Access Rights, Users, and Groups

Depending on the application, you may need something more sophisticated than what is suggested in the previous code snippets. If so, you might consider creating database tables to represent some notion of access rights, users, and groups. A typical implementation would establish a many-to-many relationship between users and groups, so that a user can be in more than one group, and each group have any number of users. In addition, a one-to-many relationship generally would exist between groups and access rights. Tables with names such as `GroupsUsers` and `GroupsRights` would maintain the relationships.

After the tables were in place, you could adapt the code examples in this chapter to enforce the rules established by the tables. For instance, assuming that you had a table called `Rights`, which had columns named `RightID` and `RightName`, you might put a query similar to the following after the `GetUser` query in `LoginCheck.cfm` (refer to Listing 21.3):

```
<!--- Find what rights user has from group membership --->
<cfquery name="getRights" >
 SELECT r.RightName
 FROM Rights r, GroupsContacts gu, GroupsRights gr
 WHERE r.RightID = gr.RightID
 AND gu.GroupID = gr.GroupID
 AND gu.ContactID = <cfqueryparam cfsqltype="cf_sql_integer"
 value="#session.auth.contactID#">
</cfquery>

<!--- Save comma-separated list of rights in session --->
<cfset session.auth.rightsList = valueList(getRights.RightName)>
```

Now `session.auth.rightsList` would be a list of string values that represented the rights the user should be granted. The user is being granted these rights because the rights have been granted to the groups they are in.

After the previous code is in place, code such as the following could be used to find out whether a particular user is allowed to do something, based on the rights they have actually been granted:

```
<cfif listFind(session.auth.rightsList, "SalesAdmin">
 <a href="SalesData.cfm">Sacred Sales Data</a>
</cfif>
```

or

```
<cfif not listFind(session.auth.rightsList, "SellCompany">
 Access denied.
 <cfabort>
</cfif>
```

NOTE

The `<cflogin>` framework discussed in the next section provides the `IsUserInRole()` function, which is a similar way to implement security based on groups or rights. In particular, the `OrderHistory4.cfm` template shown later in Listing 21.9 uses this function to provide different levels of access to different users.

Using ColdFusion's `<cflogin>` Framework

So far, this chapter has presented a simple session-based method for securing and personalizing an application, built on user names and passwords. Using the preceding examples as a foundation, you can easily create your own custom security framework. For the purposes of this section, let's call this type of security a *homegrown* security framework.

With ColdFusion, you also have the option of using a security framework that ships as part of the CFML language itself. This new framework includes a few tags; most important is the `<cflogin>` tag, which you will learn about in this section. The ColdFusion documentation refers to the new framework as *user security*. For clarity, let's call it the `<cflogin>` framework.

Because the `<cflogin>` framework boasts tight integration with the rest of the CFML language, you may want to use it to provide security for some applications. That said, you may want to stick to a homegrown approach for flexibility. In either case, you will probably end up writing approximately the same amount of code.

Table 21.1 shows some of the advantages and disadvantages of the `<cflogin>` framework versus a homegrown framework.

Table 21.1   Comparing the `<cflogin>` framework with homegrown approaches

STRATEGY	ADVANTAGES	DISADVANTAGES
Homegrown framework	Designed for your specific needs	Not immediately recognizable by other developers. Not automatically recognized and enforced by CFCs.
`<cflogin>` framework	Tightly integrated with CFCs: You just tell the component which user groups (roles) may access each method.	While open and flexible, it may not suit your particular needs. Still requires approximately the same amount of careful coding as the homegrown approach.

NOTE

One key advantage of the `<cflogin>` framework is its integration with the ColdFusion Components (CFC) system, which you will learn about soon.

→   CFCs are covered in Chapter 24, "Creating Advanced ColdFusion Components," in Volume 2.

Tags and Functions Provided by the `<cflogin>` Framework

The `<cflogin>` framework currently includes eight CFML tags and functions, as shown in Table 21.2. You will see how these tags work together in a moment. For now, all you need is a quick sense of the tags and functions involved.

Table 21.2   `<cflogin>` and Related Tags and Functions

TAG OR FUNCTION	PURPOSE
`<cflogin>`	This tag is always used in a pair. Between the opening and closing tags, you place whatever code is needed to determine whether the user should be able to proceed. In most situations, this means checking the validity of the user name and password being presented. You will often place this tag in `Application.cfc`. Code between the opening and closing tags won't be run if the user is logged in.
`<cfloginuser>`	Once the user has provided a valid user name and password, you use the `<cfloginuser>` tag to tell ColdFusion that the user should now be considered logged in. This tag always appears within a pair of `<cflogin>` tags. Like `<cflogin>`, this tag will typically get called by `Application.cfc`.
`getAuthUser()`	Once the user has logged in, you can use this function to retrieve or display the user's name, ID, or other identifying information.
`isUserInRole()`	If you want different users to have different rights or privileges, you can use this function to determine whether they should be allowed to access a particular page or piece of information.
`isUserInAnyRole()`	Allows you to check users to see if they belong to any of a set of roles.
`getUserRoles()`	Returns a list of all users roles.
`isUserLoggedIn()`	Returns `true` if the user is logged in.

Table 21.2 (CONTINUED)

TAG OR FUNCTION	PURPOSE
`<cflogout>`	If you want to provide a way for users to explicitly log out, use the `<cflogout>` tag. Otherwise, users will be logged out after 30 minutes of inactivity. This value can be modified using the `idleTimeout` value of the `<cflogin>` tag. The `<cflogin>` framework can be tied to a user's SESSION scope so that both expire at the same time. This option is enabled by using the `loginStorage` setting in the This scope in your `Application.cfc` file. This is the preferred option when using the `<cflogin>` framework.

Using `<cflogin>` and `<cfloginuser>`

The first thing you need to do is add the `<cflogin>` and `<cfloginuser>` tags to whatever parts of your application you want to protect. To keep things nice and clean, the examples in this chapter keep the `<cflogin>` and `<cfloginuser>` code in a separate ColdFusion template called `ForceUserLogin.cfm` (Listing 21.6).

Once a template like this is in place, you just need to include it via `<cfinclude>` from any Cold-Fusion page that you want to password-protect. To protect an entire application, just place the `<cfinclude>` into your `Application.cfc` template. Since it automatically executes for every page request, the `<cflogin>` and related tags will be automatically protecting all of your application's pages.

Listing 21.6 `ForceUserLogin.cfm`—Using the `<cflogin>` Framework

```
<!---
 Filename: ForceUserLogin.cfm
 Created by: Nate Weiss (NMW)
 Purpose: Requires each user to log in
 Please Note Included by Application.cfc
--->


<!--- Force the user to log in --->
<!--- *** This code only executes if the user has not logged in yet! *** --->
<!--- Once the user is logged in via <cfloginuser>, this code is skipped --->
<cflogin>

 <!--- If the user hasn't gotten the login form yet, display it --->
 <cfif not (isDefined("form.userLogin") and isDefined("form.userPassword"))>
    <cfinclude template="UserLoginForm.cfm">
    <cfabort>

 <!--- Otherwise, the user is submitting the login form --->
 <!--- This code decides whether the username and password are valid --->
 <cfelse>

    <!--- Find record with this Username/Password --->
    <!--- If no rows returned, password not valid --->

    <cfquery name="getUser">
    SELECT ContactID, FirstName, rTrim(UserRoleName) as UserRoleName
```

Listing 21.6 (CONTINUED)

```
FROM Contacts LEFT OUTER JOIN UserRoles
ON Contacts.UserRoleID = UserRoles.UserRoleID
WHERE UserLogin =
 <cfqueryparam cfsqltype="cf_sql_varchar" value="#form.UserLogin#">
AND UserPassword =
 <cfqueryparam cfsqltype="cf_sql_varchar" value="#form.UserPassword#">
</cfquery>

<!--- If the username and password are correct... --->
<cfif getUser.recordCount eq 1>
  <!--- Tell ColdFusion to consider the user "logged in" --->
  <!--- For the NAME attribute, we will provide the user's --->
  <!--- ContactID number and first name, separated by commas --->
  <!--- Later, we can access the NAME value via GetAuthUser() --->
  <cfloginuser
  name="#getUser.ContactID#,#getUser.FirstName#"
  password="#form.userPassword#"
  roles="#getUser.userRoleName#">

<!--- Otherwise, re-prompt for a valid username and password --->
<cfelse>
  Sorry, that username and password are not recognized.
  Please try again.
  <cfinclude template="UserLoginForm.cfm">
  <cfabort>
</cfif>


</cfif>

</cflogin>
```

NOTE

This template is very similar conceptually to the homegrown `LoginCheck.cfm` template discussed earlier (see Listing 21.3). The logic still centers around the `getUser` query, which checks the user name and password that have been provided. It just remembers each user's login status using `<cflogin>` and `<cfloginuser>`, rather than the homegrown `session.auth` structure.

NOTE

Whenever Listing 21.6 needs to display a login form to the user, it does so by including `UserLoginForm.cfm` with a `<cfinclude>` tag. This login form is nearly identical to the one shown earlier in Listing 21.2; the main difference is that it takes advantage of two user-defined functions to preserve any **URL** and **FORM** variables that might be provided before the login form is encountered. The actual code for this version of the login form is included at this book's companion Web site; it is also discussed in Chapter 22, "Building User-Defined Functions," in Volume 2.

The first thing to note is the pair of `<cflogin>` tags. In most cases, the `<cflogin>` tag can be used with no attributes to simply declare that a login is necessary (see the notes before Table 21.3 for information about `<cflogin>`'s optional attributes). It is up to the code inside the `<cflogin>` tag to do the work of collecting a user name and password, or forcing the user to log in. If they have already logged in, the code within the `<cflogin>` block is skipped completely. The `<cflogin>` code executes only if the user has yet to log in.

At the top of the `<cflogin>` block, a simple `<cfif>` test sees whether form fields named `userLogin` and `userPassword` have been provided. In other words, has the user been presented with a login form? If not, the login form is presented via a `<cfinclude>` tag. Note that the `<cfabort>` tag is needed to make sure that execution stops once the form is displayed.

Therefore, the code beginning with `<cfelse>` executes only if the user has not yet successfully logged in and is currently attempting to log in with the login form. First, a simple `<cfquery>` tag is used to validate the user name and password. This is almost the same as the query used in Listing 21.3. The only difference is that this query also retrieves the name of the user's security role from the `UserRoles` table.

NOTE

For this example application, the security role is conceptually similar to that of a user group in an operating system; you can use the role to determine which users have access to what. For instance, those in the `Admin` security role might be able to do things other users cannot. You'll see how this works in the `OrderHistory4.cfm` template, later in this chapter.

TIP

You don't have to use database queries to validate users' credentials and retrieve their information. For instance, if you are storing this type of user information in an LDAP data store (such as one of the Sun Java System Directory Server products, or Microsoft Windows 2003, 2008 or .NET systems), you could use the `<cfldap>` tag instead of `<cfquery>` to validate the user's security data. The ColdFusion documentation includes an example of using `<cfldap>` together with `<cflogin>` and `<cfloginuser>` in such a way.

If the user name and password are valid, the `<cfloginuser>` tag tells ColdFusion that the user should now be considered logged in. If not, the login form is redisplayed. Table 21.3 shows the attributes `<cfloginuser>` supports.

Take a look at how `<cfloginuser>` is used in Listing 21.6. The purpose of the `name` attribute is to pass a value to ColdFusion that identifies the user in some way. The actual value of `name` can be whatever you want; ColdFusion retains the value for as long as the user is logged in. At any time, you can use the `getAuthUser()` function to retrieve the value you passed to `name`. Because the various pages in the application need to have the user's `ContactID` and first name handy, they are passed to `name` as a simple comma-separated list.

NOTE

Behind the scenes, the `<cflogin>` framework sets a cookie on the browser machine to remember that a user has been logged in. The cookie's name will start with `CFAUTHORIZATION`. The `<cflogin>` tag supports two optional attributes that control how that cookie is set. The `cookieDomain` attribute allows you to share the authorization cookie between servers in the same domain; it works like the `domain` attribute of the `<cfcookie>` tag (as discussed in Chapter 19). The `applicationToken` attribute can be used to share a user's login state among several applications; normally, this attribute defaults to the current application's name (which means that all pages that use the same name in their `THIS` scope from the `Application.cfc` file will share login information), but if you provide a different value, all `<cflogin>` blocks that use the same `applicationToken` will share the login information (creating a "single sign on" effect). You can also tie the `<cflogin>` system to the application's `SESSION` scope. This is done using the `loginStorage` attribute of the `THIS` scope. If you set this attribute to `session`, then a user's "logged-in-ness" will be explicitly tied to that user session.

TIP

The `<cflogin>` tag supports an optional `idleTimeout` attribute, which you can use to control how long a user remains logged in between page requests. The default value is 1800 seconds (30 minutes). If you want users to be considered logged out after just 5 minutes of inactivity, use `idleTimeout="300"`. This attribute is used only when `loginStorage` is not set to `session` in the `Application.cfc` file.

Table 21.3 `<cfloginuser>` Tag Attributes

ATTRIBUTE	PURPOSE
name	Required. Some kind of identifying string that should be remembered for as long as the user remains logged in. Whatever value you provide here will be available later via the `getAuthUser()` function. It is important to note that the value you provide here does not actually need to be the user's name. It can contain any simple string information that you would like to be able to refer to later in the user's session, like an ID number.
password	Required. The password that the user logs in with. This is used internally by ColdFusion to track the user's login status.
roles	Optional. The role or roles that you want the user to be considered a part of. Later, you will be able to use the `isUserInRole()` function to find out whether the user is a member of a particular role. You can use `GetUserRoles()` to return all of the user's roles.

The other values passed to `<cfloginuser>` are straightforward. The password that the user entered is supplied to the `password` attribute, and the name of the role to which the user is assigned is passed as the `roles`.

NOTE

It is up to you to ensure that each possible combination of `name` and `password` is unique (this is almost always the case anyway; an application should never allow two users to have the same user name and password). The best practice would be to make sure that some kind of unique identifier (such as the `ContactID`) be used as part of the `name`, just to make sure that ColdFusion understands how to distinguish your users from one another.

NOTE

The way the Orange Whip Studios example database is designed, each user will always have only one role (or associated group). That is, they can be assigned to the `Admin` role or the `Marketing` role, but not both. If your application needed to let users be in multiple roles or groups, you would likely have an additional database table with a row for each combination of `ContactID` and `UserRoleID`. Then, before your `<cfloginuser>` tag, you might have a query called `getUserRoles` that retrieved the appropriate list of role names from the database. You would then use the `valueList()` function to supply this query's records to the `roles` attribute as a comma-separated list; for instance: `roles="#valueList(getUserRoles.userRoleName)#"`.

Now that the code to force the user to log in is in place, it just needs to be pressed into service via `<cfinclude>`. You could either place the `<cfinclude>` at the top of each ColdFusion page that you wanted to protect, or you can just place it in `Application.cfc` to protect all your application's templates. Listing 21.7 shows such an `Application.cfc` file.

Listing 21.7 `Application2.cfc`—Logging with the `<cflogin>` Framework

```
<!---
 Filename: Application.cfc
 Created by: Raymond Camden (ray@camdenfamily.com)
 Please Note: Executes for every page request
--->

<cfcomponent output="false">

  <!--- Name the application. --->
  <cfset this.name="OrangeWhipSite">
  <!--- Turn on session management. --->
  <cfset this.sessionManagement=true>
  <!--- Default datasource --->
  <cfset this.dataSource="ows">

  <cffunction name="onApplicationStart" output="false" returnType="void">

    <!--- Any variables set here can be used by all our pages --->
    <cfset application.companyName = "Orange Whip Studios">

  </cffunction>

  <cffunction name="onRequestStart" output="false" returnType="void">

    <cfinclude template="ForceUserLogin.cfm">

  </cffunction>

</cfcomponent>
```

Using `getAuthUser()` in Your Application Pages

Once you save Listing 21.7 as a file named `Application.cfc`, users will be forced to log in whenever they visit any of the pages in that folder (or its subfolders). However, the order history pages that were created above will no longer work, since they rely on the `session.auth` variables populated by the homegrown login framework. A few changes must be made to allow the order history pages with the `<cflogin>` framework. Basically, this just means referring to the value returned by `getAuthUser()` to get the user's ID and first name, rather than using `session.auth.contactID` and `session.auth.firstName`. Listing 21.8 shows the new version of the order history template.

Listing 21.8 `OrderHistory3.cfm`—Using `getAuthUser()`

```
<!---
 Filename: OrderHistory3.cfm
 Created by: Nate Weiss (NMW)
 Purpose: Displays a user's order history
--->

<html>
<head>
 <title>Order History</title>
```

Listing 21.8 (CONTINUED)

```
<!--- Apply some simple CSS style formatting --->
<style type="text/css">
BODY {font-family:sans-serif;font-size:12px;color:navy}
H2 {font-size:20px}
TH {font-family:sans-serif;font-size:12px;color:white;
background:MediumBlue;text-align:left}
TD {font-family:sans-serif;font-size:12px}
</style>
</head>
<body>

<!--- getAuthUser() returns whatever was supplied to the name --->
<!--- attribute of the <cflogin> tag when the user logged in. --->
<!--- We provided user's ID and first name, separated by --->
<!--- commas; we can use list functions to get them back. --->
<cfset contactID = listFirst(getAuthUser())>
<cfset contactName = listRest(getAuthUser())>


<!--- Personalized message at top of page--->
<cfoutput>
 <h2>YourOrder History</h2>
 <p><strong>Welcome back, #contactName#!</strong><br>
</cfoutput>



<!--- Retrieve user's orders, based on ContactID --->
<cfquery name="getOrders">
 SELECT OrderID, OrderDate,
 (SELECT Count(*)
 FROM MerchandiseOrdersItems oi
 WHERE oi.OrderID = o.OrderID) AS ItemCount
 FROM MerchandiseOrders o
 WHERE ContactID =
 <cfqueryparam cfsqltype="cf_sql_integer" value="#contactID#">
 ORDER BY OrderDate DESC
</cfquery>


<!--- Determine if a numeric OrderID was passed in URL --->
<cfset showDetail = isDefined("url.orderID") and isNumeric(url.orderID)>

<!--- If an OrderID was passed, get details for the order --->
<!--- Query must check against ContactID for security --->
<cfif showDetail>
 <cfquery name="getDetail">
 SELECT m.MerchName, oi.ItemPrice, oi.OrderQty
 FROM Merchandise m, MerchandiseOrdersItems oi
 WHERE m.MerchID = oi.ItemID
 AND oi.OrderID =
 <cfqueryparam cfsqltype="cf_sql_integer" value="#url.orderID#">
 AND oi.OrderID IN
 (SELECT o.OrderID FROM MerchandiseOrders o
 WHERE o.ContactID =
  <cfqueryparam cfsqltype="cf_sql_integer" value="#contactID#">)
```

Listing 21.8 (CONTINUED)

```
      </cfquery>

      <!--- If no Detail records, don't show detail --->
      <!--- User may be trying to "hack" URL parameters --->
      <cfif getDetail.recordCount eq 0>
      <cfset showDetail = False>
      </cfif>
    </cfif>
    <cfif getOrders.recordCount eq 0>
     <p>No orders placed to date.<br>
    <cfelse>
     <cfoutput>
     <p>Orders placed to date:
     <strong>#getOrders.recordCount#</strong><br>
     </cfoutput>

      <!--- Display orders in a simple HTML table --->
      <table border="1" width="300" cellpadding="5" cellspacing="2">
      <!--- Column headers --->
      <tr>
      <th>Date Ordered</th>
      <th>Items</th>
      </tr>

      <!--- Display each order as a table row --->
      <cfoutput query="getOrders">
      <!--- Determine whether to show details for this order --->
      <!--- Show Down arrow if expanded, otherwise Right --->
      <cfset isExpanded = showDetail and (getOrders.OrderID eq url.orderID)>
      <cfset arrowIcon = iif(isExpanded, "'ArrowDown.gif'", "'ArrowRight.gif'")>

      <tr>
      <td>
      <!--- Link to show order details, with arrow icon --->
      <a href="OrderHistory3.cfm?OrderID=#orderID#">
      <img src="../images/#ArrowIcon#" width="16" height="16" border="0">
      #dateFormat(orderDate, "mmmm d, yyyy")#
      </a>
      </td>
      <td>
      <strong>#ItemCount#</strong>
      </td>
      </tr>

      <!--- Show details for this order, if appropriate --->
      <cfif isExpanded>
      <cfset orderTotal = 0>
      <tr>
      <td colspan="2">

      <!--- Show details within nested table --->
      <table width="100%" cellspacing="0" border="0">
      <!--- Nested table's column headers --->
      <tr>
      <th>Item</th><th>Qty</th><th>Price</th>
      </tr>
```

Listing 21.8 (CONTINUED)

```
<!--- Show each ordered item as a table row --->
<cfloop query="getDetail">
<cfset orderTotal = orderTotal + itemPrice>
<tr>
<td>#merchName#</td>
<td>#orderQty#</td>
<td>#dollarFormat(itemPrice)#</td>
</tr>
</cfloop>

<!--- Last row in nested table for total --->
<tr>
<td colspan="2"><strong>Total:</strong></td>
<td><strong>#dollarFormat(orderTotal)#</strong></td>
</tr>
</table>
</td>
</tr>
</cfif>
</cfoutput>
</table>
</cfif>

</body>
</html>
```

As noted earlier, getAuthUser() always returns whatever value was provided to the name attribute of the <cfloginuser> tag at the time of login. The examples in this chapter provide the user's ID and first name to name as a comma-separated list. Therefore, the current user's ID and name can easily be retrieved with the listFirst() and listRest() functions, respectively. Two <cfset> tags near the top of Listing 21.8 use these functions to set two simple variables called contactID and contactName. The rest of the code is essentially identical to the previous version of the template (refer to Listing 21.5). The only change is the fact that contactID is used instead of session.auth. contactID, and contactName is used instead of session.auth.firstName.

Using Roles to Dynamically Restrict Functionality

So far, the examples in this chapter provide the same level of access for each person. That is, each user is allowed access to the same type of information. ColdFusion's <cflogin> framework also provides a simple way for you to create applications in which different people have different levels of access. The idea is for your code to make decisions about what to show each user based on the person's role (or roles) in the application.

NOTE

For the purposes of this discussion, consider the word "role" to be synonymous with group, right, or privilege. The example application for this book thinks of roles as groups. That is, each contact is a member of a role called **Admin** or **User** or the like. Those role names sound a lot like group names. Other ColdFusion applications might have role names that sound more like privileges; for instance, **MayReviewAccountHistory** or **MayCancelOrders**. Use the concept of a role in whatever way makes sense for your application. How exactly you view a role is up to you.

Back in Listing 21.6, the name of the role assigned to the current user was supplied to the `roles` attribute of the `<cfloginuser>` tag. As a result, ColdFusion always knows which users belong to which roles. Elsewhere, the `isUserInRole()` function can be used to determine whether the user is a member of a particular role.

For instance, if you want to display some kind of link, option, or information for members of the `Admin` role but not for other users, the following `<cfif>` test would do the trick:

```
<cfif isUserInRole("Admin")>
 <!--- special information or options here --->
</cfif>
```

Listing 21.9 is one more version of the order history template. This version uses the `isUserInRole()` function to determine whether the user is a member of the `Admin` role. If so, the user is given the ability to view any customer's order history, via a drop-down list. If the user is an ordinary visitor (not a member of `Admin`), then they only have access to their own order history.

Listing 21.9 `OrderHistory4.cfm`—Using `isUserInRole()` to Restrict Access

```
<!---
 Filename: OrderHistory4.cfm
 Created by: Nate Weiss (NMW)
 Purpose: Displays a user's order history
--->

<html>
<head>
 <title>Order History</title>

 <!--- Apply some simple CSS style formatting --->
 <style type="text/css">
 BODY {font-family:sans-serif;font-size:12px;color:navy}
 H2 {font-size:20px}
 TH {font-family:sans-serif;font-size:12px;color:white;
 background:MediumBlue;text-align:left}
 TD {font-family:sans-serif;font-size:12px}
 </style>
</head>
<body>

 <!--- GetAuthUser() returns whatever was supplied to the NAME --->
 <!--- attribute of the <cflogin> tag when the user logged in. --->
 <!--- We provided user's ID and first name, separated by --->
 <!--- commas; we can use list functions to get them back. --->
 <cfset contactID = listFirst(getAuthUser())>
 <cfset contactName = listRest(getAuthUser())>

 <!--- If current user is an administrator, allow user --->
 <!--- to choose which contact to show order history for --->
 <cfif isUserInRole("Admin")>
 <!--- This session variable tracks which contact to show history for --->
 <!--- By default, assume the user should be viewing their own records --->
 <cfparam name="session.orderHistorySelectedUser" default="#contactID#">

 <!--- If user is currently choosing a different contact from list --->
```

Listing 21.9 (CONTINUED)

```
<cfif isDefined("form.selectedUser")>
<cfset session.orderHistorySelectedUser = form.selectedUser>
</cfif>
<!--- For rest of template, use selected contact's ID in queries --->
<cfset showHistoryForContactID = session.orderHistorySelectedUser>


<!--- Simple HTML form, to allow user to choose --->
<!--- which contact to show order history for --->
<cfform
action="#cgi.script_name#"
method="POST">

<h2>Order History</h2>
Customer:

<!--- Get a list of all contacts, for display in drop-down list --->
<cfquery name="getUsers">
SELECT ContactID, LastName || ', ' || FirstName AS FullName
FROM Contacts
ORDER BY LastName, FirstName
</cfquery>

<!--- Drop-down list of contacts --->
<cfselect
name="selectedUser"
selected="#session.orderHistorySelectedUser#"
query="getUsers"
display="FullName"
value="ContactID"></cfselect>

<!--- Submit button, for user to choose a different contact --->
<input type="Submit" value="Go">

</cfform>

<!--- Normal users can view only their own order history --->
<cfelse>
<cfset showHistoryForContactID = contactID>

<!--- Personalized message at top of page--->
<cfoutput>
<h2>YourOrder History</h2>
<p><strong>Welcome back, #contactName#!</strong><br>
</cfoutput>

</cfif>


<!--- Retrieve user's orders, based on ContactID --->
<cfquery name="getOrders">
SELECT OrderID, OrderDate,
(SELECT Count(*)
FROM MerchandiseOrdersItems oi
WHERE oi.OrderID = o.OrderID) AS ItemCount
FROM MerchandiseOrders o
```

Listing 21.9 (CONTINUED)

```
 WHERE ContactID =
 <cfqueryparam cfsqltype="cf_sql_varchar" value="#showHistoryForContactID#">
 ORDER BY OrderDate DESC
</cfquery>


<!--- Determine if a numeric OrderID was passed in URL --->
<cfset showDetail = isDefined("url.orderID") and isNumeric(url.orderID)>

<!--- If an OrderID was passed, get details for the order --->
<!--- Query must check against ContactID for security --->
<cfif showDetail>
 <cfquery name="getDetail">
 SELECT m.MerchName, oi.ItemPrice, oi.OrderQty
 FROM Merchandise m, MerchandiseOrdersItems oi
 WHERE m.MerchID = oi.ItemID
 AND oi.OrderID =
 <cfqueryparam cfsqltype="cf_sql_integer" value="#url.orderID#">
 AND oi.OrderID IN
 (SELECT o.OrderID FROM MerchandiseOrders o
 WHERE o.ContactID =
 <cfqueryparam cfsqltype="cf_sql_integer" value="#showHistoryForContactID#">)
 </cfquery>

 <!--- If no Detail records, don't show detail --->
 <!--- User may be trying to "hack" URL parameters --->
 <cfif getDetail.recordCount eq 0>
 <cfset showDetail = False>
 </cfif>
</cfif>


<cfif getOrders.recordCount eq 0>
 <p>No orders placed to date.<br>
<cfelse>
 <cfoutput>
 <p>Orders placed to date:
 <strong>#getOrders.recordCount#</strong><br>
 </cfoutput>

 <!--- Display orders in a simple HTML table --->
 <table border="1" width="300" cellpadding="5" cellspacing="2">
 <!--- Column headers --->
 <tr>
 <th>Date Ordered</th>
 <th>Items</th>
 </tr>

 <!--- Display each order as a table row --->
 <cfoutput query="getOrders">
 <!--- Determine whether to show details for this order --->
 <!--- Show Down arrow if expanded, otherwise Right --->
 <cfset isExpanded = showDetail and (getOrders.OrderID eq url.orderID)>
 <cfset arrowIcon = iif(isExpanded, "'ArrowDown.gif'", "'ArrowRight.gif'")>
```

Listing 21.9 (CONTINUED)

```
<tr>
<td>
<!--- Link to show order details, with arrow icon --->
<a href="OrderHistory4.cfm?orderID=#OrderID#">
<img src="../images/#arrowIcon#" width="16" height="16" border="0">
#dateFormat(OrderDate, "mmmm d, yyyy")#
</a>
</td>
<td>
<strong>#ItemCount#</strong>
</td>
</tr>

<!--- Show details for this order, if appropriate --->
<cfif isExpanded>
<cfset orderTotal = 0>
<tr>
<td colspan="2">

<!--- Show details within nested table --->
<table width="100%" cellspacing="0" border="0">
<!--- Nested table's column headers --->
<tr>
<th>Item</th><th>Qty</th><th>Price</th>
</tr>

<!--- Show each ordered item as a table row --->
<cfloop query="getDetail">
<cfset orderTotal = orderTotal + itemPrice>
<tr>
<td>#MerchName#</td>
<td>#OrderQty#</td>
<td>#dollarFormat(ItemPrice)#</td>
</tr>
</cfloop>

<!--- Last row in nested table for total --->
<tr>
<td colspan="2"><strong>Total:</strong></td>
<td><strong>#dollarFormat(orderTotal)#</strong></td>
</tr>
</table>
</td>
</tr>
</cfif>
</cfoutput>
</table>
</cfif>

</body>
</html>
```

As you can see, the isUserInRole() function is used to determine whether the user is an administrator. If so, the <cfselect> tag is used to provide the user with a drop-down list of everyone from the Contacts table. The session.orderHistorySelectedUser variable is used to track the user's current drop-down selection; this is very similar conceptually to the way the `client.lastSearch` variable was used in the `SearchForm.cfm` examples in Chapter 19. Another variable, called `showHistoryForContactID`, is created to hold the current value of `session.orderHistorySelectedUser`.

If, on the other hand, the user isn't an administrator, the value of `showHistoryForContactID` is simply set to their own contact ID number. In other words, after the large `<cfif>` block at the top of this listing is finished, `showHistoryForContactID` always holds the appropriate ID number with which to retrieve the order history. The rest of the code is very similar to that in the earlier versions of the template in this chapter; it just uses `showHistoryForContactID` in the `WHERE` parts of its queries to make sure the user sees the appropriate order history records.

Figure 21.5 shows the results for users who log in as administrators (you can log in with user name `Ben` and password `Forta` to see these results). All other users will continue to see the interface shown in Figure 21.4.

Figure 21.5

The concept of user roles can be used to expose whatever functionality is appropriate for each one.

You may also want to know what roles a user belongs to. ColdFusion has the `getUserRoles()` function, which returns all the roles that were assigned to a user at login. Another new feature is `isUserInAnyRole()`. Before discussing this function, let's consider how `isUserInRole()` handles multiple roles. If you pass a list of roles to `isUserInRole()`, the user must be in all of the roles for the function to return a `true` value. If you want to see whether a user is any role, you would use the `isUserInAnyRole()` function. A common use for this functionality is in situations where you want to restrict access to a certain group *and* also enable a special admin group to always be allowed. Previous versions of ColdFusion required code like this:

```
<cfif isUserInRole("test") or isUserInRole("admin")>
```

Now you can simply test for either role, like this:

```
<cfif isUserInAnyRole("test,admin")>
```

You also may wonder how you can check to see whether a user is currently logged in. Our example application forced all users to log in, but you may build a Web site where login is optional. Cold-Fusion's `isUserLoggedIn()` function returns `true` or `false` based on whether or not the user is logged in.

Using Operating System Security

We've seen how you can roll your own security system so that authentication can be performed in multiple fashions. You can use a database lookup, LDAP, or any other method. One that may be particularly useful is the operating system itself. If your ColdFusion server runs on a Windows machine using domains, ColdFusion allows you to authenticate against any domain. You can not only authenticate a user, you can also get a list of groups the user is a member of. This is all possible with the <cfNTAuthenticate> tag. Table 21.4 lists the attributes for this tag.

Table 21.4 <cfNTAuthenticate> Tag Attributes

ATTRIBUTE	PURPOSE
username	Required. User name to authenticate.
password	Required. Password to authenticate.
domain	Required. The domain that the user belongs to. ColdFusion must be running on a box that has access to this domain.
result	Optional. Default: cfntauthenticate. Specifies the name of a variable that will contain the result of the authentication attempt. This structure will contain an auth key that indicates if the user was authenticated, a groups key that lists the groups the user is a member of (if the listGroups attribute is used), and a status value. Status will be success, UserNotInDirFailure (the user isn't a member of the domain), or AuthenticationFailure (password failure).
listGroups	Optional. If true, the user's groups will be returned in the structure specified by the result attribute. The default value is false.
throwOnError	Optional. Specifies if the tag should throw an exception if the authentication fails. This defaults to false.

Listing 21.10 demonstrates a simple example of using <cfNTAuthenticate>. I'm keeping this example very simple since it will only run on Windows machines, and only those machines that are part of a domain. Obviously you will need to modify the user name and password values.

Listing 21.10 DomainAuth.cfm—Using <cfNTAuthenticate>

```
<!---
 Filename: DomainAuth.cfm
 Created by: Raymond Camden (ray@camdenfamily.com)
 Purpose: Uses <cfNTAuthenticate>
--->

<!--- Change this username! --->
<cfset username="changeme">

<!--- Change this password! --->
<cfset password="changeme">

<!--- Change this domain! --->
<cfset domain="changeme">

<!--- Attempt to logon --->
```

Listing 21.10 (CONTINUED)

```
<cfNTAuthenticate username="#username#" password="#password#" result="result"
 domain="#domain#" listGroups="yes">

<cfdump var="#result#" label="Result of NT authentication.">
```

The script begins by creating variables for the three main pieces needed for authentication, user name, password, and domain. As it obviously states in the code, you will need to change these values. However, if you want to see a failed authentication result, you can leave these alone. Finally, we run the `<cfNTAuthenticate>` tag, passing in the values and telling it to return the result in a struct called result and enumerating the groups the user belongs to. Lastly we dump the result structure. Again, you will have to modify the values in order to get a valid authentication result.

Defending Against Cross-Site Scripting

One way your Web application be harmed is by cross-site scripting. This is simply the use of HTML and other codes within Web-based forms. As a simple example, imagine a forums application that lets people write their own entries. Someone could write an entry that contained JavaScript code. When someone else views that page, the JavaScript code is executed just as if you had written it yourself. This could be very dangerous. Luckily, ColdFusion provides a simple solution. In Chapter 18, you learned about the `Application.cfc` file and how you can configure Cold-Fusion applications via the THIS scope. You can simply add one more attribute to the THIS scope:

```
<cfset this.scriptProtect="all">
```

This one line will clean all FORM, URL, CGI, and COOKIE variables. So for example, this line of text:

```
<script>alert('hi');</script>
```

becomes

```
<InvalidTag>alert('hi');</script>
```

You can specify just one of the above scopes instead of "ALL" if you want to be more specific. You can also turn this feature on automatically for all files on the server. You do this by enabling Enable Global Script Protection in the ColdFusion Administrator.

PART **4**

Appendices

APPENDIX A

Installing ColdFusion and ColdFusion Builder

This appendix provides information about installing ColdFusion, ColdFusion Report Builder, ColdFusion Builder, and the sample files used in the lessons in this book.

Installing ColdFusion 9

ColdFusion 9 is supported on Windows, Mac OS X, Linux, and Unix systems. All of these platforms are supported by the exact same ColdFusion; all that differs is the installer. Thus, although the exact installation steps vary based on the platform, once ColdFusion is installed, everything about it is consistent regardless of the platform used.

NOTE

A link to download ColdFusion can be found on the book Web page at http://www.forta.com/books/032166034X/.

The Different Flavors of ColdFusion 9

ColdFusion 9 comes in three editions:

- ColdFusion Developer Edition

- ColdFusion Standard

- ColdFusion Enterprise

As already explained, there is a single ColdFusion installation program and a single ColdFusion application. The different editions are activated based on the serial number specified.

NOTE

ColdFusion Developer Edition is functionally equivalent to ColdFusion Enterprise, but has IP address restrictions.

TIP

The installation of a local ColdFusion Developer Edition is highly recommended. While you can indeed learn ColdFusion and practice on remote hosted servers, having a local unrestricted version that you can fully control will greatly improve your ColdFusion experience. All of the lessons in these books assume that you are using the free local ColdFusion Developer Edition.

Pre-installation Checklist

To be sure ColdFusion will work at peak performance on your hardware platform, make sure you follow the steps listed here:

- Check the system requirements in the installation documentation.

- Check your hardware specifications. If your RAM or disk space is inadequate, or if your processor can't handle the load, an upgrade will be necessary.

The complete list of supported platforms and the system requirements for each can be found at `http://www.adobe.com/products/coldfusion/productinfo/systemreqs/`.

Choosing Your Hardware

You probably already know which hardware platform you will use for ColdFusion: the hardware you already own. But if you're still deciding, keep the following points in mind:

- Virtually all ColdFusion code will execute perfectly across all supported platforms. So if you jump ship to another platform during or after development, your applications will require little, if any, porting.

- From a ColdFusion perspective, there is no real difference between hardware platforms. The decision as to which platform to use should be driven by cost, experience, support, and other factors.

Checking Your Web Server

As explained in Chapter 1, "Introducing ColdFusion," Web servers are separate software programs that enable two-way communication between your system and other Web servers. A great number of Web servers are available for a great number of operating systems. You must choose the Web server that is compatible with your operating system and ColdFusion.

ColdFusion is primarily used with Microsoft Internet Information Server (IIS) and Apache. In addition, an embedded Web server is available, allowing you to do development without the need to install and configure a Web server.

- Microsoft IIS is free and comes bundled with Windows. One of IIS's principal advantages is that it can use Windows' user lists and security options, eliminating the complexity of maintaining multiple lists of passwords and security privileges.

- Apache is one of the oldest and still one of the most popular Web servers. The Apache Web server is a free, open source software project available for most operating systems, including Windows, Linux, and Solaris. Despite its popularity, Apache is harder to install and manage than IIS.

Because the applications you develop with ColdFusion are portable among all supported Web servers, your production Web server can differ from the Web server used for development with minimal changes in your ColdFusion code.

After you have installed a Web server, you must verify that it is working properly. To do this, start a Web browser and go to the URL `http://localhost/`. If everything is working, your Web server's default home page should appear.

If the home page doesn't appear, you must do a little troubleshooting. First, type `ping 127.0.0.1` at a command prompt. If the ping is successful, TCP/IP is working. More than likely, the problem lies with the Web server. For more information, consult the Web server's documentation.

Installing ColdFusion on Windows and Mac OS X

You install ColdFusion on Windows and Mac OS X systems using an interactive installation program. You must have administrative privileges to install ColdFusion.

During the installation, you will be prompted for information:

- Product serial number (which will activate ColdFusion as either ColdFusion Standard or ColdFusion Enterprise). You can omit the serial number if you are installing ColdFusion Developer Edition or the 30-day free trial. (The trial edition will revert to the Developer Edition after 30 days unless a serial number is provided.)

- Installation type, if you are installing ColdFusion Enterprise or ColdFusion Developer Edition. You can install a stand-alone configuration (integrated J2EE server, single instance only), JRun plus ColdFusion, or additional instances on top of an existing J2EE server. ColdFusion Standard edition always installs using the stand-alone configuration.

- Web server to be used. ColdFusion will display a list of detected Web servers, as well as offering you the option of using the internal HTTP server (to be used on development systems only).

- Passwords to be used to secure the ColdFusion Administrator and RDS access (used by ColdFusion Builder, ColdFusion Report Builder, and Dreamweaver to provide access to databases and more).

TIP

Stand-alone mode is the simplest to use for development, as no Web server is needed. Most of the examples in this book assume that stand-alone mode is being used.

With this information complete and verified, the installer will install and configure ColdFusion and will create Start menu icons to access ColdFusion documentation and the ColdFusion Administrator.

Installing ColdFusion on Linux and Unix

To install ColdFusion on Linux and Unix systems, make sure that the appropriate attributes have been assigned to the installation file. The installation file must be made executable using the chmod command as follows:

```
chmod 755 filename
```

You must be logged on as an administrator to install ColdFusion.

During the installation, you will be prompted for information:

- Product serial number (which will activate ColdFusion as either ColdFusion Standard or ColdFusion Enterprise). You can omit the serial number if you are installing ColdFusion Developer Edition or the 30-day free trial. (The trial edition will revert to Developer Edition after 30 days unless a serial number is provided.)

- Installation type, if you are installing ColdFusion Enterprise or ColdFusion Developer Edition. You can install a stand-alone configuration (integrated J2EE server, single instance only), JRun plus ColdFusion, or additional instances on top of an existing J2EE server. ColdFusion Standard edition always installs using the stand-alone configuration.

- Location and account information for Apache (if you are not using the integrated HTTP server).

- Passwords to be used to secure the ColdFusion Administrator and RDS access (used by ColdFusion Builder, ColdFusion Report Builder, and Dreamweaver to provide access to databases and more).

TIP

Stand-alone mode is the simplest to use for development, as no Web server is needed. Most of the examples in this book assume that stand-alone mode is being used.

Installing ColdFusion Builder

ColdFusion Builder is the Eclipse-based ColdFusion development environment. It runs on Windows and Mac OS X and can be installed in two ways:

- If you already have Eclipse 3.1 or later installed (perhaps because you are using Adobe Flex Builder), then you can install ColdFusion Builder in that same Eclipse installation.

- If you do not have Eclipse installed, then perform a full ColdFusion Builder installation (which will also install Eclipse).

NOTE

For a link to download ColdFusion Builder, see the book's Web page: http://www.forta.com/books/032166034X/.

Installing ColdFusion Report Builder

ColdFusion Report Builder is a Windows application (although reports created with it can be processed by all editions of ColdFusion on all platforms).

The ColdFusion Report Builder installer can be downloaded from Adobe. You can run this installer to manually install ColdFusion Report Builder on development machines.

NOTE

For a link to download ColdFusion Report Builder, see the book's Web page: `http://www.forta.com/books/032166034X/`.

Installing Samples and Data Files

The best way to learn a product is by using it, and in this book you learn ColdFusion by building applications: some really simple and some quite sophisticated. The applications you'll create are for a fictitious company named Orange Whip Studios, or OWS for short.

Building the applications involves writing code, using databases, and accessing images and other files. You don't need to create all of these manually—they're available for download from the book's Web page. You can install all of these files or just the ones you need; the choice is yours.

NOTE

The OWS data files and links to other files that are mentioned in this appendix can be found at the the book's Web page: `http://www.forta.com/books/032166034X/`.

What to Install

The OWS files are distributed in two downloadable Zip files.

The `owsdata.zip` file contains a folder named `ows` containing the Apache Derby database used by the lessons and examples in this book.

The `ows.zip` file contains subdirectories that each contain the files that make up the applications. Note the following subdirectories:

- The `images` directory contains GIF and JPEG images used in many of the applications.

- The `sql` directory contains a SQL query utility used in Chapters 6, "Introducing SQL," and 7, "SQL Data Manipulation."

- The numbered directories contain files created in specific chapters in this book, with the directory number corresponding to the chapter number. For example, directory `8` contains the files created in Chapter 8, "The Basics of CFML."

All readers should install the database directories and the `images` directory. This book walks you through the processes for creating the tables and designing the images. Without the databases, most of the examples won't work, and without the images your screens won't look like the screen shots in the book.

The `sql` directory is optional and should be installed only if you have no other tool or utility with which to learn SQL.

CAUTION

To ensure database and server security, don't install the files in the `sql` directory on production servers.

The numbered directories should *not* be installed unless you plan to not try the examples yourself (which would be a pity). These files are provided so you can refer to them as needed, or even copy specific files to save time. To really learn ColdFusion, you'll want to complete every lesson in this book and create the files yourself.

Installing the OWS Files

The default location for ColdFusion databases is the ColdFusion database folder (the `db` folder under the ColdFusion root; on Windows machines, this will usually be `c:\coldfusion9\db`). The `owsdata.zip` file contains a folder named `ows`, which you should save in the database folder.

Install the `ows.zip` contents under the Web server root. If you are using ColdFusion in stand-alone mode (in Windows) using installation defaults, then the Web root will be

    c:\coldfusion9\db

If you are using Microsoft IIS, the Web root will likely be

    c:\inetpub\wwwroot

To install the OWS files, do the following:

1. Create a directory named `ows` beneath the Web server root.

2. Copy the `images` directory into the `ows` directory you just created. You can copy the entire directory; you don't need to copy the files individually.

3. Copy the `sql` directory, if needed.

4. Copy the chapter directories, if needed. If you plan to create the files yourself—which we recommend—you'll be creating your own files in the `ows` directory as you work through the book. Thus, you may want to copy these files to another location (not the newly created `ows` directory) so they will be readily available for browsing if needed, but not in the way of your own development.

And with that, you're ready to start learning ColdFusion.

APPENDIX B

Sample Application Data Files

Sample Database Tables

"Orange Whip Studios" is a fictitious company used in the examples throughout this book. The various examples and applications use a total of 12 database tables, as described in the following sections.

NOTE

The sample applications use Apache Derby as a database (this database engine is included with ColdFusion). Because of limitations in the data types supported by Apache Derby, all money or currency fields are represented as real types, and all bit fields are represented by single character types.

The `Actors` Table

The `Actors` table contains a list of all the actors along with name, address, and other personal information. `Actors` contains the columns listed in Table B.1.

Table B.1 The `Actors` Table

COLUMN	DATA TYPE	DESCRIPTION
ActorID	Numeric (Identity)	Unique actor ID
NameFirst	Text (50 chars)	Actor's (stage) first name
NameLast	Text (50 chars)	Actor's (stage) last name
Age	Numeric	Actor's (stage) age
NameFirstReal	Text (50 chars)	Actor's real first name
NameLastReal	Text (50 chars)	Actor's real last name
AgeReal	Numeric	Actor's real age
IsEgomaniac	Small Integer	Egomaniac flag
IsTotalBabe	Small Integer	Total babe flag
Gender	Text (1 char)	Gender (M or F)

Primary Key

- `ActorID`

Foreign Keys

- None

The `Contacts` **Table**

The `Contacts` table stores all contacts, including mailing list members and online store customers. `Contacts` contains the columns listed in Table B.2.

Table B.2 The `Contacts` **Table**

COLUMN	DATA TYPE	DESCRIPTION
FirstName	Text (50 chars)	Contact first name
LastName	Text (50 chars)	Contact last name
Address	Text (100 chars)	Contact address
City	Text (50 chars)	Contact city
State	Text (5 chars)	Contact state
Zip	Text (10 chars)	Contact ZIP
Country	Text (50 chars)	Contact country
Email	Text (100 chars)	Contact email address
Phone	Text (50 chars)	Contact phone number
UserLogin	Text (50 chars)	Contact user login
UserPassword	Text (50 chars)	Contact login password
MailingList	Small Integer	Mailing list flag
UserRoleID	Numeric	ID of the associated role

Primary Key

- `ContactID`

Foreign Keys

- The `UserRoleID` column is related to the primary key of the `UserRoles` table.

The `Directors` **Table**

The `Directors` table stores all movie directors. `Directors` contains the columns listed in Table B.3.

Table B.3 The `Directors` Table

COLUMN	DATA TYPE	DESCRIPTION
DirectorID	Numeric (Identity)	Unique director ID
FirstName	Text (50 chars)	Director first name
LastName	Text (50 chars)	Director last name

Primary Key

- `DirectorID`

Foreign Keys

- None

The `Expenses` Table

The `Expenses` table lists the expenses associated with listed movies. `Expenses` contains the columns in Table B.4.

Table B.4 The `Expenses` Table

COLUMN	DATA TYPE	DESCRIPTION
ExpenseID	Numeric (Identity)	Unique expense ID
FilmID	Numeric	Movie ID
ExpenseAmount	Real	Expense amount
Description	Text (100 chars)	Expense description
Expense Date	Date Time	Expense date

Primary Key

- `ExpenseID`

Foreign Keys

- `FilmID` related to primary key in `Films` table

The `Films` Table

The `Films` table lists all movies and related information. `Films` contains the columns in Table B.5.

Table B.5 The `Films` Table

COLUMN	DATA TYPE	DESCRIPTION
FilmID	Numeric (Identity)	Unique movie ID
MovieTitle	Text (255 chars)	Movie title
PitchText	Text (100 chars)	Movie one-liner
AmountBudgeted	Currency (or numeric)	Movie budget (planned)
RatingID	Numeric	Movie rating ID
Summary	Memo (or text)	Movie plot summary
ImageName	Text (50 chars)	Movie poster image file name
DateInTheaters	Date Time	Date movie is in theaters

Primary Key

- FilmID

Foreign Keys

- RatingID related to primary key in FilmsRatings table

The FilmsActors Table

The `FilmsActors` table associates actors with the movies they are in. `FilmsActors` contains the columns in Table B.6. Retrieving actors with their movies requires a three-way join (`Films`, `Actors`, and `FilmsActors`).

Table B.6 The `FilmsActors` Table

COLUMN	DATA TYPE	DESCRIPTION
FARecID	Numeric (Identity)	Unique film actor ID
FilmID	Numeric	Movie ID
ActorID	Numeric	Actor ID
IsStarringRole	Small Integer	Is star flag
Salary	Real	Actor salary

Primary Key

- FARecID

Foreign Keys

- FilmID related to primary key in Films table
- ActorID related to primary key in Actors table

The `FilmsDirectors` Table

The `FilmsDirectors` table associates directors with their movies. `FilmsDirectors` contains the columns in Table B.7. Retrieving actors with their movies requires a three-way join (`Films`, `Directors`, and `FilmsDirectors`).

Table B.7 The `FilmsDirectors` Table

COLUMN	DATA TYPE	DESCRIPTION
FDRecID	Numeric (Identity)	Unique films director ID
FilmID	Numeric	Movie ID
DirectorID	Numeric	Director ID
Salary	Real	Director salary

Primary Key

- `FDRecID`

Foreign Keys

- `FilmsID` related to primary key in `Films` table
- `DirectorID` related to primary key in `Directors` table

The `FilmsRatings` Table

The `FilmsRatings` table lists all movie ratings. `FilmsRatings` contains the columns in Table B.8.

Table B.8 The `FilmsRatings` Table

COLUMN	DATA TYPE	DESCRIPTION
RatingID	Numeric (Identity)	Unique rating ID
Rating	Text (50 chars)	Rating description

Primary Key

- `RatingID`

Foreign Keys

- None

The Merchandise Table

The Merchandise table lists the movie-related merchandise for sale in the online store. Merchandise contains the columns in Table B.9.

Table B.9 The Merchandise Table

COLUMN	DATA TYPE	DESCRIPTION
MerchID	Numeric (Identity)	Unique merchandise ID
FilmID	Numeric	Movie ID
MerchName	Text (50 chars)	Merchandise name
MerchDescription	Text (100 chars)	Merchandise description
MerchPrice	Real	Merchandise price
ImageNameSmall	Text (50 chars)	Item's small image file name
ImageNameLarge	Text (50 chars)	Item's large image file name

Primary Key

- MerchID

Foreign Keys

- FilmID related to primary key in Films table

The MerchandiseOrders Table

The MerchandiseOrders table stores online merchandise order information. MerchandiseOrders contains the columns in Table B.10.

Table B.10 The MerchandiseOrders Table

COLUMN	DATA TYPE	DESCRIPTION
OrderID	Numeric (Identity)	Unique order ID
ContactID	Numeric	Buyer contact ID
OrderDate	Date Time	Order date
ShipAddress	Text (100 chars)	Ship to address
ShipCity	Text (50 chars)	Ship to city
ShipState	Text (5 chars)	Ship to state
ShipZip	Text (10 chars)	Ship to ZIP
ShipCountry	Text (50 chars)	Ship to country
ShipDate	Date Time	Ship date

Primary Key

- OrderID

Foreign Keys

- ContactID related to primary key in Contacts table

The MerchandiseOrdersItems Table

The MerchandiseOrdersItems table contains the items in each order. MerchandiseOrdersItems contains the columns in Table B.11.

Table B.11 The MerchandiseOrdersItems Table

COLUMN	DATA TYPE	DESCRIPTION
OrderItemID	Numeric (Identity)	Unique order item ID
OrderID	Numeric	Order ID
ItemID	Numeric	Ordered item ID
OrderQty	Numeric	Number of items ordered
ItemPrice	Real	Item sale price

Primary Key

- OrderItemID

Foreign Keys

- OrderID related to primary key in MerchandiseOrders table
- ItemID related to primary key in Merchandise table

The UserRoles Table

The UserRoles table defines user security roles used by secured applications. UserRoles contains the columns in Table B.12.

Table B.12 The UserRoles Table

COLUMN	DATA TYPE	DESCRIPTION
UserRoleID	Numeric (Identity)	Unique user role ID
UserRoleName	Text (20 chars)	Role name
UserRoleFunction	Text (75 chars)	Role purpose

Primary Key

- `UserRoleID`

Foreign Keys

- None

INDEX

WATCH
READ
CREATE

Meet Creative Edge.

A new resource of unlimited books, videos and tutorials for creatives from the world's leading experts.

Creative Edge is your one stop for inspiration, answers to technical questions and ways to stay at the top of your game so you can focus on what you do best—being creative.

All for only $24.99 per month for access—any day any time you need it.

creativeedge.com